MANAGEMENT

Management

CONCEPTS AND APPLICATIONS

THIRD EDITION

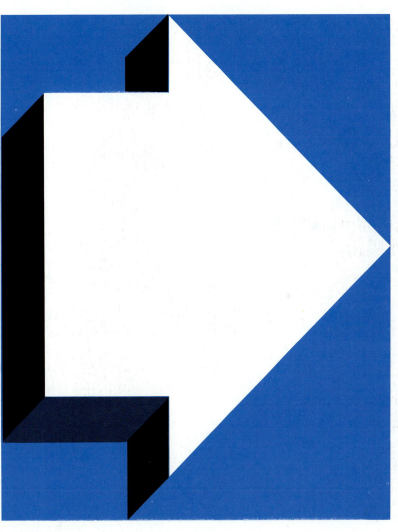

Leon C. Megginson
Mobile College

Donald C. Mosley
University of South Alabama

Paul H. Pietri, Jr.
University of South Alabama

1817

HARPER & ROW, PUBLISHERS, New York
Cambridge, Philadelphia, San Francisco, London,
Mexico City, São Paulo, Singapore, Sydney

Sponsoring Editor: Jayne L. Maerker
Project Editor: Joan Gregory
Text Design: Joan Greenfield
Cover Design: Keithley Associates, Inc.
Cover Illustration: Kyuzo Tsugami
Text Art: Hadel Studio
Photo Research: Mira Schachne
Production Manager: Jeanie Berke
Production Assistant: Paula Roppolo
Compositor: Ruttle, Shaw & Wetherill, Inc.
Printer and Binder: R. R. Donnelley & Sons Company
Cover Printer: New England Book Components

Photo Credits: *p. ii(l)* Nigel Dickson, Deluxe Photography, Inc.; *p. ii(r)* © Leinwand, Monkmeyer Press; *p. v* Mercer, Stock, Boston; *p. vi(l)* © Coletti, Stock, Boston; *p. vi(r)* © Grant, Taurus; *p. vii* © Siteman, Picture Cube; *p. viii(l)* © 1985, Hahn, Taurus; *p. viii(r)* Rice, Monkmeyer; *p. ix(l)* Conklin, Monkmeyer; *p. ix(r)* Douglas, The Image Works; *p. x* © Rutledge, Taurus; *p. xi* © Nikas, Picture Cube; *p. xii* © Hedman, Jeroboam; *p. xiv* Logan, Monkmeyer; *p. xv* Gallery, Stock, Boston; *p. 73* Harper & Row Publishers, Inc.; *pp. 78, 575* AP/Wide World.

Management: Concepts and Applications, Third Edition

Library of Congress Cataloging in Publication Data

Megginson, Leon C.
  Management concepts and applications / Leon C. Megginson, Donald C. Mosley, Paul H. Pietri, Jr.—3rd ed.
      p.   cm.
  Includes bibliographies and index.
  ISBN 0-06-044466-5 (Student Edition)
  ISBN 0-06-044473-8 (Teacher Edition)
  1. Management. I. Mosley, Donald C. II. Pietri, Paul H.
III. Title.
HD31.M394 1989   88-17676
658—dc19   CIP

88 89 90 91 9 8 7 6 5 4 3 2 1

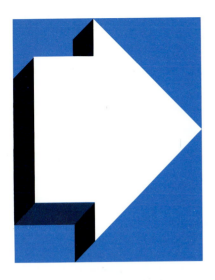

CONTENTS

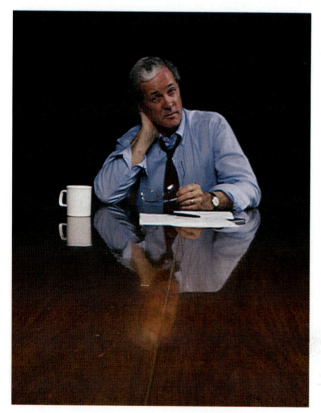

PART THREE
DESIGNING AND STAFFING AN ORGANIZATION, 176

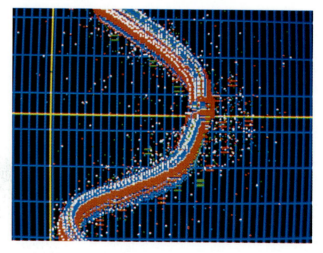

PART SIX
CURRENT ISSUES AND CHALLENGES FACING MANAGERS, 506

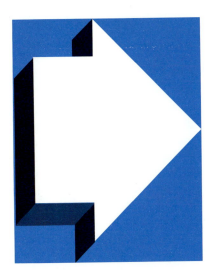

TO THE INSTRUCTOR

WHEN WE WROTE THE FIRST edition of *Management: Concepts and Applications* in 1983, we decided that certain factors would be crucial to its success:

- A clear, concise, and personal writing style
- A focus on the practical application of theory
- A strong visual appeal

This third edition of *Management* is substantially revised and updated, but we have remained committed to these key factors and think they will continue to contribute to the book's success. While many new features have been added to make this edition of *Management* even more helpful to students and instructors alike, we have retained the basic approach, structure, and writing style of the earlier editions—used by students at hundreds of colleges and universities, both in the United States and abroad, as their introductory management text.

In this edition, we continue our commitment to a book with a strong application orientation, making frequent use of examples, vignettes, incidents, and cases, both to illustrate concepts and to involve students actively in thinking about and analyzing the material. Today's students are far less insulated from the world of managers and managing than they were in earlier periods. Larger percentages of students have been—or presently are—employed. Moreover, they are bombarded from all sides with facts about organizations and managers. Professional publications such as *Business Week*, *Fortune*, and the *Wall Street Journal* are far more likely to be used in college class-

rooms today. *USA Today* and local newspapers carry stories about job opportunities, compensation, career ladders, future job growth, social responsibility and managerial ethics, and international opportunities. Corporate leaders such as Sam Walton, Ross Perot, Lee Iacocca, T. Boone Pickens, and Dr. Armand Hammer have never been so visible. Even popular television shows increasingly use the organizational world as their settings. To today's students, then, the world of organizations and management is an ever-present reality, and a textbook that fails to recognize this fact misses a teaching opportunity.

Reading about management should be dynamic, exciting, interesting, and informative, and we have tried to achieve this through the proper blend of theoretical concepts and practical applications. While application is emphasized, the text material is based upon sound current theoretical concepts. We agree with the late Kurt Lewin's observation that "nothing is so practical as good theory." The theories and concepts we present are relevant and especially applicable in the manager's world of rapid change, technological development, increasing competition, greater social responsibility, and expanding international operations. Thus, our thrust has been toward maintaining a balance between explaining relevant theories and emphasizing their applications.

SPECIAL FEATURES OF THIS EDITION

A number of special features have been incorporated into this edition to make the material come alive for the reader. Some of the special features are described here.

Chapter Opening Case. Each chapter opens with an actual case that sets the stage for the chapter material. Questions that immediately follow the case will stimulate students' thinking about the material and may serve as a basis for further discussion. There are eleven new opening cases in this edition, presenting scenarios from such well-known firms as Ford Motor Company, IBM, Apple Computer, and American Express.

What Is Your View? Appearing frequently throughout each chapter, a feature called What Is Your View? presents thought-provoking questions and problems that will stimulate students to apply key concepts presented in the text. Many instructors find these an excellent basis for broader class discussion.

Management Application and Practice (MAP). A special boxed item called Management Application and Practice (MAP) appears one or more times in each chapter to highlight a relevant concept discussed in the text and show how the concept has been applied in actual practice. Each MAP is based on data about a real-world organization, collected from *Fortune, Business Week, Forbes, USA Today*, the *Wall Street Journal*, and other professional publications.

TIPS. Most chapters also contain one or more special boxed items called TIPS, which provide helpful insights into how to perform more effectively as a manager. These helpful hints range from basic *how to's* (TIPS 9.1: "Guidance to Lawful and Unlawful Preemployment Inquiries") to instruments designed to help students gain better insights into themselves (TIPS 10.1: "Rate Your Listening Habits").

Learning Exercises. One or more Learning Exercises—consisting of cases, experiential learnings, or other structured activities—are presented at the end of each chapter to help readers apply the concepts they have learned. While more popular exercises from the previous edition have been retained, 18 are new to this edition.

Other Learning Aids. A number of other features will help students master the material. The following are a few of these.

- Each of the book's six parts begins with an introductory overview—including a concise outline of all the main concepts—to provide a framework for studying the detailed material.
- At the beginning of each chapter are learning objectives, a chapter outline, and a list of important terms that will provide direction for learning. Boldface type used for key terms in the text highlights their importance. The terms are defined in the Glosssary at the end of the text.
- Descriptive, clearly differentiated headings help students organize the material for easier learning
- Figures, tables, cartoons, and boxed materials provide visual appeal and present ideas and information in an interesting and different format.
- Photos and cartoons provide a change of pace and promote interest.
- End-of-chapter summaries reinforce major points and facilitate review.
- Review and discussion questions test students' mastery of material and stimulate further thought and learning.
- Suggested readings assist in further research.

ORGANIZATION OF THE TEXT

The book consists of 20 chapters organized into 6 parts. Part One provides the basic foundation by focusing on the reasons for studying management. The first three chapters address the issue of what management is, examine what managers do, and trace the evolution of management thought from antiquity to contemporary times.

Parts Two and Three focus on the most relevant concepts and applications involved in planning, organizing, and staffing an organization. Concepts and theories of strategic planning, departmentalization, delegation, decision making, human-resource planning, and many others come alive with numerous situations, examples, vignettes, self-insight instruments, and applications. Six chapters (4 through 9) are devoted to developing these concepts and applications.

Part Four contains some of the most current thinking in management literature, as it focuses on leading and developing an organization. Subjects covered in depth in Chapters 10 through 13 include the behavioral aspects of organization and individual behavior, such as communication, motivation, leadership, organizational culture, and change.

Part Five's three chapters focus on controlling organizational operations. A highlight of these chapters is the presentation of quantitative concepts and control techniques in a clear, easily understood manner, with many illustrations. Furthermore, there is an excellent section about using budgets and budgetary controls. Part Five also includes the newest concepts in production/operations management, covering such topics as just-in-time (JIT) inventory, robotics, and computer-assisted design (CAD) and manufacturing (CAM) systems.

Part Six presents some current issues and challenges facing today's managers. Chapter 17 is devoted to the management of international operations, and Chapter 18 explores the growing field of not-for-profit organizations. Chapter 19, completely new to this edition, addresses social responsibility and managerial ethics. Finally, Chapter 20 covers managerial careers and future trends in management.

SUPPLEMENTS

Gayle M. Ross, Kathy J. Daruty, and Elizabeth Peterson have produced excellent supplementary aids to support the text.

The *Instructor's Resource Manual*, prepared by Gayle M. Ross, Copiah-Lincoln Junior College, contains ideas for preparing and structuring a course, chapter-by-chapter teaching guide, detailed lecture outlines, supplementary lecture notes, suggestions for student involvement, suggested audiovisuals and answers to the review, discussion, and learning exercise questions. There are over 100 Transparency Masters in the *Instructor's Resource Manual*. A separate package of 70 color transparencies is also available from Harper & Row. These transparencies are all new figures.

Elizabeth Peterson, University of Northern Iowa, has provided a printed *Test Item File* with over 2,000 questions. This file includes true/false, multiple-choice, and essay questions for each chapter. The *Test Item File* is also available on Harper & Row's acclaimed microcomputerized test generation system Harper Test. It has full word-processing capabilities that permit instructors to scramble questions and add new ones. (Available IBM, Apple, and some compatibles.)

The *Student Learning Guide*, written by Kathy J. Daruty, Los Angeles Pierce College, is available for use with *Management*. It provides self-study and assessment. For each chapter the *Student Learning Guide* offers an overview, terminology review, a series of self-tests keyed to the chapter's learning objectives, and additional learning applications to enrich the students' learning.

Also available for adoption is a user-friendly software package, *Interactive Cases in Management*, by J. Daniel Sherman, University of Alabama-Huntsville. It consists of a student manual and three disks for IBM-PC.

ACKNOWLEDGMENTS

The expertise, advice, and suggestions of colleagues in our discipline, practicing managers, and students have helped us greatly to clarify our thinking about this new edition. We appreciate the perceptions, insights, and constructive contributions of our reviewers, especially Nell T. Hartley, Robert Morris College; Anthony J. Murphy, Hillsborough Community College; Alfred Rosenbloom, Lewis University; Smiley W. Weatherford, Jr., Western Carolina University; Kathy J. Daruty, Los Angeles Pierce College; Elizabeth Peterson, University of Northern Iowa; Joseph E. Cantrell, DeAnza College; Ronald B. Courchene, Community College of Allegheny County; Fred B. Hazlett, Brookdale Community College; and Gordon Heath, Rochester Community College.

We gratefully acknowledge the commitment and excellent work performed by Kay Emanuel and Rosemary Fittje in converting our dictation and original material into legible typeset. And without Suzanne S. Barnhill's editing, revising, and proofreading, this edition would not have been possible. Teresa Blakney, Lyne McMullen, Jay Megginson, and Luci Palmer provided valuable research and word-processing assistance.

We are especially indebted to Professor Emeritus Charles R. Scott of the University of Alabama, Tuscaloosa, who wrote the original chapter "Managing Operations" as it appeared in the second edition, and who updated it for this edition.

Special thanks go to Jayne Maerker, sponsoring editor of Harper & Row, for her continued original ideas, enthusiasm, and commitment to this project. All of the Harper & Row staff with whom we've worked have been especially supportive and competent, including Joan Gregory and Alice Lavin.

Our goal when we undertook the original text was to make it sufficiently successful to merit revised editions. While we have felt very positive about the first two editions, we believe that this one, above the rest, reflects our most synergistic efforts. Beginning with a foundation of clear objectives, helped by exceptionally valuable reviews, and supported by our publisher's people—especially editors and artists, and individuals who assembled supplementary material—this edition flowed remarkably smoothly. And, of course, we could not have produced this book without the wholehearted support of our wives—Joclaire, Susan, and Kathie.

We have been fortunate to have received excellent feedback from many instructors who have taught from previous editions of this book. While we appreciate positive reinforcement, it is the constructive criticism that helps us most. Will you please give us yours? We assure you that it will be appreciated and put to good use. Please write or call any of us at any time.

Leon C. Megginson (205) 675-5990
Donald C. Mosley (205) 460-6411
Paul H. Pietri (205) 460-6130

TO THE STUDENT

CONGRATULATIONS ON READING THIS PRE-FACE before setting sail on studying this third edition of *Management: Concepts and Applications.* Knowing something about where you're going and how you're going to get there always makes a voyage easier and more enjoyable.

Management is a dynamic, exciting, and rewarding field of study! That's why you'll find this text interesting to read. It will help you evaluate the effectiveness of managers and organizations for whom you presently work or have worked in the past. Although many of you may not at present aspire to a management career, one day (perhaps sooner than you think!) you may be given an opportunity to become a manager; having taken this course may help you decide whether or not management is for you. Furthermore, insights gained in this course can help you obtain more meaningful data regarding prospective employers. Recruiters don't often hear questions such as, "Do you have a formal performance appraisal system?" "What is the management philosophy of this organization?" "What types of career development opportunities do you offer?" You can learn about these and similar subjects from this text. You'll find ample charts and figures to highlight major points. Moreover, there are numerous examples involving real companies, many of which—IBM, Apple Computer, Ford Motor Company, Pizza Hut, Adidas, and others—are already familiar to you.

Briefly, here is an overview of some of the major features of this book, designed to make your reading journey more rewarding.

1. Each chapter begins with an actual case from the "real world," designed to capture some of the key issues covered in the chapter. References back to the case are made to reinforce key concepts as they are developed within the chapter.

2. Each chapter also begins with an outline, a set of learning objectives, and a list of important terms discussed in the chapter and defined in the Glossary.

3. Throughout each chapter are questions entitled What Is Your View? that challenge you to apply concepts you have studied.

4. Each chapter contains boxed segments, called either Management Application and Practice (MAP) or TIPS. Each MAP demonstrates how the concepts presented are practiced in actual organizations. TIPS gives you an insight into some aspect of your own values or behavior (such as discovering what you want from *your* job), or steps in how to handle a specific management situation (such as how to develop a contingency plan).

Other elements designed to aid the learning process include the following.

- Clear organization of material. Headings are well differentiated and follow the outlines given at the beginning of each part and each chapter.
- Ample visuals, including tables, figures, and occasional cartoons (a little humor can help

make a point, too!), complement the text and add variety.

- Important terms are in boldface type.
- End-of-chapter summaries serve as good reviews.
- Review and discussion questions follow each chapter.
- Learning exercises, such as cases and experiential learning exercises, provide opportunities for you to apply what you have learned.
- Suggested additional readings on the material presented may prove helpful if outside work is required.

An excellent *Student Learning Guide*, written by Kathy J. Daruty, is available to accompany this text. While your teacher may or may not require it, if you have found such guides helpful in past courses, then you may want to give it a try. If it's not carried in your bookstore, you may order it from:

Harper & Row, Publishers, Inc.
College Division
10 East 53rd Street
New York, NY 10022-5299

We think that you will enjoy this book and hope that you'll find its style and presentation especially helpful in mastering the material presented. Will you please write us and give us your feedback about the book—especially your suggestions for improving future editions? We wish you the best in achieving your objectives in this course, and in your managerial careers.

The Authors

MANAGEMENT

PART ONE

Why Study Management?

The difference between a company that is a leader in its industry and one that is a follower is management—superior human performance.

—RICHARD S. REYNOLDS, JR.

ACCORDING TO LAWRENCE APPLEY, former president of the American Management Association, "Management is the management of people, not the management of things." The objective of Part One is to develop that thought and to show why you should study management. In doing so, we explain what management is, what managers do, and how management thought has developed. On the facing page is an overview of what is covered in Part One.

Chapter 1 explains what management is: making things happen in an organization. Chapter 2 discusses what managers do: *how* they make things happen. Chapter 3 traces the development of management thought from ancient times to the present.

WHY STUDY MANAGEMENT?

1. What management is

Importance of management	Functions needed universally Knowledge applicable universally Managers necessary in every organization
Purposes of management	Reach objectives Maintain balance among conflicting goals Achieve efficiency and effectiveness
Meanings and applications of management	An occupational grouping An individual or a group An academic discipline A process

2. What managers do

Levels and types of management	Levels of management Types of organizational functions Types of managers	
Managerial functions	Planning Organizing Staffing	Leading Controlling
How managers spend their time		
Skills of a manager	Conceptual Human-relations	Administrative Technical

3. The evolution of management thought

Early developments	Feudal system Guild system	Cottage system Factory system
Effects of the Industrial Revolution		
Developments in the United States		
Scientific approach	Taylor's scientific approach Fayol's administrative approach	
Behavioral approach	Sheldon's philosophy Hawthorne experiments Follett's integration process Barnard's theory of authority	
Contemporary approaches	Management science Systems approach Contingency approach In search of excellence	
Evolutionary process speeding up		

1

What Management Is: Making Things Happen

Learning Objectives

After studying the material in this chapter, you should be able to do the following:
- Explain that management is found wherever people function in groups.
- Describe how management is needed to reach organizational objectives, balance conflicting goals, and achieve efficiency and effectiveness.

Some Important Terms

organization
management
universality of management
contingency approach
stakeholders
efficiency
effectiveness

concept
principle
profession
entrepreneurs
managers
intrapreneurship
supervision

Outline of the Chapter

Management is needed in all organizations
Definition of management
Management functions are universal
Management knowledge is universal
Managers are needed in every organization
Why management is needed
To reach objectives
To maintain balance between conflicting goals
To achieve efficiency and effectiveness
What management is
Management as both art and science
Management as a profession
Different meanings of the term *management*
Different applications of the term *management*
Summary

Labor can do nothing without capital, capital nothing without labor, and neither can do anything without the guiding genius of management.
—W. L. MACKENZIE KING

The Music Makers

From age 10, when he received a trumpet for Christmas, Charles Overman* had loved music. Some of his happiest moments in college were those spent playing in a small dance band, for parties and other social functions.

Charlie's work as a chemical engineer kept him busy during the week, but on weekends he was a lost sheep. One day Charlie heard that a neighborhood lounge needed a four-piece group to play on Saturday nights. He managed to sell the services of his band sight unseen and then recruited three other players to complete the group. By the next Saturday night, the Music Makers were in business. The job lasted several months, until lack of business forced the owner to discontinue the use of a band.

Because all the band's members had played music regularly at one time or another, they looked for opportunities to play again. After several informal discussions, they decided to keep the band, without appointing a specific leader. Each one would try to line up jobs, and the money would be split evenly among the members.

At first, things went very slowly, because few jobs were available. Finally, Charlie decided to assume leadership of the band. Without telling the others, he mailed form letters to clubs and organizations advertising the band, placed advertisements in local papers, bought new music and equipment, and had official contracts—with new rates—printed. Charlie's wife handled most of the bookings, kept the records, answered the telephone, and mailed out the contracts.

Charlie then announced to the band members that in the future he would handle all bookings, that any prospective clients the other members lined up would have to be submitted to him, and that he would collect the leader's share of the income and would split the rest of the money evenly among the other band members.

The band members did not like the new arrangement. It had been "our band," and now it was "Charlie's band." They also felt that since they played the same number of hours and appeared at the same places they should all get the same amount of pay.

But after Charlie began managing the band, things began to happen. Business picked up immediately. Soon the Music Makers were in great demand, with over 50 advance bookings, at much higher rates. Now the problem was how to limit engagements to Saturday nights, with an occasional Friday night or Sunday afternoon job, as Charlie had decided.

What do Charlie's actions explain about the need for—and role of—management in an organization? ■

THIS CASE ILLUSTRATES THE BASIC THEME of this book, and particularly of this chapter. Managers, who are needed in all types of organizations to make things happen, require special abilities that must be developed. In discussing this subject, we see where and why management is needed. Then we will also explain what it is.

* Name disguised.

MANAGEMENT IS NEEDED IN ALL ORGANIZATIONS

"Who needs management?" you ask. "Business!" is the reply. Of course, this answer is partially correct, but it is incomplete, because management is also needed in all types of organized activities and in all types of organizations, as shown in Figure 1.1. In fact, every time two or more people interact to achieve a common objective, an **organization** exists. And wherever there is such an organization, management is needed.

In summary, since we are constantly being managed or are managing others, a greater understanding of management should make life more predictable and comfortable for all of us. As you will see from the questions that follow, you come into contact with management many times every day.

What is your view?

Think back over the past week. How many managers have you interacted with or seen in action? How about the following examples?

1. Manager of a retail store.
2. Coach or manager of a sports team.
3. The leader of your place of worship.
4. A government official (president, governor, mayor, head of an agency).
5. Your college's president or a dean or department head.

Can you name others? In what ways were each of these people performing managerial functions?

Management is as old as humanity itself and is needed wherever there is organized human activity. However, there is still little understanding of what it is and what it is supposed to do. Management is needed for goods-producing and service-performing activities, in private and public organizations, and in other groups, both large and small.

Definition of Management

Now that we have established the need for management, we can present a working definition of the term and place it in its proper perspective for the purpose of this book. *Management can be defined as working with human, financial, and physical resources to determine, interpret, and achieve organizational objectives by performing the functions of planning, organizing, staffing, leading, and controlling* (see Figure 1.2). Notice that the purpose of management is to set and reach the organization's objective(s). In doing so, management functions are performed, and human resources (people), financial resources (money), and physical resources (facilities, equipment, supplies) are used. TIPS 1.1 can help you better understand what management is.

Management Functions Are Universal

You should be able to understand where and why management is needed if you understand the concept of **universality of management.** The universal nature of management results from this fact: The functions of management must be performed by managers in all types of organizations, in all cultures of the world.

FIGURE 1.1
Managers are needed in
all types of
organizations.

General Charles de Gaulle made a suggestion to his wife about the way she should manage the household. Mme. de Gaulle, who was noted for the care and effectiveness of her housekeeping, stared up at her tall, stern, overbearing husband and replied, "You manage France, and I'll manage my house."

Management functions found in all organizations. Many students believe that "management" only applies to business, especially big business. This is a misconception, as managerial functions must be performed in all organizations: small businesses and large ones; public, semipublic, and private organizations; profit-oriented and not-for-profit organizations; manufacturing firms, service organizations (remember the Music Makers?), and retail concerns; and American, foreign, and multinational firms. In other words, the functions of management are basically the same for any kind of organization. Although they may be applied differently by different managers—depending on variables such as the type of organization,[1] culture,[2] and types of employers and employees—the functions remain the same.

Incidentally, the world of work is constantly and drastically changing. For example, around 90 to 97 percent of the 15 million U.S. businesses are small, with fewer than 100 employees. But they hire around two-thirds of all new employees.[3] Also, 9 out of every 10 new jobs created before the year 2000

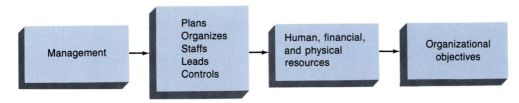

FIGURE 1.2
What management is.

will be in the service industries, such as fast foods, transportation, communications, information, trade, finance, real estate, government, health care, travel, and recreation.[4]

Because all managers operate by achieving goals through the coordinated efforts of other people, we see many instances in which managers transfer from one department to another or even from one type of organization to another and still are able to do their management jobs effectively.

Robert McNamara, an analytical "whiz kid" in the War Department during World War II, became president of Ford Motor Company, secretary of defense in the Kennedy administration, and then head of the World Bank. Arjay Miller, president of Ford Motor Company during the turbulent 1960s,

---

TIPS 1.1   Differentiating *Managing* from *Doing*

You might think of a manager's job as being somewhat similar to that of a coach. Just as there is a difference between coaching and playing, there is a distinction between managing and doing. The coach's managerial job consists of having players prepared, organizing and conducting practices, making required adjustments in game play, and making strategic decisions during games. But players perform the actual executing or *doing* activities in the game, not the coach.

Why not try your hand at differentiating between managing and doing in a business setting? Assume that Lee Iacocca, as chairman of Chrysler Motors, engages in each of the activities shown below. Check each of those in which he is *managing* as opposed to *doing*.

1. _____ Calling on a major corporate customer to try to close a sale of 300 Chrysler cars for the company's fleet.
2. _____ Meeting with union representatives to resolve an impasse in labor contract negotiations.
3. _____ Discussing with top executives the company budget for the upcoming fiscal year.

4. _____ Making a speech to a meeting of Wall Street investment analysts.
5. _____ Approving a request by one of his managers to spend $5,000,000 to upgrade plant facilities.
6. _____ Giving a motivational talk to the Chrysler marketing and sales team.
7. _____ Approving the decision by Chrysler to begin offering newer, broader, and more extensive service contract warranties on new Chrysler vehicles.
8. _____ Personally tinkering with some fender design changes for a new car model.

In the situations above, Iacocca was performing some managing activities and some doing activities. Items 1, 2, 4, and 8 were *doing* activities, and items 3, 5, 6, and 7 were *managing*. There's no question that *doing* can be very important, especially to managers who have *doing* talents. But many managers are effective *doers* who fail at their overall jobs because they perform their managerial tasks poorly. The focus in this text is on *managing*, in contrast to *doing*, activities.

served also as dean of the College of Business at Stanford University in California. He performed very successfully in both positions.

Functions cannot always be performed successfully. Chapter 3 will show that the **contingency approach** to management has somewhat weakened the universality concept. Managers must still perform the same basic functions, but the extent to which they use each one, and the manner in which they apply it, varies with differing situations.

If managers perform their functions effectively in one situation, there is some probability that they will do the same in other situations. Because of the many variables involved, however, there is no assurance of success when a given manager moves from one type of activity to another (see MAP 1.1).

What is your view?

John Harris is 27, has a high school education, and is a first-line supervisor for the Acme Manufacturing Company. He supervises 21 machinists and is the best machinist supervisor the company has ever had. Because John possesses the management skills required to do an effective job of first-line supervision, does the universality of management concept mean that he would also have the skills necessary to become an effective company president? Would he be able to become supervisor of another machinery department? Explain.

Management Knowledge Is Universal

Management is also universal in that it uses a systematic body of knowledge, including laws, principles, and concepts that tend to be true in all managerial situations. This knowledge can be applied to all organized human endeavors, whether business, government, educational, social, religious, or other. It is equally applicable at all levels of management in the same organization, from the lowest to highest levels. It can therefore be concluded that *if a manager has this fundamental knowledge and knows how to apply it to a given situation,*

Management Application and Practice 1.1   Jack Nicklaus—The Cautious Entrepreneur

Jack Nicklaus, an outstanding professional golfer and, at 47, the oldest Master's Tournament champion ever, recently said, "You shouldn't be involved with things you really don't know about. It's taken me 25 years of being on the periphery of my business to learn that." Nicklaus was referring to his decision to get out of non-golf-related businesses and concentrate on golf-oriented ones.

When he turned pro in 1961, he hired a manager to organize and manage Golden Bear International, Inc. (GBI), a vehicle for Nicklaus's businesses. While his golf winnings and endorsements made money for GBI, some of his business ventures did not. His entry into enterprises such as a Pontiac dealership, a radio station, a travel agency, a home security firm, an oil and gas general partnership, and real estate developments did not turn out well.

In November 1985, Nicklaus had to tell his bankers that he was not sure he could finish a $35 million golf community in Westchester County, New York. At that time, he took personal charge of GBI and started concentrating on activities he knew most about—golf course design, at which he is considered to be the best, and making golf gear.

SOURCE: Roger Lowenstein, "A Golfer Becomes an Executive: Jack Nicklaus's Business Education," *Wall Street Journal,* January 27, 1987, p. 37.

he or she should be able to perform the managerial functions efficiently and effectively if he or she has the flexibility to adapt to the new situation.

Dwight D. Eisenhower is a classical example of the universality concept in action. He served at various times as commander of the Allied forces in Europe during World War II, president of Columbia University in New York, commander of NATO forces, and president of the United States for two terms.

Managers Are Needed in Every Organization

What is your view?

Before reading the following material, see if you know where managers are found in the United States. Can you answer these questions about the U.S. economy?

1. What industry hires the most managers and administrators?
2. What organization is the largest employer?
3. About how many managers and administrators are there?
4. About what percentage of all employed persons are managers and administrators?
5. What percentage of private firms have sales of $1 million or more?

If you asked your friends where most managers are found, they probably would answer, "In manufacturing plants." Yet, as you can see from Table 1.1, almost twice as many managers and administrators are found in wholesale and retail trade as in manufacturing, and over half again as many are in services. Notice that 20 percent of all employees in finance, real estate, and insurance are managers. In other words, managers are needed in every organization, as was shown in Figure 1.1.

The largest employer in the United States is the federal government, with around 3 million civilian and 2.5 million military personnel. The largest nongovernmental employer in the United States was the American Telephone & Telegraph Company (AT&T), which had over 1 million employees before its breakup in 1984. About 205,000 of those employees were managers. As shown in Figure 1.3, the two largest private employers in the United States

TABLE 1.1
Numbers and Percentage of Managers Classified by Type of Industry

SOURCE: Data compiled from U.S. Department of Labor, Bureau of Labor Statistics, *Handbook of Labor Statistics* (Washington: Government Printing Office, 1985).

Type of industry	Number of managers and administrators (in thousands)	Percentage of all managers	Percentage of all employees in industry who are managers
Wholesale and retail	3,023	29	15
Services	2,563	24	8
Manufacturing	1,546	15	8
Finance, real estate, and insurance	1,257	12	20
Public administration	885	8	17
Transportation and public utilities	618	6	9
Construction	548	5	10
Mining	126	1	12
Agriculture	31	0	1

FIGURE 1.3
The five largest private
U.S. employers.
SOURCE: Copyright 1987, USA
TODAY. Used with permission.

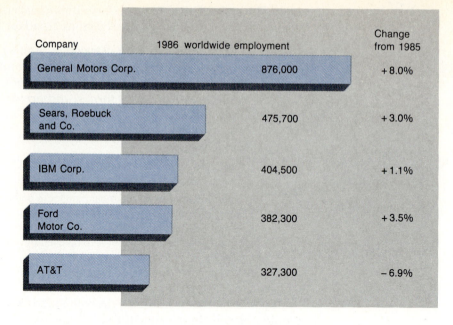

Company	1986 worldwide employment	Change from 1985
General Motors Corp.	876,000	+8.0%
Sears, Roebuck and Co.	475,700	+3.0%
IBM Corp.	404,500	+1.1%
Ford Motor Co.	382,300	+3.5%
AT&T	327,300	−6.9%

in 1986 were General Motors, with 876,000 employees, and Sears, Roebuck and Company, with 475,700. There are over 12 million executives, administrators, and managers in the United States (excluding farms). As shown in Table 1.2, they account for over 11 percent of all employees.

As indicated earlier, there are around 15 million private firms in the United States. Between 90 and 97 percent of them can be classified as "small business," and about 95 percent of the firms have annual sales of less than $1 million.

As you can see from these figures, you have the greatest chance of becoming a manager in a small company engaging in trade, services, or manufacturing.

TABLE 1.2
Employed Persons,
Classified by
Occupation

SOURCE: Compiled from data in
the *107th Statistical Abstract
of the United States,* 1987,
Table 657.

Occupation	Number employed (in thousands)	Percentage of all employed persons
Executives, administrators, and managers	12,221	11
Professional specialists	13,630	13
Technicians	3,255	3
Sales	12,667	12
Administrative support and clerical	17,309	16
Services	14,441	14
Precision production, crafts, and repair	13,340	12
Operators, fabricators, and laborers	16,816	16
Farming, forestry, and fishing	3,470	3
Total	107,150	100

WHY MANAGEMENT IS NEEDED

Management is needed in organizations because without it people would go off on their own and work toward obtaining their own objectives independently of others. Without management in organizations, effort would be wasted, as was true of the Music Makers in the opening case before Charlie became the leader. Therefore, management is needed to (1) reach objectives, (2) maintain balance between conflicting goals, and (3) achieve efficiency and effectiveness.

To Reach Objectives

Management is needed to reach organizational and personal objectives. This need was well expressed by Lawrence A. Appley, past president of the American Management Association, when he said, "The basic function of management is to attain objectives through action taken by the members of the organization. Since dynamics are the forces which produce the action and motion, it follows that the dynamics of management are those forces which produce the action which is required . . . [Those] forces of management do not just happen. They must be given impetus by . . . [managers]."[5]

The objective of most public and private organizations is to perform a service for the public. To be sure, private firms are expected to receive a profit from their operations, but in a capitalistic economy, this is acceptable and even considered to be in the public interest. Even in profit-oriented firms, however, the objective must be to perform a service for others in order to make a profit for the owners. Therefore, if you want to be a manager in a private business, you must keep in mind the need to have "profitable service" as your primary objective. The reason for this is that if the firm stops giving service, people will no longer patronize it, and profits will not result. If there are no profits, however, the company will soon be unable to perform the needed service.

To Maintain Balance Between Conflicting Goals

It should be emphasized at this point that managers need to maintain balance among the conflicting objectives, goals, and activities of the stakeholders of an organization. **Stakeholders** are all those who have a stake in the organization's success, including employees, owners, customers, government authorities, creditors, and others. There must be a balance between such things as income and expenditures, individual and internal expenditures, the services offered versus the costs involved, and the demands of different groups.

As shown in Figure 1.4, management holds in trust the interest of many different groups. It performs the function of stewardship on behalf of the *owners*, who are seeking a satisfactory return on their investment. The return may be profits (as in a business) or service (as in city, state, or federal government). It must also consider the best interests of the *employees*, who seek good pay, safe and comfortable working conditions, fair and equitable treatment, the greatest possible job security, and more time off. The interest of the *public*, including consumer groups, environmentalists, and civil rights advocates, must be looked after. Management must also please its *customers*, *clients*, and *consumers*, for without them the organization would be without

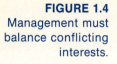
FIGURE 1.4
Management must balance conflicting interests.

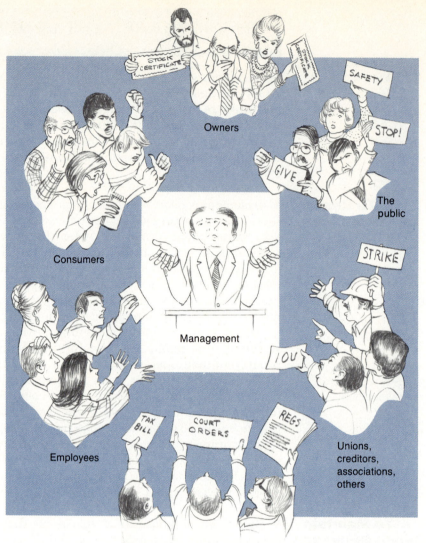

Federal, state, and local governments

purpose. Others—such as *creditors, suppliers, union leaders,* and *trade associations*—must also be considered. Finally, management must satisfy the needs and demands of various *governments*. If management favors one group at the expense of the others, it will, in the long run, tend to create an imbalance that will be detrimental to the organization.

As you can see, this challenge involves balancing the internal operations with the external environment. Because of the emphasis on social responsibility and managerial ethics (see Chapter 19), management can no longer give priority to the owners and employees. Instead, it must satisfy those on the outside whose future is tied to that of the organization.

To perform this new and more exacting role, managers have at least three sets of relationships, as shown in Figure 1.5. First, they must maintain satisfactory personal relationships with their family and friends. Then, organizational relationships must be maintained with employees and other managers. Finally, many often conflicting external relationships must be maintained with the organization's "public."

To Achieve Efficiency and Effectiveness

An organization's performance can be measured in many different ways. Two of the most common ways are in terms of efficiency and effectiveness. There is a considerable difference between these concepts.

Efficiency, the ability to "get things done correctly," is a mathematical concept—the ratio of output to input. An efficient manager is one who achieves higher outputs (results, productivity, performance) relative to the inputs (labor, materials, money, machines, and time) needed to achieve them. In other words, a manager who can minimize the cost of the resources used to attain a given output is considered efficient. Or, conversely, the manager who can maximize output for a given amount of input is considered efficient.

Effectiveness is the ability to "do the right things," or to get things accomplished. This includes choosing the most appropriate objectives and the proper methods of achieving the objectives. That is, effective managers select the "right" things to do and the "right" methods for getting them done.

One of us once heard a sergeant tell a soldier, "Sort these reports by date and number before you destroy them." The reports were sorted and then destroyed. The soldier may have been acting efficiently, *but he was far from performing* effectively!

According to management expert Peter Drucker, effectiveness is the secret of success for any organization. For managers, "the pertinent question is not how to do things right, but how to find the right things to do, and to concentrate resources and efforts on them."[6] It is much easier to say this

FIGURE 1.5
The manager's relationships.

SOURCE: Adapted from Donald C. Mosley, Leon C. Megginson, and Paul H. Pietri, Jr., *Supervisory Management: The Art of Working with and through People* (Cincinnati, OH: South-Western Publishing Co., 1985), p. 21.

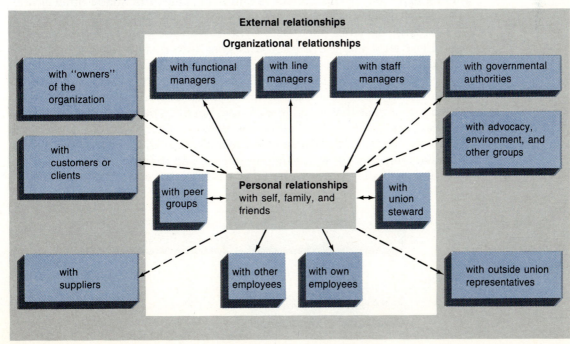

than to do it. A real stumbling block to practicing managers is knowing *what should be done* rather than *how to do* routine activities.

WHAT MANAGEMENT IS

We now come to a difficult issue: identifying specifically what management is. To do this, we must look at the following topics:

1. Management as both art and science.

2. Management as a profession.

3. Different meanings of the term *management*.

4. Different applications of the term *management*.

Management as Both Art and Science

As shown earlier, this book is based on the assumption that there is a systematic body of knowledge constituting a core of principles of management that tend to be true in most managerial situations. It is also assumed that *if managers understand this body of knowledge and know how to apply it to given situations, they should be able to perform the managerial functions both efficiently and effectively, wherever they are performed.*

Relationship between theory and practice. The need for a theory of management was expressed by Henri Fayol, a leading French industrialist, about 70 years ago, when he said, "The reason for the absence of management teaching . . . is absence of theory; without theory no teaching is possible."[7] Fayol indicated the need for a theory that would include a collection of principles, roles, methods, and procedures that were tried and checked by general experience. This lament is still being voiced by many other academicians and practitioners.

Leonardo da Vinci once said, "Those who are enamoured of practice without science are like a pilot who goes into a ship without rudder or compass and never has any certainty where he is going. *Practice should always be based upon a sound knowledge of theory.*" Thus, there is a complementary relationship between theory and practice, as shown in Figure 1.6. A theory cannot be developed in a vacuum but must be based on the practical experience and observation of practitioners. In turn, theorists develop the theory that explains the cause-effect relationships involved in a set of phenomena. From the theory, principles are derived that must be tested by the practitioner. If they prove to be false, the theorists must again attempt to

FIGURE 1.6
Management practice is based on a systematic body of knowledge.

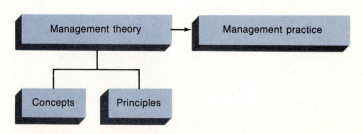

develop a new theory or enunciate new principles. Therefore, the relationship between theory and practice is: (1) a theory is developed; (2) it is applied in actual practice; (3) it proves effective and is accepted; or (4) it proves defective and so must be revised or replaced by a different theory.

In conclusion, management theory, well understood, is a basis for improving the management action of all practicing managers.

Difference between concepts and principles. It is best to start this discussion by explaining the difference between concepts and principles. A **concept** is an abstract or generic idea generalized from particular instances that serves as the basis for an action or discussion. A **principle** can be considered a general belief or proposition sufficiently applicable to a situation to provide a guide to thought or action in that situation.

What is your view?

"There is a limit to the number of subordinates a given manager can effectively manage."

Is this statement a management concept or principle? Why?

"Work expands to fill the time available to do it."

Is this statement a concept or principle? Why?

As is true in the other social sciences, management has few principles. There are, however, many useful concepts. It is believed that the lists of so-called principles found in some earlier management textbooks were not principles but generalizations, or concepts. But we do believe that there are *some* principles of management. These principles are in the form of general propositions, or statements of *probable* cause-and-effect relationships, that provide guides to thought or action in the process of making and applying management decisions.

It should be emphasized at this point that we are *not* saying that management is a science. We cannot accept the assumption of Frederick W. Taylor, "the father of scientific management," that management is the mechanical application of certain principles. Instead, we believe that Oliver Sheldon, the eminent British management philosopher and practitioner, was correct when he said nearly half a century ago that "undoubtedly, there is a science of management, but it is to be sharply distinguished from the art which employs that science."[8]

Management as a combination of both art and science. Thus it is not a question of management being either an art or a science. Instead, management is a combination of both (as shown in Figure 1.7), and this combination is not a fixed proportion but is found in varying proportions in differing situations.

In general, *effective managers use the scientific approach in making decisions. In many aspects of planning, leading, communicating, and dealing with the human element,* however, *managers must also use the artistic approach.* In short, management is not so much a hard science, like chemistry or physics, but rather it has more in common with the social sciences such as psychology and sociology.

FIGURE 1.7
Management is both an
art and a science.

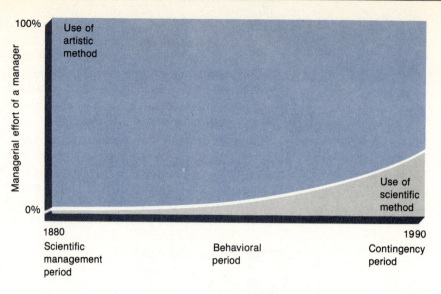

**Management as a
Profession**

Many efforts have been made to classify management as a profession. If it is one, it must meet the following criteria for a **profession:**[9]

1. A codified body of knowledge.

2. A long period of formal education and training, controlled by the profession.

3. Controlled entry, usually by means of a formal examination.

4. An enforced code of ethics, with discipline imposed on those who break it.

5. Unselfish service to others.

As indicated, there is at present a relatively uniform body of management knowledge. Also, most managers in the middle and upper levels of management have had long years of formal education and training. This trend is being assisted and enhanced by the rise in the numbers of excellent schools of business and management and by management development programs. Frequently, however, there is no prior training or education given to new managers, as shown by the following example.

At a management seminar conducted by one of us for a national company, one manager was asked to explain her first managerial position. She said: "About eight years ago, I came to work on a Monday morning as an engineer. At noon, I was no longer an engineer but a manager. I had lunch with the director of engineering services, who offered me the job of head engineer. It seems that the former head had resigned unexpectedly, and the position had to be filled quickly. I had no management training or experience and was in a state of shock. It took me a few years to learn the difference between being an engineer and being a manager, but things seem to have worked out."

There is little effort to control entry into management, but several management groups do have accreditation programs. Also, many professional organizations, companies, and managers are striving for greater social responsibility and more ethical behavior.

For example, the Administrative Management Society has a Certified Administrative Manager program. The American Society of Personnel Administrators also has a rigorous certification program for its members.

The professions of law, medicine, and accountancy are licensed, and serious infractions of the professional codes may result in disbarment from practice in a given profession. At present, management has no such professional monitoring body or agency and therefore cannot be classified as a profession in the strictest sense of the word. It can, however, be considered a profession in the same general sense that allows engineers, teachers, writers, and other educated and dedicated workers to be considered professionals.

Different Meanings of the Term Management

Definitions in management theory and practice are neither constant nor universally accepted. This is particularly true of some of the most frequently used terms, such as *management*, *entrepreneurship*, and *supervision*, which are often used to mean different things to different people in different organizations. But the following are our definitions.

Management as distinct from entrepreneurship. In economics, the factors of production are land, labor, capital, and entrepreneurship (ownership). (The labor factor includes both the workers who produce and distribute the goods and services and the managers who make the decisions to produce and distribute the products.) **Entrepreneurs,** by definition, conceive of, gather the resources for, organize, and run businesses. They tend to be risk takers who are motivated by the desire for profit.

Management, by contrast, involves organizing and running businesses and other organizations, but it is usually not concerned with conceiving or owning them. **Managers,** therefore, are high-level employees who identify more closely with other employees than with the owners.

With the rapid explosion of innovation in small, service-type organizations, one of the most pressing problems facing executives of large organizations is how to develop the new products and services needed to compete. One answer may be the introduction of **intrapreneurship**—allowing people the freedom to take an entrepreneurial role in large, bureaucratic groups.[10] This arrangement involves executives encouraging their employees and managers to come up with new product and business opportunity ideas.

IBM used the intrapreneurial approach when developing and introducing the IBM-PC. It asked a group of its executives and employees to set up an entirely new division—separate and distinct from the existing organization—to develop the new consumer product. A new organization was formed, a separate headquarters and plant were established, and new research, design, production, and marketing divisions were organized. The reason for this arrangement? The "old" IBM was oriented toward selling its products to commercial, industrial, and not-for-profit buyers. The PC was oriented toward the consumer.

Management as distinct from supervision. Generally, **supervision** is leading and directing lower-level employees in the organization. (The word *supervise* is derived from the Latin words *super* and *videre*, that is, to "see from above," or oversee.) Common names for the supervisory position are *foreman* and *first-line supervisor*. (Foremen were originally the biggest and strongest workers, who walked in front of the other workers to see that they did their share.) In most economic systems, foremen and supervisors are not included as part of management. Instead, these positions are considered the top level that operative or hourly employees normally can reach. Managers come in at the next highest level and progress upward from there.

From a practical point of view, however, foremen and first-line supervisors do perform the same managerial functions as upper-level managers. Therefore, we think it is important to treat them as part of management, and we do so in this book.

Different Applications of the Term Management

Much confusion also arises from the fact that there are at least four different applications of the term *management*. Management can be used to refer to any one of the following:

1. An occupational grouping within an organization.
2. An individual who is a part of that group.
3. An academic discipline.
4. A process.

An occupational grouping. Management can mean a group of people performing managerial tasks and functions. It is used collectively to include all the individuals in that group.

The employees of a chemical plant went on strike; the managers lived in the plant while they ran it. Newspaper headlines read: "Management Runs Plant While Workers on Strike."

An individual. Any individual who performs managerial functions or is part of that overall group is considered to be part of management.

Bill, a premed student at a small college, worked as an orderly in a nearby hospital. At the end of the first day on the job, a friend asked how things were going. "I like it fine," said Bill. "I had some problems, but I took them up with management [the head nurse] and she solved them."

An academic discipline. Management is an area of academic specialization, a concentration of courses, or a field of study.

Several students were discussing their majors during registration. One was studying history, another sociology, and John was "going into management."

A process. Management is also a process, because it involves performing a series of specific activities or functions.

Gayle is sometimes asked what she does as department head at Women's Fashions, a large retail store. She answers this way: "I oversee 15 salespersons in three departments here at the store. In addition, I coordinate with our buyers in making decisions about styles and fabrics that we will carry. I handle complaints that my salespeople can't handle, and my biggest responsibility is keeping my salespeople motivated to do a good job."

Having explained what management is, we must further examine the nature, concepts, and functions of management to answer questions such as: What do managers do? How do they perform their job? What skills are required? What are the characteristics of successful managers? These concerns are discussed in the next chapter. The terms *administration, management,* and *supervision* will be used interchangeably to denote both the process of management and those who perform it.

SUMMARY

People form organizations because they can accomplish more by cooperating with one another in groups than they can by working alone. An organization is a group of two or more people working together to achieve a common objective. Management is needed whenever people work together in an organization, and this is particularly true in the increasing number of small businesses and service industry companies.

The managerial functions of planning, organizing, staffing, leading, and controlling must be performed by anyone who manages any type of organized activity, whether it is a business enterprise or not. These functions are performed at *all* levels of an organization, regardless of its type or size. This truth is called the principle of universality of management.

Management achieves its objectives through coordinating the development and use of scarce financial, physical, and human resources. Yet management itself is the most important of those resources. Managers must balance the conflicting demands made by stakeholders such as owners, employees, customers, creditors, and government authorities with a stake in the organization.

Management is an art based on the scientific method of operating. It is an art in the human-resources area, but it uses the scientific approach in the quantitative and mathematical areas. There is some inherent quality found in good managers that permits them to move from one managerial situation to another and still operate efficiently.

The term *management* is confusing because it may refer to an occupational grouping, an individual, an academic discipline, or a process. Management is also performed differently at different levels and for different organizational functions. As indicated, management is needed in all human groupings, and the more successful organizations tend to be those that have more dynamic management.

Similarly, effective managers must be constantly alert for new and better ways to perform their managerial activities. They must be willing to adjust and adapt to a variety of situations, such as improvements in technology and the changing social, political, religious, technological, and economic environments in which they operate. Those who are unable to make these transitions will not remain competitive for long.

REVIEW QUESTIONS

1. Is it true that managers are needed in all organizations? Explain.
2. What does the universality of management concept mean?
3. In what types of organizations are managers needed? Explain.
4. Why is management needed?
5. Distinguish between (a) entrepreneurship and intrapreneurship, and (b) management and supervision.
6. What are the four different applications of the term *management*?

DISCUSSION QUESTIONS

1. Do you think the universality of management concept is valid? Explain.
2. Is management really as important as the authors claim? Explain.
3. Are entrepreneurs managers? Explain.
4. Can you think of areas of organized human activity that do not need management? Explain.
5. Is management (a) an art, (b) a science, or (c) a profession? Discuss.

LEARNING EXERCISE 1.1

The Technical Expert*

Walter White is a new manager of a group of research engineers. He is young, but in addition to having an excellent technical background, he is also sensitive to people.

Bill Wilson is a subordinate of Walter White and a supervisor of a work group of 12 engineers. Bill was promoted to a supervisory position before Walter became his manager. Bill has 20 years' experience with the company, and his peers marvel at his technical abilities.

However, since Bill was made supervisor, about a year ago, there have been problems in his group. His subordinates complain: "Bill doesn't always tell us what he wants done. Then he gets mad if we don't do it"; "He seems to be too secretive. We want to know what's going on"; "Bill is such a perfectionist that you can never do your work well enough, but he sure is quick to point out your mistakes."

Walter decided he should have a talk with Bill. He began by asking Bill to identify his strong points as a supervisor. To Walter's surprise, Bill said, "I think I am good at communicating with my people. I can motivate them to get the job done. When they slack off, I know how to perk them up."

After some discussion, Walter suggested that Bill might be happier in a research position. Bill, who apparently enjoyed the power of the supervisory position, said, "I like being a manager. I don't intend to go back to being just an engineer."

Walter faces a dilemma. He could force Bill to accept a nonsupervisory position without cutting his pay. But he is afraid that Bill would quit. The company badly needs his technical expertise, and he has been with them for 20 years. However, if Bill continues as a supervisor of the group, the whole division will suffer.

Questions

1. How much consideration does the company owe Bill for his 20 years of service?
   _____very much _____some _____a little _____none at all
2. Should Walter try to spend time training Bill to be an effective supervisor?
   _____yes _____no. If you answered "yes," how long should Walter allow for Bill's training and improvement? _____
3. Assuming that Bill does not respond to supervisory training, what do you recommend that Walter do?
   _____ A. Continue to work with Bill and keep him in his supervisory position. He is too valuable to the company to lose. Maybe you could get him an assistant to help with the people problems.

* Published with permission of National Association for Management, 1983.

_____ B. Force Bill to accept a nonsupervisory position. Even though you realize that he has been with the company 20 years and he might quit, you must do this for the benefit of the division.

NOTES

1. Myron D. Fottler, "Is Management Really Generic?" *Academy of Management Review* 6 (January 1981): 1–12.
2. Uma Sekaran, "Are U.S. Organizational Concepts and Measures Transferable to Another Culture? An Empirical Investigation," *Academy of Management Journal* 24 (June 1981): 409–417.
3. Constance Mitchell, "3 Million More Jobs Forecast," *USA Today*, March 31, 1986, p. 1B.
4. "Work in the Future," *AARP Bulletin*, July 1987, pp. 13–14.
5. Lawrence A. Appley, quoted in *Management News*, November 1953, p. 1.
6. Peter F. Drucker, *Managing for Results* (New York: Harper & Row, 1964), p. 5.
7. Henri Fayol, *General and Industrial Management*, trans. Constance Storrs (New York: Pitman, 1949), pp. 14–15.
8. Oliver Sheldon, *The Philosophy of Management* (London: Sir Isaac Pitman & Sons, 1923), pp. 33–34.
9. Paul Donham, "Is Management a Profession?" *Harvard Business Review* 40 (September–October 1962): 60–68; and Nancy G. McNulty, "And Now, Professional Codes for the Practice of Management, But Not in the U.S.," *Conference Board Record* 12 (April 1975): 23.
10. For more details, see "Secrets of Intrapreneurship," *Inc.*, January 1985, pp. 69–76.

SUGGESTIONS FOR FURTHER STUDY

BARNARD, CHESTER I. *The Functions of the Executive*. Cambridge: Harvard University Press, 1938.

CARLAND, JAMES W., et al. "Differentiating Entrepreneurs from Small Business Owners: A Conceptualization." *Academy of Management Review* 9 (April 1984): 354–359.

DRUCKER, PETER F. *Management: Tasks, Responsibilities and Practices*. New York: Harper & Row, 1974.

———. *The Practice of Management*. New York: Harper & Row, 1954.

FOLLETT, MARY PARKER. "Management as a Profession." In *Business Management as a Profession*, edited by Henry C. Metcalf. Chicago: A. W. Shaw, 1927.

GRIBBONS, RONALD E., and HUNT, SHELBY G. "Is Management a Science?" *Academy of Management Review* 3 (January 1978): 139–144.

HESKETT, JAMES L. *Managing in the Service Economy*. Boston: Harvard Business School Press, 1986.

HITT, MICHAEL A., and IRELAND, R. DUANE. "Peters and Waterman Revisited: The Unended Quest for Excellence." *Academy of Management Executive* (May 1987): 91–98.

KOONTZ, HAROLD. "The Management Theory Jungle." *Journal of the Academy of Management* 4 (December 1961): 174–188.

MEE, JOHN F. "Management Philosophy for Professional Executives." *Business Horizons* 1 (December 1956): 5–11.

MILLS, PETER K. *Organizational Practices in a Postindustrial Economy*. Cambridge, MA: Ballinger, 1986.

PETERS, THOMAS J., and WATERMAN, ROBERT H., JR. *In Search of Excellence: Lessons from America's Best-Run Companies*. New York: Harper & Row, 1982.

RYAN, WILLIAM G. "Management Practice and Research—Poles Apart." *Business Horizons* 20 (June 1977): 23–29.

2

What Managers Do: How They Make Things Happen

Learning Objectives

After studying the material in this chapter, you should be able to do the following:

□ Discuss how different organizational levels—and types of activities—affect managers' performance.
□ Describe the overall functions performed by managers.
□ Identify and explain the specific activities engaged in by managers when performing these functions.
□ Describe how managers spend their time.
□ Describe some skills used by managers.

Outline of the Chapter

Levels and types of management
Different levels of management
Different types of organizational functions
Functional and general managers
Functions performed by managers
Definitions of the functions
Relationships among the functions
Managers perform all the functions
What managers actually do
The activities approach
Activities performed by managers
How managers spend their time
With whom do managers spend their time?
How do managers spend their time?
Managerial skills used
Conceptual skills
Human-relations skills
Administrative skills
Technical skills
Summary

Some Important Terms

administrative management
operative management
primary functions
service functions
functional managers
general managers
planning
organizing
staffing
leading (directing, activating, influencing)
controlling
positive control
negative control
administrative activities
interactional activities *or* roles
informational roles
entrepreneurial role
conceptual skills
human-relations skills
administrative skills
technical skills

OPENING CASE

Clyde Kirkland—Hospital Administrator

Linda Culver was studying the performance of managerial personnel at Capital City General Hospital as the basis of her doctoral dissertation at State University. She was interviewing Clyde Kirkland, the hospital administrator, to find out what his duties and responsibilities were.

Kirkland had grown up in Smalltown, where he had been active in school athletics and politics, as well as civic, social, and religious activities. Upon graduation from college, he returned to Smalltown, married, started an insurance agency, and later acquired an automobile agency.

After that, he moved to Capital City to head an agency of the state government for four years. Finally, he became chief executive officer of the hospital, a position he had occupied for five years when he was interviewed by Linda.

"How does your job here differ from your previous positions?" she asked.

"Very little," he answered. "It took me a while to learn the essential details of operating a health care facility, but the basic functions are the same. I have to select assistants, plan new facilities, meet the public, prepare and follow up on a budget, make changes in the organization, meet with my staff, send out memos, and sometimes even solve 'personnel problems.'"

AS YOU CAN SEE, this case illustrates many of the concepts developed in Chapter 1. Kirkland had successfully owned and managed two different private firms, had then served as administrator of a large public agency, and was at the time of the interview operating a hospital. As a manager, he had the job of making things happen in each of these organizations.

The case also illustrates the subjects to be covered in this chapter: what managers do and how they make things happen. As previously shown, managers' functions and activities differ according to their level in the organization and the type of position held. The way managers spend their time is described, as are some of the skills needed by managers and how those skills can be developed.

LEVELS AND TYPES OF MANAGEMENT

There are many levels and types of management. In general, management performance differs at different organizational levels and by different organizational functions.

Different Levels of Management

As you have just seen, the terms *administration* and *management* are virtually synonymous in general usage. But in practice there are some important differences between them. Essentially, **administrative management** is more concerned with setting objectives and then planning, organizing, staffing, and controlling activities in a coordinated manner so that the organization's objectives are attained. **Operative management** is more involved with supervising, motivating, and communicating with employees to lead them to

FIGURE 2.1
Administrative and operative managers differ in the extent to which they perform the management functions.

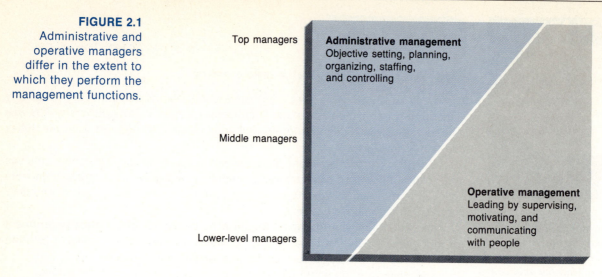

Top managers

Administrative management
Objective setting, planning, organizing, staffing, and controlling

Middle managers

Operative management
Leading by supervising, motivating, and communicating with people

Lower-level managers

achieve effective results. At lower levels of an organization, managers are more concerned with operative management. As they rise to higher levels, they become more involved with administrative management.

As you may already have concluded, no management position is exclusively either operative or administrative; all positions have elements of both. Figure 2.1 shows some of the differences between these two types of management.

Number of people supervised differs at different levels. The usual way of showing the different levels of management is with a pyramid, as shown in Figure 2.2. As you can see, the number of people at each level decreases as employees move from the nonmanagerial level up through the managerial levels.

Nonmanagerial personnel represent the bulk of an organization's employees, and there is great variation regarding their status and pay. This level includes low-skill-level positions, such as physical laborers and assembly line operators, as well as high-skill-level positions, such as engineers, scientists, and technologists.

Within the managerial ranks, the number of managers at each level decreases as individuals move up from the operative to the administrative level. Finally, at the apex of the organization, there is normally only one person, the chief executive officer (CEO), whatever his or her title may be.

Activities differ at different levels. In general, people in the lower levels of management spend most of their time directly supervising and working with their subordinates to meet the operating goals of higher management. People in the higher levels spend more time setting objectives and goals, determining policies and programs, setting operating goals and standards, establishing and controlling budgets, and making long-range forecasts.

Titles differ at different levels. Another generalization is that titles and designations differ at successively higher levels. At the first and lowest level, managers are typically referred to by titles such as *supervisor, head nurse,*

FIGURE 2.2
Management levels in an organization.

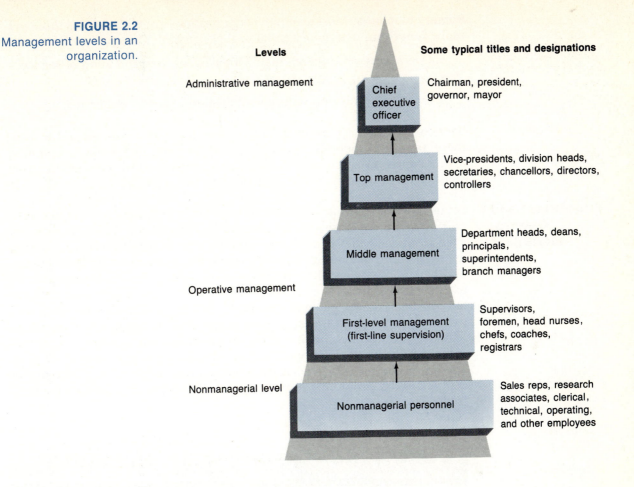

Levels   Some typical titles and designations

Administrative management   Chief executive officer — Chairman, president, governor, mayor

Top management — Vice-presidents, division heads, secretaries, chancellors, directors, controllers

Middle management — Department heads, deans, principals, superintendents, branch managers

Operative management

First-level management (first-line supervision) — Supervisors, foremen, head nurses, chefs, coaches, registrars

Nonmanagerial level

Nonmanagerial personnel — Sales reps, research associates, clerical, technical, operating, and other employees

or *chief.* At the second level, managers may be called by titles such as *superintendent, department head,* or *dean.* At the third level, managers have titles such as *division head, director,* and *vice-president.* The individual at the apex of the pyramid may be called the *chief executive officer, president, chairman of the board, governor,* or *administrator.*

In summary, managers are given more authority and responsibility at higher levels. They perform different organizational functions and engage in different activities depending on their level; also, the time and the skills required of them differ according to their level. (These points are discussed later in this chapter and throughout the text.)

What is your view?
What are the titles of some of the managers you come in contact with at your school?

Different Types of Organizational Functions

The way managers perform their jobs tends to vary according to the organizational function performed. The missions or purposes of organizations vary greatly. There are, however, many similar functions that all organizations must perform in carrying out their missions. Basically, these functions can be classified as either primary or service functions.

Primary functions. Most economic organizations are built around three **primary functions** that are essential to their survival. These are as follows:

1. *Operations:* production, manufacturing, or the generation of service.
2. *Marketing:* distribution, sales, or service.
3. *Finance:* acquisition of funds, utilization of funds, budgeting.

Service functions. Some of the major **service functions** needed to keep these primary functions operating effectively are personnel; accounting; maintenance; research and development; legal; clerical; engineering; purchasing; and public, community, and legislative relations.

Functional and General Managers

Let us now clarify some additional terms used to designate types of managers and management positions. In general, **functional managers** are responsible for the activities of only one of these primary or service functions, such as production, marketing, finance, personnel, or accounting. The activities of other functions are the responsibility of other functional managers. For example, the marketing manager is responsible for all distribution activities but must call on the personnel manager for help with personnel problems.

At higher levels in the organization, **general managers** oversee a total operating unit or division, including all the functional activities of that unit. Figure 2.3 illustrates these relationships. Most business schools and divisions are now reemphasizing the basics, such as operations and production, and companies are promoting executives with broad-based rather than specialized skills.

FUNCTIONS PERFORMED BY MANAGERS

In Chapter 1, *management* was defined as working with human, financial, and physical resources to determine, interpret, and achieve organizational objectives by performing the functions of planning, organizing, staffing, leading, and controlling. Generally, there is agreement about what these functions are. One of the earliest classifications of managerial functions was made by Fayol, who suggested that planning, organizing, coordinating, commanding, and controlling were the primary functions.[1]

FIGURE 2.3
Relationship between functional and general managers.

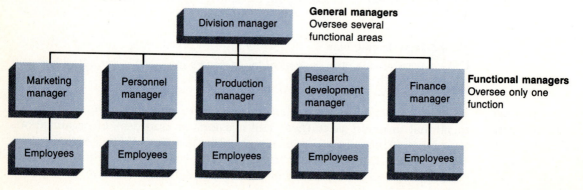

Definitions of the Functions

Regardless of the type of industry, the organizational level, or the organizational function involved, at least five functions must be performed by anyone who is a manager—planning, organizing, staffing, leading, and controlling organizational activities.[2] At this time, we present only a general overview of these functions; they will be discussed in detail in Parts Three through Five.

Planning. **Planning** is (1) choosing or setting an organization's mission, or purpose, and objectives and then (2) determining the policies, projects, programs, procedures, methods, systems, budgets, standards, and strategies needed to achieve them. As you can see, decision making is heavily involved in this function as well.

Beginning with Frederick W. Taylor's work in the late 1800s, there has been a tendency to transfer the planning function from operating employees to their managers. Although planning cannot be entirely separated and isolated from the employees' activities, it is such an integral part of any manager's job that to speak of management is to include planning as well. In essence, creative planning is the work of determining and specifying the factors, forces, effects, and relationships needed to accomplish the designated objectives.

All other functions depend on this one, for they cannot succeed without sound, thorough, and continuous planning and decision making. In turn, good planning relies on effective execution of the other functions as well.

Organizing. **Organizing** is (1) determining what resources and activities are required to achieve the organization's objectives, (2) combining them into workable groups, (3) assigning the responsibility for accomplishing them to responsible subordinates, and (4) delegating to those individuals the authority necessary to carry out their assignments. This function provides the formal structure through which work is defined, subdivided, and coordinated.

There are several facets of organizing. First, there are many activities that must be done first in order to perform other functions. These include selecting capable people, training and developing them, and rewarding their performance. Organizing also includes establishing authority-responsibility relationships among members of the organization, setting up work groups, providing for intergroup activities, and providing systems for communicating with different organizational levels. Second, it is necessary to accumulate a plant, machinery and equipment, capital, and the latest technology and arrange them so that they will be most productive. Third, the financial, physical, and human resources should be integrated into an overall productive scheme.

Staffing. **Staffing** is planning personnel needs; recruiting, selecting, training, and developing capable employees; placing them in productive work environments; and rewarding their performance. In performing this function, management determines the mental, physical, and emotional requirements of work positions through job analyses, job descriptions, and job specifications and then finds the necessary employees with the personal characteristics—such as abilities, education, training, and experience—needed to accomplish the job. This function includes activities such as establishing rewards for effective job performance; evaluating employees for promotion, transfer, or even discharge; and training and developing employees.

The importance of this function was emphasized by two highly successful retired chief executive officers. Irving Shapiro, of Du Pont, said, "The greatest satisfaction is being able to identify talent and develop it and get people into positions where their talents can be used constructively." David Rockefeller, of the Chase Manhattan Bank, said, "I suppose that's one of the best tests of a chief executive—whether [he or she is] good at delegating and equally good at picking the right people to whom to delegate."[3]

Leading. Plans—and the organization and staff that result from them—are useless without the function of leading and supervising employees. The **leading** function, simply stated, is getting employees to do the things you want them to do. Therefore, it involves the leader's qualities, styles, and power, as well as the leadership activities of communication, motivation, and discipline.

This function—often called *directing*, *actuating*, or *influencing*—may be performed in the face-to-face manner of assigning tasks and issuing instructions, transmitting goals and objectives, requesting cooperation, asking for ideas, or otherwise communicating directly with employees. Communication can also be achieved indirectly through publishing standing orders, standard operating procedures (SOPs), and job descriptions, or by means of some other impersonal communiqué. It may be suggested that the higher managers move in the organization, the more impersonal are their methods of communication; the lower the position they occupy, the more personal are their methods.

Controlling. All these functions are ineffective without the last one, which is controlling. **Controlling** is devising ways and means of assuring that planned performance is actually achieved. It can be either positive or negative. **Positive control** tries to see that the objectives of the organization are efficiently and effectively reached; **negative control** tries to insure that unwanted or undesirable activities do not occur or recur. The concept of control is probably easy for you to understand, for you encounter it in nearly all of your activities.

For example, control is involved in (1) traffic lights, (2) the refrigerator, water heater, and air conditioner in homes, (3) examinations and grades, (4) the automatic transmission in cars, and (5) your music and other electronic systems.

What is your view?

Can you identify other familiar examples of control?

1. Positive controls

2. Negative controls

In essence, control involves (1) setting up standards of performance, (2) determining methods for measuring performance, (3) measuring actual performance, (4) comparing it with the established standards, and (5) taking corrective action to bring actual performance into conformity with the standard when necessary. Therefore, for effective control, there must first be planning, organizing, staffing, and leading.

Relationships Among the Functions

One of the oldest and most frequently asked questions about management is: What is the relationship among the functions? Many efforts have been made to answer this question. The only honest answer is they are all necessary and are related to each other as shown in Figure 2.4. While they can be performed in any order or sequence, they tend to be performed in the planning, organizing, staffing, leading, and controlling sequence.

The relationship among all these functions can be compared to taking a trip in an automobile. That is:

Planning = studying a road map

Organizing = getting into the vehicle

Staffing = getting qualified drivers

Leading = encouraging others to go on the trip

Controlling = reading the road signs

Thus, you can't say one function is more important than another; they are all needed, but they must be coordinated to achieve the optimum level of performance.

Figure 2.5 shows that the five functions are like the layers of a cake. They

FIGURE 2.4
Relationships among the management functions.

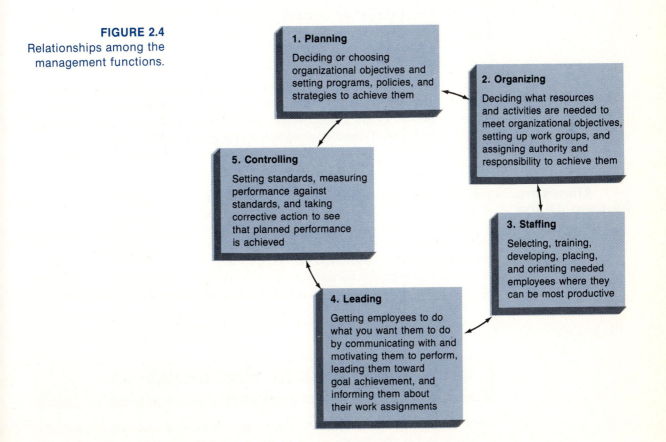

FIGURE 2.5
Relationship between management functions and types of management, according to organizational functions.

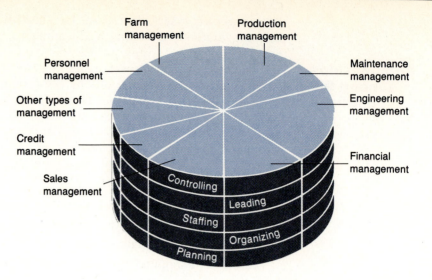

are common to all types of management, as shown by the slices of the cake. In other words, farm managers, maintenance managers, and all others perform all of the functions.

 What is your view?

Notice that one slice is labeled "Other types of management." What types of management would you put there? Office? Military? Hospital? Health care? City? Fast-food restaurant? Research lab? Do these types of management use the five functions?

It should be emphasized that although management functions are the same in different types of enterprises, for different functional jobs and at different levels they are not given the same emphasis. One or more functions may be emphasized more than others when performed at different levels of management. For example, planning is a primary concern of top management, whereas first-line supervisors are more concerned with leading.

Managers Perform All the Functions

The functions of management must be performed by someone whenever and wherever there are organized groups. The responsibility for *all* these activities falls on the managers' shoulders. In carrying out these responsibilities, managers (1) plan and organize the physical, financial, and human resources of the organization, (2) secure the necessary staff, (3) lead, direct, or supervise the performance of essential activities, and (4) measure, evaluate, appraise, and control the execution of these activities. As you can see, the success or failure of an organization depends heavily on the ability of its managers to perform these functions effectively.

WHAT MANAGERS ACTUALLY DO

What do managers do? The Opening Case illustrates some of the specific activities managers engage in and provides a glimpse of the characteristics of managerial work. As indicated earlier, managers such as hospital administrators *do* plan, organize, staff, lead (or direct), and control organizational activities. And these functions *do* form a sequence of interdependent, interacting, and interrelated events, from goal setting to controlling, that assures performance of purposeful, goal-oriented activities.

The Activities Approach

We frequently find in executive development programs that some practicing professional managers have difficulty relating the managerial functions named to what they actually do in their jobs. Instead, these managers say they spend most of their time attending meetings, talking on the telephone, writing or reading memos and reports, having visitors, touring the organization's property, and the like. As you think about it, these activities are not managerial functions, but they are in fact the *means* by which these functions are carried out. They are the many tasks, duties, and assignments that give meaning to the overall functions, as shown in the following details of the Opening Case.

As Culver's interview continued (in the Opening Case) Linda asked Kirkland, "What are some specific things you do in performing the managerial functions?"

Kirkland replied: "Let me answer by describing some of the things I've done recently. This will give you some idea of what I do.

"I submitted the architectural plans for our new wing to the board for approval. Then the chairperson and I arranged for its financing at a meeting of several bankers. William [the vice-president in charge of supervising the physical plant] and I got the approval of the regional medical planning group and discussed the plans with the architect and contractor.

"I have met several times with Mary [the vice-president in charge of clerical work, communication systems, housekeeping, personnel, and training] about a new organization plan we are putting into effect—and the training program you're going to put on for our supervisors. We have just created a new vice-presidency to handle several areas that were being neglected. Mary and I discussed plans for an executive development program that will begin after the study and training are complete.

"Last week I presided at the party for our retirees and presented awards to those who are retiring, and this morning I served as a pallbearer for the mother of one of our nurses.

"I'm going to a church budget planning meeting at 4:00 P.M. today. Then I have to meet with the repairman about the air conditioning at my house.

"I had to meet with the doctors in charge of the pathology and X-ray departments to resolve a conflict between them and their technicians.

"Monday I met with the staff physicians about the new Medicare requirements set up by HHS [Health and Human Services]. I have to see that the physicians work with the business office and the board to meet those guidelines.

"What else? Oh, yes! We had to fire an employee for stealing and using drugs."

The activities approach versus the functional approach. Here is a dilemma for management writers and teachers, as well as for practicing managers.

The functional approach provides the most logical way of organizing and discussing management. It is of little help, however, in explaining what managers actually do. And if we don't understand what they do—the activities approach—how can we improve the teaching and practice of management?

Many studies have examined what managers actually do and how they spend their time. Many of these, which will be mentioned later in this chapter and throughout the text, were concerned with positions such as supervisor, general manager, hospital administrator, company president, production manager, and sales manager in the United States and other countries. Although questionnaires were often used to ask managers what they did, more useful information has been obtained by actually observing managers at work.

Mintzberg's synthesis. Henry Mintzberg, noted researcher, studied a variety of managerial jobs and found no inherent conflict between the functional and activities approaches, finding instead that they complement each other.[4] Management teaching and practice have been radically changed by Mintzberg's findings, which form the basis of the following discussion.

We have organized the material in this book into parts and chapters on the basis of the functional approach, but we have also included as much of the activities approach as was feasible.

Activities Performed by Managers

In the previous example, Kirkland, in his job as hospital administrator, engaged in several activities, which can be classified into four loose groups: (1) personal, (2) technical, (3) administrative, and (4) interactional. Most of these activities are related to, and can be studied in terms of, the managerial functions. By comparing these activities with the function, you get a better overall view of the manager's job.

Figure 2.6 illustrates how these personal, technical, administrative, and interactional activities are related in defining the manager's job according to the functions performed by managers. As with the management functions, these activities are so interrelated, interdependent, and interacting that they form an integrated system. Yet, for discussion purposes, they are presented separately.

Personal activities. We tend to think of managers as part of an organization that is independent of their own personal interests, families, and social life. Yet, if we ignore these personal elements, the real picture of what managers do will be distorted. Managers bring their own problems, perceptions, goals, ideals, values, biases, and practices into their organizations, and these personal elements affect the way jobs are done, but the functions do not change because of these personal influences. Notice that Kirkland related how he was engaged in many church-related activities, was concerned about the air conditioning in his home, and performed other personal tasks.

Because a manager's personal goals are sometimes different from the organization's objectives, these goals may even conflict with those of the organization. For example, some managers might try to increase their power at the expense of others in the group and thereby reduce everyone's effectiveness. Managers should become concerned with employees' personal goals if they are in conflict with those of the organization.

FIGURE 2.6
Activities performed by managers.

SOURCE: Adapted from Kae Chung and Leon Megginson, *Organizational Behavior* (New York: Harper & Row, 1981), p. 12.

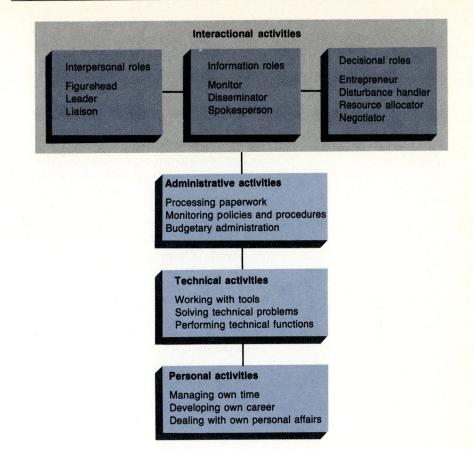

Bob West, a plant manager for a large manufacturing firm, was generally considered a good choice to succeed the vice-president of manufacturing, who was slated to retire in two or three years. Bob's quest for the position began to show, however, in his efforts to cut down others whom he saw as potential contenders. He bickered with other plant managers at group meetings, spent more time "politicking" with higher-ups at the home office, and even put pressure on his own plant to increase its productivity. Bob's efforts alienated his peers, and performance at his plant began to drop. The company eventually selected an outsider to fill the position of vice-president.

Technical activities. Technical activities include such endeavors as working with tools, solving technical problems, and performing the specialized activities found in the various departments of an organization. These activities are related directly to the specific tasks being performed in each respective department. The amount of time managers spend in such activities tends to decrease as they progress into higher positions and perform other managerial activities. Regardless of level, however, effective managers need at least a sufficient knowledge of the technical activities they supervise to be able to tell when the job is being done properly.

For example, when serving as a financial manager, a person is primarily required to know the techniques involved in financial operations. But when that person becomes the general manager, he or she should understand something about the technical functions of the total organization. This does not mean that the individual should become a technical expert in each area. Instead, he or she must have a working knowledge of how the technical parts fit into the whole operation, the results to be expected, and how to achieve those results.

> *A supervisor with a large paper company shocked his associates at a management development program when he said that he did not know how to operate a front-end loader, a skidder, or even a chain saw, all of which were equipment used by his employees. "What's important to me as a manager," he stated, "is that I understand what results each of these pieces of equipment can get for me."*
>
> *"How do you go about training new employees if you don't know the equipment?" he was asked.*
>
> *He replied, "I have my senior people break them in. That's their job."*

What is your view?

Do you agree with the supervisor? Why? Why not? How much technical knowledge should a manager have? Should Kirkland, as hospital administrator, know how to perform lab work? Understand surgery? Be familiar with computers and pricing of services?

Technical activities are especially important to supervisors and junior executives, because most organizations prefer to hire people at the entry

"In this organization, Challis, middle management uses only blue highlighting markers."

(Reprinted from The Wall Street Journal *by permission of Cartoon Features Syndicate.)*

level to perform specific technical functions and then promote them to managerial positions on the basis of their managerial potential. Therefore, these lower-level managers are generally hired on the basis of their scientific, professional, or technical competence and are initially assigned to positions according to their technical expertise. Thus, although some specialists gradually become generalists as they are promoted, their technical background allows them to get involved in technical activities and show special interest in their favorite projects.

Administrative activities. The activities that, for want of a better term, are labeled **administrative activities** include processing paperwork, preparing and administering budgets, monitoring policies and procedures, and maintaining the stability of operations. Many managers dislike these activities and spend only a relatively small portion of their time performing them; they usually complain that as managers they waste too much time on these administrative tasks.

> *At a low point in his administration, President Jimmy Carter said that one of his greatest failings was spending too much time on "administrative matters" and not giving enough attention to "providing leadership." A former U.S. Navy engineering officer, he sought to master the details of the presidency. The results? His administration generated more paperwork than any one-term presidency in history. It took archivists in Atlanta six years to whittle down the 50 million pieces of paper to 27 million pages, and only 6 million were available to the public in early 1987.[5]*

Adding to managers' administrative burden is the increasing number of laws, regulations, and court decisions that they are expected to be familiar with, understand, and comply with.

> *For example, it requires a great deal of time, physical and emotional energy, money, and paperwork to comply with laws such as the Civil Rights Act of 1964, the Age Discrimination in Employment Act of 1967, the Environmental Protection Act, the Occupational Safety and Health Act, the Consumer Protection Act, and the 1986 Immigration Reform and Control Act, to name just a few. It is estimated that small firms alone spend $12.7 billion annually on forms for 103 separate federal agencies.[6]*

Functional managers usually delegate most of their paperwork to administrative assistants, secretaries, and/or other managers in service departments such as personnel, accounting, and legal. They must be aware of these laws and guidelines and comply with them, however, because any failure to comply, or even any suspicion of noncompliance, can be very costly to a firm.

> *A reverse form of this practice is now occurring in many legal offices. Persons without law degrees are being hired by law firms as office managers to relieve lawyers of the job of handling administrative matters such as personnel, billing, purchasing, and payroll. Although many large firms have traditionally employed such administrators, many others have relied on managing partners or management boards.*

Interactional activities (roles managers play). As a result of studying several executives at work, Mintzberg classified their behaviors into three distinct **interactional activities,** or **roles,** that managers play: interpersonal, informational, and decisional.

Figure 2.7 shows that managers have formal authority over their units and derive their status from this authority. Authority and status cause managers to get involved in performing the interpersonal, informational, and decision-making roles. Managers then use their personal and managerial skills and abilities to perform the roles most effectively.

Interpersonal roles. These activities result in managers performing the roles of (1) *figurehead,* (2) *leader,* and (3) *liaison.* This set of roles derives directly from the manager's formal position. As the *figurehead* for their units, managers are called on to perform certain ceremonial functions associated with being the formal representatives of their organizations. These include greeting visitors and attending social functions involving their subordinates (weddings, funerals, and the like). Notice that Kirkland played the figurehead role when he presided at the dinner for retirees and presented awards to those who were retiring from the hospital, and as a pallbearer.

In playing the role of *leader,* managers relate to members of the group. Managers motivate and encourage subordinates to achieve organizational objectives. In return, the managers help subordinates to satisfy their own needs. Employee evaluations and performance appraisals are also involved. Kirkland played the role of leader when he submitted the architectural plans to the board.

Managers play the *liaison role* when they serve as a connecting link between their organization and others or between their units and other organizational units. For example, a department head plays this role when serving on the college's United Fund committee. The mayor performs this function when serving on a regional planning committee. Notice that Kirkland served as liaison between the staff physicians and HHS representatives.

Informational roles. Managers play **informational roles** by (1) monitoring the information flow, (2) disseminating information to other people, and (3) serving as the spokespersons to people outside their units. By maintaining a network of interpersonal contacts, managers act as the nerve centers of their organizational units. By being in the center of the information system, they are in a position to collect, monitor, and disseminate more information than any other person on the staff. They tend to have access to more and better sources of data, which they store for future use.

Since managers need information to make decisions, and since others

FIGURE 2.7
Roles played by
managers.

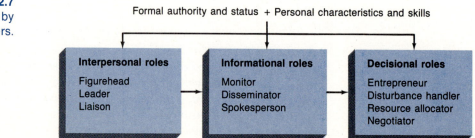

depend on them as a source of useful information, managers must be information disseminators by providing needed data to employees. Managers use memos, orders, letters, and personal communication such as informal discussions and formal speeches to convey these ideas.

As the unit's *spokesperson* or representative, a manager must keep influential people informed about what is going on in the unit. People outside the organization—and superiors—look to managers to find out what is going on inside the group. But information is not an end in itself: it is collected and distributed to facilitate making the right decisions, as shown in the following situation.

> *A recent study found that dealing with individuals and organizations outside the company—such as community groups, the media, investors and lenders, and government agencies—consumes as much as 50 percent of a CEO's time. Some 90 percent of the executives interviewed said they had been unprepared for that aspect of their job and that it took from one-and-a-half to three years to learn to cope with it.*[7]

Decisional roles. In performing the decision-making role, managers act as (1) entrepreneur, (2) disturbance handler, (3) resource allocator, and (4) negotiator. In playing the **entrepreneurial role,** managers actively seek to improve their units' performance by initiating planned changes to adapt to environmental changes. Some examples are instituting a new motivational system, acquiring a new word processing system, or revising the organizational structure.

As *disturbance handlers*, managers deal with the problems and pressures imposed on them, such as personality clashes, interpersonal conflicts, strikes, breaches of contract, shortages of materials, and complaints and grievances. This role is probably the most unpopular one that managers have to perform. Notice that Kirkland used the pronoun "I" until the last sentence of the case, when he said, "*We* had to fire an employee." Do you think the change in wording was unconscious or deliberate?

As *resource allocators*, managers decide why, when, how, for what, and to whom the scarce organizational resources are to be allocated. Preparing the budget is an example of this.

As *negotiators*, managers carry out negotiations with people outside their units. They arrange for transfer of resources, information, and activities between organizational units.

> *"Not too long ago," said Kirkland, (in the Opening Case), "we had the opportunity to buy a CAT scanner on most attractive terms—if we acted immediately. I called all of the board members to get them to agree to invest the $1 million needed.*
>
> *"On another occasion, an extended health care center near us became available. My assistants and I looked into the possibilities of using it for some of our patients, the aging, and other activities. We explored sources of funds, called a special board meeting, and obtained approval for buying the property."*
>
> *Notice that Kirkland played the roles of entrepreneur, resource allocator, and negotiator.*

HOW MANAGERS SPEND THEIR TIME

As shown in Chapter 1, most managers spend considerable time, effort, and energy interacting with other people, both inside and outside the organization. Included are suppliers, customers, union leaders, community leaders, subordinates, peers, superiors, and government personnel. Did you notice how many different types of people Kirkland had been in touch with while performing his activities? He usually interacted directly with at least 25 or 30 different individuals, in groups, in person, or on the phone, in the course of a day.

Is it any wonder, then, that so many writers and speakers define management as working with and through other people?

With Whom Do Managers Spend Their Time?

With whom do managers interact? As shown in Figure 2.8, the chief executives studied by Mintzberg spent less than half (48 percent) of their contact time with their subordinates, while spending 52 percent with outsiders. Notice that they spent 20 percent of their time with clients, suppliers, and professional associates, 16 percent with peers, 7 percent with directors, and 9 percent with others.

The findings are somewhat different for foreign managers, especially those at lower levels. One study examined how British senior and middle managers spent their time with other persons. It found that they spent 40 percent of their time with subordinates, 19 percent with colleagues, 13 percent with fellow specialists, 12 percent with superiors, 8 percent with people in other organizational units, and 8 percent with people outside their organization.[8]

How Do Managers Spend Their Time?

Other studies confirm that managers spend a great deal of time interacting with other people. For example, chief executives in one study spent 78 percent of their time in oral communication activities such as attending meetings, talking on the telephone, and touring their plants.[9] Another study found that a sample group of middle managers devoted 80 percent of their

FIGURE 2.8
Chief executives' contacts.
(Note: The top figure indicates the proportion of total contact time spent with each group, and the bottom figure the proportion of mail from each group.)

SOURCE: Henry Mintzberg, "The Manager's Job: Folklore and Fact," *Harvard Business Review* 53 (July–August 1975):57.

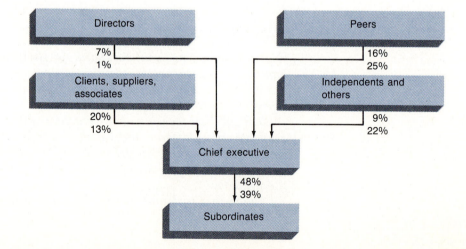

FIGURE 2.9
How managers spend
their time—what
activities they participate
in.

SOURCE: Adapted from Henry
Mintzberg, *The Nature of
Managerial Work* (New York:
Harper & Row, 1973), p. 39.

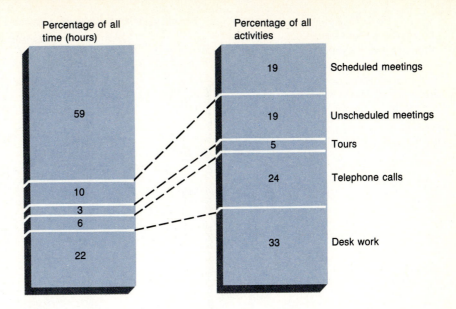

time to oral communication,[10] while a third group of middle managers spent 78 percent.[11]

Figure 2.9 shows the time required for some of management's activities. While the activities in this study are different from those activities discussed in the text, the findings are significant. For example, notice the tremendous amount of time spent in meetings—69 percent of the total time spent—and the much smaller amount of time spent in contacts with other groups or individuals—31 percent. Another interesting finding is the large number of interruptions by the telephone.

Another study of how managers from low, medium, and high levels in their organizations used their time performing several management activities is summarized in Figure 2.10. Once again, the activities are different from those discussed in the text.

In summary, it appears that managers at all levels tend to spend about 80 percent of their time working with other people and consider such activities the most important element in effective management.

MANAGERIAL SKILLS USED

What managerial skills are generally used by effective managers? A study of 2000 executives found that "superior managers" have 64 basic skills (see MAP 2.1). These can be grouped into 18 general "competencies," which form the major management functions.

Other authorities reduce these to four, which are:

1. Conceptual skills

2. Human-relations skills

3. Administrative skills

4. Technical skills[12]

FIGURE 2.10
How managers at
different levels spend
their time.

SOURCE: Adapted from
T. A. Mahoney, T. H. Jerdee, and
S. J. Carroll, "The Job(s) of
Management," *Industrial
Relations* 4 (February 1965):103.

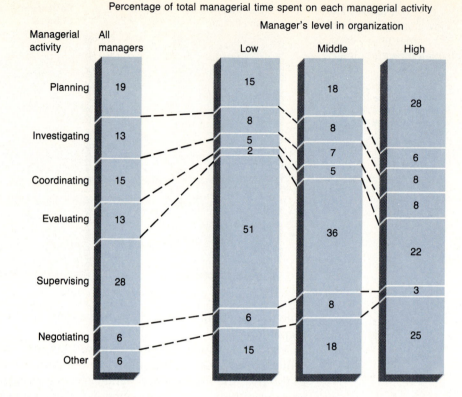

The relative importance of any one of these skills to a given manager at a given time depends on the type of organization, the managerial level, and the function being performed (see Figure 2.11). While each of these skills is required to some degree by all managers, you can see that top managers use the conceptual skills more than middle and first-level managers. Yet first-level managers use the technical skills more than the other two levels of managers do. Human-relations and administrative skills are used about the same by all managers.

Conceptual Skills

Conceptual skills, which include diagnostic skills, are the mental abilities needed to acquire, analyze, and interpret information received from various sources and to make complex decisions. They involve the ability to understand the relationship of the parts to the whole and, conversely, to understand the whole by breaking it into parts. Thus, effective managers are able to obtain meaning from inadequate—and often conflicting—data. Managers who are unable to do so tend to respond alike to all inputs without considering their relative importance. Consequently, they lose a sense of control and direction.

Managers need to develop conceptual skills that will enable them to see what goes on in their work environment and help them to react appropriately. In essence, this is the ability to "see the big picture," to plan ahead rather than to react.

A survey of the *"Fortune"* 500 companies tends to confirm the conclusion (as shown in Figure 2.11) that these conceptual skills are used more by

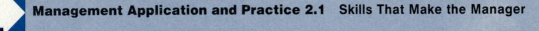

Management Application and Practice 2.1   Skills That Make the Manager

Good management is a matter of choice, not chance. When the American Management Association, based in New York City, commissioned a study of 2000 executives, the group discovered that superior managers have 64 basic skills. These fall into 18 general "competencies," or facets of management. Those, in turn, form the major management functions. But the most heartening information for less-than-superior managers is that these skills can be learned. Here's a sampling.

Goal and action management

Efficiency orientation. Skills: Sets challenging goals or deadlines for tasks; plans logical action steps, and supplies resources and other means for overcoming obstacles; emphasizes a clear standard of excellence.

Proactivity. Skills: Initiates action to accomplish tasks; gathers information from a variety of sources; takes calculated risks and accepts responsibility.

Concern with impact. Skills: Expresses concern with his image and the image of his company.

Diagnostic use of concepts. Skills: Uses theories and past events to explain current situations.

Directing subordinates

Use of unilateral power. Skills: Gives directions based on rules, procedures, or personal authority to get results.

Developing others. Skills: Gives constructive performance feedback; provides resources and delegates authority so employees can complete tasks.

Spontaneity. Skills: Acts from feelings without considering the consequences; makes hasty decisions. Note: Superior managers know that spontaneity can jolt employees into action.

Human-resource management

Accurate self-assessment. Skills: Evaluates strengths and weaknesses objectively; seeks to improve shortcomings.

Self-control. Skills: Overrides an impulse for the good of the company; holds back anger or other emotions in arguments.

Stamina and adaptability. Skills: Maintains high performance standards on prolonged tasks; remains flexible to accommodate changes in work load.

Perceptual objectivity. Skills: Accurately restates conflicting opinions during discussions and arguments.

Positive regard. Skills: Expresses belief in a person's ability to complete a task or improve his performance.

Managing group process. Skills: Formally and informally communicates a need for teamwork; creates symbols that identify his team, and actively promotes cooperation with other work groups; lets group share credit for successes.

Use of socialized power. Skills: Uses a broad network of contacts to complete tasks, accomplish goals, and influence the outcome of disputes.

Leadership

Self-confidence. Skills: Is forceful, assured, and unhesitating; expresses little ambivalence over past decisions.

Conceptualization. Skills: Identifies meaningful patterns in events; develops new concepts to explain situations; uses illustrative metaphors and analogies.

Logical thought. Skills: Extrapolates cause-and-effect relationships in a series of past or hypothetical events.

Use of oral presentation. Skills: Speaks clearly and convincingly; uses objects, diagrams, and other visual aids to reinforce concepts; asks audience if his points are clear.

SOURCE: *Success,* May 1987, p. 49.

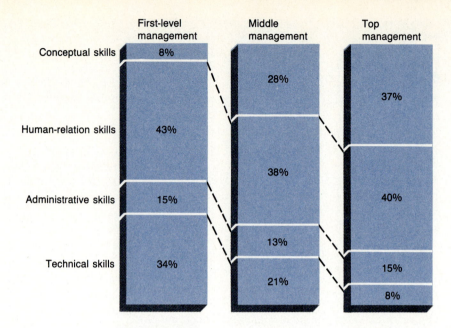

people in top management than in any other level of management in an organization.[13]

Human-Relations Skills

Managers need a network of contacts and human relationships to achieve organizational goals by using the efforts of other people. Therefore, they need to possess many different behavioral and analytical skills to work with people in and out of their organizations.

> *Realizing that the high-tech world of tomorrow will require "high-touch" executives adept at leading workers into uncharted waters, Ford Motor Company set up a one-week training program at its Executive Development Center. The program's objective is to polish managers' skills in getting along smoothly with workers.*[14]

Human-relations skills consist of the many diverse abilities required to understand other people and to interact effectively with them. Interpersonal skills are needed to create and maintain a network of contacts with people outside one's own chain of command. For example, interpersonal skills are needed in leading, motivating, and communicating with subordinates, peers, bosses, and even outsiders. One problem with these skills is that most managers think they have all of them that they need.

> *In 1985, as a consultant to two divisions of Citibank, Robert Lamb found frustration and fear among employees who believed that management was "too political." It was who you knew that counted rather than what you knew. Top management did not believe him but passed out buttons saying, "We're number one in employee work environment." Only when a large percentage of employees refused to fill out confidential surveys for fear of reprisal did management change its tune.*[15]

Administrative Skills

The term **administrative skills** refers to the whole range of skills associated with planning, organizing, staffing, and controlling. These skills include an

TIPS 2.1 Taking a Managerial Skills Inventory

By this time in the course, you may have begun to ask yourself how well qualified you are to be a manager and how you can become qualified for such a position while you are still in school. This exercise is designed to help you take stock of your current qualifications and to show you what managerial skills you may need to acquire in the years ahead. Even if you are not interested in becoming a manager, the qualifications in the checklist are applicable to most professional positions.

The procedure

1. Take an inventory of your managerial qualifications, using the checklist that follows.
2. Prepare a profile of your qualification inventory. It will reveal your strengths and weaknesses.
3. Think about how you are going to remedy any weaknesses in your qualifications. This may help you better plan your college program.

The managerial qualification checklist

Instructions: Each of the following items concerns managerial qualifications. Respond to each item by placing an X in the column that indicates your assessment of your own qualities and skills.

Items	Low 1	2	3	4	High 5
Personal qualities:					
1. *Motivation to manage:* The desire to manage an organizational unit.					
2. *Motivation to lead:* The desire to have an influence on other people.					
3. *Capacity for empathy:* The capacity to put oneself in another person's shoes.					
4. *Tolerance for ambiguity:* The capacity to tolerate ambiguity.					
5. *Emotional strength:* The emotional strength to function under pressure.					
6. *Risk-taking behavior:* The capacity to take risks.					
Managerial skills:					
7. *Interpersonal skills:* The ability to create and maintain personal contacts.					
8. *Leadership skills:* The ability to motivate and lead other people.					
9. *Communication skills:* The ability to collect and disseminate information.					
10. *Group process skills:* The ability to use work groups to solve problems.					
11. *Entrepreneurial skills:* The ability to take advantage of business opportunities.					
12. *Analytical skills:* The ability to understand what goes on in the organization.					
13. *Resource decision skills:* The ability to make correct resource decisions.					
14. *Negotiation skills:* The ability to negotiate differences with others.					
15. *Administrative skills:* The ability to plan, organize, and execute activities.					
16. *Technical skills:* The ability to solve technical problems.					

SOURCE: Adapted from Kae H. Chung and Leon C. Megginson, *Organizational Behavior: Developing Managerial Skills* (New York: Harper & Row, 1981), pp. 524–526.

administrator's ability to follow policies and procedures, process paperwork in an orderly manner, and manage expenditures within the limits set by a budget. In this sense, administrative skills are an extension of conceptual skills; they implement these decisions by using administrative (and human-relations) skills.

Technical Skills

Technical skills include the ability to use the knowledge, tools, and techniques of a specific discipline or field, such as accounting, engineering, production, medicine, or sales. Managers still need some knowledge of the technical functions they are supervising, although the amount of time they spend performing technical activities decreases as they move up the organizational ladder. In summary, technical skills pertain to the knowledge of, and the ability to perform, the mechanics of a particular job. Some examples of these skills with which you may be familiar are the ability to program a computer, operate a machine (such as a lathe, printing press, or typewriter), or prepare financial statements.

As indicated earlier, these skills are relatively more important for first-line supervisors than for top managers. First-line supervisors are closer to the actual work being performed, often must tell—or show—employees how to perform it, and must know when it is done properly. Every industry, every company or enterprise, and every job has its special technical skill requirements.

Some words of caution are needed here. First, do not assume that an employee who is highly skilled, and who has been able to perform technical jobs, also has the requirements and characteristics to become a supervisor or manager. That is an invalid assumption, for a good producer is not necessarily a potentially effecive supervisor or executive.

Second, do not let this list of managerial skills overwhelm you! Provided that you have the natural abilities required to be a manager (which are discussed in Chapter 12), you can learn most of these skills in school or later through experience. See TIPS 2.1 for a checklist to indicate what managerial qualifications you have and to what extent they need developing.

SUMMARY

In this chapter we have presented an overall view of what managers do and how they make things happen. First, we saw how organizational levels and types of managerial activities caused differences in performing the managerial function. Then we looked at the functional approach and saw that managers get things done through other people by planning, organizing, staffing, leading, and controlling their activities. This approach has been widely accepted by both practicing managers and scholars in the field for several decades. The approach is simple and readily understood and presents an excellent overview of the managerial process. Yet it does not describe in detail what managers *actually do* in the real world of managing.

On the other hand, the activities approach to studying management does describe what managers actually do in performing their jobs. It identifies a set of activities that managers engage in while carrying out their daily operations. These activities include personal, technical, administrative, and interactional activities. In performing the interactional activities, managers play the interpersonal, informational, and decisional roles, including the roles of figurehead, leader, and liaison.

We then analyzed how managers spend their time. We reached the conclusion that managers spend about 80 percent of their time working with and through other people. This constitutes the core of managerial emphasis. CEOs tend to spend over half their time with people outside their organization.

Finally, we identified a set of skills that managers need in order to do their jobs effectively. Those skills include conceptual, human-relations, administrative, and technical skills. We suggested that these skills can be acquired through education and experience.

We have also shown the relationship between these functions, activities, and skills.

REVIEW QUESTIONS

1. What is the difference between administrative management and operative management?
2. What is the difference between primary functions and service functions?
3. What are the five management functions identified in the chapter? Explain each of them.
4. Explain the relationships among the functions.
5. What is the difference between the management functions approach and the management activities approach in studying management?
6. What are the four classifications of management activities developed by Mintzberg?
7. How would you explain each of the interactional roles played by managers?
8. How do managers spend their time?
9. What are the managerial skills used by effective managers? Explain each.

DISCUSSION QUESTIONS

1. Would a highly successful college football coach have the necessary skills to make an effective bank president? Discuss.
2. What managerial function is being performed when sales managers go over their salespersons' reports to see how they are doing? Discuss.
3. Of the types of skills required by managers, which, if any, are more desirable for the president of a college fraternity; the head of a large church; a drill sergeant in the U.S. Army?
4. Do you think the size of an organization influences the way managers spend their time? Discuss.
5. Is there an inconsistency between the theoretical functions of management and what managers actually say they do on their jobs? Discuss.
6. Should a top manager be a generalist or a specialist? Explain.
7. Are the conceptual, human-relations, administrative, and technical skills as important to managers as claimed? Why or why not?

LEARNING EXERCISE 2.1

The Choice*

Jack Dufton is the director of a medium-sized agricultural experiment station that has 10 staff members doing research in several disciplines. There are also about 35

* Prepared by Gayle M. Ross, Copiah-Lincoln Junior College, Wesson, Mississippi.

employees carrying out this research under the direction of George Smith, who is classified as a "farm manager" in the state classification system.

George, aged 62, has completed 35 years of service and plans to retire in a year. He has a difficult job, since he is responsible for assigning work to all 35 employees, helping make decisions about field plot locations, translating the desires of staff members into practical field operations, and in general making the routine decisions required to keep the field research operations running smoothly.

George is the key man, and Jack Dufton is concerned about who his replacement will be. The job qualifications for a farm manager specify a B.S. degree or its equivalent. Jack is doubtful that a young, recent graduate would know or understand how to handle the group of workers involved. Further, the salary level is set too low to attract the top graduates; so the applicants would more than likely be in the lowest level of academic and practical achievement.

Jack has a young man presently on the payroll, Fred Monroe, who he thinks might be able to fill George Smith's position. Fred is 30 years old, married, and has been employed at this station for the past six years. He is hardworking and conscientious and can operate most of the equipment and machinery used on the experiment station. On the negative side, he has only a high school diploma, is loud, jokes with his coworkers more than he should, and is younger than most of those he would be supervising.

Jack Dufton would like to know whether to try to recruit a new person as farm manager or promote Fred Monroe from within the organization and hope that he will grow into the job.

Questions

1. What would you do if you were Jack Dufton? Why?

2. Is there another alternative Jack has not considered? What?

3. Could Jack help Monroe to become more promotable? If so, how?

LEARNING EXERCISE 2.2

Understanding the Job of Managing*

Managers perform a great variety of activities on their jobs. These activities can range from simple telephone calls to major investment decisions. They can also vary in relative importance and in the time they consume. This exercise is designed to help you gain some first-hand knowledge of managerial work.

The procedure

1. Find a manager (supervisor, plant manager, office supervisor, general manager, personnel manager, production manager, or the like) whose job primarily involves supervising the work of other people. Then arrange an interview to obtain information regarding that person's job.

2. Ask the manager to identify the activities that he or she considers important and those that are time-consuming. The following managerial job questionnaire can be a guide.

3. Prepare a managerial job profile by compiling your findings and those of other students. The average scores for the relative importance and the time consumption of each item can be the basis of the profile. Rankings can be made from these average scores.

4. Make comparisons among managers in different functional groups and in different hierarchical levels.

5. Discuss the implications of these findings for improving managerial performance and for managerial education.

* Kae H. Chung and Leon C. Megginson, *Organizational Behavior: Developing Managerial Skills* (New York: Harper & Row, 1981), pp. 23–25.

The managerial job questionnaire

Managerial activities	Importance	Time consumed
Interpersonal roles *Figurehead:* Activities involving ceremonial, social, or legal duties (dinners, luncheons, signing contracts, civic affairs, etc.)		
Leader: Motivating, guiding, and developing subordinates (staffing, training, and rewarding employees)		
Liaison: Maintaining contacts with people outside your chain of command (staff meetings, lunches with peers, customers, and suppliers)		
Informational roles *Monitor:* Seeking and obtaining information through verbal and written communication media (meetings, memos, reports, telephone calls)		
Disseminator: Transmitting information to subordinates (through meetings, memos, briefings, and telephone calls)		
Spokesperson: Transmitting information to people outside the work group (speaking to groups, reporting to outsiders, and briefing stockholders)		
Decision roles *Entrepreneur:* Searching for business opportunities and planning new activities for performance improvement (new venture, new product, and planning)		
Disturbance handler: Taking corrective actions on problems or pressures (labor strikes, material shortages, and personal conflict resolutions)		
Resource allocator: Deciding which organizational units get what resources and how much (budgeting, capital expenditure decisions, and personnel assignment)		
Negotiator: Negotiating with employees, customers, suppliers, and unions (sales negotiations, labor contract negotiations, and salary negotiations)		
Administrative activities: Processing paperwork, budgetary administration, and monitoring rules and regulations		
Technical activities: Solving technical problems, supervising the technical work, and working with tools and equipment		
Organizing activities: Organizing or reorganizing group activities, reassigning tasks, and defining authority and responsibility relationships		

The managerial job questionnaire
Instructions: The items in the managerial job questionnaire on page 47 concern the activities you perform as a manager. This survey is to identify the relative importance you attach to various managerial activities and the amount of time per week you devote to each activity or role. Enter an appropriate number for each activity on the basis of a 5-point scale, with *1* representing *least important* or *least time-consuming* and *5* representing *most important* or *most time-consuming.*

NOTES

1. Henri Fayol, *General and Industrial Management,* trans. Constance Storrs (New York: Pitman, 1949), p. xxi.
2. These five categories (plus environment) are those used in the functional analysis performed by the *Wall Street Journal* to classify its articles dealing with the discipline of management.
3. "Life at the Top—What It Takes to Run a Big Business," *U.S. News & World Report.* June 15, 1981, p. 39.
4. Henry Mintzberg, *The Nature of Managerial Work* (New York: Harper & Row, 1973). See also Mintzberg, "The Manager's Job," *Harvard Business Review* 53 (July–August 1975): 49–61.
5. *U.S. News & World Report,* March 9, 1987, p. 21.
6. *Wall Street Journal,* June 18, 1981, p. 17.
7. Robert B. Lamb, *Running American Business* (New York: Basic Books, 1987).
8. Rosemary Stewart, *Managers and Their Jobs* (New York: Macmillan, 1967).
9. Mintzberg, *Nature of Managerial Work,* p. 38.
10. E. E. Lawler, L. W. Porter, and A. S. Tannenbaum, "Managers' Attitudes Toward Interaction Episodes," *Journal of Applied Psychology* 52 (1968): 432–439.
11. E. E. Jennings, *The Mobile Manager* (Ann Arbor: University of Michigan Bureau of Industrial Relations, 1967).
12. This list of managerial skills was derived from Robert Katz, "Skills of an Effective Administrator," *Harvard Business Review* 52 (September–October 1974): 90–102; and Mintzberg, *Nature of Managerial Work,* pp. 188–193.
13. P. J. Guglielmino, "Developing the Top-Level Executive for the 1980's and Beyond," *Training and Development Journal* 33 (April 1979): 12–14.
14. Michael Schiffres, "Challenges Future Managers Will Face," *U.S. News & World Report,* December 23, 1985, p. 46.
15. Lamb, *Running American Business.*

SUGGESTIONS FOR FURTHER STUDY

Bowman, James S. "The Meaning of Work and the Middle Manager." *California Management Review* 19 (Spring 1977): 63–70.

Drucker, Peter F. *Management: Tasks, Responsibilities and Practices.* New York: Harper & Row, 1974.

Ford, Jeffrey D., and Hegarty, W. Harvey. "Division Makers' Beliefs About the Causes and Effects of Structure: An Exploratory Study." *Academy of Management Journal* 27 (June 1984): 271–291.

Keller, Robert T., and Holland, Winford E. "Communicators and Innovators in Research and Development Organizations." *Academy of Management Journal* 26 (December 1983): 742–749.

Kiechel, Walter, III. "How Executives Think." *Fortune,* February 4, 1985, pp. 127–128.

McCarthy, Michael J. "A CEO's Life: Money, Security, and Meetings." *Wall Street Journal,* July 7, 1987, p. 31.

Mills, Peter K. *Managing Service Industries: Organizational Practices in a Postindustrial Economy.* Cambridge, MA: Ballinger, 1986.

ROETHLISBERGER, FRITZ J. "The Foreman: Master and Victim of Double Talk." In *Man in Organization.* Cambridge, MA: Harvard University Press/Belknap Press, 1968.

TSUI, ANNE S., and GUTEK, BARBARA A. "A Role Set Analysis of Gender Differences in Performance, Affective Relationships, and Career Success of Industrial Middle Managers." *Academy of Management Journal* 27 (September 1984): 619–635.

WATERS, JAMES A. "Managerial Skill Development." *Academy of Management Review* 5 (July 1980): 449–453.

3

The Evolution of Management Thought

Learning Objectives

After studying the material in this chapter, you should be able to do the following:

□ Explain the importance of studying the evolution of management thought.

□ Understand that the development of management thought has been a slow evolutionary process.

□ Describe the early beginnings of management knowledge.

□ Distinguish among the scientific, behavioral, management science, systems, and contingency approaches to management.

□ Explain the basis and characteristics of the scientific approach, the reasons for using it, and the reason for its decline in popularity.

□ Explain the basis and characteristics of the behavioral approach, the reasons for using it, and the reason for its decline in popularity.

□ Explain the basis and characteristics of the contemporary approaches and the reasons for using them.

Outline of the Chapter

Management knowledge has evolved slowly
Some early developments
How the Industrial Revolution affected management
Development of management in the United States
The scientific approach
Forerunner of the scientific approach
Frederick W. Taylor's scientific management
Henri Fayol's administrative management
The contributions of Fayol and Taylor compared
Other contributors to the scientific approach
The scientific approach in perspective

The behavioral approach
Forerunners of the behavioral approach
Oliver Sheldon's philosophy of management
The Hawthorne experiments
Mary Parker Follett's integration process
Chester Barnard's acceptance theory of authority
The behavioral approach in perspective
Some contemporary approaches
The management science approach
The systems approach
The contingency approach
Evaluation of the contemporary approaches
In search of excellence
The evolutionary process now speeding up
Summary

Some Important Terms

Industrial Revolution
feudal system
guild system
cottage system
factory system
laissez-faire, laissez-passer
trial-and-error approach
scientific approach
scientific management movement
behavioral (humanistic, organic) approach
human-relations movement
management science (quantitative methods) approach

systems approach
contingency approach
principle of the transfer of skill
mental revolution
administrative management
economic man concept
Hawthorne effect
social ethic
integration process
acceptance theory of authority
operations research (OR)
system
closed system
open system
eclectic approach

What is past is prologue.
—WILLIAM SHAKESPEARE

To understand what is happening today or what will happen in the future, I look back.
—JUSTICE OLIVER WENDELL HOLMES

OPENING CASE

The Decline of the Roman Empire

Arnold Toynbee, the great British historian, believed that there were recognizable cycles in the rise and decline of organizations. For example, take the Roman Empire. During its ascendancy, Rome went through a period of expansion through arms, diplomacy, and building—especially of roads and aqueducts. The empire was successful for many years because of its intelligent rule of its conquered peoples.

Most provincials found life better under Roman rule than previously. They were allowed to retain their language and were granted Roman citizenship. After a long period of growth characterized by innovation, development, and a high energy level of the people, the empire began to stagnate and decline. As the "wealthy elite" moved into the so-called good life, they gained a reputation for hedonism, depravity, and corruption. Under the rule of the wealthy aristocracy, they became conservative and resisted change because they felt the old ways were best. Bribery of officials was rampant, and there was widespread scheming for power and control. Eventually, the leader lost control and the decline accelerated.

Some experts believe there are many parallels between the rise and fall of civilizations and the rise and fall of large organizations such as governments and conglomerates. Certainly, there are many lessons we can learn from historical developments. In fact, some experts, such as Lawrence Miller, author of *American Spirit*,[1] and John W. Gardner, maintain that stagnancy and decline are not inevitable and that organizations can go through processes of renewal and have the ability to offset stagnation and decline.

To what extent do you think there are parallels between the growth, stability, and decline of the Roman Empire and of organizations today? ∎

THIS CASE REINFORCES the conclusion of the writer George Santayana that "those who cannot remember the past are condemned to repeat it." Modern managers face many new, bewildering, and often contradictory ideas and situations. In order to handle them, managers need to understand not only *what* is happening but also *why* it is happening. And that *why* can best be understood when placed in historical perspective. Therefore, reviewing the evolution of management thought from the earliest days to the present should help you understand what is happening in the managerial world of today. In summary, a study of the unfolding drama of managerial relationships of the past should contribute greatly to our understanding of how to practice the dynamic, evolving process called *management*.

MANAGEMENT KNOWLEDGE HAS EVOLVED SLOWLY

Management, management concepts, and management techniques have always been used, either consciously or unconsciously. For example, Moses used the "span of management" and "delegation" principles in the exodus from Egypt around 1250 B.C.[2] Yet management thought was slow to develop for several reasons. First, from the days of the Greek philosophers through the Middle Ages, and even into the early modern period, business was not accepted as a respectable occupation. Second, early economists and political scientists were interested primarily in the national and international levels of analysis and did not concern themselves with the managerial or entre-preneurial aspects of business activities. Third, business people themselves did not aid the development of management thought, since they considered their profession an art rather than a science, explaining that principles cannot be applied to management as they can to sciences. Fourth, business, up to the last third of the nineteenth century, was operated principally on a small personal basis, as a sole proprietorship or partnership. Thus, there was little real incentive for management theory to develop.

Some Early Developments

There were, however, some early developments in the practice of manage-ment, with many of these developments still in use today.

Early civilizations. The great civilizations of Sumer, Babylon, Egypt, Assyria, and Persia had expert managers, as evidenced by their achievements. Many of these—such as the great pyramids of Egypt (see Figure 3.1)—cannot be duplicated with today's technology. The walled cities and canals of Sumer (whose builders relied on the use of merit wages); the hanging gardens, irrigation system, and astronomical and mathematical achievements of Bab-ylon; the highway and library systems of Assyria; and the great cities and wealth of Persia required organization and managerial genius to achieve. The Code of Hammurabi included incentive and minimum wages as early as 1800 B.C.

FIGURE 3.1
The Great Pyramid of Egypt.
SOURCE: Courtesy of The National Archives, The Egyptian Tourist Bureau.

Greece. The name *Greece* still brings visions of sophisticated art, architecture, literature, and civil government. These accomplishments required the application of involved and complex management knowledge. The citizens of Greek cities worked under the piecework system on government contracts.

Rome. As shown in the opening case, Rome once controlled the world from England to Asia and is still known for its systems of roads (many of which are still in use), elaborate construction of public buildings, commercial ventures, civil government, and the *Pax Romana* ("Roman peace"). These were developed and maintained by a military system that is still a model for today's armies. All these required the application of highly developed management knowledge. As early as 300 B.C., Rome used maximum wage laws to try to compensate for a shortage of labor (it didn't work then, either!).

China. China's Great Wall (see Figure 3.2), massive armies, intercontinental road system, and silk trade required considerable management expertise. The principle of specialization (division of labor) was used as early as 1650 B.C., and labor turnover was understood as early as 400 B.C. In 1978, an all-weather road was opened between China and northern Pakistan. It was built by hand by Chinese laborers along the original "silk route."

FIGURE 3.2
The Great Wall of China.
SOURCE: Roger Whittaker.
Copyright Camera Press (Text & Illustrations) Ltd., London.

Machiavelli. Over 400 years ago, a diplomat and civil servant in the city-state of Florence wrote a book called *The Prince.* His name was Niccolò Machiavelli, and he was an experienced observer of the intrigues of state. His book was a how-to-do-it treatise for a ruler or aspiring ruler. It focused on how to rule—not how to be good or wise—but how to rule successfully.

Machiavelli's beliefs about the nature of people of that time are illustrated by his famous statement, "Whoever desires to found a state and give it laws, must start with the assumption that all men are bad and ever ready to display their vicious nature whenever they may find occasion for it."[3] Consequently, a leader is justified in using any leadership style or tactic to cope with these types of people. That is, the end (maintaining power) justifies the means. Moreover, should a leader have to choose between being feared and loved, she or he should choose fear, since he can control fear but not love, which is changeable. In the late 1960s, Anthony Jay took many of Machiavelli's ideas and applied them to success in large organizations. He concluded that "Machiavelli ... is bursting with urgent advice and acute observation for the management of the great private and public corporations all over the world."[4]

> **What is your view?**
> Do you think Machiavellianism is prevalent in some of today's organizations? Give some examples or evidence to support your view.

The Catholic church. The Roman Catholic church has contributed greatly to the evolution of management thought. As Christianity spread and different sects emerged, the church needed to define more clearly its mission, purpose, objectives, policies, rules and regulations, and organizational hierarchy. It developed a strong centralized authority-responsibility relationship. However, the conflict between centralized and decentralized church authority has continued to present times. This issue, along with the extent of enforcement of policies, procedures, doctrines, and rules and regulations, is one of the major differentiating factors among the Christian denominations.

How the Industrial Revolution Affected Management

The systematic development of management theories, principles, and practices increased slowly until the **Industrial Revolution,** which began during the eighteenth century. The revolution in Europe actually occurred in two stages, over a period of one and one-half centuries (1700–1850).

Some of the forerunners of the Industrial Revolution were the **feudal system** in the rural areas and the **guild system** in the urban areas. These later merged into the **cottage system** of production, which, in turn, was supplanted by the **factory system** that was the heart of the Industrial Revolution.

The feudal system. The feudal system evolved and reached its peak of development in Europe during the Middle Ages. The *serfs,* who constituted the lowest order of workers, were neither slaves nor hired laborers. Economically, the serfs were bound to the land, but they had certain privileges (they could not be sold, and they received part of their produce) that generally corresponded with their responsibilities. This arrangement gave the serfs a status superior to that offered to slaves in most societies. The lords, for their part, were responsible for protecting the serfs from bandits, hostile lords, and other dangers.

The feudal system was principally designed to be a form of land tenure and was best adapted to rural and agrarian production. With the emergence of manufacturing and commercial industries as dominant economic forces, serfdom declined in importance and had largely disappeared from Europe before the end of the Middle Ages.[5]

The guild system. The development of crude manufacturing brought the laborers to cities and led to the guild system. Within the guild itself there were clear-cut differences among master craftsmen, journeymen, and apprentices. The *master* was the owner of the shop who employed the traveling *journeyman* to work for him. The *apprentice* was a young learner who usually worked for his board, lodging, and a small allowance. During the initial stages of the system, all three classes of workers were a closely knit social group, since they had to work closely together. This was the beginning of personnel management, since it involved selecting, training, and developing the workers, as well as wage and salary administration.

The cottage system. At the beginning of the eighteenth century, the cottage system was the most common form of industrial organization. Under that system, work was performed in the homes of the workers in rural areas. An independent merchant would pay the master craftsman on a piecework basis, and he, in turn, would pay the workers who did the actual production in their homes. The merchant capitalist had few management problems, since the place and conditions of work were not his concern. (With some modifications, this system is still used in places such as Hong Kong, Italy, and some parts of New England and Appalachia for producing handcrafted items such as clothing and wooden products.)

What is your view?

In the future, larger numbers of workers may be employed to do assigned work in their own homes. They will be linked to their companies by computers. What would be the impact of such a return to the home as a primary workplace? (Consider the effect on traffic patterns, child care, the garment industry, energy use.)

A new productive system. The Industrial Revolution was precipitated by a new productive system founded on the concept of economic freedom and by the invention and use of new tools, processes, and machines for manufacturing cotton and woolen products. The latter were made possible by a new energy source—the steam engine, using coal, a fossil fuel. All these factors indirectly resulted from the growth of knowledge during the great period of vigorous intellectual activity called the First Intellectual Revolution of the sixteenth and seventeenth centuries.

A new economic doctrine. The new system was based on the French concept of **laissez-faire, laissez-passer,**[6] the forerunner of the free enterprise system. Adam Smith, the noted economist, felt that if entrepreneurs were left alone to pursue their own self-interests they would be guided by an "invisible hand." According to Smith, this hand directs "the private interests and passions of men" toward that "which is most agreeable to the interest of the whole society."[7] Also, there were natural laws, such as the law of supply and demand, that would regulate economic relationships to the benefit of society. Finally, Smith said there was a mutual interest between the workers, who worked harder for more money, and the owners, who benefited from the profits derived from the extra production.

What is your view?
Do you see a similarity between these concepts and today's supply-side economics, with its emphasis on lower taxes and increased incentives to produce?

The factory system. The new economic doctrine and the invention of numerous machines to improve manufacture led to the factory system of production and eventually resulted in mass production processes. This was especially true of Eli Whitney's method of using interchangeable parts in production that made the assembly line possible.* These changes allowed people to have a higher standard of living, but the introduction of the factory system brought about extensive and intensive changes in the performance of managerial activities and functions.

Moreover, many psychological problems resulted from excessively long working hours, monotony, fatigue, noise, strain, and the ever-present danger of accidents. The workers lost the gratifying feeling of being individually important in their jobs. Employers could then hire women and children to run the machines, often replacing men.

The Industrial Revolution shifted production from the homes of the employees to the factories. This was possible because the fuel- and water-generated power systems supplanted the effort and energy of human and animal power. The master craftsmen and merchants became employees of the emerging group of capitalists, and the skill of employees was transferred to the newly developed tools and machines. *The need for capable managers was accelerated.*

Development of Management in the United States

Within a short period of time, the new factory system made obsolete the production and distribution activities in use in Europe at the time. Entrepreneurs became aware of problems they had not faced before the factory system emerged. But in most cases, they did not realize the relationship between the changing environment and their activities, nor did they understand the nature of the new managerial problems.

Early management practices. By the middle of the nineteenth century, business people in the United States began to have some serious human problems. Managers tended to exploit workers, for they assumed that labor was a commodity that could be bought and sold like other products and resources. Consequently, the gap between managers and workers widened as the factories enlarged.

Performance of the managerial activities, which was based on a **trial-and-error approach,** became increasingly lacking in accuracy and effi-

---

*Whitney lost money on his more famous cotton gin. Since it was so readily copied, he had to spend a great deal of time and money to protect his patents. He made his fortune by demonstrating the value of interchangeable musket parts to the U.S. Army.

ciency. Thus managers had to rely on their own judgment, their intuition, and their business records to remedy the immediate and critical problems, for they could not consider the long run. They were concerned primarily with the problems of machines, material, and equipment rather than with management activities as such.

How management has evolved. Management developed differently in the United States than in Europe, primarily because of the scarcity of human resources in the United States. Some of the possible approaches to the use of these resources in producing goods and services are shown in Figure 3.3. It shows a continuum of the possible approaches to managerial behavior in an organization. These approaches are based primarily on two dimensions: (1) the manager's concern with production and operations and his or her use of authority to obtain it, as opposed to (2) concern for subordinates and the human relationships with which they are involved. During later periods, the effects of the external environments became important.

We have made an effort to develop these thoughts in chronological order. The trial-and-error approach deserves no more coverage. Therefore, the next section traces the development of the **scientific approach,** which sought efficient operations and regarded workers as just another factor of production, like land or equipment. The **scientific management movement** that tried to increase production while improving the employees' working conditions and increasing earnings is an example of an enlightened scientific approach.

The **behavioral approach** (also called **humanistic** and **organic**), which emphasized favorable treatment of employees rather than their output or performance, is covered next. The movements beginning in the Hawthorne experiments are first described, and then the **human-relations movement** is discussed more fully.

The reaction to these two movements resulted in the development of several contemporary approaches, especially the **management science**

FIGURE 3.3
Management
approaches used.

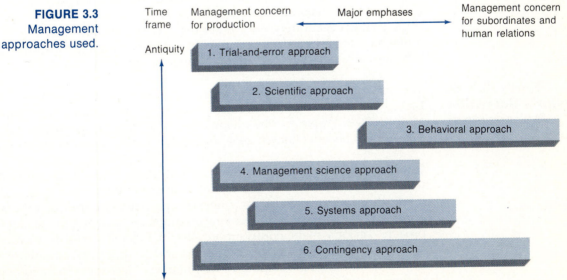

(**quantitative methods**) **approach,** the **systems approach,** and the **contingency approach.** These were a rational synthesis of the two previous approaches, using the better elements of each one. We believe that the approach most commonly used in the future will be a contingency approach, whereby management decisions and actions are determined by the prevailing situational elements.

THE SCIENTIFIC APPROACH

It was not difficult for early American entrepreneurs and managers to supervise small groups and obtain the desired results under the trial-and-error management system. Each business could be directed personally, and what little planning and control was needed could be done when necessary. As organizations grew larger, however, managerial problems became more significant, and the way the organization was managed determined the success or failure of the enterprise. However, during the last half of the nineteenth century, with the expansion of transportation (railroads) and communications (telegraph, telephone, and postal systems), the development of the western frontiers, and the mechanized plants and factories in the East, the need for more systematic management became evident. The people shown in Figure 3.4 were largely responsible for the development of this type of management—the *scientific approach.*

Forerunner of the Scientific Approach

Charles Babbage, a Cambridge professor and eminent mathematician, is given credit for writing the first treatise on management in the machine age. Babbage's work, entitled *On the Economy of Machinery and Manufacturers,* was published in 1832. The author is known primarily, however, for his formulation of the **principle of the transfer of skill,** namely: To the extent that a machine becomes more automatic and is able to produce large quantities of goods accurately, the worker using it requires less skill and becomes a machine tender rather than a skilled worker. Babbage also invented the differential calculating machine that foreshadowed the computer.

Frederick W. Taylor's Scientific Management

The earliest concepts of the scientific approach were introduced into the United States by Frederick W. Taylor (1856–1915), an engineer who joined the Midvale Steel Works in Philadelphia as a machine shop laborer in 1878.[8] These ideas became known as the *scientific management movement.*

Origin of his ideas. Although the origin of many of his ideas can be traced to other American, British, and French thinkers of the period, Taylor saw the implications of these ideas for American management and took the lead in improving the current management methods by applying the scientific approach. Taylor's main contribution was in making available to American factories, by codifying certain principles and stating them coherently, practices that had been developing in well-managed factories over a long period of time.

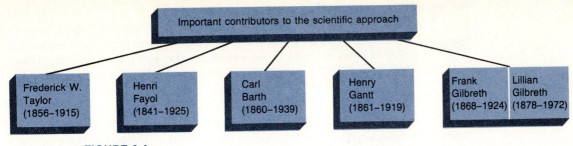

FIGURE 3.4
Important contributors
to the scientific
approach.

"Mental revolution" involved in the new system. Taylor considered the heart of his management approach to be a **mental revolution.** This meant that managers would want to increase productivity and share those gains with the workers through easier work and improved material well-being. Unfortunately, some of the systematizers, or efficiency experts, who sprang up in the early 1900s were among those who made use of the mechanics and techniques of scientific management without understanding and using the mental revolution. Being primarily concerned with speeding up production and increasing output, they often neglected to pay proper attention to the human element involved. It was this type of thinking that aroused opposition to Taylor's system from the labor movement and government officials.

Frederick Winslow Taylor (1856–1915).
(Courtesy of Ronald G. Greenwood.)

What is your view?

Have you seen the classic silent movie *Modern Times*, starring Charlie Chaplin? The film is a satire on the scientific approach. The manager has Chaplin, the worker, use his right hand to run a machine, then both hands, then both knees. Finally, the actor is using both hands, both knees, both elbows, and his head to run the machine. Do you think this is a valid use of the scientific approach?

Management responsibilities under the system. On the basis of his philosophy and experiments with selected workers, Taylor developed the following approach, which constituted the new duties of the professional manager under his system. Each manager would (1) develop a science for each element of a person's work that would replace the old rule-of-thumb method; (2) scientifically select, train, teach, and develop the workers (in the past, workers had chosen their own work and trained themselves as best they could); (3) heartily cooperate with the employees to ensure that all the work was done in accordance with the best available methods of operation; (4) divide the work and the responsibility almost equally between management and the workers; and (5) use incentive wages to motivate workers to produce more.

> *Taylor used his methods to improve the handling of pig iron. Having determined the best way to do the work, he sought "high-priced" men to demonstrate the improvements. A man called Schmidt was selected, was trained in the new method, and did exactly what he was told to do. He was told when—and how—to pick up the slab of iron (called a pig), when and how to walk, and when and how to put it down, as well as when and how long to rest. The results were impressive. Schmidt increased his daily output from 12.5 tons to 47 tons, for which his daily pay increased from $1.15 to $1.85.[9]*

Evaluation of Taylor's contributions. Taylor designed better work methods to enable workers to produce more. His research, experiments, speeches, and writings were directed toward the *lowest operating level* of the organization rather than higher management levels. The emphasis Taylor and his followers placed on small work groups at lower levels of the organization caused middle and top management to receive little attention in the United States and therefore to make little improvement.

Taylor actually did much more than he is given credit for. He developed an entire production (and management) system that was far ahead of its time. That system was partially responsible for our great productive systems during World Wars I and II.

Henri Fayol's Administrative Management

While Taylor's scientific management movement was being studied, praised, criticized, and expanded on in the United States, Henri Fayol (1841–1925) was revolutionizing management thinking in France with his studies and writings concerning universal principles of **administrative management** that could be applied to the entire organization.[10] He was Europe's most distinguished contributor to the field of management theory and practice up to the middle of the present century. Trained as a mining engineer, he

Henri Fayol (1841–1925).
(Courtesy of Ronald G. Greenwood.)

worked his way up to be the head of Comambault, a coal mining and iron foundry combine. He brought it from near bankruptcy to an extremely strong position. Whereas Taylor's focus was the bottom of the organization, Fayol zeroed in on management principles from the chief executive's point of view.

His two main concepts. Fayol's most important thesis concerned the universality of principles that may be applied to the functions of administration in all forms of organized human endeavor (see Chapter 1). His second major thesis was that there is a theory of management made up of a body of knowledge that can—and should—be taught. This led to the development of a management discipline that can validly be taught at the college level.

Basic principles of management. Fayol then developed 14 general principles of management (Figure 3.5) that applied to all types of human organizations. These were considered to be flexible and capable of meeting every managerial need, if one had the intelligence, experience, decision-making ability, and sense of proportion to use them properly and effectively. Many of these principles have lasted through time and will appear in this book, including (1) division of work, (2) authority and responsibility, (3) unity of command, and (4) the scalar chain.

FIGURE 3.5
Fayol's 14 principles of
management.

SOURCE: Henri Fayol, *General
and Industrial Management*.
Copyright 1987 by David S.
Lake Publishers, Belmont, CA.

1. **Division of work.** By performing only one part of the job, a worker can produce more and better work for the same effort. *Specialization* is the most efficient way to use human effort.

2. **Authority and responsibility.** Authority is the right to give orders and obtain obedience, and responsibility is a corollary of authority.

3. **Discipline.** Obedience to organizational rules is necessary. The best way to have good superiors and clear and fair rules and agreements is to apply sanctions and penalties judiciously.

4. **Unity of command.** There should be one and only one superior for each individual employee.

5. **Unity of direction.** All units in the organization should be moving toward the same objectives through coordinated and focused effort.

6. **Subordination of individual interest to general interest.** The interests of the organization should take priority over the interests of an individual employee.

7. **Remuneration of employees.** The overall pay and compensation for employees should be fair to both the employees and the organization.

8. **Centralization.** There should be a balance between subordinate involvement through decentralization and managers' retention of final authority through centralization.

9. **Scalar chain.** Organizations should have a chain of authority and communication that runs from the top to the bottom and should be followed by managers and subordinates.

10. **Order.** People and materials must be in suitable places at the appropriate time for maximum efficiency—that is, a place for everything and everything in its place.

11. **Equity.** Good sense and experience are needed to ensure fairness to all employees, who should be treated as equally as possible.

12. **Stability of personnel.** Employee turnover should be minimized to maintain organizational efficiency.

13. **Initiative.** Workers should be encouraged to develop and carry out plans for improvements.

14. **Esprit de corps.** Management should promote a team spirit of unity and harmony among employees.

Basic functions of management. The functions (elements) of management required to apply these principles effectively were (1) planning, (2) organizing, (3) commanding, (4) coordinating, and (5) controlling. Fayol explained each of these in detail, but they are not discussed in detail here, since they were essentially covered in the previous chapter.

What is your view?

Recall the functions of management we discussed in Chapter 2. How do these compare with those of Fayol?

The Contributions of Fayol and Taylor Compared

The concept of "universality of management" is the primary common ground between Fayol and Taylor, although they started from opposite ends of the organizational hierarchy. Taylor's main contribution to the field of management theory was his emphasis on rational analysis of problems, but he contributed little to the specific management principles that since have been demonstrated by Fayol and his followers. In fact, Fayol was inclined to be unsympathetic to Taylor's views, although both men were engineers, scientists, and managers, and both dedicated their lives to advancing the idea of applying science to administration. Fayol accepted Taylor's contributions when he realized that their work was complementary in the advancement of the science of managing.

Other Contributors to the Scientific Approach

The associates of Taylor who contributed most to the scientific approach in industry were Carl G. Barth, Henry L. Gantt, Frank and Lillian Gilbreth, and Henry Ford.

Carl Barth (1860–1939). Carl G. Barth, who worked closely with Taylor, had as much to do with developing, testing, and perfecting the mechanisms of scientific management as Taylor himself. Barth's greatest contribution was the development of the slide rule that bears his name. This was a predecessor of the computer.

Henry Gantt (1861–1919). Henry L. Gantt's greatest contribution was the extension of the use of graphic methods, now called the "Gantt chart" (see Fig. 15.8 for a modification of this chart), for recording performance. Gantt also began the production scheduling methods on which modern scheduling techniques are based.

Frank and Lillian Gilbreth. Frank and Lillian Gilbreth were a husband and wife team who expanded Taylor's ideas. Frank B. Gilbreth (1868–1924), a pioneer in developing time and motion studies, arrived at some of his management techniques independently of Taylor. He was interested in efficiency, especially in finding the "one best way to do the work." He was able to obtain—without undue fatigue—outputs that, according to one authority, trade union bricklayers in England considered impossible nearly 50 years later.[11]

Lillian Gilbreth (1878–1972) was most interested in the human aspects of work, such as the selection, placement, and training of personnel. She made a contribution to management by publishing the first book on management psychology.[12]

What is your view?

Perhaps you have read the book (or seen the movie) *Cheaper by the Dozen*. This story, based on the lives of the Gilbreths, was written by 2 of their 12 children, whom Frank and Lillian regimented into an efficiency that could be envied by any manager! Do you think organizational and management principles apply to family and/or home situations?

Frank Bunker Gilbreth (1868–1924) and
Lillian Gilbreth (1878–1972).
(Courtesy of Ronald G. Greenwood.)

Henry Ford (1863–1947). No discussion of the evolution of management thought would be complete without mentioning Henry Ford. In 1913 and 1914, he modified the assembly line that had been used in the meat-packing industry (based on Whitney's concept of interchangeable parts) and began the mass production of automobiles.

The Scientific Approach in Perspective

Under the scientific approach, managers' main responsibilities were to plan, direct, and control the actions of their subordinates to obtain the highest output from them. The goal was to achieve production objectives on schedule. Subordinates were expected to carry out the plans, directions, and controls imposed on them without question, since this type of supervision resulted from the valid use of authority by the manager and obedience on the part of subordinates.

Reasons for using the approach. The scientific approach did have many benefits and may still apply to certain types of work. Under this approach, subordinates tend to comply with the policies, job procedures, and rules and regulations that are imposed on them, making management's job easier. This type of system can be useful (1) when time is a critical factor in accomplishing the task, (2) when the number of people involved is high relative to the space available to bring them together, and (3) under conditions of stress or where survival is involved. For example, one study found that leaders who maintained an authoritative type of structure tended to be more effective under stress conditions than leaders who were more permissive.[13]

Reasons for the declining use of the approach. A basic assumption in this type of management is that there is little chance of, or need for, social groupings, since it is desirable to prevent the interactions of subordinates from interfering with their work. The primary concern for subordinates was in designing the workplace for the individual to minimize effort and fatigue so that maximum output could be obtained. Rewards under this system were based on the **economic man concept,** which assumed that motivation and rewards were achieved through providing employees with "a fair day's wage for a fair day's work."

Workers were seen as "biological machines." Yet, when work is completely planned for an employee, it becomes mechanical and fails to provide for the person's psychological needs, such as the desire for responsibility and meaningful, creative, satisfying work. Also, because of the dominance of power and authority, the employee's feeling of personal worth was essentially eliminated.

In effect, what happened under this form of management was that managers were prescribing to individuals what their needs were and also how they were to be satisfied. Consequently, the only thing the workers had to do was submit to management's dictates. Creativity ends not to flourish in this type of environment, particularly at lower levels.

In all deference to Taylor, Fayol, and their colleagues, although managers applying their principles often obtained increased production, they frequently failed to take sufficient account of the human factors present in the organization. The approach worked up through the Great Depression of the 1930s, with its massive unemployment and poverty, but failed with the advent of World War II, with its increased demand for, and declining supply of, workers.

What is your view?

Under what conditions, if any, would the scientific approach most likely be effective today? Why? Do you see any evidence that this approach is being used in industries (such as the auto, textile, or steel industries) that are faced with foreign competition?

THE BEHAVIORAL APPROACH

By the 1920s, the mechanization resulting from the Industrial Revolution, the assembly line technology introduced in the meat-packing industry and later perfected by Henry Ford, and the "mental revolution" of Taylor's scientific management combined to create the period of "perpetual prosperity," as the decade was designated. Yet the majority of entrepreneurs and professional managers still used the trial-and-error approach to managing that was almost universally practiced before the introduction of the scientific approach. Some of the leading entrepreneurs had accepted the new approach and were using it or introducing it into their operations. Yet criticisms were

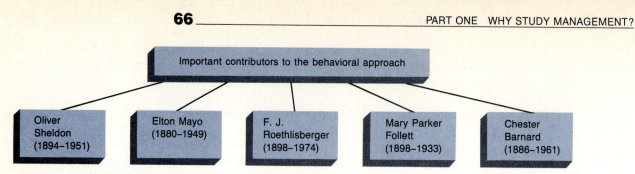

FIGURE 3.6
Important contributors
to the behavioral
approach.

already being directed toward the principles, at least in the form in which they were being practiced.

Many critics found contradictions among the various principles. Some showed that inadequate attention had been given to the concept of motivation. Other thinkers felt that these principles were only a part of management thought, and some were already suspecting that many of the assumptions on which these principles were apparently based might not necessarily be true. Some critics felt that it had been erroneously assumed that motivation was unrelated to job content, methods, and procedures.

Forerunners of the Behavioral Approach

The *behavioral* approach, which is also called the *organic* or *humanistic* approach, did not really begin in the 1920s. Instead, there were at least three outstanding forerunners of the approach. First, Robert Owen, a Scottish mill owner, socialist, reformer, philanthropist, and humanitarian, had been an early practitioner of this approach.[14] He believed that to abolish poverty it was necessary to eliminate the influences of a hostile environment. To improve the individual as a person and as an employee, and thereby achieve increased productivity, it was necessary either to remove him or her from an adverse physical, social, and economic environment or to change that environment by providing more satisfactory living and working conditions.

Owen therefore organized model villages next to his cotton mills in Scotland from 1800 to 1828 and had the employees plant trees, shrubs, flowers, and gardens around their homes. He introduced into his factories such unheard-of facilities as shower baths and toilets, and the factories themselves were cleaned and painted and had windows for light and ventilation. Day schools were organized for the children, and night schools for the workers. Later Owen abolished child labor altogether.

Hugo Munsterberg, the "father of industrial psychology," emphasized as early as 1913 the need for studying human behavior, in addition to scientific management.[15] Max Weber, an early sociologist, had shown that bureaucracy was an ideal way to ease the transition from small-scale entrepreneurial management to professional management of large-scale enterprises.[16] Based on these beginnings, the group of pioneers shown in Figure 3.6 drastically changed the direction of management theory and practice.

Oliver Sheldon's Philosophy of Management

The main questions about the scientific method focused on the objectives of management, the methods of motivation, and the nature of organizational relationships. Thus, a major contribution to the development of management thought was made by Oliver Sheldon with his statement in 1923 of a philosophy of management. Sheldon anticipated the activists of the 1960s and 1970s by emphasizing that a business has a "soul"' and that management has social responsibilities "as a major partner in the community, alongside capital and labour."[17] Furthermore, he thought of management in a much broader sense than did Taylor, or even Fayol, for he included the determination and execution of policy, coordination of functions, and other organizational processes as valid and integral activities of management.

Sheldon's ideas set the stage for introducing a new approach to solving management's problems. This came in the form of the *human-relations movement*—the process of motivating individuals in a given situation to achieve a balance of objectives that would yield greater human satisfaction *and* achieve organizational goals.

The Hawthorne Experiments

The behavioral approach is generally considered to have started with the experiments conducted at the Hawthorne plant of the Western Electric Company near Chicago from 1924 to 1932. A series of studies there led to the discovery of the new dimensions in the meaning of work, motivation, and organizational and interpersonal relationships. The studies revealed that the powerful incentive toward increased production was not due to physical working conditions or financial rewards but was the result of the **Hawthorne effect,** whereby workers felt important and appreciated because they were chosen as subjects for a scientific study.

Background. The Western Electric Company was a progressive organization that had applied many of the philosophies, theories, and principles of scientific management. Despite all its progressiveness, however, worker dissension and dissatisfaction were quite prevalent. In fact, the streetcar conductor announced "All out for the jail" when unloading workers at the plant (see Figure 3.7). Researchers from the National Research Council of the National Academy of Sciences began a series of experiments in 1924 in an attempt to find a causal relationship between the physical environment and improved performance.

The original experiment focused on the relationship between lighting intensities and productivity. Two groups of workers were selected, one group in which experiments would be conducted and one to be used as a control group. Illumination was increased for the experimental group, and productivity increased. This was consistent with the experimenters' original expectations and hypotheses. The experimenters were surprised, however, to discover that the productivity of the control group (whose lighting had not been changed) had also increased! To test the findings further, the illumination of the test group was lowered, and to the amazement of the researchers, the productivity of the test group increased again. The group of researchers withdrew from the experiments, completely baffled.

What is your view?

If the changed illumination level wasn't responsible for the increases in productivity in the experimental and control groups, what do you think was the actual cause?

The relay-assembly test group. Later, in 1927, a group of industrial psychologists led by George Elton Mayo (1880–1949), an associate professor of the Harvard Graduate School of Business, began a series of experiments at Hawthorne. F. J. Roethlisberger (1898–1974), one of Mayo's colleagues, related

FIGURE 3.7
The telephone apparatus building of the Hawthorne plant of Western Electric Company in 1931.

SOURCE: Courtesy of Western Electric Photographic Services.

that in the beginning the inquiry was concerned primarily with the relation between conditions of work—such as shorter workdays and workweeks, rest periods, company-provided lunches, and varied starting and stopping times and the resulting fatigue and monotony—and hourly and total output.

Later, six 15- to 16-year-old girls were carefully selected and put in a separate room (see Figure 3.8), each girl performing the same job—one that could be completed in a short time. The operators were selected because they were experienced, willing, and cooperative. There were five assemblers and one layout operator (far left in the photograph), who assigned work and obtained parts. They were observed, and their output was measured and recorded. Their output, attendance, and morale increased steadily over a period of two and one-half years.

Other experiments were performed with the relay-assembly group, a mica-splitting group, and a bank-wiring group. An interview program—emphasizing the nondirective, listening approach—involved the supervisors and subordinates.

As a result of the magnitude of the studies, the inquiry stretched on until 1932, when the experiment was suspended for external reasons—including the Great Depression. From an original observation of six workers, the investigation at one stage expanded to include a variety of studies (including an

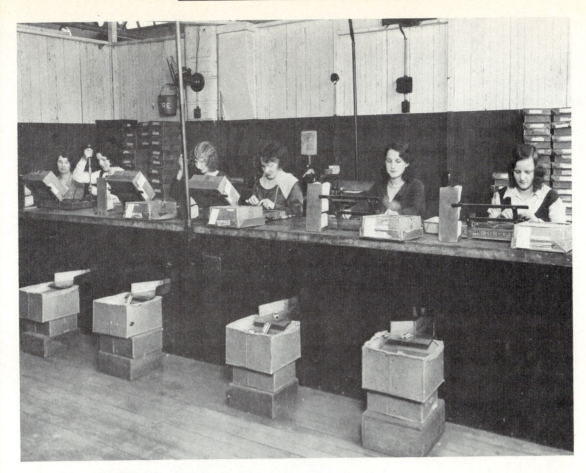

FIGURE 3.8
The relay room of the
Hawthorne plant in 1927.

SOURCE: Courtesy of Western
Electric Photographic Services.

interview and counseling program) involving approximately 21,000 individual employees.[18]

What is your view?

Are you curious about what became of the six girls? In 1932 the girls' jobs were terminated because of the depression, but many went back to work during World War II. One of them, Theresa Layman Zajas (fourth from the right in the photograph), was still employed at the time of the celebration of the 50th Anniversary of the Hawthorne studies in 1974. Three of the others attended the anniversary banquet, one was in a nursing home, and one had returned to Europe. Did you think they were older?

Results of the experiments. These studies served to upset some of the traditional principles of industrial efficiency. They also became the stimulus to the humanistic approach to management and provided its conceptual framework—namely, that increased morale results in increased productivity. However, subsequent experiments supported the finding that the workers' productivity increased simply because they felt that someone was taking an interest in them, making them feel important in their jobs. (Had you already guessed this?) Another result was a shift away from the individualistic ethic toward the **social ethic,** which has as its foundation the corporate well-being of society, and toward the value of harmony in interpersonal and intergroup relationships.

Mary Parker Follett's Integration Process

Mary Parker Follett (1868–1933) served as a link between the scientific and humanistic periods. Yet she leaned toward the latter. Ignored for a long time, her ideas are found in many management and psychology textbooks today. One of her contributions was her analysis of how to deal with conflict. She believed that any conflict of interest could be resolved by (1) voluntary submission of one side, (2) struggle and victory of one side over the other, (3) compromise, or (4) integration (today we call it joint problem solving).

The preferred solution would be an **integration process,** whereby everyone wins, as opposed to a win-lose situation, or a watered-down compromise where neither side gets what it wants. An example she gave to illustrate the concept of integration was an incident that occurred when she was working in a small room in the Harvard library. The other person in the room wanted the window open, while Follett wanted it closed. After discussion, integration was achieved when they opened a window in the next room. This solution was not a compromise, since both got what they wanted: The other person got fresh air, but Follett did not have a cold draft on her back.[19]

Follett also believed that the essence of good human relations was cre-

Mary Parker Follett (1868–1933).
(Courtesy of Ronald G. Greenwood.)

ating the feeling of working *with* someone rather than *over* or *under* some-one—the notion of "power with" rather than "power over." For example, if an accounting manager discovered that a person working in the office was making a mistake, instead of giving a direct order and specific instructions on how to correct it, he or she might say, "We seem to be short $5000. Let's look at the statement and see what needs to be done to correct it." Thus, instead of giving a direct order, the manager works with the other person, and the order (correction) is derived from the situation.

Chester Barnard's Acceptance Theory of Authority

Chester Barnard (1886–1961), president of the New Jersey Bell Telephone Company, wrote widely on a variety of management subjects, but his most influential book was *The Functions of the Executive*, written in 1938.[20] He saw organizations as systems of goal-directed activities. Management's primary functions, in Barnard's view, are formulating objectives and acquiring the resources required to meet the objectives.

Barnard emphasized communication as an important means of achieving group goals. He also introduced a new **acceptance theory of authority.** According to his theory, subordinates will accept orders only if they understand them and are able and willing to comply with them. Barnard was a pioneer in advocating the "systems approach" to managing.

The Behavioral Approach in Perspective

Like the scientific management movement, the human-relations movement was not immediately recognized and accepted for what it was—namely, another revolution in management philosophy, theory, and practice. The national environment of the early 1930s—the deepening depression, massive unemployment, new political experiments, the expanding labor movement, and an economy based on restricting output, increasing demand, and sharing the work—did not encourage the acceptance of the new approach. Hence general implementation of the approach came during the period from World War II until the late 1950s. Although it is still quite prevalent and will continue to be for some time, the approach is gradually being replaced by the newer approaches discussed in the next section.

Basic model. Under the behavioral approach, managers tend to be more concerned with morale building and maintenance of social interactions than with improving operations and output. Managers reason that high morale is a desirable objective and that it results from having good working conditions and congenial coworkers and being treated humanely.

The model for this approach was employee participation → job satisfaction → increased productivity. Yet there are at least three possible relationships between satisfaction and performance:

1. Satisfaction can contribute to, or influence, performance (satisfaction → performance).
2. There may be an uncertain relationship between satisfaction and performance, whereby it could go in either direction (satisfaction ⇆ performance).
3. Performance itself may contribute to satisfaction (performance → satisfaction).

Basic assumptions. The behavioral approach assumes that two insights are needed by management in all organizations. First, managers must regard the organization as a system designed to produce and distribute a product or service at a reasonable cost-price-profit relationship. And second, the organization is to be viewed as a social system through which individuals try to find expression for their hopes and aspirations, as well as to satisfy their economic needs. The two basic functions of management are to maintain the cost-price-profit relationship and to keep people working effectively while allowing individuals to develop their potential and find their place in society.

Some of the practitioners, however, have either been ignorant of or tended to ignore this dual basic philosophy. Consequently, in many organizations, "good" interpersonal and intergroup relationships were seen as most important, while the direct concern for efficient production was minimal. Major emphasis was placed on relationships, and inadequate concern was given to accomplishing other organizational objectives.

Reasons for the decline in the use of the behavioral approach. The behavioral approach has had its share of critics. Malcolm McNair, a vocal critic, and many others have frequently attacked human relations as representing "sloppy sentimentalism," "warm-feeling management," and even worse.[21] As with the scientific approach, however, most of the attacks seem to have come as a result of overzealous advocates using the form and techniques of the school of thought but disregarding its underlying philosophy. Regardless of the justice of criticism of the general theory, the fact remains that the humanistic approach has served to broaden the concepts of management theory and practice.

Types of organizations using the behavioral approach. There are at least five types of organizations in which the behavioral approach operates more efficiently. First, this approach may be effective in companies that operate on a cost-plus basis, such as defense and space program industries, and others with government contracts. Second, this approach is used in firms in which profits are so easy to make that operating efficiency is not an important objective. Third, the behavioral approach is used extensively in religious, educational, governmental, and other not-for-profit organizations. Fourth, organizations, or divisions, that are highly research oriented use this approach, since creative people are likely to object to the authority-obedience assumptions usually associated with other approaches. Fifth, it is used in situations in which workers have a strong internalized drive toward reaching the objective. For example, researchers and professionals (who say, "Treat me nicely and let the work take care of itself") tend to be highly committed workers.

To summarize, then, the organizations most likely to use the behavioral approach are:

1. Firms operating on cost-plus contracts.
2. Firms to which profits come easily.
3. Not-for-profit organizations.
4. Organizations or units that are highly research oriented.
5. Organizations in which workers have strong motivation and drive.

SOME CONTEMPORARY APPROACHES

Several *contemporary approaches* that have evolved since World War II resulted from a blending, meshing, or *synthesis*, of the scientific and behavioral approaches.

The quantitative theorists of the scientific movement were predominantly engineers, whereas the behavioral theorists were mainly industrial psychologists. The engineers studied the work areas for more efficient production; the psychologists made studies of job satisfaction, morale, productivity, and conflict resolution.

The contemporary approaches have included researchers from varied disciplines—behavioral science (psychology and sociology), systems theory, operations research (quantitative experts), decision theory, statistics, computer sciences, and other areas of research methodology. These unique combinations are providing greater validity in research, resulting in the evolution of a strong management science. With the strengthening of the basic disciplines underlying management science and an increased understanding of the use and application of behavioral, statistical, and mathematical techniques, we have seen the development of better management theory, one based on rigorous testing of propositions and more reliable knowledge of management processes and techniques.

The starting point for the contemporary approaches was dissatisfaction with the principles proclaimed by the scientific management and human-relations writers. Today's scholars believe that neither of these early movements was sufficiently rigorous in its methods to provide valid principles and theories.

The most popular contemporary approaches are (1) the management science (quantitative methods) approach, (2) the systems approach, and (3) the contingency approach. The influence of Peter Drucker runs through all these approaches, as shown in MAP 3.1. Drucker contributed to the development of these approaches through his insightful studies, writings, and consulting.

Management "guru" Peter F. Drucker.

Management Application and Practice 3.1   Peter F. Drucker—Management Popularizer

Peter F. Drucker can be called "the father of modern management" for his pioneering work in the 1940s and 1950s. His lengthy study of General Motors in 1943 was the first detailed study of the inner workings of a major U.S. corporation. From this and later studies by Drucker grew the concept that management is a job separate and distinct from other activities in an organization.

Drucker's greatest contribution to the evolution of management has been to codify, popularize, and institute some of today's basic management concepts and practices. For example, in the 1950s, he formulated the concept of *management by objectives (MBO)*, a method of redesigning an organization to allow managers and subordinates to set their own goals. He also applied the military concept of strategy to other organizations. And his idea that innovation can be fostered by management within an organization is a cornerstone of today's concept of *intrapreneurship.*

How does Drucker manage to have companies lining up to pay him fees two or three times as high as those charged by other consultants and to have people clamoring to get into his courses and management seminars at Claremont Graduate School? His success is probably based on his ability to see the world differently from the way others see it and to arrive at practical solutions to difficult problems.

But his scholarly and freewheeling approach to problems is not without its critics. For example, some academics find his analysis insufficiently rigorous, and some consultants find it impractical. But despite what admirers and critics say about him, he has greatly influenced the evolution of management thought.

SOURCE: Peter F. Drucker, *The Practice of Management* (New York: Harper & Row, 1954); Amanda Bennett, "Management Guru: Peter Drucker Wins Devotion of Top Firms with Eclectic Counsel," *Wall Street Journal*, July 28, 1987, pp. 1 and 12; and Kathy Rebello, "Peter Drucker: His 'Management by Objectives' Is a Commandment for Execs," *USA Today*, October 26, 1987, p. 4B.

The Management Science Approach

As you remember from the earlier discussion, Taylor's scientific management approach was a systematic way of making management decisions instead of using a seat-of-the-pants approach. Scientific management was primarily applied to production and operations problems but was limited in its use of mathematics and statistics. On the other hand, the *management science* (or *quantitative methods*) *approach* refers to decision-making techniques developed over the past 45 years that involve the use of mathematical models and usually require the use of a computer. Management science techniques can be used to help managers solve problems in a broad range of management situations, such as decision making and operations management.

Management science approaches originated during World War II in the form of **operations research (OR).** Basically, OR involved pulling together teams of scientists—such as mathematicians, physicists, and statisticians—rather than military experts to help the Allied forces make certain strategic operating decisions. OR was highly successful and was given marked credit for Allied successes. After World War II, many OR specialists returned to their positions in U.S. universities, businesses, and government organizations and applied some of the OR techniques to a wide variety of business problems.

Some of the kinds of problems they had successfully resolved during the war were:

1. What distribution of ground antiaircraft batteries and what firing patterns would maximize protection against enemy air raids?

2. What cluster of bombing patterns would inflict maximum damage on enemy targets?

3. What deployment of depth charges would result in the greatest number of enemy submarine "kills"?

In management science and operations research, specialists pool their knowledge to develop quantitative models. Mathematical models are designed to represent the behavior of the variables in each situation. Once the models are designed, they can be manipulated to reflect changes in the variables and to select solutions for optimum results.

This approach is used in most high-tech, transportation, automobile manufacturing, and aerospace industries today. It is used for activities such as finding the optimum location and layout of facilities improving sequencing of operations, and designing products.

The techniques and applications of the management science approach are covered in detail in Chapters 15 and 16.

The Systems Approach

Change is probably the most critical factor affecting the lives of individuals as well as the operations of a business enterprise. Those who can adapt to it survive; those who cannot, stagnate and may even die. The relative stability of the 1950s was shattered by the activism of the 1960s. Management of organizations found the external social, political, and legal environments influencing almost every decision. Previous approaches to managing no longer worked. A new approach—the *systems approach*—was mandated. It integrated the universal management functions, the managerial activities approach, and strategic planning with the importance of external factors.

What is a system? The leading pioneers in the development of the systems approach were Richard Johnson, Fremont Kast, and James Rosenzweig. They define a **system** as "an organized or complex whole; an assemblage or combination of things, or parts forming a complex or unitary whole."[22] A system is made up of (1) inputs, (2) operations (or processes), and (3) outputs, as shown in Figure 3.9. A management system can be compared to the human body, in which each organ is related to, interacts with, and is depen-

FIGURE 3.9
The systems approach.

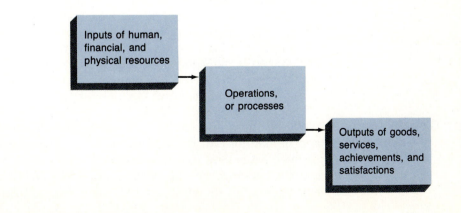

dent on the proper functioning of the other organs. If something happens to one part of the body, the other parts are affected.

Systems can be either closed or open. A **closed system** tends to move toward a static equilibrium, as, for example, does a heat pump. On the other hand, an **open system,** such as an organization, tends to be in a dynamic relationship with its environment, receiving various inputs, transforming them in some way, and producing outputs. The receiving of inputs in the form of material, energy, and information, along with feedback regarding outputs, allows the open system to offset the process of decline. Moreover, the open system adapts to its environment by changing the processes of its internal components or structure as the need arises. For example, an organization adds people and modifies its organization on the basis of increased demand and sale of its products and services.

An organization is a system. The systems approach to management has three goals: (1) to define relationships both internal and external to the business organization, (2) to see the pattern of these relationships, and (3) to see the overall purpose of the relationships. As stated, the systems approach is essentially a way of thinking about the organization—its goals, objectives, and purposes—and the relationships among its parts.

The concept of the business organization as a system is not new, since many successful business people have used the approach that is now called the systems concept. For example, many of the builders of great corporations, such as Theodore Vail of AT&T and Alfred Sloan of General Motors, had the ability to view the business as an integrated whole, or system. They were able to identify strengths and weaknesses and to see how those factors were critical to success. This approach was the basis of their genius for organizing their companies and developing their management capabilities.[23]

On the other hand, many of the 100 largest corporations in 1900 are not around today because their top managers ignored the systems concept. One was a manufacturing company that moved South to avoid labor unions. It was a family-owned concern that had been producing quality products for several generations; yet, within two decades of moving south, it was nearly bankrupt and was forced to sell out to a larger corporation. The company's decline was not caused by declines in quality of its product; rather, the decline resulted from an obsolete and inefficient marketing system and a closed-minded top management that would not accept suggestions for improvement from lower-level managers and professionals.

As we discussed in Chapter 1, conceptual skill, or the ability to see the big picture—to take a systems approach—is very important for top management. Today, more than ever before, automation, computerization, and the tremendous changes occurring in society have made a systems point of view necessary in managing a company. Systems thinking on the part of top management can protect a company from the same circumstances that caused buggy manufacturers to go bankrupt.

The Contingency Approach

While all these approaches have some validity, they also have weaknesses and limitations. We do not believe there is one best method of managing. Instead, we believe that now and in the near future effective managers will use the *contingency approach*. Combining the best aspects of the other approaches (as shown in Figure 3.10), the contingency approach theorizes

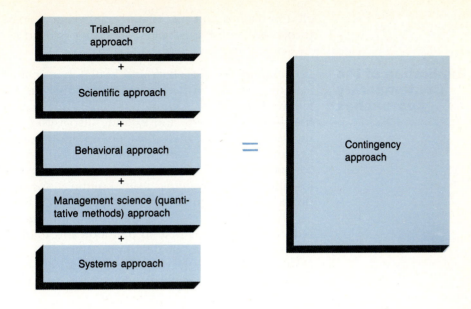

FIGURE 3.10
The contingency approach combines aspects of the other approaches.

that different conditions and situations require the application of different management techniques.[24]

Advocates of the contingency approach say there are few if any universal truths, concepts, or principles that can be applied under all conditions. Instead, every management situation must be approached with an "it all depends" attitude. Contingency theorists attempt to explain what styles or approaches would best apply under different circumstances, as shown in the TIPS 3.1.

Contingency theories have been developed in such areas as organization design, leadership, motivation, strategic planning, and group dynamics. We look at many of these in this book. In addition to the contingency approach, the **eclectic approach,** which draws on the best available information from

TIPS 3.1   Which Leadership Style to Use

"You have to know your people," said Ann Wardlow, principal of Emerson Elementary School. "I use a different leadership style with my experienced teachers, whom I know well and who are very capable. I seldom have to emphasize lesson plans, adherence to school policies, and so on. But I keep a close eye on my new teachers, especially a couple who seem very shaky. One in particular seems a bit headstrong in his dress and behavior, as if he's trying too hard to be one of the kids. Another is constantly in my office, afraid to make decisions on her own. But there's no doubt that you must know your people—their capabilities, experience, and knowledge, their role, attitudes, and relationships with peers and their students—to be able to handle each effectively. A subtle suggestion from me will get the message to some; with others I must be perfectly blunt and direct. The trick is in being skilled enough to know which approach works with whom. To use the same approach with every person would be disastrous."

all approaches and disciplines (such as sociology, psychology, cultural anthropology, and industrial engineering), is used in this text.

Evaluation of the Contemporary Approaches

Contemporary researchers and writers have contributed important insights into the practice of management, and the ideas of these professionals are followed closely throughout this book. They perceive that management is on the threshold of new and exciting discoveries in the fields of organization theory, strategic planning, leadership, motivation, conflict resolution, management of change, general systems theory, interpersonal competence, organizational development and effectiveness, decision theory, group dynamics, information systems, team building, operations research, matrix and project management, and the quality of work life of employees.

The new theorists, who are quoted throughout the book, use the most recent advances in research methods and mathematics and computers for making many kinds of decisions. The mark of the new approach is its emphasis on sophisticated research methods, empirical investigation (based on observation and experience), and rigorous testing of hypotheses.

What is your view?

What effect(s) do you think the computer is having on contemporary management theories and practice? What effect(s) do you expect it to have in the future?

In Search of Excellence

Successful managers are constantly looking for ways to improve organizational effectiveness. They have to because of increasing international competition and the increasing rate of innovation and change. As we saw in the opening case, organizations go through periods of stagnation and decline just as civilizations do. However, more and more U.S. organizations are fighting back by undergoing renewal processes and achieving productivity increases. For example, in a survey of 1598 firms, the American Productivity Center and the American Compensation Association found that today's com-

Thomas J. Peters and Robert Waterman.

panies are using innovative reward systems and more supportive human-resource practices to increase productivity. Most of these programs have been instituted recently and run the gamut from gain sharing and small-group incentive plans to employee involvement programs encompassing participative management concepts.

We believe that the current approaches to the practice of management are best exemplified by *In Search of Excellence*, by Thomas J. Peters and Robert Waterman. This widely quoted book is causing many firms to examine past practices and initiate renewal processes.[25]

The attributes of excellent companies. The attributes, or characteristics, that distinguish the excellent and innovative companies in America, according to Peters and Waterman, are these:[26]

1. *A bias for action.* These companies "get on with it." They don't let bureaucracy, such as market research, keep them from making decisions.

2. *Closeness to the customer.* They love their customers and learn from the people they serve.

3. *Autonomy and entrepreneurship.* They have "product champions" who generate new products or services. They encourage these people to "make sure you generate a reasonable number of mistakes."

4. *Productivity through people.* They treat the rank and file as the source of quality and productivity gain. They love their people, or, better, they respect the individual.

5. *Hands-on, value-driven.* Company values and philosophy are more important than organizational structure.

6. *"Stick to the knitting."* They never acquire a business they don't know how to run.

7. *Lean staff, simple form.* They have simple organizational structures and lean top-level staffs.

8. *Simultaneous loose-tight properties.* They are both centralized (about the few core values) and decentralized (product development and "product champions").

Criticisms of *In Search of Excellence*. As with all management approaches, questions have been raised over the lack of specifics from Peters and Waterman as to how the excellent firms were analyzed and how the eight attributes of excellence were identified. Some have raised questions as to whether the same eight attributes would apply to firms operating in different environments. Peters and Waterman propose the same attributes of excellence for all firms competing in all types of environments.

A study by Michael Hitt and Duane Ireland raises the question of whether other factors, such as quality of technology development, efforts, and marketing, may be involved in excellence. They also indicate that the idea of contingency management is ignored in the book and warn managers to be cautious of concepts that propose a "quick fix."[27] Without question, Peters and Waterman have had a significant influence on the thinking of many managers.

THE EVOLUTIONARY PROCESS NOW SPEEDING UP

Although management philosophies, and the resulting improved practices, have been developing for centuries, the pace has quickened during the last four decades. During that time, many major progressive organizations tried to apply some of the newer management concepts to improve performance. There are, however, many differences, variations, and inconsistencies in the theories, concepts, and programs these organizations are presenting to their employees—as well as in the reactions of employees to these new ideas.

SUMMARY

Today's concepts of management are the product of a long and complicated evolutionary process, one that is still under way and is revolutionizing management theory and practice. Many traditional ways of dealing with employees, customers, and the public are being questioned; many things assumed to be true about management theories are being challenged; and traditional management theories are in a state of confusion. In the past few decades, many writers have proclaimed that the traditional theories and concepts should be subordinated to the newer behavioral theories of administration, as well as the newer systems and contingency theories. The stated reason for these challenges is to see whether the older theories will stand up under the newer methods of the behavioral and quantitative sciences that study behavior in organizations.

The human-relations approach that developed from the Hawthorne experiments attempted to fill the gaps in the scientific approach fostered by the practitioners of scientific management. The discovery of new factors affecting employee productivity and morale opened up broad new fields for research and experimentation. The scientific theories of management were essentially nonpsychological, and the practitioners of theories paid little attention to the human element.

The main contributions of the behavioral scientists to management were the identification, isolation, and revelation of the importance of the human and social factors in organizational relationships. The development of realistic "scientific" techniques that were applicable to the study, as well as the management, of human and social behavior was also a major contribution of the humanists. Another major contribution was the demonstrated evidence that motivation involved multiple variables and was not solely a function of satisfying economic needs. Finally, it was learned that managers, instead of dealing with discrete individuals, had to operate within cultural and social systems and subsystems.

With the increasing professionalization of management since the 1930s, a most significant development has been the tendency of professional managers to be concerned with human and social relations as well as with maximizing profits. Constant and swift technological changes have necessitated that management thinking be geared to evolutionary—and even revolutionary—situations. Therefore, today's managers must be ready to face new problems and make rapid decisions involving more systematic and longer-range planning and development. Therefore, the contemporary approaches to management created a rational synthesis of the scientific and behavioral approaches to be applied to varied and changing situations. These situations are now viewed from a systems approach that considers the effects of the environment on management decisions.

Yet none of these approaches is completely acceptable in today's rapidly changing, and often hostile, environment. None of them fits all situations, so future managers must use a contingency approach; that is, every management situation must be approached with an "it all depends" attitude.

REVIEW QUESTIONS

1. What management developments occurred in the following countries?
   a. Greece
   b. Rome
   c. China
2. What is (or was) each of the following?
   a. The scientific approach
   b. The scientific management movement
   c. The behavioral approach
   d. The management science (quantitative methods) approach
   e. The systems approach
   f. The contingency approach
3. On what bases was the Industrial Revolution founded? Explain each.
4. What were the management responsibilities under Taylor's scientific management?
5. What was the relationship between Taylor's and Fayol's contributions to management?
6. What were some of the results of the Hawthorne experiments?
7. What were the primary contributions of the following?
   a. Carl Barth   g. Mary Parker Follett
   b. Henry Gantt   h. Chester Barnard
   c. Frank Gilbreth   i. Peter Drucker
   d. Lillian Gilbreth   j. Johnson, Kast, and Rosenzweig
   e. Mayo and Roethlisberger   k. Peters and Waterman
   f. Oliver Sheldon
8. What is the contingency approach?

DISCUSSION QUESTIONS

1. (a) Why has management knowledge evolved so slowly? (b) Why is the evolution now speeding up?
2. How did the Industrial Revolution affect management?
3. (a) Why did the scientific approach succeed? (b) Why did it fail?
4. (a) Why did the behavioral approach succeed? (b) Why did it fail?
5. To what extent have contemporary approaches succeeded? Failed?
6. Do you think the contingency approach will succeed? Why or why not?
7. Which of the three possible relationships between job satisfaction and performance do you think best explains what happens in work situations?
8. What caused the decline and fall of the Roman Empire? How could it have been prevented?

LEARNING EXERCISE 3.1

Employee Ownership

Municipal Steel was founded in 1917 by Henry Cooper. The company grew from a one-person operation to its present 1500 employees.

Henry Cooper was a devout Christian who was dedicated to the welfare of his employees. In the early years, religious prayer services were conducted on company time; today, there is a chapel on the premises and numerous religious maxims are displayed in signs throughout the plant. The plant medical clinic provides free medical care for employees and their immediate families, and the firm provides generous pensions and vacation plans and was one of the first to provide dental coverage for employees. Displayed in the major foyer are the pictures of 15 "employees of the month." The company provides a social and educational outlet for wives and families of employees, sponsoring bridge clubs, educational programs, recreational teams, and social gatherings.

"Mr. Henry" was highly respected by all employees. He spent one day each month performing one of the operative-level tasks alongside the other employees. From doing this, he got a "feel" for things and earned his employees' respect. He knew most of the employees by name. When Mr. Cooper died in 1957, his will stipulated that the company be left in a trust to be owned by its employees—one share per worker. The trust is governed today by a board of directors that includes company managers, key outsiders, and several employee representatives. Dividends are paid out directly to employees from profit and are based on salary. In a good year, employees might earn as much as 30 percent of their annual salary.

The company annual report emphasizes loyalty to employees and includes a reference to "doing whatever we can for our employees' welfare." Among the new programs recently mentioned are a free tuition refund program for attendance at local universities and the creation of a "company store," where grocery items can be bought at 10 to 15 percent less than in regular grocery stores. The company is nonunion with a financial performance rated "average" for the industry. Turnover is slightly below average.

Questions

1. Would you enjoy working for Municipal Steel? Why or why not?
2. Under which of the management approaches is the organization apparently operating?
3. Why do you suppose that it is only an "average" performer in the industry?

NOTES

1. Lawrence M. Miller, *American Spirit—Visions of a New Corporate Culture* (New York: Warner Books, 1985).
2. See Chapter 18 of the Book of Exodus.
3. Niccolò Machiavelli, *Discourses on Living,* trans. Alan H. Gilbert, repr. in *Machiavelli: The Chief Works and Others* (Durham, NC: Duke University Press, 1956), I: 203.
4. Anthony Jay, *Management and Machiavelli: An Inquiry into the Politics of Corporate Life* (New York: Bantam Books, 1968).
5. As late as 1861, however, there were still 20 million serfs in Russia. See W. Bowden, M. Karpovich, and A. P. Usher, *An Economic History of Europe Since 1750* (New York: American Book Co., 1937), p. 600.
6. Alfred Marshall, *Principles of Economics*, 8th ed. (New York: Macmillan, 1948). The term meant that people should be permitted to make what they want and to go where they please.
7. Adam Smith, *An Inquiry into the Nature and Causes of the Wealth of Nations* (New York: Modern Library, 1937; originally published in 1776).
8. L. Urwick, ed., *The Golden Book of Management* (London: Newman Neame, 1956), p. 76. Most of the material in this section is taken from pages 72–79 of that source

and from Frederick W. Taylor, *The Principles of Scientific Management* (New York: Harper & Row, 1947).

9. Taylor, p. 47.

10. Henri Fayol, *General and Industrial Management*, trans. Constance Storrs (New York: Pitman, 1949). The French original was published in 1916.

11. E. F. L. Brech, *Management: Its Nature and Significance* (New York: Pitman, 1948), p. 209.

12. Lillian M. Gilbreth, *The Psychology of Management* (New York: Sturgis and Walton, 1914; reissued by Macmillan, 1921).

13. F. E. Fiedler et al., "An Exploratory Study of Group Creativity in Laboratory Tasks," *Acta Psychologica* 18 (1961): 100–119.

14. Elbert Hubbard, *Little Journeys to the Homes of the Great*, anniversary ed. (New York: Wm. H. Wise & Co., 1916), pp. 9–49, esp. pp. 38–40.

15. Hugo Munsterberg, *Psychology and Industrial Efficiency* (Boston: Houghton Mifflin, 1913).

16. Max Weber, *The Protestant Ethic and the Spirit of Capitalism*, trans. Talcott Parsons (New York: Scribner, 1958). Originally published in German in 1905 and revised in 1920.

17. Oliver Sheldon, *The Philosophy of Management* (New York: Pitman, 1939), p. 2. First published in 1923.

18. F. J. Roethlisberger and W. J. Dickson, *Management and the Worker* (Cambridge: Harvard University Press, 1939), p. 1.

19. Henry C. Metcalf and Lyndall Urwick, eds., *Dynamic Administration: The Collected Papers of Mary Parker Follett* (New York: Harper & Row, 1940), pp. 32–37.

20. Chester Barnard, *The Functions of the Executive* (Cambridge: Harvard University Press, 1938).

21. Malcolm P. McNair, "Thinking Ahead: What Price Human Relations?" *Harvard Business Review* 35 (March–April 1957): 15–18.

22. Richard A. Johnson, Fremond E. Kast, and James E. Rosenzweig, *The Theory and Management of Systems* (New York: McGraw-Hill, 1963), p. 4.

23. Allen Harvey, "Systems Can Too Be Practical," *Business Horizons*, Summer 1964, p. 63.

24. See Fred Luthans, *Introduction to Management: A Contingency Approach* (New York: McGraw-Hill, 1976), for an excellent expression of this approach.

25. Thomas J. Peters and Robert Waterman, *In Search of Excellence: Lessons from America's Best-Run Companies* (New York: Harper & Row, 1982).

26. As summarized by Thomas L. Wells in a presentation to the Alabama Banking School, Mobile, Alabama, August 1986.

27. Michael A. Hitt and R. Duane Ireland, "Peters and Waterman Revisited: The Unended Quest for Excellence," *Academy of Management Executive* 1 (May 1987): 91–97.

SUGGESTIONS FOR FURTHER STUDY

BEHLING, ORLANDO, and MILLER, MABRY. "An Alternate Approach to the History of Management Thought." *Proceedings of the Academy of Management* (1978).

COOKE, MORRIS L. *Academic and Industrial Efficiency.* New York: Carnegie Foundation for the Advancement of Teaching, Bulletin No. 5, 1910.

FRY, LOUIS. "The Maligned F. W. Taylor: A Reply to His Many Critics." *Academy of Management Review* 1 (July 1976): 124–129.

FULMER, ROBERT, and WREN, DANIEL. "Is There Anything 'New' in Management?" *Journal of Management* 2 (Fall 1976): 71–75.

GILBRETH, FRANK B., JR. and CARY, ERNESTINE GILBRETH. *Cheaper by the Dozen.* New York: Crowell, 1948.

GULICK, LUTHER, and URWICK, LYNDAL, eds. *Papers on the Science of Administration.* New York: Institute of Public Administration, 1937.

HAMBRICK, DONALD C. "High Profit Strategies in Mature Capital Goods Industries: A Contingency Approach." *Academy of Management Journal* 26 (December 1983): 687–707.

LEE, SANG M.; LUTHANS, FRED; and OLSON, DAVID L. "A Management Science Approach to Contingency Models of Organizational Structure." *Academy of Management Journal* 25 (September 1982): 553–566.

LOCKE, EDWIN A. "The Ideas of Frederick W. Taylor: An Evaluation." *Academy of Management Review* 7 (January 1982): 14–24.

LONGENECKER, JUSTIN, and PRINGLE, CHARLES. "The Illusion of Contingency Theory as a General Theory." *Academy of Management Review* 3 (July 1978): 679–683.

LORSCH, JAY W., and MORESE, JOHN J. *Organizations and Their Members: A Contingency Approach.* New York: Harper & Row, 1974.

LUTHANS, FRED, and STEWART, TODD. "A General Contingency Theory of Management." *Academy of Management Review* 3 (July 1978): 683–687.

MEE, JOHN. *A History of Twentieth Century Management Thought.* Columbus: Ohio State University Press, 1959.

SHEPARD, JON, and HOUGHLAND, JAMES, JR. "Contingency Theory: 'Complex Man' or 'Complex Organization'?" *Academy of Management Review* 3 (July 1978): 413–427.

SMIDDY, H. F., and NAUM, LIONEL. "Evolution of a 'Science of Managing' in America." *Management Science* 1 (October 1954): 4.

WEISS, RICHARD M. "Weber on Bureaucracy: Management Consultant or Political Theorist?" *Academy of Management Review* 8 (April 1983): 242–248.

WREN, DANIEL A. *The Evolution of Management Thought,* 2d ed. New York: Wiley, 1979.

PART TWO

Planning Organizational Operations

Plan your work; work your plans.
—HENRY FAYOL

PLANNING IS REQUIRED in performing the other managerial functions. In fact, planning and controlling are so closely related that they have been called "the Siamese twins of management." The main aspects of planning covered in this part—the organizational mission, objectives, and strategic planning, the fundamentals of planning and decision making—are shown on the opposite page.

Chapter 4 covers the fundamentals of planning. Some of the more important subjects you will find are what planning is, reasons for planning, the relationship between planning and other management functions, how time affects planning, types of planning and plans, criteria for evaluating the effectiveness of a plan, barriers to effective planning, and management by objectives.

Strategic planning, including the organizational mission, objectives, and strategies, are covered in Chapter 5. Important topics included are the strategic planning process, the role of organizational mission, some internal and external variables affecting strategic planning, and some strategic options.

Chapter 6 discusses decision making, covering the steps in decision making, the involvement of subordinates in decision making, and problem-solving types of decision making.

4. Fundamentals of planning

What planning is	Where planning is done Reasons for planning
How planning relates to other functions	Relationships to organizing, staffing, leading, and controlling
Planning and the time factor	Short-, intermediate-, and long-range plans How management levels affect planning
Types of planning and plans	Strategic, standing, and single-use
Criteria for evaluating effectiveness of plans	Usefulness, accuracy, objectivity, scope, cost effectiveness, accountability, and timeliness
Barriers to planning	Forecasting problems, tendency to become inflexible, cost, and inhibiting effects
Management by objectives (MBO)	Objectives Key aspects Concepts Problems

5. Strategic planning: mission, objectives, and strategies

Strategic planning process	What it is Strategic planning steps
Organizational mission	Role of mission
Organizational objectives	Need for balancing objectives Areas needing objectives
Internal and external variables	Planning premises SWOT analysis Growth/share matrix
Strategic options	Concentration Turnaround/retrenchment Vertical integration Divestment/liquidation Diversification Combination of strategies

(continued)

6. Decision making

What decision making is	Individual and managerial decision making Involves all employees Programmed and unprogrammed decisions
Steps involved	Understand and define problem Generate and evaluate alternatives Make and implement decisions Evaluate results
Role of subordinates	What group decision making is When to use subordinates
Problem-solving types	Myers-Briggs Type Indicator The Jungian Framework

Fundamentals of Planning

Learning Objectives

After studying the material in this chapter, you should be able to do the following:
- ☐ Define what planning is.
- ☐ Explain where planning is done.
- ☐ Discuss the relationship between planning and the other management functions.
- ☐ Relate how time affects planning.
- ☐ Identify the three basic types of plans.
- ☐ Name and explain the criteria for evaluating the effectiveness of a plan.
- ☐ Discuss the barriers to effective planning.
- ☐ Define management by objectives.
- ☐ Identify the steps in management by objectives.

Outline of the Chapter

What planning is
Definition of planning
Where is planning done?
Reasons for planning
Relationship between planning and other management functions
Organizing and staffing
Leading
Controlling
The time factor and planning
Short-, intermediate-, and long-range plans
Effects of management level on timing of planning
Types of planning and plans
Ways of classifying planning and plans
Strategic plans
Standing plans
Single-use plans

Criteria for evaluating the effectiveness of a plan
Usefulness
Accuracy and objectivity
Scope
Cost-effectiveness
Accountability
Timeliness
Barriers to effective planning
Impossibility of forecasting effectively
Difficulty of planning for nonrepetitive operations
Tendency toward inflexibility
Cost
Possible stifling of initiative
Management by objectives (MBO)
Objectives of MBO
Underlying concepts of MBO
Requirements for successful use of MBO
Key aspects of the MBO process
Some problems encountered in MBO programs
Summary

Some Important Terms

planning
short-range plans
intermediate-range plans
long-range plans
strategic plans
mission
objectives
strategies
standing plans
single-use plans
policies
procedures
rules *and* regulations
programs
projects
budget
budgetary control
self-fulfilling prophecy *or* Pygmalion effect
management by objectives (MBO)

Plan ahead—it wasn't raining when Noah built the ark.

—ANONYMOUS

The Registration Fiasco

Dr. Bob Oldham, chairman of State University's newly formed registration committee, was looking over the results of a survey that the student senate had just completed. It showed that students were highly dissatisfied with registration, which involved long lines, long hours, and loads of frustration. In fact, during the registration three weeks previous, a local television reporter had experienced such frustration while attempting to register that he had recorded live interviews with students engaged in the process and then he showed them on his evening news show. The students had vented their frustrations, which included some not-so-favorable comments about the university's administrators. The whole affair was not a model of university public relations. The president had appointed a registration committee to examine the registration process and make recommendations for improvements.

As Oldham sifted through the survey, he reflected on the major causes of the recent fiasco.

1. There was an unexpected enrollment increase of 4 percent, when in fact stable enrollment or even a slight decrease had been expected.
2. Many of the new students were transfers who were unfamiliar with State's registration system and therefore required more advising time than regular students.
3. Because of the large enrollment increase, many popular classes and courses were closed out earlier than usual, resulting in disgruntled students and drastic changes in course schedules.
4. Computer problems shut down many stations, such as financial assistance, housing assignments, and fee payment, whose systems were electronically dependent.
5. Professors, advisors, and registration workers were upset because the process problems required them to work three hours past the 6 P.M. close of registration each evening in order to accommodate the increased student numbers and overcome the system's breakdowns.

As one student had written on the survey, "I thought I was back in the Army with all the lines, lines, lines! You'd spend 15 minutes in one line only to end up being told that you didn't need to be there. They'd tell you a class was closed; so you'd go back, wait in line 30 minutes to see your advisor, get him to sign a new schedule, and go fight another line for 40 minutes to get a class card, only to find that by the time you got there, that class was closed. So it was back to the advisor. Many people ended up saying the heck with it and just took fewer courses than they wanted to."

What do you think was the real problem?
What could have been done to improve the situation?

THE NEED FOR EFFECTIVE PLANNING is illustrated by this case. Planning is an activity that managers at all levels of an organization must perform well in order to be effective. This chapter looks at what planning is, the relationship between planning and the other management functions, types of plans, how time affects planning, criteria for evaluating the effectiveness of a plan, some barriers to effective planning, and an integrated planning system—MBO.

WHAT PLANNING IS

The term *planning* is an old one, found in many languages for many centuries. Planning has also been practiced since people first began thinking of the future implications of current choices of action. What else can explain the building of the pyramids and the other great wonders of the ancient world? The concept of planning, however, has changed over time.

In its earlier forms, planning was a simple device used by individuals and small groups. When societies became more highly organized, planning came to be considered an integral part of leadership and management. The usefulness of planning as a management tool has also changed. In the past, managers and leaders considered planning a luxury or something extra used to bring about change. Planning gave managers and leaders a considerable advantage over their competitors in the search for greater challenges to be met. In those days, though, planning could not be called an indispensable function, for, more often than not, organizations succeeded without it.

Following the Industrial Revolution, and particularly after the revolution was modified in the United States by assembly line techniques and the introduction of Taylor's principles of scientific management, it was inevitable that planning would become a necessity. This trend emerged because of the growing demands on resources, because of the longer lead times required by modern technology, and because the people and organizations had come to depend so heavily on each other. Thus, as institutions became more interrelated and interdependent, and as they began decentralizing into numerous subdivisions, planning became necessary for the organization's existence.

Definition of Planning

Planning, which is future oriented, is choosing a course of action and deciding in advance what is to be done, in what sequence, when, and how. Good planning attempts to consider the nature of the future environments in which planning decisions and actions are intended to operate, as well as the current period when plans are being made.

Planning provides the basis for effective action resulting from management's ability to anticipate and prepare for changes that might affect organizational objectives. Thus, it is the basis for integrating the management functions and is especially needed for controlling the organization's operations.

Figure 4.1 illustrates some of the key questions that must be addressed if planning is to be effective. Note that the "Why" question should be asked first; this addresses the issue of management effectiveness discussed in Chapter 1.

Where Is Planning Done?

The question of where planning is to be done in an organization can be approached from several different angles. First, planning can be "centralized" so that the major planning work in the organization is done from a central

FIGURE 4.1
The six planning
questions.

> 1. *Why* should the work be done? 4. *When* does the work have to be done?
>
> 2. *What* has to be done? 5. *How* will the work be done?
>
> 3. *Where* will the work be done? 6. *Who* is going to do the work?

point, such as a corporate planning department. It is not unusual for large organizations to have over 50 employees in such departments.

Second, "decentralized" planning may be used, whereby each division or department is responsible for planning all its own operations, without regard to the central planning unit. Thus department managers plan for their departments, unit managers for their units, and so forth. In 1981, Texas Instruments announced that it was abandoning digital watches and certain electronic components. According to the company, this was an example of a management system that "pushes strategic planning down to the lowest levels of the company."[1]

Third, under a modified arrangement, the central planning department does the original long-range planning, and each department and unit then does the detailed planning of its own activities needed to implement the long-range plan.

What is your view?

Assume that you are in charge of corporate planning for one of the "big three" American automakers. The president has asked you to make a sales forecast for next year so that budgets can be planned. Which of the three approaches indicated above would you use in arriving at this forecast? Why?

At General Electric (GE), strategic planning is handled in each of the company's 40-plus business units, under the umbrella of corporate plans laid out by the central planning department.[2]

The planning policy to be followed generally depends on the type of enterprise that is to use the plans. It is important to note, however, that many plans—even long-term ones—originate at lower levels and work their way upward. This is often called "the bottom-up approach."

Reasons for Planning

There are many reasons for planning. First, it prepares the organization for continuous change. While planners cannot control the future, they should at least attempt to *identify and isolate present actions and changes that can be expected to influence the future*. A second purpose of planning is to see that current programs and findings can be used to increase the chances of achieving future objectives and goals—that is, to increase the chances for making better decisions today that help improve tomorrow's performance.

To improve performance. Unless planning leads to improved performance, it is done in vain. So, to help an organization and its managers anticipate the future so that they can stay alive and prosper in a changing world, there must be active, vigorous, continuous, and creative planning—that is, *proactive planning*. Otherwise, management will be *reactive*—only reacting to its

FIGURE 4.2
Management can either
react to or plan to adapt
to the environment.

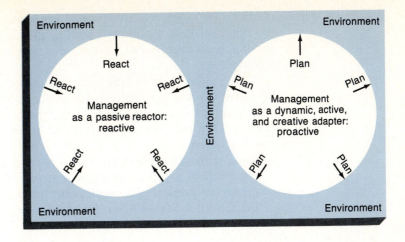

environment and not being an active participant in the competitive world,
as shown in Figure 4.2.

Some managers and organizations that plan poorly constantly devote
their energies to solving problems that would not have existed, or at least
would be much less serious, with better and earlier planning. Thus, they
spend their energies putting out brushfires rather than preventing or at least
anticipating the fires in advance. Figure 4.3 shows how this tendency de-
prives an organization of the positive benefits of planning.

Advantages of planning. Planning has many advantages. For example, it (1)
helps management to adapt and adjust to changing environments, (2) assists
in crystallizing agreements on major issues, (3) enables managers to see the
whole operating picture more clearly, (4) helps place responsibility more
precisely, (5) provides a sense of order to operations, (6) assists in achieving
coordination among various parts of the organization, (7) tends to make
objectives more specific and better known, (8) minimizes guesswork, (9) saves
time, effort, and money, and (10) helps reduce errors in decision making.

Disadvantages of planning. Planning also has several disadvantages. Some
of these are that (1) the work involved in planning may exceed its actual
contributions, (2) planning tends to delay actions, (3) planning may unduly

FIGURE 4.3
Cycle of the nonplanner.

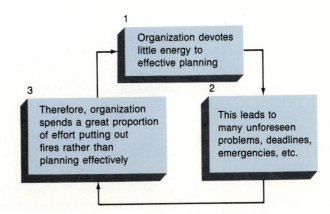

restrict management's exercise of initiative and innovation, (4) sometimes the best results are obtained by an individual appraising the situation and tackling each problem as it arises, and (5) few plans are followed consistently anyway.

Yet, in spite of these and other disadvantages, the advantages of planning far outweigh any problems involved. Firms that do even a poor job of planning tend to do better than those that do no planning at all. Planning therefore not only *should* be done but *must* be done!

Note in the Opening Case how poorly State University had planned the registration process. Without actively planning for the enrollment increase or preparing a contingency plan in the event of computer system malfunction, State University could only passively react to the unexpected variables that arose.

RELATIONSHIP BETWEEN PLANNING AND OTHER MANAGEMENT FUNCTIONS

In some respects, planning is the most basic and pervasive of all management functions. It and the other managerial functions and activities are interrelated, interdependent, and interacting, as shown in Figure 4.4. Notice that each of the functions affects the others and is in turn affected by them.

Organizing and Staffing

Organizing is the process of seeing that the organization's financial, physical, and human resources work together. Planning provides the facts and estimates how to put these resources together for the greatest effectiveness. For example, could you really staff the organization effectively without effective personnel planning?

Leading

The function of leading is always closely associated with planning. Planning determines the best combination of factors, forces, resources, and relationships needed to lead and motivate employees. The leading function involves putting those elements into effect, as the following example illustrates.

FIGURE 4.4
How planning is related to other management functions.

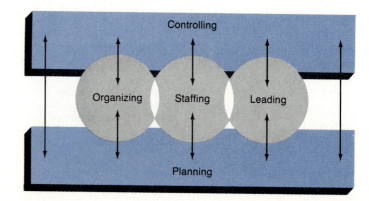

Dr. Jean Ward, head of the Management Department at State University, was thinking about how to open her session with her secretary, Joyce. "Joyce, your work has been pitiful lately, and you've got to improve, or else." No, she mused, that opening might be too strong and offensive. Perhaps she could be more tactful: "Joyce, two weeks ago you and I discussed the importance of meeting your deadlines. But you haven't been doing it, and last week you were way behind schedule. What is the problem?" Then, thought Dr. Ward, I'll offer her some specific suggestions for improving her work. Dr. Ward thought she preferred the latter approach, since it would be less likely to put Joyce on the defensive. Then she pondered, "Should I do this in my office or Joyce's? Or maybe over coffee in the cafeteria?"

Dr. Ward was planning the approach she would take with Joyce. But notice how closely the planning function ties in with leading. When Dr. Ward does meet with Joyce, she will be performing the leading function. But the quality of leading is tied closely to the quality of the planning that preceded it. Seeing that Joyce actually improves her performance is control.

Controlling Planning and controlling are so closely related that they have been called "the Siamese twins of management."[3] Control is an important by-product of effective planning, for it shows managers if their plans are unrealistic or if poor management practices have caused the plans not to work out as expected. Therefore, control acts as a means of evaluating actual performance against plans. Control then also becomes part of the new plan; or:

$$\text{Plan} \longrightarrow \text{(synthesis)} \longrightarrow \begin{matrix} \text{new plan} \\ \text{control} \end{matrix} \longrightarrow \text{(synthesis)} \longrightarrow \begin{matrix} \text{new plan} \\ \text{control} \end{matrix}$$
$$\text{Control}$$

The purpose of a plan is to assure that resources contribute positively toward achieving the organization's goals and objectives. Yet planning is unique in that it, in turn, establishes the objectives toward which all group effort is directed. Plans must be made to accomplish the organization's goals before managers can determine what kinds of organizational relationships to establish, what qualifications are sought in employees, how they are to be led, and what kinds of controls are to be applied.

THE TIME FACTOR AND PLANNING

Time affects planning in three ways. First, considerable time is required to do effective planning. Second, it is often necessary to proceed with each of the planning steps without full information concerning the variables and alternatives because of the time required to gather the data and calculate all the possibilities. Third, the amount (or span) of time that will be included in the plan must be considered, as shown in Figure 4.5. Most firms mesh their short- and long-term plans. For example, Texas Instruments is renowned for its long-range planning; yet it is a "90-day company as well. It often used quick fixes to keep its earnings and stock prices up during bad times."[4]

FIGURE 4.5
Planning at different management levels and time frames.

Management levels

Planning period (in years)

Top Managers
Chief executive officer, chairman, president, general manager, division heads

Long-range plans of 2–5 or more years, such as: What new products? What rate of growth? What broad competitive strategies?

Middle Managers
Functional managers, department heads, product managers

Intermediate-range plans from 1 to 3 to 5 years. For example: How to improve scheduling coordination? How to better utilize lower managers?

Lower-Level Managers
Supervisors, unit managers, group leaders

Short-range plans—daily, weekly, monthly (from daily to 1 year). These include: How to implement new policies, work assignments, work methods? How to increase efficiency?

Short-, Intermediate-, and Long-Range Plans

Short-range plans cover anywhere from a day to a year; **intermediate-range plans** have a time span of from one to five years; and **long-range plans** involve activities of two to five years, with some plans projected 25 or more years in advance. Long-range planning is now usually referred to as *strategic planning.* Utilities, real estate operations, and government agencies have developed plans that project even farther into the future. In fact, companies such as International Paper and Weyerhaeuser plant timber stands in the 1980s that will be harvested around the year 2030 or later.

Since time ranges for planning differ so from organization to organization, it is hard to say exactly whether a given plan is long-, medium-, or short-range. Also, plans change from long-range to medium-range to short-range as time passes.

What is your view?

Reflect for a moment on your own career. Give an example of some of your short-, intermediate-, and long-range plans. Which of the three types of plans are people least likely to have a clear picture of? Why?

Another time factor affecting planning is how often plans are to be reviewed or revised. This depends on the resources available and the degree of accuracy management seeks from planning in the first place. The usual relationship is this: *the longer the time span of the plan, the longer the period between reviews and revisions.* Conversely, *the more important the plan is to the organization's immediate success, the more closely it will be watched and checked.* MAP 4.1 shows that this futuristic aspect of planning is requiring a new type of specialist.

Management Application and Practice 4.1   Corporate Futurists

Today, many of the country's largest corporations employ in their planning departments specialists called corporate futurists. Their job is to try to peer into the future—as much as 30 years ahead—and evaluate the influence of numerous social and political factors on the corporation. Their backgrounds are usually in economics or market research, but through prolific reading they are broad and visionary, with insights combining multiple disciplines. In some companies their work is called social and political forecasting; in others it's known as environmental scanning.

Gillette's Joseph Shapiro reads three newspapers daily and 30 to 40 magazines monthly. Like other futurists, he often asks upper-level executives "what if?" questions, such as, "If fewer families eat their meals together, will formal dinnerware sales decline?" or, "What if the average age of living Americans continues to increase?" Shapiro's questioning and information were instrumental in Gillette's broadening its product base in the 1970s.

SOURCE: Donald Moffett, ed., *The Wall Street Journal Views America Tomorrow* (New York: Dow Jones, 1977), pp. 12–17.

Effects of Management Level on Timing of Planning

All managers plan, but they spend different amounts of time planning and plan for different time periods. Figure 4.6 shows that as managers move up in the organization they spend an increasing proportion of their time planning. Notice that the percentage increases significantly when moving from middle to top levels.

Planning is a function of every manager in an organization, but the character and breadth of planning vary with each manager's authority-responsibility relationship and the nature of policies and plans outlined by the individual's superior. Therefore, the nature and timing of planning changes as managers move into higher organizational levels, as shown in Figure 4.7.

FIGURE 4.6
Time spent planning varies according to management level.

SOURCE: Adapted from T. A. Mahoney, T. H. Jerdee, and S. J. Carroll, "The Job(s) of Management," *Industrial Relations* 4 (February 1965):103.

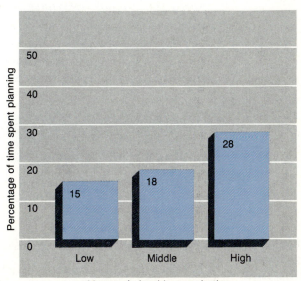

Manager's level in organization

Percentage of planning for:

	Today	1 week ahead	1 month ahead	3–6 months ahead	1 year ahead	2 years ahead	2–3 years ahead	5–10 years ahead
President	1	2	5	10	15	27	30	10
Executive vice-president	2	4	10	29	20	18	13	4
Vice-president of functional area	4	8	15	35	20	10	5	3
General manager of a major division	2	5	15	30	20	12	12	4
Department manager	10	10	24	39	10	5	1	1
Section supervisor	15	20	25	37	3			
Group supervisor	38	40	15	5	2			

FIGURE 4.7
Time frame of planning changes with different organizational levels.

SOURCE: George A. Steiner, *Top Management Planning* (New York: Macmillan, 1969), p. 26. Reprinted by permission.

Notice that lower-level managers tend to plan for the day or week. Consider, for example, the case of this first-line supervisor:

Planning? Sure, I spend time planning. But most of our goals and objectives—and even schedules—are handed down from above. So my planning is mostly short run, like deciding who I'm going to put in what job, planning for maintenance, scheduling vacations, and deciding how I can cut scrap and improve quality. Our turnover is pretty high; so I'm also working on a plan to improve the rate in our department. But I don't really get into any heavy planning—mostly just the short-run stuff.

Middle managers plan on a weekly, monthly, quarterly, and semiannual basis. Top managers make plans—such as budgets, programs, and projects—for one to five years into the future. These conclusions are, of course, generalizations, and there are many exceptions to this rule of thumb.

TYPES OF PLANNING AND PLANS

Planning and the resulting plans may be classified in many different ways. The way planning is classified will determine the content of the plans and how the planning is done.

Ways of Classifying Planning and Plans

There are at least five ways to classify plans. They are as follows:

1. *Functional area* covered—such as personnel, production, marketing, and finance. Each of these functions requires a different type of planning.

2. *Organizational level*—including the entire organization, or units and subunits of the organization. Different techniques and content are involved at different levels.

3. *Characteristics* of the plans—such factors as the completeness, complexity, formality, and cost involved.

4. *Time* involved—such as short, medium, or long range.

5. *Activities* involved—including the most frequently performed activities, such as operations, advertising, personnel selection, and research and development.

For the purposes of this book, a more general classification of planning, or plans, is used. The classification includes (1) *strategic plans*, or those that fix the nature of the organization, (2) *standing plans*, or those that tend to remain fixed for long periods of time, and (3) *single-use plans*, or those that serve a specific purpose for a limited period and are then changed, modified, or discarded (see Figure 4.8).

Strategic plans include (1) the **mission,** or definition of the organization (Shell is now an "energy" company, whereas it used to be an "oil" company); (2) **objectives,** meaning the ends toward which all organizational activities are aimed, since they represent the end point of planning and the goal toward which the other management functions are aimed; and (3) **strategies,** which include plans that cover the overall general activities of the organization, especially interpretive plans made in the light of the plans of competitors. Strategies can be considered the mechanisms that help the organization adapt to its environments and integrate its internal operations.

Standing plans include (1) *policies*, or those general statements and understandings that are guides to, or channels of, thinking and decision making by managers and subordinates; (2) *procedures* that establish a standard or routine method or technique for handling recurring activities; and (3) *rules and regulations* that state mandatory courses of action chosen from among available alternatives.

FIGURE 4.8
Types of plans.

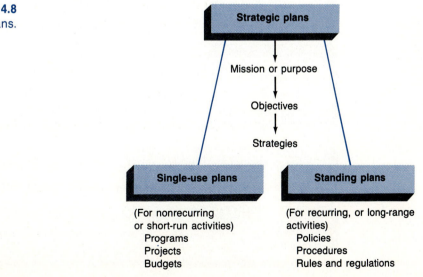

Strategic plans

Mission or purpose

Objectives

Strategies

Single-use plans

(For nonrecurring
or short-run activities)
  Programs
  Projects
  Budgets

Standing plans

(For recurring, or long-range
activities)
  Policies
  Procedures
  Rules and regulations

Single-use plans include (1) *programs* that involve the entire complex of activities necessary to carry out a given course of action, (2) *projects*—that is, plans for the accomplishment of a specific objective, and (3) *budgets*, which are usually financial statements of expected results in numerical terms. Budgets are usually included in all three of the types of plans discussed.

Strategic Plans

Since we shall discuss the major elements of strategic plans in Chapter 5, the focus here will be upon standing and single-use plans.

Standing Plans

The most common standing plans are (1) policies, (2) procedures, and (3) rules and regulations. These plans, once established, continue to apply until they are modified or abandoned. They are thus fixed in nature and content.

Policies. **Policies** are broad, general statements of expected actions that serve as guides to managerial decision making or to supervising the actions of subordinates. Some examples of policies are given in Figure 4.9. Sometimes policies are formally determined and announced; they may also be informally

FIGURE 4.9
Some examples of policies.

Purchasing policy. "We shall have several sources of supply so as not to be totally reliant on only one."

Wage policy. "Wages shall be established and maintained on a level favorable to that found for similar positions within our industry and the community."

Marketing policy. "Only a limited number of dealers will be selected to distribute and sell the company's product lines in a given territory."

Hiring policy. "We are an equal opportunity employer."

Communications policy. "Managers should periodically hold group meetings with subordinates for the purpose of discussing objectives of the department, discussing new developments that may be of interest to or may affect subordinates, answering questions, and, in general, encouraging more effective and accurate communications within the organization."

Promotion policy. "We shall promote from within, whenever possible."

Open-door policy. "Every employee has the right to discuss with any higher-level manager any concerns he or she has about management actions or decisions."

FIGURE 4.10
Policies may orginate at
any organizational level.

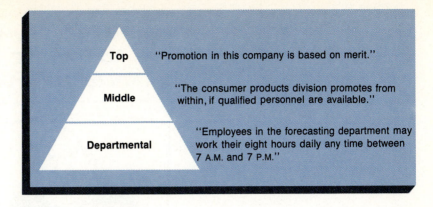

set by the actions of superiors, who may not intend for them to become policies. They may be written or unwritten, spoken or even unspoken. As shown in Figure 4.10, they may be initiated at any level of the organization.

Purpose of policies. The one characteristic of a policy is that it becomes a guideline to help managers decide what to do when there is no one else to decide for them or when there is no other way for them to know how to decide or to act.

Once the overall policies are set, managers have the job of formulating the less significant, but often more urgent, policies. These are broad in nature and tend to cross departmental lines.

> *For example, when a company decides to add a new product line, it is confronted with new problems in the sales, purchasing, production, finance, and personnel departments. After a decision has been made about the exact nature of the new product and what it will consist of, each department has to revise its policies to conform to the new situation. Another set of plans that usually comes under the jurisdiction of a company's board of directors is the set of policies about the organization's competitiveness, aggressiveness, and expansion. Then the policies regarding the stockholders' equity and rights to earnings must be considered. Finally, the board has the additional job of coordinating the departmental plans through review and approval of the master budget.*

Functional policies. Once the broad organizational policies are set by the administration, the functional departments (such as production, sales, finance, and engineering) set forth their policies. These policies must conform and contribute to the ultimate organizational objectives. These functional departments usually establish policies pertaining to research, quality, distribution, procurement, and personnel, as well as planning and control policies.

A growing area of concern for management is establishing uniform personnel policies, especially those affected by public policy in the form of laws, court decisions, and administrative rules and regulations. Some new policy areas facing managers include providing equal employment opportunities for all groups, maintaining occupational safety and health, improving the quality of work life, providing comparable pay for comparable work, and securing employees' privacy.

In short, policies are relatively permanent, general plans of action used to guide managerial decision making or other activities required to achieve

TO ERR IS HUMAN
TO FORGIVE IS
NOT COMPANY POLICY

(Reprinted from The Wall Street Journal *by permission of Cartoon Features Syndicate.)*

organizational objectives. They are helpful in securing uniform performance and are used to guide management toward reaching the goal of efficient and effective operations.

Procedures. When it is important that certain steps be taken in a given sequence and that work be done accurately, management may establish detailed plans called **procedures,** which are to be followed in all instances.

What is your view?

Can you think of some examples of procedures in your school, or where you work or shop?

Procedures should be designed to ensure that pertinent information flows to the people needing such data and that each person involved in the process understands just what he or she is to do with it. The transfer and manipulation of written information can be coordinated and simplified through the use of standard forms and procedures. Standardizing forms, in turn, leads to the standardization of information storage facilities.

Need for coordination of procedures. Many procedures affect several departments. This often causes a problem of coordination of effort. MAP 4.2 shows a typical grievance procedure for a student's final grades at a Texas university.

Some problem areas. As with all planning, several problems arise when procedures are being designed or modified. Some procedures are traditional or have been copied from other organizations and have become useless. Also, procedures may lose their relevance simply by not being modified as conditions warrant. Often there is duplication of effort caused by the desire for

Management Application and Practice 4.2 Procedures in Action: Grievance Procedures for Final Grades*

If a student believes that a final course grade is unfair, these procedures will be followed:

1. The student shall consult the instructor as soon as possible to seek explanation.
2. If the disagreement remains unresolved, the student shall submit a written complaint to the chair of the department in which the course is taught. The complaint must be made within the first four weeks of the following quarter, except summer. A copy of the complaint will be forwarded to the instructor.
3. The department chair will act as negotiator in attempting initially to resolve the dispute between student and instructor.
4. If the matter cannot be resolved, each side will submit to the department chair a formal written statement representing his or her viewpoint. The student will file a "Final Grade Grievance Form," which will include the student's request that the grade be changed and the specific reason (or reasons) the student believes justifies the change of grade. This form will be supplied to the Departmental Grievance Committee for the purpose of its preliminary review. Once the need for a hearing has been established, the statements from both student and instructor will be supplied to the individuals involved and to the committee at least two days in advance of the hearing.
5. Once a grievance has been filed, the committee will review the Final Grade Grievance Form filled out by the student. Based on this information alone, the committee will determine whether the grievance is frivolous; if not, it will proceed to a hearing.
6. The hearing will be conducted with both the student and instructor present; either party may call a witness or witnesses as deemed appropriate by the committee chair.
7. At the conclusion of the hearing, the committee shall meet alone and deliberate on the case.
8. If the committee finds that the final course grade is unjust or incorrect, it may change the grade and determine to what it shall be changed.
9. The chair shall forward the committee's decision to the student and instructor concerned, the department chair, and the dean of the college. The decision should be sent out within a week of the committee's reaching a decision.
10. If either the instructor or the student wishes to challenge the procedure involved in the committee's recommendation, he or she may appeal in writing to the appropriate dean for a procedural review.
11. If the dean determines that the procedures followed were invalid, the dean will direct that a rehearing be held.

* At a state university that wishes to remain anonymous.

secrecy or by ignorance of what others are doing. Procedures tend to become obsolete without being discontinued. TIPS 4.1 identifies some practical pointers for making procedures more practical.

During World War II, firms had to make a weekly report, with several copies for wide distribution, on the amount of gasoline used and the vehicles using it. This was the basis for firms' receiving ration coupons. A forms-control expert for a large oil company found that this procedure was still being used at one of its refineries as late as 1953, eight years after rationing ended.

In summary, the most important advantages of procedures are that they (1) conserve managerial effort, (2) facilitate delegation of authority and placement of responsibility, (3) lead to development of more efficient methods of operation, (4) permit significant personnel economies, (5) facilitate control, and (6) aid the coordination of activities.

TIPS 4.1   Making Procedures More Effective

Procedures are an essential part of an organization's plans since they affect so many people and processes. The following are some important principles to keep in mind regarding procedures.

1. *Restrict procedures to critical areas.* Procedures should be established only when they are clearly called for. Remember, good reasons for procedures are consistency, coordination, and efficiency. Overuse of procedures—or poorly designed procedures—creates needless red tape, wastes time and energy, and stifles imagination and creativity.
2. *Keep procedures simple.* Procedures should be easy to read and simple to follow. Where possible, use itemized lists or steps, with short paragraphs and sentences, in simple, clear language.
3. *Put procedures in writing.* Having procedures in written form provides an available reference source and helps promote consistent interpretation.
4. *Publicize procedures.* It's important for people to understand that procedures exist. For new procedures, or those that modify or replace earlier ones, it may be necessary not only to promote them through written documents but also to follow up with meetings or briefings.
5. *Don't allow procedures to eliminate flexibility.* Recognize that sometimes emergencies, changed conditions, or unusual circumstances may require circumventing procedures.
6. *Evaluate and revise procedures as needed.* Procedures tend to survive even when outdated. Therefore, they should be reviewed periodically, revised as needed, and discarded if they have become unnecessary.

Rules and regulations. The simplest yet usually the most detailed of all standing plans, **rules** and **regulations** specifically state what can and cannot be done under a given set of circumstances. Thus, they are used to implement other plans and are usually the result of a policy being adhered to in *every* instance. When no variations are permitted, the plan becomes a rule or regulation, often carrying a negative outcome if it is violated. Some examples of rules are these:

No drugs permitted on the premises.

No smoking permitted in this area.

Hard hats must be worn in the plant at all times.

All checks for over $25.00 must be approved by a department head.

A student may enroll for no more than 21 hours of course credit in a given semester.

What is your view?

What are some other rules and regulations at your school? Which of them are really needed? Which of them do you consider too rigid?

Single-Use Plans   Standing plans, in the form of policies, procedures, and rules and regulations, help give continued guidance to the actions or expected actions of organization members. But organizations also use other types of plans that you might think of as one-shot, or single-use plans—that is, they are essentially nonrecurring. The most prevalent single-use plans are programs, projects, budgets, and organizational plans.

Programs. **Programs** are a mixture of objectives, goals, strategies, policies, rules, and job assignments, as well as the fiscal, physical, and human resources required to implement them. A distinguishing feature of this type of plan is the commitment (usually on a long-term basis) of these resources in the form of capital, developmental, and operating budgets.

A program usually includes the objectives of the program and the principal steps that must be taken to achieve the objectives—with the approximate timing of each—as well as the resources required to accomplish the stated objective. Considerable effort and expertise are required to design and implement a comprehensive program. Managers should therefore understand a program's nature and benefits so that they can decide whether its preparation is worth the expected expenditure of time, effort, and resources.

Major programs are usually found in an organization in the form of (1) the research, development, and initiation of new products or services; (2) the budgeting of sales, inventories, production requirements, and financial needs; and (3) the training and development of personnel to cope with some major change in the organization.

Some examples of specific programs are:

1. *The Penn Central Corporation was armed with much cash as the result of a settlement with the U.S. government over the value of the bankrupt Penn Central's railroad assets that were taken over by the government. The new company has embarked on an acquisition program that has resulted in its acquiring several other firms.*
2. *General Motors has set aside huge sums to prepare its obsolete workers for new jobs in areas such as servicing robots.*
3. *A major university seeks to attract 300 new minority students as part of its new minority student commitment.*

Projects. Frequently, individual segments of a general program are relatively separate and clear-cut, so they can be planned and executed as distinct **projects.** For example, an energy firm may have a program to reduce its reliance on imported petroleum from OPEC. Specific projects within the program may be to develop gasohol or extract oil from shale. Furthermore, each of these projects may have numerous subprojects.

Project planning is a flexible type of planning that may be adapted to a variety of situations. If operations can be easily divided into separate parts with a clear termination point, the project is a natural and effective planning device.

Budgets.

What is your view?

What normally comes to your mind when you hear the word *budgeting*?

Almost every individual, family, or organization uses some form of budgeting, either formally or informally. A well-planned budget serves as both a planning and a control device and should express realistic goals that can be achieved. Only when these goals are realistic and satisfactory will the budget serve as an effective measure of managerial performance.

A **budget** is a detailed plan or forecast of the results expected from an officially recognized program of operations, based on the highest reasonable expectations of operating efficiency. It is generally expressed in monetary terms.

By itself, a budget is merely a collection of figures or estimates that indicates the future in financial terms. **Budgetary control,** on the other hand, involves careful planning and control of all the activities of the organization. It assumes a genuine desire on the part of management to keep as close to the previously charted course as possible, to check actual performance against the plans, and to use the budget as a road map to reach the previously established goals. We cover budgeting in greater depth in Chapter 15.

CRITERIA FOR EVALUATING THE EFFECTIVENESS OF A PLAN

As with other management functions, it should be possible to evaluate the effectiveness of planning. Figure 4.11 shows some criteria that can be used to do this, such as (1) usefulness, (2) accuracy and objectivity, (3) scope, (4) cost effectiveness, (5) accountability, and (6) timeliness.

One authority has found that the planning system best fitting those criteria is a three-year plan, consisting of a one-year operating plan, with the development of a forward plan for the next two years.[5]

Usefulness

To be most useful to management in performing its other functions, a plan should be flexible—yet stable—continuous, and simple.

Flexibility. Flexibility, essential to successful strategic planning, results from careful analysis and forecasting, developing contingency plans, and making planning a continuous process. The plan should therefore be capable of quick and smooth adjustment to changing environmental conditions without serious loss of effectiveness.

Stability. If plans change too often, managers don't become familiar with them as an operating tool and don't use them effectively. A stable plan, then, is one that will not have to be abandoned or modified extensively merely because of changes in the long-run trend of the organizational environment.

FIGURE 4.11
Criteria for evaluating a plan's effectiveness.

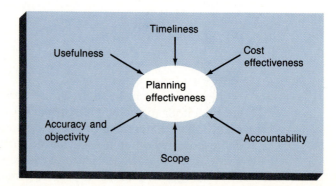

Continuity. Planning should have continuity. However, when a plan has outlived its usefulness, it is replaced by another so that the guiding concepts provided by planning may be continuous.

Simplicity. The larger and more complex an organization and its environment are, the more complex the plans must be. Sometimes, however, the plans may be more complicated than they need to be. The more complex plans are, the more difficult they are to implement and monitor. Thus, a simple plan provides for the accomplishment of its objective with the fewest possible variables, so that the chance of complications is minimized.

Accuracy and Objectivity

Plans should be evaluated to see whether they are definite, clear, concise, and accurate. Decisions and other management actions are only as effective as the information on which they are based. Thus planning must be based on factual and realistic thinking about the requirements needed to reach objectives rather than on the personal objectives of those doing the planning. To achieve this goal, planning should be based on objective thinking, and emotional and personal objectives should not be permitted to interfere with the factual, logical, and realistic requirements of the plan.

Scope

Plans should be evaluated in terms of their scope: How comprehensive are they? What do they include? What range of activities is included? What units or departments are concerned?

Comprehensiveness. A plan should adequately cover all the action that will be required of individuals and organizational elements to reach objectives. Yet it should not specify the nature and conditions of the action in such minute detail that it will be unduly restrictive. That is, it should not put limitations on the nature and conditions of actions to such an extent that loss of initiative and freedom of action may result. Instead, it should enable managers at every level to coordinate the action on the lower levels for which they are responsible.

Unity. Unity implies that, if possible, only one plan should be put into operation at a time in order to prevent confusion and inconsistency. This does not imply that there should not be subdivisions of the overall plan or other contingency plans, for there may be several parts to a plan. It does mean that each plan should be designed to achieve one central objective and to be consistent and complete in itself.

Consistency. Each administrative unit of an organization is related to, and depends on, the other units. These units each have managers who plan their operations and actions in terms of the special objectives of their units. The effectiveness of these managers may be lost if the various unit plans lack consistency, cooperation, and coordination. Therefore, there must be unity and consistency, at least in the overall objectives of the planning units and the organization itself.

Cost-Effectiveness

Planning is costly in terms of the time, effort, and emotional drain on those doing it. Therefore, the guideline in planning is: *Unless the results increase*

"Things must be going badly—he keeps referring
to it as my plan."
(Reprinted from The Wall Street Journal by
permission of Cartoon Features Syndicate.)

revenues or reduce costs by more than the cost of the planning and its
implementation, don't do it.

Accountability   There are two aspects of accountability: (1) responsibility for doing the planning and (2) responsibility for implementing the plans.

As we mentioned earlier, planning is generally not the job of any one
person designated as "the planner" but rather is part of the job of all the
managers in an organization because it must reflect the ideas and commitments of those responsible for implementing the plans if they are to be
successful. Yet those managers also need overall guidance, coordination, and
direction in their own efforts from someone higher in the organization who
has specific authority and experience in planning. This guidance can take
the form of guidelines, specific measures of performance, and timetables
provided by top management.

Timeliness   Forecasting the future with any reasonable degree of accuracy presents a
problem because of the vast number and variety of events that may take
place over which management has little, if any, control. Organizations are
affected by many things, such as major catastrophes, technological changes,
or even changes in the weather. Such events are difficult to predict, but the
planners must attempt to make such important predictions.

    What is your view?

Perhaps you have been to Disney World, Six Flags, or another large theme park.
To these organizations, timeliness of plans is very critical. For example, certain
key weekends (Labor Day, Fourth of July, and Memorial Day) result in increased
crowds and require additional park personnel to work refreshment counters,
games, rides, cleanup detail, and so on. Can you think of some other organizations where timeliness is very important?

BARRIERS TO EFFECTIVE PLANNING

Although its use is inevitable to a certain degree, planning is not an unmixed blessing, for there are some liabilities and disadvantages to the extensive use of this management function. According to a retired executive who is now a worldwide consultant and college teacher, one barrier to planning that is not often recognized is mental laziness. Planning is difficult, since it requires a search for data, a rigorous analysis of those data, and concentrated mental effort. Many otherwise successful managers find this effort just too much for them.

Effective planning can be obstructed by various barriers. Some of these are (1) the impossibility of forecasting effectively; (2) the presence of nonrepetitive factors and operations that are difficult to plan for; (3) the tendency toward inflexibility in administering plans; (4) the cost in time, effort, and money of making effective plans; and (5) a possible inhibiting effect on creativity and innovation.

Impossibility of Forecasting Effectively

A plan is useful only so long as the bases of the plan prove to be substantially correct. It is difficult, if not impossible, for planners to forecast economic conditions, government policies, or human behavior with any great degree of accuracy, although there are attempts, such as the *Kiplinger Letter* and lobbying organizations. Moreover, the reliability of such forecasts diminishes as they are projected farther into the future. The negative effect of time on predictability is one of the primary reasons it is practical to plan in considerable detail only for activities in the relatively near future and not for the distant future. That is why most plans seem to be based on "last year's experience."

Managers may limit unreliable forecasting through extensive research or by detouring around the areas of greatest uncertainty. The latter is accomplished by establishing alternate programs during the strategic planning phase and then following the most effective alternate program to its conclusion when the operating conditions are actually known. Even this is not always successful.

Instead of relying on only one corporate strategic plan, many companies, such as Dow Chemical, Chevron, and GE, establish alternate plans that are activated according to changes in the external environment. In 1975, for example, Mead Corporation had three short-term contingency plans, A, B, and C, that stood for "aggressive," "basic," and "conservative." Given the conditions of the economy, Mead eventually scrapped its original C plan in favor of an even more conservative one.[6]

Difficulty of Planning for Nonrepetitive Operations

Repetitive operations are essential for formulating standing plans; so planners seek out and maintain standard operations. Some ways of accomplishing this are (1) to isolate the repetitive aspects of a situation and standardize their treatment and (2) to control the situation so that there is greater repetitiveness.

Tendency Toward Inflexibility

The establishment of, and excessive adherence to, standing plans tends to force managers to be inflexible. Further, the more detailed and widespread the plans, the greater the inflexibility tends to become. Executives who make the original plans may want to change them, but there is a tendency toward inflexibility due to the psychological reluctance to change a decision. Once a person's mind is set on a given course of action, it is difficult for him or her to maintain an objective viewpoint because of the phenomenon of the **self-fulfilling prophecy** (also called the **Pygmalion effect**).

A well-developed plan encourages executives to make commitments in advance and thereby makes changes more difficult. Periodic reviews of existing plans may aid in minimizing this tendency toward inflexibility.

Cost

Planning is quite costly, since it uses extensive financial, physical, and human resources. Someone must therefore be responsible for doing a cost-benefit analysis and determining at what point the cost becomes greater than the benefits derived. This must be done even though both costs and benefits are often difficult to specify and quantify. Because of these tendencies, considerable managerial judgment is required to determine to what extent planning will be profitable. The important question is whether the additional expense of planning, or additional planning, will be greater or less than the additional benefits to be derived.

A survey done by Odiorne Associates shows some of the reasons managers seem to be opposed to planning. More than 40 percent say planning takes too much time, uses methods that are mysterious, and is useless because of an unpredictable future.[7]

The time requirements of planning may also be detrimental, for when time is pressing, detailed planning may not be profitable. Usually, time is not a limiting factor in formulating standing plans, since they are intended for repeated use.

Possible Stifling of Initiative

Planning that is extensive in scope and detail tends to inhibit the initiative of individual managers and operative personnel. Planners may overcome this disadvantage by consulting supervisory and operative employees regarding decisions affecting their work and then incorporating their suggestions into the plan from the start. Another possible solution is to identify and transfer those individuals with considerable initiative, innovativeness, creativity, and sound judgment to positions where those abilities may be utilized more fully.

MANAGEMENT BY OBJECTIVES (MBO)

Earlier in this chapter, you saw how planning was closely related to the other management functions of organizing, staffing, leading, and controlling. Management by objectives (MBO), while strongly emphasizing managerial planning, is an excellent example of the close relationship among the managerial functions.

Management by objectives (MBO) was first publicized by Peter Drucker in his book *The Practice of Management*, published in 1954.[8] The process also goes by other names, including *management by results* and *joint target setting.* MBO has grown to be quite popular, especially in larger organizations. It has certainly called much attention to the role of planning and setting objectives.

MBO is hard to define, for organizations use it in different ways and for different reasons. In general, **management by objectives** involves the superior and subordinate managers of an organization jointly setting its overall common goals, defining each individual's major area of responsibility in terms of the results expected of him or her, and using those measures as guides for operating the unit and assessing the contribution of each of its members.

Objectives of MBO

A study of the application of a MBO program in one organization disclosed that the 48 managers who participated felt that the program served several varying purposes. As you can see from Table 4.1, the objectives ranged from linking the evaluation process to worker performance (35.4 percent) to enabling managers to know what their jobs are (12.5 percent).

Underlying Concepts of MBO

MBO's success is based on two underlying hypotheses. First, *if one is strongly attached to a goal, one is willing to expend more effort to reach it than if one were less committed to it.* The second hypothesis, the principle of the self-fulfilling prophecy, is that *whenever we predict that something will happen, we will do everything possible to make it happen.*

These hypotheses explain why MBO is having such success in reaching the objectives set for it. Another reason for its success is that it tends to incorporate the better parts of several motivational and leadership theories. For example, it incorporates Maslow's self-fulfillment need; McGregor's Theory Y; Herzberg's motivational factors of achievement, recognition, challenging work, and responsibility; and McClelland's need for achievement. (You'll become familiar with these concepts in later chapters.)

MBO is also based on the concept that people prefer to be evaluated according to criteria that *they* perceive to be realistic and standards that *they* view as reasonably attainable. Under this method, people participate in setting the goals and identifying the criteria that will be used to evaluate and reward their performance. Some of the goals may be measurable in quantitative terms (such as sales—or production—volume, expenses, or profits), whereas others may be assessed qualitatively (such as customer relations, a marketing plan, or employee development).

**TABLE 4.1
Philosophy and
Rationale of MBO**
*(As seen by 48 managers in
one organization)*
SOURCE: Steven Carroll and
Henry L. Tosi, Jr., *Management
by Objectives* (New York:
Macmillan, 1973), p. 23.

Objective of program	Percentage naming objective
To link evaluation process to worker performance	35.4
To aid managers in planning	25.0
To motivate managers	22.9
To increase boss-subordinate interaction and feedback	22.9
To develop management potential	16.6
To link company objectives to department objectives	16.6
To enable managers to know what their jobs are	12.5
No mention	14.5

TABLE 4.2
Interpretations of MBO by 38 "Experts"

SOURCE: Mark L. McConkie, "A Clarification of the Goal Setting and Appraisal Processes in MBO," *Academy of Management Review* 4 (January 1979): 31–32.

Characteristics of objectives set under MBO	Percentage agreeing
Be stated specifically	97
Be defined in measurable ways	97
Integrate individual and organization goals	97
Involve superior and subordinate jointly	92
Be reviewed periodically	82
Specify target dates for completion	71
Be verifiable and quantifiable whenever possible	68
Be flexible—change as conditions warrant	68
Include a "plan of action"	55
Be assigned priority rankings	50

Requirements for Successful Use of MBO

Regardless of how deeply committed management is to the use of MBO, and regardless of what form the use of MBO takes within a given setting, management by results requires a unique approach to the appraisal of managers. That approach is geared to assessing these executives' managerial performance rather than their personal qualities and potential.

In essence, MBO stresses the importance of managers' setting (with the aid and concurrence of their immediate superiors) specific objectives that they intend to reach in the next period and then measuring performance against the standard of those preset objectives. Table 4.2 shows what 38 "experts" thought the characteristics of these objectives should be.

In the more successful applications, the approach extends beyond the objectives-results-objectives setting and implementing cycle into a process of ongoing career planning and development that is carefully integrated into the organization's overall development program.

Key Aspects of the MBO Process

MBO basically consists of the six steps shown in Figure 4.12. The following aspects of the MBO process are critical for its success.

Linking organizational goals. The first step of the MBO process enables the subordinate to understand his or her supervisor's objectives. An effective

FIGURE 4.12
Steps in the MBO process.

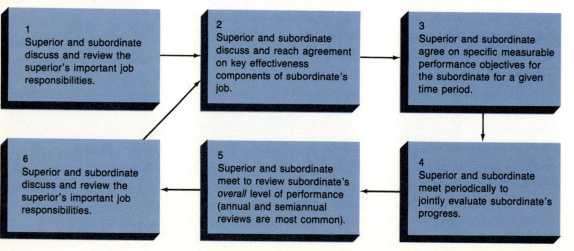

MBO program can produce a clear understanding of how division, department, section, and individual objectives are related.

Forcing managerial planning. In steps two and three of the MBO process, employees are required to think their own jobs through. They are more likely to visualize the big, overall picture and to focus on the truly important performance areas. Instead of wasting their energies working on minor, less important activities, managers direct their efforts toward achieving the major performance targets they have established jointly with their superiors.

Increasing communication and interaction. Properly executed, MBO establishes more direct, even daily, communication between boss and subordinates. As one manager reported after completing stages one and two:

> *The thing I liked best was the way our session cleared the air. If we accomplish nothing else, it's been helpful. I learned more about my department head's problems in that 45-minute meeting than I had in the two previous years I'd worked for her. I just wasn't aware of how crucial some things were to her. In the meeting, I learned why my superior and I had some disagreements and why she gets so uptight about some things that I haven't considered important at all. And some things that I place high priority on in my job weren't given high priority by Janet. There's no doubt that she and I have a much better picture of each other's jobs.*

Involving subordinates in objective setting. Perhaps the unique feature of MBO is the active role that subordinates play in helping to establish their own objectives. It is based on the assumption that individuals are more likely to be highly committed to objectives that they have had a hand in setting. Note that MBO doesn't give subordinates blanket privilege in setting their own objectives; the supervisor also provides his or her inputs. MBO emphasizes the jointness of the objectives and indicates that both parties can play an active role. The final decision for approval, of course, rests with the supervisor.

Establishing specific, measurable performance objectives. Important to MBO programs is the need for objectives that are specific and measurable. Some examples of "weak" and "improved" statements of objectives are given in Table 4.3. Well-stated objectives facilitate the evaluation and reward processes, which are the final stages of the MBO cycle.

 What is your view?

If you are presently employed, think about your job for a moment. What are two specific, measurable performance objectives that you can establish for your job next year?

If you are not presently employed, think about your academic career. What are two specific, measurable performance objectives you can establish for your schoolwork in the next year?

Figure 4.13 shows an actual MBO format as used by one organization. Note that the subordinate is required to identify the basic objective and also must state the key action plans that will be taken toward completion of the

**TABLE 4.3
Examples of MBO
Statements of
Objectives**

Weak	Improved
To improve communication with employees	To implement a system of weekly departmental meetings by June
To stress individual development of my subordinates	To have each employee attend a professional development program of one day or more in his or her field during the year
To better the safety record in the department	To reduce lost work hours due to accidents from 1200 to 1020, or by 15 percent
To improve the quality of nursing service from the patient's standpoint	To average a score of 80 percent on the 'quality of nursing service' questionnaires filled out by all hospital patients during the next year
To improve relationships and attitudes among my employees	To reduce the number of supervisory-related grievances filed in my department by 20 percent next year
To increase sales	To have each salesperson make 10 additional sales calls per month and to gain a 10 percent increase in sales in the new territory by the end of the fiscal year

objective. The supervisor's completed evaluation ultimately serves as the basis for determining the employee's annual performance rating and, ultimately, the merit increases or other rewards given by the organization.

Some Problems Encountered in MBO Programs

Many organizations look to MBO as an instant solution to their problems. They fail to realize that MBO programs require careful planning and implementation to be successful. The following problems are frequently listed as preventing MBO from achieving its best results, and they often cause entire programs to fail.

Takes time. The MBO process can be very time-consuming, especially during the first cycle. Since subordinates are usually unsure of the new system, they are more likely to request meetings with their superiors to receive reassurance. The formal, periodic progress and end-of-period evaluations also consume time, especially for managers who have broad spans of control.

Increases paperwork. MBO sometimes results in a great deal of extra paperwork. Since management allows subordinates to function largely on their own in determining how objectives will be achieved, many managers attempt to stay abreast of what's going on by having lower-level personnel submit regular reports, data, and performance indicators.

May overlook qualitative objectives. The need for specific, measurable objectives in MBO means that there exists a built-in emphasis on activities such as sales, profits, costs, production turnover, and objectives that are readily convertible into numbers. Factors such as employee attitudes and job satisfaction are more difficult to measure but must also be included in objective setting.

FIGURE 4.13
MBO in action.
(Names of
organization and
individuals are
disguised.)

CHARITY HOSPITAL
MANAGEMENT OBJECTIVE STATEMENT (A)

Name: Larry C. Henderson   Title: Human Resource Manager

Objective Number: 1 of 7   Initials: (Supervisor) *P.R.J.*   Initials: (Employee) L.C.H.

Objective Statement (What)

To complete by Dec. 1, 1988 a Feasibility report regarding establishment
of an In-House-Physical Fitness Program for all employees of the hospital.

Action Plan (How) (give broad overview only)	Date Due	Responsibility Assigned To:
1. Interview a minimum of five responsible PFP directors in organizations which have established similar programs.	September 15, 1988	Henderson, Sanchez
2. Conduct written survey of all hospital employees to determine interest level in a PFP.	September 30, 1988	Henderson
3. Create a PFP task force of persons from key departments to generate ideas, handle feedback regarding feasibility.	October 15, 1988	Henderson

---

CHARITY HOSPITAL
SEMI-ANNUAL PERFORMANCE EVALUATION (B)
Supervisor: Evaluate the employee's attainment of the work objectives shown
on Form A. Your evaluation should be discussed with your employee.

Supervisor's Evaluation of Employee's Attainment of Work Objectives

Employee achieved objective well. Final report was exceptionally thought out,
documented, and presented. Hospital administrator was highly pleased with the
work done. Moreover, the employee's presentation to the administrator's staff
was polished and professional.

Final Performance Rating (Check One)

☐ Unsatisfactory   ☐ Satisfactory   ☐ Competent   ☐ Commendable   ☒ Superior

Employee's Signature (I acknowledge having read and discussed the comments and
performance rating noted above.)
Larry C. Henderson

Supervisor's Signature   *Perry R. Jackson*   Date *Jan. 15, 1989*

May have poor or inadequate top-management support. For an MBO program to succeed, it *must* have top management's wholehearted commitment
and support. Sometimes top management does not set overall objectives at
all but delegates the responsibility for MBO to a staff department, such as

personnel. This seldom works! Top management must be committed to the implementation of a MBO program and through its actions set an example for other units of the organization.

Is poorly communicated and misunderstood. Much apprehension usually exists when MBO is first introduced. Some see the process as a threat to their authority; others misinterpret the intent of MBO. Still others lack understanding of the procedure to be followed. Meetings and reports outlining MBO's philosophy, procedure, and manner of implementation are essential to the success of the program.

Is inconsistent with managerial philosophies. For many managers, MBO signals a 180-degree turn from their present ways of thinking and acting. These managers have always established objectives for subordinates. Suddenly, under MBO, subordinates are to have strong input in helping establish these objectives *jointly* with their superiors.

SUMMARY

Planning is choosing a course of action and deciding in advance what is to be done, in what sequence, when, and how. Planning can be centralized so that the major planning work of an organization is done from a central point. It may also be decentralized, whereby each division or department essentially does its own planning without a single central planning unit at the top of the organization. A combination of the two systems results in the central planning unit doing the original umbrella planning, with each unit working so as to complement the central unit's plans.

Planning is closely related to all of the other management functions but is most closely related to controlling. From a time standpoint, long-range plans cover periods of two to five or more years; intermediate-range plans vary from one to five years; and short-range plans range from daily plans to those covering a year. Top managers typically devote a greater proportion of time to long-range plans, and lower managers are typically more involved in short-range plans.

Three main types of plans are strategic, standing, and single-use. Strategic plans include mission, objectives, and strategies and serve as the basis for deriving other plans. Standing plans, including policies, procedures, and rules and regulations, tend to be fixed in nature. Single-use plans, including programs, projects, and budgets, are nonrecurring.

Some criteria for evaluating the effectiveness of plans are usefulness (including flexibility, stability, continuity, and simplicity), accuracy and objectivity, scope (including comprehensiveness, unity, and consistency), cost-effectiveness, accountability, and timeliness.

Some barriers to effective planning are the impossibility of forecasting effectively, the difficulty of planning for nonrepetitive operations, the tendency of plans, once made, to be inflexible, the high cost of planning, and the possibility that making plans will stifle initiative.

Management by objectives (MBO) is the managerial process by which supervisors and subordinates jointly set performance objectives for each subordinate; the objectives thus established then become the basis for measuring and rewarding performance. MBO (1) links objectives set by different levels of management, (2) forces managers to plan, (3) provides increased communication between manager and subordinate, (4) involves subordinates in the goal-setting process, and (5) requires that specific, measurable performance objectives be established. MBO is no panacea, however, and several potential problems in MBO's implementation must be overcome to maximize its effectiveness.

REVIEW QUESTIONS

1. What are the "six planning questions"?
2. What are some of the advantages of planning?
3. What are some of the disadvantages of planning?
4. What is the relationship between planning and each of the other management functions?
5. (a) What is the difference between strategic plans, standing plans, and single-use plans? (b) What are some examples of each?
6. What is a budget? What is its relationship to planning?
7. How would you explain the relationship between management levels and the timing of planning?
8. What are short-, intermediate-, and long-range plans?
9. What are some examples of standing plans?
10. What are the primary criteria for evaluating the effectiveness of a plan?
11. What steps are involved in the process of management by objectives?
12. What are some problems encountered in implementing MBO programs?

DISCUSSION QUESTIONS

1. Some organizations may have as many as 50 to 100 individuals who work in corporate planning; others may have many fewer. Assume that two large organizations are about the same size, competing within the same industry. Company A has a corporate planning staff of 30 people; Company B has only 5. Does this mean Company B will be less effective in accomplishing its objectives than Company A? Discuss.
2. At a management seminar, when shown Figure 4.3, "Cycle of the nonplanner," one manager stated: "This definitely characterizes me, but I can never find the time to plan. I'm just *too* busy putting out fires. How can I get off the treadmill?" How would you answer this manager?
3. A manager says, "We don't need written policies around here. We're a small outfit with little turnover, and everyone knows what he or she's supposed to do. Once these things got put in writing, we'd be locked into them, and we'd lose our flexibility." Discuss this manager's view.
4. Explain the differences in the time factor in planning for top, middle, and lower-level managers.
5. Do you think that MBO is more applicable for large or small organizations? Or does the size of organization not make any difference? Discuss.
6. Are the barriers to effective planning really *barriers*, or are they merely excuses?

LEARNING EXERCISE 4.1

Practice in Policy Writing

The purpose of this exercise is to give you practice in developing and writing policies.

Instructions: Refer to the Nekoosa Papers philosophy statement below. Using the company statement as your reference, write five policies that would serve as guides to decision makers throughout the company. The policies you write must reflect the philosophy contained in the company statement.

Nekoosa Papers Performance Improvement Process
Mission Statement*

Nekoosa is committed to being the best in the paper industry in the quality of its products and services. We will judge our progress by how much better we anticipate and satisfy our customer needs than our competition. Our mission is to improve continually our products and services to meet our customer needs and, by doing so, to prosper as a business and to provide a reasonable return on our investment.

How we accomplish our mission is as important as the mission itself. Fundamental to success for Nekoosa are certain basic values:

1. We serve ourselves best by serving the customer first. Without him we have no business. He is an irreplaceable partner and, above anything else, we must treat him as such.
2. Our people are our source of strength. They provide our corporate intelligence and determine the reputation, the strength and the vitality of our company. Employee involvement and teamwork are our key human values as is the recognition that intelligence, skills and creativity exist at all levels in our organization.
3. Our products are the end result of our efforts, and they should be the best that exist. As our products are viewed so is Nekoosa viewed.
4. Profits are the life-blood of any business and the ultimate measure of the strength and viability of the company and its ability to grow. Profits also reflect how efficiently we produce and sell products to our customers....

We will call our process the Nekoosa Performance Process (NPI Process) and we are pledging the leadership and resources to make it a success. We wish to instill Quality as the basic business principle in Nekoosa, and to ensure that total quality improvement becomes the job of every Nekoosa person. By quality we mean quality of products and services for internal as well as external customers, and the quality of work life for all employees.

In support of this process, Nekoosa will commit to the following operating principles:

1. As a part of this new process, Nekoosa will do everything reasonable to provide pleasant and efficient working conditions and continue to provide a safe work environment.
2. Nekoosa will allocate resources to provide the most up-to-date production equipment available to the industry and will maintain its equipment to the highest industry standards.
3. Nekoosa will use the highest quality raw materials available, and will, as an integral part of this process, work actively with all of its suppliers in developing suitable raw materials for use in producing Nekoosa quality products.
4. Nekoosa will help employees increase their skills and knowledge through company support of training programs and education as needed to fully support the NPI Process.

We believe that Nekoosa's performance improvement is best accomplished under a system of participative management and employee involvement which emphasizes teamwork, trust, respect and recognition as the normal way to do business. Improved

---

* SOURCE: Nekoosa Papers, Inc.; used by permission.

performance will be an ongoing, never-ending effort, and we will know if we are achieving this goal when:

1. Each one of us enjoys our work and is proud of his or her own personal contribution to product quality and production efficiency.
2. Everyone is knowledgeable about company plans and goals and its progress toward fulfilling them.
3. All of our customers always receive excellent product quality and fast and considerate service at competitive prices.
4. Each of our competitors regard us as *his* toughest competitor.
5. Our neighbors continue to regard us as a good neighbor and a responsible member of the community.
6. Our profitability provides not only a good and secure living for all of us, but also provides funds to improve our plants' competitiveness through better economies and new products.

This is a new and different way of managing a company for most of us. We will not accomplish our mission quickly. It will take time, and it will require training for all of us. Products and people come and go and the challenge of new technology and changing economic conditions will always be with us, and these will impact our business. However, with the Nekoosa Performance Improvement Process functioning, we'll face these challenges and many others as we succeed in our objectives and bring meaningful rewards to ourselves and our company.

LEARNING EXERCISE 4.2

Practice in Objective Setting

An important part of MBO is to establish quantifiable, verifiable performance objectives. To give you experience in writing such objectives, write two performance objectives that could be established for each of the following positions:

Position

a. New car salesperson   1. _____
                          2. _____

b. Police officer (patrol car assignment)   1. _____
                          2. _____

c. Campus bookstore manager   1. _____
                          2. _____

d. City playground manager (oversees recreational playgrounds)   1. _____
                          2. _____

NOTES

1. "Technology: When Marketing Failed at Texas Instruments," *Business Week*, June 22, 1981, p. 91.
2. "Corporate Planning: Piercing the Future Fog in the Executive Suite," *Business Week*, April 28, 1975, p. 49.
3. Donald C. Mosley and Paul H. Pietri, *Management: The Art of Working With and Through People* (Encino, CA: Dickenson Publishing, 1975), p. 27.
4. "Technology: When Marketing Failed," p. 92.
5. T. G. Morford, "Long-Range Planning—An Evaluative Approach," *Managerial Planning* 27 (January–February 1979): 13–15.
6. "Corporate Planning: Piercing the Future Fog," p. 48.
7. J. Bologna, "Why Managers Resist Planning," *Managerial Planning* 28 (January–February 1980): 23–25.
8. See Peter Drucker, *The Practice of Management* (New York: Harper & Row, 1954), p. 62, for further details.

SUGGESTIONS FOR FURTHER STUDY

Genero, Guy, and Johnston, Russell A. "How to Assess Your On-Going MBO Program." *SAM Advanced Management Journal* 50 (Winter 1985): 40–46.

Gouindarajan, Vijay. "Decentralization, Strategy and Effectiveness of Strategic Business Units in Multibusiness Organizations." *Academy of Management Review* 11 (October 1986): 844–857.

Larson, Erik. "The Best-Laid Plans." *Inc.* 9 (February 1987): 60–65.

Leonard, Joseph W. "Why MBO Fails So Often." *Training and Development Journal* 40 (June 1986): 38–40.

McCartney, William W., and Callerman, William G. "Improving Productivity: Why Not Try MBO?" *Supervisory Management* 29 (October 1984): 17–23.

Pearce, John A., and David, Fred. "Corporate Mission Statements: The Bottom Line." *The Academy of Management EXECUTIVE* (May 1987): 109–115.

Richards, Bob. "Three Classes of Objectives and Plans Make MBO More Effective." *Personnel Journal* 65 (December 1986): 28–31.

Strategic Planning: Mission, Objectives, and Strategies

Learning Objectives

After studying the material in this chapter, you should be able to do the following:
- Define strategic planning.
- Identify the key steps in strategic planning.
- Explain what an organization's mission is.
- Identify the major performance areas in which an organization should establish objectives.
- Explain what is meant by the organizational hierarchy of objectives.
- Identify key internal and external environmental variables in strategic planning.
- Identify the major types of corporate strategy.

Outline of the Chapter

The strategic planning process
What is strategic planning?
Components of strategic planning
Organizational mission, or "What are we about?"
Role of organizational mission
Role of customers in determining mission
Organizational objectives
How the mission affects objectives
Some examples of organizational objectives
Need for balancing objectives
Why objectives are important
Setting overall objectives: Which areas?

Internal and external variables affecting the strategic plan
Planning premises
SWOT analysis
Strategic planning growth/share matrix
Some strategic options
Concentration
Vertical integration
Diversification
Turnaround/retrenchment strategies
Divestment/liquidation strategies
Combination of strategies
Summary

Some Important Terms

strategic planning
organizational objectives
organizational mission
productivity *or* efficiency
planning premises
uncontrollable factors
controllable factors
SWOT analysis

strategic business unit (SBU)
concentration
vertical integration
diversification
turnaround/retrenchment strategies
divestment/liquidation strategies

If you don't know where you are going, then any road will get you there.
—LEWIS CARROLL

Only a clear definition of the mission and purpose of the business makes possible clear and realistic objectives.... Strategy determines what the key activities are and strategy requires knowing "what our business is and what it should be."
—PETER DRUCKER

People Express—Growing Too Fast, Too Soon

People Express Inc. (now part of Continental Airlines) began operations on April 30, 1981, with 250 employees and three aircraft serving four cities. Within five years, it had grown to be the fifth largest airline in the United States, with 117 jetliners flying to 107 cities.

People began operations with a "keep it simple" philosophy. As a relatively small airline, People Express could maintain a lower cost structure than the majors. It achieved this competitive edge by maintaining its own reservation system, encouraging passengers to carry their luggage on board, buying used aircraft, cross-utilizing its employees (who were not unionized), and keeping a simple organizational structure. Net income of $1,002,000 in 1982 increased to $10,434,000 in 1983, but then decreased to $1,648,000 in 1984 and was followed by a loss of $17,537,000 in 1985.

In 1986, Donald Burr, People's cofounder and chairman, sold it to archrival Texas Air Corp., where it became part of Continental Airlines.

What had happened in such a short time period? For one thing, People's purchase of Frontier Airlines had turned out to be a mistake. Frontier's employees were unionized, enjoying higher wage rates than People's, and their labor contract limited cross-utilization of employees. Moreover, Frontier's customers, primarily in the Northwest, were not so enamored of the no-frills service that had been People's initial formula for success. Also, the purchase of additional new aircraft produced a heavy debt burden on the company and diminished its financial flexibility. Numerous overbookings, lost luggage, and flight delays resulted in customer dissatisfaction.

The company's management structure, which allowed workers a say in managerial decisions, was unable to handle the rapid growth. People was forced to raise prices to strengthen its financial picture, but this resulted in lost customers. Moreover, as a result of deregulation, larger airlines also cut prices, thereby increasing competition. People had just grown too fast, too soon.

To what extent did Burr's managerial philosophy contribute to People's demise? His goal was to "make a better world," which included giving employees a chance for development not found elsewhere. While his primary goal of "service, growth, and commitment to the individual" was instrumental in People's initial success, the fact that "maximizing profit" was his last goal may have helped cause its financial problems. ∎

THIS CASE ILLUSTRATES THE IMPORTANCE of strategic planning—especially the role of organizational mission and objectives and choice of strategy. In this chapter, we will introduce you to the concept of strategic planning, then discuss some of the key elements of the process, including organization mission, organizational objectives, assessing the organization's environment, and some of the key forms of strategy.

THE STRATEGIC PLANNING PROCESS

The concept of strategic planning has become exceptionally important in management circles today. This is due in large part to the increasing complexities of both external and internal environments, as well as growing management sophistication. The term *strategy* is derived from the Greek word *strategos*, which means "a general." In ancient times, it meant the art and science of managing military forces to victory. Today, business and not-for-profit organizations engage in strategy when choosing the best options for accomplishing their purposes for existence.

What Is Strategic Planning?

Strategic planning consists of those activities leading to the definition of the organization's mission, the setting of objectives, and the development of strategies that enable it to function successfully in its environment. Strategic planning can be differentiated from other types of organizational planning (discussed in Chapter 4) by the following criteria:

1. It involves decisions made by top management.
2. It involves ultimate allocation of large amounts of resources, such as money, labor, or physical capacity.
3. It has significant long-term impact.
4. It focuses on the organization's interaction with the external environment.[1]

Components of Strategic Planning

Figure 5.1 shows the basic components of strategic management, which underlies strategic planning. First, a clear understanding of the organizational mission is essential to permit development of objectives and formulation of strategies. Second, objectives must be established—the organization must decide what it wants to accomplish, including overall objectives regarding profitability, market share, and so on. Third, management identifies the strategic alternatives available to achieve its objectives. This step entails examining its strengths and weaknesses, forecasting the future environment, and so on. Finally, in Step 4, strategic choices are made.

Note that our focus in this chapter is upon strategic *planning*. Management must also be concerned, however, with strategic implementation and control processes once strategic plans have been established.

We will now discuss strategic planning.

ORGANIZATIONAL MISSION, OR "WHAT ARE WE ABOUT?"

Organizations simply cannot survive if they take a posture such as this chapter's opening quotation by Lewis Carroll, from *Alice in Wonderland*. They *must* know where they're going and what they are all about. An organizational mission identifies the fundamental, unique purpose that the organization attempts to serve and identifies its products or services and customers. Thus, the mission identifies the organization's reason for existence—that is, what it stands for. For example, MAP 5.1 gives the mission statement for Rochester (Minnesota) Community College. Note that the statement clearly defines the school's purpose, the programs it offers, the clientele it seeks.

What is your view?

Examine the mission statement of Rochester Community College. In what ways is Rochester's mission likely to be different from that of a major state university such as the University of Minnesota, which offers a full array of B.A., M.A., and Ph.D. degrees?

Role of Organizational Mission

Suppose you were named president of a firm such as Mobil Oil, the Chase Manhattan Bank, or International Paper. Would you have to concern yourself with the corporate mission? Probably not in the short run, since missions don't change very often. You would inherit an organization, products or services, and customers. But the mission would be very important to you as a new president. What business are you in? Where are you headed? Where *should* you be headed? It is in seeking answers to questions such as these that top managers should spend their time.

The history of the Tennessee Valley Authority (TVA), the public utility and public works complex, also illustrates the problems caused by lack of a clear mission. When TVA was created in the 1930s, some saw government ownership as but the first step in the nationalization of electric energy in the United States. Others, however, welcomed it for its promise of cheap electricity and free fertilizer for the Tennessee Valley, which was primarily agricultural. Others saw it as a provider of flood control and navigation.

There was such a conflict in expectations that TVA's first head floundered completely. Unable to decide what TVA's business ought to be and how varying objectives might be balanced, he accomplished little. Finally, he was replaced by an almost totally unknown young lawyer with little previous experience as an administrator, David Lilienthal.

Lilienthal, facing the need to define TVA's business, concluded that the first objective was to build truly efficient electric plants and to supply an energy-starved region with cheap and plentiful power. All the rest, he decided, hinged on attaining this first goal.

Today, TVA has accomplished many other objectives as well—flood control, navigable waterways, fertilizer production, and even balanced community development. But it was Lilienthal's insistence on a clear definition of TVA's business that resulted in TVA's now being taken for granted, even by those who, 50 years ago, were its enemies.[2]

FIGURE 5.1

The strategic process.

SOURCE: Adapted from Lloyd L. Byars, *Strategic Management* (New York: Harper & Row, Publishers, 1984), p. 10.

A good example is the railroad industry. If you were responsible for determining the mission of a large railroad, what would it be? Unfortunately,

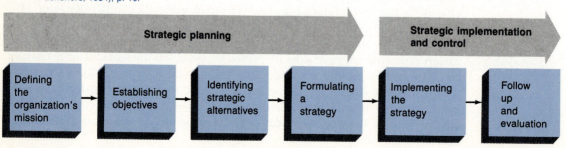

Strategic planning | Strategic implementation and control

Defining the organization's mission → Establishing objectives → Identifying strategic alternatives → Formulating a strategy → Implementing the strategy → Follow up and evaluation

Management Application and Practice 5.1   Mission Statement of Rochester (Minnesota) Community College

Rochester Community College is dedicated to carrying out a commitment to lifelong learning. As an equal opportunity, open access institution, it serves people with varying interests, aspirations, and abilities, reaching many who otherwise would not have the option to pursue higher education.

Rochester Community College provides quality programs and services on an affordable, convenient basis. Helping people realize their potential, further their ambitions, and improve their lives is the purpose of Rochester Community College.

In carrying out its mission, Rochester Community College provides:

1. *Transfer education in the Liberal Arts and Sciences* by offering instruction at the freshman and sophomore levels of undergraduate education enabling the individual to earn a baccalaureate degree.
2. *Career education* of a technical or semiprofessional nature offering certificates and/or associate degrees that upon completion permit the individual to secure employment in the occupational field for which preparation is sought. These programs address the latest technological innovations in the occupational field for which preparation is offered.
3. *General education* by expanding the individual's social, cultural, ethical, and intellectual horizons through the investigation of broad areas of human knowledge and achievement and by aiding the individual to explore possible career and life choices.
4. *Continuing education* by enabling the individual to advance, as well as maintain, certification in an occupational field and by providing personal growth and cultural enrichment.
5. *Community services* by offering cultural and recreational activities that encourage community, as well as student, involvement; providing access to college facilities for community activities; and assisting in the promotion of the social and economic well-being of the community.
6. *Developmental education* by recognizing the needs of some individuals to improve their basic learning skills in order to make satisfactory progress toward their educational objectives.
7. *Cooperative programs with services* for school systems, businesses, industries, community agencies, and other institutions of postsecondary education.
8. *Student support services* that enable individual students to formulate and carry out their educational objectives through quality, advising, counseling, financial aid, child care, and placement services.
9. *Student activities* encouraging students to participate in experiences geared to their vocational, social, cultural, and recreational interests.

The college implements these services by articulating its instructional programs, student services, and continuing education/community service functions with the secondary schools, vocational schools, colleges and universities, businesses and industries of its service area.

SOURCE: Courtesy of Dr. Geraldine Evans, President, Rochester Community College, Rochester, Minnesota.

many railroads saw their mission quite narrowly as being in the "railroad business" instead of thinking in terms of "transporting people and products." This narrow view of their mission spelled doom for many railroads, for they failed to examine the key issues involved and failed to change the nature of their economic mission.

The question "What business are we in?" is deceptively simple, for it is, in effect, quite difficult to answer. Robert Townsend, Chairman and CEO of Avis, highlighted the difficulty when he said it took Avis six months to define one objective: "To become the fastest growing company with the highest profit margin in the business of renting and leasing vehicles without drivers." He added that "this let us put the blinders on ourselves and stop considering the acquisition of related businesses like motels, hotels, airlines, and travel agencies. It also showed us that we had to get rid of some limousine and sight-seeing companies that we already owned."[3]

Having an unclear, unidentified mission can ultimately lead to disaster. As one insider put it, a prime factor underlying the failure of W. T. Grant, a retail giant with over 1000 stores, was internal dispute over whether Grant should be a full-service store like J. C. Penney and Sears or a discounter like Kmart.[4] Boise Cascade, the highly profitable forest products company, shifted its mission in the 1970s by acquiring companies in unrelated fields. These fields included modular housing construction, real estate, pleasure cruise lines, mobile home manufacturing, and building and office construction. The inability to manage such unrelated firms effectively was disastrous and led to a deficit of $250,000,000 over a two-year period. Then, under new management, the company retrenched by disposing of its non–forest-related acquisitions and returning to its narrower mission, thus regaining profitability.

So, whether you're a manager in a large, multibillion-dollar firm such as GM or an officer of a not-for-profit organization such as the student Accounting Club, you should have a clear picture of just "what our reason for existence is."

An organization's mission statement often goes beyond defining its products or services, markets, and customers. Frequently it contains an outline of the organization's values and beliefs or general guidelines that it will use in pursuing its mission. These are sometimes referred to as *credos* or *company creeds*.

A good example of a broader—yet concise—mission statement is the one developed by Mary Kay Cosmetics.

THE MARY KAY MISSION
To achieve preeminence in the manufacturing and marketing of personal care products by providing personalized service, value, and convenience to Mary Kay customers through our independent sales force.
                   —Richard C. Bartlett, President
                   Mary Kay Cosmetics, Inc.

Role of Customers in Determining Mission

A key aspect of an organization's mission is to identify the persons who will be the ultimate users of the services or products. Just who is the customer? People Express tried to get the less affluent travelers to change from cars and buses to planes. Radio Shack pursued a different type of customer by marketing home computers and electronics for individuals. Different missions, though, lead to different objectives, strategies, programs, policies, and plans. For example, IBM focused on large businesses as customers for its computers and business products. But when it introduced the IBM-PC, it set up an entirely new unit to produce and sell it to individual purchasers.

What is your view?
Head Ski Company originally manufactured skis, then moved into ski clothing, then tennis rackets, and finally sportswear in general. To what extent are these customer groups similar or different? How far could this expansion be carried?

Some organizations, such as Gulf + Western, LTV, and Teledyne, serve a variety of customers with broad product lines, while others concentrate on a single line. For example, Texaco, one of the largest energy firms, focuses on locating, producing, refining, and marketing petroleum products and chemicals. But Tenneco, one of Texaco's competitors, is not only in the petroleum business but also in shipbuilding, farm equipment, automotive parts, gas pipelines, agriculture, real estate development, and insurance. Tenneco's mission has gradually changed to allow for diversification.[5] Similarly, Ford Motor Company is not only in automobile manufacture but also in aerospace, electronics, and many other activities.

A model of the key steps an organization must take in determining its economic mission is shown in Figure 5.2. When the Salk and Sabin polio vaccines were perfected and the spread of polio halted, the Polio Foundation didn't go out of business. Instead, it examined its resources and society's needs and formulated a new mission—financing research to prevent birth defects. We know the organization today as the March of Dimes.

ORGANIZATIONAL OBJECTIVES

FIGURE 5.2
Formulating an economic mission, or answering the question: "What kind of business should we be in?"

Organizational objectives are similar to railroad tickets—they indicate destinations or ends that the organization seeks to achieve. They are the targets toward which managers move in order to fulfill the organization's mission. In summary, they are performance targets. Organizations have numerous higher-level, overall objectives, among them profitability, market share, good labor relations, and others, as will be discussed later.

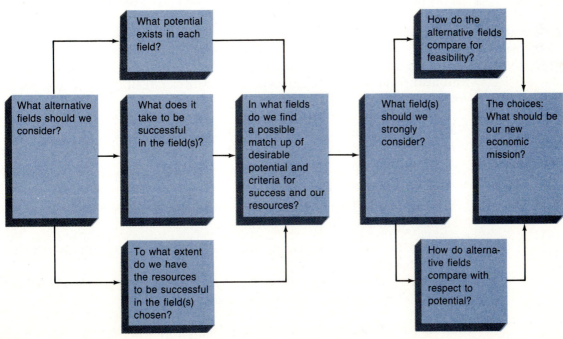

Does an objective differ from a goal? It is important to note that semantics often leads to dispute in answering this question. Some management writers and practitioners say goals are broad and general, whereas objectives are specific (recall our discussion of MBO in Chapter 4). Others say just the reverse, such as "The nature of objectives is general, whereas goals connote greater degrees of specificity and consequently are more operative in everyday activities, including decision making."[6] Goals and objectives both have value orientations and reflect desired conditions considered necessary to improve the overall performance of the organization. Keep in mind, then, that while some writers and managers do make this distinction between the two, it is much more common *not* to make such a distinction. We shall simply say that the terms *objective* and *goal* are used interchangeably in this book to indicate an end result to be sought and accomplished.

How the Mission Affects Objectives

The **organizational mission** identifies the function that the organization intends to perform within its social or economic system. As shown in Figure 5.3, only after the basic mission is established can specific objectives, strategies, programs, policies, and plans fall into place. Let's examine such a mission by looking at that of People Express Inc., mentioned in the Opening Case. People's mission was to make a better world by providing mass transportation to less affluent customers. This mission, therefore, required overall organizational objectives to be set regarding service, growth, and individual performance. Then, specific objectives had to be set to have lower costs and a higher-than-average ratio of passengers to seats than other airlines. These objectives of high volume and low costs required subplans and strategies such as cross-training of employees, limiting frills in flight, scheduling services only on high-traffic routes, and charging lower fares so as to attract the high volume needed. People also had "wheel and spoke routes," with all flights originating in, or returning to, its Newark, New Jersey, terminal.

Some Examples of Organizational Objectives

Objectives go beyond and are more specific than answers to "What is our business?" At the same time, however, an organization's long-term, ongoing objectives are usually stated in broad terms rather than in the specific terms you learned about in management by objectives (MBO) in Chapter 4. Some examples follow.

PepsiCo. Following is the statement of objectives of PepsiCo, the large food and beverage company.

> PepsiCo's efforts in all its activities are predicated on the fulfillment of three fundamental objectives:
>
> To earn the highest possible return on its shareholders' investment consistent with fair and honest business practices.
>
> To ensure steadily increasing per-share profits and dividends paid to shareholders.
>
> To perform consistently better than the industry in every market where PepsiCo products and services compete.[7]

Norton Company. Here is another statement, from the Norton Company, a large manufacturer of abrasives, tubing, gaskets, and safety products:

FIGURE 5.3
Relationships among
mission, objectives, and
other organizational
plans, as applied to
People Express (now
Continental Airlines).

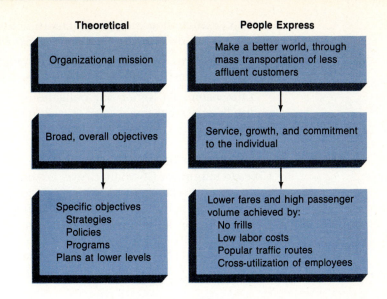

To manage the business in a manner which will enable Norton Company to remain the worldwide leader in the field of abrasives.

To improve our product portfolio or mix by balancing abrasives with a limited number of diversified product lines and without conglomeration.

To maintain and build Norton's reputation as a responsible corporate citizen, which at times means accepting a lower profit.

To maintain a working environment equal to the best for all our employees at all levels. This includes providing employees with individual freedom to act, opportunities for personal growth, and protecting health, safety, and security.

To preserve and enhance the value of Norton stock and improve its marketability.[8]

Hewlett-Packard. Hewlett-Packard (HP), founded in 1939, is a major designer and manufacturer of precision electronic equipment, including computers, calculators, medical and scientific instruments, and other products. The company's corporate objectives are summarized in these seven objectives:

Profit: To achieve sufficient profit to finance our company growth and to provide the resources we need to achieve our other corporate objectives.

Customers: To produce products and services of the greatest possible value to our customers, thereby gaining and holding their respect and loyalty.

Fields of interest: To enter new fields only when the ideas we have, together with our technical, manufacturing, and marketing skills, assure that we can make a needed and marketable contribution to the field.

Growth: To let our growth be limited only by our products and our ability to develop and produce technical products that satisfy real customer wants.

Our people: To help HP people share in the company's success, which they make possible; to provide job security based on their performance;

to recognize their individual achievements; and to help them gain a sense of satisfaction and accomplishment from their work.

Management: To foster initiative and creativity by allowing the individual great freedom of action in attaining well-defined objectives.

Citizenship: To honor our obligations to society by being an economic, intellectual, and social asset to each nation and each community in which we operate.[9]

ServiceMaster Industries. ServiceMaster Limited Partnership, based in the Chicago suburb of Downers Grove, is America's leading provider of management support services to health care, educational, and industrial facilities. Its return on equity averaged an amazing 30.1 percent from 1974 to 1984. Consistently near the top of analysts' lists of best performers among service companies, ServiceMaster (Service to the Master) has a firm spiritual and ethical focus. Its Bible Belt values resulted in four fundamental aims, namely:

To honor God in all we do.

To help people develop.

To pursue excellence.

To grow profitably.[10]

Note that some of these objectives are very specific and others are rather general. PepsiCo says its objective is "to earn the highest possible return." But just what is "the highest possible return"? HP aims to "produce products and services of the greatest possible value to our customers." ServiceMaster's "to honor God in all we do" is certainly general. On the other hand, Norton says it seeks "to remain the worldwide leader in the field of abrasives," which is more specific. But even though most of these statements are fairly general, they provide direction in the form of a set of end points toward which the organization will be aimed.

Need for Balancing Objectives

Most organizations have multiple objectives that require them to make trade-offs in order to accomplish all the objectives. These trade-offs, in turn, cause conflict in the ends and means necessary for achieving them. In short, multiple goals require balancing, or accommodating, the wants, needs, and requirements of such diverse groups as those shown in Figures 1.4 and 1.5.

Management must determine the optimum balance or mix of these objectives. For example, as shown in the statements of overall objectives of Hewlett-Packard, the interests of shareholders, workers, and society may be quite different. Shareholders or owners want larger dividends or increased stock prices; customers want better-quality products or services at lower prices; workers want higher salaries and benefits, with more paid time off; and society expects high standards of social conduct. Consequently, management must exercise considerable judgment in setting multiple overall objectives that allow for some flexibility and trade-offs in reflecting the interests of each key group.

Why Objectives Are Important

Objectives are important to management for several reasons, the most important of which are that objectives (1) permit unified planning by all de-

The Objectives of ServiceMaster

To honor God in all we do

To help people develop

To pursue excellence

To grow profitably

ServiceMaster Industries Inc.

Objectives based on religious values.
(Source: "ServiceMaster: The Protestant Ethic Helps Clean Hospitals Better,"
Business Week, February 19, 1979, p. 58. Reprinted by permission.)

partments, (2) serve as a basis for employee motivation, and (3) enable management to perform the function of control. Thus, they should be integrated, challenging, achievable, and measurable.

Objectives permit unified planning. Top management establishes overall objectives that are integrated into the framework within which lower-level managers and employees establish their own subobjectives and plans. This creates a hierarchy of objectives. Let's look at an example of a hierarchy of objectives in a hypothetical organization, Hertex Inc.

Hertex Inc. continuing objective: To earn the highest profit possible consistent with fair business practices.

1989 overall profit objective: $300,000,000

1989 Sales Division objective: $32,000,000

1989 Western Region sales objective: $14,000,000

1989 California state sales objective: $9,000,000

1989 California sales representative individual objective: $450,000

Objectives provide motivation and a sense of achievement. Objectives that are achievable, by being set realistically, serve as the basis for group and individual motivation. The Sales Division manager of Hertex gears his or her entire efforts toward accomplishing the $32 million sales goal against which his or her performance will be measured. This is true throughout the entire hierarchy of objectives.

But note an important qualifier in the example. To have the maximum effect, the $32 million sales objective must be perceived by the division manager as challenging, but realistic. Objectives that are set too low don't provide a challenge; objectives that are unrealistically high may not be accepted or may even be counterproductive.

Objectives serve as a basis for control. Measurable objectives enable managers to perform the control function of management more effectively. As you will learn in Chapter 14, the control process involves (1) setting performance targets or standards, (2) measuring performance, (3) comparing actual performance with present standards, and (4) taking corrective action if needed. You will note that the first step of controlling, then, is having a goal or objective to shoot for.

When information indicates that objectives are *not* being met, a manager must examine the situation and determine whether corrective action is necessary. If corrective action is needed, he or she must decide what form the action will take. But, again, the corrective action is aimed at making the actual performance conform to the objective.

Setting Overall Objectives: Which Areas?

What is your view?

Suppose you were planning to open a small business of your choice, such as a gift shop, hobby shop, or bookshop. What would you say is your business's primary objective? Think about your answer for a few seconds before reading the following material.

What was your answer to the question just posed? If you're like most people, you probably said your primary objective would be to make a profit. Businesses certainly need to make a profit to stay in business. But should the sole underlying purpose that guides a firm's daily activities be just to make a profit? The answer is no. However, it should be emphasized that *an organization's primary objective is survival.*

Profit alone? Although profits are the primary objective, look how easily you and other business people with such a single mission could get into trouble.[11] Would you, for the sake of profits, refuse to accept merchandise returns? Would you be reluctant to invest in new equipment? What about contributing to local charities? Would you be tempted to cut corners in a variety of areas, such as store attractiveness, in order not to each up your profits?

Larger firms with the same primary profit objective might avoid sinking money into research and development because the costs would reduce the profit picture in the short run.

Profit and service? Through the concentration of economic power in the hands of corporate managers, which has occurred in the last half-century,

(Reprinted from The Wall Street Journal *by permission of Cartoon Features Syndicate.)*

management has largely turned away from primary allegiance to the shareholders and to the sole necessity of making a profit. This thought was expressed by Irving Shapiro on his retirement as chairman of the board of Du Pont, when he said that "earning a profit—*staying in business*—is still the No. 1 thing. Unless you can earn money, you cannot do any of these other things. The economic mission is of great importance, but *it's not of sole importance.*[12]

Since economic activities are influenced by the society and culture in which they are performed, a realistic management philosophy today is based on *balancing objectives* in the search for optimum profits with the fulfillment of the service objective. W. J. Cross, vice-president and treasurer of Reader's Digest, one of the largest and most profitable book and magazine publishers, record distributors, and direct mail marketing houses, stated this belief when he said, "Profits are secondary to providing a good product, at a reasonable price, and making this a good place to work."[13]

We conclude, therefore, that corporate managers should have the dual objective of *optimizing long-term profits* for the stockholders and at the same time *performing a needed service* for the public. This conclusion is based on the theory that a long-range concern for optimum profits provides a clear measure of managerial efficiency and effectiveness. It is further assumed that, in the long run, managers concerned with seeking to achieve such a profit must provide a service needed by the public or they will lose their main constituents, the customers.

A test of reality is that if managers do *not* accomplish this they will fail, for most business firms are customer oriented, which distinguishes them from other social institutions. Conversely, those executives whose objective is to maximize short-term profits will not long provide an *efficient economic* organization that will effectively serve its customers and the public. Since the perspective of the economic function is the primary difference between business enterprises and other types of organizations, the dual objective of profit achievement and service performance should remain a primary concern.

What is your view?

Which chief executives do you think are most likely to say that their overriding objective is profits—those from large, publicly owned corporations or those from smaller, family-owned businesses? Why?

Increasing awareness of social responsibility. One question that is being asked more frequently is whether management should take a leading role in achieving broad social goals. Because modern business corporations have become such power centers in the economic, social, and political realms, many people—especially the opinion makers—apparently feel that the range of corporate actions should be limited, as will be shown in Chapter 19. It is now accepted by most corporate managers that they have a social responsibility. This means that corporate managers have a responsibility to employees, consumers, and the general public, as well as to the owners, and that the owners have no special priority.

One reason for this trend is that Americans have increasingly accepted private business enterprise as the best tool for providing the material things of life. The corporation itself has evolved as a powerful—and generally efficient—semipublic, *economic* institution rather than a private venture. A similar development is the public's acceptance of executives of big business as members of the nation's leadership. Yet the public, in general, tends to distrust business in general, especially big business.

What is your view?

Do you think the public distrusts only business, or is there a tendency to distrust large organizations and institutions in general—unions, governments, and the media?

Areas needing objectives. Peter Drucker, while working as a consultant for GE, identified eight major areas in which businesses should set objectives. As shown in Figure 5.4, these areas are (1) market standing, (2) productivity, (3) physical and financial resources, (4) profitability, (5) innovation, (6) manager performance and development, (7) worker performance and attitudes, and (8) public and social responsibility.[14]

Market standing. A business must set objectives concerning what share of the market it will try to capture. The best market share requires careful analysis of (1) customers and products or services, (2) market segments (what groups are buying the product or service), and (3) distribution channels (who is getting the product to the customers). Before its breakup by the government, AT&T had defined its target market: "No longer do we perceive that our business will be limited to telephony, or for that matter, telecommuni-

FIGURE 5.4
Areas that need objectives.

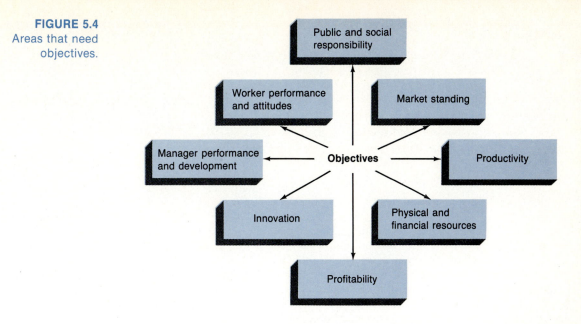

cations. Ours is the business of information handling, the knowledge business. And the market we seek is global."[15] Note that Norton Company in its statement of objectives indicated that it sought to remain the market leader in abrasives.

Productivity. Productivity, or **efficiency,** is the ratio of an organization's inputs to its outputs. What inputs of labor, equipment, and finances are necessary to produce the firm's outputs? For example, when a firm cuts its employee turnover rate, the costs of hiring and training new employees drop, resulting in increased productivity. Productivity improvement objectives can be set in several areas, including work methods, machinery and equipment advances, and increased worker efficiency.

Physical and financial resources. How will the organization's financial resources be generated and utilized? Objectives should be established regarding plant and equipment and supply of raw materials.

Profitability. Profit objectives are important to accomplish other objectives, including (1) the research and development needed for innovation, (2) the financial strength to update plant and equipment, and (3) the salaries needed to attract outstanding personnel.

Innovation. There is a great need for new and innovative products and services. Although there is a certain risk in being the first with something new, there are also potentially high rewards.

What is your view?
Ted Turner's 24-hour Cable News Network (CNN) wasn't given much chance by experts to succeed, nor was Gannett's *USA Today*. Why do you think Turner and Gannett would take such risks when most experts were highly skeptical?

Manager performance and development. The survival of many organizations depends on strong, innovative management. Smaller firms are especially vulnerable, since the management expertise often rests with one or a few talented managers. But organizations both large and small must set objec-

TIPS 5.1   Guidelines for Effective Objective Setting

Objective setting in the real world is often a poorly understood, poorly implemented process. Properly done, however, it leads to more effective management. The following guidelines—which apply to all management levels—will help you become more effective in setting objectives.

1. *Limit objectives to selected performance areas.* Many managers establish far too many objectives for their personnel. Since the nature of objective setting is to stimulate and direct attention and energy, critical objectives lose some of their luster when thrown in with many others. Instead of setting 15 objectives for your people, it is better to select five or six that address key performance areas that really count, such as profitability, quality, cost control, and/or customer relations.

2. *Be specific.* If you can't count, measure, or describe an objective in some specific way, forget about it. Vague objectives not only are subject to misinterpretation by personnel but don't provide tangible satisfaction when they are achieved. Consider, for instance, this objective: "The Division X objective is to show good profitability in 1992." This statement is vague on several counts: (a) What is "good" profitability? (b) What measure—return on assets, return on equity, return on sales, and so forth—will be used to determine profitability? (c) Will profitability be determined before or after taxes? A better statement would be: "The Division X objective for 1992 is to earn a 20 percent return on average assets after taxes."

3. *Set challenging objectives.* Objectives should not be set so low that they can be met by "average" effort, nor should they be unrealistically high. For instance, it is unrealistic for Chrysler to set an objective of gaining 50 percent of the U.S. auto market by 1990. This not only would serve no useful purpose, it would also demoralize personnel who know there is no reasonable hope of achieving it.

4. *Keep objectives in balance.* Key performance areas tend to be interrelated, so managers must consider the impact objectives have on one another. For example, quality of work influences quantity of output; profitability and cost control may not always be consistent with customer service or maintenance of physical assets.

5. *Set realistic deadlines.* Objectives, properly set, should establish time frames for completion. This holds individuals accountable over a period of time and allows for periodic assessment of their performances.

6. *Involve subordinates.* Since people are more committed to what they themselves establish, try to get them to set objectives and performance levels. As a manager, you're not necessarily committed to what they feel are reasonable objectives, but the level they establish will frequently surprise you. The major premise of MBO is based on this principle.

7. *Establish results-oriented objectives.* Since objectives are end results, they should be desirable levels of achievement within themselves. For example, the objective "To increase advertising by 10 percent in 1990" measures the amount spent on advertising, not the *end result* that the advertising is designed to achieve. A better objective would focus on the number of new customers, size of customer orders, or increased sales attributable to advertising, rather than the *level* of advertising itself.

8. *Follow up.* Don't wait until the end of the performance period to determine whether objectives are being met. Use intermediate performance reports or progress checks to see how your people are doing. If they're doing well, praise and reinforce their performance; if they're on the wrong track, coach them as needed.

tives relating to the quality of management performance and to ensuring the development of managers at all levels.

Worker performance and attitudes. Operative-level employees do most of the routine work in every organization. The operations of many large and small firms have been disrupted by labor strife; managers of smaller nonunion firms become alarmed when their workers begin talk of organizing or joining a union. Having objectives established regarding such factors as output per employee, quality of product, and morale level should benefit management in its search for effectiveness.

Public and social responsibility. Public boycotts, legal actions, and governmental actions face firms that do not adopt and implement social and public objectives. Some companies, such as General Mills, Armco, and many others, have what they call standing "public responsibility" committees that advise their boards of directors on social issues. Standard Oil of Indiana (AMOCO), Du Pont, and Bethlehem Steel are among several firms that include social responsibility information in their annual reports.

TIPS 5.1 presents some guidelines for setting objectives more effectively.

INTERNAL AND EXTERNAL VARIABLES AFFECTING THE STRATEGIC PLAN

Strategic planning does not take place in a vacuum, but should consider many variables that affect the organization. Thus, identification of key variables, awareness of their impact, and the ability to predict their future potential impact is essential to effective strategic planning. In the early 1980s, the U.S. auto industry failed to predict Americans' desire for smaller vehicles that get higher gas mileage. Customers' tastes, however, were ripe for change as a result of increasing gasoline costs, fuel shortages resulting from the oil embargo by OPEC, and uncertainty over future oil supplies. In foreign countries, smaller autos had already captured a high market share, and their U.S. share had been increasing. Yet, American manufacturers persisted in focusing on large cars. As a result, in 1980, American auto manufacturers lost $4.2 billion primarily because of the popularity in the United States of small vehicles offered by foreign manufacturers.

FIGURE 5.5
Assessing internal and external environments.

SOURCE: Adapted from Lloyd L. Byars, *Strategic Management* (New York: Harper & Row, 1984), p. 66.

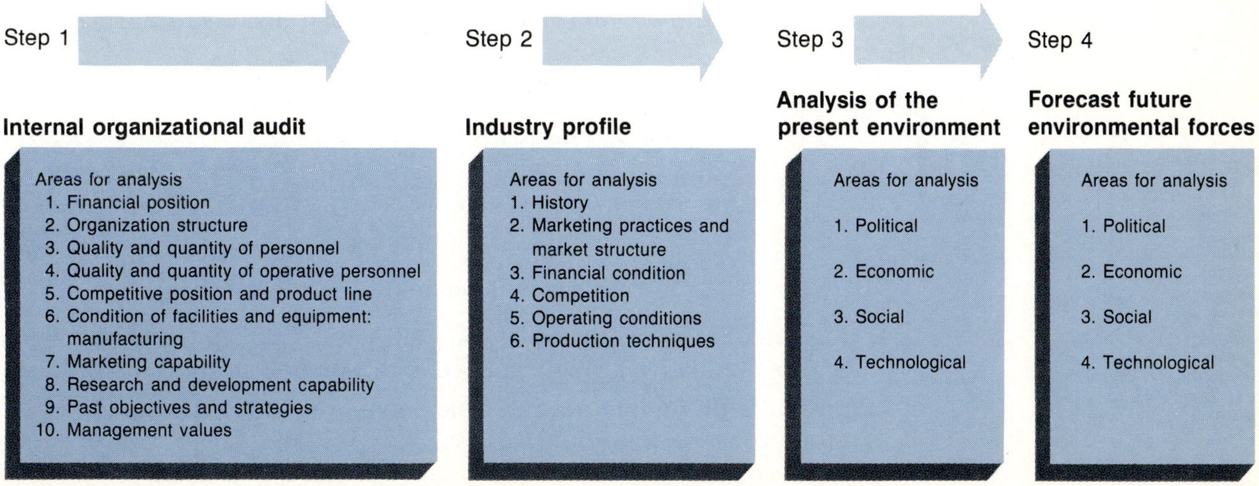

Figure 5.5 shows the areas for analysis that an organization must consider. Basically, these consist of four distinct analyses:

Step 1	Step 2	Step 3	Step 4
Internal organizational audit	**Industry profile**	**Analysis of the present environment**	**Forecast future environmental forces**
Areas for analysis 1. Financial position 2. Organization structure 3. Quality and quantity of personnel 4. Quality and quantity of operative personnel 5. Competitive position and product line 6. Condition of facilities and equipment: manufacturing 7. Marketing capability 8. Research and development capability 9. Past objectives and strategies 10. Management values	Areas for analysis 1. History 2. Marketing practices and market structure 3. Financial condition 4. Competition 5. Operating conditions 6. Production techniques	Areas for analysis 1. Political 2. Economic 3. Social 4. Technological	Areas for analysis 1. Political 2. Economic 3. Social 4. Technological

1. Internal organizational factors, such as management values, quality of personnel, competitive position and product line, and research and development.

2. Industry profile, which includes factors such as the industry's history, competitive forces, and financial condition.

3. Present external environmental factors, including political, economic, social, and technological forces.

4. Forecast of future external environmental factors, which involves predicting accurately the changes that are foreseen in present external environmental variables.

Planning Premises

As you can see, forecasting is extremely important to strategic planning. The information derived from forecasting leads to **planning premises,** which are those assumptions made about future environments. Thus, premises are established for external political, social, technological, and economic variables, as well as internal variables such as development of new products, research and development breakthroughs, production capacity, levels of personnel proficiency, and so on.

In the early 1970s, the athletic running shoe industry was dominated by one firm—Adidas. By 1980, however, four upstart firms that had come into existence since 1970 had captured over 75 percent of the market in the United States, led by Nike with over 50 percent. What had caused this disaster for Adidas? At least three of the firm's planning premises were at fault:

1. Adidas had failed to forecast the tremendous boom in popularity that jogging and fitness were to play in this country.

2. It had not anticipated the technological breakthroughs in athletic shoes introduced by the new competition, such as light weight, increased flexibility, and increased comfort.

3. It assumed that the upstart firms could not pose a short-term threat because they lacked the physical base to produce a high volume of shoes. They were shocked when Nike contracted with firms in the Far East to manufacture its shoes.

Nike's newfound dominance was relatively short-lived, however, since it failed to anticipate the aerobics craze and allowed Reebok to upstage it in the mid-1980s.[16]

What is your view?

In 1980, Ford, GM, and Chrysler all committed themselves heavily to small, 4-cylinder, front-wheel-drive vehicles. What do you think were some of the critical planning premises on which these decisions were based? Have those assumptions proven to be accurate?

There are two groups of factors affecting the planning process:

1. **Uncontrollable factors,** or those that have no direct, traceable cause, such as population growth, political environment, and social pressures.

2. **Controllable factors,** or those elements over which the organization, through the decision of its managers, has at least some control, such as research, building sites, and organizational relationships.

Another factor to be considered is that the planning process requires many assumptions that cannot possibly take into account all the events in the future, but these premises do provide management with an orderly path to follow, and they *can* be changed as changing conditions might warrant. Strategic planners must monitor these changes and modify the planning premises as conditions dictate.

SWOT Analysis

One useful format for helping organizations identify key internal and external variables, as well as identify potential opportunities, is called SWOT analysis. **SWOT analysis** is the process of systematically identifying an organization's *s*trengths, *w*eaknesses, *o*pportunities, and *t*hreats. An example of SWOT analysis for Winnebago Industries in the 1970s is found in Figure 5.6. By using SWOT analysis, organizations may obtain a clearer picture of their strategic position. But SWOT analysis consists of more than just formal list making, as the example implies. It is essential that weights, probabilities, and other evaluative measures be used to analyze the items identified.

What is your view?

Presumably, you are studying this book in conjunction with a course offered by an educational institution. Since you have some familiarity with the institution's setting, identify some strengths, weaknesses, opportunities, and threats associated with the institution.

FIGURE 5.6
SWOT analysis of Winnebago Industries, early 1970s.

SOURCE: Adapted from Heinz Weihrich, "The TOWS Matrix—a Tool for Situational Analysis," *Long Range Planning* 15 (April 1982):58.

Strengths

1. Strong corporate image and reputation
2. Good service and warranty
3. Established dealer network and good relations
4. Automated, economical plant
5. Solid research and development capabilities
6. Capable of manufacturing most parts of product

Weaknesses

1. Vulnerable as a one-product company
2. Focus mainly on high-priced products
3. Cost of model changes will be high due to heavy toolmaking investment
4. Plant located in single community
5. No preparation for transition from family to corporation management

Opportunities

1. Demand for smaller recreational vehicles
2. Development of international market
3. Demand for low cost, modular housing (FHA subsidy for mortgage loans)

Threats

1. Higher gas prices/gasoline shortage
2. Slackening demand for RVs
3. Increased competition by GM, Ford, VW, Toyota, others
4. Impending safety regulations
5. Possible governmental action against low mpg vehicles (gas guzzler taxes)

Strategic Planning Growth/Share Matrix

Most large corporations have a number of products in one or more industries. It can be said, then, that each such company consists of a portfolio of several distinct smaller businesses, called strategic business units. A **strategic business unit (SBU)** consists of a unique company business that has its own mission, product or service lines, competition, customers, threats, and opportunities. Thus, a diversified corporation such as General Electric has over 40 SBUs in such areas as refrigerators, gas turbines, aircraft equipment, televisions and stereos, and others. At a state university, colleges of arts, business, education, engineering, and science each has its own mission, faculty, students, and external environmental factors to monitor; each of these could be considered as a separate SBU.

One of the most publicized techniques in strategic planning for diversified corporations is a four-quadrant matrix developed by the Boston Consultant Group (BCG) and shown in Figure 5.7. The BCG matrix is based on two strategic factors: the industry's growth rate and the SBU's relative market share.

> *Stars* are SBUs in fast-growth markets with large market share. In order to support their dominant position, substantial resources are required. Stars, however, are excellent opportunities for future growth and profitability.
>
> *Question marks* are SBUs in high-growth industries, but with a small market share. They have appeal because of their high growth potential. However, in order to maintain their position in a growing industry, or to attempt to increase it, they normally require strong financial outlays.
>
> *Cash Cows* are high market share SBUs, but compete in mature, low-growth industries. Contrary to stars, cash cows typically do not require commitments of great financial resources; thus, their profits can be "milked" and allocated to stars and question marks.
>
> *Dogs* are SBUs with low market share, which compete in industries with little growth. Their industry is mature and saturated and typically has strong competition with low profit margins.

FIGURE 5.7
The growth/share matrix.

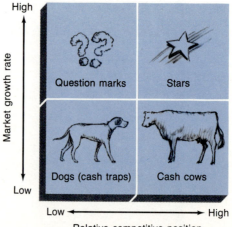

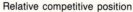

A major advantage of growth/share analysis is the visual representation of the mix of SBUs within a company's portfolio. Also, a number of strategic options have been generalized for effectively managing SBUs in each quadrant, but that is beyond the scope of our presentation here.

SOME STRATEGIC OPTIONS

After a company has identified the internal and external variables and attempted to forecast their impact, it may consider the options available. Basically, several generic options for corporate strategy have been identified.[17] These are as follows.

Concentration

Concentration refers to a firm that operates within a single line of business, such as McDonald's, Polaroid, or Dr. Pepper. Advantages of concentration include relative simplicity of management, clarity of objectives, and a singular organizational focus. Danger, however, can be associated with a firm's putting all its eggs in one basket.

Vertical Integration

Vertical integration is extending a business's scope by taking on an activity or function backward toward sources of supply or forward toward the end user. Integrating backward assures a reliable source of supply, as in a paper manufacturer's decision to own timberlands or a food processing firm's decision to own cattle- or poultry-producing firms. The big advantage of forward integration is a greater control of a business's distribution channel. Examples of forward integration include a book publisher's decision to own bookstores or a clothing manufacturer's decision to establish its own retail clothing outlets. The major disadvantages of vertical integration are the increased complexity of management and the requirement of additional capital.

Diversification

Diversification involves deciding whether to enter a business different from the present one(s). The advantages are the protection afforded by dividing risks or by selecting industries that are countercyclical. *Related* diversification means retaining a common thread throughout the various businesses, such as Weyerhaeuser's pulp, paper, lumber, newsprint, and timber businesses. *Unrelated* diversification means that the various businesses have few similarities. ITT follows a highly unrelated diversified strategy; its business segments consist of hotels (Sheraton), insurance (Hartford), telecommunications, fertilizers, perfume, and many others. Acquisition of existing businesses is a very popular way to achieve diversification. The disadvantage associated with diversification, especially into nonrelated fields, is the additional complexity of management.

Turnaround/ Retrenchment Strategies

Turnaround and **retrenchment strategies** are used to nurse a poorly performing company back to health. Problems causing the poor performance, such as poor management, changing markets, increased competition, or outdated products, must be identified and addressed. Turnaround may focus on replacement of management (frequently done!), attention to cost controls,

In 1984, *Business Week* assessed the outcome of strategies embarked upon by a number of companies featured in its earlier 1979 and 1980 issues. The examples below identify some of the successful and unsuccessful strategies, as determined by *Business Week*.

PLANS THAT DIDN'T WORK . . .

Strategy	BW assessment
American Natural Resources	
Offset sagging natural gas sales by diversifying into trucking, coal mining, oil/gas exploration, and coal gasification.	Ran into trouble because anticipated gas shortages and higher prices failed to materialize.
Ashland Oil	
Sell off energy exploration/production business and diversify into insurance and other nonoil areas.	Largely unsuccessful, partly because of industry problems in refining and insurance.
Campbell Soup	
Diversify away from food.	Abandoned by new CEO who successfully expanded into new food products.
Church's Fried Chicken	
Build modular, efficient fast-food outlets aimed at the lower end of the market.	Failed because upscale chicken restaurants are capturing most of the market growth.
Adolph Coors	
Regain lost market share and become a national force in the beer industry.	Largely unsuccessful because of weak marketing clout.
Exxon	
Diversify into electrical equipment and office automation, offset shrinking U.S. oil reserves by investing in shale oil and synfuels.	Failed because of poor acquisitions, management problems in office automation, and falling oil prices.
Foothill Group	
Diversify from commercial financing into leasing—especially oil-field drilling equipment.	Failed because the equipment market slumped and the company failed to obtain adequate collateral from borrowers.
General Motors	
Gain market share by outspending U.S. competitors in the race to offer more fuel-efficient, downsized cars.	Failed as import market share grew. Modified strategy to pursue diversification.
International Multifoods	
Diversify away from flour milling by developing niche products in consumer foods and expanding restaurant business.	Largely unsuccessful because of management timidity, problems overseas, and the recession.

. . . AND PLANS THAT DID

Strategy	BW assessment
Abbott Laboratories	
Become less vulnerable to cost-containment pressures in traditional hospital products.	Won a leading share of the diagnostic-products market through acquisitions and internal development and built a highly profitable dietary supplements business.
American Motors	
Capitalize on a consumer shift to small cars by building autos designed by Renault to broaden its product line.	New Renault cars perked up AMC, breaking 14 quarters of consecutive losses. Product timing still a threat.
Bausch & Lomb	
Regain dominance in soft contact lenses through intense marketing and aggressive pricing. Become a major force in lens solutions.	Boosted share of daily-wear lens market to 60%.
Bekins	
Return to profitability by selling real estate, building market share in basic moving business, and remedying poor diversification moves.	Increased moving's market share through improved marketing. Divested bad businesses.
Borg-Warner	
Offset the cyclicality of manufacturing-related businesses.	Expanded into financial and protective services through acquisitions and internal development; services now account for a third of earnings.
Dayton Hudson	
Maintain impressive sales and earnings growth by diversifying retail operations.	Jumped to No. 5 in retailing by dramatically expanding Target, Mervyn's promotional apparel, and B. Dalton Booksellers chains.
Gould	
Move from an industrial and electrical manufacturer into an electronics company via divestitures and acquisitions.	Built electronics to 100% of earnings by buying nine high-tech companies and divesting old-line operations

PLANS THAT DIDN'T WORK ...

Strategy	BW assessment

Lone Star Industries

Strategy	BW assessment
Focus entirely on cement-related businesses and sell off other operations.	Ran into trouble because cement shortages and higher prices did not materialize.

Napco Industries

Strategy	BW assessment
Become the dominant distributor of nonfood items to grocery stores.	Ran into trouble through bad acquisitions, logistical and management problems, and the recession.

Oak Industries

Strategy	BW assessment
Diversify into subscription TV and cable TV equipment.	Failed because cable TV competition was underestimated; it also did not keep abreast of TV equipment technology.

Shaklee

Strategy	BW assessment
Streamline product lines and become the leading nutritional products company.	Ran into trouble because of the recession and sales-force turnover.

Standard Oil (Ohio)

Strategy	BW assessment
Use the cash flow from giant Prudhoe Bay oilfield to expand energy base and diversify into nonoil businesses.	Largely unsuccessful so far. Kennecott acquisition is still a big loser, and efforts to find new oil have met with mixed success.

Toro

Strategy	BW assessment
Capitalize on brand recognition and reputation for quality in mowers and snowblowers by expanding into other home-care products.	Failed because of snowless winters and distribution mistakes; new management changed strategies.

Trailways

Strategy	BW assessment
Survive in the bus business by striking alliances with independent carriers and persuading regulators to hold Greyhound to 67% of intercity bus traffic.	Failed because of deregulation and Greyhound's market-share war.

Union Carbide

Strategy	BW assessment
Reduce dependence on commodity chemicals and plastics and build up six faster-growing, higher-margin lines.	Deep economic slump hit all chemical markets and delayed sale of undesired businesses.

U.S. Home

Strategy	BW assessment
Use economies of scale in land development and financial clout to take a commanding position in homebuilding.	Ran into trouble when interest rates rose and its home sales sank.

... AND PLANS THAT DID

Strategy	BW assessment

Hershey Foods

Strategy	BW assessment
Diversify into noncandy foods, nonchocolate candy, and food services.	Reduced dependence on chocolate via new candies and snack foods. Expanded pasta and restaurant divisions.

National Intergroup

Strategy	BW assessment
Improve efficiency of and reduce dependence on steel operations.	Became an efficient steelmaker by modernizing. Diversified into financial services, sold a steel plant to workers, and sold a 50% share of steel operations to Nippon Kokan.

New England Electric System

Strategy	BW assessment
Reduce dependence on oil by switching to coal, developing other fuel sources, and promoting conservation.	Switch to coal saved over $200 million, cut oil consumption 58%.

Ralston Purina

Strategy	BW assessment
Refocus on basic grocery-products and feed business.	Shed mushroom and European pet food divisions, revitalized core business through product development and improved marketing.

Southern California Edison

Strategy	BW assessment
Reduce dependence on oil and gas.	Developed alternate energy sources and is well on the way to generating 2,200 megawatts from new sources by 1992.

Triangle Pacific

Strategy	BW assessment
Become less vulnerable to swings in housing market.	Sold off wholesale lumber business and expanded kitchen cabinet fabrication operations.

Uniroyal

Strategy	BW assessment
Revive ailing tire business and abandon lackluster businesses.	Shut two U.S. tire plants, shed many foreign and U.S. operations, and is expanding in specialty chemicals.

* Companies were selected from those whose strategies were described by *Business Week* in 1979 and 1980 and reassessed since by *Business Week*.
SOURCE: Reprinted from "The New Breed of Strategic Planner" in the September 17, 1984, issue of *Business Week*, by special permission. Copyright 1984 by McGraw-Hill, Inc.

disposing of unprofitable segments, or shifting resources from some segments to others. Chrysler Corporation, under Lee Iacocca's leadership, is one of the most visible examples of a successful retrenchment/turnaround strategy.

Divestment/ Liquidation Strategies

Divestment, or **liquidation, strategies** are taken in those instances where an organization's business is felt to have lost its appeal. In each case, it means a decision to sever the particular business entity. Divestment involves selling off the business, or a component of it. What is one company's albatross, because of mismanagement, poor strategic position, or changing market, may become another's silver lining. Liquidation involves terminating its existence by either shutting it down or disposing of the assets.

Combination of Strategies

A *combination of strategies* involves using several of the strategies mentioned above, as is frequently the case with large firms. Within a year, for instance, a large, diversified firm may make several acquisitions which diversify, or vertically integrate, other SBUs in the portfolio; it may also sell off, or prune, other SBUs and may choose to liquidate another.

MAP 5.2 (pages 142–143) provides some examples of successful and unsuccessful business strategies that have been tried by some well-known companies. Note that a number of the examples refer directly to some of the strategies referred to in this section.

A final word on strategy is in order. This chapter has provided a broad overview by focusing on some of the key elements in strategic planning. Once overall strategic plans are determined, other segments must in turn generate their own planning so as to adequately reflect those higher-level strategic plans. Planning will occur within various functional departments such as operations, marketing, finance, personnel, research and development, and others. Furthermore, once plans are implemented, they must be monitored and evaluated and, where necessary, corrective actions must be taken.

The strategic planning process is an ongoing one, for in today's organizational climate, the winds of change shift rapidly. Every organization must constantly monitor its environment and be alert to the threats and opportunities that it faces.

SUMMARY

Strategic planning consists of activities leading to the definition of the organization's mission, the setting of objectives, and the development of strategies that enable it to function successfully in its environment.

The organizational mission identifies the function the organization intends to perform within society. The statement of mission typically identifies the organization's products or services, markets, and customers. Thus, a clear mission enables the organization to establish its overall objectives.

Objectives are essential to organizations, because they establish the end results sought. Profit is only one of several objectives that businesses should try to achieve. They also need objectives in the key areas of market standing, productivity, physical and financial resources, innovation, manager performance and development, worker performance and attitudes, and public and social responsibility. Three important advantages of objectives are that they (1) permit unified planning throughout the organization, (2) serve as a motivator and provide a sense of achievement, and (3) serve as a basis for managerial control.

A number of important internal and external variables affect an organization's strategy. Planning premises, or assumptions about future conditions affecting the firm's environment, must be made. Analysis must also be made of the firm's strengths, weaknesses, opportunities and threats. The growth/share matrix indicating the relative market share and growth of the industry within each strategic business unit (SBU) is helpful in assessing the various businesses in a diversified firm's various lines.

Six broad strategic options available to businesses are concentration, vertical integration, diversification, turnaround/retrenchment, divestment/liquidation, and some combination of the above.

REVIEW QUESTIONS

1. What is an organizational mission?
2. What are objectives?
3. How do objectives, goals, and organizational mission differ?
4. What are the three reasons objectives are important as a management tool?
5. What is meant by the concept of "balancing objectives"?
6. What is a hierarchy of objectives?
7. What is meant by SWOT analysis?
8. What is a SBU?
9. Identify the major types of corporate strategy.

DISCUSSION QUESTIONS

1. Evaluate the following statement by the president of a medium-sized furniture company with 300 employees: "My great-grandfather, my grandfather, and my father have operated this company in our family for over 100 years. In all that time, we've made nothing but Early American furniture, and we've done very well. The mission we have remains what it has been through the years, and we never really even think about changing it." Is the president's view a healthy one? Discuss.
2. Business organizations have become aware of "social responsibility" objectives in the past 25 years. Do you think that this objective will become more or less important in the United States in the next 25 years? Explain.
3. Do you think that a small business or a large one is more likely to survive and prosper with a "profit at all costs" objective? Discuss.
4. Do you think the strategic planning process is more important for organizations today than 20 years ago? Discuss.
5. What are the pros and cons of a highly diversified strategy such as that followed by ITT? How can a company effectively manage so many diverse business segments including hotels, bakery products, frozen foods, publishing, lawn care, soft drinks, communications equipment, and others?

LEARNING EXERCISE 5.1

Pizza Hut's New Sales Strategy: Faster Service, Expanded Menus*

Pizza Hut was a bigger headache than Donald Smith, the 40-year-old crackerjack PepsiCo hired in May 1980 to fix its ailing restaurant chain, had imagined. Smith was

* Condensed from Gay Sand Miller, "Pizza Hut's New Sales Strategy: Faster Service, Expanded Menus," *Wall Street Journal*, November 20, 1980, p. 29.

lured from Pillsbury's Burger King by pay rumored to be $350,000 a year, an increase of at least one-third, and what he described as his fondness for "doing something with unfulfilled potential."

Attention to detail helped Smith rejuvenate Burger King during his 3½ years as president, and before that to climb to one of the highest posts at McDonald's, where he'd started as a management trainee 11½ years earlier.

After six months of nibbling pizzas and poking around 300 of Pizza Hut's 4000 outlets, Smith was ready to start his toughest—and most sweeping—turnaround campaign at the nation's sixth-largest fast-food operation and its largest pizza chain. He planned to test more than 100 changes, including new menu and decor ideas, before starting a 2½-year, $100 million overhaul.

When PepsiCo bought Pizza Hut in 1978 for more than $300 million, the restaurant chain, then 18 years old, was thriving. But then unit sales stagnated as customers fled from the restaurant's inconsistent quality and relatively high prices. Operating profits of the 2009 company-owned Pizza Huts (the rest are franchised) fell to $43.7 million in 1978 and $26.4 million in 1979 from the 1977 peak of $56.6 million, according to an estimate. Per-store sales of $250,000 were well below the fast-food industry average of $434,823.

By 1980, the decline had been arrested, largely because of a deep-dish pizza introduced by Frank Carney, the Pizza Hut founder. But competition was increasing from smaller chains that were invading the company's Midwest stronghold and from independent mom-and-pop pizzerias that still claimed more than half the market.

To fulfill Pizza Hut's potential, Smith wanted to create two restaurants in one: a speedier lunch plate and an expanded-menu and quality dinner house. He would test the ideas at Pizza Hut in Gainesville, Florida, and Binghamton, New York. The units in which sales flourished most would give Smith clues about how to combine new lunch and dinner formats in about six restaurants in Spokane, Washington, the final test site, before installing them nationally in 1981.

A major feature of the plan was a breakthrough: acceleration of pizza cooking time—to about 5 minutes from 12 to 18—that Smith hoped would transform lunch into truly fast food. To further speed the midday flow of customers, Smith would experiment with cafeteria-style, instead of sit-down, ordering. Supper menu additions to be tested included sundae bars and pasta.

Smith's objectives were (1) to add $100,000 to the average Pizza Hut's annual sales, (2) to increase the chain's less-than-5 percent return on assets to more than 10 percent by 1983, and (3) to add roughly $80 million to PepsiCo's pretax profits that could restore some of the prestige Pizza Hut had cost its parents on Wall Street.

Questions

1. Which of the six corporate strategies discussed in the chapter can you identify in this case?

2. Why would a large soft drink manufacturer acquire a firm such as Pizza Hut?

3. Examine PepsiCo's three fundamental objectives, as stated in the text. Which of these three is the Pizza Hut division satisfying?

4. What is your evaluation of the strategic actions taken by Smith? Explain.

NOTES

1. John Pearce II and R. B. Robinson, *Strategic Management*, 2nd ed. (Homewood, IL: Richard D. Irwin, 1985), p. 7.
2. Peter Drucker, *An Introductory View of Management* (New York: Harper's College Press, 1977), p. 150.
3. Robert Townsend, *Further Up the Organization* (New York: Alfred A. Knopf, 1984), p. 155.
4. "How W. T. Grant Lost $175 Million Last Year," *Business Week* February 25, 1975, p. 75.

5. See J. E. Blankenship, "Goal Setting in the Diversified Company," *Managerial Planning* 25 (November–December 1977): 14–18.

6. Frances Bridges, Kenneth Olm, and J. Alison Barnhill, *Management Decisions and Organizational Policy* (Boston: Allyn & Bacon, 1971), p. 54.

7. PepsiCo, Inc., *Annual Report*, 1977, p. 1.

8. Norton Company, *Annual Report*, 1975, pp. 6–12.

9. Hewlett-Packard Company, *Annual Report*, 1979, pp. 6–24.

10. "ServiceMaster: The Protestant Ethic Helps Clean Hospitals Better," *Business Week*, February 19, 1979, p. 58; and Rod Willis, "ServiceMaster: The Details Make the Whole Thing Work," *Management Review*, October 1987, p. 26.

11. See Robert N. Anthony, "The Trouble with Profit Maximization," *Harvard Business Review* 38 (November–December 1960): 126–135, for a good perspective on the role of profits.

12. "Life at the Top—What It Takes to Run a Big Business," *U.S. News & World Report*, June 15, 1981, p. 39. Emphasis added.

13. "Reader's Digest: Modernizing the Beat of a Different Drummer," *Business Week*, March 15, 1979, p. 98.

14. See Peter F. Drucker, *The Practice of Management* (New York: Harper & Row, 1954), p. 62, for further details.

15. AT&T, *Annual Report*, 1980, p. 7.

16. Robert F. Hartley, *Management Mistakes*, 2nd ed. (New York: John Wiley & Sons, 1986), pp. 44–55.

17. Based on Arthur A. Thompson, Jr., and A. J. Strickland, *Strategic Management*, 3rd ed. (Plano, TX: Business Publications, Inc., 1984), pp. 79–96.

SUGGESTIONS FOR FURTHER STUDY

CARROL, PETER J. "The Link Between Performance and Strategy." *Journal of Business Strategy* 2 (Spring 1982): 3–20.

DAVID, FRED R.; COCHRAN, DAN; and GIBSON, K. "A Framework for Developing an Effective Mission Statement." *Journal of Business Strategies* (Spring 1986): 4–17.

DRUCKER, PETER A. "The Meaning of Corporate Social Responsibility." *California Management Review* 26 (Winter 1984): 53–63.

HUNTER, J. C. "Managers Must Know the Mission: If It Ain't Broke, Don't Fix It." *Managerial Planning* 33 (January–February 1985): 18–22.

LARSON, ERIK. "The Best-Laid Plans." *Inc.*, February 1987, pp. 60–64.

LEONTIADES, MILTON. "A Diagnostic Framework for Planning." *Strategic Management Journal* 4 (January–March 1983): 11–26.

PEARCE, JOHN A., II. "The Company Mission as a Strategic Tool." *Sloan Management Review* (Spring 1982): 15–25.

ROBINSON, R. B., JR., and PEARCE, JOHN A., II. "Research Thrusts in Small Firm Strategic Planning." *Academy of Management Review* 9 (January 1984): 45–52.

STEINER, GEORGE A. *Strategic Planning.* New York: Free Press, 1984.

THOMPSON, ARTHUR A., JR., and STRICKLAND, A. J., III. *Strategy Management.* 3rd ed. Plano, TX: Business Publications, 1984.

6

Decision Making

Learning Objectives

After studying the material in this chapter, you should be able to do the following:

□ Define what decision making is.
□ Distinguish between programmed and unprogrammed decisions.
□ Identify the five steps of the decision-making process.
□ Explain what variables help determine the extent to which a manager should involve subordinates in the decision-making process.
□ Explain some different types of problem solving.

Some Important Terms

decision making
programmed decisions
unprogrammed decisions
decision tree
satisficing
bounded rationality
maximizing
optimizing
creativity
Delphi technique
nominal grouping technique (NGT)
brainstorming
Myers-Briggs Type Indicator
sensing
intuition
thinking
feeling
Jungian Framework

Outline of the Chapter

What is decision making?
Individual decision making
Managerial decision making
All employees must make decisions
Programmed and unprogrammed decisions
Steps in decision making
Step 1: Understand and define the problem
Step 2: Generate alternatives
Step 3: Evaluate alternatives
Step 4: Make the decision and implement it
Step 5: Evaluate the decision results
Involvement of subordinates in decision making
Group decision making
When to use subordinates
Problem-solving types
The Myers-Briggs Type Indicator
The Jungian Framework
Summary

OPENING CASE

The Frustrating Engineer[1]

When a California electronics firm was expanding its technical force, it screened applications from dozens of graduating engineers until it had selected the ten best prospects for personal interviews. Bill Brown was one of these hopefuls; he had an outstanding record at State Tech, including some of the highest academic honors in his class.

The vacancy required a topnotch technical person, and Bill's record placed him among the most promising prospects. He had an exceptionally high mental ability score and had chosen a rigorous college curriculum, indicating that he had outstanding ability as well as an interest in the field. In addition to his studies corresponding with the job requirements, Bill appeared to be an enthusiastic person and eager for the job.

He was interviewed by a department manager who was 42 years old, with one B.S. degree in electrical engineering and another in mathematics. The manager, Frank Ernest, gave Bill a short, written quiz and discovered not only that Bill's handwriting was illegible but also that he could hardly spell. Yet, during the discussion, Bill answered difficult questions easily and confidently.

The interview revealed that Bill was 23 years old and the only child from a socially prominent family. Although his father was a professional man, his mother had tended to dominate the family during Bill's childhood and youth. Now Bill was married to a girl he had met while attending college.

Bill was hired and assigned to a section of the plant as an "engineer in training." He learned quickly, asking questions of everyone and seeking to understand why things were done as they were. However, when he didn't receive adequate answers to complicated technical problems, he responded with caustic criticisms, often in group discussions, and caused antagonism.

Bill liked responsibility, but he felt he was not being given enough scope in his work to accomplish what he wished. Frank, however, was doubtful about releasing too much authority to him because of his inexperience and his radical approach to many problems. As the months passed, the young man revealed gross immaturity in his dealing with others. Bill's unpredictable outbursts entertained colleagues who did not have to work with him but presented a real problem to his superiors and peers. It also seemed that Bill was suffering from a certain inability to communicate: He could sell his ideas orally, but he could not convey ideas in written reports.

During his training period, Bill had considerable counseling from Frank and other managers. They tried to help him recognize the extent to which his actions were negatively affecting his work and the work of his fellow employees. He was assigned to other special, highly technical projects so that he could best apply his remarkable skills. In these activities, however, he would remain apart from most of the other engineering personnel. Eventually, he would become dissatisfied with the limits of the assignment and would have to be changed to another one.

Bill, it appeared, would never develop to his fullest potential; he would never become the well-rounded supervisor that the firm needed.

Bill posed a difficult personnel problem: his technical skills were superior, but in the area of employee relations, Bill would lose out to others who had greater managerial abilities.

What would you do about Bill if you were his boss?

SEVERAL ASPECTS OF DECISION MAKING are illustrated by this case, such as what decision making is, steps in decision making, and involving subordinates in decision making.

Keep in mind that effective decision-making skills are a very important factor in advancing to higher levels of management. In a study by Norma Carr-Ruffino, 110 women managers identified problem-solving and decision-making skills as the second most important factor in reaching their present positions.[2] This and other findings are shown in Table 6.1.

WHAT IS DECISION MAKING?

Decision making is required of everyone, individuals as well as managers. Let us first see how individuals make decisions and then discuss managerial decision making in greater detail. Then we'll concentrate on the more difficult, nonroutine decisions that managers must make. It should be emphasized that decision making applies to taking advantage of opportunities as well as to solving problems.

Individual Decision Making

Each of us makes many decisions every day. We have to decide whether and when to get up, what clothes to wear, what to eat, where to go, and how to get there; and we face countless job or school decisions every day. Most of these decisions fall into the "routine" category. That is, they do not involve a great deal of analytical effort to arrive at a final course of action. Occasionally, though, a choice comes along that has much greater stakes.

Sharon Jeffers was in a quandary as she left the office of Dr. Figures, the head of the university's accounting department. As a graduating senior, she was undecided about what type of accounting position to accept. An excellent student, she had received two offers from accounting firms, one from a bank, and another from a large utility. She had assured all of these that she would let them know her decision in another week. Now she

TABLE 6.1 Strategies or Techniques Cited by 110 Women Managers as Helpful in Getting to the Top

SOURCE: *USA Today,* August 17, 1987, p. 2D. Copyright USA Today, 1987. Used with permission.

Strategy or technique	Percent choosing
Communication skills	89
Problem-solving/decision-making skills	**85**
Understand the organization and its people	81
Personal power (poise, serenity, command of inner resources)	78
Cooperating as a team member	75
Knowing how to motivate people to perform	71
Savvy in organizational politics	63
Delegation/supervisory skills	63
Mentor	54
Charisma, charm, social skills	53
Technical skills (computer, financial, etc.)	44
Support network	37

Note: Respondents could choose more than one.

had just received a fifth alternative—an assistantship in the accounting department at the university to pursue work on her master's degree. She had said she'd let Dr. Figures know within a week.

The decision that Sharon makes will have a significant long-range impact on her life and require greater energy than the routine decisions that she ordinarily makes.

Managerial Decision Making

Decision making can be defined as the conscious selection of a course of action from among available alternatives to produce a desired result, as shown in Figure 6.1. As such, it is a way of life for managers, and the quality of the decisions made is a predominant factor in determining how upper management views a lower manager's performance. Books, movies, television series, and news documentaries dramatize decisions made by top managers. Whether it is the decision of President Ronald Reagan to help free the hostages in Lebanon by selling military spare parts to Iran or of Lee Iacocca to have Chrysler buy American Motors, decisions receive much attention in the media and play a key part in our lives.

But top managers are not alone in making decisions that are often very important. Middle and lower managers also face such decisions, as the following example shows.

Gilbert, an environmental manager, had just ordered a shutdown and evacuation of his firm's nuclear research department. The shutdown involved the movement of over 110 persons and required at least 12 hours of corrective steps and tests before the area could be reopened. The cost of this decision was a minimum of $300,000, plus the load of paperwork, interviews, unfavorable publicity, and investigation by various federal and state officials. And there was a 30 percent chance that Gilbert's decision was an incorrect one. Still, on the basis of instrument readings and other evidence, Gilbert believed that everyone's safety was jeopardized by possible contamination in a radioactive area, and he could take no chances.

All Employees Must Make Decisions

Managers are not the only ones who make critical decisions in organizations. Surgeons, for instance, make life-and-death decisions daily. So do air traffic controllers and aircraft inspectors. Computer maintenance technicians often

FIGURE 6.1
Decision making.

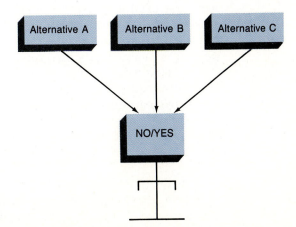

make million-dollar decisions. Secretaries decide who and what gets to their supervisors, and accountants decide what value to place on certain assets. We can say that every person's job in an organization—even the most routine one—involves some degree of decision making.

J. Georg Bednorz and K. Alex Mueller, researchers at IBM's Swiss laboratory, began working on an idea so big that they were loath to share the details with IBM officials. When they mentioned to an IBM official their research to find a cheap, simple substance to conduct electricity with little, if any, resistance, they got a skeptical reaction. So they hunted quietly, telling a supervisor a half-truth and steering a curious visitor off the track. But their breakthrough with superconductors in January 1986, stunned the scientific world. It also earned them the 1986 Nobel Prize in Physics.[3]

What is your view?

Figure 6.2 shows the "10 most boring jobs" and the "boredom factor" in 23 typical jobs. Even though the boring jobs are routine, can you think of decisions that people performing them must make?

Programmed and Unprogrammed Decisions

One broad method of classifying decisions is to examine whether a decision is programmed or not. **Programmed decisions** are those that are routine and repetitive. The manager (or organization), to facilitate decision making, has devised an established, systematic way to handle the decision situation. Examples of programmed decisions include the following:

1. A grocery store manager's decision about how many items to reorder when the stock level reaches a given count.
2. A university's decision about how to process a student's request to drop or add a course.
3. A hospital's process for admitting new patients.
4. A maintenance department's decision about the frequency of maintenance servicing of machinery and equipment.
5. A manager's disciplinary action when a worker reports to work in an intoxicated condition.

These examples are handled in a systematic way, and a decision framework (for example, a set of policies) has been established for the decision maker to follow. Perhaps the handling of an intoxicated employee appears to you to be different from the other four examples. But if the company policy manual prescribes a given penalty for intoxication, the decision about the penalty the supervisor should impose tends to be a programmed or predetermined one.

Unprogrammed decisions are those that occur infrequently and, because of differing variables, require a separate response each time. Examples of unprogrammed decisions might include the following:

1. Whether to buy a new car and which make of car to buy.
2. Which job offer to select from the many received.
3. Where to locate a new company warehouse.

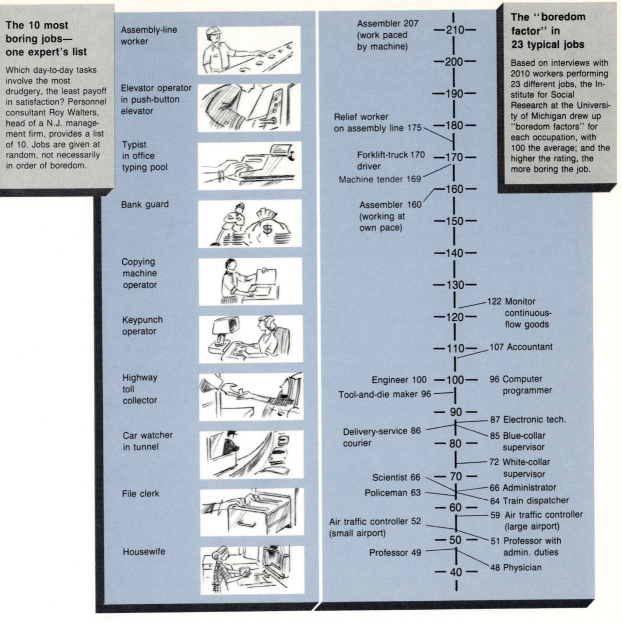

FIGURE 6.2
Jobs and boredom.

SOURCE: Reprinted from "Those 'Boring' Jobs—Not All That Dull," *U.S. News & World Report*, December 1, 1975, pp. 64–65. Copyright 1975 U.S. News & World Report, Inc.

4. Whom to promote to the vacant position of plant manager at one of the company's plants.

5. How a supervisor should schedule workers' vacations, given their requests, so that the department can operate at 90 percent of capacity each week during the summer.

What is your view?

Review the chapter's opening case. Is the decision of what to do with Bill Brown a programmed or an unprogrammed decision? Why?

STEPS IN DECISION MAKING

The decision-making process that you will study in this chapter consists of the following steps, as shown in Figure 6.3.

1. Understand and define the problem.
2. Generate alternatives.
3. Evaluate alternatives.
4. Make the decision and implement it.
5. Evaluate the decision results.

Step 1: Understand and Define the Problem

If you're like most people, when you are first faced with a decision, you tend to wade right into it without thinking much about it. Suppose, for instance, that your car's "high temperature" light comes on while you are driving. You pull off to the side of the road to find your car's radiator steaming. In what ways do you think of the problem? Do you think of it as, "My car needs water"? If you do, and make a decision to find water, refill your radiator, and go on your way, you may be in trouble. You may (1) have wasted your time filling the car because it will overheat again shortly, or (2) face a more costly problem later. The odds are that you will have only treated a *symptom* of the problem in refilling the car with coolant. The possible *causes* of the problem that need to be treated may include such things as a broken thermostat, a leak in the radiator or a hose, or possibly that you are pulling too heavy a load.

Mistaking symptoms for causes. A frequent mistake is to observe a problem's symptoms and treat them as underlying causes. Let us look at a business example. Assume that you own a small business and your profits have been down sharply for the last several months. You would be very naive to make assumptions about the causes without some investigation of the problem (unless there is some strong evidence that an obvious factor has caused it—for instance, a natural disaster or a competitor who has located next door to your store). Possible causes might include the following:

1. Changes in the competitive situation (such as new competitors, disruptive competitor price policies, competitor product advantages).
2. Higher costs (increased rent, utilities, payroll, overtime).
3. Employee inefficiency (poor motivation, poor sales technique, pilferage).

FIGURE 6.3
The decision-making process.

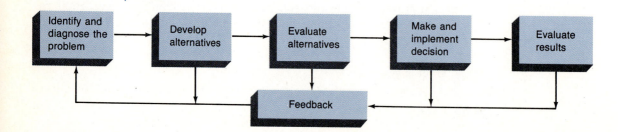

4. Changes in traffic patterns (new thoroughfares, interstate highway, closed roads).

5. Seasonal shifts (many businesses, such as gift shops, ice cream parlors, and photography stores routinely experience drops in sales—and profits—at certain times of the year).

6. Store policy (no credit, no returns on merchandise).

In addition to the foregoing, there may be other possible causes that you could think of. Effective decision makers are keenly aware of the importance of properly identifying the problem and understanding the problem situation, as shown in the following example.

The Kepner-Tregoe method of problem analysis teaches that the first step in decision making, recognizing the problem, is the most important step. Getting a good definition of the real problem is critical for making an intelligent, valid decision about a solution. This method teaches that it is often easier to define what the problem is not, rather than what it is. Also, the problem—and its solution—is prioritized with other problems, to clarify its relative importance. The final step is searching for cause-effect relationships. In summary, their method includes:

> 1. *Problem recognition.*
> 2. *Definition of what the problem is and is not.*
> 3. *Prioritizing the problem.*
> 4. *Testing for cause-effect relationships.*
> 5. *Making the decision.*[4]

This method has been taught to managers in some of the largest organizations in the world for the last quarter century. One aspect of this difficulty in defining and understanding the problem is poor framing of the problem and/or alternatives. Decision makers often allow a problem to be "framed" by the language or context in which it is presented instead of exploring it from every angle.[5] For example, at the Center for Decision Making at the University of Chicago, students were split into two groups to make a decision. One group was told that a business decision had an 80 percent chance of success; the other group was told that the decision had a 20 percent chance of failure. The first group gave the decision a green light, while the second group turned it down, even though both groups had actually been given the same information. The key variable was the form in which the data had been presented.

How managers identify problems. Managers gain insight into problem identification in several ways.[6] For one, they systematically examine cause-effect relationships. They also look for major variances or changes from what is considered normal. And, perhaps most important, they consult others who are capable of giving them different perspectives and insights into a problem or opportunity. In many respects, American managers are far behind their Japanese counterparts in handling this first step of decision making. Drucker explains it this way:

The Westerner and the Japanese mean something different when they talk of making a decision. In the West all the emphasis is on the answer to the question. To the Japanese, however, the most important element in decision making is defining the question. The important and crucial steps are to decide whether there is a need for a decision and what the decision is about.... It is in this step that the Japanese aim at attaining consensus. Indeed, it is this step that, to the Japanese, is the essence of decision making.

The Japanese process is focused on understanding the problem. The desired end result is action and behavior on the part of people.... Japanese managers may come up with the wrong answer to the problem, but they rarely come up with the right answer to the wrong problem.[7]

Step 2: Generate Alternatives

Once you have a clear definition and understanding of the problem, you are prepared to generate alternatives. Remember from the definition that if there is no choice of alternatives there really is no decision to be made. The use of staff groups and the counsel of others may lead to the development of certain alternatives that the manager might not have been able to identify alone. In the **decision tree** shown in Figure 6.4, alternative five (A_5) represents such an "unknown" alternative.

Should a manager identify *all* feasible alternatives? Perhaps this sounds

FIGURE 6.4
Role of alternatives in the decision process.

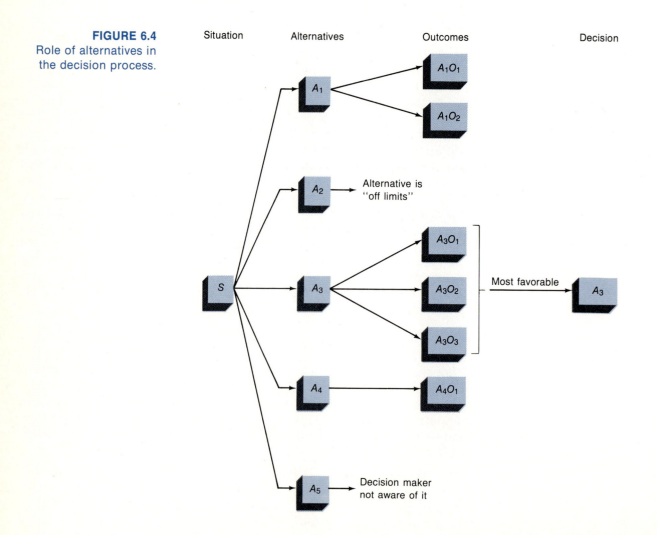

good in theory, but in practice it is frequently difficult to achieve. This is true for several reasons. For example, consider the following points.

Knowledge of alternatives is limited. Managers do not usually have complete information at their disposal when making decisions. Yet some books and courses in decision making still advise the decision maker to get "all the facts" before considering alternatives in making a decision. Consider the following example of the selection of a controller for a large organization.

> *The person in charge of selecting a new controller indicated that the objective was to obtain "the most highly qualified person in the country," since some of the decisions to be made would be "of critical importance to the future of the company."*
>
> *An intensive search for candidates within the company was undertaken. In addition, an executive search consultant was engaged to find suitable candidates from outside the firm. All possible candidates from these sources were evaluated, but the total number of persons seriously considered was limited to 12. Eventually, a person from within the company was selected for the position.[8]*

How close was the organization able to come to an "optimum solution" to the problem? Was the person making the decision able to obtain all the facts? Although the individual selected may have been a satisfactory choice for the position, "the most highly qualified person in the country" probably wasn't even contacted. Instead, the search for candidates probably uncovered a group of "satisfactory" or at least "minimally qualified" individuals.

A better person than the one selected might have been found through more search activity, but the extra cost might have exceeded the benefits obtained. In general, managers can rarely make decisions based on *complete* information and *perfect* foresight. Herbert Simon, a noted management scholar, calls this concept **satisficing,** meaning that the decision maker selects an alternative that is reasonably good, although not necessarily the perfect or ideal one.[9] According to his concept of **bounded rationality,** Simon considered the range of satisfaction in relationships to be **maximizing** (most or greatest), **optimizing** (best), and **satisficing** (satisfactory).

Reasons alternatives are restricted. The following are some factors that might restrict the search for alternatives.

1. Some alternatives may be ruled out because they are too costly even to be considered.
2. The organization's physical facilities may eliminate certain alternatives from consideration.
3. The time constraints for making the decision may not allow a thorough search for alternatives.
4. Higher management may already have indicated to the decision maker that certain alternatives are "off limits" (A_2 in Figure 6.4).

You need to keep in mind that *the search for alternatives is greatly influenced by the way you go about defining or thinking about the problem.* Suppose, for example, that a retailer's sales are down and the cause of the problem is found to be poorly motivated sales personnel. The available alternatives will focus on ways to motivate the present sales force—incentives, pep talks, trips to Hawaii, and the like. But let's take it one step further. Suppose the problem solver raises the fundamental question, "What function do my salespeople perform; why do I need them in the first place?" Now the retailer is able to get to the core of the problem. Some other available alternatives to be considered are (1) reaching customers not only through sales personnel but also through other methods, such as direct mail catalogs, and (2) the possibility of eliminating salespeople altogether and using only direct mail catalogs.

Role of creativity in generating alternatives. Nearly all managerial decision making requires a measure of **creativity,** which uses knowledge, evaluation, innovation, imagination, and inspiration to convert something into something else. The greater our knowledge, the more ideas we have; the wider our experience, the more imagination we have; and the freer our mind is to explore new ideas, the greater is our creativity. Then the new idea must be evaluated and developed into a useful idea.

Step 3: Evaluate Alternatives

Assuming that alternatives have been derived, the next step is for you to evaluate them. A given alternative can have more than a single outcome (as shown earlier in Figure 6.4). It is important to understand not only the benefits of each alternative and how such benefits may influence the decision objective but also the potential negative side and costs of each alternative.

> *Alfred Sloan, as head of GM, supposedly would defer any major decision that his staff unanimously agreed on. It is reported that on one critical decision, after hearing only favorable discussion of one alternative, he said, "Gentlemen, I take it we are all in complete agreement on the decision here?" They all nodded. "Then," he continued, "I propose that we postpone further discussion of this matter until our next meeting to give ourselves more time to develop some disagreement and perhaps gain some understanding of what the decision is all about." At the next meeting, the proposal was voted down.*[10]

In a survey of 469 senior managers in the United States and Europe, one researcher found the following:

1. Managerial decision making at the senior executive level tends to be dominated by individual preferences when the decision maker has a strong personal preference. One executive, for example, decided to locate corporate headquarters near his home rather than another location, where an extensive staff survey indicated it should have been located.

2. Managers generally tend to make decisions themselves and then try to convince others that they are correct instead of using a "participative" approach. The process of reaching decisions involves communication with subordinates but is more often in the form of "influence" by the top manager rather than subordinate "participation" in the decision process.

One approach to evaluating alternatives is for one or more alternatives to be assigned to an individual, who then identifies their pros and cons and presents these to the decision maker. In this way, one person, or perhaps a team, will be responsible for fully exploring the decision potential of a given alternative.

As will be shown in Chapter 16, there are many types of management science tools, such as linear programming, queuing theory, network modeling, and regression analysis, that may be used to evaluate alternatives. But, as will be shown later in this chapter, intuition can also be effective.

Step 4: Make the Decision and Implement It

This fourth decision-making step causes problems for many managers. After getting the facts, the managers may still not be able to decide, for the analysis and interpretation of the facts may make it more difficult to make a clear-cut decision.

Some managers won't make a decision, even with all the facts. This may cause others to feel unsure and insecure about a decision maker's ability to make the right decision.

Many managers straddle the fence on an important decision, leaning one day in one direction, another day in the opposite. This creates uncertainty in the minds of others and may cause greater resistance to the decision than if it were made quickly and decisively. Sometimes decisions are announced in a halfhearted, almost apologetic manner.

"I wish he'd make up his mind," said Dennis Unser, "so that we could let our people know something. There're all kinds of uncertainties, and it seems like he's waffling on this one."

The process of making a decision.

Management Application and Practice 6.1   "I Have That 'Gut Feeling'!"

They hire consultants, badger assistants, and study management books. But when it comes right down to it, 43 percent of American executives say it's those old "gut feelings" they rely on most when making tough decisions. So reports the Pinnacle Group, a consortium of public relations firms that polled 349 executives.

"You always suspect that many decisions are made based on gut feelings, but I didn't think many executives would actually admit it," said Darryl Lloyd of Darryl Lloyd Inc., a North Hollywood, California,

public relations firm and Pinnacle member. Of those who don't rely on gut feelings, 37.2 percent indicated that they prefer to base decisions on staff recommendations; 30.9 percent turn to numbers or statistics; and 7.4 percent say they prefer to use consultants' opinions. Pinnacle surveyed executive vice presidents and above for the survey.

SOURCE: Mark Memmott, "It Takes Guts for Executives to Make the Tough Decisions," *USA Today*, July 21, 1987, p. 7B.

What Unser was referring to was the proposed merger of Drexel Company, his own firm, with another firm noted for its progressiveness in the field. Harold Barnes, president of Drexel, had indicated at a press conference for financial reporters three weeks earlier that the merger appeared to be on, with only details needing to be worked out. Later he told a meeting of 150 Drexel managers that the merger was being studied but definitely had strong possibilities. Yesterday a newspaper quote attributed to him said that "merger at this point may not be in Drexel's best interests."

"So nobody really knows where we stand," Unser stated. "I just wish he'd hurry up and get it over with, one way or another."

How *do* American managers actually make decisions? According to a recent study, a large percentage use their "gut feeling," as shown in MAP 6.1.

Effective decision making doesn't stop when the decision is made. It also entails good follow-through and implementation by the parties involved. In fact, many good decisions may be ruined by ineffective implementation, but the decision maker is most often held responsible.

One college football team had just lost an important game to a cross-state rival. With 20 seconds left and losing by three points, the team went for a win instead of a tying field goal with the ball on the opponent's 4-yard line. In the postgame interview, the coach said, "Given the circumstances, I'd do exactly the same thing again. We've run that play over and over. It's been our bread and butter all season long. It was my decision to go for it. How could I know that our quarterback would mishandle the center snap and we'd lose the game? No, I didn't make the wrong decision. I made the right decision, but we muffed the execution."

Step 5: Evaluate the Decision Results

After making and implementing the decision, you still have not finished your job. Now you must perform the "control" function of management. That is, you must evaluate whether the implementation is proceeding smoothly and the decision is attaining the desired results. If the decision turns out to have been a poor one, you aren't bound by any rule to stick with it. You have perhaps heard the expression, "Don't throw good money after bad." In many cases, it is less costly for a manager to admit having made a poor decision and to reverse it than to try to save face by riding out a decision that doesn't accomplish its objective. This assumes, of course, that the decision is not irreversible. If it is irreversible, then you will have to stick it out and try to make it succeed.

The five decision-making steps presented here represent the most common type of decision model. You should also find the "Rules for Ulcerless Decision Makers" (Figure 6.5) an extremely helpful decision-making guide.

What is your view?

Think of an important decision you have recently made, such as buying a car, beginning or ending a romance, selecting an elective course, or choosing a career or job. To what extent did you consciously follow the five decision-making steps in making your decision?

As you may have discovered in answering the previous question, there are situations that arise every day that do not lend themselves to this decision model. In a crisis, the decision must be made quickly, and this approach may be too time-consuming or the decision may involve variables that do not lend themselves to a rational approach.

INVOLVEMENT OF SUBORDINATES IN DECISION MAKING

It is difficult for managers to make decisions without bringing in subordinates in one way or another. This involvement may be formal, such as the use of group decision making shown in Table 6.2, or informal, such as asking for ideas. The assistance may occur at any of the decision steps. Also, as will be shown in Chapter 18, it involves the effective use of committees.

Group Decision Making

Some managers feel strongly that decisions made by groups such as committees are more effective because they use the knowledge of others. Other managers completely avoid group involvement, feeling that it is slow and cumbersome and often leads to watered-down decisions that attempt to accommodate all points of view.

Why use? There are many reasons for and against involving others in decision making. Table 6.3 shows some of the advantages and disadvantages of group decision making. The characteristics of decision situations and styles of management decision making will influence whether group decision making should be used.

There is no question that on certain occasions a manager will not have the expertise or information available to make an intelligent decision without the assistance of others. In other decision situations, the manager may be thoroughly knowledgeable about the decision situation and would gain little by involving others.

FIGURE 6.5
Rules for ulcerless
decision makers.

SOURCE: Adapted from
Lawrence Steinmetz and Ralph
Todd, *First Line Management:
Approaching Supervision
Effectively* (Dallas: Business
Publications, Inc., 1975).

1. **Differentiate between big decisions and little problems.** The first rule to follow is to determine what *big* problems merit real decision concerns and what are the *little* problems that shouldn't be worried over.

2. **Rely on established policy when possible.** Have preestablished policies as a guide for action in routine situations. You should be prepared to implement preconceived, thought-out policies that are known to work in overcoming problems of a particular (but relatively routine) nature.

3. **Consult and check with others.** Other people who are well informed— supervisors, specialists, customers, friends—cannot make a decision for you, but they can provide useful insight and data.

4. **Avoid crisis decisions.** Deciding under stress is not an ideal situation. You can avoid crisis decisions to some extent by anticipating problems and also by avoiding procrastination. Going systematically (if only for 1 or 2 minutes) through the decision-making steps helps you think more clearly.

5. **Don't try to anticipate all eventualities.** Many poor decision makers spend most of their time thinking about *everything* that can possibly go wrong. Stick instead to the probable outcomes. Overconcern with negatives about different alternatives leads to a negative rather than a positive decision approach.

6. **Don't expect to be right all the time.** A good decision maker recognizes that poor decisions are a fact of life. There is usually a middle ground where one may not have elected the *best* of alternative decisions, but the choice made was not the worst either. A good decision maker recognizes when a decision is less satisfactory than the optimum one, is not overly defensive about it, and has enough self-confidence to admit it.

7. **Be decisive.** Indecision creates tensions in most people. *Procrastination* is the failure or inability to make a decision when all the inputs are there and a decision should be made. *Vacillation* is switching from one alternative to another and even back again to the original after a decision has been halfheartedly implemented. This "on again, off again" waffling may cause a decision maker to lose the respect of others and to feel that decision making is a more painful process than it is.

8. **Once the decision is made, implement it.** Most good decision makers agree that once a decision has been made the implementation of the decision becomes critical for success. Good leadership must be demonstrated. Decisions must be communicated and people motivated to do what is necessary. A halfhearted implementation is often responsible for many decisions being ultimately labeled wrong or poor decisions when, in fact, *poor implementation* has ruined a *good decision!*

Some techniques to use. Some of the techniques used in group decision making are (1) the Delphi technique, (2) the nominal grouping technique, and (3) brainstorming.

The **Delphi technique** involves sending a series of questionnaires to a group of volunteer respondents who do not meet with the other participants—or even know who they are. The responses are tabulated and returned to the respondents for further response and so on until a consensus

TABLE 6.2
What Group Decision Making Is and Is Not

Group decision making is	Group decision making is not
Being fair to all members of the group	Giving each individual what he or she wants
A means of getting together different attitudes	Manipulating group members to reach the "right" decision
Letting members tell what they think should be done to solve a problem	Selling the ideas of the superior manager to the members of the group
Group discipline through social pressure and persuasion	Throwing discipline to the wind and permitting anarchy
Solving problems cooperatively	Appearing to seek advice, without planning to use it

is reached. This technique reduces the influence of personalities on the decision.

The **nominal grouping technique (NGT)** is a structured process in which small groups of around five to nine members make suggestions in writing and then discuss *all* suggestions to reach a decision. All suggestions are silently recorded by each participant, listed on a board one at a time, discussed, and voted on by secret ballot until a consensus is reached.

Brainstorming involves a small group of creative employees in an idea-generating session under rigidly controlled conditions. Everyone is encouraged to present ideas—however unusual—and to refrain from criticizing or even adapting the ideas of others. The ideas are recorded and discussed at subsequent meetings until a decision is reached.

TABLE 6.3
Important Advantages and Disadvantages of Group Decision Making

SOURCE: J. L. Gibson, J. M. Ivancevich, and J. H. Donnelly, Jr., *Organizations: Behavior, Structure, Processes*, 3d ed. (Dallas: Business Publications, Inc., 1979), p. 117.

Advantages	Disadvantages
1. In developing objectives, groups provide a greater amount of available knowledge.	1. The implementation of a decision, whether or not it is made by a group, must be accomplished by individual managers. Since a group cannot be held responsible, group decisions may result in a situation in which no one is responsible and buckpassing occurs.
2. In developing alternatives, the individual efforts of group members can enable a broader search in the various functional areas of the organization.	
3. In evaluating alternatives, groups have a wider range of viewpoints.	2. Considering the value of time as an organizational resource, group decisions are costly.
4. In selecting alternatives, groups are likely to accept more risk than are individual decision makers.	3. Group decision making is inefficient if a decision must be made promptly.
5. Because of participating in the decision-making process, the individual members of groups are more likely to be motivated to carry out the decision.	4. Group decisions may in some cases be the result of compromise and indecision on the part of group members.
6. Greater creativity results from the interaction of individuals with different viewpoints.	5. If superiors are present, or if one member has a dominant personality, the decision of a group may in reality not be a group decision.

When to Use Subordinates

The extent to which subordinates should be involved in decision making has been studied by several scholars and consultants. Two particular researchers, Vroom and Yetton, have developed a "decision tree approach" for identifying the particular "optimum" decision style that a manager would find appropriate in a given situation.

Characteristics of a given situation. The key characteristics of a decision situation, Vroom and Yetton say, are the following:

1. Is there a quality requirement such that one solution is likely to be more rational than others?
2. Does a manager have sufficient information to make a high-quality decision?
3. Is the decision situation structured?
4. Is acceptance of the decision by the manager's subordinates critical to effective implementation of the decision?
5. Is it reasonably certain that the decision would be accepted by subordinates if the manager were to make it alone?
6. Do the manager's subordinates share the organizational goals to be achieved if the problem is solved?
7. Is the preferred solution likely to cause conflict among the subordinates?[11]

In other words, these key variables should determine the extent to which a manager involves subordinates in the decision process or makes the decision alone, without their input.

Management decision-making styles. The second element in the Vroom-Yetton decision tree is the particular management decision-making "style." Many styles are possible, but the following five are the most common:

1. The manager makes the decision alone, using information available at the time.
2. The manager obtains the necessary information from subordinates and then determines the appropriate decision. The role played by others is that of providing the manager with the necessary information rather than of generating or evaluating alternatives.
3. The manager shares the problem with subordinates individually and obtains individual ideas and suggestions, without bringing subordinates together as a group. The manager then makes the decision, which may or may not reflect the subordinates' input or feelings.
4. The manager shares the decision situation with subordinates as a group and solicits their ideas and suggestions in a group meeting. The resulting decision may or may not reflect the subordinates' input or feelings.
5. The manager shares the decision situation with subordinates as a group, and the group generates and evaluates alternatives. The manager does not attempt to influence subordinates and is willing to accept and implement any solution on which there is consensus.[12]

Choosing the appropriate style. We are now ready to combine the key problem aspects with the appropriate decision-making style to be used for a given decision situation. In Figure 6.6, the characteristics of the decision situation appear at the top. To use the model for a particular decision situation, you should start at the left-hand side and work toward the right. When you encounter a box, answer the question above it. When you finally reach a letter, the letter corresponds to the optimum decision-making style to use. There are other parts of Vroom and Yetton's theory that are too detailed to present here. The model has been the subject of much attention and is being tested and evaluated by many management researchers.[13] TIPS 6.1 gives an example of how you might use the Vroom-Yetton decision tree to determine the optimum decision style to use in a hypothetical decision situation.

TIPS 6.1   The Vroom-Yetton Model: Which Decision Style to Use*

Decision problem

As president of the Student Management Club at State University, you must make a decision concerning a date for the annual student banquet.

Q1   Is there a quality requirement such that one solution is likely to be more rational than another?
Ans   Yes. One solution is likely to be more rational because there are various dates that will be unsatisfactory because of competing activities.

Q2   Do you have sufficient information to make a high-quality decision?
Ans   No. You may have certain information on competing dates for some officially scheduled university activities, but there may be some other kinds of activities going on that you are unaware of.

Q3   Is the problem structured?
Ans   Yes. Selection of a given date for a banquet to be held within the next month is a well-structured decision problem.

Q4   Is acceptance of the decision by your subordinates critical to implementation?
Ans   Yes. If the subordinates (and others) don't show up, the banquet is a failure.

Q5   Is it reasonably certain that the decision would be accepted by your subordinates if you were to make it by yourself?
Ans   No. You might accidentally select a date that would not be suitable to your subordinates. For example, the day you select could be one on which subordinates have a major exam or term papers due the following day.

Q6   Do members share the view that the banquet date is important?
Ans   Yes. Members have shown good attendance at meetings and consider the banquet the highlight of the year. Awards are presented, next year's officers announced, and so on.

Optimum decision style

As president, you should share the problem with members as a group, with the group generating and evaluating alternatives, and should attempt to arrive at a consensus decision.

* For decision styles, see the list on page 164 under ''Management decision-making styles.''

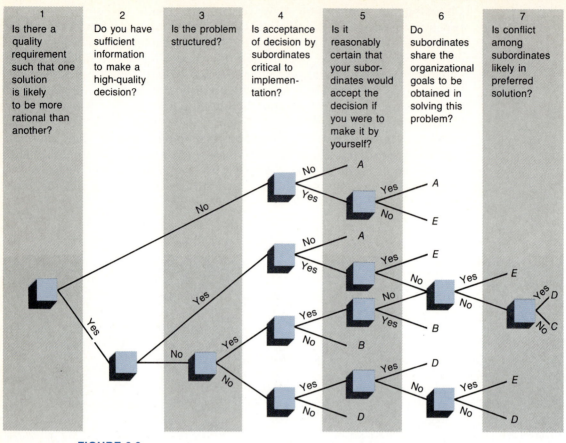

FIGURE 6.6
Effective decision styles.

PROBLEM-SOLVING TYPES

Another concept that is important in decision making is a person's problem-solving type or preference. In fact, a manager's problem-solving type can influence the degree to which he or she may wish to involve others in the decision-making process. The two most popular such processes are the Myers-Briggs Type Indicator and the Jungian Framework.

The Myers-Briggs Type Indicator

The Myers-Briggs concept is based on the work of the scholar-physician Carl Gustav Jung, born in Switzerland and a contemporary of Sigmund Freud.[14] Isabel Myers-Briggs further refined and added to the basic theory and has developed the 126-item **Myers-Briggs Type Indicator,** which helps identify an individual's problem-solving type.[15]

Although the Myers-Briggs indicator focuses on measuring eight dimensions of types of decision making, we will concern ourselves with only the four internal dimensions, which are (1) sensing versus (2) intuition and (3) thinking versus (4) feeling. They are directly related to problem solving and decision making. Figure 6.7 indicates the continuum of the four dimensions. Although everyone uses all four dimensions, each of us tends to develop and

FIGURE 6.7
Continuum of
information-gathering
and information-
evaluating dimensions.

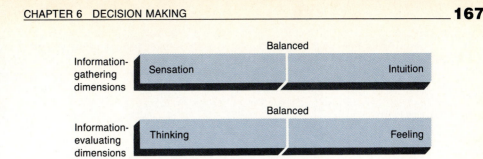

use one information-gathering dimension and one information-evaluating dimension more than the others.

The ideal is to maintain a balance by developing capability in all four dimensions. Although experience and growth opportunities can help develop weaker dimensions, most people have developed two of the dimensions more than the others. An analogy can be drawn by thinking of the four dimensions or functions as four people in a family—two adults and two children. When the family has a problem, the members may discuss it together, but the adults have more influence and probably make the final decision. The same reasoning applies to the four functions. Two of the functions have much greater influence in the development of perception and making judgments.[16]

Two ways of perceiving information and gaining insights. Human beings are equipped with two distinctly different ways of perceiving or gathering information and insights. One is through the process of **sensing** or becoming aware of things through the five senses. The other is through **intuition,** the ability to know things without the use of rational thinking processes. Intuitive understanding may range from a hunch to waking up at night with a creative solution to a problem you have been working on for days.

According to Myers-Briggs, people who rely primarily on sensing tend to be patient, practical, and realistic. Those who rely primarily on intuition tend to be impatient, idea- and theory-oriented, and creative. Although everyone uses both ways of perceiving, Myers-Briggs indicates that at an early age we develop a preference for one method over the other. Therefore, we tend to use our favorite function and slight the function we enjoy less. With the benefits of practice, the preferred function tends to become trustworthy, and individuals may develop along different paths in approaching problem solving and gaining insights. Thus, people develop a set of traits that is based on whether they prefer sensing or intuition.[17] These two contrasting sets of traits and characteristics are shown in Table 6.4.

Two ways of deciding. Just as there are two ways of perceiving, there are two ways of deciding or evaluating. One way is to decide through **thinking,** whereby one uses a logical process and a rational—or sometimes legalistic—reasoning in arriving at impersonal conclusions. The other way is to decide through **feeling,** whereby one uses innate processes that include values and beliefs in arriving at conclusions that take other people's actions or beliefs into consideration. People with a feeling orientation tend to be humanistic, sympathetic, and sometimes subjective in their approach to problem solving and decision making.

**TABLE 6.4
Sensing and Intuitive
Characteristics**

SOURCE: Isabel Myers-Briggs, *Introduction to Type* (Palo Alto, CA: Consulting Psychologists Press, 1980), p. 18.

Sensing types	Intuitive types
Dislike new problems unless there are standard ways to solve them.	Like solving new problems.
Like an established way of doing things.	Dislike doing the same thing repeatedly.
Enjoy using skills already learned more than learning new ones.	Enjoy learning a new skill more than using it.
Work more steadily, with realistic idea of how long it will take.	Work in bursts of energy powered by enthusiasm, with slack periods in between.
Usually reach a conclusion step-by-step.	Reach a conclusion quickly.
Are patient with routine details.	Are impatient with routine details.
Are impatient when the details get complicated.	Are patient with complicated situations.
Are not often inspired, and rarely trust the inspiration when they are.	Follow their inspirations, good or bad.
Seldom make errors of fact.	Frequently make errors of fact.
Tend to be good at precise work.	Dislike taking time for precision.

People who trust and prefer thinking are quite skillful in dealing with matters that require logic, objectivity, and careful examination of facts. On the other hand, if you trust and prefer feeling, you tend to be adept at working with other people and successful in applying skills in interpersonal and human relations. For example, you are normally tactful and appreciative and have the ability to empathize with other people's problems and feelings.

In the world of business, there seem to be many more thinking types than feeling types. This is probably true because there is a need for logic, objectivity, and decision making based on concrete facts and weighed alternatives. For example, in the opening case, Bill Brown was a thinking type. As we shall see later, the predominance of thinking types in the business world often causes human problems to develop because the human factor has not been adequately considered in the problem-solving process. Table 6.5 compares the thinking and feeling types.

Relationship of the four dimensions to problem solving. When experts talk or write about the decision process or the problem-solving process, they are basically talking about the scientific method. As discussed earlier, the first four steps are (1) understanding and defining the problem *(sensing)*, (2) generating alternative solutions and possibilities *(intuition)*, (3) evaluating alternatives *(thinking)*, and (4) making and implementing the decision *(feeling)*. Although the functions overlap somewhat in the process, each internal dimension adds a special insight for each step.

Sensing is invaluable in developing and facing facts as well as being realistic about the nature of the problem or opportunity.

Intuition is utilized in areas where one needs to be creative in seeing possibilities and developing opportunities. Some of the most creative final solutions go beyond the known facts and are the ideas behind brainstorming sessions.

Thinking is most helpful in focusing on impersonal analysis in weighing

TABLE 6.5
Thinking and Feeling
Characteristics

SOURCE: Isabel Myers-Briggs, *Introduction to Type* (Palo Alto, CA: Consulting Psychologists Press, 1980), p. 17.

Thinking types	Feeling types
Do not show emotion readily and are often uncomfortable dealing with people's feelings.	Tend to be very aware of other people and their feelings.
May hurt people's feelings without knowing it.	Enjoy pleasing people, even in unimportant things.
Like analysis and putting things into logical order. Can get along without harmony.	Like harmony. Efficiency may be badly disturbed by office feuds.
Tend to decide impersonally, sometimes paying insufficient attention to people's wishes.	Often let decisions be influenced by their own or other people's personal likes and wishes.
Need to be treated fairly.	Need occasional praise.
Are able to reprimand people or fire them when necessary.	Dislike telling people unpleasant things.
Are more analytically oriented—respond more easily to people's thoughts.	Are more people oriented—respond more easily to people's values.
Tend to be firm-minded.	Tend to be sympathetic.

and considering the alternatives. It considers consequences of cause and effect from an impersonal standpoint in the evaluation step.

Feeling is most important because we need to consider values, ethics, and the impact on other people of our final decision.

Since most of us are strongest in only two of the four functions, there is a tendency to slight the contributions the other two make in problem solving.

A nonunion manufacturing plant was composed of managers who were sensing-thinking types. The firm was quite profitable, and things were dealt with in a businesslike, impersonal, matter-of-fact manner. Most decisions were made on the basis of what effect they would have on efficiency and profits.

A union attempted to organize the plant and, much to the surprise of management, was successful in its efforts. The personnel manager informally discussed the reasons with several operative employees. He was told that although employees were pleased with the pay, they were insecure because they had no appeal process in disciplinary matters. They cited the example of an employee who had been summarily fired because her production had fallen below standard for a month. This employee had met the standard for three years and had only suffered a drop when personal problems intervened. Her 14-year-old daughter had recently been diagnosed as having leukemia.

This incident is not intended to downgrade the contributions of people with a sensing-thinking orientation. Many business people in the United States have this orientation, and this is perhaps one of the reasons we have achieved such outstanding economic success. The incident does, however, highlight the need for a balance in utilizing the four primary internal dimensions in problem solving and decision making.

FIGURE 6.8
MBTI decision styles.

SOURCE: Ben Roach, *Strategy Styles and Management Types* (Notre Dame, IN: Proactive Management Associates, 1987), Transparency IV-7.

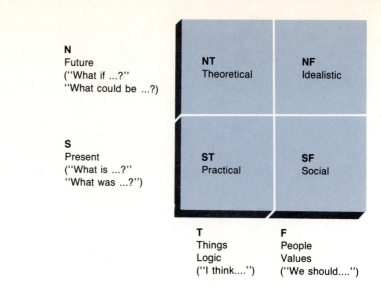

N
Future
("What if ...?"
"What could be ...?)

S
Present
("What is ...?"
"What was ...?")

NT Theoretical	**NF** Idealistic
ST Practical	**SF** Social

T
Things
Logic
("I think....")

F
People
Values
("We should....")

The Jungian Framework

Ben Roach, former management professor and now full-time consultant, has studied decision styles using the **Jungian Framework,** which is a matrix of four key elements:[18] the present (S), the future (N), things and logic (T), and people and values (F), as shown in Figure 6.8.

Roach explains the system by showing that the ST is a practical, matter-of-fact decision maker who makes logical decisions about the present state of affairs. The SF is a sympathetic and friendly decision maker who considers the present motives and values of people. The NF decision maker is an idealist who is enthusiastic and insightful about the future value of people. And the NT decision maker is a theoretical person, who is logical and ingenious about the future state of the organization's affairs.

The four decision styles are different, but all four are necessary in an organization if high-quality and effective decisions are to be made.

SUMMARY

This chapter focused on the decision-making process of management. Decision making was defined as the conscious selection of a course of action from among available alternatives to produce a given result.

Programmed decisions are routine and repetitive and enable management to develop a systematic way to make them. Unprogrammed decisions occur relatively infrequently, and a separate decision must be undertaken each time.

The five steps in decision making are (1) understanding the problem, (2) selecting alternatives, (3) evaluating alternatives, (4) making and implementing the decision, and (5) evaluating the decision results.

To what extent should a manager involve subordinates in the decision-making process? The Vroom-Yetton decision tree helps answer the question by (1) examining the key characteristics of given decision situations and

(2) identifying various decision-making styles. A particular decision style can be selected on the basis of answers to questions about the characteristics of the given situation. Some techniques for involving subordinates are (1) the Delphi technique, (2) the nominal grouping technique (NGT), and (3) brainstorming.

We stressed that, according to the Myers-Briggs Type Indicator, individuals have two ways of perceiving information and two ways of evaluating information. The four combinations of sensing-thinking, intuitive-thinking, sensing-feeling, and intuitive-feeling have a definite influence on problem solving and decision making. Ideally, a balance may be developed by using all four functions in decision making.

Another way of classifying decision-making styles is using the Jungian Framework. According to it, managers may be (1) practical, (2) social, (3) idealistic, or (4) theoretical.

REVIEW QUESTIONS

1. What is managerial decision making?
2. What is the difference between programmed and unprogrammed decisions?
3. What are the steps involved in management decision making? Briefly explain each.
4. What is group decision making?
5. Discuss some techniques for involving subordinates in decision making.
6. In what way is the Vroom-Yetton decision tree of value to managers?
7. Give a brief description of each of the following:
   a. Sensing
   b. Intuition
   c. Thinking
   d. Feeling
8. What are the types of decision makers as defined by the Jungian Framework?

DISCUSSION QUESTIONS

1. Peter Drucker states that a big decision-making error that managers frequently make is to fail to get a handle or grasp on the problem. Instead, managers plunge in prematurely. Why do you think many managers make this common mistake?
2. "It's better for a manager to try to carry out a poor decision for the sake of worker confidence. You can't build worker confidence by continually admitting the poor decisions you make." Discuss this statement.
3. What are the pros and cons of decisions made by groups such as committees and task forces as compared to decisions made by one person?
4. Is it possible for someone to be a good decision maker but a poor manager? Explain.
5. One manager says that he finds procrastination to be a big help in his decision making. Do you agree or disagree? Why?

LEARNING EXERCISE 6.1

Between a Rock and a Hard Place

"This is a rough decision," said Frank Owens, store manager and vice-president of Amalgamated Department Store, a large urban retailer with 350 employees. Amalgamated was a family-owned business that had operated in Philadelphia for over 30 years. Owens seriously believed in delegating authority to lower levels of management, but this latest problem had been referred to Owens by Lucille Hearns, manager of the women's sportswear department.

Six weeks ago, Susan Ayres, aged 23, had been hired as a temporary employee. She had an outstanding personality and immediately made friends with the senior workers in the department, as well as with other salespersons and clerks in the store. Moreover, she was an exceptional salesperson who related so well to customers that many had gone out of their way to tell Hearns how much they enjoyed dealing with Susan.

After the 2-week temporary period, Hearns requested that Susan be hired on a full-time basis; Susan's husband had recently undergone major surgery, so Susan desired full-time work.

Four days ago, Bill Jacobs, personnel manager of the store, realized that Susan had not been asked to take the medical exam required of all full-time employees. Susan took the exam that afternoon but didn't pass it because of a heart condition. Under the terms of the company's medical insurance program, she could not be hired, and Jacobs told Hearns that Susan would have to be terminated. Not only did Hearns argue strongly for an exception being made in Susan's case, but several employees also saw Jacobs and told him that since it was his oversight it was unfair to Susan to release her now. Moreover, they said that the company should be willing to help people like Susan, since they had EEO programs and had even hired some physically handicapped employees in the past. But Jacobs said that Susan must go; the rule was that all permanent employees must pass the physical, and Susan had not.

Hearns appealed the decision to Owens, who said he would let her know something the next day. As he pondered a way out of the dilemma, Owens noted the results of a survey on his desk: 42 percent of the employees had said that they would consider joining a union if one attempted to organize the store.

Questions

1. What are the key issues in the case?

2. Develop the realistic alternatives that Owens has in selecting a decision. How would you go about determining the probable outcomes of each decision?

3. What decision do you recommend that Owens make?

<table>
<tr><td>**LEARNING**
EXERCISE 6.2</td><td>

Determining Your Decision-Making Preferences

1. Examine Tables 6.4 and 6.5. Place a check (√) by each statement that you feel best describes your own characteristics. If you come out with more checks for one type than its opposite, this indicates your preferred style. Circle your problem-solving type below.

</td></tr>
</table>

Sensing	or	Intuitive
Thinking	or	Feeling

2. Break into groups of five and compare your problem-solving type with other students in your group. How many perceive information through sensing? Intuition? How many decide through thinking? Feeling?

3. If your team members were asked to make a team decision or arrive at a consensus regarding a given situation or case assignment, what are the implications of your team's particular problem-solving profile? Discuss.

LEARNING
EXERCISE 6.3

Chris, Cerise, and Klaus*

Chris and Cerise are secretaries in a small office. They operate word processors and other automated equipment, answer telephones, greet visitors to the office, and

_____

* This case was developed by organization development consultants Adam Yagodka, Ph.D., and Sue Clancy and presented at a workshop at the Association of Psychological Type Conference, Gainesville, Florida, June 1987.

generally assist the professional staff in the day-to-day operations of the office. Klaus is the office manager and is responsible for the performance appraisal of Chris and Cerise.

Chris has been working in the office for about three years; she was the first secretary hired when the office opened. Cerise came to work in the office about two years ago. Both received superior performance ratings on their last annual performance review. For the first year, Chris and Cerise seemed quite friendly with each other, often socializing together after work. During the past year, friction and tension between them has been building. Klaus recognizes the conflict brewing and knows he will have to do something about it or both may have to seek jobs elsewhere. He has spoken to both Chris and Cerise (separately) about the conflict between them, but so far he hasn't made any progress in resolving or managing it.

The main problem seems to be in the differences in how the women approach their jobs. Chris has established what she considers efficient methods and procedures for getting the work done, but Cerise doesn't want to follow them all the time. Cerise seems to delight in finding new, innovative ways to do the work (and expand her job), while Chris likes things the way they are.

Chris prides herself on having a tidy workstation. The only decorations in her workspace are pictures of her family. She arrives at work 10 to 15 minutes early and frequently opens the office. She takes pleasure in organizing her work for the day and almost always has it finished by quitting time. She works at a steady pace and deals efficiently with interruptions. Klaus considers her a stabilizing, responsible, productive member of the office. Chris has a husband, two children, and a home in the suburbs, which are her highest priorities.

Cerise doesn't seem to mind having a messy workstation. Instead of filing papers, she stacks them in piles (though she rarely loses anything). She has pictures of animals everywhere. She has smudges on her terminal. Cerise usually arrives at work on time but is well-known for staying late to finish projects. She is well liked by all the professionals in the office, freely offering to do special projects for them. Cerise seems to have a knack with people and brings out their best when she works on group projects. Klaus finds her very easy to talk to and frequently uses her as a sounding board when he has to make difficult decisions. He thinks she makes a very positive contribution to the office, though it is different from Chris's. Cerise is unmarried but has a steady boyfriend. The most important thing in her life is developing herself for future challenges. She is attending a local college part-time and plans eventually to finish graduate school. She has a strong career orientation.

Klaus attended a management development course about three months ago in which the Myers-Briggs Type Indicator (MBTI) was used. He was very much impressed with the insights he gained about his own and others' behavior. He came out INFP (intuitive/feeling type). Other professional staff in the office have taken the MBTI and frequently "talk type." Chris and Cerise have not yet taken the Indicator.

Klaus has concluded that he needs to have a meeting with Chris and Cerise to iron out their differences and restore harmony to the office. He has asked you, as a consultant qualified in using the MBTI, whether you think type might be helpful in this case. If so, he would like you to administer the Indicator to Chris and Cerise. After giving them feedback on their MBTI results, he would like you to help plan and facilitate a meeting with the three of them next week in an effort to resolve the conflict.

Questions

1. Identify the problem-solving styles of Chris and Cerise.
2. Diagnose the causes of the conflict between the two women.
3. If you were the consultant in this case, how would you handle the meeting to resolve the conflict?

NOTES

1. Esther Dyson, "Should We Move to Milpitas?" *Forbes*, August 10, 1987, pp. 102ff.
2. Kathleen Cook, "Why Aren't Women in the Top Jobs?" *USA Today*, August 17, 1987, p. 2D.
3. Richard L. Hudson, "Scientific Saga: How 2 IBM Physicists Triggered the Frenzy over Superconductors," *Wall Street Journal*, August 19, 1987, pp. 1 and 6; and *USA Today*, December 18, 1987, p. 5A.
4. C. H. Kepner and B. B. Tregoe, *The Rational Manager* (New York: McGraw-Hill, 1985).
5. John McCormick, "The Wisdom of Solomon," *Newsweek*, August 17, 1987, p. 62.
6. Even ESP is being accepted more by researchers and managers as part of decision making and planning, but there are many skeptics. See C. B. Cheatham, "ESP: A Useful Planning Tool," *Managerial Planning* 25 (November–December 1976): 38–40.
7. Peter F. Drucker, *An Introductory View of Management* (New York: Harper & Row, 1977), pp. 28–29.
8. Max Richards and Paul Greenlaw, *Management Decision Making* (Homewood, IL: Irwin, 1966), pp. 28–29.
9. Herbert Simon, *Administrative Behavior* (New York: Macmillan, 1957), p. xxv.
10. Drucker, p. 398.
11. V. H. Vroom and P. W. Yetton, *Leadership and Decision Making* (Pittsburgh: University of Pittsburgh Press, 1973); and V. Vroom, "A New Look at Managerial Decison Making," *Organizational Dynamics* 1 (Spring 1973): 66–80.
12. Ibid.
13. See, for example, G. Jago and Victor H. Vroom, "An Evaluation of Two Alternatives to the Vroom/Yetton Normative Model," *Academy of Management Journal* 23 (June 1980): 347–355.
14. Carl G. Jung, *Psychological Types* (Princeton: Princeton University Press, 1971; original edition 1921).
15. Isabel Myers-Briggs, *Gifts Differing* (Palo Alto, CA: Consulting Psychologists Press, 1980). We recommend that students take the Myers-Briggs Type Indicator from the university's counseling center. It can be helpful in identifying problem-solving type and in career choice consideration.
16. Edwin N. Barker and Mary H. McCaulley, "The Myers-Briggs Type Indicator in Management and Technology," Level I Workshop, Orlando, Florida, November 3–5, 1983.
17. Myers-Briggs, pp. 2–3.
18. Ben Roach, *Strategy Styles and Management Types* (Notre Dame, IN: Proactive Management Associates, 1987), Chapter 4.

SUGGESTIONS FOR FURTHER STUDY

Byrne, John A. "Searching for Failure in the Executive Suite." *Business Week*, July 20, 1987, pp. 16 and 18.
"Computer Familiarity Still Runs Low in the Executive Suite." *Wall Street Journal*, July 7, 1987, p. 1.
Gordon, J. J. *Synectics: The Development of Creative Capacity.* New York: Macmillan, 1961.
Heenan, D., and Addleman, R. "Quantitative Techniques for Today's Decision Makers." *Harvard Business Review* 54 (May–June 1976): 32–62.
Kiechel, Walter, III. "How Executives Think." *Fortune*, February 4, 1985, pp. 127–128.
McGrail, G. R. "The Decision-Making Process in Small Business." *Managerial Planning* 26 (January–February 1978): 19–25.
McKenney, James L., and Keen, Peter G. W. "How Managers' Minds Work." *Harvard Business Review* 52 (May–June 1974): 79–90.
Parnes, Sidney J. "Learning Creative Behavior." *The Futurist* 18 (August 1984): 30–31.

SCHULER, RANDALL S. "A Role and Expectancy Perception Model of Participation in Decision Making." *Academy of Management Journal* 23 (June 1980): 331–340.

SIMON, HERBERT A. *The New Science of Management Decison* (Englewood Cliffs, NJ: Prentice-Hall, 1960), pp. 5–8.

WILLIAMS, MARJORY. "How I Learned to Stop Worrying and Love Negotiating." *Inc.* September 1987, pp. 132–133.

PART THREE

Designing and Staffing an Organization

Take away all our factories, our trade, our avenues of transportation, and our money, but leave me our organization, and in four years I will have reestablished myself.

—ANDREW CARNEGIE

THIS STATEMENT BY ONE of America's pioneer industrialists emphasizes that organizations are more than just physical facilities using financial resources to achieve objectives. Instead, organizations are people, working together in a structure with authority-responsibility relationships, and led by capable managers. These key elements are found in all effective organizations.

The main objective of most organizations, as discussed in Part Two, is to produce goods or provide services effectively. Most organizations also seek to provide employment and satisfaction to employees, benefits to clients and the public, and satisfactory returns to owners. These objectives can best be achieved by combining the available resources into an effective system. Part Three shows how this can be done.

You can see from the opposite page that Chapter 7 covers some fundamental concepts involved in designing an organization. Topics such as division of labor, bureaucracy, span of management, types of organization, and departmentalization are discussed.

Chapter 8 explains how to make the organization more effective through the judicious use of delegation, authority, power, responsibility, accountability, centralization—or decentralization—of authority, committees, and informal organizations.

Chapter 9 reemphasizes that people are the most important element in any organization. Only through recruiting, selecting, developing, compensating, and maintaining the health and safety of capable employees can an organization expect to be effective. The chapter also covers the important role of equal employment opportunity laws.

7. Fundamentals of organizational design

Some basic concepts	Division of labor, use of organization charts, and bureaucracy
Types of organizations	Line, line and staff, and functional
Span of management	Span and organizational levels related Different spans at different levels Span, levels, and employee satisfaction Factors affecting span
Departmentalization	Functional, product, territorial, customer, process, and matrix

8. Using delegation to make organizations more effective

Role of delegation	Reasons for delegating Why managers fail to delegate Why employees don't accept delegation	
Role of authority	Sources of authority	Types of authority
Role of power	Sources of power How power expands power	Limits on use of authority and power
Role of responsibility and accountability	Responsibility and accountability can't be shifted Authority and responsibility aren't equal	
Role of centralization	Centralization versus decentralization Factors affecting degree of centralization	
Role of committees	Types of committees Advantages and disadvantages Using task forces	
Role of informal organizations	Functions performed	Problems created

(continued)

9. Staffing and human-resource management

Role of staffing

How EEO laws affect staffing	Laws providing for EEO Enforcing EEO laws
Planning human-resource needs	Determining job needs Developing sources of employees
Recruiting and selecting employees	Recruiting employees Selecting right person for the job Orienting new employees
Training and developing employees	Reasons for training and development Training and development methods
Compensating employees	Importance of compensation Income differentials How compensation is determined How employees are paid Role of employee benefits

Maintaining health and safety

7

Fundamentals of Organizational Design

Learning Objectives

After studying the material in this chapter, you should be able to do the following:

□ Define and explain some basic concepts of organization.
□ Describe the different types of organizations.
□ Recognize the variables in determining the span of management.
□ Discuss the six major forms of organization departmentalization.
□ Explain the concept of *bureaucracy* and explain how it operates.

Outline of the Chapter

Some basic concepts of organization
Division of labor, or specialization
Use of formal organization charts
Bureaucracy
Types of organizations
The line organization
The line-and-staff organization
The functional organization
Span of management
Effects on organizational levels of varying the span
Using different spans at different levels
Spans, levels, and employee satisfaction
Factors affecting span
Departmentalization
Functional departmentalization
Product departmentalization
Territorial departmentalization
Customer departmentalization
Process or equipment departmentalization
Matrix departmentalization
Other bases of organizing activities
Summary

Some Important Terms

organizing
synergy
division of labor
specialization
chain of command
unity of command
span of management
  (control, authority)
bureaucracy
red tape
line organization
line-and-staff organiza-
  tion
functional organization
contingency approach

departmentalization
functional departmental-
  ization
product departmentali-
  zation
territorial (regional, area,
  geographic) depart-
  mentalization
customer departmentali-
  zation
process (equipment) de-
  partmentalization
matrix departmentaliza-
  tion
facilitators

The effort of two or more individuals working as a unit toward a common goal is greater than the sum of the effort of the individuals working as individuals.

—WILLIAM B. CORNELL

IBM—A Changing Organization

When you think of IBM, you think of computers, right? Well, yes and no. Although computers are now IBM's most visible product (with the possible exception of typewriters), this was not always the case. Few people realize that for several years after the computer's introduction in the late 1940s, IBM resisted developing computers of its own, since it controlled 97 percent of the tabulating equipment business.

IBM actually began in 1884 when Herman Hollerith patented an automatic punch-card tabulating machine and won a contract to process the U.S. census in 1890 and again in 1900. Losing the 1910 census contract, he sold the company to Computer-Tabulating-Recording Company (CTR), a maker of time clocks, butcher scales, and tabulators.

Thomas J. Watson was hired to run CTR in 1914. He revitalized the company by transforming its sales force into dedicated supersalesmen wearing dark suits, white starched shirts, and conservative striped ties. Each day began with a pep rally where Watson gave a motivational speech to the salesmen and led them in singing from the company's songbook, *Ever Onward*. After 1920, CTR concentrated on tabulators, and, having changed its name to International Business Machines Corporation in 1924, the firm totally dominated its field until the early 1950s. Then came the computer, and Watson wasn't interested in the newfangled "electrical brains."

After Remington Rand placed the first giant computer (the Univac) at the U.S. Census Bureau in 1951 and another at General Electric in 1954, IBM sold its first commercial computer to Monsanto in 1955. Though a late starter, IBM soon took the lead in the computer field and, thanks to its organizational principles, managed to hold it until 1977, when smaller, more innovative firms such as Apple, Commodore (Pet), and Tandy (Radio Shack) began selling desktop computers, As in the 1950s, IBM had to change its mission and organizational principles in order to survive.

William C. Lowe, a typical IBM executive, but also a risk-taking "intrapreneur," led an independent 12-person team to develop the IBM-PC in an obscure laboratory in Boca Raton, Florida—far away from IBM's other operations. An autonomous division—Entry Systems Division (ESD)—was set up to design, develop, manufacture, and sell the new tool, which IBM hoped would become a centerpiece of its office automation system.

This change in mission and strategy led to many fundamental changes. As an independent unit, ESD was spared many of the controls and formal reporting structures of other divisions. Thus, the original PC took only 13 months from preliminary planning to introduction in 1981, whereas most IBM products took years to develop. The PC was built from off-the-shelf parts instead of parts designed and produced by IBM. ESD used software from an outsider, Microsoft, instead of developing its own. Instead of having only highly trained salespeople and commercial users, ESD sells computers to millions of customers through its own retail stores and other dealers such as Computerland outlets and Sears, Roebuck's new nationwide chain of business machines stores. IBM also uses massive advertising blitzes to sell to the public.

Like all large organizations, IBM had become bureaucratic. For example, although it was "America's most admired" corporation for several years, it had fallen to fourth (out of 10) in its industry in "innovativeness." By 1987, however, new management was trying to change things. New products were introduced, personnel costs were cut through attrition and employee buyouts, the force of 40,000 managers was cut and management layers reduced to lower costs and permit quicker response to marketplace demands, 22 percent more sales and marketing jobs were created by transferring headquarters and factory personnel to those areas, and a new strategy of emphasizing more profitable software and services was introduced. ■

SEVERAL CONCEPTS ABOUT ORGANIZING that are discussed in this chapter are illustrated by this case. As you learned in Chapter 1, there are three primary functions—operations, marketing, and financing—that must be performed in all organizations. The first two of these are covered in the IBM case.

In Chapter 5, you learned that an organization has (1) a mission, which defines its purpose; (2) objectives, which are the goals management tries to reach; and (3) strategies, which are the plans for the overall activities of the firm. These were also featured in the case.

Now, this chapter discusses some basic concepts of organization, looks at the different types of organizations, explains how many people managers can supervise effectively, and shows how organizations can be divided into smaller operating units by a process of departmentalization.

SOME BASIC CONCEPTS OF ORGANIZATION

As shown in Chapter 1, organizations, which are groups of individuals with a common goal bound together by a set of authority-responsibility relationships, are required wherever groups of people work together to reach common goals. One of management's functions is to coordinate available organizational resources for effective operations.

The term **organizing** has various meanings. It can be used to refer to the following:

1. The way management designs a formal structure to use most effectively the financial, physical, material, and human resources of the organization.

2. How the organization groups its activities, with each grouping being assigned a manager with the authority to supervise group members.

3. Establishing relationships among functions, jobs, tasks, and employees.

4. The way given managers subdivide the tasks to be done in their departments and delegate the necessary authority to accomplish the tasks.

There are some well-defined concepts affecting the organization and the organizing process. The most important ones are (1) division of labor, or specialization, (2) use of formal organization charts, (3) chain of command, (4) unity of command, (5) departmentalization, (6) levels of hierarchy, (7) span of management, (8) authority-responsibility relationships, (9) bureaucracy, (10) use of committees, and (11) the inevitability of informal groupings.

Concepts 1 through 9 are covered in this chapter; concepts 10 and 11 will be discussed in Chapter 8.

Division of Labor, or Specialization

The goal of an organization is to accomplish some purpose that individuals cannot achieve by themselves, acting alone. As the chapter opening quotation indicates, groups of two or more persons, working together in a cooperative, coordinated way, can accomplish more than each could do independently. (See Figure 7.1 for an example of how this principle operates.) This concept is called **synergy.** The cornerstone of organizing is the principle of **division of labor** that allows synergy to occur. The management word for this principle is **specialization,** whereby employees (and managers) carry out the activities they are more qualified for and adept at performing.

We live in an era of specialization, not only of employees and managers, but also of professionals, who must cooperate and coordinate their activities.

In a hospital of 300 employees, there are doctors, nurses, technicians, food service personnel, receptionists, guards, laundry workers, custodians, clerks, and many other types of employees. When the job is divided into components, more can be accomplished by the total group than would be possible for even 300 doctors if each ran his or her own separate medical facility with no support personnel or assistance. Can you imagine how important it is for them to cooperate and how difficult it is to coordinate their activities?

 What is your view?

Can you think of some other task situations with which you are familiar in which "specialization" allows a strong synergistic effect to occur?

Examples of specialization. You can see examples of specialization in many different areas—for example, on the football field: A team may consist of a head coach, assistants, a trainer, a water boy, and a sideline statistician, as well as blocking backs, offensive linemen, defensive linemen, and other "specialized" players, such as field-goal kickers.

Reasons for its effectiveness. Division of labor is effective because, since only a small part of a job is performed by each worker, less-qualified personnel may be used and job training is easier. Moreover, the wasted motions and movement that occur when a person performs two or more parts of a job are minimized. Finally, division of labor usually leads to the invention of efficient equipment and machinery that increases productivity.

How many straight pins could you and nine of your friends make in a day, assuming that you were using no automatic equipment? The answer depends on whether all of you would make entire pins or each would perform a specialized job—drawing the wire, rounding the body, sharpening the point, or shaping the head. Adam Smith argued the case for division of labor, or specialization, in his book The Wealth of Nations, *published in England in 1776, when he addressed the issue of a small pin-making shop with 10 workers. Each person, working independently to do the whole job, could have made no more than 20 pins daily, for a maximum of 200. But the shop, by employing specialization, produced about 4800 pins daily.*[1]

FIGURE 7.1
"It pays to cooperate!"

Some negative consequences. As you will see later, however, there are severe behavioral consequences resulting from the division of labor when it is carried to extremes. It can lead to fatigue, monotony, boredom, and loss of motivation, which can result in inefficiency rather than efficiency.

Use of Formal Organization Charts

A formal organization chart represents the organizational game plan for division of work. An organization chart shows several key aspects of organization. These are (1) chain of command, (2) unity of command, (3) departmentalization, (4) levels of hierarchy, (5) span of management, and (6) division of labor. It cannot, however, show how informal groups operate within the formal structure. This topic is discussed in the next chapter.

Chain of command. The **chain of command** depicts the authority-responsibility relationships that link superiors and subordinates together throughout the entire organization. It flows from the chief executive officer down to the lowest worker in the organization, as shown in Figure 7.2. Therefore, each organization member has some linkage with the top manager of the organization—in this case, the president of the university.

What is your view?

Assume you are taking this management course from the professor of management theory shown in Figure 7.2. What would be the chain of command from the chairman of the board to you? What is the chain of command from the CEO of your school?

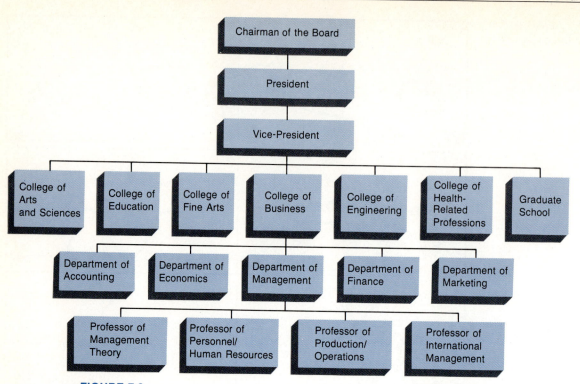

FIGURE 7.2
Organization chart for
Union State University.

Unity of command. Christ said, "No man can serve two masters."[2] Henri Fayol advanced this principle as one of his principles of management.[3] According to the principle of **unity of command,** each individual employee in an organization reports to and is accountable to only one immediate superior. This means that the chain of command should be so clear that a subordinate will receive assigned duties and delegated authority from only one manager and be accountable to only one superior.

Unity of command is desirable because it simplifies communication and the placement of responsibility. Yet, in today's complex organizations, most employees receive instructions from many managers, especially when there is functional authority, as we show in the next chapter. This practice, although necessary, results in many negative consequences, as will become evident in this and subsequent chapters.

Departmentalization. Large groups are impossible to work with unless they are divided into smaller groupings. In organizations, this is the process of departmentalization, which will be discussed later. By examining an organization chart, you can see how the organization groups its activities to best accomplish its goals. As you will see in the chapter, several patterns of groupings exist.

Levels of hierarchy. An organization chart shows the levels of management that exist in a given structure, in addition to the chain of command and reporting relationships. Notice that the vertical lines from one level to another reflect different degrees of authority and responsibility—as will be shown in the next chapter. A tall structure portrays a large number of levels, as shown

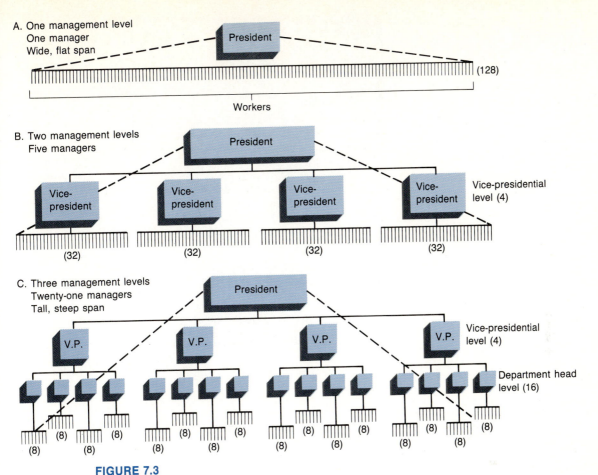

A. One management level
One manager
Wide, flat span

President

(128)

Workers

B. Two management levels
Five managers

President

Vice-president   Vice-president   Vice-president   Vice-president   Vice-presidential level (4)

(32)   (32)   (32)   (32)

C. Three management levels
Twenty-one managers
Tall, steep span

President

V.P.   V.P.   V.P.   V.P.   Vice-presidential level (4)

Department head level (16)

(8) (8) (8) (8)   (8) (8) (8) (8)   (8) (8) (8) (8)   (8) (8) (8) (8)

FIGURE 7.3
How span of management and levels of hierarchy are interrelated.
(You would rarely find the span of management the same for each position on a given level, but we have made them equal in this chart for comparative purposes.)

SOURCE: Prepared by Allan Mazur, *The Bureaucrat*, Spring 1978.

in Figure 7.3C, and a flat structure a smaller number of levels, as shown in Figure 7.3A.

Span of management. As will be shown later, **span of management** refers to the number of subordinates reporting to a given supervisor. A tall structure portrays a narrow span of management (Figure 7.3C) and a flat structure a wide span (Figure 7.3A).

Division of work (specialization). An organization chart also shows the degree to which specialization is used. The horizontal lines connecting the positions on the same level reflect specialization, or performing specialized activities. Although the chart reflects the overall division of work, it does not include the informal organization.

We might say that the formal organization structure (as represented by the organization chart) represents a type of game plan management has set up to reach the organization's objectives. But just as numerous game plans are never put into practice, formal organization charts often only remotely describe the important relationships that exist. Frequently, the pecking order of the informal organization is completely out of line with the formal organization chart that hangs in top management's office. In such cases, the

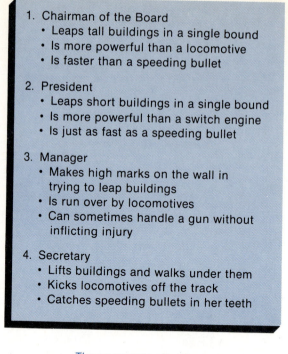

1. Chairman of the Board
   • Leaps tall buildings in a single bound
   • Is more powerful than a locomotive
   • Is faster than a speeding bullet

2. President
   • Leaps short buildings in a single bound
   • Is more powerful than a switch engine
   • Is just as fast as a speeding bullet

3. Manager
   • Makes high marks on the wall in trying to leap buildings
   • Is run over by locomotives
   • Can sometimes handle a gun without inflicting injury

4. Secretary
   • Lifts buildings and walks under them
   • Kicks locomotives off the track
   • Catches speeding bullets in her teeth

The corporate structure.

informal organization (discussed later) carries a greater weight, since it describes the way things actually get done in the organization.

Bureaucracy

You have probably heard various candidates for national and local office lambasting federal and state bureaucracies and bureaucrats. There are strong negative connotations associated with bureaucracy today. Let us now examine the meaning of this form of organization.

The concept of bureaucracy was advanced by the German writer Max Weber.[4] Under a **bureaucracy,** the organization structure has the following characteristics:

1. Tasks are divided into very specialized jobs.
2. A rigorous set of rules must be followed to ensure predictability and eliminate uncertainty in task performance.
3. There are clear authority-responsibility relationships that must be maintained.
4. Superiors take an impersonal attitude in dealing with subordinates.
5. Employment and promotions are based on merit.
6. Lifelong employment is an accepted fact.

Most of us criticize unyielding bureaucracies, but in certain circumstances bureaucratic structures may be very effective, for they do provide order and guidance. Yet highly specialized tasks become monotonous; rules are often unnecessarily restrictive; managers can't always be impersonal; and it is often difficult to identify clearly the more capable workers. Thus, management in the organization tends to become rigid, inflexible, and heavily reliant on **red tape,** or official routines and procedures marked by excessive complexity, resulting in unnecessary delay.

In summary, as organizations become older and larger, they tend to become more bureaucratic. Notice that IBM, in the opening case, suffered from that malaise.

TYPES OF ORGANIZATIONS

Any discussion of organizational design should begin with an explanation of the most popular types of organizations. The main types are (1) the line organization, (2) the line-and-staff organization, and (3) the functional organization.

The Line Organization

In general, the **line organization** refers to those departments that are directly responsible for accomplishing the major activities of the organization (called *primary functions* in Chapter 1). If the objective of the organization is to produce and sell goods, then the line organization would consist of at least the president, a sales manager, and a production manager, together with the employees who perform production and sales work in these departments. Figure 7.4 presents the organization chart of a small manufacturing company that operates as a pure line organization. As shown, individuals in each department perform the major activities of the enterprise—production and sales. Each person has a reporting relationship to only one superior, so there is a unity of command.

The Line-and-Staff Organization

Suppose the small line organization shown in Figure 7.4 grows to the point where it makes sense to hire certain persons who do not directly perform sales or production work. Instead, they assist the line managers or departments to operate more effectively. Perhaps the position is that of an accounting specialist who will perform certain services for the line organization. These services might be keeping the books, preparing cost reports, billing customers, and so forth. Another position might be that of a personnel specialist who will perform personnel recruiting, interviewing, and screening of potential job candidates. Another specialist might be an industrial engineer who will aid the line organization by seeking to find improved work methods and practices. Another might be a purchasing specialist who will

FIGURE 7.4
A simple line organization.

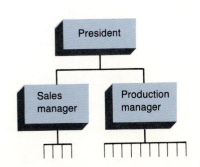

follow through and serve the line by handling all the orders for materials, equipment, and supplies. And another might be a maintenance specialist who will aid the line departments by servicing and maintaining equipment. These new personnel, who do not perform line activities, are referred to as "staff."

This new organization structure will reflect the presence of staff as well as line, as shown in Figure 7.5. Notice that an additional staff position, legal, is also shown. The result is what is called a **line-and-staff organization,** in which staff positions have been added to serve the basic line departments and help them accomplish the organization's objectives more effectively.

Essentially, *staff* employees or *staff* departments are those that are not directly involved in the organization's or department's mainstream activity. For example, maintenance specialists do not create a product or sell it. Neither do accountants, purchasing agents, computer programmers, industrial engineers, public relations people, or personnel specialists.

Distinction not always clear. Sometimes it is difficult to tell whether a department or position is line or staff. Some departments are so intimately related to obvious line work that they are considered part of the line. To make the distinction, you must ask the question, "What is the business of the firm?" Line activities are the organization's fundamental reason for existence—the bread-and-butter activities, so to speak.

> *Ordinarily, maintenance is considered a staff function in a manufacturing facility; the company is not in the business of providing maintenance. At an airline, however, airplane maintenance is so critical that it is considered a line activity.*
>
> *Auditing, for instance, is normally considered staff in most organizations, but when a junior partner at Price Waterhouse, the well-known*

FIGURE 7.5
A simplified line-and-staff organization.
(Staff positions are shown by broken lines.)

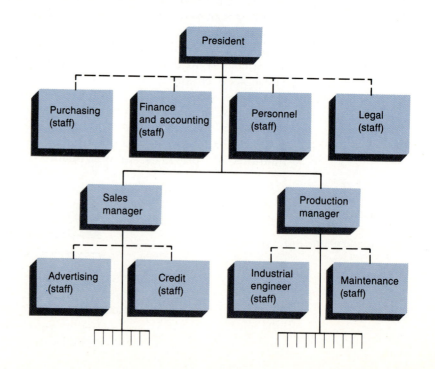

accounting firm, undertakes an auditing service for a customer, he or she is engaged in a line activity.

An editor at a publishing house is doing a line activity, but an editor at a manufacturing plant, editing the employee newsletter, is doing a staff function.

What is your view?

Which of these is line and which is staff in a university?

registrar's office	student financial aid
admissions	department of management studies
student counseling	payroll office
library	personnel office

In the example above, only one of the entries listed is clearly and directly engaged in the business of education, the major reason for the university's existence, and that is the department of management. All the others are supportive—important, but still supportive. There would perhaps be some question about the library. Since it is such an integral part of education (especially if there is a school of library science), some experts would consider the library line. But others would not, reasoning that the library exists primarily to serve the line teaching and research departments. The other functions are definitely staff, serving the line organization and facilitating its job.

Reasons for making the distinction. Why do we make such a distinction between line and staff activities? First, since line activities represent the fundamental activities of the organization, management must be especially aware of the need to preserve the integrity and influence of those departments. To restrict the performance of line departments by granting too much authority or influence to staff can erode the ultimate morale and efficiency of line departments. Second, organizational cutbacks made in times of crisis are largely determined by whether departments are line or staff. For example, when demand for products or services is down, you are apt to see cutbacks primarily in line departments. When General Motors laid off workers because of unfavorable economic conditions in 1982–1983 it took the workers mostly from the line. In other words, GM did not need to manufacture cars when no one was buying them. But when demand for the organization's products or services is still strong but the organization must cut costs, the cutbacks are most likely to be in staff. Notice that IBM moved employees from its headquarters staff into sales when it had to cut expenses in 1986–1987.

Types of staff. The two main types of staff employees are personal staff and specialized staff.

Personal staff is created to provide advice, help, and service to an individual manager. Sometimes referred to as the "assistant to" or "staff assistant," this person works on a variety of tasks for the manager and is usually a generalist.

Specialized staff, on the other hand, advises, counsels, assists, and serves the line and all elements of the organization. It is referred to as "specialized" staff because its function is narrow, and the processor is viewed as an expert;

Management Application and Practice 7.1   Lean Staff, Simple Form

In their highly popular book, *In Search of Excellence*, Thomas Peters and Robert Waterman identified the eight attributes of the excellently managed companies of the United States. One of these attributes particularly relates to the principles of this chapter: *lean staff, simple form.*

According to Peters and Waterman, those companies known for their excellence tend to have relatively few staff personnel at corporate headquarters but rely more on line personnel. As large as most of the excellent companies were (Du Pont, General Motors, Kmart, McDonald's, and some 60 others), top-level corporate staffs rarely consisted of more than 100 persons. For example, Schlumberger, the $6 billion diversified oil service company, runs its worldwide empire with a corporate staff of 90. ROLM man-

ages a $200 million dollar business with only 15 or so people located at corporate headquarters.

What is the effect of this lean corporate staff? What does it mean for the company? It means that these firms rely more on line activities and less on staff. This practice enhances the integrity of the various line divisions or units. Product development, usually a corporate or group activity, is wholly done at the division level in companies like Johnson & Johnson, 3M, Hewlett-Packard, and others. None of these companies, for example, have corporate planners at the corporate level!

SOURCE: Thomas J. Peters and Robert H. Waterman, Jr., *In Search of Excellence* (New York: Harper & Row, 1982), pp. 306–317.

the specialist's expertise is made available throughout the organization. Examples of specialized staff include personnel specialists, safety specialists, legal specialists, and so on. Specialized staff may report to various levels of the organization, such as the corporate level, the division level, or the decentralized facility level, as shown in MAP 7.1.

The Functional Organization

Whenever a staff function or activity becomes so important that its performance is critical to the organization's success, it is given a special status. It becomes a **functional organization,** and its manager has the authority to see that it is performed correctly in *all* parts of the organization (see Chapter 8 for more details). Examples of this type of organization are the personnel department, which must enforce the many laws described in Chapter 9, and the accounting department, which must see that all records are maintained according to legal requirements. Those departments see that the laws, regulations, policies, and procedures are uniformly enforced everywhere in the organization.

SPAN OF MANAGEMENT

The principle of span of management has to do with the number of subordinates a manager can effectively supervise. It was this problem that confronted Moses in the following example. According to the theory of the *span of management*, sometimes referred to as the *span of control* or *span of* *authority*, there is a limit to the number of subordinates a manager can effectively supervise.*

> *The Old Testament account of the exodus from Egypt tells that the progress of the Israelites had ceased. The people were "wallowing in the wilderness." They "stood by Moses from the morning unto the evening" while Moses sat judging them. At that point, this discussion took place between Moses and his father-in-law, Jethro:*

> JETHRO: *What is this that you are doing for the people? Why do you sit alone and all the people stand about you from morning till evening?*
> MOSES: *Because the people come to me to inquire of God; when they have a dispute, they come to me, and I decide between a man and his neighbor.*
> JETHRO: *What you are doing is not good. You and the people with you will wear yourselves out, for this thing is too heavy for you; you are not able to perform it alone.... Choose able men from all the people ... and place such men over the people as rulers of thousands, of hundreds, of fifties, and of tens. And let them judge the people at all times; every great matter they shall bring to you, but any small matter they shall decide themselves; so it will be easier for you, and they will bear the burden with you.*

> *Moses took his father-in-law's advice, the plan worked, and the Israelites came out of the wilderness and reached their objective, the Promised Land.[5]*

The optimum span of management depends on several variables, such as the size of the organization, technology, specialization, and routines of activities.[6] In general, the optimum span depends on the supervisor's "burden": the greater the burden, the smaller the span; the less the burden, the greater the span.

Effects on Organizational Levels of Varying the Span

From Figure 7.3 (page 185) you can see how varying spans of management influence the organization structure. In the top example, *A*, the executive has an extremely wide span of 128 employees. In reality, it would be practically impossible for him or her to manage such a large group without additional managerial assistance. Assume that it is decided to reduce the president's span to only 4. Positions for 4 vice-presidents are created, and managers are selected to fill the position, as shown in *B*. The organization now has a total of 5 managers. The span of the president is 4 and each vice-president 32. Finally, management decides to reduce the spans of the vice-

---

* This generalization is based on the work of V. A. Graicunas, the noted French consultant, who wrote in 1933 that a given manager's span of management could be computed as follows: $R = n (2^{n-1} + n - 1)$, where R = the number of relationships, and n = the number of subordinates. Because a manager has three potential types of relationships—direct, group, and cross relationships—his or her span increases as new workers are added. Thus, two workers = 6 potential relationships, three workers = 18 potential relationships; and eighteen workers = 2,359,602 potential relationships.

For further information, see V. A. Graicunas, "Relationship in Organization," *Bulletin of the International Management Institute* (Geneva: International Labour Office, 1933), in *Papers on the Science of Administration*, ed. L. Gulick and L. Urwick (New York: Institute of Public Administration, 1937), pp. 181–187.

presidents to 4 also, as shown in C. So 16 new department head positions are created and managers selected. Each department head now has a span of 8 workers.

Note that as the span of management decreased, the number of required managerial positions increased, along with the number of hierarchical levels. Thus organizations with increasing numbers of employees have three organizational options:

1. Increase managerial spans.
2. Increase levels of hierarchy.
3. Increase both managerial spans and levels of hierarchy in some combination.

Reasons for using a wider span. Hierarchical levels tend to reduce the timeliness of information circulated from top to bottom in the organization. Furthermore, the greater the number of levels through which information must pass, the greater the chance for distortion. Finally, adding levels is expensive in that it requires additional managerial salaries. Notice that when IBM wanted to cut costs, the number of executives and management levels was reduced.

Having too small a span may result in the inefficient use of the manager's resources. Organizations therefore do not hastily make the decision to add levels. Instead, the foregoing arguments lead to wide spans and fewer levels.

The Japanese tend not to employ many managers to review and pass on the work of other managers. Instead, they trust employees to be competent and to have the company interest at heart. This leads to a simplified organizational structure that has helped many such companies become low-cost producers by reducing overhead and red tape.

For example, at one time Ford Motor Company had 11 layers of managers between the factory worker and the chairman, whereas Toyota Motor Company got by with only 6.[7]

Between 1940 and 1947, IBM completely eliminated one level of management in order to improve efficiency. What happens to the authority previously held by a position when a level is eliminated? In IBM's case, the authority was transferred to the level beneath the one eliminated.

At some point, though, the strains of increasingly large managerial spans ultimately result in managerial inefficiency and require a move to additional hierarchical levels.

Reasons for using a narrower span. Managers who have too broad a span of management will not have time to do the productive activities that make their organization successful.

Sometimes a narrow span results from reducing the work force at lower levels while retaining managers. For example, when New York City was in a fiscal crisis some years ago, it eliminated lower-level jobs but kept its supervisors. The result was a span of 1 to 5 instead of the 1 to 8–15 usually found in city government. In one department, 28 second-level managers supervised 29 workers.[8]

With too broad a span, a manager has little opportunity to devote much personal attention to individual subordinates. Subordinates may feel insecure not having close contact with their supervisors if they are on their own most of the time. But if the manager spends too much time interacting with subordinates in order to maintain a personal approach, he or she will have little opportunity to plan.

Using Different Spans at Different Levels

Does the span have to be the same throughout the organization? The answer is, "Certainly not!" In fact, the span may vary widely. Generally, the span of management becomes narrower as one moves from the bottom to the top of the organization. Studies of the span have shown that you are likely to find a span of 5 to 12 executives reporting to the chief executive officer, as shown in Table 7.1.

At the first-line management level, spans are much broader, commonly exceeding 30 to 40 subordinates when the work is routine, repetitive, unskilled, standardized, and manual.

> *At one time, the president of International Telephone and Telegraph (ITT) had the widest span shown in a National Conference Board listing of over 60 large manufacturing firms. The chief executive of ITT had 38 executives reporting to him.*[9]

Spans, Levels, and Employee Satisfaction

We have found from our studies of the effect of hierarchical levels on employee satisfaction that employees at higher levels of organizations are more satisfied then employees at lower levels. Also, higher-level managers in tall, steep organizational structures (see Figure 7.3) are more satisfied than higher-level managers in flat organizational structures. Conversely, lower-level managers in flat organizational structures are more satisfied than lower-level managers in tall ones.

What is your view?

Why do you think that lower-level managers in organizations with flat structures are more satisfied than their counterparts in organizations with tall, steep structures?

TABLE 7.1
Span of Management of Company Chief Executives in 93 Large Companies

Number of executives reporting to the chief executive	Number of companies
1	2
2	1
3	4
4	1
5	8
6	8
7	13
8	8
9	10
10	7
11	8
12	5
13	4
14	3
15 and over	11

Factors Affecting Span

Several years ago, a group with Lockheed attempted to develop a contingency approach to determining the correct span for a given manager's job.[10] Basically, these factors and their effect on the span were considered:

1. *Similarity of functions:* the more similar the functions performed by the work group, the larger the span.
2. *Geographic proximity:* the closer a work group is located physically, the larger the span.
3. *Complexity of functions:* the simpler and more repetitive the work functions performed by subordinates, the larger the span.
4. *Degree of direct supervision required:* the less direct supervision required, the larger the span.
5. *Degree of supervisory coordination required:* the less coordination required, the larger the span.
6. *Planning required of the manager:* the less planning required, the larger the span.
7. *Organizational assistance available to the supervisor:* the more assistance the supervisor receives in functions such as training, recruiting, and quality inspection, the larger the span.

What is your view?

What factors do you think influence the number of students that a teacher can effectively teach? Can a teacher's span of management (class size) ever be too small or too large? What happens in each case?

In summary, there is no magic formula for determining the correct size of a manager's span. The **contingency approach,** in which span size varies depending upon the particular situation, makes the most sense, according to Lawrence and Lorsch, who studied the organizational structure of firms in different industries. They found that the type of industry and related factors showed no consistent pattern as far as organizations were concerned.[11] The study of organizational design, especially the relationship between size and technology as determinants of an organization's structure, has been a favorite topic of discussion for a long time. Still, there is no one best design, size, or shape.

DEPARTMENTALIZATION

There are several ways in which organizations decide on the organizational pattern that will be used to group the various activities to be performed. Again, as mentioned earlier, the organizational process of determining how activities are to be grouped is called **departmentalization.** We will now discuss several forms of departmentalization. These forms, with some examples of each, are as follows:

1. *Function:* sales, accounting, production, customer service, or credit department.

2. *Product or service:* a bank's loan department, a hospital's coronary care unit, a state highway department.

3. *Territory:* Southwest Division, Northern Zone, International Operations.

4. *Customer:* industrial sales, retail sales, governmental sales, consumer sales.

5. *Process:* cutting department, relay assembly group, mailroom.

6. *Matrix:* used by many high-technology, energy-oriented, and consulting firms.

It should be noted, however, that most organizations use a combination of these forms; that is, most organizations will use more than one of these approaches in their groupings. However, most organizations use the functional approach at the top and others at lower levels.

Functional Departmental- ization

Functional departmentalization groups together common functions or similar activities to form an organizational unit. Thus, all individuals performing similar functions are grouped together, such as all sales personnel, all accounting personnel, all secretarial personnel, all nurses, all computer programmers, and so on. Figure 7.6 shows how functional departmentalization would be used at the top management level in dividing the three major business functions—production, sales, and finance.

Functional departmentalization may occur at any level of the organization and is normally found very near the top.

Advantages. The primary advantages of the functional approach are that it maintains the power and prestige of the major functions, creates efficiency through the principles of specialization, centralizes the organization's expertise, and permits tighter top-management control of the functions. For example, having all library-related activities on a college campus reporting to a common "library director" permits unified library policy to be carried out.

This approach also minimizes costly duplications of personnel and equipment. Having all computers and computer personnel in one department is less expensive than allowing several departments to have and supervise their own computer equipment and personnel.

Disadvantages. There are also many disadvantages to a functional approach. Some of these are that responsibility for total performance rests only at the top, and, since each manager oversees only a narrow function, the training of managers to take over the top position is limited. Organizations attempt

FIGURE 7.6
Functional departmentalization at the top management level.

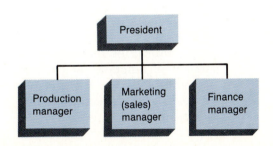

to remedy this by transferring managers so that they become "rounded," with experience in several functions.

Coordination between and among functions becomes complex and more difficult as the organization grows in size and scope. Finally, individuals identify with their narrow functional responsibilities, causing subgroup loyalties, identification, and tunnel vision.

Product Departmentalization

At some point, the problems of coordination under a functional approach become extremely complex and cumbersome, especially when rapid, timely decisions must be made. Since the functional approach is slow and cumbersome, some products that top management feels have the most potential may not receive the attention they deserve. And no one person is accountable for the performance of a given product line. What can be done to resolve this dilemma? One solution for many organizations is to shift to smaller, more natural semiautonomous miniorganizations built around specific products, each with its own functional capabilities. This is known as **product departmentalization.**

To capitalize on the information processing market in the 1980s, IBM reorganized its management structure. It changed from a functional orientation in which centralized manufacturing, marketing, and product development served all products to a product orientation, thereby placing functions in product groups.[12]

Examples of product approach. You have all observed examples of the product approach. For example, in department stores products may be grouped into departments such as sporting goods, housewares, appliances, furniture, and so on.

Consider these examples:

1. General Motors has the Saturn, Chevrolet, Pontiac, Oldsmobile, Buick, and Cadillac divisions.

2. The school you attend is probably grouped according to different "products," or areas of study: business, engineering, chemistry, computer science, and so forth.

3. A hospital's departments may be grouped by services rendered, such as surgery, obstetrics, coronary care, and so on.

Figure 7.7 demonstrates the grouping of major business activities of General Electric (GE). Note that each general business group is further broken down into various products, each with its own activities, such as manufacturing, sales, finance, and engineering. In essence, each group is run as a network of smaller companies within the policy guidelines and controls established by top management.

Advantages. Some of the advantages of the product approach are that attention can be directed toward specific product lines or services, coordination of functions at the product division level is improved, and profit responsibility can be better placed. Also, it is easier for the organization to develop several executives who have broad managerial experience in running a total entity.

Disadvantages. Some of the disadvantages of the product approach are that it requires more personnel and material resources, unnecessary duplication of resources and equipment may result, and top management shares a greater burden of establishing effective coordination and control. What a disaster it would be for the next economy-priced Chevrolet to have a body style almost identical to the top-priced Cadillac! Top management must utilize staff support to create and oversee policies that guide and limit the range of actions taken by its divisions.

Territorial Departmentalization

Territorial departmentalization, sometimes referred to as **regional, area,** or **geographic departmentalization,** is grouping activities according to the places where operations are located. A large company may group its sales activities into areas of the United States such as the Northeast region, Southeast region, and Southwest region. Branch banks are often set up this way, and athletic conferences are often at least nominally geographic. The old American Telephone & Telegraph Company (AT&T) had set up its major divisions this way—South Central Bell, New England Bell, Pacific Bell, Mountain Bell, and so on. When it was broken up in 1984, the seven new Bell companies were organized on this same basis. An example of territorial departmentalization in a large public school system is shown in Figure 7.8.

The advantages and disadvantages of this method are similar to those given for the product method. Such a grouping enables a division to focus on the unique needs of its area, but requires considerable top management coordination and control of each region.

Customer Departmentalization

Customer departmentalization is grouping activities in such a way that they focus on a given use of the product or service. This method is used primarily in grouping sales or service activities. Department stores, for example, may have a teen shop, a junior shop, or a bridal shop, not to mention infants' and children's departments. In each case, the sales effort can be focused on the specific attributes and needs of the client. Another example of customer departmentalization is the social service agency shown in Figure 7.9.

The major advantage of customer departmentalization is adaptability to a particular clientele. The disadvantages are difficulty of coordination, underutilization of resources, and competition among managers for special concessions for their own customers.

Process or Equipment Departmentalization

Process or **equipment departmentalization** is a grouping of activities that focuses on production processes or equipment. It is most frequently found in production. A manufacturing plant's activities may be grouped into drilling, grinding, welding, assembling, and finishing departments.

You will notice a modification of this organizational grouping when you buy food at a fast-service hamburger restaurant. Notice that some people are cooking the meat; others are cooking french fries; and others are preparing the drinks. There is usually a separate order taker, who accepts payment and assembles the order.

The process approach is advantageous when the machines or equipment used require special operating skills or are of such large capacity that to be

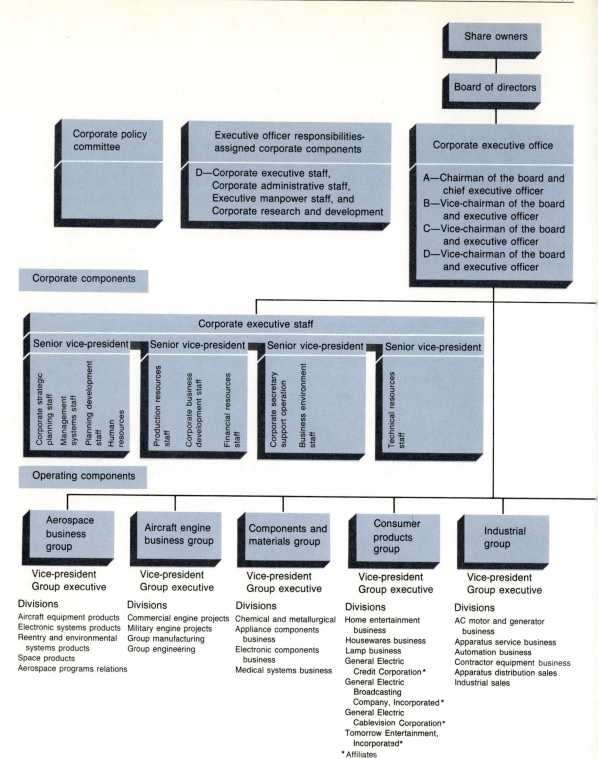

FIGURE 7.7
General Electric (GE)
organization chart.

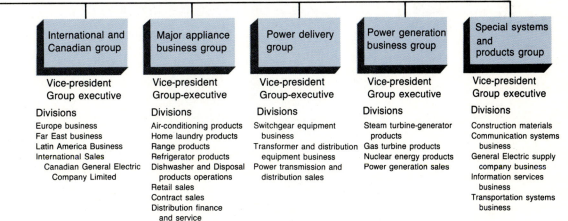

Executive officer responsibilities-assigned operating groups

A—Power delivery group and Power generation business group

B—Components and materials group, Consumer products products group, Industrial group, Major appliance business group

C—Aerospace business group, Aircraft engine business group, International and Canadian group, and Special systems and products group

Corporate administrative staff

Senior vice-president

- Corporate accounting operation
- Corporate consulting services
- Corporate education services
- Corporate employee relations operation
- Corporate facilities services
- Corporate legal operation
- Corporate public relations operation
- Corporate treasury operation
- Trust investment operations
- Washington corporate office

Executive manpower staff

Vice-president

Corporate research and development

Vice-president

Regional vice-presidents and commercial vice-president report to vice-president-corporate public relations

International and Canadian group

Vice-president
Group executive

Divisions

Europe business
Far East business
Latin America Business
International Sales
 Canadian General Electric
  Company Limited

Major appliance business group

Vice-president
Group-executive

Divisions

Air-conditioning products
Home laundry products
Range products
Refrigerator products
Dishwasher and Disposal
 products operations
Retail sales
Contract sales
Distribution finance
 and service
Customer relations
 and sales
  support operation

Power delivery group

Vice-president
Group-executive

Divisions

Switchgear equipment
 business
Transformer and distribution
 equipment business
Power transmission and
 distribution sales

Power generation business group

Vice-president
Group executive

Divisions

Steam turbine-generator
 products
Gas turbine products
Nuclear energy products
Power generation sales

Special systems and products group

Vice-president
Group executive

Divisions

Construction materials
Communication systems
 business
General Electric supply
 company business
Information services
 business
Transportation systems
 business

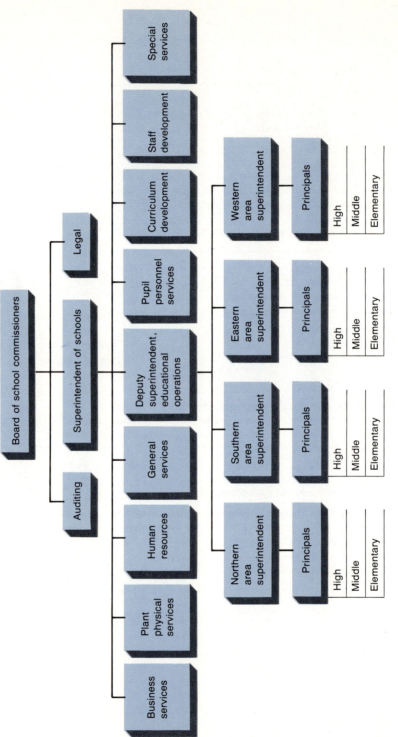

FIGURE 7.8
Example of geographic departmentalization in a public school system.

FIGURE 7.9
Example of customer or
client
departmentalization.

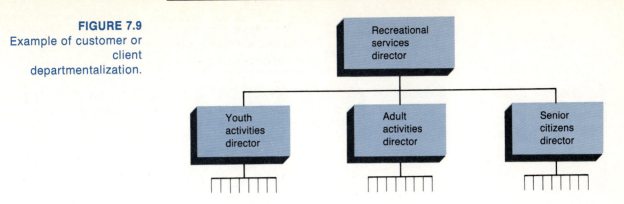

used economically they must be used all the time. This departmentalization approach is determined mainly on the basis of economic considerations.

Matrix Departmentalization

Matrix departmentalization is a hybrid type of departmentalization. It usually evolves from one or more of the other types of departments and is used in response to demands for unique blends of skill from different specialties in the organization. Say, for example, that a company had to complete a project that required close, integrated work between and among numerous functional specialties. The project could be designing a weapons system or building a prototype for a supersonic aircraft. The traditional approaches to organization we have discussed do not easily provide the flexibility to handle such complex assignments, which involve expertise from numerous functional areas of the organization. But the matrix approach involves ways to bring together organizational personnel from several specialties to complete limited-life tasks. As shown in Figure 7.10, matrix organizations result from the information of independent, limited-life teams of specialists necessary to achieve a specific goal. As shown in Figure 7.10, a project manager is given line authority over the team members during the life of the project.

Characteristics of matrix departmentalization. The matrix organization provides a hierarchy that responds quickly to changes in technology.[13] Hence, it is typically found in technically oriented organizations, such as Boeing, General Dynamics, NASA, and GE, in which scientists, engineers, or technical specialists work on sophisticated projects or programs. It is also used by companies with complex construction projects, such as Ebasco Services, Incorporated.

Under this system, team members' functional departments maintain personnel files, supervise administrative details, and assemble performance reports while their members are on assignment.

Advantages of the matrix approach. One advantage of the matrix approach is that it permits open communication and coordination of activities among the relevant functional specialists. Another advantage is that its flexibility enables the organization to respond rapidly to change. This response to change is the result of a self-imposed, professional desire to respond—not a response to hierarchically managed change effort. The use of this approach is essential in technologically oriented industries.

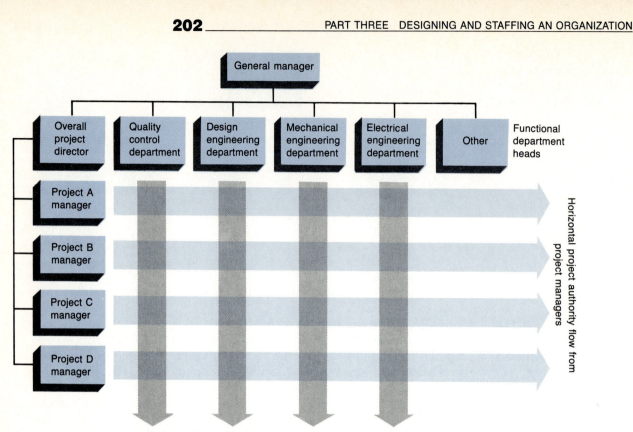

FIGURE 7.10
Example of matrix
departmentalization.

Disadvantages of the matrix approach. One disadvantage of matrix depart-mentalization relates to the lack of clarity and coordination in assigned roles. This, in turn, requires **facilitators,** who intervene to resolve clashes resulting from conflicting priorities.[14] This may place strong demands on team mem-bers in terms of the relative time devoted to each project.

> *Jean Johnson was a professor of management at Mid-Atlantic University.*
> *For the past year, she had been teaching in the management department*
> *and working half time on an interdisciplinary project within the university*
> *to improve the university computer system. For the life of the project, she*
> *had two bosses—the project director and the chairman of the manage-*
> *ment department. Until recently, this dual reporting had not caused any*
> *problem, but within the last month, the chairman of the management*
> *department had been putting increasing pressure on Jean to teach an*
> *additional course for the fall term. A professor had resigned suddenly,*
> *leaving the department shorthanded. The dilemma was that the computer*
> *study was nearing completion and required a major commitment of time*
> *and effort from all project members.*

In a matrix structure, who will decide on the members' advancement and promotion? Moreover, who will assign them to their next projects? Normally, the functional department head will make these decisions, based in part on reports received from project managers for whom the persons have worked. But functional specialists are often caught in the middle in disputes and torn between loyalties to project managers and to their functional department heads.

Finally there are disadvantages relating to the temporary nature of assignments under this form of departmentalization. Psychologically, one may never feel that one has "roots" while drifting from one project to another—perhaps unrelated—project. Moreover, the close personal ties formed while working on a project team may be severed by the project's completion, in which case an individual's reassignment requires a new set of working relationships with strangers.

Special managerial abilities required. Because of the complexities of the matrix approach, managers should have special abilities if they are to be successful. They should be adept at teamwork and coordination, but also be competitive; they should have the intrapreneurial viewpoint, and have persuasive and negotiating skills; and they should be opportunistic, fast reacting, and visionary.

Other Bases of Organizing Activities

Some other bases of organizing work and related activities could be time and numbers. For example, when employees perform shift work, each shift is headed by a supervisor. In the Social Security system, organization of work may be based on the Social Security numbers of cases being handled.

SUMMARY

This chapter has focused on the organizing function of management. Basically, the organizing process involves design of organization structure, grouping of activities, establishing the relationships among functions and tasks, and delegating the necessary authority to accomplish each task (to be covered in Chapter 8).

First, some basic concepts of organization were discussed. A formalized organization structure, often shown on an organization chart, represents the official organizational game plan for accomplishing work. Several key aspects of organizing shown by a formal organization chart are chain of command, unity of command, departmentalization, levels of hierarchy, span of management, and division of work.

Bureaucracy is a specific form of organization with a high degree of division of labor (or specialization), rigorous rules, clear authority-responsibility relationships, impersonal attitudes toward subordinates, employment and promotions based on merit, and lifelong employment. But it also tends to become rigid, inflexible, and burdened with red tape.

The types of organizations were then discussed. The line organization was shown to consist of those departments that directly accomplish the organization's objectives of producing and selling a product. The addition of staff specialists who also interact with line personnel results in a line-and-staff organization. Staff departments ordinarily advise, recommend, counsel, and serve line departments. They may also become functional departments with authority over an activity or function wherever it is found in the organization.

The principle of span of management states that there is a limit to the number of subordinates a manager can effectively supervise. Generally, spans are broader at lower levels of management and narrower at the top. Factors affecting span size include the similarity of the functions supervised, the geographic proximity of subordinates, the degree of direct supervision required, the degree of coordination necessary, and the managerial assistance available to the supervisor.

Organizations departmentalize their activities along several lines, using one of the following approaches: (1) function, (2) product, (3) territory or geography, (4) customer, (5) process or equipment, and (7) matrix departmentalization. The matrix form is a hybrid in that it is a temporary structure designed to utilize personnel specialties from various functional areas of the organization.

REVIEW QUESTIONS

1. What is an organization?
2. How does *organizing* differ from *organization?*
3. What role does division of labor play in the organizing function?
4. What do formal organization charts show?
5. What is the chain of command?
6. What is meant by unity of command?
7. What is bureaucracy?
8. How would you describe the *(a)* line, *(b)* line-and-staff, and *(c)* functional organization?
9. What is meant by *span of management?*
10. In what ways does the matrix organization differ from the more traditional approaches to departmentalization?

DISCUSSION QUESTIONS

1. In a large department store, there are three different shoe departments—men's, women's, and children's. They are located in the parts of the store devoted to these three types of customers. Should these three departments report to a single shoe manager, or should they report to the men's department manager, women's department manager, and children's department manager? What are the pros and cons of each reporting relationship?
2. From an employee's standpoint, what are the pros and cons of the supervisor having a very large span of management—say, 25 to 30 persons? What are the pros and cons of a very small span—6 to 8 persons?
3. Is bureaucracy all bad? What are some advantages of bureaucracy?
4. "The best way to make sure something gets done is to put two people in charge of it instead of one." Discuss this statement.
5. If a formal organization chart is needed to show how the organization is supposed to work, why is it that so many small- and medium-sized organizations do not have a formal chart drawn up? Explain.
6. Why do so many excellent companies use ad hoc task forces rather than matrix organizations?

LEARNING EXERCISE 7.1

Alternative Organization Structures*

Assume that an organizational unit has five basic functions or job activities to perform. The end result is a product or service consisting of activities, *V, W, X, Y,* and *Z.* These activities could, for example, be accounting, sales, engineering, manufac-

---

* This case adapted from George Strauss and Leonard Sayles, *Personnel* (Englewood Cliffs, NJ: Prentice-Hall, 1967), pp. 421 and 422.

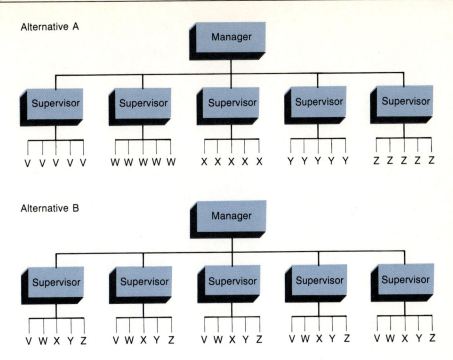

Alternative organization structures.

turing, and maintenance. Or perhaps they could be five subcomponents of manufacturing, such as receiving, cutting, sanding, assembling, and painting. There is a
total of five different sets or resources available to complete the task. One approach
is to place all V work under a common supervisor, all W work under a common
supervisor, and so on, as shown in alternative A. Another approach is to have five
supervisors, each of whom directs V, W, X, Y, and Z, as shown in alternative B.

Questions

1. Examine each of the organizational alternatives, pointing out the effect on such
   activities as coordination, innovation, personnel training required, quality of personnel, manager development, and others that you can identify.
2. In which situation would you prefer to be the manager? Why? In which would
   you prefer to be supervisor? Why?

**LEARNING
EXERCISE 7.2**

Change of Organization

Starting by himself in 1959, Jim Hardy built Hardy Pest Control until it operated in
four states and employed over 1000 persons.

In 1978, Hardy hired Derek Temple as vice-president of marketing. Temple, exceptionally bright and articulate, had previously owned an advertising agency. Before
Temple was hired, all the employees in each local area reported to the local manager,
and the service personnel were also the salespeople for the firm.

Temple persuaded Hardy to specialize by separating sales from service and
placing all sales personnel under Temple. Under this new arrangement, even though
sales personnel operated from the local manager's office, they reported organizationally to a district sales manager, usually located in another city (see Hardy organization chart). The sales manager positions, since they were new, had to be staffed
with office help and supplied with office space.

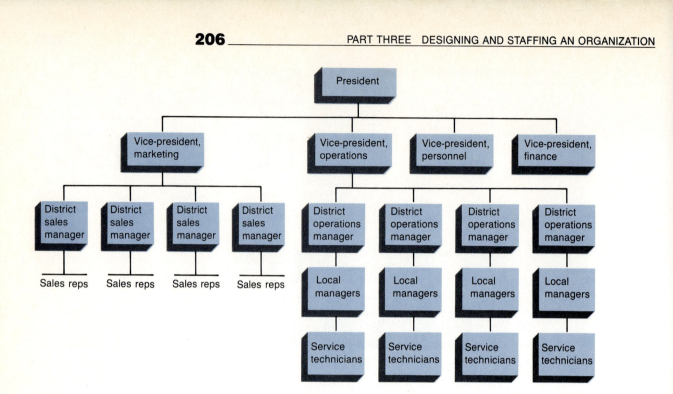

Hardy organization chart.

Questions

1. Does the new organizational structure for Hardy Pest Control result in a more logical arrangement of activities? Why?
2. What do you see as the pros and cons of the new structure?
3. What do you think will be the position of *(a)* the local managers and *(b)* the vice-president for operations under the new structure?
4. Do you think the organizational change will be effective? Why?

NOTES

1. Adam Smith, *An Inquiry into the Nature and Causes of the Wealth of Nations* (1776).
2. Matthew 6:24.
3. Henri Fayol, *General and Industrial Management,* trans. Constance Storrs (New York: Pitman Publishing, 1949).
4. Max Weber, *The Theory of Social and Economic Organization* (New York: Oxford University Press, 1947).
5. Adapted from Exodus 18:13–27.
6. Robert D. Dewar and Donald P. Simet, "A Level Specific Prediction of Spans of Control Examining the Effects of Size, Technology, and Specialization," *Academy of Management Journal* 24 (March 1981): 5–24.
7. "Trust: The New Ingredient in Management," *Business Week,* July 6, 1981, pp. 104–105.
8. "NYC Management Study Finds Unnecessary Jobs," *Mobile Press,* February 20, 1978, p. 9-A.
9. "Corporate Organization Structures," Conference Board Report No. 598, 1973, p. 56.
10. C. W. Barkdull, "Span of Control—a Method of Evaluation," *Michigan Business Review* 15 (May 1963): 27–29; and Harold Steiglitz, "Span of Control," *Management Record* 24 (September 1962): 27.

11. Paul R. Lawrence and Jay W. Lorsch, *Organization and Environment* (Boston: Graduate School of Business Administration, 1967).

12. "No. 1's Awesome Strategy," *Business Week*, June 8, 1981, pp. 84–90.

13. "How to Stop the Buck Short of the Top," *Business Week*, January 16, 1978, pp. 82–83. This is an excellent article on the matrix organization and should be read if you are really interested in this subject.

14. "How Ebasco Makes the Matrix Method Work," *Business Week*, June 15, 1981, pp. 126–131.

SUGGESTIONS FOR FURTHER STUDY

AIKEN, MICHAEL; BACHARACH, SAMUEL B.; and FRENCH, J. LAWRENCE. "Organizational Structure, Work Process, and Proposal Making in Administrative Bureaucracies." *Academy of Management Journal* 23 (December 1980): 631–652.

BOBBITT, H. RANDOLPH, JR., and FORD, JEFFREY D. "Decision-Maker Choice as a Determinant of Organizational Structure." *Academy of Management Review* 5 (January 1980): 13–23.

COHEN, ALLEN R. et al. *Effective Behavior in Organizations*, rev. ed. Homewood, IL.: Irwin, 1980, pp. 121–122.

EGAN, JACK. "What Makes Giant GE Keep on Growing." *U.S. News & World Report*, November 23, 1987, pp. 48–49.

GLISSON, CHARLES A., and MARTIN, PATRICIA YANCEY. "Productivity and Efficiency in Human Service Organizations as Related to Structure, Size, and Age." *Academy of Management Journal* 23 (March 1980): 21–37.

GRIFFIN, RICKY W. "Relationships Among Individual, Task Design, and Leader Behavior Variables." *Academy of Management Journal* 23 (December 1980): 665–683.

GRINYER, PETER H., and YASAI-ARDEKANI, MASOUD. "Dimensions of Organizational Structure: A Critical Replication." *Academy of Management Journal* 23 (September 1980): 405–421.

PAULSON, STEVEN K. "Organizational Size, Technology, and Structure: Replication of a Study of Social Service Agencies among Small Retail Firms." *Academy of Management Journal* 23 (June 1980): 341–347.

PEREIRA, JOSEPH. "Gillette Co. Sets Reorganization." *The Wall Street Journal*, November 20, 1987, p. 14.

WALTON, ERIC J. "The Comparison of Measures of Organization Structure." *Academy of Management Review* 6 (January 1981): 155–160.

8

Using Delegation to Make Organizations More Effective

Learning Objectives

After studying the material in this chapter, you should be able to do the following:
- ☐ Explain what delegation is and how it is done.
- ☐ State why managers are reluctant to delegate authority.
- ☐ Define authority and explain its use.
- ☐ Describe line, staff, and functional types of authority, and identify causes of line-staff conflict.
- ☐ Explain where power comes from and how it can be used.
- ☐ Describe responsibility and accountability and understand that they can't be delegated.
- ☐ Discuss the factors that determine the extent of centralization and decentralization.
- ☐ Explain why and how committees are used.
- ☐ Describe how informal organizations are formed and operate.

Outline of the Chapter

The role of delegation
How delegation occurs
Reasons for delegating
Why managers fail to delegate
Why employees don't accept delegation
The role of authority
What is authority?
Sources of authority
Types of authority
The role of power
How power is obtained
How power can be used
Limits on the use of authority and power

The role of responsibility and accountability
Responsibility and accountability can't be delegated
Equality of authority and responsibility?
The role of centralization
Centralization versus decentralization
Factors affecting the degree of centralization
The role of committees
Types of committees
Advantages of committees
Disadvantages of committees
Use of task forces
The role of informal organizations
Functions performed
Problems created
Summary

Some Important Terms

delegation	referent power
authority	expert power
responsibility	responsibility
formal authority	accountability
acceptance theory of authority	centralization
line authority	decentralization
staff authority	committees
functional authority	standing committees
power	ad hoc committees
reward power	hidden agenda
coercive power	logrolling
legitimate power	task forces
control-of-information power	informal organization

OPENING CASE

Markham's Lumber—Delegation at Work

James Markham had grown up in the lumber business, and Markham's Lumber had served the community since 1943. A year ago the company had consisted of two lumberyards with 19 employees, as the following chart shows:

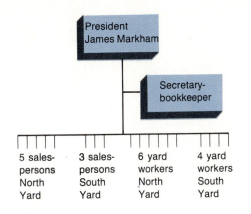

The salespersons took orders on the phone and served customers who came to the business. Yard workers cut lumber to customer specifications, loaded and unloaded trucks, delivered lumber to customers, and did other odd jobs.

Markham usually spent his mornings in the larger North Yard and his afternoons at the South Yard. He took the South Yard's daily receipts and paperwork home with him and gave them the next morning to the secretary-bookkeeper, who billed customers and paid invoices.

Markham did all the lumber buying for the two yards. He especially enjoyed getting out and calling on several major accounts who were old friends, but recently the demands of the job had caused him to curtail these activities.

The major part of Markham's time was spent directly supervising each yard. A problem that often arose was that salespeople (who received a commission on sales) took orders and made delivery promises that the yard couldn't meet. This was a constant source of conflict, and Markham frequently had to intervene to resolve the situation. Moreover, turnover of sales and yard people had increased to the point where Markham had to devote much time to interviewing, hiring, and orienting the new personnel.

Last year, a banker friend suggested that Markham's Lumber had outgrown its original organization structure. He suggested that each yard be run as a separate profit center, with a yard manager reporting to Markham. Each manager would make the major supervisory decisions at his yard, including coordination of the sales and yard activities and orienting and training new employees, and would be responsible for results. Markham would still do the wholesale buying and sell to the major external accounts, and he would have more time with his friends in the business.

Six months ago, Markham made the change, as shown in the following chart, promoting one of his salespeople to the South Yard manager position and hiring a new person to run the larger North Yard. Things have run so well that Markham has been considering something he'd given up on for years—acquiring from a friend another small yard in the western part of town.

209

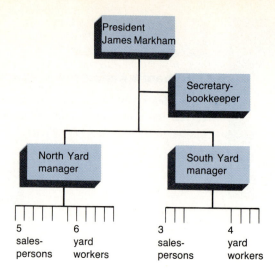

Do you think the banker's analysis of the situation was correct? If so, what do you think of his suggested solution? ■

THE IMPORTANCE OF DELEGATION in organizations is shown by this case. In the previous chapter, we discussed some of the basic concepts of organizing human endeavors into formal organizations. As was indicated, an organization's success is based on people's knowing what its objectives are, understanding what activities they are to perform, and then performing those activities effectively.

But how do people know what their duties are? Those duties must be delegated to them by their managers. That's what this chapter is about: explaining how delegation makes organizations more effective.

THE ROLE OF DELEGATION

Delegation is the process by which managers allocate authority downward to the people who report to them and assign responsibility for how authority is used. **Authority** is the _right_ to do something, or to tell someone else to do it, in order to reach organizational objectives. **Responsibility** is the obligation that is created when an employee accepts the manager's delegation of authority.

How Delegation Occurs

Delegation occurs when the following actions take place:

1. The manager assigns objectives or duties to the lower-level employee.
2. The manager grants the authority needed to accomplish the objectives or duties.
3. The employee accepts the delegation, whether implicitly or explicitly, thereby creating an obligation or responsibility.
4. The manager holds the employee accountable for results.

Effective delegation is a major difference between successful managers and unsuccessful ones.

Captain William Jones was a West Point graduate with many excellent characteristics needed for effective leadership. He was conscientious and energetic and had a fine mind. Jones's unit, however, was considered the poorest in the regiment, even though Jones devoted 14 to 16 hours each day to carrying out his duties.

The amount of time Jones spent on the job was symptomatic not of inefficient troops or officers but of Jones's inability to delegate. When the captain did delegate, which was not very often, he would constantly check to see if things were being done properly and in general "breathe down the necks" of those to whom he had supposedly given authority. Consequently, Jones's troops were continually frustrated in using their own ideas and methods and took the attitude, "Well, let's not worry about it, because no matter what we do, he'll probably come back and do it over anyway."

Reasons for Delegating

There are many reasons for delegating. For one, delegating tasks enables managers to accomplish more than if they attempted to handle every task personally. Also, delegation allows managers to focus their energies on the most crucial, high-priority tasks and the things they want to do. Notice in the opening case that, after delegating some authority, Markham had time to consider acquiring another lumberyard.

Delegation also enables subordinates to grow and develop, even if this means learning from their mistakes. Failure to delegate may result in lack of preparation for future managerial responsibilities. For example, when Robert Ingalls, founder of Ingalls Industries, died of a stroke in 1951, his once-proud shipbuilding company ran into heavy seas and began to founder. Ingalls' son had not been prepared to assume command, and the organization went steadily downhill until the shipbuilding subsidiary was purchased at a very low price by Litton Industries in 1961.

The Japanese have used delegation in the form of quality circles to improve performance and output. See TIPS 13.2 for suggestions for the effective use of quality circles.

Delegation is needed because managers do not always have the knowledge needed to make decisions. They may see "the big picture" but not know enough about the problem to act intelligently, as the following example shows.

The U.S. Postal Service is usually viewed as a surly, stodgy bureaucracy with a vast disregard for its clients. In recent years, though, Postmaster General Preston R. Tisch has tried to revitalize the USPS by emphasizing concepts such as "service" and "marketing" and using computer-based automatic letter sorters to boost productivity and lower labor costs.

But Tisch, who was formerly president and chief operating officer of Loews Corporation, a conglomerate owned by his family, has been criticized for his relaxed management style at the Postal Service. He is charged with not being enough of a strong, hands-on manager. At congressional hearings, he passes off to subordinates questions requiring detailed responses. He defends his lack of involvement in the details of the mail system by saying, "My approach is to really understand what's going on and to direct people to make things happen."[1]

Why Managers Fail to Delegate

Delegation is critical to effective management, but some managers may fail to delegate, or may delegate weakly, for several reasons. Some of the more important reasons are listed here.

1. Managers may feel more powerful if they retain decision-making privileges for themselves.

2. Managers do not care to face the risk that employees will exercise authority poorly.

3. Managers believe that employees lack the ability to exercise good judgment—that "I can do it better myself." The "indispensable tiger" described in Figure 8.1 is an example of the way many managers act toward their employees.

4. Managers feel that workers would prefer not to have broader decision-making latitude.

5. Managers fear that employees will perform tasks so effectively that their own positions will be threatened.

What is your view?

Can you think back to a situation in which you were reluctant to delegate authority to someone else? The person may have been an employed subordinate, a friend, a little brother or sister, or perhaps your spouse or child. Why were you unwilling to delegate?

On the other hand, can you think of a situation in which authority was delegated to you, but you felt uneasy about your new responsibility or even turned it down? Why?

Why Employees Don't Accept Delegation

Not all the barriers to effective delegation are found in superiors, however. Employees themselves may resist accepting delegation of authority. First, delegation adds to their responsibilities and accountabilities. It is sometimes easier to go to your manager to resolve a problem than to make the decision yourself.

Second, there is always the chance that you will exercise your new authority poorly and receive criticism, as was frequently the case with subordinates in Captain Jones's command. Third, some employees lack self-confidence and feel much pressure when granted greater decision-making authority.

Ted Augusta* had 42 years' seniority with the railroad. Every time a supervisory or management job opened up, he had to refuse it before it could be offered to the person with the next highest seniority, and he always did. "I have enough problems of my own without having to worry about other people's," he said in explanation of his unwillingness to accept responsibility.

Delegation is fundamental to effective management. If an employee can answer affirmatively the questions in TIPS 8.1, it can be assumed that delegation is being used effectively.

* Name disguised.

FIGURE 8.1
The indispensable tiger.

SOURCE: *Management Review* 50 (October 1961):46–47. Copyright 1961 by the American Management Association, Inc. Reprinted by permission of the publisher. All rights reserved.

A powerful old tiger, the leader of his pack, was preparing to go on a hunt. Gathering the other tigers about him, he said, ''We must go out into the plains and hunt, for the winter is coming. You young fellows come with me; perhaps you will learn a thing or two.''

The young tigers were pleased to hear this, for the old fellow had hitherto shown no interest in tiger development. He usually left them behind when he went foraging, and they were tired of doing nothing but keeping order among the cubs and performing other routine tasks.

The first day out, the old tiger spotted a herd of elephants. ''Here's your chance, Bernard,'' he said to one of the younger tigers. ''Look at it as a challenge.''

But Bernard had no idea how to go about hunting. With a roar, he rushed at the elephants, who ran off in all directions. ''It looks as though I'll have to do the job myself,'' said the leader philosophically. And so he did.

The next day, the tigers came upon a herd of water buffalo. ''Suppose you take over now, Jerome,'' said the old tiger, and Jerome, reluctant to ask silly questions but determined to do his best, crept up on the grazing buffalo. He leaped straight at the largest of them, but the big buffalo tossed him to the ground, and Jerome was lucky to escape in one piece. Mortified, he crept back to the group.

''No, no, no!'' said the old tiger. ''What's happening to performance around here?''

''But you never taught us how to do it,'' cried one of the young tigers. The old tiger was in no mood to listen. ''The rest of you stay where you are,'' he growled, ''and I will do the job myself.'' And so he did.

''I can see,'' said the old tiger, as the others gathered admiringly about him, ''that none of you is yet ready to take my place.'' He sighed. ''Much as I hate to say it, I seem to be indispensable.''

Time brought little change. The old tiger sometimes took the younger ones along with him on hunts, and occasionally he let one of them try to make a kill. But having received no instruction, they were unequal to the task. And the old tiger still made no effort to teach the others his tricks; he had forgotten that he himself was a product of tiger-to-tiger coaching.

One day, when he had grown quite old, the tiger met a friend—a wise lion he had known for years. Before long, the tiger was launched on his favorite topic of conversation: the lack of initiative in the younger generation.

''Would you believe it?'' he asked the lion. ''Here I am, getting a bit long in the tooth, and I still have to do all the hunting for my pack. There seems to be no one of my stripe around.'' ''That's odd,'' said the lion. ''I find the younger lions in my pack take well to instruction. Some of them are carrying a good bit of responsibility. In fact,'' he continued, ''I'm thinking about retiring next year and letting the younger fellows take over.''

''I envy you,'' said the tiger. ''I'd take things easier and relax myself if I only saw a little leadership material around me.''

The old tiger sighed and shook his head. ''You can't imagine,'' he said, ''what a burden it is to be indispensable.''

MORAL: Managers who won't share the burden must bear the burden.

TIPS 8.1   Test of Effective Delegation

Effective delegation occurs when a subordinate can answer all the following questions affirmatively.

1. Is there at least one written record to which I can refer to determine my authority?
2. Did I participate in establishing my authority?
3. Is my authority tailored to my accountabilities?
4. Can I plan ahead to accomplish my accountability with the knowledge that I have the requisite authority?
5. Can I normally act without fear of exceeding my authority or having my action reversed by higher authority?

6. Do my superiors, subordinates, and peers have sufficient knowledge of the authority I enjoy?
7. Has an adequate control and feedback system been established—for both my boss's benefit and mine—about how I am carrying out my authority?

If it is not possible to answer these questions positively, the requisite authority is probably lacking, and the weakness should be remedied before proceeding.

SOURCE: Dale D. McConkey, *No Nonsense Delegation* (New York: AMACOM, a division of American Management Association, 1974), p. 154. Reprinted by permission.

As has been shown, or implied, there are at least four factors involved in delegation. Those factors are authority, power, responsibility, and accountability. These interact to make delegation effective—or ineffective. We now discuss each of these.

THE ROLE OF AUTHORITY

Authority is constantly being used, but its nature and role are not well understood. We need to start by seeing what authority is and where it originates.

What Is Authority?

As shown earlier, authority is the right to do something, or get someone else to do it, in order to reach organizational objectives. It can be compared to the nervous system of the human body. Without the brain and nerves, the body could not function. Without a system of authority, an organization could not function. The following are some common examples of the use of authority.

A police officer gives a motorist a ticket for driving 45 mph in a 30-mph zone. The officer's authority derives from the city council.

In 1978, Henry Ford, chairman of Ford Motor Company, fired Lee Iacocca as its president. Ford's authority came from the company's board of directors, which got its power from the stockholders.

The department manager at Macy's assigned the work shifts for her personnel during the Christmas holidays. Her authority was delegated by the store manager.

In each of these examples, the individual exercised the right to exert authority over others. Authority results from the delegation or shifting of authority from upper to lower positions in the organization.

Sources of Authority

Basically there are two contradictory views regarding the source of a manager's authority: the formal theory and the acceptance theory.

Formal authority view. According to the **formal authority** concept, authority is conferred; authority exists because someone was granted it. This view traces the origin of authority upward to its ultimate source, which for business organizations is the owners or stockholders. The head nurse in a hospital has authority granted by the nursing director, who has been granted it by the hospital board, which has been granted it by the stockholders (if a private hospital) or the public (if a public hospital). The formal theory is consistent with the definition of authority we presented in the previous section.

What is your view?

You are probably reading the material in this textbook because it has been assigned by an instructor. What is the source of the instructor's authority to make such an assignment, to give exams, and to assign you a grade in this course?

Acceptance of authority view. The **acceptance theory of authority** disputes the idea that authority can be conferred. Acceptance theorists (chiefly behaviorists) believe that a manager's authority originates only when it has been accepted by the group or individual over whom it is being exercised. Chester Barnard stated this position when he wrote: "If a directive communication is accepted by one to whom it is addressed, the authority for him is confirmed or established."[2] Thus acceptance of the directive becomes the basis of action. Disobedience of such a communication by an employee is a denial of its authority for him or her. Therefore, under this definition, as shown in Figure 8.2, the decision about whether an order has authority lies with the persons to whom it is addressed and does not reside in "persons of authority" or those who issue those orders, as the following example implies.

The Jena High football team, which had lost all its games the past year, was having a tough preseason conditioning drill under its new head coach, Joe Wakefield. Wakefield was an exacting taskmaster known for his ability to build winners. Of the original 60 players, 30 had quit, primarily as a result of the two daily practice drills in 98-degree heat.

After a grueling three-hour workout, Wakefield blew his whistle and assembled the team, telling them that they were now in good enough

FIGURE 8.2
Differences in emphasis of formal and acceptance views of authority.

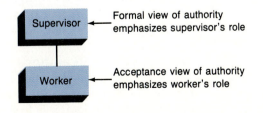

physical condition for him to institute a new daily drill—a one-mile run in full pads and helmet. Hank Fellows, the previous year's team captain, told Wakefield that this was too demanding and that the players were too exhausted to do it. Wakefield chewed the group out for several minutes and indicated that anybody who didn't run the mile could quit the team. He blew his whistle, and every player began to jog around the field. To Wakefield's amazement, however, on reaching the end of the field, all but 3 of the 30 players went straight to the dressing room.

Formal authority view generally accepted. We have defined authority in line with the position taken by the formal theorists—that authority is a right a manager has been formally granted by the organization. As we will shortly point out, though, the acceptance theorists seem to be confusing authority with power or leadership, which involves the ability of a manager to influence employees to accept his or her authority.

But the behaviorists do make the point that *to be effective,* managers are certainly very dependent on acceptance off their authority.

In the early 1950s, Howard Hughes's capricious leadership chased off from Hughes Tool Company many outstanding managers and scientists who refused to accept his authority. Many of them achieved outstanding success, and one, Tex Thornton, founded Litton Industries, today one of the nation's top industrial firms.

In the example given earlier, Coach Wakefield exercised authority, but the team's failure to accept his authority may cost him his job or at least place him in a very embarrassing position.

What is your view?
Two ways subordinates resist authority are by quitting or by refusing to perform duties. Can you think of other ways that subordinates might resist a manager's authority?

In Chapter 12, we will examine some of the ways in which managers can gain acceptance of their authority through the use of effective leadership.

Types of Authority

At this point, we must add a complicating factor to the discussion—that is, the distinction between types of authority. This problem is a major source of misinterpretation and confusion among managers and students of management.

Line authority. **Line authority** is the authority that managers exercise over their immediate subordinates. It is command authority and corresponds directly to the chain of command. It is directed downward through the organizational levels. As shown in Figure 8.3, both line and staff department managers exercise line authority over their immediate subordinates. In fact, all managers exercise line authority over their employees.

Staff authority. **Staff authority** is the right possessed by staff units or specialists to advise, recommend, or counsel line personnel. It does not give the staff members the authority to dictate to the line or command them to take certain actions. In fact, it is frequently directed upward, toward those above

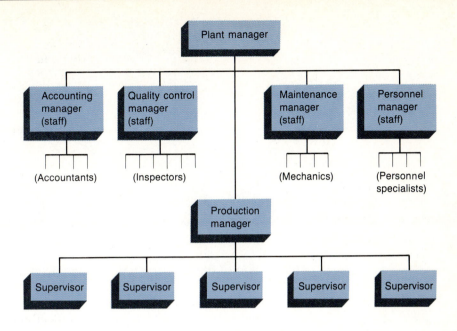

FIGURE 8.3
Staff and line department heads have line authority within their departments.

the staff members. This is the most common type of staff relationship with the line departments and is dependent on staff's degree of influence.

Functional authority. **Functional authority** is the strongest relationship staff can have with line units. When granted functional authority by top management, a staff specialist has the right to command line units in matters regarding the functional activity in which the staff specializes. Some examples of different staff specialists exercising functional authority are as follows:

1. A safety specialist may have authority to command line laboratory managers to shut down a lab when noxious fumes reach a certain level.

2. The quality control inspector may have authority to require production departments to complete satisfactorily a production run that is felt not to meet standards.

3. The legal department may be able to modify or alter the wording of all contracts that obligate the organization to outside entities such as dealers, suppliers, or contractors.

4. Personnel departments have functional authority to tell managers of other departments how to implement Equal Employment Opportunity (EEO) and affirmative action programs (AAPs).

As shown in Figure 8.4, functional authority, when granted to staff units, may violate the principle of unity of command and in so doing cause many organizational conflicts. The *overuse* of functional authority also undermines the integrity of the line departments that are held accountable for results. For this reason, functional authority should be granted to staff to be exercised only in crucial matters.

Sources of line-staff conflict. Several factors may cause conflicts between and among line and staff departments and personnel (see Chapter 7 for the

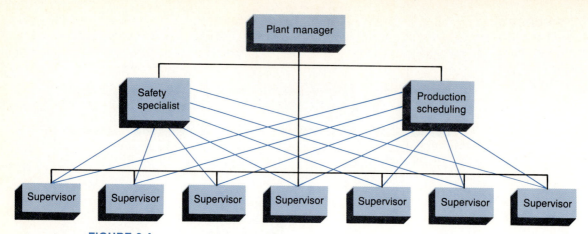

FIGURE 8.4
Organization chart showing functional authority of staff.

discussion of the different types of organizations). These include the following:

1. Staff personnel are frequently younger and more highly educated than line employees, which may create a generation gap.

2. Staff personnel may exceed their authority and attempt to give orders directly to line personnel.

3. Line personnel may feel that staff specialists do not fully understand line problems and think their advice is not workable.

4. Staff may attempt to take credit for ideas implemented by line; conversely, line may not acknowledge the role staff has played in helping it resolve problems.

5. Because staff is highly specialized, it may use technical terms and language that line cannot understand.

6. Top management may not have clearly communicated the extent of authority staff has in its relationship with line.

7. Organizationally, staff departments are placed in relatively high positions close to top management; lower-level line departments tend to resent this.

If it is to resolve conflicts of this nature, top management must clearly convey the extent of its delegation to staff departments. Moreover, to be effective, *staff departments must realize that their job is to sell, not to tell*—that is, to sell a line department on their ideas, not tell them how to function.

Staff specialists often operate as if the line were there to assist them instead of the other way around. They often forget that staff is merely personnel added to help the line be more effective. Staff specialists must keep in mind that they are useless if they do not do this. Management can help by constantly emphasizing that the only real results are the results of line activities. Many companies, including American Telephone & Telegraph Company (AT&T), Exxon, and IBM, systematically rotate line and staff personnel among the production, sales, accounting, engineering, purchasing, and other departments. This enables managers to better appreciate the roles of line and staff and allows them to work smoothly with each.

THE ROLE OF POWER

The manager's possession of authority is not always sufficient in itself to assure that subordinates will respond as the manager desires. In such cases, a manager must use some other approach, as the following example illustrates.

Mary Fleming was named supervisor of the Number 2 paper machine at the Northern Mill. She was the first female supervisor to be named to such a traditionally male position. The position carried much authority with it, but Mary was intelligent enough to realize that her authority alone wouldn't get her workers to accept her and meet performance standards.

Several of the employees tested her immediately by taking extended work breaks and making some snide remarks within her hearing range about the department's "skirt supervisor." Mary ignored this behavior the first few days and felt that the worst thing she could do was to overreact and come on too strong. But the resistance persisted. Mary had a meeting with Carl White and Pete Antheim, the two senior members of the department, and asked for their advice about handling the situation. White and Antheim seemed flattered by being consulted and told Mary they'd handle the situation. The problems never recurred, and, six months after the incident, Mary's group was highly supportive of her leadership, and the "female department head" issue had been forgotten.

In this case, Mary used both authority and the human-relations approach to support her position. But what could she have done if the employees had still not accepted the authority of her position? To be effective, a manager must sometimes also exercise **power,** which is the ability to influence individuals, groups, decisions, or events. As shown in Figure 8.5, there are various combinations of power and authority. Effective managers find the combination that is best for them and their people.

FIGURE 8.5
The authority-power
combinations.

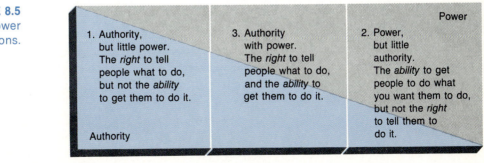

1. Authority, but little power. The *right* to tell people what to do, but not the *ability* to get them to do it.

Authority

3. Authority with power. The *right* to tell people what to do, and the *ability* to get them to do it.

Power

2. Power, but little authority. The *ability* to get people to do what you want them to do, but not the *right* to tell them to do it.

The belief of Sir Dalberg Acton that "power tends to corrupt, and absolute power corrupts absolutely" is widespread in our culture. In recent years, however, there has been an increasing awareness that power is not necessarily all bad—that the use of power may be essential for the effective accomplishment of individual, organizational, and social goals. In fact, several best-selling books have been published with such titles as *Power: The Inner Experience*,[3] *Power! How to Get It, How to Use It*,[4] and *Winning Through Intimidation*.[5] Interest has also revived in the seventeenth-century classic treatise on power *The Prince*, by Niccolò Machiavelli. According to Machiavelli, leaders can be effective by (1) winning people's love or (2) acting forcefully in order to make people respect them.[6] Interest in power has also been generated by David McClelland's research (covered in Chapter 12) showing that a high need for power is an important characteristic of successful managers.

How Power Is Obtained

As shown by French and Raven, there are many sources from which power can be obtained.[7] Six of these sources have been translated into types of power, as shown by Figure 8.6. They are classified as follows:

1. **Reward power** arises from the number of positive rewards (money, protection, etc.) that people perceive a potential leader to control.

2. **Coercive power** results from people's perceived expectation that punishment (being fired, reprimanded, etc.) will follow if they do not comply with the aims of a potential leader.

3. **Legitimate power** develops from internalized values that dictate that a leader has a legitimate right to influence subordinates. Under this view, one has an obligation to accept that influence simply because a person is designated boss or leader.

4. **Control-of-information power** derives from knowledge that others do not have. Some people use this method by either giving or withholding needed information, as shown in MAP 8.1.

5. **Referent power** is based on people's identification with a potential leader and what that leader stands for or symbolizes. Personal charisma, charm, courage, and other traits are important factors in the exercise of referent power.

6. **Expert power** results from a potential leader's having expertise or knowledge in an area in which that leader wants to influence others.[8]

FIGURE 8.6
Sources of managerial power.

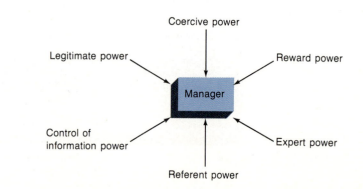

Management Application and Practice 8.1   Information Is Power

A recent arrival on the information technology scene is the "executive information system." Executive information systems, as offered by a number of firms, allow executives to bypass the usual information system channels and quickly discover the answers to their own data needs. Suddenly, these systems allow the CEO to go outside the "palace guard" to obtain his or her own information. Executives using the new systems typically use an assistant to fetch the data they want. However, some executives sit right down at the computer terminal in their office and run it themselves.

This has made life uncomfortable for staff departments such as accounting, inventory control, marketing research, and electronic data processing. Whereas personnel in these departments once controlled what executives saw and heard, the advent of these information systems has allowed executives to avoid dependency on these departments. As a result,

staff groups and electronic data processing (EDP) managers fear that their influence may drop. For example, John Rockart, director of the Sloan School of Management's Center for Information System Research at MIT, says, "If you believe information is power, anytime you change the information flow, you change the power structure."

At Westinghouse, the system has removed a favorite excuse of staff officers. In the past, when a senior executive called and asked about a report requested several weeks earlier, the answer often was, "We haven't seen the figures yet." Now the top executive can challenge that excuse: "Why haven't you seen them? You've had them for two days, and I'm looking at them right now."

SOURCE: "Some Chief Executives Bypass and Irk Staffs in Getting Information," *The Wall Street Journal,* January 12, 1983, p. 1.

Table 8.1 gives some examples of these power sources. Do not infer from this discussion or from Figure 8.6 that a given manager draws upon all of these sources of power. Rather, each manager finds his or her own source of strength from one or more sources.

Ed McMahon proclaimed on the Tonight Show *that G. Dale Murray is "a ball of fire who lights up everything he touches." Whether that is true or not, Murray has the uncanny ability to create an image of Murray Industries' Chris-Craft as "a high-glamour business [with] real charisma." He and associates such as McMahon and General Alexander Haig have led Chris-Craft from sales of $26 million in 1981 to around $200 million in 1986.[9]*

What is your view?

What kind of power is being exercised when (1) a masked gunman orders people in a bank to face the wall with their hands over their heads and they do it, and (2) three of the players on Coach Wakefield's team obediently run the 20 laps as ordered?

How Power Can Be Used

Some managers believe that if a manager has power (the wherewithal to influence others, such as knowledge sources or access to authority) and shares it with others, it is diminished. Actually, the best way to expand power

**TABLE 8.1
Examples of Power
Sources**

Situation	Source of power
1. Jones volunteers for weekend work because supervisor promises him a highly desirable job assignment.	Reward
2. Supervisor directs employee to comply with company policy or be fired. Employee complies.	Coercive
3. Visitor stops car at the company gate in response to a uniformed security officer's upraised hand.	Legitimate
4. Graduate assistant quiets the class, telling them that the professor is out ot town, and since he (the assistant) wrote the final exam, he will now review how to study for it.	Control of information
5. Company president and founder is hard-driving, innovative, and outspoken, puts in 75 hours a week on the job, and has a charismatic personality and the ability to inspire others.	Referent
6. Crucial piece of equipment breaks down. Junior machinists quickly follow the orders barked out by senior mechanic Barkley, widely respected as one of the most knowledgeable in the industry.	Expertise

is to share it, for power can grow, in part, by being shared. Sharing power is different from giving or throwing it away, for delegation does not mean abdication.[10]

Effective managers have a high need for power, but that need is oriented toward the benefit of the organization as a whole. In addition, the need for power is stronger in these managers than the need to be liked by others. Thus, as a manager you must be willing to play the influence game in a controlled way. This does not imply that you need to be authoritarian in action. On the contrary, it appears that power-motivated managers make their subordinates feel stronger rather than weaker. A true authoritarian would have the reverse effect, making people feel weak or powerless.

Another important element in the profile of a manager is her or his managerial style. In a firm studied by David McClelland, a Harvard psychologist, those managers whose employees had higher morale scored higher on the democratic or coaching styles of management.[11] That the managers were also higher in power motivation implies that they express their power motivation in a democratic way, which is more likely to be effective.

Limits on the Use of Authority and Power

All organization members have certain restrictions or limitations placed on their authority, as shown in Table 8.2. The president of the United States cannot legally declare war; only Congress has that authority. The chief executive officers of major corporations, even though they may be very powerful, lack absolute authority. Some of these limits are imposed by external factors such as agencies of federal, state, and local governments, contracts with dealers and suppliers, collective bargaining agreements, and so on.

Internal factors may also limit managerial authority. These include the organization's charter and bylaws, policies, rules, procedures, budgets, and position descriptions. A vice-president may have the authority to spend, say, $250,000 without consulting the president, whereas a first-line supervisor

TABLE 8.2
Internal and External
Limits to Authority

External	Internal
Government rules and regulations	Corporate bylaws and charter
Collective bargaining agreements	Budgets
Dealer, supplier, and customer agreements	Policies, rules, procedures
	Position descriptions

may be permitted to spend only $100 for needed supplies without first clearing it with the department head.

As shown in Figure 8.7, the scope of authority is broader at the top of an organization and narrower at the lower levels of the chain of command. Yet there are restrictions or limits on the authority of even the stockholders. For example, they can do only those things permitted by the corporation's charter, and they cannot do things that are illegal—such as refusing to pay valid taxes.

THE ROLE OF RESPONSIBILITY AND ACCOUNTABILITY

Responsibility is the obligation that is created when an employee accepts the manager's delegation of authority. Another frequently used term is **accountability,** which refers to the fact that employees will be judged by the extent to which they have fulfilled their responsibilities. Being accountable implies that one's supervisor can confer either punishment or reward, depending on how well one has exercised the responsibility to use the delegated authority.

Responsibility and Accountability Can't Be Delegated

Can a person escape his or her own responsibility or accountability by shifting it to another person? The following example furnishes a partial answer.

Bill Jones walked into the teacher's office very upset about the F he had received on his term paper. He had put a lot of work into the paper and felt that it deserved at least a B.

Dr. Hanna explained: "You knew the date the paper was due and that the penalty for lateness was one letter grade for each day it was late. Your paper was a B—a good, solid paper, Bill—but I received it four days late. This gave you a grade of F. I'm sorry that you couldn't get it in on schedule."

Bill explained that Edith Evans, a secretary at the university, had typed up the paper and said she would give it to Dr. Hanna on the due date. Bill argued that he shouldn't have been penalized by Dr. Hanna, since the paper's lateness was not his fault but the secretary's.

What is your view?

Do you think that Bill has a good case—that *he* isn't responsible for the delay and shouldn't be held accountable? If Bill isn't accountable, then is Edith Evans, on whom Dr. Hanna has no authority to impose sanctions?

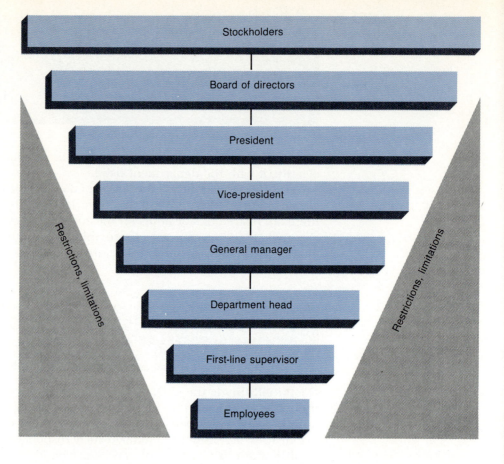

If you agree with Bill, you've overlooked a major organizational principle: No one can assume—or accept—another person's responsibility for performing a duty. Delegating your authority to another person does not relieve you of the original responsibility and accountability. In fact, as shown in Figure 8.8, a whole network of responsibility-accountability transactions can occur when authority to carry out tasks is delegated to lower organizational levels.

Equality of Authority and Responsibility?

An important principle of organization is that individuals should be assigned or delegated sufficient authority to carry out their responsibilities. For example, if a manager's responsibility is to maintain a certain production capacity, he or she must be given sufficient latitude to make decisions that affect production capacity. Also, you wouldn't tell a coach that you expect him or her to win the championship but that you will make all the decisions concerning which players are to be used.

Equality of responsibility and authority is good in theory, but it is difficult to achieve in practice. In fact, many experts argue that in today's management world it is unrealistic even to attempt to achieve it. Some reasons for this are government laws and regulations, the presence of unions, and the network of dependence that exists in organizations. Most managers—even efficient ones—have more responsibility than authority.

Another major reason for inequality of authority and responsibility is the reluctance of higher-level managers to delegate to their subordinates. It's like

FIGURE 8.8
Flows of authority,
responsibility, and
accountability.

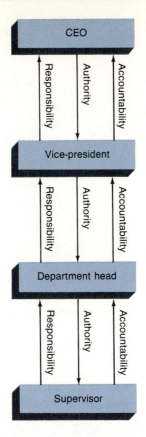

saying, "You're responsible for getting results, but I'll call all the shots." It is fundamental that people should have a range of authority to exercise judgment and latitude in making decisions about those major results for which they will ultimately be held accountable.

> *Hal Bankston, an insurance company branch manager, is responsible for reaching the sales and profit goals that have been established for his branch office. While he's accountable for these results, he certainly doesn't have a free hand to accomplish them. For example, before he can hire a promising new sales representative, the employee must be screened by the home office personnel executives. In fact, they've turned down some people that Hal was really impressed with. Moreover, what Hal can offer a new employee in salary and benefits is established by top management. Before Hal can purchase equipment or supplies over $100, the purchasing department must approve the vendor and price. Hal doesn't have the authority to determine his own pricing, either, since that is also done by the home office. As Bankston notes, "You don't have a totally free hand in running the branch, but they sure do hold you responsible for results."*

In conclusion, there are two frequent violations of the principle of equality of authority and responsibility that lead to ineffective management. First, giving a person little authority but much responsibility can result in frustration and inefficiency. Conversely, if authority is greater than responsibility, it can lead to abuses and arrogance.

VIETOR'S   **FUNNY BUSINESS**

**From now on, you will be in charge of a department
for which you have total responsibility and zero authority. Good luck.**

(Source: Copyright 1987, USA TODAY. Reprinted with permission.)

THE ROLE OF CENTRALIZATION

Another important factor leading to effective management is the degree of centralization of authority within the organization. Actually, authority can be centralized or decentralized.

Centralization Versus Decentralization

The concept of centralization, like the concept of delegation, has to do with the degree to which authority is concentrated or dispersed. Whereas the term *delegation* usually refers to the extent to which individual managers delegate authority and responsibility to people reporting directly to them, *decentralization* is a broader concept and refers to the extent to which upper management delegates authority downward to divisions, branches, or lower-level organizational units.

     Centralization is concentrating the power and authority near the top, or in the head, of an organization. **Decentralization** is dispersing the power and decision making to successively lower levels of the organization (see Figure 8.9). *No organization is completely centralized or decentralized; the extent ranges along a continuum from high centralization to high decentralization.*

Factors Affecting the Degree of Centralization

The extent of centralization or decentralization within a given organization depends on several interrelated factors as shown in Table 8.3. These are:

     1. The management philosophy of the organization.

     2. The history of organizational growth.

3. The geographic dispersion of the organization.

4. The availability of effective controls.

5. The quality of managers at different levels.

6. The diversity of products or services offered.

Influence of management philosophy. Some top managers are highly autocratic and desire strong central control. They surround themselves with a strong central staff and reserve most major decisions for the highest organizational levels. On the other hand, some managers believe strongly in the virtues of a decentralized organization. An excellent proponent of a decentralized managerial philosophy is Ralph J. Cordiner, former president and chairman of the board of General Electric (GE). Although Cordiner made his comments several years ago, his philosophy is still followed by GE today.

> At General Electric, decentralization is used as a way of preserving and enhancing the contributions of a large enterprise, while achieving the flexibility and the "human touch" popularly associated with, but not always achieved by, smaller organizations.
>
> Under this concept, GE has decentralized according to products, geography, and functional types of work. But the company has also decentralized the responsibility and authority for making business decisions.[12]

The practical result of GE's philosophy is to put the responsibility for making decisions not with a few top executives but with individual managers and functional employees who have the most information needed to make sound decisions and take prompt action. When such authority is delegated—along with the required responsibility and accountability—and according to carefully planned organization of work, employees have challenging and dignified positions that bring out their full resources and enthusiastic cooperation.

History of organizational growth. Organizations that expand internally tend toward centralization because this was their approach initially. For example, Ford Motor Company and National Cash Register (NCR) grew internally and

FIGURE 8.9
Centralization-
decentralization and the
chain of command.

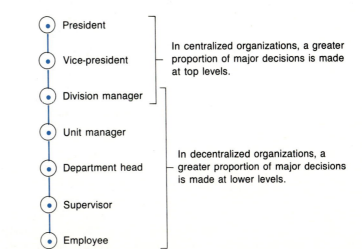

TABLE 8.3
Factors Affecting
Degree of Centralization

Condition favorable for centralization		Condition favorable for decentralization
No	Is top management's philosophy consistent with strong delegation?	Yes
No	Has organization grown externally through merger and acquisition?	Yes
No	Is organization widespread geographically?	Yes
No	Are effective controls available to monitor lower levels?	Yes
No	Is there an adequate number of highly qualified managers?	Yes
No	Does organization have a diverse product-service line?	Yes

now tend to have higher degrees of centralization than organizations that have grown externally through merger with and acquisition of other firms. Sometimes, however, moderately or marginally effective (or sometimes even unprofitable) firms that are loosely managed are acquired by strong companies with the idea that strong centralization from the parent company will turn them around.

Geographic dispersion of the organization. Generally, the more widely dispersed organizational units are, the more likely it is that decentralization will be practiced. For example, Nestlé Corporation, which operates through-

"As you can see, we have
a highly centralized organization."

out the world, is highly decentralized. Decentralization allows lower-level managers to have a greater degree of decision-making latitude and to adapt to local conditions affecting their units.

> *Thom McAn shoe stores are located all over the country and face their stiffest competiton not from other national retail shoe store chains like Jarman, Baker's, or Kinney's but from locally owned, owner-managed stores. Decentralization allows the local Thom McAn units to have greater authority regarding such matters as promotions, pricing, and inventory.*
>
> *Large grocery chains such as A&P and Safeway have tough competition from smaller chains operating in a relatively compact geographic area and need to have some flexibility to adapt to local conditions.*

What is your view?

Walgreens, the national drug chain, decided to open five stores in New York City. Drug chains haven't had much success in New York, partly because of the traditional patronage of independent drugstores, particularly in ethnic neighborhoods. What are some examples of how decentralization might be used by Walgreens to make these stores successful?

Availability of effective controls. Organizations that lack effective means of controlling lower-level units will tend toward higher centralization since they cannot easily monitor the performance of lower-level units. This generalization is true of most maintenance departments.

In 1958, management theorists Harold Leavitt and Thomas L. Whisler published an article, entitled "Management in the 1980's," that shocked the business world. They predicted that by the 1980s large organizations would have gone through a process of recentralization and that the trend toward decentralization would be reversed. They also predicted that most middle-management jobs would become highly structured and routinized, with the majority of middle-management jobs moving downward in status and pay. They based their predictions on the increasing use of the computer and what they called "information technology."[13]

Leavitt and Whisler seem to have erred in some of their predictions, since middle managers have increased in number, status, pay, and in many cases, responsibility. However, the authors were partially correct in that information technology has enabled top management to move toward larger amounts of centralized decision making. Conversely, the availability of more effective controls for top management has also made possible a greater degree of decentralized decision making.

Quality of managers. Decentralization requires greater numbers of more qualified managers, since managers will be allowed greater latitude in making their own decisions at lower levels. This practice is followed by 3M, which encourages innovation and creativity on the part of its personnel. In organizations in which there is a scarcity of highly qualified managers and specialists, the strategy followed is to maintain decision-making authority at higher organizational levels.

Diversity of products and services. The more diverse the range of products or services offered, the greater the tendency toward decentralization. Conversely, the narrower the product and service range, the more feasible centralization is. For example, some years ago, when Exxon Chemicals produced over 750 items, it was highly decentralized.

In summary, several factors affect the degree of centralization and decentralization in an organization. Moreover, the degree may vary within different divisions or departments of the organization and must change according to the organization's internal and external environment. Thus a contingency approach is the most logical approach for organizations to follow.

> *When Lee Iacocca took over as head of a beleaguered Chrysler Corporation in the late 1970s, he changed to a highly centralized organization, making all the important decisions himself and tightening the reins on expenditures at the division levels. But as Chrysler began to turn around and pull itself out of the hole, Iacocca began to move slowly toward less-centralized decision making. This game plan has apparently worked, and Chrysler survived a close call with bankruptcy.*
>
> *The recession in the early 1980s saw many companies cutting costs by reducing the number of staff personnel in corporate headquarters. The result was frequently a move toward greater decentralization.*[14]

THE ROLE OF COMMITTEES

If you were president of a large company such as U.S. Steel or Du Pont, how would you go about coordinating the work of those under you? If your span was large, say 10 to 15, you would probably have some difficulty doing all the coordinating needed; so you would have to make some provision for it. Moreover, there might be some important decisions to be made—decisions in which the inputs of several persons were necessary. Should you spend a million dollars on a plant expansion? Should you reorganize the company?

For reasons such as these, committees are formed. **Committees** are groups of persons from more or less the same level. Table 8.4 shows that the purpose of committees is to coordinate and exchange information, advise top management, or even to make decisions themselves. Most banks, for example, have "loan committees" that meet regularly to decide whether to

TABLE 8.4
Three Basic Committee Functions

Committee purpose	Nature and examples	Examples
1. Coordinating	Permit communication, integration of various departments and activities that are interrelated	New product planning committee
2. Advising	Provide advice or make recommendations to management	University faculty senate Budget committee Advisory councils
3. Decision making	Make decisions and see that they are carried out	Corporate board of directors Bank loan committee Executive compensation committee

approve loan applications in excess of certain amounts. Hospitals have boards that do the same when approving large expenditures for medical equipment.

Committees are usually characterized by a designated membership, a chairperson, somewhat regular meetings, and a secretary. Frequently, the chairperson ranks a notch higher than the membership and may even be their immediate superior.

Committees are a fact of organizational life. Approximately 80 percent of top-management executives serve on at least one committee; about 75 percent of middle managers do so, as do 50 percent of lower-level managers and over 30 percent of nonmanagers.[15] Perhaps you have served on some kind of committee and have some experience of how they function. Since committees are a major part of the structure of organizations, it is important that you understand what they are and how they work.

Types of Committees

Committees are of two types: standing committees and ad hoc committees. **Standing committees** are a permanent part of the structure of an organization, such as a corporate finance committee, a compensation or salary committee, or a research and development committee. **Ad hoc committees** function similarly to a task force in seeking to accomplish a specific purpose and then being disbanded; they are not permanent.

Advantages of Committees

When several people with different experience and backgrounds are brought together, there is a greater amount of knowledge, and usually more alternative approaches will be identified in problem solving than would be found by a single individual. In many cases, several people with different experience and backgrounds working together will come up with a better solution than the same number of people working individually.

Increases acceptance. Participation tends to increase acceptance of new ideas or programs. Persons who have participated in a decision usually have a proprietary feeling about it (called *ownership*) and therefore an interest in seeing that the decision is effectively implemented. Even if their viewpoints do not prevail, participants at least understand the reasoning behind the decision.

Prevents abuse of power. Another possible advantage is the dispersion of power that occurs through committee assignments. For example, an assistant director of a federally funded manpower program took away the authority of the personnel director to make the sole recommendations on applicants for key jobs. She appointed a committee to carry out that task because she suspected the personnel director of prejudice in the recommendations.

Avoids unpleasant consequences. Still another advantage is that an executive may use a committee to kill an idea or proposal. This situation occasionally occurs when an executive is faced with a decision that will be unpopular and for political or public relations reasons prefers not to have the decision associated with him or her. It is a simple tactic to "seed" the committee with people who are instructed to kill the proposal. This tactic should be used very cautiously, since it may backfire. For example, the dean of a graduate school didn't like a proposal made by the Graduate Council.

He appointed a committee that felt as he did about the proposal. The committee's report was negative. The Graduate Council rejected the committee's report and fought the dean after that.

Training ground for aspiring managers. Work on a committee can serve as a training ground for aspiring managers to learn such tactics as bargaining, teamwork, and human relations.

Disadvantages of Committees

The possibility of domination by one or two strong-willed, assertive personalities is one of the hazards of using a committee. This situation is especially damaging if the committee is dominated by a strong-willed chairperson. Unless the dominant person is the best problem solver, a committee will not normally achieve synergy when there is domination. Another possible disadvantage is the reverse; that is, with most committee actions, no one individual is held responsible for those actions or their consequences.

Sometimes committees, to achieve unanimity, will resort to social pressure and compromise instead of coming up with the best recommendation. In this situation, the recommendation is watered down to get everyone "on board."

Committees are also time-consuming and expensive. Committee work takes longer than individuals working alone and involves proration of the salaries of the participants. In addition, there is the matter of opportunity

(Source: Courtesy of USA TODAY. Printed with special permission. November 11, 1984, p. 2B.)

costs, since, while working on the committee, members cannot work on other projects and activities.

Two other problems may reduce a committee's effectiveness. First, there may be a **hidden agenda.** The committee members may appear to be focusing on an item on the agenda, but in reality their attitudes—and possibly even their decisions—are being influenced by some other item, issue, or personality that is not mentioned by name. The other problem is **logrolling,** whereby members exchange assistance and/or favors with others in order to get what they want.

Many people resent poorly run, ineffective committees. The committee chairperson plays a key role in a committee's effectiveness through his or her leadership—creating a climate in which synergy is likely to occur.

Use of Task Forces

Task forces are teams that usually consist of volunteers, are of limited duration, and set their own goals. They are usually found to be much more productive than other types of committees.

In their influential book, *In Search of Excellence*, Thomas Peters and Robert Waterman emphasize the fact that America's best-run companies tend to avoid using a matrix organization and instead utilize task forces.[16] Although these companies recognize the need for multifunctional problem solving and implementation, they try to stay away from adding more levels to the company's formal organization. Members of task forces tend not to be interested in how they fit into the organizational structure; rather, they are interested in being given important assignments, thus allowing for a "fluid project-oriented environment."

As Peters and Waterman indicate, the effective use of such teams in the top companies matches the findings on the makeup of effective small groups. They found, for instance, that effective new product teams in the top companies usually range in size from five to ten members. Our experience has shown that the optimal group size is about seven. Other findings also support that conclusion.

Characteristics of effective task forces.
The characteristics of successful ad hoc task forces as seen in the best-managed companies are as follows:

1. There are usually 10 or fewer members on these task forces.
2. The task force reporting level, and the seniority of its members, are proportional to the importance of the problem.
3. The duration of the task force is very limited.
4. Membership is usually voluntary.
5. The task force is pulled together rapidly, when needed, and usually not accompanied by a formal chartering process.
6. Follow-up is swift.
7. No staff members are assigned.
8. Documentation is informal at most, and often scant.

The basic idea of task forces is to focus on results and solutions. At Texas Instruments, senior management experts expect results within three months of the task force assignment. Without question, task forces are an excellent way to improve organizational effectiveness without adding new departments or positions.

Additional advantages. In addition to the advantages of group decision making listed in Chapter 7, there are other advantages of task forces that make them an exceptional tool in organization design. Some of these are:

1. The group usually focuses its efforts on a single issue, problem, or opportunity at a time.
2. Usually a small task force is given an assignment whose results are important to the company. As a result, there is a strong sense of "ownership" and commitment to doing a good job.
3. Because it is a small group, there is less chance of one person dominating.
4. In the majority of cases, small ad hoc task forces achieve synergy while working on an assignment. That is, they develop a better solution than the most creative person in the group could develop working alone.
5. Being assigned to a task force working on an important problem is a powerful motivational vehicle. The individual's need for achievement, autonomy, power, competence, responsibility, and affiliation can all be triggered by being given such an assignment.
6. Finally, because the task force is given an assignment and then disbanded, there is a sense of completion and closure. The most capable people have a tendency toward spurts of creative energy, especially when they can see light at the end of the tunnel.

As plant manager, Tim White had a difficult technical problem that was adversely affecting plant productivity. White's top engineer had studied the problem, but his recommendation did not entirely solve the problem. Although generally skeptical about the usefulness of committees, Tim, in desperation, appointed a task force of five people from different areas to study the problem and develop a proposed solution. The solution not only solved the productivity problem but provided a solution that should enable the plant to increase the quality of its product as well.

THE ROLE OF INFORMAL ORGANIZATIONS

An important part of organization is the **informal organization,** consisting of groupings and relationships of personnel that may be more influential than the formal relationships shown on the organization chart. Informal groups inevitably emerge whenever people come together and interact in social groupings.

In formal organizations—especially large ones—these informal organizations often grow out of ad hoc committees and task forces. As organizational members interact in these groups, they tend to develop the sentiments and loyalties needed to form the informal groups.

Functions Performed

Informal groups perform three important functions: (1) to establish, enforce, and perpetuate social and cultural norms and values important to group members; (2) to stimulate effective and dynamic communication; and (3) to provide the members with the social satisfaction and status the formal organization may not give.

In performing these functions, informal groups tend to increase innovation, dynamism, vitality, and creativity within formal organizations. The formal structure, though, provides for order and longevity—since informal groups may be disorderly and short-lived.

Members of these informal groups tend to subordinate some of their individual needs to achieve organizational objectives. In return, the organization supports, protects, and rewards these individuals. Informal groups may further the interests of the organization by strengthening their members' ties to the organization. They may also oppose organization objectives, however, such as achieving high productivity, when these are considered harmful to the interests of the group.

Problems Created

These informal groups, although not part of the formally established organization, can cause managers many problems. For example, they may create conflict, especially with organizational goals, generate and spread rumors, encourage resistance to change, and lead to conformity among members, including restricting performance, as shown in the following example.

It was Fred's first day on the job as one of some 20 "parts pickers" at a regional parts warehouse for one of the Big Three automakers. Fred's job was to push a four-wheel truck throughout the warehouse and "pick" the parts ordered by various automotive dealers. A given order might include fan belts, rubber hoses, washers, bolts, gaskets, mirrors, and larger items such as doors, hoods, and engine blocks. In warehouse jargon, each different item picked was a "line" because each item number, with the quantity needed and a brief description of the item, was listed on a separate line of the order sheet.

Phil Hargen, a senior picker who was assigned to break Fred in, was laying out some of the ground rules for him. "First," he said, "the senior pickers get the cleaner jobs; so if you pull an easy order, with smaller, lighter items, you'd better give it to a senior man. Second," he continued, "don't ever make the mistake of picking more than 300 lines in one day. The supervisor will talk to you about 300 to 400 lines a day, but just ignore him. It's kind of a quota we pickers have set among ourselves, and you'd do best to remember it. We can make things plenty rough for somebody who tries to come on as a real hot shot."

What is your view?

Have you ever been in a situation where some students put pressure on others not to excel? Perhaps a teacher was grading on a curve and average or poorer students didn't want the curve dislocated. In your experience, are ambitious, eager students often unpopular? Why or why not?

In spite of these problems, informal groups are inevitable, and management must learn to live with them. Any effort to stamp these groups out only results in the formation of new ones.

SUMMARY

This chapter, building on Chapter 7, has discussed how delegation can be used to make organizations more effective. Delegation is the process by which a manager assigns authority downward in the organization. Several reasons for delegating are that it allows managers to focus their energies on the most critical, high-priority tasks; it enables subordinates to grow and develop; and it enables managers to accomplish much more than if they attempted to do all tasks themselves. Managers fail to delegate for many reasons, including fear of employee failure or the desire to retain their own power by keeping on top of all activities. Some employees resist delegation because it means added responsibility and because they lack the self-confidence to handle a larger decision-making role.

Authority is defined as the right to do something or tell someone else to do it in order to reach organizational objectives. The legitimacy of a manager's authority is received from formal delegation by higher levels. The acceptance theory disputes that formal view, arguing that authority exists only when it is accepted by others. We feel that the formal theory is more appropriate for organizations, but we also feel that, to be effective, managers should spend a portion of their efforts trying to get subordinates to accept their authority.

The three basic types of authority used by managers are (1) line authority, which is the right to tell someone what to do, (2) staff authority, which is the right to advise someone on what *should* be done, or how it is to be done, and (3) functional authority, which gives a staff person a limited amount of line authority over a specialized function.

Conflicts often occur in line-staff relations as the result of numerous factors, many of which are interpersonal and result directly from the relationships required of the two types of positions. Staff are typically younger, better educated, and less experienced than line. They may look down on line, deal with line condescendingly, and fail to appreciate line's point of view. Conversely, line may see staff's legitimate advisory role as unnecessary and resent staff members' usually having easier access to top management.

Power is the ability to influence others; it exists as a corollary of the concept of authority. There are a number of types of power: reward, coercive, legitimate, control-of-information, referent, and expert. Effective managers seem to possess a strong need for power, but they orient their use of power toward the goals of the organization rather than solely for their personal, selfish needs.

There are limits to every manager's ability to delegate authority. The scope of delegated authority is broadest at top-management levels and narrowest at the lower levels of the chain of command. When managers are granted authority—or acquire power—they soon find that responsibility and accountability follow. But, even though managers may delegate their authority, they cannot escape their responsibility and accountability to their own superiors.

Centralization and decentralization in an organization refer to the extent to which delegation has been granted to lower levels of the organization. The degree of centralization and decentralization is affected by (1) top-management philosophy, (2) the history of the organization's growth, (3) the geographic dispersion of the organization, (4) the availability of effective controls, (5) the diversity of products and services offered, and (6) the number of qualified managers and specialists at different levels.

The use of committees is another way to make organizations more effective. They can be standing committees or ad hoc committees. It has been shown that in actual practice the most successful companies stay away from matrix organization but do use task forces extensively. Standing committees are permanent; ad hoc committees accomplish a specific purpose and are then disbanded. Task forces may be used for the same purpose. A major advantage of committees is that they bring together persons with different viewpoints.

Informal organizations frequently grow out of ad hoc committees and task forces. They are informal groupings that provide innovation, dynamism, vitality, and creativity in formal organization structures. They can be disruptive if they interfere with organizational goals.

REVIEW QUESTIONS

1. What is delegation and how does it operate?
2. What is the difference between the formal authority concept and the acceptance theory of authority?
3. What are the differences between (a) line authority, (b) staff authority, and (c) functional authority?
4. What are some causes of conflict between line and staff personnel? What steps might organizations take to enable line and staff to work together more harmoniously?
5. In what way, if any, does *authority* differ from *power*?
6. What are the six sources of power? Explain each.
7. Why does power tend to expand?
8. What are (a) responsibility and (b) accountability?
9. What does it mean when an organization says that it is *decentralized*?
10. Why are committees used?
11. What are informal organizations, and what can managers do about them?

DISCUSSION QUESTIONS

1. Suppose a supervisor who reported to you had excellent managerial potential but refused to delegate to subordinates. In fact, several of the subordinates had mentioned this to you. What steps might you take to help your supervisor become a more effective delegator?
2. Perhaps against your better judgment, you accept a staff person's recommendation and make a decision to purchase some expensive new equipment that has just come on the market. It turns out that the equipment is inferior and doesn't work as well as what you had before. In explaining the situation to your boss, you say, "It's not my fault. Henderson recommended that I buy it, and he's our resident expert. If I were you, I'd really knock him down a peg or two. He cost me about $3800 with his most recent recommendation. He's accountable, not me." Are you correct in saying that you're not accountable? Discuss.
3. Of the six power sources, which do you feel is the most effective? Least effective? Why?
4. Can authority and responsibility really be equal in practice? Explain.
5. In a large auto manufacturer such as General Motors, which is organized by divisions, to what extent can auto design be decentralized to the various divisions? Discuss.
6. Where should admissions be administered in a university? Should each college

set its own admissions criteria, or should admissions be centralized in a single, central admissions office? Discuss.

7. What are some examples of informal organizations among your friends? At your school? In other organizations?

Who's in Charge?

A small government unit consisted of four women, all college graduates aged 26 to 35. The women were supervised by a man in the home office in another city who also supervised five other offices in different locations throughout the state. This supervisor visited the office at random intervals and could be called when problems arose. The unit was new, but all the employees had worked at least five years for the parent organization.

When the unit was first formed, no one was appointed manager, all duties were divided equally, and there was no clerical staff. After a few months, the central office felt that communications with the branch offices would be improved if one worker, called a contact person, was responsible for all telephone messages between the central office and the branch office. The contact person was chosen on the basis of chronological age, and the appointment was informal.

As responsibilities and paperwork increased, the central office, feeling the need for more control, designated the contact person the "worker-in-charge." This person was given control over many facets of the office, including supervision of the recently added clerical staff, but did not actively supervise the rest of the staff. She was given authority to sign all leave requests and to help the home office with evaluations of the other workers.

After about a year, the worker-in-charge was named office manager, and it was understood that she was, in effect, the supervisor.

This gradual concentration of power and authority in one member caused tension and anxiety in the office. All four workers had been hired as equals, had been working together as such, and were accustomed to a merit system in which most promotions were based on tests. Furthermore, the worker who had been appointed did not wish to be office manager and had repeatedly informed her superior and her fellow workers that she did not like the added responsibility and intended to do as little work as possible.

Several months later, the office manager resigned. Another worker who had wanted to be manager and could have done a good job, when asked, decided to refuse the position because she felt that the position and its accompanying authority and responsibility were "too unclear." She had talked with the other workers, and together they had agreed to refuse if the job were offered them, for the title was still unofficial, and no increase in pay was involved.

Questions

1. What would you have done if you had been the first office manager?
2. How would you have reacted if you had been the second person offered the job?
3. What is needed to make the position "valid"?
4. What does the case show about authority, responsibility, and power?

The Making of a College Dean[17]

Dr. Donald Singleton was the newly appointed dean at an eastern university. After serving as program director of an educational foundation for five years, he had decided to return to academia. Since he was an articulate individual, he made a good impression on the people he met. He was therefore well received by the faculty, as well as university and community leaders.

Within a few months of his arrival, Dr. Singleton recruited several of his old acquaintances as full professors with very little consultation with the faculty. When he did consult with some of them, he selected a few individuals who he knew would support his views. The faculty protested this practice, but nothing happened.

Dean Singleton was highly sensitive to external politics. He participated actively in community affairs and engaged in activities that would give him noticeable recognition and news coverage. He promised to institute several educational programs at the university that would please local professional and trade groups. In the past, these programs had been resisted by the faculty as being nonacademic. The faculty usually learned of these promises through the local newspaper and the university's press releases.

The faculty moaned and grumbled but did not know how to handle the dean. They complained about his insensitivity to the collegial form of university governance, but nothing happened until they learned through the media that he was raising funds by selling honorary professorships. The price would range from $1,000 to $40,000, depending on the rank. This angered the faculty, and they called a series of meetings to discuss issues ranging from honorary professorships to recruiting. The fund-raising project was immediately dropped, and the faculty began to propose and pass new procedures for recruiting and for instituting new academic programs.

In the months following, a series of meetings was held to negotiate the procedures for recruiting and instituting new programs. Once these procedures were developed, the dean and the faculty were able to work together again in the process of serving the college.

Questions

1. What were the dean's assumptions about his job?
2. (a) What type of authority did the dean have? (b) What kinds of power did he have?
3. How would you evaluate the way this problem was handled by the university's administration?
4. What does the case illustrate about the roles of authority and power?

NOTES

1. Jeanne Sadler, "Postal Service Seeks to Dispel Bad Image," *The Wall Street Journal*, May 27, 1987, p. 6.
2. Chester Barnard, *The Functions of the Executive* (Cambridge, MA: Harvard University Press, 1938).
3. David C. McClelland, *Power: The Inner Experience* (New York: Halsted Press, 1975).
4. Michael Korda, *Power! How to Get It, How to Use It* (New York: Random House, 1975).
5. Robert J. Ringer, *Winning Through Intimidation* (New York: Fawcett, 1979).
6. See Richard H. Buskirk, *Modern Management & Machiavelli* (New York: New American Library/Mentor Books, 1975), for a good explanation of this concept.
7. Based in part on J. R. P. French, Jr., and Bertram Raven, "The Bases of Social Power," in *Studies in Social Power*, ed. D. Cartwright (Ann Arbor, MI: Institute for Social Research, 1959).
8. For an interesting study of the role of expertise and other forms of power, see Charles J. Fombrun, "Determinants of Perceived Power: Individual or Context?" in *The Academy of Management Proceedings*, ed. Kae H. Chung (Academy of Management, 1981), pp. 254–258.
9. Amy Saltzman, "Full Speed Ahead," *Venture*, March 1986, pp. 54–56.
10. Rosabeth Moss Kanter, "Power Failure in Management Circuits," *Harvard Business Review* 57 (July–August 1979): 73.
11. David C. McClelland and David H. Burnham, "Power Is the Great Motivator," *Harvard Business Review* 54 (March–April 1976): 105.

12. Ralph J. Cordiner, "Decentralization: A Managerial Philosophy," in *New Frontiers for Professional Managers* (New York: McGraw-Hill, 1956), pp. 40–79.

13. Harold Leavitt and Thomas L. Whisler, "Management in the 1980s," *Harvard Business Review* 36 (November–December 1958): 41–48.

14. David P. Garino, "Some Companies Try Fewer Bosses to Cut Costs, Decentralize Power," *The Wall Street Journal*, April 10, 1981, p. 27.

15. R. Tillman, "Committees on Trial," *Harvard Business Review* 40 (May–June 1962): 8.

16. Thomas J. Peters and Robert H. Waterman, Jr., *In Search of Excellence: Lessons from America's Best-Run Companies* (New York: Harper & Row, 1982), pp. 127–130.

17. Adapted from Kae H. Chung and Leon C. Megginson, *Organizational Behavior: Developing Managerial Skills* (New York: Harper & Row, 1981), p. 359.

SUGGESTIONS FOR FURTHER STUDY

ALLEN, LOUIS A. *The Professional Manager's Guide.* Palo Alto, CA: Louis A. Allen Associates, 1981.

CAVANAUGH, GERALD F.; MOBERG, DENNIS J.; and VELASQUEZ, MANUEL. "The Ethics of Organizational Politics." *Academy of Management Review* 6 (July 1981): 363–374.

COBB, ANTHONY T. "Informational Influence in the Formal Organization: Perceived Sources of Power Among Work Unit Peers." *Academy of Management Journal* 23 (March 1980): 155–161.

FORD, JEFFREY D. "The Administrative Component in Growing and Declining Organizations: A Longitudinal Analysis." *Academy of Management Journal* 23 (December 1980): 615–630.

GARINO, DAVID P. "Some Companies Try Fewer Bosses to Cut Costs, Decentralize Power." *The Wall Street Journal*, April 10, 1981, p. 27.

PETERS, THOMAS J., and WATERMAN, ROBERT H., JR. *In Search of Excellence.* New York: Harper & Row, 1982. See especially chapters 7, 11, and 12.

SAUNDERS, CAROL STOAK. "Management Information Systems, Communications, and Departmental Power: An Integrative Model." *Academy of Management Review* 6 (July 1981): 431–442.

WILSON, SLOANE. *The Man in the Gray Flannel Suit.* New York: Pocket Books, Inc., 1955.

9

Staffing and Human-Resource Management

Learning Objectives

After studying the material in this chapter, you should be able to do the following:
- Discuss the importance of staffing and human-resource management.
- Describe some of the laws providing for equal employment opportunity (EEO).
- Explain why an organization needs capable employees.
- Discuss how to plan for future personnel needs.
- Name the usual sources from which to recruit potential employees.
- Outline the procedure for recruiting and selecting new employees.
- Explain how to train and develop employees.
- Outline some of the problems involved in compensating employees.
- Discuss the need for improved health and safety in business firms.

Outline of the Chapter

The role of staffing
How equal employment opportunity (EEO) laws affect staffing
Laws providing equal employment opportunity
Enforcing EEO laws
Planning human-resource needs
Determining job needs
Developing sources of supply of employees
Recruiting and selecting employees
Recruiting personnel
Selecting the right person for the job
Orienting new employees

Training and developing employees
Reasons for training and development
Training and development methods
Compensating employees
Importance of compensation
Importance of income differences
How compensation is determined
How employees are paid
Role of employee benefits
Maintaining health and safety
Summary

Some Important Terms

staffing
equal employment op-
  portunity (EEO)
affirmative action pro-
  grams (AAPs)
handicapped person
human-resource plan-
  ning
career management
job analysis
job descriptions
job specifications
upgrading
transferring
promoting
temporaries
recruitment
employee referrals
selection
polygraph
training
development

education
coaching
planned progression
job rotation
temporary *or* anticipa-
  tory assignments
performance appraisal
  (evaluation, review)
mentor
executive development
  programs
laboratory training
organization develop-
  ment (OD)
compensation
wages
benefits
comparable worth
time (day) wages
incentive wage
commission
profit-sharing plan

Management is the management of people, not the management of things. . . . [It] is getting things done through people.
—LAWRENCE APPLEY

Corporate Women—Breaking Through to the Top

According to writer Laurie Baum, there are "few women in America with wide-ranging, high-level line responsibilities at a major corporation, performing tough, general management jobs." And it is from this small group that many major companies will select the next generation of CEOs and other top managers. This group is in the vanguard of a new era for women managers. As you can see from Table 9.1, 37 percent of women are now in management and administrative jobs, as compared to 20 percent in 1972. Their progress in management has paralleled their progress in education. As shown, more than a third of the 70,000 MBAs graduating each year are women, as opposed to 4 percent in 1972.

More important than their increasing numbers is the fact that women managers are now moving beyond staff and mid-level management jobs, where they staked their claims in the 1960s and 1970s.

There are several reasons for the rapid progress of these women managers. First, as indicated, they are better educated and more determined to advance. Second, the broad economic shift from manufacturing to services—which more readily accept women as managers—provides them more opportunities to land top jobs. Third, many managers working their way up in American business are accustomed to having women as peers, having gone to school with women and worked with women as colleagues and supervisors. Finally, the wave of restructurings, spin-offs, and leveraged buyouts—with huge personnel reshufflings, breaking up long-entrenched male cultures—favors women's progress. For example, before International Harvester (now Navistar International Corporation) ran into financial problems in the late 1970s, female managers existed in only narrowly defined, specialized areas. But, as division after division was peeled off, a new corporate culture developed. Now, one of Navistar's top managers is Roxanne J. Decyk, 34 years old, with a law degree from Marquette University, who started as corporate secretary in 1981. After four promotions, she's senior vice-president for administration and plays a pivotal role in everything from strategic direction to labor relations.

But these women still face many hurdles. They still encounter old-fashioned prejudice and resistance at some companies. Also, they still earn around 42 percent less than their male counterparts. Finally, according to Laurie Baum, "Many women simply don't want to make the family sacrifices generally required in the highest ranks of America."

TABLE 9.1
As More Women Get MBAs, Their Role as Managers Increases

SOURCE: Reprinted from June 22, 1987 issue of *Business Week* by special permission. Copyright 1987 by McGraw-Hill, Inc.

Year	% of women among graduating MBAs[a]	% of women in management and administrative jobs[b]
1972	4	20
1976	12	24
1987	33	37

[a] Data from Center for Education Statistics, U.S. Education Department.
[b] Data from Bureau of Labor Statistics, BW estimates.

If this estimate of progress for women managers is true, what does it portend for staffing and managing human resources in the future? ■

THIS CASE AND THE APPLEY quotation illustrate the importance—and changing nature—of one of the major problems facing management today: staffing and managing human resources. How effectively managers perform this function will determine their success or failure as managers. This chapter looks at the most important aspects of staffing and managing human resources.

THE ROLE OF STAFFING

When the entertainer Art Linkletter, owner of over 75 companies, was asked the secret of his success, his answer was, "I bet on people." And, as noted earlier, the great industrialist Andrew Carnegie once said, "Take away all our factories, our trade, our avenues of transportation, and our money, but leave me our organization, and in four years, I will have reestablished myself." By this he meant that an organization is not the factories, trade, transportation, money, or other financial and physical resources. Rather, it is made up of the people or human resources who are linked together in a formal structure, guided by managerial leadership. People are vital for an effective organization, as the following example shows:

> *The American Telephone & Telegraph Company (AT&T) 1980 annual report said, "We have even greater strength than our technology: Bell System people. It is not only their skills but their spirit that makes our business great—and will keep it great." That strong group of people carried AT&T through the 1984 breakup and now is making it and the seven regional Bell System companies dynamic growing firms.*

Staffing—which is planning personnel needs; recruiting, selecting, training, and developing capable employees; placing them in productive work environments; and rewarding their performance—is a very important management function. Often called *human-resource management*, staffing has increased in significance with the impact of labor unions, the human rights movement, growing government regulation, and escalating technology. High-tech demands are causing great concern for management. People are literally being displaced at a rate faster than they can be retrained, so that adequate skills can't be obtained to meet the demand. The human-resource management system suggested in this book is shown in Figure 9.1. Notice that it is performed in two different types of environment: the external environment, consisting of all the factors outside the organization that directly or indirectly affect it, and the internal environment, made up of all the elements within the organization.

The staffing function must be performed by all managers, whether they run the largest corporations or are the owners of small businesses, whether they manage private or public corporations, profit-oriented or not-for-profit organizations.

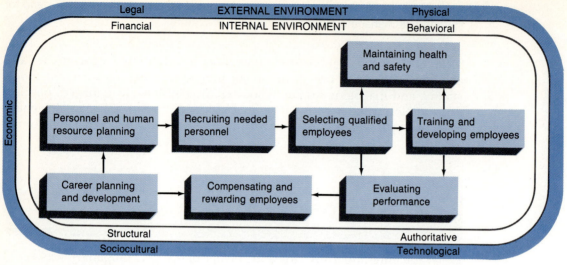

FIGURE 9.1
A model human-resource management system.

Effective staffing cannot be done with a quick, simple one-shot approach. Instead, it is a continuous activity, requiring the best efforts of capable people. Increasingly, CEOs are saying, "Check it out with our human-resource people" before instituting new programs, locating a new facility, or making other major decisions.

HOW EQUAL EMPLOYMENT OPPORTUNITY (EEO) LAWS AFFECT STAFFING

Almost every aspect of employment—from personnel planning to retirement—is now affected by **equal employment opportunity (EEO)** laws, which prohibit employment decisions based on race, color, religion, sex, national origin, age, or disability. We are putting this discussion early in the chapter so you can refer to it as you study the various subjects involved in human-resource management.

It might surprise you to learn that, until the 1960s, employment discrimination was generally accepted. Most managerial and other desirable jobs were held by white males. Women, minorities, the aged, and the handicapped were placed in jobs with lower status—and lower pay—and remained there. Now, for moral, economic, and legal reasons, EEO is generally accepted.

What is your view?

Do you agree that EEO is generally accepted? Why or why not?

Laws Providing Equal Employment Opportunity

The specific requirements of the most important EEO laws are shown in Table 9.2. The laws apply to (1) hiring and firing, (2) wages, terms, conditions, or privileges of employment, (3) classifying, assigning, or promoting employees, (4) assigning the use of facilities, and (5) training or retraining.

TABLE 9.2
Legal Influences on Equal Employment Opportunity (EEO) and Affirmative Action (AA)

Laws	Coverage	Basic requirements	Agencies involved
Title VII of Civil Rights Act of 1964, as amended	Employers with 15 or more employees, engaged in interstate commerce, federal service workers, and state and local government workers	Prohibits employment decisions based on race, color, religion, sex, or national origin	Equal Employment Opportunity Commission (EEOC)
Executive Order 11246, as amended	Employers with federal contracts and subcontracts	Requires contractors who underutilized women and minorities to take affirmative action, including setting goals and timetables, to recruit, select, train, utilize, and promote more minorities and women	Office of Federal Contract Compliance Programs (OFCCP), in the Labor Department
Age Discrimination in Employment Act of 1967, as amended	Employees from age 40	Prohibits employment discrimination, including mandatory retirement (except for some high-salaried executives and tenured faculty)	EEOC
Vocational Rehabilitation Act of 1973	Employers with federal contracts or subcontracts	Prohibits discrimination and requires contractor to develop AAPs to recruit and employ handicapped persons	OFCCP
Veterans' Readjustment Act of 1974	Employers with federal contracts or subcontracts	Requires contractors to develop AAPs to recruit and employ Vietnam-era veterans, and to list job openings with state employment services, for priority in referrals	OFCCP

Women and minorities. EEO began when Congress passed the *Civil Rights Act* in 1964.[1] Then President Johnson issued Executive Order 11246 in 1965 (amended by Executive Order 11375 in 1967), and Congress passed the *Equal Employment Opportunity Act* in 1972. As a result, employers had to do more than just see that their employment practices were not unfair. They had to develop **affirmative action programs (AAPs)** to actively seek out women and minorities and promote them into better positions.

Older workers. During the 1960s, there was a decline in the hiring—and an increase in forced retirement or discharge—of older workers. To protect older workers, Congress passed the *Age Discrimination in Employment Act* (ADEA) to prevent discrimination against employees who are 40 and above, including forced retirement (except for tenured faculty and some high-salaried executives).

The handicapped. The *Vocational Rehabilitation Act*, passed in 1973, prohibits employers with federal contracts from discriminating against the handicapped. A **handicapped person** is defined as anyone with a physical or mental disability that substantially restricts major normal activities such as walking, seeing, speaking, working, or learning.

Veterans. The *Veterans' Readjustment Act* of 1974 provides for job counseling, training, and placement service for Vietnam-era veterans. In addition, it requires firms with federal contracts to have AAPs for recruiting and hiring disabled veterans.

Enforcing EEO Laws

Enforcement of the EEO laws is spread over several agencies. The most important ones, however, are the Equal Employment Opportunity Commission (EEOC) and the Office of Federal Contract Compliance Programs (OFCCP). The EEOC has overall responsibility for coordinating enforcement. A set of *Uniform Guidelines on Employee Selection Procedures* that helps employers comply with EEO provisions is used by all agencies.[2]

Affirmative action programs (AAPs). In general, AAPs should include (1) making concerted efforts to recruit and promote women, minorities, the handicapped, and veterans, including recruiting through state employment services and at minority and women's colleges; (2) limiting the questions that may be asked in employment applications and interviews; (3) determining available percentages of women, minorities, and the handicapped in the local labor force; (4) setting up goals and timetables for recruiting women, minorities, the handicapped, and veterans; and (5) avoiding testing unless it meets established guidelines.

Religious minorities. The EEOC's proposed rules on religious accommodations are particularly troubling to managers. First, they require the employer to go out of his or her way to avoid assigning employees to work on any day that violates their religious beliefs. Second, the definition of religion includes "sincerely held moral or ethical beliefs." This concept seems to be harder to administer than the others.[3]

PLANNING HUMAN-RESOURCE NEEDS

An organization cannot wait to find competent people as they are needed to fill specific positions. Instead, it must make an effort to plan for future needs and to decide where to find the right people to fill those needs. This requires **human-resource planning,** which includes all those activities needed to provide the right types and numbers of employees to reach the organization's objectives. Keep in mind that an important aspect of personnel planning is **career management** (covered in Chapter 20), which integrates the individual's career planning and development into the organization's personnel plans.

There are three parts to personnel planning: (1) determining the jobs to be performed, the abilities needed by employees to do the jobs, and how many employees will be needed; (2) knowing where to look for the potential employees; and (3) considering the demand for and supply of workers.

Determining Job Needs

How do large companies go about staffing an expanded or start-up operation, such as a hotel, hospital, or research lab? Simply stated, they begin by determining the organization's objectives and plans. Next, they determine the types of jobs to be performed and the skills needed to perform them. Third, they estimate the total number of employees needed for a given period in the future. Fourth, they make an inventory of the people who are already available to perform the jobs. This is followed by an estimate of how many new people must be hired and when they will be needed. Finally, some type of action program for filling the needs must be set up.

Determining types of jobs and skills needed. This starts with **job analysis,** which is the process of gathering information and determining the elements of the job by observation and study and presenting the results in written form. From these data, management prepares **job descriptions,** which outline the skills, responsibility, knowledge, authority, environment, and interrelationships involved in each job. These are then written up as job specifications that become the basis for hiring new people. **Job specifications** are

"I CAN REMEMBER WHEN ALL WE NEEDED WAS SOMEONE WHO COULD CARVE AND SOMEONE WHO COULD SEW."

(Source: Phi Kappa Phi Journal, *Spring 1985, p. 14.)*

written statements about the job and the personal qualifications required of a person to perform the job successfully.

The specifications should provide a statement of the minimum acceptable standards the person should meet to perform the job satisfactorily. For dead-end, routine, and low-level jobs, it may also be desirable to state the maximum acceptable standards to prevent an overqualified person from taking the job and being dissatisfied (see Figure 9.2 for a sample of these specifications).

Determining objectives and plans. The next step is to decide where the organization wants to go. What does it plan to do? What new products or services are going to be introduced? Are new markets or clientele going to be opened up? The answers to these and related questions will influence the number and types of people to be hired.

In general, the growth in new jobs is now occurring in service-performing industries rather than goods-producing ones. These service jobs account for around three-fourths of all jobs. Retail and wholesale trade, together with finance, insurance, and real estate, create around 2 million new jobs each year.[4]

Determining overall personnel needs. Next, management must decide the overall number of employees needed to perform the jobs, and what skills

FIGURE 9.2
A sample job description, with job specifications included.

SOURCE: Robert L. Mathis and John H. Jackson, *Personnel: Human Resource Management,* 4th ed. (St. Paul: West Publishing Co., 1985), p. 197. Used with permission.

Job Description

Job Title: Accounting/Settlement Clerk

Department: Accounting

Position of Immediate Supervisor: Accounting Supervisor

I. GENERAL SUMMARY OF RESPONSIBILITIES

Prepares, checks, and distributes various accounting reports and statements to clients and internal staff. Posts to and prepares reports from general ledger accounts and performs other clerical duties as required.

II. SPECIFIC JOB RESPONSIBILITIES

1. Prepares bank reconciliation statements and other financial summary statements for distribution to clients and internal staff.
2. Posts entries in various general ledger journals.
3. Prepares special reports from information generated from computer printouts and accounting statements.
4. Prepares, on a monthly basis, complete financial reports and related trial balances for internal reporting purposes.
5. Performs certain routine office duties such as mailing, typing, report verification, and copy work.

III. JOB SPECIFICATIONS

High school degree required, with knowledge of accounting or previous accounting experience. Position requires intensive knowledge of financial summary and bank reconciliation statements. Detailed accuracy of prime importance. Prepares and produces confidential information.

and abilities they will need. Therefore, the firm's *overall personnel needs* must be estimated in terms of occupational specialties, job skills, personal characteristics, and number of employees needed.

Colleges go through this process annually. On the basis of the expected number of students, the courses to be offered, the number of sections of each course, and class sizes, the deans and department heads must decide the total number of faculty needed to satisfy the students' needs. Of course, this decision—like any manager's decision—is restricted by the resources available.

Studying present personnel. Once the number of future employees is known, management must see how many people it already has who can perform those jobs. This requires an inventory of present personnel with the required abilities who can do the jobs adequately. This inventory will enable management to match the skills of the people in the organization with the overall personnel needs. This inventory provides an overview of the present work force.

Determining net personnel needs. The difference between the overall needs and present employee inventory is the *net new personnel requirement* that must be filled by recruitment. This becomes the organization's hiring objective. Although the net requirement is the number of people needed, other factors such as occupational choices, experience, age, sex, race, and expected retirements, terminations, and transfers should be considered.

Setting up an action program. Management can start some type of action program to recruit and select employees once it knows the net need for new people. An *action program* involves all the personnel functions needed to fill the firm's personnel needs and objectives, including recruiting, selecting, developing, maintaining, and rewarding personnel.

Developing Sources of Supply of Employees

If you want to buy an item of clothing, where do you go to find it? If you go to several stores selling the item, your selection will be better, and your chances of getting the exact garment you want will be increased. On the other hand, what if there is only one store handling a limited line of that item? The selection you make will probably be very limited.

The same holds true for developing sources from which to recruit personnel. In general, the larger the number of sources of supply, the greater the chances of finding a person with the needed qualities. Most effective managers, realizing this, develop and maintain many different sources of supply. For example, most of them maintain an ongoing relationship with college and university faculties to know when capable employees are available.

The accounting firm of Lawton, Burton, and Bunge (LB&B) has developed excellent rapport with the accounting faculties in the major state universities. It sponsors social functions, provides guest speakers for classes, and even flies faculty members to its main office for tours or special occasions. Each year LB&B has had much success in hiring the top accounting graduates in the state.

Which source to use? There are really only two sources from which employees can be recruited to fill specific jobs—from within the organization and from outside (see Figure 9.3). *Each source* shown in the figure *has disadvantages, as well as advantages.* Therefore, care should be taken to weigh the advantages *and* disadvantages when using any of these sources.

Managers prefer to use the internal source because it serves to motivate present personnel. If you do an effective job for your employer and are then promoted to a higher job, your morale is boosted and you are motivated. Furthermore, as you see others promoted internally, this also encourages you. You too could get a promotion!

Some jobs, however, require going outside to find the right people. When a new technological development is introduced—say, when a computer is installed—management must look outside if present personnel can't be trained to do the job. Also, if the internal source is used exclusively, there is the risk of "inbreeding." Everybody will be familiar with the way everybody else thinks, and there will be few new ideas. Therefore, most organizations use a combination of promoting from within and hiring from without, but there are exceptions.

FIGURE 9.3
Where to find needed employees.

SOURCE: Leon C. Megginson, Lyle R. Trueblood, and Gayle M. Ross, *Business* (Lexington, MA: D. C. Heath, 1985), p. 239.

Promotion from within is "the gospel" at Minnesota Mining and Manufacturing (3M) Company. The last time it hired a vice-president from the outside was in the 1940s. The last time one left the firm to work elsewhere was in the 1960s. As a result, 111 of 3M's executives have risen through

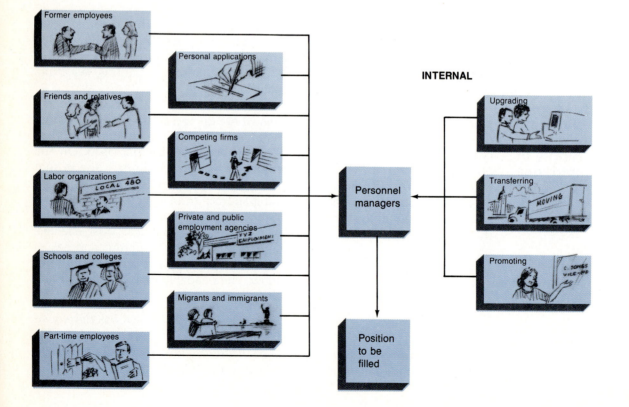

the ranks. The last four chairmen had spent their entire careers with the company. Inbreeding isn't a problem here, however, because of transfers among diversified divisions.[5]

In general, if the organization is growing in size, management must go outside to hire people. But if it is remaining the same—or even declining—it will probably only promote from within. Ideally, capable people from within will be promoted into the higher-level positions, whereas the lower, entry-level jobs will be filled by recruiting from the outside.

Internal sources. There are three methods of obtaining employees internally. First, they can be obtaining through **upgrading,** whereby the employee currently holding the position is educated, trained, or developed to perform the job better as the situation demands. For example, a large church changed from doing accounting by hand to doing it by computer. It was possible to train the current bookkeeper to use the computer instead of having to go outside to hire someone else.

Second, jobs can be filled by **transferring** or moving employees from less desirable or less rewarding jobs in the organization to others that better satisfy their needs.

Third, jobs can be filled by **promoting** employees from a lower-level job to a higher-level one. This usually carries with it a higher salary, a new job title, and added duties and responsibilities. This is a form of reward that serves as a good motivator.

External sources. When going outside, the supply source to be used will depend on the job to be filled, the type of worker desired, and economic conditions. Some of these external sources of employees, as shown in Figure 9.3, are (1) former employees who left with a good record, (2) personal applications, (3) friends and relatives of present employees, (4) competing firms, (5) labor organizations, (6) private and public employment agencies, (7) schools and colleges, (8) migrants and immigrants, and (9) part-time employees.

Employers are now using many part-time employees, or **temporaries,** such as students, retirees, and parents with school-aged children who want to work for only limited hours each week. Also, many organizations hire employees from outside concerns that specialize in performing a given service. This method is particularly useful in clerical, custodial, and maintenance operations for which an employee with a given specialty can be hired by the hour or day, as the situation dictates. They now provide about 20 percent of the work force.[6]

In 1987, Mary Ann Padilla was honored by the Small Business Administration and Avon Products Inc. as one of their "Women of Enterprise" for the work of her small business—Sunny Side/Temporary Side Inc. When the oil industry started declining in 1984, it pulled her Denver employment service down with it. So she started providing temporary help for the jobs still available and transformed her business. It's now her biggest revenue producer—$1 million in 1987.[7]

RECRUITING AND SELECTING EMPLOYEES

You are probably familiar with the recruitment of athletes for college sports. The coaches or managers determine what positions need filling, look over the potential players in selected high schools and junior colleges, select the players they want, and then go out and recruit them.

Employers do much the same, with one exception. They recruit the potential employees first. Then they select the workers they want from this pool of recruits. That's what this section is all about. We now look at recruitment and discuss selection.

Recruiting Personnel

Recruitment refers to reaching out and attracting a pool of potential employees from which to select the ones needed to satisfy the organization's needs. Recruiting, then, involves attracting the right number of people with the abilities needed to fill the available jobs.

The methods used to recruit personnel vary with different employers, in different industries, and in different localities. Some managers passively wait for applicants to come to them. Others, using a more aggressive approach, go out seeking and searching for potential employees. The usual methods of recruitment involve employee referrals, advertising, college recruiting, and the use of the computer.

Employee referrals. If used properly, **employee referrals** are an excellent method of recruiting personnel. Since current employees know the job to be filled and the personal abilities needed to fill it, they may be able to recruit a relative or friend for it. In fact, many firms give bonuses to employees who attract new employees. For example, a division of Loral Electronics offers a $5000 bonus for finders of engineers with a minimum of four years of experience. One General Electric (GE) unit pays a $500 finder's fee and gives the finder a "GE name-dropper" T-shirt.

Advertising. The most common form of recruiting is the use of want ads in newspapers. In fact, Sears, Roebuck and Company began when Alvah Roebuck answered a want ad placed by Richard Sears in the *Chicago Daily News* of April 11, 1887.

Other forms of advertising include billboards, radio, and professional journals, as shown in Figure 9.4.

College recruiting. College graduates provide the best source of scientific, technical, professional, and managerial personnel. Therefore, the larger, more successful firms generally do some type of campus recruiting.

Using the computer. You are probably familiar with the use of computers to provide dates for individuals. Computers are also used in a similar way to find employees. For example, the Department of Labor has a *Job Bank* that uses a computer to match jobs and people.

Selecting the Right Person for the Job

Selection is choosing from a group of potential employees the specific person to perform a given job. In theory, selection is simple. As shown earlier, management decides what the job involves and what abilities the individual

FIGURE 9.4
A typical ad in a
professional journal.

> **POSITION AVAILABLE**
> **EXECUTIVE**
> **VICE-PRESIDENT**
>
> An aggressive northeastern corporation headquartered in Stamford, CT, with a sound financial base and growing market share seeks an executive vice-president who will have responsibility for corporate planning, diversification, acquisition, and merger programs. Will work closely with the president and board of directors.
>   Salary in the 80K range with outstanding company benefits. If you are qualified and interested, please send résumé and references to:
>
> Management Search Incorporated
> P.O. Box 1507
> New York, NY

must possess to perform the job effectively. Then the manager looks at the applicants' past performance records and selects the one whose abilities, experiences, and personality most nearly conform to the job requirements. Unfortunately, selection is not that simple! It is much more complicated than it appears.

Past performance is still the best indicator of future performance. What a person has done in the past, as evidenced by school records, work experience—including part-time and summer jobs—and extracurricular activities, is the best predictor of what he or she will *probably* do in the future. Hiring the "right" person for the "right" job can greatly improve employees' performance.

What to look for. It is impossible to state exactly what to look for in a potential employee. Yet there are some factors that tend to affect an employee's performance. They are the following:

1. *Personal background,* including education and work history, to show what the person has done in the past.

2. *Aptitudes and interests,* to estimate the person's interests and capacities.

3. *Attitudes and needs,* to predict the person's responsibility and authority.

4. *Analytical and manipulative abilities,* to study thinking and evaluating abilities.

5. *Skills and technical abilities,* to judge the ability to perform the technical aspects of the job.

6. *Health, energy, and stamina,* to see the person's physical ability to perform the work.

What is your view?

In looking at graduates from a local community college or university, one recruiter said, "I place the heaviest weight by far on grades. They are the equivalent of on-the-job performance and, to me, the best indicator of a person's future success." Do you agree or disagree? Why?

Selection procedure. The actual selection of people is a continuous process and can never be thought of as completed. The procedure shown in Figure 9.5 is suggested as an effective way of choosing people. The usual steps are preliminary interview, biographical inventory, testing, in-depth interview, checking performance references, physical examination, and personal judgment. See TIPS 9.1 for questions you can and cannot ask an applicant.

Preliminary interview. During the preliminary interview, the less capable applicants are rejected because of poor appearance, physical disabilities that would prevent them from doing the job they are applying for, or lack of serious interest in the job. This interview is usually conducted at the organization's offices. In college recruiting, however, it is typically done at the applicant's campus.

Biographical inventory. Probably the most frequently used step in the selection procedure is looking for evidence of past performance in a person's record. This can be found from an application blank, a personal data sheet or résumé, work records, school records, military records, and similar biographical sources.

Testing. Testing provides the only *objective* basis for gathering information about the applicant. With well-developed and well-administered tests, one can estimate the individual's ability to perform the job. Tests are not being used very much now because it is difficult to develop reliable and valid tests

FIGURE 9.5
Procedure for selecting employees.

SOURCE: Leon C. Megginson, *Personnel Management: A Human Resources Approach,* 5th ed. (Homewood, IL: Richard D. Irwin, 1985), p. 203. Copyright 1985 by Richard D. Irwin, Inc. Reprinted by permission.

Applicants who are available as potential employees

Instruments used to gather data

Characteristics to look for

Preliminary screening or interview — Obvious misfit from outward appearance and conduct

Biographical inventory from application blank, BIB, resumé, etc. — Lacks adequate educational and performance record

TESTING
Intelligence test(s) — Fails to meet minimum standards of mental alertness
Aptitude test(s) — Lacks specific capacities for acquiring particular knowledges or skills

Proficiency or achievement test(s) — Unable to demonstrate ability to do job

Interest test(s) — Lacks significant vocational interest in job

Personality test(s) — Lacks the personal characteristics required for job

In-depth interview — Lacks necessary innate ability, ambition, or other qualities

Verifying biographical data from references — Unfavorable or negative reports on past performance

Physical examination — Physically unfit for job

Personal judgment — Overall competence and ability to fit into the firm that do not discriminate against minorities or that would hold up in a lawsuit.

One type of test—the **polygraph,** or lie detector—is not permitted in many states because its findings are inconclusive. It is at this point that an employer may begin to run afoul of the EEO laws. So the interviewer should avoid questions (see TIPS 9.1) that might indicate an intent to discriminate.

In-depth interview. The in-depth interview is a very important step in the selection procedure, for all the other information about the applicant is brought together at that point. In reality, it is an effort to get information about the person's attitudes, feelings, and abilities. It is a *two-way exchange of information* between the potential employee and management. It requires the applicant to do a great deal more talking about a variety of things than an interviewer-dominated, highly structured interview. See MAP 9.1 for the types of questions actually asked during these interviews.

Performance references. By checking with previous employers, the personnel manager can obtain information about the applicant's past performance. But care must be taken to protect the individual's personal rights. One of the great problems today is the invasion of privacy by employers and the government. Another problem is the refusal of former employers to provide a reference.

Physical examination. Physical exams are given to see whether the person has a contagious disease that might jeopardize other employees. They are

"We asked your previous employers for references but you've been erased from their memory banks!"

(*Source:* The Wall Street Journal, October 8, 1987.)

also used to decide whether the person can do the work and to serve as a defense in case of worker's compensation charges.

Two burning issues now challenging employers are (1) testing and treatment for drug and alcohol abuse and (2) testing and treatment for AIDS (acquired immune deficiency syndrome). One survey showed that 15 percent of the firms queried were testing applicants and employees, while 5 percent planned to start within a year.[8] Those not testing said employees' lawsuits—or the threat of them—as well as the attitude of state officials prohibited them.

Subject of inquiry:	It is not discriminatory to inquire about:	It may be discriminatory to inquire about:
10. Relatives	a. Names of relatives already employed by the organization b. Name and address of person or relative to be notified in an emergency	a. Name and/or address of any relative of applicant
11. Organizations	a. Applicant's membership in any union, professional, service, or trade organization	a. All clubs, social fraternities, societies, lodges, or organizations to which the applicant belongs where the name or character of the organization indicates the race, creed, color, or religion, national origin, sex, or ancestry of its members
12. Arrest record and convictions		a. Number and kinds of arrest and convictions unless related to job performance
13. Photographs		a. Photographs with application or before hiring b. Résumé with photo of applicant
14. Height and weight		a. Any inquiry into height and weight of applicant, except where it is a bona fide occupational requirement
15. Physical limitations	a. Whether applicant has the ability to perform job-related functions	a. Whether an applicant is handicapped, or the nature or severity of a handicap
16. Education	a. Training an applicant has received if related to the job applied for	a. Educational attainment of an applicant unless there is validation that having certain educational backgrounds (i.e., high school diploma or college degree) is necessary to perform the functions of the job or position applied for
17. Financial status		a. An applicant's debts or assets b. Garnishments

SOURCE: Used with permission of Omaha, Nebraska, Human Relations Department.

There is growing controversy over testing for the virus that causes AIDS. Those who favor it say there's a need to track its spread in an effort to contain it. Opponents claim testing invades privacy, is prohibitively costly, and is invalid because there are so many testing errors.[9] These two problems will challenge managers for years to come, and solutions to them are nowhere in sight.

Personal judgment. When all else has been done, some manager must make a personal decision to accept or reject the person for employment.

Management Application and Practice 9.1   Typical Questions Asked During an Employment Interview

Indicated below is a general classification of those questions that, in one form or another, were reported as being used by at least three or more companies. These were indicated as the most helpful questions asked by employers during the initial interview with graduating college seniors as reported by 170 companies.

	Number of companies
1. What are your long-range goals? Ambitions? Future plans? Basic objectives? What do you want to be doing 5–10–15 years from now? What are your immediate objectives?	93
2. Why did you choose your field of special study? How have you prepared yourself for work in your chosen field? What subjects have you enjoyed most? Least? Do you have plans for graduate study?	74
3. What type of work do you want to do? Why? Why do you think you qualify for this type of work? In what type of job would you like to start?	60
4. Why do you think you might like to work in our type of industry? Our company? Why did you select this company? What can you contribute to a company such as ours?	53
5. What were your extracurricular activities? What have you gained from your activities? What leadership office(s) have you held? What are your hobbies—your interests out of school?	40
6. What is your scholastic record? Where do you stand in your class? Explain your academic record. In what courses have you earned your best grades? How well did you apply yourself in your studies?	37
7. Do you like to travel? Are you willing to travel? To relocate? Have you geographical preferences? Would you like to live in our community?	36
8. What are your major strengths and weaknesses? Your accomplishments to date? Major achievements in college? Any plans for improvement?	30
9. What work experience have you had? Summer jobs? Part-time work? What experiences did you like the best? Why?	28
10. What do you know about our company? What questions would you like to ask? Is the size of a company important to you?	15
11. How was your education financed? What part did you earn?	9
12. Tell me about your background and experience.	11
13. What is your draft status? What service experience have you had?	5
14. Are you interested in a training program?	5
Total number of questions summarized above	496

SOURCE: Frank S. Endicott, *Endicott Report—1980: Trends in the Hiring of College Graduates* (Evanston, IL.: The Placement Center, Northwestern University, 1979). Reprinted by permission.

Job offer. If the person is selected, a job offer is made. Yet about half of all job offers to college graduates are turned down. Then the procedure must start all over again!

What is your view?

Would all these selection procedure steps be used by a small firm? If not, which ones would probably be omitted? What other steps (or methods) could be used?

There is no perfect selection procedure. As shown in Figure 9.6, each of the steps can have a potentially adverse effect on one or more of the types of employees sought. Therefore, once again, a contingency approach must be relied on; that is, each employer should develop the procedure that delivers the best results.

Orienting New Employees

After being selected, the employee is placed on the job and introduced to the organization through some form of orientation. This process is important because a new job is difficult and frustrating for a new employee.[10] The new employee may be qualified for the job, but the new situation is different and strange, and poor orientation can squelch enthusiasm and effort right from the start! About half of labor turnover occurs during the first pay period.

Research has shown that an effective orientation program can (1) reduce labor turnover, (2) reduce employee anxiety and uncertainty, (3) save time of fellow employees and supervisors, and (4) instill more positive work values and improve the motivation and job satisfaction of the new worker.[11]

The orientation process can be a very simple introduction to present employees or a lengthy process of informing the employee of the employer's policies, procedures, and employee benefits.

What is your view?

Think about your most recently held job. It might be one you presently hold or one you had during summers or perhaps it was only part time. To what extent were you "oriented" to your job and the organization? If you have never held a job, did you go through an orientation when you came to college?

FIGURE 9.6
Adverse impact of screening techniques on minorities.

SOURCE: Richard D. Arvey, *Fairness in Selecting Employees,* copyright 1979, Addison-Wesley, Reading, MA. Fig. 9.1, p. 236. Reprinted with permission.

	Blacks	Females	Elderly	Handicapped
Intelligence and verbal tests	√√	+	√	?
Work sampling tests	+	NE	NE	NE
Interview	+	√√	√	√
Educational requirements	√√	+	√	?
Physical tests (height, weight, etc.)	+	√√	?	√√

Key
√√ = Fairly established evidence of adverse impact
√ = Some evidence of adverse impact
? = No data which bears direct evidence of adverse impact, but seems likely depending on type of handicap or type of test
NE = No or little evidence to indicate one way or the other
+ = Evidence indicates that particular minority group does as well as or even better than majority members

TRAINING AND DEVELOPING EMPLOYEES

New employees usually already have the basic education and training needed. They are a product of an educational system and experience that have given them a certain level of ability and competence. Managers must begin with the employee's present level of development and build on that to make the person a more productive worker.

For the purpose of this discussion, **training** is attaining specific, detailed, and routine job skills and techniques. **Development** is the broader scope of improvement and growth of abilities, attitudes, and personality traits.

In general, society is responsible for providing potential employees with a general **education,** which is the acquisition of generalized knowledge. Then the organization is responsible, along with the individual, for providing training for specific jobs or positions. Development can occur formally or informally as the person grows and learns to adapt by using his or her education and training.

Reasons for Training and Development

Development is important for the individual, for the organization, and even for the country. You are probably aware from observing team sports that a major way to improve the team is to improve the individual players or to improve the level of coaching. The same holds true in other organizations. An organization that is to grow and develop must have within it people who grow and develop. In fact, employers always pay the cost of developing employees, even if the company has no formal training program. If they don't spend for development, they pay the price in poor work, waste, grievances, absenteeism, and labor turnover.

Development is needed to meet technological advances. In general, today's unemployed workers are those who do not have the training and education to hold down technically oriented jobs. A person who was an effective electrician a few years ago probably needs to learn how to become an electronics technician. Today, the accountant needs to understand computer programming and capabilities.

Development leads to greater personal satisfaction. As people become better educated, trained, and developed, they have a greater sense of worth, dignity, and well-being. They also become more valuable to their employers and society. In general, the better-developed employees cause fewer problems and have greater job satisfaction.

Development must be dynamic and continuous. Learning is a lifelong process. As the Red Queen admonishes Alice in *Through the Looking Glass*, "It takes all the running you can do, to keep in the same place." Margaret Mead, the noted anthropologist, said the same when she wrote, "No one will live all his life in the world into which he was born, and no one will die in the world in which he worked in his maturity.... Learning ... must go on not only at special times and in special places, but all through production and consumption."[12] We no longer assume that learning stops when people leave school. People must keep learning and developing if they are to remain effective and satisfied employees.

Training and Development Methods

There are so many methods used for training and developing employees that it is not possible to discuss all of them. In general, employees learn on the job and off the job.

On-the-job methods. The usual on-the-job methods are (1) **coaching,** whereby superiors provide guidance and counsel to subordinates in the course of their regular job performance; (2) **planned progression,** or moving subordinates in well-ordered channels through different levels of the organization; (3) **job rotation,** or moving people through highly diversified and differentiated jobs; (4) **temporary** or **anticipatory assignments,** in which the subordinate serves in management positions for short periods; and (5) **performance appraisals** (**performance evaluations** or **reviews**) systems.

An important aspect of coaching is providing a **mentor**—an individual who will systematically develop and promote a subordinate's abilities through intensive tutoring, coaching, and guidance. Often women and minorities, still breaking into fields previously dominated by white males, are the ones who need mentors the most; unfortunately, they also have more difficulty finding them.[13]

As shown in Figure 9.7, the typical performance appraisal system requires a manager to rate each employee's performance according to preestablished performance criteria over a given period of time (normally six months or a year). Note the focus on ways that the employee can grow and develop in his or her present position. Performance appraisal systems also provide a basis for coaching and planned progression (1 and 2 in the foregoing) as well as means for determining merit increases, transfers, and even dismissals.

Many large companies have had excellent success with their on-the-job management development programs.

Bethlehem Steel's "Operation Loop" is one example of how a large company develops managerial talent among its new college recruits. Bethlehem's three-phase program loops trainees through all of Bethlehem's operations, from steelmaking to accounting to public relations. The first phase is a two-week orientation session at corporate headquarters that gives participants an overall look at the company. Extensive movement through the recruit's assigned plant or office follows. Then there's on-the-job training for two years, with quarterly evaluations. The aim is to have participants rise at least as high as the department head level during their careers. Of Bethlehem's 270 top managers and executives, 152, or 56 percent, were participants in the Loop.[14]

Off-the-job methods. Off-the-job development takes place in (1) **executive development programs** at universities or other educational institutions, where managers participate in generalized programs using case analysis, simulation, and other learning methods; (2) **laboratory training,** where one learns to be more sensitive to other people and more aware of one's own feelings; and (3) **organization development (OD),** which emphasizes

Employee Name _Fred Willis_ Position _Chief Engineer, Materials Research_

Period covered by evaluation: from _1/1/81_ to _7/1/82_

	(1) Unsatisfactory	(2) Meets minimum	(3) Average	(4) Above average	(5) Outstanding	Score
1. Quality and thoroughness of work		✓				2
2. Volume of work				✓		4
3. Knowledge of job, methods, and procedures				✓		4
4. Initiative and resourcefulness				✓		4
5. Cooperation, attitude, and teamwork			✓			3
6. Adaptability and ability to learn quickly					✓	5
7. Ability to express self clearly in speaking and writing			✓			3
8. Planning, organizing, and making work assignments		✓				2
9. Selection and development of subordinates		✓				2
10. Morale and loyalty of subordinates			✓			3

Total score _32_

What steps can this employee take to improve his work?

Employee is an eager, innovative, resourceful person whose eagerness sometimes causes him to sacrifice quality of work. While highly talented, he must learn to delegate more technical work to subordinates and assume more managerial tasks himself.

Other comments:

Employee has been in position about 7 months. This is his first managerial job and some problems in making the adjustment were expected.

Total score:
10–15 Unsatisfactory
16–25 Meets minimum
26–35 Average
36–45 Above average
46–50 Outstanding

Supervisor's signature _Paul Batson_
Title _Head Engineering Research_
Employee's signature _Frederick R. Willis_
Approved by _Ann Wilhelm_
Title _Director, Research and Development_

FIGURE 9.7
Employee evaluation form.

change, growth, and development of the entire organization (see Chapter 13 for a detailed discussion of OD).

What is your view?

Suppose that you owned your own business, with 800 employees, that manufactures and sells den furniture. You want to retire in five years and have your son or daughter succeed you as president. What kind of ''development'' program would you establish for your successor, who has just turned 23 and joined the company as a college graduate last month?

COMPENSATING EMPLOYEES

> He got a fair raise; or, to be precise,
> Just half what he estimated
> He well deserved—and easily twice
> What the boss believed he rated.[15]

This doggerel helps explain why the question of compensation is one of the most difficult and perplexing employee problems management has to deal with. Although wages must have some logical and defensible basis, they involve many emotional factors from the point of view of employees. **Compensation** is providing employees with a financial payment as a reward for work performed and as a motivator for future performance.

Compensation takes two forms—wages and benefits. **Wages** are the reward one receives for working for someone else. They take the form of an hourly wage, salary, bonus, tips, or commission. **Benefits** are what one is entitled to because of being employed. They take the form of paid holidays, vacations, insurance, retirement, and pensions.

Importance of Compensation

Compensation is very important to individual employees because it is a measure of their worth to themselves, fellow workers, families, and society. Thus employees' absolute level of income determines their scale of living, and their relative income indicates their status, prestige, and worth.

Compensation is also important to the organization, for the amount it pays its employees in the form of salaries and benefits is usually its most important (and frequently the greatest) cost item. Since the turn of the century, employee costs for the average firm have been about 50 percent of sales, in spite of wars, depressions, inflation, and unionization.[16]

Compensation is important to the economy also, as about 80 percent of the nation's income comes from this source. Also, employee income is the largest part of the purchasing power that is used to buy the goods and services produced by business firms.

Importance of Income Differences

Employees usually judge the fairness of their pay by comparing it with that of other employees. Whether they think their income is fair or not will depend on how they see its value relative to that of others. Most employee dissatisfaction is over differences in pay between jobs and individuals.

What is your view?

You are undoubtedly familiar with many star athletes who become upset when another high-priced athlete joins their team and receives greater compensation than they do. Are they really concerned about the economic difference? If not, what *is* it that upsets them so much?

Acceptable differences. In general, employees will accept pay differences based on greater responsibility, ability, knowledge, productivity, job differences, or managerial activities. But they bitterly resent differences that cannot be justified on the basis of one of the factors just named. For example, college professors tend to be unconcerned if they earn less than plumbers, electricians, truck drivers, or bricklayers. But they will become upset if the professor down the hall, with less experience and fewer publications, gets a larger salary increase than they do.

Unacceptable differences. There have been differences in pay based on race, ethnic group, and sex; these are now prohibited by law and public policy. For example, the EEO laws discussed earlier in the chapter prohibit such discrimination. In addition, the *Equal Pay Act of 1963* makes it illegal to pay women less than men for the same general type of work. A big issue now is whether comparable pay should be given for jobs of "comparable worth."

Comparable worth means paying employees for a given job according to points arrived at by a formula that considers education, effort, skill, and responsibility required for the job. It goes beyond paying equal salaries for equal jobs, and requires equal salaries for women performing jobs that are different from, but just as demanding and valuable as, those performed by men.[17]

Women's earnings were only about 69 percent of men's earnings in 1986. And, as you can see from Figure 9.8, the difference was found in some of the

FIGURE 9.8
Women earn 69 percent of men's pay. Comparison of weekly salaries in top-paying jobs.

SOURCE: *USA Today*, April 24, 1987, p. 1B. Data from the Bureau of Labor Statistics. Copyright 1987, USA TODAY. Used with permission.

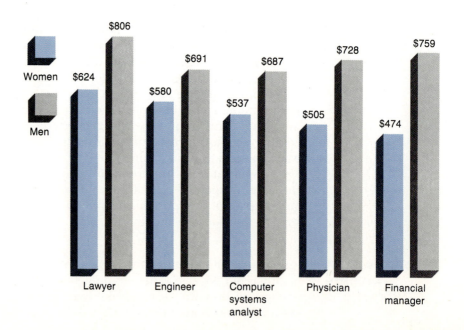

top-paying jobs for women. There are many reasons for this, including the fact that about two out of three new employees are women. Women come into companies at the entry level and receive lower rates of pay in those low-level jobs. Also, in spite of public policy, women still tend to be employed in the lower-paid industries and jobs.

A similar situation exists for black and Hispanic workers. Figure 9.9 shows that while the median weekly income for white workers is $402, income for blacks and Hispanics is $307 and $300, respectively.

How Compensation Is Determined

Management's compensation policies and practices are determined by the interaction of three factors: what it is *willing* to pay, what it is *able* to pay, and what it is *required* to pay.

What management is willing to pay. It is no exaggeration to say that most managers *want* to pay fair salaries. Yet managers also feel that employees should do "a fair day's work for a fair day's pay." So they first try to improve employee performance and output. Then they encourage employees to increase their output so that higher wages and salaries can be paid.

What management is able to pay. Regardless of all other factors, in the long run a private employer can only pay salaries based on employee output—in spite of other factors. As indicated earlier, there must be income before there can be wages. There must be profits for the owners if wages are to continue to be paid. Real wages of employees are based on employee productivity. In the last few years, although salaries and wages have been increasing in dollar amount, employees' real earnings have been declining because of declining productivity and inflation.

What management is required to pay. In the short run, wages and salaries are based on external pressures from governments, unions, and competitors to pay "prevailing" wages.

Government factors. There are several state and federal laws dealing with employee income, in addition to the ones already discussed. The best known is the *Fair Labor Standards Act of 1938*, as amended. This act sets the minimum wages for employees and the maximum number of hours (40) they can work per week without receiving overtime premium pay. In 1981, the

FIGURE 9.9
Comparing earnings. Median weekly income for full-time employees; 1986 data.

SOURCE: *USA Today*, June 8, 1987, p. 1A. Data from U.S. Department of Labor. Copyright 1987, USA TODAY. Used with permission.

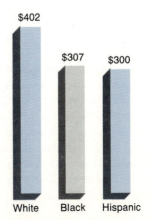

minimum wage was raised to $3.35 per hour, where it remained until 1987, when Congress proposed raising it to $4.50.

Collective bargaining. Unions have great effect on wages and salaries, whether the employer is unionized or not. Through strike activities, legislative lobbying, and informing the public, unions tend to increase the wages of their members and others.

Comparable wages. An organization's wage and salary practices must conform to wage patterns in its industry and in its community. Sears, Roebuck, for example, must pay salespeople about the same as J. C. Penney and Montgomery Ward. Local hospitals must pay about the same for nurses and banks about the same for tellers. This is caused by competition as well as trade associations.

Certain occupations also have relatively the same earnings. Doctors, lawyers, and other professionals tend to have fee structures that are generally the same for everyone in the profession.

How Employees Are Paid

At one time, employees were paid in cash at the end of the day on the basis of the number of hours worked. Many are still paid an *hourly wage* but receive it in a check at the end of the week. This is called **time** (or **day**) **wages.** Other employees are paid a *fixed salary* per week, month, or year.

What is your view?

What are the advantages and disadvantages of a daily pay system being used today?

About 25 percent of production employees and most sales personnel are also paid some form of **incentive wage,** whereby their earnings are directly related to the amount they produce or sell above a predetermined standard. For example, the people who sell refreshments at sports events are paid according to the number of units they sell. Automobile and real estate salespersons receive a percentage of their sales as a **commission.**

Many firms have a **profit-sharing plan** under which employees receive a definite, prearranged percentage of the firm's profits as extra income. According to the American Productivity Center in Houston, this method was used by 32 percent of a group of 1600 firms surveyed.[18]

Role of Employee Benefits

One of the fastest-growing parts of compensation is the amount paid for *employee benefits* above and beyond the basic salary paid. Originally called "fringe benefits," these benefits now cost about 37 percent of an organization's payroll, or, to put it another way, for every dollar paid to an employee in salary, an *additional $0.37* is provided for various benefits! This now amounts to over $7500 per employee per year. Some of these benefits are *legally required.* For example, the *Social Security Act* requires retirement pay, disability pay, and survivors' benefits. *Unemployment compensation* is also required by the act. All states have *workers' compensation* laws that provide for industrial illness and accidents.

There are also many *voluntary* benefit programs, and they take many forms. The most popular ones include pay for time not worked, pay for overtime and special activities, retirement pay, health protection, and others. Some of the more popular benefits are hospitalization insurance, legal services, dental services or insurance, paid vacation and holidays, educational benefits, and discounts on purchases of goods and services. Management feels that these voluntary benefits are essential for attracting and retaining employees.

MAINTAINING HEALTH AND SAFETY

An increasingly important area of management is maintaining employee health and safety. Business is doing much to improve the situation, but the *Occupational Safety and Health Act of 1970* (OSHAct) has speeded up these activities. OSHA inspectors are concentrating on those industries with the highest accident rates. The law, which is administered by the Occupational Safety and Health Administration (OSHA), is forcing employers and employees to provide even safer and more healthful working conditions and to be more responsible for these activities.

OSHA (1) develops standards, (2) conducts inspections to see that standards are being met, and (3) enforces standards by issuing citations and imposing penalties for violations. For instance, IBP Inc., the largest U.S. meat packing company, was fined a record $2.59 million for failing to report more than 1000 cases of employee injuries and illnesses.[19]

SUMMARY

Effective employees are required if an organization is to succeed. But an effective work group doesn't just happen. Therefore, staffing and human-resource management are essential to effective performance in organizations.

Management must plan for its human-resource needs. It must decide how many workers of each type are needed and where they can be recruited. In general, workers for new jobs and those in the lower levels are recruited from outside the organization. Higher-level jobs are filled by upgrading, transferring, or promoting present employees.

Individual employers must compete with others for new employees; new employees are, after all, a scarce resource. Therefore, managers need to study the national labor market to see what the overall supply and demand picture looks like. In general, the newer jobs are in the service-performing industries rather than the goods-producing ones. Around three-fourths of all workers now perform services; only about 25 percent produce goods.

Another trend is the increasing number of workers who were previously not employed in the better jobs. The modern work force has more women, especially as high-level managers.

Employers must now have affirmative action programs to actively recruit minorities, women, veterans, the handicapped, and older persons. The most common forms of recruiting are advertising, college recruiting, and employee referrals.

The usual procedure for selecting employees involves some combination of the following steps: preliminary interviewing, studying past performance, testing, in-depth interviewing, checking references, and giving (or requiring) a physical exam. Two big issues now are testing for drugs and AIDS.

Both new and old employees should be trained and developed. Otherwise, the organization pays a high cost in the form of poor performance, complaints and grievances, absenteeism, and labor turnover.

Employee compensation is important to employees, employers, and the nation. Management should try to set its wage rate high enough to attract capable employees, yet low enough to allow the price of the firm's product to be competitive. Also, the owners must make a profit to remain in business.

The health and safety of employees are now requiring much of management's time, effort, and money.

REVIEW QUESTIONS

1. What is staffing?
2. (a) What are some of the laws providing for equal employment opportunity? (b) What employers are covered by each? (c) What protection does each provide and for whom is it provided?
3. What is an AAP? Explain.
4. (a) What is human-resource planning, and why is it so important to management? (b) What is career management, and how is it related to the management of human resources?
5. (a) What are the most important internal sources of supply of personnel? Explain. (b) What are the most important external sources of supply of personnel?
6. (a) What is recruitment? (b) What are some of the methods used to recruit personnel?
7. (a) What is selection? (b) What are the usual steps in the selection procedure?
8. What three factors help determine management's compensation policies and practices? Explain.

DISCUSSION QUESTIONS

1. Are staffing and human-resource management really as important as the authors claim? Explain.
2. Why are employee training and development so important? What are some of the more popular ways of developing managers? Explain.
3. What are some acceptable income differentials? Unacceptable? What is being done to remove the unacceptable ones?
4. What is your opinion of "comparable worth"?
5. What are some reasons for and against drug testing?

LEARNING EXERCISE 9.1

Merit or Seniority?

Many people who lacked the qualifications normally required of new employees were hired by Purity Chemicals, an old, established firm, during World War II. Because of the manpower shortage, it was necessary to hire those who were available. Following the war, additional employees were hired as production was increased, and the overall qualifications of these employees were much higher than those of earlier employees.

Since it was company policy to promote production supervisors from the wage-roll ranks, many highly qualified supervisors were promoted from among the ranks of these newer employees. According to a union-manager agreement, all production supervisors retained and continued to accrue plant seniority in the bargaining unit from which they had been promoted.

In the late 1950s, the company found it necessary, because of technological changes and a decrease in demand for its products, to reduce the number of its employees. Seniority was the primary guide in determining who would be terminated. It was apparent that the company's younger—and in many cases better—supervisors, would be involved in the layoff as a result of this seniority clause. The union agreement was followed, however; and the younger supervisors were terminated according to their seniority.

A few years later, following a change in top management, great efforts were made to make Purity the leader in its field. In addition, the company began to expand and diversify into other related fields.

Shortly after this new era of growth began, the production manager asked his subordinate, the production superintendent, for a list of employees whom he considered to be potential supervisors since additional ones would be needed for the new production facilities. The superintendent had thought about this many times and had already made a survey of those employees who had some of the more desirable qualities of leadership. For reasons such as health, age, and lack of education, however, he no longer had employees he felt could be promoted. He informed the manager of this problem. The latter had received similar reports from other superintendents.

Some of the new units could be run without hiring new wage-roll personnel by redistribution of existing personnel, but additional supervisors would be required in some cases.

Questions

1. What does this case show about the relationship between the organization and its environment?
2. What does it illustrate about the importance of the human resource?
3. What would you do now if you were the production manager? The production superintendent?
4. (a) What caused the real problem? (b) How do you think the problem can be corrected? (c) Is your answer a feasible one?
5. What does the case illustrate concerning the use of (a) merit, (b) seniority, and (c) outside recruiting in selecting personnel for management positions?

LEARNING EXERCISE 9.2

The New Director of Human Resources

As the new director of human resources at City Hospital, Shelly Adams was told by the hospital administrator, "Your principal authority and responsibility will be for human-resource planning, recruitment, selection, and training, as well as coordination of company personnel practices in areas such as discipline and wage and salary management." In announcing Adams's appointment to the new position several months earlier at a meeting of the line department heads, the administrator had emphasized the advantages of the new position and urged all managers to give Shelly their full cooperation.

It hasn't worked out that way, however. Department managers have continued to interview and hire their own employees just as in the past. Some send Shelly a memo after the fact, but a number have hired new people and have yet to inform her. Three employees have been dismissed from their jobs, and not only was Shelly not consulted in any case, but, in her opinion, one of the dismissed workers has an excellent case if she chooses to file a discrimination suit against the hospital. Shelly has avoided going to the administration with her problem of gaining compliance from the other department heads, as she feels the situation will improve, given time.

Recently, the administrator announced that an employee performance appraisal system was to be implemented in the hospital. He named five department managers to serve on the committee to design the system, with Shelly serving as chairperson. After consultation with the department heads, Shelly sent them a memo announcing a date and time for the first committee meeting. To her dismay, no one showed up! Hurt and angry, she marched up the stairs to the administrator's office.

Questions

1. Who do you think is responsible for the problem?
2. What caused the problem?
3. What do you think the administrator is going to do? Why?
4. What would you do if you were the administrator? Explain.

NOTES

1. Actually, there have been state and federal laws, executive orders, and regulations affecting discrimination since the 1930s, but they were primarily passive or designed to *prevent discrimination, not to require positive, affirmative action.*
2. See "Adoption by Four Agencies of *Uniform Guidelines on Employee Selection Procedures,*" *Federal Register* 43 (August 25, 1978): 38290–38315, for these guidelines.
3. See John M. Norwood, "But I Can't Work on Saturdays," *Personnel Administrator* 25 (January 1980): 25–30.
4. "Services Are Still Buoying the Economy," *Business Week,* June 23, 1987, p. 39; and "Where the New Jobs Will Be," *USA Today,* March 20, 1987, p. 1B.
5. Lawrence Ingrassia, "3M Uses Promote-from-Within Policy to Breed Managers Like Chairman Lehr," *The Wall Street Journal,* July 7, 1980, pp. 15–16.
6. Leon C. Megginson, *Personnel Management: A Human Resources Approach,* 5th ed. (Homewood, IL: Richard D. Irwin, 1985), p. 172.
7. "A Temporary Solution," *USA Today,* June 18, 1987, p. 9B.
8. Mark Memmott, "Employers Must Weigh Pros, Cons of Drug Tests," *USA Today,* July 1, 1987, p. 4B.
9. "Debate Rages Over AIDS-Test Policy," *The Wall Street Journal,* June 18, 1987, p. 33.
10. O. C. Brenner and J. Tomkiewicz, "Job Orientation of Males and Females: Are Sex Differences Declining?" *Personal Psychology* 32 (Winter 1979): 741–750.
11. Megginson, pp. 246–248.
12. Margaret Mead, "Thinking Ahead: Why Is Education Obsolete?" *Harvard Business Review* 36 (November–December 1958): 34.
13. David M. Hunt and Carol Michael, "Mentoring: A Career Training and Development Tool," *Academy of Management Review* 8 (July 1983): 475–485.
14. Douglas R. Sease, "Grads Trained for Fast Track at Bethlehem," *The Wall Street Journal,* July 29, 1980.
15. George S. Galbraith, "Salary Adjustment," *Management Review* 52 (May 1963): 17.
16. Sidney Weintraub, "A Law That Cannot Be Repealed," *Challenge* 10 (April 1962): 17–19.
17. See "A Business Group Fights 'Comparable Worth,'" *Business Week,* November 10, 1980, pp. 100–105, for the issues involved. Further, the Supreme Court has moved in the direction of favoring comparable pay by saying that women can sue their employers for sex discrimination even if the jobs are not identical. See "A Fresh Round in Fight over Equal Pay," *U.S. News & World Report,* June 22, 1981, pp. 81–82.
18. Beth Brophy, "Thanks for the Bonus, but Where's My Raise?" *U.S. News & World Report,* July 20, 1987, pp. 43–44.
19. Ruth Sinai, "OSHA Cites IBP; Record Fine Sought," *Mobile* (Alabama) *Register,* July 22, 1987, p. 2-A.

SUGGESTIONS FOR FURTHER STUDY

BENNETT, AMANDA. "As Big Firms Continue to Trim Their Staffs, 2-Tier Setup Emerges." *The Wall Street Journal,* May 4, 1987, p. 12.

BREAUGH, JAMES A. "Relationship Between Recruiting Sources and Employee Performance, Absenteeism, and Work Attitudes." *Academy of Management Journal* 24 (March 1981): 142–147.

FREEDBERG, SYDNEY P. "Forced Exits? Companies Confront Wave of Age-Discrimination Suits." *The Wall Street Journal*, October 13, 1987, p. 37.

HARAYDA, JANICE. "Exploding Myths about Women's Success—Mostly." Review of *Her Own Business: Success Secrets of Entrepreneurial Women*, by Joanne Wilkens (McGraw-Hill, 1987). *USA Today*, July 10, 1987, p. 7B.

KUCHEROV, ALEX. "10 Forces Reshaping America." *U.S. News & World Report*, March 19, 1984, pp. 40–52.

LEVINSON, HARRY. "Criteria for Choosing Chief Executives." *Harvard Business Review* 58 (July–August 1980): 113–120.

LONGNECKER, CLINTON O.; SIMS, HENRY P., JR.; and GIOIA, DENNIS A. "Behind the Mask: The Politics of Employee Appraisal." *The Academy of Management Executive* (August 1987): 183–193.

MCMASTER, JOHN B. "Designing an Appraisal System That Is Fair and Accurate." *Personnel Journal* 57 (January 1979): 38–40.

MARTIN, JAMES E., and PETERSON, MELANIE M. "Two-Tier Wage Structures: Implications for Equity Theory." *Academy of Management Journal* 30 (June 1987): 297–315.

MEMMOTT, MARK. "Child-care Plans Take 1st Steps." *USA Today*, June 17, 1987, p. 1B.

———. "More Companies Are Calling On Retirees." *USA Today*, June 30, 1987, p. 1B.

MOORE, LYNDA L. "From Manpower Planning to Human Resource Planning Through Career Development." *Personnel* 56 (May–June 1979): 9–16.

PERLMAN, ITZHAK. "Judge People by Their Ability, Not Disability." *USA Today*, February 10, 1984, p. 9A.

SCHILLER, BRADLEY R. "Training Keeps the Job Machine Running." *The Wall Street Journal*, June 24, 1987, p. 26.

SHENKAR, ODED, and ZEIRA, YORAM. "Human Resources Management in International Joint Ventures: Directions for Research." *Academy of Management Review* 12 (July 1987): 546–557.

PART FOUR

Leading and Developing an Organization

Any use of human beings in which less is demanded of them and less is attributed to them than their full status is a degradation and a waste.

—NORBERT WIENER

AS SHOWN IN PART THREE, success in management results from choosing capable people, assigning them definite work to do, giving them adequate authority, and holding them accountable for the use of that authority. Yet an organization and its plans will be ineffective until the leading or directing function is performed. This function sets the organization in motion and gives life and meaning to its plans and strategies.

While human resources are an organization's most precious asset, leading those resources is the very heart of management. It is the dynamic, energetic, and enthusiastic force driving the members of the organization to achieve organizational and personal goals. The leading function involves guiding and supervising people to perform assigned duties and responsibilities so that the desired performance is achieved. It also involves both managers and workers striving to achieve the desired goals and objectives.

You can see from the opposite page that leading involves communicating with people, motivating employees, exercising leadership, and bringing about change and development in the organization's culture. Communicating with people is covered in Chapter 10; motivating employees is discussed in Chapter 11; the various aspects of managerial leadership are examined in Chapter 12; and the need for, and methods of bringing about, change and development within the organization's culture are explored in Chapter 13.

272

10. Communicating with people

What is communication?	Definition Role in organizations
How communication flows in organizations	Downward Lateral Upward Diagonal
The communication process	Source → encoding → transmitting → receiving → decoding → feedback
Role of informal communication	Purposes served Inevitable and effective
Role of nonverbal communication	Forms of nonverbal language How to use nonverbal language
Barriers to effective communication	Organizational barriers Interpersonal barriers
Increasing communication effectiveness	Using feedback Being an effective listener

11. Motivating employees

Need for positive motivation	Definition Purposes of motivation
Motivation is the essence of management	How motivation and ability affect performance How human behavior affects motivation Results of effective motivation
Content theories of motivation	Maslow's hierarchy of needs Herzberg's motivation-maintenance McClelland's need for achievement
Process theories of motivation	Expectancy theory Equity theory Operant conditioning
Role of money and occupation in motivation	How money affects motivation How occupational level affects motivation
Motivation is more than mere techniques	

(continued)

273

12. Leadership in action

What is leadership?	Leadership not same as management
Traitist approach to studying leadership	Research on traits Limited applicability
Behavioral approach to studying leadership	Kurt Lewin's small group behavior McGregor's Theory X and Theory Y Likert's System 4 Blake and Mouton's Managerial Grid® Ohio State's initiating structure/consideration Japanese style leadership
Is there an ideal leadership style?	Support for ideal style Support for a contingency-situational approach
Contingency-situational approach	Tannanbaum and Schmidt's continuum Fiedler's contingency theory Hersey-Blanchard's life-cycle theory
Factors affecting leadership behavior	General factors Specific factors
Applying leadership theory	

13. Organizational culture and change

Why study organizational culture?	Role of values Elements of organizational culture Problems related to organizational culture Participative management and organizational culture Functions performed by organizational culture	
Managing organizational change	Forces causing change Ways of dealing with change What should be changed?	Reactions to change How to manage change
Using organizational development (OD) to promote change	What is OD? A basic OD model	Selected OD strategies Promise and limitations of OD
Conflict management	Causes of conflict Conflict resolution: What works?	

10

Communicating with People

Learning Objectives

After studying the material in this chapter, you should be able to do the following:

□ Recognize the important role that communication plays in an organization.

□ Identify the four basic flows of formal organizational communication.

□ State the purposes served by informal communication.

□ Describe the major elements in a communication model.

□ Describe the main types of nonverbal communication.

□ Show how certain organizational and interpersonal factors act as barriers to effective communication.

□ Discuss how feedback and active listening help communication effectiveness.

Outline of the Chapter

What is communication?
Definition
Role of communication in organizations
How communication flows in an organization
Downward communication
Upward communication
Lateral or horizontal communication
Diagonal communication
How the communication process operates
An interpersonal communication model
The source
Encoding the message
Transmitting the message
Receiving the message
Decoding the message
Feedback

Role of informal communication
Purposes served by informal communication
Informal communication is inevitable and effective
Role of nonverbal communication
Forms of nonverbal language
How to use nonverbal communication
Barriers to effective communication
Organizational barriers
Interpersonal barriers
Increasing communication effectiveness
Awareness of the need for effective communication
Use of feedback
Be a more effective listener
Summary

Some Important Terms

communication
downward communication
upward communication
lateral (horizontal) communication
diagonal communication
feedback
informal communication
grapevine
nonverbal communication
sign language

action language
object language
paralanguage
noise
jargon
perception
selective perception
stereotyping
credibility
connotative meaning
denotative meaning
active listening
reflective statements

Meanings are not in words, but in us.
—SENATOR S. I. HAYAKAWA

Beauty is altogether in the eye of the beholder.
—LEW WALLACE

Nature has given to men one tongue, but two ears, that we may hear from others twice as much as we speak.
—EPICTETUS

At Cross Purposes

BILL EVANS (SUPERVISOR): You wanted to see me, sir?

CARL ODOM (SUPERINTENDENT): Yes, I did. I'll be right with you. Have a seat. *(He talks on the phone for about four minutes, his tone of voice showing that he is upset about something, then hangs up. He takes off his watch and places it face up on the desk in front of him.)* Bill, I hate to call you in to criticize you like this, but I'll get right to the point. I just checked with Quality Inspection, and the situation on those rejects coming out of your department is getting really intolerable. What's going on? I've never seen anything like it!

EVANS *(Fidgeting)*: Well, I think it's mostly these new people I got last week during the rush. I talked with them about it, for whatever good that'll do.

ODOM: So what am I supposed to do? You want me to put an inspector directly in your department? The other departments have had a lot of new people in the last few weeks, too, but they don't seem to be having problems. Bill, it's your job to get quality work from these people; you know that!

EVANS: Well, usually there'd be no trouble, but those guys got only one week's training instead of three. I help them when I can, naturally, but I've got twenty others to worry about, too, you know.

ODOM: I think one week is probably time enough, and, anyway, these reject errors are things almost anybody would probably catch, even with one *day's* training.

EVANS: Well, I only want to say . . .

ODOM *(Interrupting)*: Look, this big rush with three shifts has caused us all some problems, Bill . . . *(Phone rings)* Odom speaking. Yes sir, I'll bring the reports right up. *(To Evans)* I've got to go upstairs for a second. I know you can straighten this thing out. *(Picks up watch, rises, and walks toward Evans, who rises also. Both start for the door.)* I told Quality Inspection to get the information to you more quickly when bad units come up, and I know you'll take care of this matter. Listen, neither of us likes to have to talk about this, but you know we just can't operate this way at this time of year. *(Pats Evans on shoulder, and both turn and walk away.)*[1]

Do you think communication was effective in this situation? Why or why not? Would Odom and Evans answer this question differently? ■

COMMUNICATING EFFECTIVELY IS a problem that plagues many organizations and individual managers. In this chapter, you should gain a better perspective on the communication process and things that can be done to help managers communicate more effectively.

WHAT IS COMMUNICATION?

The term *management communication* is relatively new. *Communication* itself was not an important part of management's vocabulary until the late 1940s and early 1950s. But, as organizations became more "people conscious" in the behavioral approach (see Chapter 3) and as social scientists began to apply their research to organizations, communication became one of management's chief concerns. The billions of dollars spent on company communication programs and communication specialist positions, as well as the numerous seminars and workshops offered by associations, universities, and consultant firms, reflect management's current concern about this important activity. Communication, however, is still just a management *tool* designed to accomplish objectives and should not be considered an end in itself.

Definition

Communication is the process of transferring meaning in the form of ideas or information from one person to another. A true interchange of meaning between people includes more than just the words used in their conversations. It includes shades of meaning and emphasis, facial expressions, vocal inflections, and all the unintended and involuntary gestures that suggest real meaning.[2] An effective interchange requires more than just the transmission of data. It requires that the person sending the message and receiving it rely on certain skills (speaking, writing, listening, reading, and the like) to make the exchange of meaning successful.

Communication is the chain of understanding that links the members of various units of an organization at different levels and in different areas. This concept has the following elements: (1) an act of making oneself understood, (2) a means of passing information between people, and (3) a system for communicating between individuals. This traditional view of communication, however, as occurring between two or more individuals is being modified by the technological revolution to include communication between people, between people and machines, and even between machines and other machines.

Role of Communication in Organizations

Communication is important to managers, and it is needed by all employees. Readers of the *Harvard Business Review* chose "the ability to communicate" as an executive's most essential qualification for promotion to higher levels.[3] In one survey, 252 personnel and marketing managers in New York and Hawaii were asked to rank in order of importance the skills they felt every business administration graduate should have. The results, as shown in Table 10.1, show that communication is widely accepted as an important function of management.

A large part of the typical manager's time is spent in some form of communication—writing, reading, speaking, or listening. It was shown in Chapter 2 that managers spend about 80 percent of their time communicating (see Figures 2.8, 2.9, and 2.10). Similar results are shown in Table 10.2, in which managers are shown to spend from 57 to 89 percent of their time in performing oral communications alone.

HOW COMMUNICATION FLOWS IN AN ORGANIZATION

You can better understand organizational communication if you examine the basic directions in which it moves. Formal communication channels are

**TABLE 10.1
Relative Importance of
Skills Needed by
Business Graduates**

*(As ranked by four groups
of managers in
New York and Hawaii)*

SOURCE: Alfred G. Edge and
Ronald Greenwood, "How
Managers Rank Knowledge,
Skills and Attributes Possessed
by Business Administration
Graduates," *AACSB Bulletin* 2
(1974): 32. Reprinted by
permission.

Skills	Personnel managers		Marketing managers	
	New York	Hawaii	New York	Hawaii
Communicating	1	1	2	1
Working with and using skills of others, motivating	2	3	3	2
Planning, developing, organizing, and coordinating	3	2	1	3
Analyzing data, proposing solutions, and making decisions	4	4	4	4
Analyzing financial data	5	6	5	5
Applying quantitative techniques	6	7	6	7
Analyzing accounting data	7	5	7	6
Utilizing a computer	8	8	8	8

dictated by the organization's structure or are prescribed by some other formal means. As shown in Figure 10.1 (page 280), these basic channels are upward, downward, lateral, and diagonal.

Downward Communication

Downward communication is generally thought of as following the organization's formal chain of command from top to bottom. It tends to follow and reflect the authority-responsibility relationships shown in the organization chart. Some examples of downward communication are listed here:

1. Information related to policies, rules, procedures, objectives, and other types of plans.
2. Work assignments and directives.
3. Feedback about performance.
4. General information about the organization, such as its progress or status.
5. Specific requests for information from lower levels.

Downward messages may be in either written or oral form. They are typically passed through bulletin boards, memos, reports or other documents, conferences, meetings, and speeches and in small groups or person to person. Management traditionally concentrates most of its communication effort on downward communication. But the important point is that the results are usually alarmingly ineffective! An exception to this tendency was Lee Iacocca's efforts to get Chrysler workers to make concessions to save the company, as shown in MAP 10.1 (page 281).

What is your view?

An example of downward communication was demonstrated in the Opening Case when superintendent Carl Odom called supervisor Bill Evans in to notify him of the poor work being done in Evans's department. There were several other examples of downward communication in this case. Can you identify the examples?

TABLE 10.2
**Percentage of Time
Spent by Managers in
Oral Communication**

SOURCE: James Powell and
Edward Goodin,
"Organizational
Communication: Are We
Meeting the Need?" Arthur G.
Bedeian, Achilles Armenakis,
William Holley, Jr., and Hubert
Field, Jr., eds., *Proceedings of
the 35th Annual Meeting of the
Academy of Management* (New
Orleans: Academy of
Management, August 10–13,
1975), p. 39. Reprinted by
permission.

Researchers	Subjects	Percentage of time spent in oral communication
Carlson	12 German executives	70
Stogdill and Shartle (cited by Dubin)	470 navy officers	60
Burns	4 engineering executives	80
Kelly	10 middle managers	67
Guest	Supervisors	57
Sayles	First-line supervisors	50–80
Mintzberg	5 executives	89

Upward Communication

Upward communication may be viewed as a feedback of data or information from lower levels to upper-management levels. But, whereas progress and performance reporting are perhaps the major forms of upward communication, other forms are also vital to management. These include the following:

1. Ideas and suggestions for improvements and problem solving.
2. Requests for assistance, information, or resources.
3. Expression of attitudes, feelings, and gripes that influence performance directly and indirectly (see Figure 10.2, page 282).

From an organizational standpoint, the principal forms of upward communication are the various types of performance reports that indicate employees' progress toward their work goals. The "open door" policy, grievance systems, attitude surveys, employee-management councils, or the military's inspector general system are designed to provide upward communication to top management.

 What is your view?

Supervisor Evans's explanations to his superintendent in the Opening Case about the causes of poor performance in his department reflect the upward communication process (although we might question its effectiveness in Odom's case!). Can you identify other examples of upward flows in this incident?

Lateral or Horizontal Communication

Lateral or **horizontal communication** includes the following:

1. Communication among peers within the same work group.
2. Communication that occurs between and among departments on the same organizational level.

This form of communication is essentially coordinative in nature and results from the concept of organizational *specialization*. That is, if you are to function effectively in your own job, you will most likely need to interact with, and be dependent on, other organizational units. Moreover, organizations today seek to use the abilities of specialists by creating special project teams, task forces (recall the matrix form of organization discussed in Chapter 7), or committees that pull together representatives from various specialties. Communication helps coordinate these lateral activities.

Diagonal Communication

Diagonal communication includes communication that cuts diagonally across an organization's chain of command. It most frequently occurs as a result of line and staff department relationships. Recall from Chapter 8 that several different relationships may exist between line and staff personnel. These may range from a purely advisory staff relationship to one in which staff exerts strong functional authority over line.

HOW THE COMMUNICATION PROCESS OPERATES

People, not organizations, communicate! An organization's communication system, therefore, reflects a variety of individuals with different backgrounds, education, beliefs, cultures, moods, and needs. But, when individuals in an organization communicate, what takes place? Let's examine a basic communication model so that you will be better able to understand the discussion of why communication fails so frequently and some actions that managers may take to improve their communication effectiveness.

FIGURE 10.1
The flows of formal communication in a hypothetical organization.

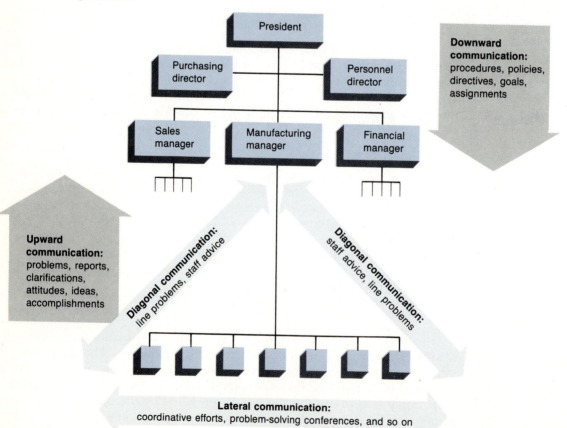

Management Application and Practice 10.1   "Communication at the Highest Level"

In 1979, Lee Iacocca became chairman and CEO of Chrysler at the lowest point in its history. After deciding not to declare bankruptcy, he set out to save the financially embattled company. Among the many things he accomplished was getting the unionized employees to agree to a $2.00-an-hour cut in income and to other concessions.

One of Iacocca's first steps was to cut his own salary to $1.00 a year. He also cut the salaries of executives—by 10 percent. Then he started on the unions. Talking tough to them, he said, "Hey, boys, . . . I've got a shotgun at your head. I've got thousands of jobs available at seventeen bucks an hour. I've got none at twenty. So you better come to your senses."

A year later, he had to go back to the unions for more concessions. At 10 P.M. on a bitter night, he made "one of my shortest speeches" to the union negotiating committee: "You've got until morning to make a decision. If you don't help me out, . . . I'll declare bankruptcy in the morning and you'll all be out of work. You've got eight hours to make up your minds. It's up to you."

The workers (and the union) made many concessions. First, they took a $1.15-an-hour cut in pay, then up to a $2.00-an-hour cut. Over a 19-month period, the average worker gave up nearly $10,000 in income. How did Iacocca do it?

"During 1980, I went to every Chrysler plant to speak directly to the workers. At a series of mass meetings, I thanked them for sticking with us during these bad times. I told them that when things got better, we'd try to get them back to parity with Ford and GM workers, but that it wouldn't happen overnight. I gave them my pitch, and they hooted and hollered, and some of them applauded and some of them booed.

"I also conducted sessions with the plant supervisors. I'd ask if anybody had questions . . . we didn't always agree on the answers, but just having the chance to talk together was a big step forward.

"That's communication at the highest level: the chairman talking to the guy on the floor."

SOURCE: Lee Iacocca with William Novak, *Iacocca: An Autobiography* (New York: Bantam Books, 1984), pp. 232–234.

An Interpersonal Communication Model

There are many different models of communication, depending on the context of communication involved. We will concentrate on the interpersonal communication model shown in Figure 10.3. This model illustrates the most important elements involved in communication between and among organization members:

1. The source of the communication message.
2. Encoding the message.
3. Transmitting the message.
4. Receiving the message.
5. Decoding the message.
6. Feedback to the source.

Later in the chapter, you will see how communication barriers affect various stages of the communication model.

The Source

The *source* or originator of the message occupies the first step in the communication process. The source controls the type of message sent, the form in which it is sent, and frequently the channel through which the eventual message passes.

FOSTER LTD. ATTITUDE SURVEY

We are interested in how you feel about your company, its policies, your supervisor, and your job. Will you please help us by providing your honest answers to the questions below?

INSTRUCTIONS: Read each statement carefully, then indicate how you feel about each statement by circling the appropriate answer. For example, if you strongly agree with statement #1, "The quality of services offered by Foster is excellent," then circle the 1; if you agree, circle the 2; if you're undecided, circle the 3; if you disagree, circle the 4; and if you strongly disagree, circle the 5.

	Strongly agree	Agree	Undecided	Disagree	Strongly disagree
1. The quality of services offered by Foster is excellent.	1	2	3	4	5
2. I feel very good about the growth prospects of Foster Ltd.	1	2	3	4	5
3. This company uses efficient work methods in getting the job done.	1	2	3	4	5
4. This company is a pleasant place to work.	1	2	3	4	5
5. The company encourages people to find new and better ways to do things.	1	2	3	4	5
6. Equipment is well maintained throughout the company.	1	2	3	4	5
7. I have a lot of pride in working for Foster Ltd.	1	2	3	4	5
8. This company is very quality conscious.	1	2	3	4	5
9. This company is a high-pressure place to work.	1	2	3	4	5
10. I feel good about my own job security.	1	2	3	4	5
11. Other employees have a lot of pride in working for Foster Ltd.	1	2	3	4	5
12. Top management of this company is very competent.	1	2	3	4	5
13. Overall, the company facilities are well maintained.	1	2	3	4	5
14. This company highly values its employees' opinions.	1	2	3	4	5
15. There is a sufficient number of rest-room facilities in this company.	1	2	3	4	5

FIGURE 10.2
Example of upward communication.

Let us place you in the source's predicament so that you are able to examine this first element. The intended communication is based on satisfying some internal need in which someone else (a receiver) plays some role. The first step is that something happens to stimulate the thought processes. You receive an order, or perhaps your boss enters the room, or you observe a slowdown in production. The event stimulates you to recognize the need for transmitting your feelings and ideas to someone else. The stimulation creates in you a desire to communicate and helps provide a need or purpose for your communication, whether it reflects your need to offer advice, to solicit an opinion, to create a given impression, or to take a given action.

FIGURE 10.3
The communication
process.

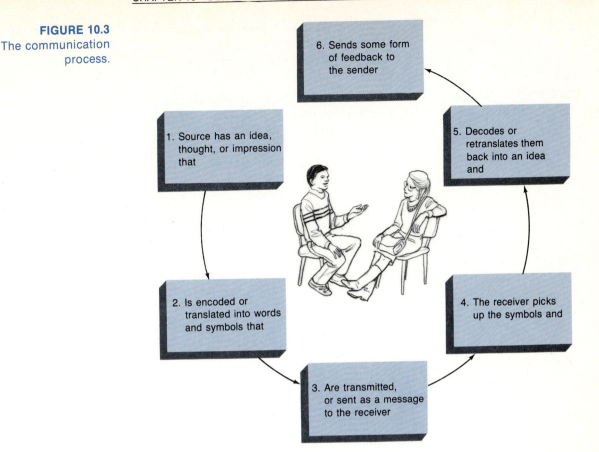

1. Source has an idea,
   thought, or impression
   that

2. Is encoded or
   translated into words
   and symbols that

3. Are transmitted,
   or sent as a message
   to the receiver

4. The receiver picks
   up the symbols and

5. Decodes or
   retranslates them
   back into an idea
   and

6. Sends some form
   of feedback to
   the sender

Encoding the Message

The second step—*encoding*—involves choosing some form of verbal or non-verbal *symbol* that is capable of transferring meaning, such as spoken or written words, gestures, or actions.

From among the available symbols, the person transmitting a message selects the ones that will fulfill a specific need and arranges them in some sequence of significance. One must think not only of *what* is going to be said but also of *how* it will be presented to have the desired effect on the receiver. Thus the message must be adapted to the level of understanding, interest, and needs of the receiver to achieve the desired consequences. It is also important, however, to consider possible unintended consequences and to present the message so that these are avoided.

The language of a given culture originates in people's interactions with each other. Prehistoric people used picture symbols; the American Indian used smoke signals; some Arab cultures use gestures. Spoken symbols were developed as a means of transmitting ideas, feelings, and attitudes as the need to communicate with others increased. These symbols are modified to meet particular needs at a given time.

Even in today's organizations, whenever managers write letters or memos, compile figures, issue orders, solve problems orally, or answer employees' questions, they are using symbols to communicate. Symbols should be selected on the basis of the meaning they will have for the listeners or readers.

That is, effective managers need to understand human nature and develop sensitivity not only to the meaning of words but also to the effects those words and symbols might have on others.

Transmitting the Message

The third step—*transmitting*—is sending the symbols from the source to the receiver and reflects the communicator's choice of medium or "distribution channel." Oral communication may be transmitted through many channels— in person, by telephone, by dictating machine, or by videotape. It may take place privately or in a group meeting of many persons. In fact, one of the most important decisions the source has to make is determining the appropriate channel for transmitting a given message.

Table 10.3 shows that, in addition to its speed, a fundamental advantage of oral, person-to-person communication is the opportunity for interaction between source and receiver, commonly known as *feedback*, the final step.

Written communication may be transmitted through channels such as memos, letters, reports, notes, bulletin boards, company manuals, and newsletters. Written communication has the advantage of providing a record for future reference, but the major disadvantage is that it does not allow spontaneous, face-to-face feedback.

What is your view?

What are some examples of communication that you feel are best handled *(a)* by a written medium (letter, memo), *(b)* by telephone, or *(c)* face to face?

Receiving the Message

The fourth step is *receiving* the symbols. How do people receive messages? Basically, people receive messages through their five senses—seeing, hearing, tasting, touching or being touched, and smelling. Full transmission has not occurred unless a party actually *receives* a message. Many important attempts at communication have failed because the message was never received!

Decoding the Message

The fifth step of the communication process is *decoding*, which involves giving meaning to the symbols the receiver receives. The receiver searches his or her memory bank for a translation of the symbols received. This, in turn, is the result of the receiver's heritage, culture, education, environment, prejudices and biases, and distractions in the surroundings. There is always

TABLE 10.3
Advantages of Written and Oral Messages

Written	Oral
1. Provides a record	1. Lends itself to more immediate feedback—questions, clarifications
2. Allows greater attention to organization and wording of message	2. Allows nonverbal communication—tone of voice, inflection, body language
3. Enables receiver to interpret at own pace	3. Is transmitted rapidly

the possibility that the source's message, when decoded by the receiver, will yield a meaning far different from the one the sender intended. The receiver thus shares a large responsibility for communication effectiveness, for *communication is a two-way street.* Managers and subordinates may occupy both source and receiver roles throughout an interaction. Moreover, they engage in a variety of interactions of different scope, importance, and duration.

What is your view?

What evidence of these types of reactions did you see in the Opening Case?

Feedback

After the message has been received and translated, the receiver may transmit a return message that stimulates the original communicator or someone else. Communicating is thus a continuous and never-ending process. A person communicates, the receiver responds by further communicating with the original sender or another person, and so forth. The response is called *feedback.*

Management might distribute a policy bulletin to a group of supervisors, but until there is a response in the form of questions, agreement, comment, or behavior, or until there has been a check to see whether the policy is being followed, management does not know how effective the statement has been.

Communication is an exchange, and, if it is to be successful, information must flow back and forth from the originator to the receiver—or at least the originator must have some knowledge of the receiver's reaction. Although the term **feedback** may be new, its importance is not.

What is your view?

Lincoln thought he had failed in his address at Gettysburg because of the silence that greeted his immortal words. Because there was no immediate feedback, he had no idea of the historical impact of his brief address.

Was the audience's silence feedback? Explain.

ROLE OF INFORMAL COMMUNICATION

Thus far, the communication flows you have studied have been what we call "formal" communication. That is, the channels carrying messages have been *designed* by the original managers to carry job-related messages. **Informal communication,** however, which is communication other than through formal channels, is also an important part of an organization's communication flow. This form of communicating serves a variety of purposes, as shown by the following examples.

Beverly, a design engineer, asked the senior design engineer how best to approach her supervisor for a change in job assignment.

Joan, a bank teller, told her associates that she would leave the bank rather than wear the uniform the bank would require beginning the next month.

Harold joined his company's "management fitness program," a group of nine managers who jogged and exercised daily during the lunch hour. "It's good for my health," he said. "And I enjoy the idea of getting together with others."

Purposes Served by Informal Communication

Informal communication channels, then, accomplish a variety of purposes, including these:

1. Satisfying personal needs, such as the need for relationships with others.
2. Countering the effects of boredom or monotony.
3. Attempting to influence the behavior of others.
4. Serving as a source of job-related information that is not provided by formal channels.

The best-known type of informal communication is referred to as the **grapevine** (or the "rumor mill"), which, like its namesake, is twisted, tangled, and hard to follow. Yet research has demonstrated that communication grapevines function rapidly, selectively, and effectively. We tend to think of the grapevine as being inaccurate because its errors are more dramatic than the normal day-to-day information it carries accurately. Yet, according to Keith Davis, an authority on human relations, research on grapevine activity shows that in normal work situations over 75 percent of grapevine information is correct.[4]

Informal Communication Is Inevitable and Effective

Effective managers recognize that informal communications, and especially the grapevine, cannot be eliminated. Moreover, it is even possible that the grapevine, if properly understood and used, can be complementary to management's goals. Consider this example:

One manager used the grapevine as a "trial balloon." He would drop a piece of information at a strategic point on the grapevine, watch it spread through the organization, and then observe how well it was received by subordinates. The manager would say something like, "Oh, yes, I am seriously considering that, and we'll probably do it"—if the subordinates accepted the information favorably. But he could deny the information by simply asking, "Where did you ever get such an idea?"—if the subordinates' responses were negative—further adding, "It's amazing how these silly rumors get started."[5]

Most staff positions require movement among, and interactions with, personnel in other departments. For this and other reasons, staff personnel tend to be better informed through informal communication channels than are line managers. Other organization members act as liaison in relaying information from group to group. This enhances their own status in addition to providing others with information about matters that affect and interest them.

Most managers are aware of the part that informal communication plays in their units. The less informed subordinates are about matters they consider important, the greater the chance that the informal system will generate its own information—correct or incorrect—about such matters. This, of course, can have either desirable or undesirable consequences.

ROLE OF NONVERBAL COMMUNICATION

Nonverbal communication is very important as it frequently carries more weight in a message outcome than verbal communication. Facial expressions, clothes, posture, tone of voice, or body movements may loudly or subtly communicate messages. In fact, nonverbal messages cannot be as readily disguised or controlled as verbal ones. Accordingly, nonverbal messages often contradict verbal messages.

Hal Langston, a highly motivated young assistant vice-president of a large bank, had recently completed a report for James Nabors, the bank's executive vice-president of commercial loans. The meeting to discuss the report was held several days after Nabors had been sent the report. When Hal entered Nabors's office, the VP remained seated on his side of the desk and motioned toward a smaller chair across from it. Hal sat down. As Hal went through his three-minute prepared presentation, he noted that Nabors did not once look directly at him, but instead thumbed somewhat slowly through the report. His jaw seemed stiff, and he nodded slightly from time to time. When Hal completed his statement, the VP placed the report on a stack of other papers, face down, and rested his hands on the desk in a steeple fashion.

"Your report looks very interesting, Hal," he stated. "I'm sure we'll want to give it some consideration."

Hal left the office dejectedly. He felt that he hadn't gotten a fair hearing at the meeting. On entering the elevator, he met a colleague who asked where he'd been. Hal replied, "I just got two weeks of work shot down the tubes by Nabors."

It turned out that he was absolutely right.

What is your view?

What nonverbal messages were being transmitted to Hal during the meeting with the vice-president? What could the VP have done to make Hal feel that he'd received a fairer hearing?

Have you ever been in a similar situation, perhaps with a professor, an attorney, a politician, or someone else who exuded power and authority? If so, you may have received some clear, nonverbal messages. These probably had a significant effect on you, for it has been shown that only about 7 percent of the meaning in face-to-face communication is directly carried by words.[6] The remainder is carried by tone of voice and facial and body expression. Notice in Figure 10.4 that only the eyebrows and lips are changed on each face.

FIGURE 10.4
Nonverbal communication: What does each face express?

Forms of Nonverbal Language

There are several forms of nonverbal messages. The most important are (1) sign language, (2) action language—how we move, how we look, (3) object language, and (4) paralanguage—how we sound (see Figure 10.5).

Sign language. **Sign language** takes the form of nonverbal messages that literally replace words. For example, workers at construction sites use flags to signal motorists to slow down, halt, or proceed; a nod of the head indicates "yes," a shake, "no"; shrugged shoulders and uplifted palms indicate "I don't know"; a military salute demonstrates respect for a higher-ranking officer.

Action language. **Action language** consists of those body movements or actions that are not specifically intended to replace words but nevertheless transmit meaning. Rising and walking toward the door indicate readiness to terminate a conversation. Opening a door for a woman sends a message about one's upbringing. Walking at a quick pace communicates that one is in a hurry. A sharply pointed finger may convey a scolding. A blank stare when someone speaks to you may communicate that your mind is elsewhere (or that you would like to be!).

What is your view?

Notice in the Opening Case how the exchanges between the supervisor and the superintendent carry nonverbal messages. What do Evans's nervousness and Odom's hurriedness and preoccupation, his standing when he wants the interaction to end, and his patting Evans's shoulder indicate? Can you find any other important action language in the meeting?

FIGURE 10.5
Forms of nonverbal language.

Sign language

Paralanguage → Nonverbal ← Action language

Object language

(Copyright 1987 by United Feature Syndicate, Inc.)

Object language. Object language consists of physical items such as clothes, furniture, physical possessions, or other *things* that convey messages. Thus, a classroom communicates a certain atmosphere of formality or informality. Awards displayed in an office indicate the occupant's accomplishments, while the size, furnishings, and location of the office indicate the occupant's status. Even the arrangement of furnishings can act as object language (see MAP 10.2). Some objects worn by individuals, such as clothing, jewelry, and other accessories, communicate strong messages to others. Clothing with signatures and logos (such as the alligator, polo player, swan) is an example of object language. IBM, known for years for its conservative attire, believes that its success is directly related to the image of "competence" and that the conservative attire of its personnel is vital to this image. Even IBM's "customer engineers" (service personnel) arrive in a car (not a van) wearing a jacket and tie. Now IBM itself is becoming a status symbol—people will pay hundreds or thousands of dollars more to purchase those "three little letters."

Paralanguage. You've heard the expression, "It's not what you say, it's the way you say it." **Paralanguage** is related to vocal sounds that influence *how* words are expressed. Paralanguage may be things such as vocal pitch, tone, volume, pace, and other delivery-related factors.

What is your view?

Consider the words, "Nice job, Sal." Can you say these words so that they communicate a compliment? Could you also say these words so that they convey a put-down?

How to Use Nonverbal Communication

According to Michael Korda, author of the book *Power! How to Get It, How to Use It*, nonverbal meanings have much to do with the amount of power you are perceived to have.[7] He suggests, among others, the following ways of exerting power:

1. Don't be the first to leave a meeting to make a restroom visit, because others perceive this as a weakness.

2. When engaged in a power play with other power players on their own turf, assert your power by intruding on their territory: Use one of their

Management Application and Practice 10.2   Desk and Chairs Communicate!

There is no question that the physical setting of a communication situation has a large impact on the ensuing communication process. One important variable is furniture arrangement, which in itself can establish a cold, formal, authoritative environment or a warmer, informal, more relaxed setting. Examine the three desk-chair arrangements shown below.

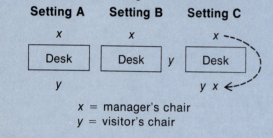

Setting A   Setting B   Setting C

x = manager's chair
y = visitor's chair

Setting A maximizes the manager's authority and dominance. Setting B, on the other hand, allows the visitor to feel more like an equal. Finally, Setting C allows the manager to use Setting A for more serious, formal situations and to step from behind the desk and assume an "equal" status with his visitor if desired. As Korda points out, one executive he knows has an arrangement similar to Setting A but has *his* desk and chair placed on a platform to enable him to peer down at visitors. Moreover, visitors sit in an extremely soft chair, into which they sink to their chins, amplifying their feelings of submissiveness.

SOURCE: Michael Korda, *Power! How to Get It, How to Use It* (New York: Random House, 1975), pp. 194–197.

possessions, such as their telephone to make a call, or doodle with their pen, to unnerve them psychologically.

3. The most powerful man's suit, Korda believes, is a navy or black pinstripe. You are apt to be perceived as authoritative and competent in those colors.

In summary, then, nonverbal communication plays an important role in the communication process. Managers should be conscious not only of the

FIGURE 10.6
Communication barriers (noise) at various stages of the communication process.

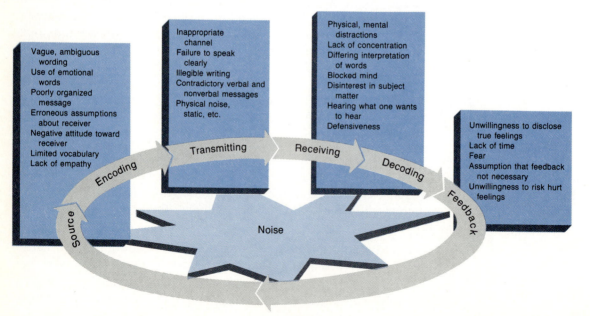

nonverbal language they use but also of the nonverbal messages others transmit to them—whether intentional or unintentional.

BARRIERS TO EFFECTIVE COMMUNICATION

Communication is vital, and managers spend a great deal of their time doing it, but research shows that as much as 70 percent of all business communication fails to achieve the intended objectives.[8] The interference that impedes communication effectiveness is commonly known as **noise,** which may interfere with communication at various stages of the process, as shown in Figure 10.6. We shall present several important barriers to effective communication, classified as (1) organizational barriers and (2) interpersonal barriers, as shown in Figure 10.7.

Organizational Barriers

A communication consultant once examined the organization chart of a firm and immediately remarked, "I see at least three communication barriers already." What she was referring to was that organizations, by their very nature, tend to inhibit effective communication. Three organizational barriers are (1) hierarchical levels, (2) managerial authority, and (3) specialization.

Hierarchical levels. As pointed out earlier, when an organization grows, its structure expands, creating many communication problems. If a message must pass through added levels, it will take longer to reach its destination and will tend to become distorted on the way.

As a message goes up or down through organizational levels, it passes through several "filters," each with its own perceptions, motives, needs, and

FIGURE 10.7
How barriers affect the communication process.

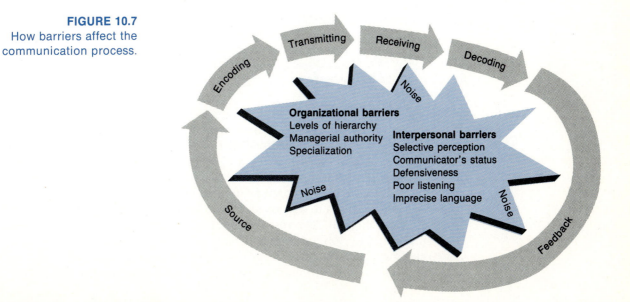

FIGURE 10.8
Loss of information in
the chain of command.

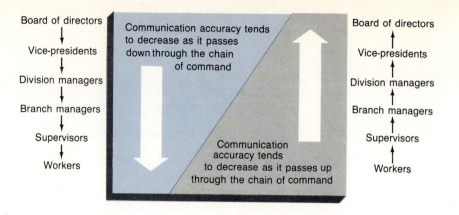

relationships with the nature of the message (see Figure 10.8). Each level in the communication chain can add to, take from, modify, or completely change the intent of a given message, as shown in Figure 10.9. A study of the accuracy of messages going from the top to the bottom of an organization in 100 companies found that the vice-presidential level understood 67 percent of what it heard from the board of directors; at the division manager level, 56 percent of the same information survived; at the plant manager level, 40 percent survived; at the supervisor level, 30 percent; and at the operating level, only 20 percent.[9]

One explanation for this tendency is that messages are usually broader and more general at higher levels of management. As author Chester Barnard noted, "It follows that something may be lost or added by transmission at each stage of the process. . . . Moreover, when communications go from high positions down they often must be made more specific as they proceed."[10]

What is your view?

When you miss a class, you probably check with a fellow student to get the class assignment. But have you ever completed the assignment only to arrive in class and find that it was not what the teacher wanted? Dependence on others' interpretations of firsthand communications, even though it risks loss of accuracy and interpretation, is an important part of organizational communication. Can you think of some real or hypothetical cases in which one *must* rely on an intermediary either to send or receive information in an organization?

Managerial authority. Authority is a necessary feature of any organization. It would simply be impossible to accomplish much without certain persons having the right to make decisions. Yet the very fact that one person supervises others creates a barrier to free and open communication. Many bosses feel that they cannot fully admit problems, conditions, or results that may make them look weak. Many subordinates, on the other hand, avoid situations that require them to disclose information that might make them appear in an unfavorable light. As a result, there is a lack of "leveling" between boss and subordinates. Job problems, frustrations, below-standard work, disagreements with the superior's policies, and other types of unfavorable information tend to be withheld or are changed to look more favorable.[11]

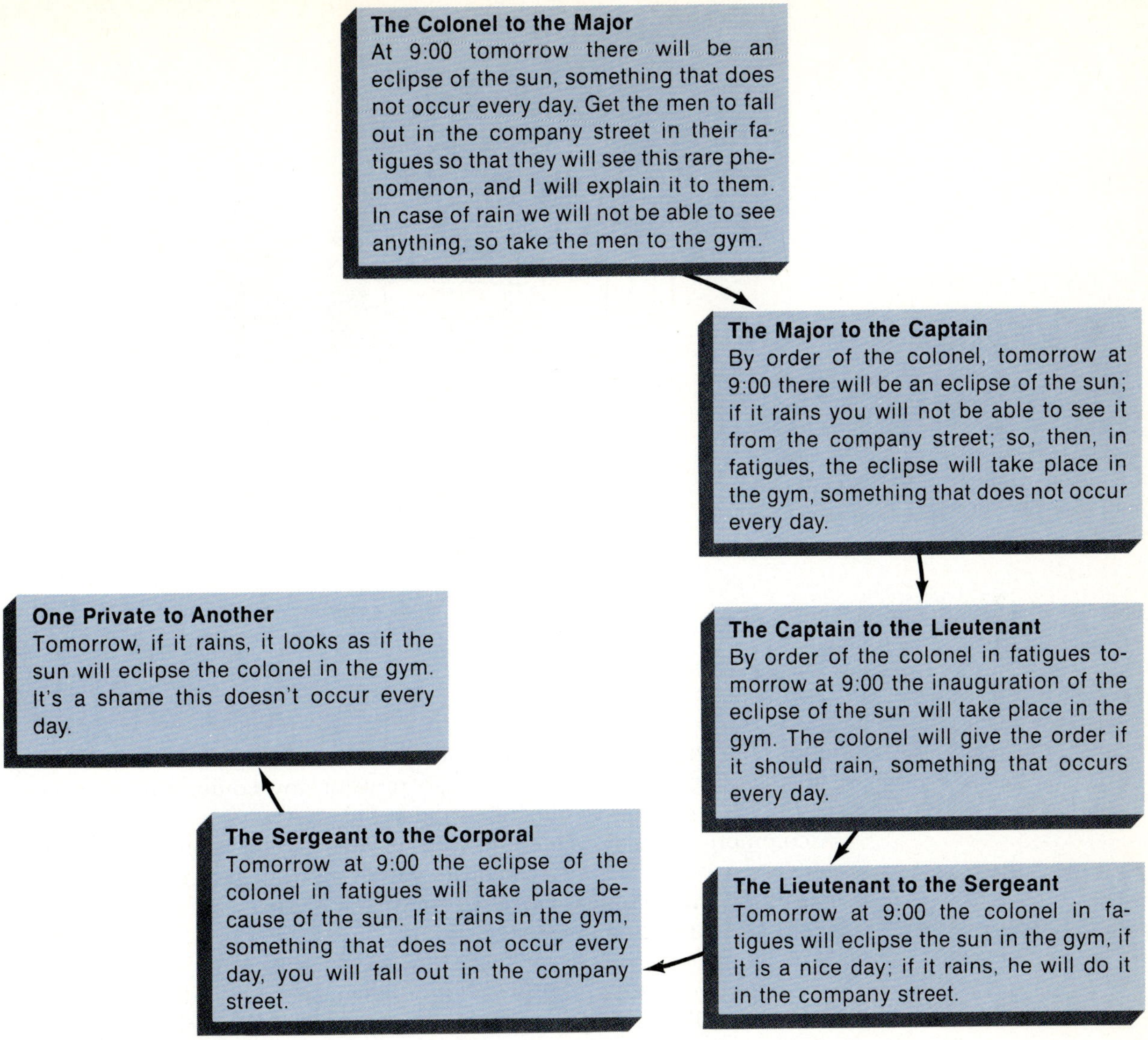

The Colonel to the Major
At 9:00 tomorrow there will be an eclipse of the sun, something that does not occur every day. Get the men to fall out in the company street in their fatigues so that they will see this rare phenomenon, and I will explain it to them. In case of rain we will not be able to see anything, so take the men to the gym.

The Major to the Captain
By order of the colonel, tomorrow at 9:00 there will be an eclipse of the sun; if it rains you will not be able to see it from the company street; so, then, in fatigues, the eclipse will take place in the gym, something that does not occur every day.

One Private to Another
Tomorrow, if it rains, it looks as if the sun will eclipse the colonel in the gym. It's a shame this doesn't occur every day.

The Captain to the Lieutenant
By order of the colonel in fatigues tomorrow at 9:00 the inauguration of the eclipse of the sun will take place in the gym. The colonel will give the order if it should rain, something that occurs every day.

The Sergeant to the Corporal
Tomorrow at 9:00 the eclipse of the colonel in fatigues will take place because of the sun. If it rains in the gym, something that does not occur every day, you will fall out in the company street.

The Lieutenant to the Sergeant
Tomorrow at 9:00 the colonel in fatigues will eclipse the sun in the gym, if it is a nice day; if it rains, he will do it in the company street.

FIGURE 10.9
Eclipse of the sun: The workings of communication channels.

Anna Stephenson was a highly autocratic upper-level manager in a large utility. Stephenson's middle managers spent a lot of time complaining among themselves, but in Stephenson's presence they pretended that they were "one happy, hard-working team" and that everything was "going just fine." They kept to a minimum any communication with Stephenson that might be taken as pressure. They reported only the information that might be detrimental to others and favorable to themselves, thereby furthering their own causes in the competition for the boss's approval.

Specialization. Although specialization, also known as division of labor, is a fundamental part of organizations, it also creates problems, for it tends to separate people even when they work side by side (see Chapter 7). Different

"If 18% credit-card interest is 'reasonable,'
how come 5¼% interest on deposits is
'generous?' "

(Reprinted from The Wall Street Journal *by
permission of Cartoon Features Syndicate.)*

functions, special interests, and job jargon can make people feel that they
live in different worlds. The result can prevent any community of feeling,
make understanding very difficult, and lead to errors.

A common problem created by specialization is the **jargon** or technical
vocabulary used by various specialists. Much resistance to data processing
is caused by the technical language that its specialists use. And the social
sciences and government agencies are bywords for the production of seem-
ingly meaningless gobbledygook, as shown in Figure 10.10.

But even deeper than the problem of language are the differing perceptions and conflicting frames of reference involved when sales, credit, production, quality control, finance, personnel, and research departments interact with one another. These departments have their own subgroup
loyalties, interests, attitudes, and ways of looking at things that frequently
create strains between individuals and departments.

**Interpersonal
Barriers**

Managers would still face the possibility that their messages would become
distorted, even if organizational communication barriers did not exist. Many
miscommunications are caused not by organizational factors, but by problems of human and language imperfections. Managers need to be aware of
interpersonal barriers such as (1) selective perception, (2) status of the communicator, (3) defensiveness, (4) poor listening, and (5) imprecise use of
language. Figure 10.6 shows how these barriers affect the communication
process.

Selective perception. **Perception** is a complicated process by which we
select, organize, and give meaning to the world around us. As soon as we

FIGURE 10.10
Cut the jargon!

SOURCE: Adapted from Stuart
Chase, *Power of Words* (New
York: Harcourt, Brace & Co.,
1953), p. 259.

A plumber of foreign extraction wrote the National Bureau of Standards and said he found that hydrochloric acid quickly opened plugged drainage pipes and inquired if it was a good thing to use. A scientist at the Bureau replied:

```
Dear Sir:

While the efficacy of hydrochloric acid is undoubtedly in-
disputable, dysfunctional coincidental effects render its
commercial utilization in said writer's case a hazardous
undertaking which this office cannot endorse.
```

The plumber wrote back thanking the Bureau for telling him that hydrochloric acid was good to use. The scientist was disturbed about the misunderstanding and brought the situation correspondence to his boss—another scientist—who wrote the plumber:

```
Dear Sir:

Hydrochloric acid, while a highly efficacious atomistic
debilitator, imposes a strongly noxious residue when in-
teracting with metallic-based substances, introducing per-
manencial structural damage and eliciting a definitive
negative endorsement of your request.
```

The plumber wrote back that he agreed with the Bureau—the hydrochloric acid really seemed to "clean out pipes real good"—and thanked the Bureau for its helpfulness. Greatly upset about their communication breakdown, the two scientists brought the problem to the top boss, who was *not* a scientist. He shook his head in dismay and wrote the plumber:

```
Dear Sir:

Don't use hydrochloric acid. It eats the hell out of
pipes!
```

Shortly thereafter, the Bureau received another letter from the plumber. It read:

```
Dear Sir:

Thanks! But I found that out for myself.
```

perceive something, we organize it into some type of significant information. Experience teaches us certain reactions; we expect to see a train when we hear a train whistle. We automatically become defensive when called into the boss's office (or the dean's!). In other words, the expectations we have lead us to see events, people, objects, and situations the way *we want* them to be. This is called **selective perception.**

Professor Higgins tried an experiment in his organizational communication class one day. Instead of a long oral introduction about the guest speaker, he passed out a written biographical sketch. Half of the class received information suggesting that the guest speaker had an education, occupation, and values that were generally consistent with those of the class. The other half of the class received information that was just the opposite, proclaiming the speaker to be, among other things, an avid Marxist. The speaker, following a brief oral introduction by the professor, then gave his speech on the theme of "Why business students need to get involved in their communities." After the speech was over, the speaker left, and the professor handed out evaluation forms. When those were completed, the results were tabulated and put on the board: Half the class rated the speaker highly; the other half did not. The speaker then returned, and, to the class's amazement, the professor explained the experiment and gave a lecture on "selective perception."

Stereotyping. The tendency to structure the world into a predictable pattern creates a process known as **stereotyping.** Thus we have stereotypes for certain groups—union leaders, business leaders, politicians, engineers, and even teachers and students! We then treat members of each group according to our perceptions of that stereotype.

What is your view?

What is your stereotype of the following groups: (*a*) first-year college students, (*b*) varsity football players, (*c*) members of social fraternities, (*d*) premed majors, and (*e*) professors? In what ways might your stereotype affect your communications with members of each group?

How selective perception occurs. Selective perception occurs because your perception is limited. A limiting factor is that you cannot grasp the whole of a stimulus at a given instant of time. Some parts of an event receive greater attention than others, and some receive no attention at all. Those parts focused on usually serve some immediate purpose. Your needs, moods, cultural and social influences, and attitudes interact to determine which stimuli are important and the role assigned to them. Consider, for example, an accident occurring on the job. All those involved viewed the accident differently. The supervisor saw the loss of a valuable worker; the safety engineer saw a blot on the safety record; the fellow workers saw a friend injured; the company physician saw an injured person to be treated; and the personnel manager saw the need to find a replacement for the injured worker. Reports of the accident were colored by those selected stimuli, and different versions resulted.

Another limiting factor is that when we perceive an object or person, our evaluation is frequently colored by the larger attributes of which that object or person is a part. The way you perceive your boss's messages is influenced not only by your relationships with the boss but also by your attitudes toward management in general. Much depends on the subordinates' seeing their bosses as members of a larger structure labeled "management."

Significance for managers. Managers should allow for three distinct aspects of selective perception:

1. Receivers will interpret the message in terms of their own experience and how they have learned to respond to it.
2. Receivers will interpret the message in such a way as to resist any change in strong personality structures.

3. Receivers will tend to group characteristics of their experience so that they can make whole patterns.

The lesson for managers is to know their people—understand as much as possible about their frames of reference, needs, motives, goals, language levels, and stereotypes.

Status of the communicator. Another major communication barrier is the tendency to size up, evaluate, and weigh a message in terms of the characteristics of the person who sends it, especially his or her **credibility.** Credibility is based on the person's "expertness" in the subject area being communicated and on the degree of one's confidence or trust that the person will communicate the truth.

Research has shown that we are more likely to accept a given message when we have a favorable attitude toward a sender.[12] When they perceive managers as having a high credibility rating, subordinates are more likely to accept their messages, sometimes even blindly.

According to "Ripley's Believe It or Not," Napoleon Bonaparte, as a French general fighting in the Middle East in 1799, was about to release 1200 Turks captured at Jaffa when he was seized by a fit of coughing. "Ma sacré toux [My confounded cough]!" he exclaimed. Bonaparte's next-in-command thought he had said "Massacrez tous [Massacre all of them]"—and all 1200 prisoners were executed!

It follows, then, that managers must be viewed by their subordinates as credible and trustworthy. Otherwise, attempts to motivate, persuade, and direct the work efforts of subordinates are greatly handicapped from the very start.

Defensiveness. A feeling of defensiveness on the part of a message sender, receiver, or both creates a severe communication barrier. Defensiveness in one person causes certain facial expressions, body movements, and speech that, in turn, increase the defense levels of the other party. Thus, a defensive chain reaction begins. This defensive listening causes us to concentrate more on what we are going to say than on what we are hearing. When we feel defensive, we also distort what we do receive and are less likely to perceive accurately the motives, values, and emotions of our receiver.

Because managers have status and exercise authority, they must be especially aware of those situations that are likely to make subordinates feel defensive.

Poor listening. We are able to recall about 50 percent of what we have heard immediately after we hear it and only about 25 percent at the end of two months. Therefore, managers must learn to listen effectively. Before reading further, complete the questionnaire in TIPS 10.1.

Some poor listening habits include (1) listening only on the surface, with little attempt to consider seriously what the other person is saying; (2) giving the impression, through either speech or manner (glancing at watch, staring into space, fidgeting), of eagerness to end the conversation; (3) showing signs of annoyance or distress over the subject matter being discussed; and (4) inactive listening or failing to understand the frame of reference of the person speaking.

What is your view?

What specific poor listening habits did superintendent Odom display in his meeting with Evans?

But more basic than good listening itself are managers' attitudes toward listening. Are they willing to spend time with employees? Do they make themselves available?

Because we naturally defend our actions, managers as well as employees resent unfavorable communication. Also, many superiors are reluctant to listen for fear of becoming involved in a subordinate's personal problems. A poor reception in one instance, however, may affect a subordinate's willingness to communicate job-related problems in the future. Finally, listening consumes time; therefore, a manager whose span of control is too large is limited in his or her listening opportunities.

Imprecise use of language. One of the biggest mistakes we make in communicating is to assume that all meaning lies in the words we use. For example, a supervisor who tells a subordinate to "clean up around here" (meaning only a five-minute cleanup of scraps near the worker's drill press) will be quite distressed to return an hour later to find the worker "cleaning up" the entire department area, at the expense of a backlog of production work. To blame the worker for the communication breakdown may protect the supervisor's ego, but it represents a poor approach to a manager's communication responsibilities.

Studies of the *Oxford English Dictionary* show an average of over 25 different meanings for each of the 500 most frequently used words in the English language.[13] Furthermore, words can also arouse feelings, emotions, and attitudes within people. This is what we refer to as the **connotative meaning** of a word, as compared with its **denotative meaning,** or dictionary definition. Thus, the supervisor who says, "Well, boys, let's get on with this job" may be unaware that the word *boy* is strongly offensive to black employees, since it was used when blacks were slaves and still connotes servanthood, or at the least seems patronizing.

What is your view?

Superintendent Odom began his communication to Evans with "Bill, I hate to call you in to criticize you like this, but . . ." What effect do you think the word *criticize* had on Evans? Can you think of a better choice of words?

A study by the Opinion Research Corporation of Princeton, New Jersey, investigated the effect on 488 industrial employees (unsalaried) of 61 terms commonly used by management. The word capitalism, *as harmlessly used by management, connoted to these workers such feelings as "the wealthiest people take over," "big business has so much money it freezes the*

TIPS 10.1   Rate Your Listening Habits

Listening habit	Very seldom 10	8	6	4	Almost always 2
1. Faking attention, pretending to be interested when you're really not.	____	____	____	____	____
2. Being passive—not asking questions or trying to obtain clarifications even when you don't understand.	____	____	____	____	____
3. Listening mainly to what a speaker *says* rather than his or her feelings.	____	____	____	____	____
4. Allowing yourself to be distracted easily.	____	____	____	____	____
5. Not being aware of the speaker's facial expressions, nonverbal behavior.	____	____	____	____	____
6. Tuning out material that is complex or contrary to your own opinion.	____	____	____	____	____
7. Drawing conclusions, having your mind made up before hearing the speaker's full line of reasoning.	____	____	____	____	____
8. Allowing yourself to daydream or wander mentally.	____	____	____	____	____
9. Feeling restless, impatient, eager to end the conversation.	____	____	____	____	____
10. Interrupting the speaker, taking over the conversation to get in your own side of things.	____	____	____	____	____

Your total score: _____
                        100

Scoring

0–49	=	Far below average
50–59	=	Below average
60–69	=	Average
70–79	=	Good
80–89	=	Very good
90–100	=	Exceptional

SOURCE: Based on Donald C. Mosley, Leon C. Megginson, and Paul H. Pietri, *Supervisory Management*, 2d ed. (Cincinnati, OH: South-Western Publishing Co., 1989), Chapter 6.

little fellow out," and "a dictatorship by the rich." The word corporation *aroused a strong image of "money," "power," and "selfishness";* company *was much more favorably accepted. The term* work stoppage *was identified as "unfair";* strike, *however, was accepted as a "practical, fair means to an end."*[14]

INCREASING COMMUNICATION EFFECTIVENESS

So far, we have pointed out several causes of communication problems and the difficulty of effective communication. Now we would like to present some ways in which managers can increase their communication effectiveness. These techniques are essentially ways to overcome some of the difficulties presented.

Awareness of the Need for Effective Communication

Because of the many organizational and interpersonal barriers, effective communication cannot be left to chance. Managers must first appreciate the important role that communication plays, for only then can steps be taken to increase communication effectiveness.

As evidence of top management's recognition of the importance of communication, many large organizations today employ "communication specialists." These specialists help improve communication by helping supervisors solve internal communication problems; devising company communication strategy regarding layoffs, plant closings or relocations, and terminations; and measuring, through interviews or surveys, the quality of communication efforts.

Several other changes reflect management's constant search for improved communication effectiveness. For example, Texas Instruments, Westinghouse, Gulf Oil, and other firms have adopted videotaped television broadcasts to present information to employees. Bethlehem Steel had only one newsletter in 1973; in 1979, it had 23 different publications tailored to the needs of its individual plants.

Top management is also acknowledging the key communication linkage represented by first-line supervisors in their organizations. After all, it is this level that works directly with the great bulk of operative employees. In one company, the plant manager meets for half an hour every week with six to eight of the company's first-line managers, discusses key issues with them, and gets their input. The discussions range from dealing with rumors to company profitability, new equipment, problems with line-staff departments, and handling supervisory problems faced by the supervisors. The plant manager, by example, encourages each supervisor to have similar meetings with his or her own personnel.

Use of Feedback

Another important means of improving communication is to use the feedback from messages sent.[15] Managers can do at least two things to encourage feedback and use it effectively. They can create an environment that encourages feedback, and they can solicit feedback by their own actions.

Creating an encouraging environment. The way managers communicate with subordinates determines, to a large extent, the amount of feedback they receive. The type of communication used and the communication environment are important in determining what feedback is obtained, but the managers' responsibility for generating feedback goes beyond these factors. Managers must take an active role in soliciting feedback from others. For example, after communicating a job assignment, you might ask, "Do you understand?"

or "Do you have any questions?" or "Did I leave anything out?" But these questions do not encourage answers; a more direct approach would be to say: "This is quite important; so, to make sure we understand each other, tell me what you are going to do." Frequently, this produces clarification of points that a subordinate might otherwise be unwilling to mention for fear of appearing stupid. Remember, though, that you must also provide subordinates with pertinent feedback.

Actively seek feedback. Participative management consists of two-way communication, a form of feedback. Therefore, a manager who allows employees to make decisions or express opinions receives helpful responses from them. These responses serve as a form of feedback that helps the manager better understand the employees' thinking. Also, participation, or even the unused opportunity to participate, makes employees feel a greater responsibility to "make things go right." Cobe Laboratories, Incorporated, holds buffet lunches each week for 50 of its 1600 employees. Top managers learn about employee gripes and give updated data on profits and sales. The practice makes workers feel that "the company does listen to us."[16]

We all have a tendency to ignore feedback, and this increases when we find ourselves in positions of power. High-level managers may therefore have a stronger tendency than others to practice one-way communication.

TIPS 10.2   Suggestions for More Effective Listening

1. *Stop talking!*
   You cannot listen if you are talking.
   Polonius (*Hamlet*): "Give every man thine ear, but few thy voice."
2. *Put the talker at ease.*
   Help a person feel free to talk. This is often called a permissive environment.
3. *Show a talker that you want to listen.*
   Look and act interested. Do not read your mail while someone talks. Listen to understand rather than to oppose.
4. *Remove distractions.*
   Don't doodle, tap, or shuffle papers. Will it be quieter if you shut the door?
5. *Empathize with talkers.*
   Try to help yourself see the other person's point of view.
6. *Be patient.*
   Allow plenty of time. Do not interrupt a talker. Don't start for the door or walk away.
7. *Hold your temper.*
   An angry person takes the wrong meaning from words.

8. *Go easy on argument and criticism.*
   This puts people on the defensive, and they may "clam up" or become angry. Do not argue. Even if you win, you lose.
9. *Ask questions.*
   This encourages a talker and shows that you are listening. It helps to develop points further.
10. *Stop talking!*
    This is first and last, because all other guides depend on it. You cannot do an effective listening job while you are talking.
    Nature gave people two ears but only one tongue, which is a gentle hint that they should listen more than they talk.
    Listening requires two ears, one for meaning and one for feeling.
    Decision makers who do not listen have less information for making sound decisions.

SOURCE: Keith Davis, *Human Relations at Work*, 5th ed. (New York: McGraw-Hill, 1978), p. 387. Reprinted by permission.

Be a More Effective Listener

Poor listening techniques plague many managers, just as they plague many of us in our nonwork relationships with others. We are more likely to be interested in ourselves, to be thinking about what we are going to say, instead of really hearing what others tell us. Moreover, although most of us have had some formal training in writing and speaking, few have had training in effective listening.

One company, Sperry Corp., made effective listening its company theme. It conducted listening training on a companywide basis. Even its national advertising programs promoted the company's willingness to listen. Spots showed, for example, Sperry managers attending listening classes, Sperry managers listening to employee's views on various subjects, and a Sperry salesperson listening to a customer's point of view. The idea being communicated was "At Sperry, we listen."

Keith Davis has developed 10 guides to effective listening. These suggestions are summarized in TIPS 10.2.

Active listening is a tool that is used effectively by psychologists, counselors, and others whose professions require a deep understanding of their clients. It is taught in parent-child seminars, marriage seminars, and leader-effectiveness seminars throughout the country. Managers who can understand and use active listening can definitely add a new dimension to their management skills.

FIGURE 10.11
Examples of active listening.

MANAGER: Art, what I wanted to talk to you about was your being away from your desk for about 20 minutes this afternoon. I noticed that we had a buildup of five or six clients to be processed, and this caused some confusion in the waiting area.

EMPLOYEE: Well, I know it happened, but there wasn't anything I could do about it at the time.

*MANAGER: So you were aware of it, but couldn't remedy the problem?

EMPLOYEE: Yeah. I really had no choice in the matter. Huggins said she needed some help upstairs clarifying some expense items we'd submitted last month, and she was going to be out of town for two weeks. It was do it right then or wait till she got back.

*MANAGER: So it was a budget item from Huggins, and you had to do it right then. . . .

EMPLOYEE: Well, she'd called me twice before and I'd been too busy, and she seemed boxed in; so I felt I'd better do it then. We do owe her a few favors, and I didn't want to risk offending her, even if a few clients had to wait a while.

*MANAGER: So, under the circumstances, you felt a client buildup was a lower-priority item?

EMPLOYEE: Well . . . no, not really. I didn't expect it to take as long as it did. There were several interruptions. Once I was there, I really couldn't leave. I probably could have asked someone else to cover for me, just in case. I know client processing is the most important part of my job. When I saw the line, I knew I'd made a mistake.

MANAGER: You're right about the importance of smooth client processing, Art, and, in retrospect, having someone fill in would have been appropriate. Let's keep that in mind when something like this comes up again.

EMPLOYEE: Sure thing.

* Examples of reflective statements demonstrating active listening.

A principal active listening technique is the use of **reflective statements** by the listener. A reflective statement demonstrates that the listener has heard what the sender said and bounces the communication ball back to the speaker. For example, if superintendent Odom in the Opening Case had been actively listening when Evans said, "Well, I think it's mostly these new people I got last week. I talked with them about it, for whatever good that'll do," how could he have responded? Had he used active listening, a reflective statement might have been: "You seem to doubt that talking with them did any good," or "You think it's mainly the new people who are the problem?"

Some examples of active listening are given in Figure 10.11.

Managers who use the active listening approach, however, must be willing to pay a price for the benefits gained. First, use of the approach is time-consuming. Second, when a superior encourages subordinates to "open up," he or she may be placed in the uncomfortable position of hearing things that are discomforting or embarrassing. It may even place the manager in a disturbing ethical position. When a subordinate seems likely to disclose something in confidence that the superior feels cannot be treated confidentially, he or she should warn the subordinate of that fact.

SUMMARY

The typical manager spends a large percentage of the workday in some form of communication with others. Communication is linked closely to the managerial functions of planning, organizing, staffing, leading, and evaluating.

Downward communication consists of policies, rules, procedures, and the like that flow from top management to lower levels. Upward communication consists of the flow of performance reports and other information from lower to higher levels. Lateral or horizontal communication is essentially coordinative and occurs between and among individuals or departments on the same level. Diagonal communication cuts across the organization's chain of command because of line-and-staff relationships.

The components of a communication model are the source, encoding the message, transmitting the message, receiving the message, decoding the message, and feedback.

Informal as well as formal channels are important to organizational communication. Important messages are passed not only by verbal means but by nonverbal ones as well. Nonverbal communication consists of sign language, action language, object language, and paralanguage.

Some organizational barriers to communication are levels of hierarchy, managerial authority, and specialization. Interpersonal barriers include selective perception, the status of the communicator, defensiveness, poor listening habits, and imprecise use of language.

To improve the effectiveness of organizational and interpersonal communication, organizations must first develop and maintain awareness of the need for effective communication. The use of feedback and active listening techniques is among the effective communication tools at a manager's disposal.

REVIEW QUESTIONS

1. How do you define *communication?*
2. Explain the steps in the communication process.
3. What are examples of the four types of communication flows found in an organization?
4. What are the four forms of nonverbal communication discussed in the text? Explain.
5. What are five interpersonal communication "barriers" discussed in the chapter? Explain them.
6. What is "active listening"? What would be an active listening response to a worker who says, "I hate the job. It seems that other people get all the praise when things go right, but when things get screwed up, I'm the one who takes all the flak."

DISCUSSION QUESTIONS

1. *Communication* may be defined as the process by which a message sender converts ideas and thoughts into words and symbols and forwards them to a receiver, where a satisfactory interpretation occurs. How does this definition differ from that given in the chapter?
2. A recent survey of 101 chief executive officers of banks conducted by one of the authors showed that almost half (43 percent) felt that the biggest communication flow problem was lateral-diagonal. Why do you think these bankers selected this flow rather than upward or downward communication as their most important problem?
3. Recently an employee of an industrial firm received a severe electric shock while performing a job in the field. A paramedic team that was rushed to the scene administered artificial respiration, but en route to the hospital emergency center, the patient lost his vital signs. Upon arrival at the hospital, he was pronounced dead, and his body was "released to the morgue," which was the common hospital terminology used. In all the excitement of the accident, no one had called the employee's spouse, who heard about the the accident shortly after it happened. When she called the company, the company spokesperson indicated that he knew nothing of the accident. Quickly investigating, he placed a call to the hospital and learned the employee's status. He then called the employee's wife and indicated to her that her husband was apparently in good shape, as a hospital spokesperson said that he had apparently been "released." How did this miscommunication occur? Upon whom would you place blame? Why?
4. Some managers are firm believers in "putting it in writing." Others favor oral, face-to-face communication. What are the relative strengths and weaknesses of oral and written communication? Which do you prefer? In which situations would each form seem to be more appropriate or effective?
5. When he was owner and CEO of Apple Computer, Steven Jobs often dressed very casually at work, frequently wearing jeans; a coat and tie were exceptions rather than standard attire. Jobs said it was just his personal style. What do you think about this type of dress for the top official in a company? Discuss.

LEARNING EXERCISE 10.1

Developing a Communication Strategy

Assume that you are a branch manager for a large national organization. The branch for which you are responsible has 120 employees. There are two levels of managers—department heads and supervisors—between you and most of the employees. All employees work at the branch location. For each of the situations shown, develop in writing a communication plan or strategy for dealing with each, and clearly support your reasons for selecting the strategy that you recommend.

    1. One of your new department managers has been badly off the mark in keeping the departmental budget under control. A report from the branch controller's

department showed that two months ago the department head exceeded the budget by 40 percent. You said nothing, since it was the department head's first month in the new position. But this time you feel that you must take some action, for last month the department's budget was exceeded by 55 percent. These are items such as supplies and equipment, overtime, maintenance and repairs, telephone; you name it, the department head spent it. Other departments did not have this difficulty.

2. You have just learned from your regional manager via a telephone call that your company has been bought by a firm from Saudi Arabia. The sale will be announced to the financial community within the hour. The division manager knew little of the details but wanted you to get the word to your people as soon as possible.

3. A new overtime system will be installed, effective in four weeks. In the past, supervisors would get in touch with workers—by seniority—either in person or by telephone to make sure that the most senior workers would have first opportunity for overtime work. This has proved slow and ineffective, since some senior workers have declined overtime for several years. The new system will give each supervisor more flexibility in overtime assignments by getting monthly advance overtime commitment from workers. You find that your department managers and supervisors definitely prefer the new system and feel that most employees will, too, although several of the more senior people will probably get upset.

4. You learn that your own boss, who held your position several years ago, has been bypassing you and communicating directly with two of your department managers. The managers have reported to your boss several negative things about you, for which you received a slight reprimand. You were caught by surprise, because the facts reported to your boss were true, but he did not get the total explanation that would have put you in a favorable rather than unfavorable light. You will clear this matter up with your boss, who is due for a branch visit in two days.

LEARNING EXERCISE 10.2

The Ineffective Committees

The Evans Company, plagued by increasing costs and labor unrest at its major plant site, decided to go to its employees for assistance. Top management were proud of their brainchild, the "Productivity Improvement Committee Concept," or "PIC," as it was called. They had high hopes that the PIC, based on the Japanese quality circle approach, would result in not only increased efficiency but also improved morale.

Basically, the PIC would be implemented in the following manner. Each department of the plant would become a productivity improvement committee (PIC), with all employees in the department serving on it. Committee leadership was to consist of three people per department. One leader was the department supervisor, another the union shop steward, and the third an employee elected by members of the department. The number of committee members varied from 6 to 31 people, depending on the number of people in the department. Each committee was to meet for 30 minutes a week and address situations in which improvements could be made. The committee's recommendations went directly to the plant manager.

After a month of functioning, only three recommendations had been generated by any of the 18 PICs. Of these, none was judged feasible by the plant manager, who was disappointed with the poor quality of the recommendations. Accordingly, he named another committee, consisting of the union president, the director of human resources, and the head of engineering, to investigate the PIC situation. After meeting with PIC leaders, this committee presented the plant manager with a list of five reasons the PIC concept wasn't working as planned:

1. Fear among employees and leaders that people would lose jobs as a result of the PIC program.
2. Inexperience of leaders in conducting PIC meetings.
3. Feeling that top management wouldn't seriously consider PIC recommendations.
4. Difficulty of resolving matters within the 30-minute PIC format.
5. Lack of understanding among employees and leaders as to what their role was as PIC members.

Questions

1. What barriers to communication do you see reflected in the five reasons given for failure of the PIC?
2. What changes, if any, would you recommend in the PIC format?
3. Assume that you are the plant manager. What action will you take, based on the five reasons given for failure of the PICs?

NOTES

1. Adapted from Donald C. Mosley and Paul H. Pietri, *Management: The Art of Working With and Through People* (Encino, CA: Dickenson Publishing, 1975), pp. 134–135.
2. For example, Laurens van der Post, *The Dark Eye in Africa* (New York: Morrow, 1955), pp. 116–117, tells of the time when the Dutch in Java realized for the first time that the Indonesians wanted them to leave. The Dutch governor-general asked the author why the people wanted the Dutch to leave, although they had abolished disease and brought prosperity. The answer was this: "I'm afraid it's because you've never had the right look in the eye when you spoke to them."
3. John Fielden, "What Do You Mean I Can't Write?" *Harvard Business Review* 42 (May–June 1964): 144–156.
4. See Keith Davis, *Human Behavior at Work*, 5th ed. (New York: McGraw-Hill, 1978), p. 280.
5. Richard K. Allen, *Organizational Management Through Communications* (New York: Harper & Row, 1977), p. 68.
6. Albert Mehrabian, *Tactics of Social Influence* (Englewood Cliffs, NJ: Prentice-Hall, 1970).
7. Michael Korda, *Power! How to Get It, How to Use It* (New York: Ballantine Books, 1976).
8. Ralph W. Weber and Gloria E. Terry, *Behavioral Insights for Supervisors* (Englewood Cliffs, NJ: Prentice-Hall, 1975), p. 138.
9. Roderick Powers, "Measuring Effectiveness of Business Communication," *Personnel Administration* 36 (July–August 1973): 47–52.
10. Chester Barnard, *The Functions of the Executive* (Cambridge, MA: Harvard University Press, 1938).
11. See Karlene Roberts and Charles O'Reilly, "Failures in Upward Communication in Organizations: Three Possible Culprits," *Academy of Management Journal* 17 (June 1974): 205–215.
12. Roberts and O'Reilly, "Failures in Upward Communication."
13. Davis, *Human Behavior at Work*, p. 381.
14. Martin Wright, "Do You Need Lessons in Shop Talk?" *Personnel* 42 (July–August 1965): 60–61.
15. We are focusing here on feedback as a clarifying tool, but research has shown that feedback to subordinates regarding their performance has a positive effect on their subsequent performance. See Wayne Nemeroff and Joseph Cosentino, "Utilizing Feedback and Goal Setting to Increase Performance Appraisal Interviewer Skills and Managers," *Academy of Management Journal* 22 (September 1979): 566–576.
16. *The Wall Street Journal*, December 2, 1980, p. 1.

SUGGESTIONS FOR FURTHER STUDY

ALLRED, HILDA F., and CLARK, JOSEPH F. "Written Communication Problems and Priorities." *Journal of Business Communication* 15 (Winter 1978): 31–35.

BAIRD, JOHN G., JR., and WIETING, GRETCHEN K. "Nonverbal Communication Can Be a Motivational Tool." *Personnel Journal* 58 (September 1979): 607–610.

D'APRIX, ROGER. "The Oldest (and Best) Way to Communicate with Employees." *Harvard Business Review* 60 (September–October 1982): 30–31.

DAVIS, T. "The Influence of the Physical Environment in Offices." *Academy of Management Review* 9 (April 1984): 271–284.

GOLDHABER, GERALD. *Organizational Communication.* 3d ed. Dubuque, IA: W. C. Brown, 1983.

GUZZARDI, WALTER, JR. "How Much Should Companies Talk?" *Fortune,* March 4, 1985, pp. 64–68.

HUNSAKER, PHILLIP L., and COOK, CURTIS W. *Managing Organizational Behavior.* Reading, MA: Addison-Wesley Publishing Co., 1986. See especially Chapter 6, "Communication," pp. 196–229.

LEWIS, PHILLIP V. *Organizational Communication.* 3d ed. New York: John Wiley & Sons, 1987.

MISCHKIND, LOUIS A. "No Nonsense Surveys Improve Employee Morale." *Personnel Journal* 62 (November 1983): 906–914.

PENLEY, L. E., and HAWKINS, B. "Studying Interpersonal Communication in Organizations: A Leadership Application." *Academy of Management Journal* 28 (June 1985): 309–326.

SAUNDERS, CAROL STOAK. "Management Information Systems, Communications, and Departmental Power: An Integrative Model." *Academy of Management Review* 6 (July 1981): 431–442.

SUNDERLIN, REED. "Information Is Not Communication." *Business Horizons* 25 (March–April 1982): 40–42.

TAVERNIER, GERARD. "Improving Managerial Productivity—The Key Ingredient Is Better Communication." *Management Review* 70 (February 1981): 12–16.

11
Motivating Employees

Learning Objectives

After studying the material in this chapter, you should be able to do the following:

☐ State the purposes of motivation in organizations.
☐ Discuss why the study of motivation is so important.
☐ Describe how human behavior affects motivation.
☐ Distinguish among the different classifications of motivational theory.
☐ Explain the operations of some content theories of motivation.
☐ Explain the operations of some process theories of motivation.
☐ Recognize that money is involved in many aspects of motivation.
☐ Describe how occupational levels affect motivation.
☐ State that motivation is more than mere techniques.

Outline of the Chapter

Need for positive motivation
Definition
Purposes of motivation
Motivation is the essence of management
How motivation and ability affect performance
How human behavior affects motivation
Results of effective motivation
Some popular motivational theories
Content theories of motivation
Maslow's hierarchy of needs
Herzberg's motivation-maintenance theory
McClelland's achievement theory

Process theories of motivation
Expectancy theory
Operant conditioning
Equity theory
Role of money and occupation in motivation theory
How money affects motivation
How occupational level affects motivation
Motivation is more than mere techniques
Summary

Some Important Terms

motivation
motive
goal
desire
incentive
job burnout
content theories
process theories
hierarchy of needs
motivators
maintenance (hygienic) factors

need for achievement
expectancy theory
operant conditioning
positive reinforcement
behavior modification
law of effect
reinforcement
punishment
equity theory
dual allegiance

Give me enough medals and I'll win you any war.
—NAPOLEON BONAPARTE

Always dream and shoot higher than you know you can do. Don't bother just to be better than your contemporaries or predecessors. Try to be better than yourself.
—WILLIAM FAULKNER

The Demotivated Researcher

Jo Brown, a chemical engineer, was pleased with the potential of an environmental control project. She set out to "learn everything there is to know about it" and half-jokingly said to Larry Roberts, the assistant technical director, "I'm going to make myself an expert in this field."

Brown became completely absorbed in extensive research into the project. In her mind, the results were well worth the effort. After about six months, however, she sensed that her work was being taken for granted and that Roberts was not giving the project the importance it deserved. She did not let this lack of recognition affect her work, however, and continued to do high-quality work and research. She expressed her feelings to some associates, but since they were not close to the problem, their replies were more humorous than serious.

These reactions caused Brown to increase her efforts, and over the course of a year she did an excellent research job. The results were completely and thoroughly presented in a well-written and well-documented report. She made several copies of the report and gave them to Roberts, who was to review the report, present it to top management, and arrange several meetings to discuss practical applications of the findings.

Brown did routine work for about a month while awaiting some reaction. Whenever she asked Roberts about the report, she was brushed off.

When Roberts took his vacation, Brown was assigned his duties. One day, when Jo was asked to get a file from Roberts' desk, she found all the copies of her report lying in a drawer—apparently unread and obviously uncirculated. This caused Brown considerable trauma, for she had been confident that by this time some of the copies of the report had been delivered to top management.

Brown was so shaken by this experience that she resigned from the company and was immediately hired by a competitor. Since then, her success has been outstanding.[1]

How do you explain the change in her?

THIS CASE DRAMATIZES the need for effectively motivating employees. It also illustrates many of the points to be covered in discussing that topic in this chapter.

NEED FOR POSITIVE MOTIVATION

Motivation is a subject about which there is very little, if any, common understanding. This fact is evidenced by the jargon in use today. Yet you would find some terms that are fairly common to motivational literature. We use the following working definitions of the most frequently used terms:

Definition

1. **Motivation** is inducing a person or a group of people, each with his or her own distinctive needs and personality, to work to achieve the

organization's objectives, while also working to achieve his or her own objectives.

2. A **motive** is an internal stimulus that directs conscious behavior toward satisfying a need or reaching a goal.

3. A **goal** is the end toward which motivated behavior is directed.

4. **Desire** refers particularly to goals of which we are fully aware.

5. An **incentive** (often referred to as a *reward*) is an external stimulus that induces one to attempt to do something or to strive to achieve something.

What is your view?

Before reading any further, look at TIPS 11.1, and complete the form in Figure 11.1 as a basis for understanding the following material. What does the exercise tell you about your own motivation?

Purposes of Motivation

The exercise you have just done partially explains some of the confusion about motivation, for managers use different types of motivation and incentives to achieve different objectives.

What is your view?

Where did you rank ''good salary'' in column 1 of the exercise you just completed?

How to motivate people.
(Copyright 1971 by King Features Syndicate, Inc. World Rights reserved.)

TIPS 11.1 What Do You Want from Your Job?

Rank the employment factors shown in Figure 11.1 in their order of importance to you at three points in your career. In the first column, assume that you are about to graduate and are looking for your first full-time job. In the second column, assume that you have been gainfully employed for 5 to 10 years and that you are presently employed by a reputable firm at the prevailing salary for the type of job and industry you are in. In the third column, try to assume that 25 to 30 years from now you have found your niche in life and have been working for a reputable employer for several years. (Rank your first choice as "1," second as "2," and so forth through "10.")

Questions

1. What does your ranking tell you about your motivation now?
2. Is there any change in the second and third periods?
3. What are the changes, and why do you think they occurred?

Most students put salary as their number one desire. That is what people need most after being in school for several years, especially if they had to work to pay all or part of their school expenses. That is what people look for when deciding to join an organization. Yet factors such as promotion possibilities, working conditions, and the chance to do creative work become important for those already gainfully employed. Safety, security, and employee benefits become more important for older employees nearing the end of their working careers.

Thus, if you have a steady job, with a "satisfactory" income, you may not consider money—in the form of salary—as important to you as challenging and rewarding work. But, if you are seeking employment or do not have the material benefits, or if you perceive your financial position to be declining or threatened, you may regard money—in the form of benefits or security—as most important.

What is your view?

Did your rankings stay the same for all three columns of the exercise, or did your priorities change?

What we're trying to say is that motivation is highly individualistic; it is the essence of human behavior. You will find that your classmates, having different backgrounds, needs, and aspirations, probably ranked the items differently. But certain underlying principles and theories of motivation enable managers to better understand and predict people's responses to performing their tasks, despite the uniqueness of human beings. We expose you to these underlying concepts of motivation in this chapter.

There are at least three primary purposes of managerial motivation, each of which requires different approaches, tactics, and incentives. These purposes are:

1. To encourage potential employees to join the organization.
2. To stimulate present employees to produce or perform more effectively.
3. To encourage present employees to remain with the organization.

Employment factor	As you seek your first full-time job	Your ranking 5–10 years later	Your ranking 25–30 years later
Employee benefits			
Fair adjustment of grievances			
Good job instruction and training			
Effective job supervision by your supervisor			
Promotion possibilities			
Recognition (praise, rewards, and so on)			
Job safety			
Job security (no threat of being dismissed or laid off)			
Good salary			
Good working conditions (nice office surroundings, good hours, and so on)			

FIGURE 11.1
Ranking of selected employment factors.

We concentrate on the second motivational objective—improving employee performance—in this chapter, but, as you prepare yourself to manage in an organization, keep all three of these objectives in mind.

MOTIVATION IS THE ESSENCE OF MANAGEMENT

The problem of motivation would be a simple one if it were merely a question of whether managers should or should not motivate their subordinates. This is not the case, however; new employees are already motivated, and managers *continually* generate either positive or negative responses from employees. Production results when managers obtain a positive response; it is withheld when the response is negative. In other words, *the essence of management is motivation.* The real question is *what type of motivation* managers can use most effectively to stimulate improved performance.

Motivation is also needed to overcome the hazard of **job burnout,** which is physical or mental depletion significantly below your capable level of performance. It's a major cause of absenteeism, alienation, and worksite antagonisms. To combat it, employers need to design jobs with periods of rest from responsibility, to rotate employees into less pressured positions, or to otherwise motivate them to operate more effectively. Motivation is also needed because of employees' increasing awareness of their individual rights, which can lead to negative attitudes toward the job.

There is no question that one of the primary challenges facing organizations is the objective of improving employee performance. This challenge is highlighted by a study that discovered that fewer than one of every four jobholders felt they were working at full potential. Half said they did not put any more effort into their job than was necessary to keep it. The vast majority, 75 percent, said that they could be significantly more effective than they were.[2]

Just imagine what would happen to performance and productivity in the United States if that 75 percent became significantly more effective! Perhaps Tom Peters and Nancy Austin were correct when they observed that a group of 100 motivated people "can do the same work, faster and of higher quality, than several thousand are able to accomplish."[3]

A 1985 Bureau of Labor Statistics (BLS) survey of some 60,000 households reached a slightly different conclusion. It found that Americans "are strongly attached to their jobs" and that many would like to work more rather than less. The study showed that the commitment to work is greater than many people think.[4]

How Motivation and Ability Affect Performance

The relationship would be simple if productivity were a function of ability alone, for employees' output would vary directly with increases in their abilities, as shown by performance curve 1 in Figure 11.2. Since this is the performance curve that would result *if productivity were based on ability alone, performance should increase directly and proportionately as ability increases.* But, because of the employees' freedom of choice to perform effectively, ineffectively, or not at all, motivation is necessary to increase output. Thus the employees' actual performance curve is also related to the type and extent of motivation involved.

You can see from performance curve 2 that the employee's *output increases at an increasing rate* when there is *increasing ability and/or strong positive motivation.* The person's *performance level will continue to be low* when there is *strong negative or weak positive motivation*, regardless of changes in ability, as shown by performance curve 3.

It can be concluded from this discussion that *employee performance is a function of ability times motivation* that can be represented by the equation $P = f(A \times M \times R)$, where P represents performance; f, function; A, ability,

FIGURE 11.2
How ability and motivation affect performance.

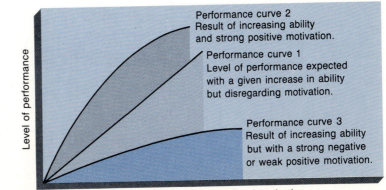

Performance curve 2
Result of increasing ability and strong positive motivation.

Performance curve 1
Level of performance expected with a given increase in ability but disregarding motivation.

Performance curve 3
Result of increasing ability but with a strong negative or weak positive motivation.

Level of performance

Level of ability and intensity of motivation

M, motivation; and *R*, role perception. Thus not only ability and motivation affect our output, but also the way we view our role in the organization.

> *Jim Jackson entered college with a score of 29 on his ACT. His performance in the first semester resulted in four Fs and one D. At that time he dropped out and spent two years in the airborne infantry. He then returned to college, and in his initial semester his performance resulted in four As and one B.*

What is your view?

Drawing on the performance equation P = f(A × M × R), speculate as to what caused Jim's performance to improve so dramatically after two years in the service.

This example highlights the fact that, although teachers and managers can certainly create a climate of positive motivation, in the final analysis, motivation comes from within each person.

The performance equation and derived curves are oversimplified, for both a person's ability and motivation are the result of many other factors.

Motivation occurs through the interaction of intrinsic and extrinsic rewards with employee needs, as modified by the employee's expectations. You can see from the relationship between these variables shown in Figure 11.3 that motivation is very complex. Notice that managers *can* motivate

FIGURE 11.3
Variables affecting ability and motivation.

SOURCE: Kae H. Chung, *Developing a Comprehensive Model of Motivation and Performance* (Ph.D. dissertation, Louisiana State University, 1968), p. 172.

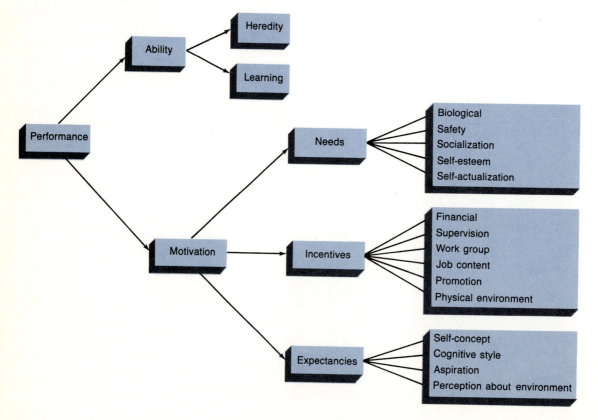

Management Application and Practice 11.1   Creating a Positive Climate Where People Are Motivated from Within

Bill Black revitalized Teleflex, a $150 million applications engineering company, by eliminating bureaucracy and developing a decentralized, entrepreneurial, participative climate. A strong people philosophy was the basis for the change. This philosophy emphasized that:

People are people, not personnel.

People don't dislike work. Help them to understand mutual objectives, and they'll drive themselves to unbelievable excellence.

The best way to really train people is with an experienced mentor—and on the job.

People have ego and development needs, and they'll commit themselves only to the extent that they can see ways of satisfying these needs.

People cannot be truly motivated by anyone else; that door is locked from the outside. They should work in an atmosphere that fosters self-motivation, self-assessment, and self-confidence, as opposed to external motivation.

People should work in a climate that is challenging, invigorating, and fun, and the rewards should be related as directly as possible to performance.

When people are in an atmosphere of trust, they'll put themselves at risk; only through risk is there growth, reward, self-confidence, and leadership.

SOURCE: Tom Peters and Nancy Austin, *A Passion for Excellence* (New York: Random House, 1985), p. 206.

employees toward improved performance by creating a positive climate where people can be motivated from within (see MAP 11.1).

What is your view?

As you are introduced to the forthcoming theories of motivation, identify what theories relate to the people philosophy of Teleflex.

What is your view?

What other variables could you add to the list in Figure 11.3 from your own knowledge and experience? Which ones would you, as a manager, be able to influence in your subordinates? Why?

How Human Behavior Affects Motivation

We indicated earlier that many people believe management can never become a science because managers have to deal with (1) human behavior that often seems unpredictable and irrational and (2) human beings, who often act from emotions rather than with reason. Without denying that people do sometimes act emotionally, we still contend that most human behavior is rational and relatively predictable (except for that of the mentally ill). Therefore, human behavior should seem less irrational and unpredictable if we understand the *why* of it.

What is your view?

In the Opening Case, Brown regarded Roberts's failure to circulate her report as irrational. Can you think of some rational reasons (at least from Roberts's point of view) for his failure to circulate the report? What about Brown's behavior? Was it rational? How would you have acted? Why? Would your behavior seem rational to Roberts?

We would like to make three basic assumptions about human behavior that form the basis for the following discussion. First, *human behavior is caused.* Second, *human behavior is goal directed.* Third, *human behavior does not occur in isolation.*

The conscious actions that we as people take are caused both by forces in our environment and by our heredity. Human behavior is not only caused, but it is also pointed toward something; that is, *human behavior is goal directed.*

In essence, individuals' behavior (1) may be caused by the way they perceive the world, (2) is directed toward achieving a certain goal, and (3) results in motivation to achieve that goal, as shown in Figure 11.4. Therefore, the motivational process is basically one of causation. *Needs* (motives) cause an inner *desire* to overcome some lack or imbalance. *Stimuli,* in the form of *incentives,* are then applied to cause a person to respond and behave so that performance results. Thus, the *goal* of satisfying the person's needs is achieved, and the organization achieves its desired output. There is a certain degree of predictability throughout the chain of events, and actions are not completely random.

> *Sally Bartow spent all of last night burning the midnight oil in preparation for her certified public accountant's (CPA) exam. In fact, many of her friends were disappointed when she did not accompany them to a benefit being staged by the local high school they had attended. Sally's choice was a conscious one, however: The CPA certification was a goal that had brought her through four years of college course work in accounting as well as her choice of which job offer to accept. So attaining the CPA designation had figured strongly in the last seven years of her life and could be brought about by her passing the exam next week. Yet Sally's friends were bewildered by her choice of priorities.*

Motivation assumes that if you understand human behavior you can better predict that behavior; if you can predict human behavior, you can better control it. Consequently, understanding this process contributes to success in seeing that organization members contribute their joint efforts to generate productivity.

FIGURE 11.4
Motivation is goal directed.

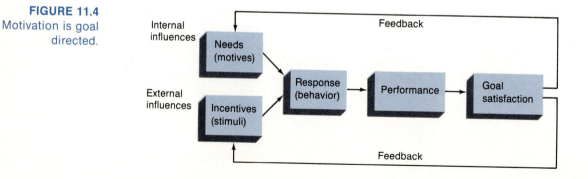

What is your view?

To what extent did this process work in Brown's case? What caused Brown's behavior? Toward what goal was it directed? Could you have predicted Brown's behavior?

Results of Effective Motivation

Although motivation provides the best potential source of increased productivity and profitability, it does not necessarily mean a greater expenditure of energy on the part of the worker. Instead, it implies that employee abilities will be used more efficiently with the same—or less—expenditure of effort. This, in turn, should lead to improved job satisfaction.

What is your view?

Did you notice how Jo Brown became ''completely absorbed'' in her work when she was motivated to use her well-developed abilities? What were the results? Why did Brown do this?

SOME POPULAR MOTIVATIONAL THEORIES

Some students do not enjoy studying theory because they feel that it is abstract and unrelated to the real world. Actually, whatever the discipline, good theory provides a basis for understanding, explaining, and predicting what will happen in the real world. In fact, as sociologist Kurt Lewin once said, nothing is more practical than good theory.[5] Moreover, whether they realize it or not, students and managers, in working with and through people, must operate from some theory.

It is difficult to condense and compare the prevailing theories of motivation, since they are based on different assumptions and often focus on different aspects of performance. For discussion purposes, however, the theories can be classified into two categories—content and process.

Content theories (sometimes called *need theories*) are concerned with the question of *what causes behavior*—such as needs that employees try to satisfy on the job. The most popular of these are (1) psychologist Abraham H. Maslow's hierarchy of needs, (2) Frederick Herzberg's motivation-maintenance theory, and (3) researcher and author David McClelland's need-for-achievement theory.

Process theories deal with *how behavior originates and is performed.* The currently accepted ones are (1) expectancy theory, (2) operant conditioning, and (3) equity theory. We turn first to content theories and then to process theories of motivation.

CONTENT THEORIES OF MOTIVATION

Content theories of motivation focus on this question: *What causes behavior to occur and stop?* The answers usually center on (1) the needs, motives, or desires that drive, pressure, spur, and force employees to action and (2) employees' relationships to the incentives that lead, induce, pull, and persuade them to perform. The *needs* or *motives* are internal to the individual. They cause people to choose a specific course of action. *Incentives* are external factors that give value or utility to the goal or outcome of the employees' behavior.

Maslow's Hierarchy of Needs

Maslow based the concept of a **hierarchy of needs** on two principles.[6] First, *human needs may be arranged in a hierarchy of importance* progressing from a lower to a higher order of needs, as shown in Figure 11.5. Second, *a satisfied need no longer serves as a primary motivator of behavior.*

How it functions. Maslow points out that needs can be thought of as being ranked in a hierarchy in which one need is more important than others until it is satisfied. Once that need is satisfied, the next higher need becomes predominant. The order, however, can be reversed and even swing back and

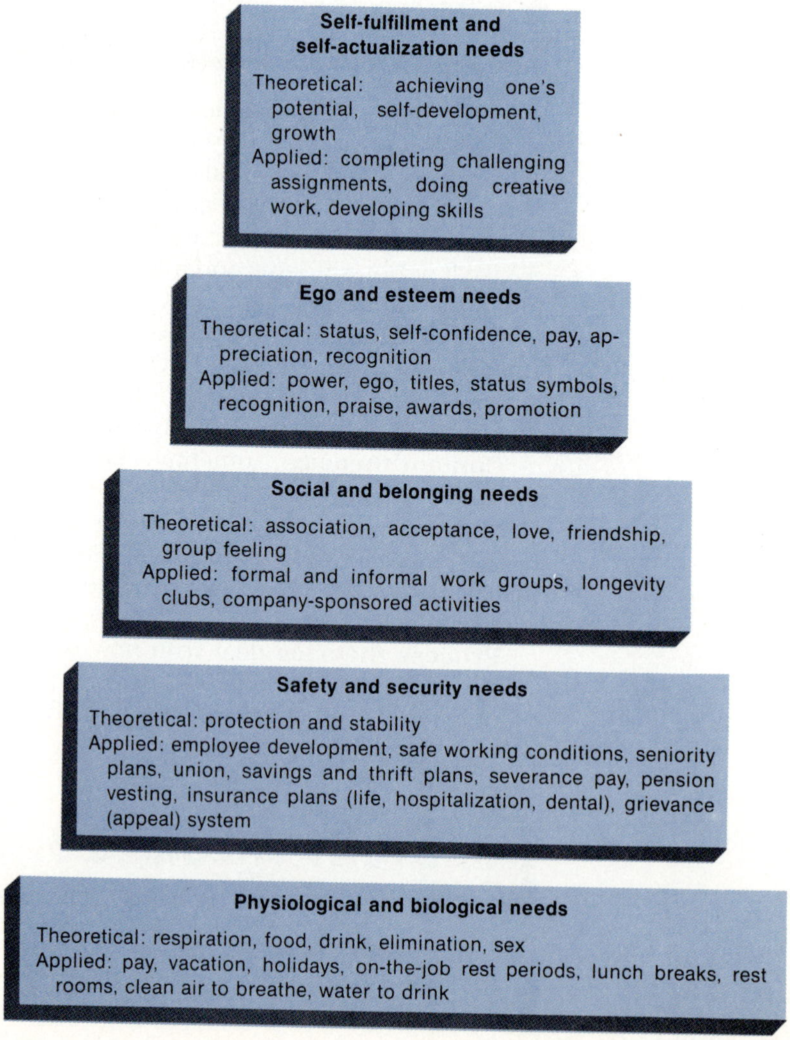

FIGURE 11.5
Maslow's hierarchy of needs, in theory, and as applied to managerial motivation.

Self-fulfillment and self-actualization needs

Theoretical: achieving one's potential, self-development, growth
Applied: completing challenging assignments, doing creative work, developing skills

Ego and esteem needs

Theoretical: status, self-confidence, pay, appreciation, recognition
Applied: power, ego, titles, status symbols, recognition, praise, awards, promotion

Social and belonging needs

Theoretical: association, acceptance, love, friendship, group feeling
Applied: formal and informal work groups, longevity clubs, company-sponsored activities

Safety and security needs

Theoretical: protection and stability
Applied: employee development, safe working conditions, seniority plans, union, savings and thrift plans, severance pay, pension vesting, insurance plans (life, hospitalization, dental), grievance (appeal) system

Physiological and biological needs

Theoretical: respiration, food, drink, elimination, sex
Applied: pay, vacation, holidays, on-the-job rest periods, lunch breaks, rest rooms, clean air to breathe, water to drink

forth. Once satisfied, a given need no longer motivates behavior. Only when one is deprived of something, and therefore craves it, can it be used as an incentive. (The threat of deprivation of need is also an incentive.) This concept is significant, for it effectively limits the frequency of use of certain incentives and restricts the use of others.

> *Joe Harris just received a call from Fred Wilson, coach of the company's softball team. Fred asked Joe if he would play for the team that played on Tuesday and Thursday evenings in the industrial league. "You'd get a chance to meet a lot of people and have fun," said Fred. "We also have several parties, and everyone has a good time." Little did Fred realize that he was using the wrong sales pitch with Joe, who, while he enjoyed softball, was already heavily involved in social activities in the community. The need for more "people relationships" did not exist, and so he politely turned Fred down.*

Now let us look at the hierarchy of needs, as shown in Figure 11.5, and then elaborate on each of the levels. The general idea is that as soon as a need at a lower level is relatively well satisfied we attempt to satisfy the needs at progressively higher levels. We now discuss each of these needs.[7]

Physiological and biological needs. At the lowest level, but of primary importance when they are not met, are our physiological or biological needs. "Man does not live by bread alone," says the Bible, but anything else is less important when there is no bread. Unless the circumstances are unusual, the need we have for love, status, or recognition, for example, is inoperative when our stomach has been empty for a while. But when we eat regularly and adequately, we cease to regard hunger as an important motivator. The same is true of other physiological needs, such as for air, water, sex, rest, exercise, shelter, and protection from the elements.

Safety and security needs. When the physiological needs are reasonably satisfied, safety and security needs become important. These protect us against danger, threat, or deprivation. When we feel threatened or dependent, our greatest need is for guarantees, for protection, for security.

Most employees are in a dependent relationship in their work environment; therefore, they may regard their safety needs as being very important. Arbitrary management actions (such as favoritism or discrimination) and unpredictable application of policies can be powerful threats to the safety needs of any employee at any level.

CROCK by Bill Rechin & Brant Parker

(Copyright 1977 by Field Enterprises, Inc.)

Social and belonging needs. Social needs include the need for belonging, association, acceptance by colleagues, and giving and receiving friendship and love.

Management knows that these needs exist, but it often assumes—quite wrongly—that these needs represent a threat to the organization. Therefore, fearing group hostility to its own objectives, management may go to considerable lengths to control and direct human efforts in ways that are detrimental to cohesive work groups. When people's social needs—as well as their safety needs—are frustrated, they may behave in ways that tend to defeat organizational objectives. They become resistant, antagonistic, and uncooperative. But this behavior is a consequence of their frustration, not a cause.

Ego and esteem needs. Above the social needs—in the sense that they do not become motivators until lower needs are reasonably well satisfied—are the *egoistic needs.* These are of two kinds: (1) those that relate to one's self-esteem—needs for self-confidence, independence, achievement, competence, and knowledge—and (2) those that relate to one's reputation—needs for status, recognition, appreciation, and the deserved respect of one's colleagues.

Unlike the lower needs, these are rarely fully satisfied, since people seek indefinitely for more satisfaction of these needs once they have become important to them. The typical organization offers few opportunities for the satisfaction of these egoistic needs for people at lower levels in the hierarchy. The conventional method of organizing work, particularly in mass-production industries, gives little consideration to these aspects of motivation.

"It's hard to get your kicks doing a routine job like I have," said Marge Powell, a sewing machine operator for a garment manufacturer. "My operation is to stitch a false pocket on men's sport coats, and each pocket takes only a few seconds. After doing a few thousand of these a day, I don't exactly go home at night thinking, 'Gee, I can't wait to get back to work tomorrow!'"

Self-fulfillment and self-actualization needs. Finally, there are needs for self-fulfillment, for realizing one's own potentialities, for continued self-development, and for being creative in the broadest sense of that term.

It is clear that the quality of work life in most organizations gives only limited opportunity for fulfilling these needs. When other needs are not satisfied, workers attempt to satisfy those lower-order needs, and the needs for self-fulfillment remain dormant.

How managers can use this theory. Figure 11.5 provides insight into how the needs hierarchy can be used in management motivation. The first three levels are self-explanatory; this chapter, Chapter 12 (on leadership), and Chapter 13 (on organizational culture and change) provide greater insight on tapping the higher-level needs.

What is your view?

What needs in Maslow's hierarchy are being satisfied by the students taking this course? Might the need for satisfaction be different for different individuals? How can the instructor attempt to satisfy the needs at various levels for different students?

Qualifications to Maslow's theory. Maslow's theory should be considered a general guide to managers, for it is a relative concept, not an absolute explanation of all human behavior. There are, therefore, some important qualifications you should be aware of.

First, there are many exceptions to the theory—for example, "starving artist" types, who make sacrifices in their personal comfort while trying to achieve self-actualization through creating their masterpiece. Moreover, some people are much less security oriented or achievement oriented than others.

Second, the two highest levels can hardly ever be fully satisfied, for there are many new challenges and opportunities for growth, recognition, and achievement. In creative organizations, people may remain in the same job position for years and still find a great deal of challenge and motivation in their work.

Making the theory come to life. Several points about Maslow's theory need to be reemphasized. This can best be accomplished through two examples.

First, the theory indicates that when the lower-level needs are relatively well satisfied they cease to be important motivators of behavior. However, when they are threatened, these needs may suddenly become important again.

Hank, a middle-level manager working for a large company in his hometown, was from an old and respected family, a graduate of a prestigious university, and happily married, with a daughter who had recently been selected as a debutante.

In 20 years with the firm, he had steadily advanced. He had a yearly salary of $50,000 and had social standing as a key member of an important company. He received much satisfaction from his work and from community activities. He rarely thought about security or social needs because he took them for granted.

Several years ago, a recession caused the unemployment of many people, including some managers. Although Hank was somewhat shaken by this development, he believed that he was secure in his position. Soon afterward, however, a large corporation purchased the company, and one of its first moves was to terminate several middle managers, including Hank.

What is your view?

What needs are important to Hank now? Why? What is Hank's primary motivation?

Second, the theory can be used to explain and predict not only *individual* but also *group* behavior. This is especially so for those whose work is closely related to that of others and whose work brings them into contact with others. It can also explain what happens as people's desire for the good life increases. When people are operating below, or near, subsistence level, they will be motivated to work for low wages and even be satisfied with poor working conditions. They may even be satisfied to continue under such conditions—for a while. But, once they are made aware that there is more to life—once they feel reasonably well satisfied at the lowest level—they naturally want, expect, and demand more. The so-called carrot-and-stick approach does not work very well once a person moves beyond the subsistence level.

Herzberg's Motivation-Maintenance Theory

In general, new employees tend to focus upon lower-level needs, particularly security, in their first job. But, after those are satisfied, they try to fulfill higher-level needs, such as initiative, creativity, and responsibility. It is by appealing to these needs that real achievement in efficiency, productivity, and creativity can be made, although managers do not always do this.

Several motivation research experiments, including those of Herzberg, have demonstrated the importance of these higher-level needs as motivators.

What is your view?

Now think of a job you have held—either full or part time—and then answer these two questions:

1. What specific event, incident, or series of related events *made you feel unusually good* about your job?
2. What specific event, incident, or series of related events *made you feel unusually bad* about your job?

The original study on job satisfaction. In the initial study, Herzberg and his associates conducted in-depth interviews with over 200 engineers and accountants.[8] These professionals were asked—as you were—to recall events or incidents from the past year that had made them feel unusually good or bad about their work. They were also asked to speculate on how much the events had affected their performance and morale.

The interviews were assessed, and, in almost all cases, the factors causing job satisfaction had a stimulating effect on performance and morale, whereas the factors causing job dissatisfaction had a negative effect. Another important finding was that *the positive factors were all intrinsic to the job, whereas the negative factors were all extrinsic.* That is, when the people felt good about their jobs, it was usually because they were doing their work particularly well or were becoming more expert in their professions. Favorable feelings were related to the specific tasks performed, such as designing a bridge, meeting a deadline, or making a big sale, rather than to background factors such as money, security, or working conditions. Conversely, unfavorable feelings resulted from some disturbance in these factors that caused the people to feel that they were not being *treated* fairly, such as poor wages, unsafe conditions, or fear of losing their jobs.

What is your view?

To what extent were your answers to the two previous questions consistent with Herzberg's findings?

Motivators and maintenance factors. On the basis of these findings, the researchers made a distinction between what they called *motivators* and what they called *maintenance factors*, as shown in Figure 11.6. **Motivators** have uplifting effects on attitudes or performance. **Maintenance factors** (sometimes called **hygienic factors**) prevent losses of morale or efficiency, and although they cannot motivate by themselves, they can forestall any serious dissatisfaction or drop in productivity and allow the motivators to

FIGURE 11.6
Herzberg's motivating and maintenance factors.

Motivating factors

Achievement
Responsibility
Recognition
Advancement
Creative and challenging work
Possibilities for growth on the job

Maintenance factors

Company policies and administration
Quality of technical supervision
Interpersonal relationships
Salary
Job security
Working conditions
Employee benefits
Job status
Personal life

operate. These factors can be compared to dental hygiene. Brushing your teeth regularly does not *improve* them, but it helps to *prevent* further decay.

These factors parallel Maslow's concept of a hierarchy of needs. The motivators relate to the two highest levels (esteem and self-fulfillment), and the maintenance factors relate to the lower-level needs, primarily the security needs (see Figure 11.7).

What this indicates is that employees today expect to be treated fairly by their managers so that their individual rights will be maintained. They expect decent working conditions and pay comparable to that of people doing similar work. They expect company policies to be consistently and equitably applied to all employees. When these expectations are not realized, employees are demotivated (or negatively motivated). This condition is usually reflected in inefficiency and a high turnover rate. But fulfilling these expectations does not necessarily motivate employees. As Maslow's theory maintains, it is only when the lower-level needs are satisfied that the higher-level needs can be used most effectively in motivating employees. The key is for the manager to tap the motivating factors. The following are some of the things a manager can do to create a motivating environment:

1. Send employees to training courses for skill upgrading and management development.

	Maslow's needs hierarchy theory	Herzberg's motivation-maintenance theory
Motivational factors	Self-fulfillment/self-actualization Ego/esteem	Creative and challenging work Achievement Possibility of growth Responsibility Advancement Recognition

Maintenance factors	Ego/esteem
	Social/belonging
	
	Safety/security
	
	Physiological/biological
		Status
		Interpersonal relations
		  Superior
		  Subordinates
		  Peers
		Supervision
		Company policy and administration
		Job security
		Working conditions
		Salary
		Personal life

2. With trained and motivated employees, delegate authority and supervise by results.

3. With new and untrained employees, assign experienced employees to assist in training and development.

4. Compliment and recognize employees for good work.

5. In dealing with complex problems or special projects, call employees in and get their ideas.

6. Assign employees to special ad hoc task forces for developing recommendations on key issues.

Evaluation of the theory. After the original study, critics of Herzberg's theory were quick to point out that, although the findings might apply to professionals who sought creativity in their work, they would not apply to other groups of employees. Herzberg, however, found similar results in 12 studies involving various groups.[9] Similar studies by different investigators in different countries *using the same research method* have shown surprisingly similar results (except for minor variations).

In a study in New Zealand, using Herzberg's methodology, findings similar to those of previous studies were reached.[10] The comments of one employee show that supervision is one of the major influences on whether higher-level need satisfaction can be realized by employees in their work.

> I was given complete responsibility for performance on a temporary job. I was to "report back at a later date and tell the boss how I was getting on." When a couple of hours later the boss came down and asked me how I was doing, I was glad he appeared to be taking an interest. But when he came back again every two or three hours, I got fed up and looked for ways of palming the job off on someone else. I wondered why I was given the job in the first place if the boss thought I couldn't do it right.
>
> I started taking longer on the job than I should have and couldn't have cared

less if what I was doing was right or wrong, since this boss was constantly checking to see if I made any mistakes.

> ### What is your view?
> Using theories discussed so far, explain what was going on in this situation. What do you predict will probably happen now?

On the other hand, studies *using a different research method* have, in the majority of instances, failed to support Herzberg's theory.[11] This fact has led some researchers to conclude that the theory is "method-bound"; that is, when Herzberg's research method is followed, the theory is supported; when his method is not followed, the theory fails. In other words, you are more likely to mention something that *you did* when mentioning a satisfying experience. You are more likely to mention something that *you could not control* when mentioning a dissatisfying work experience.

We conclude that the jury is still out regarding the absolute validity of the theory. Nevertheless, we believe that the theory is valuable as a general guide to understanding motivation at work. Two weaknesses are the conclusions that money is always a maintenance factor and that recognition and achievement are always motivators. Later, we develop the thesis that money can be a powerful motivator when it is used as a recognition of and reward for achievement. Money also has symbolic meaning. Also, lack of recognition can cause considerable dissatisfaction when one is convinced that one's performance deserves recognition and it is not forthcoming.

> ### What is your view?
> How would you explain Brown's reactions to Roberts's actions (in the Opening Case) in terms of this generalization?

McClelland's Achievement Theory

At a management conference in Helsinki in 1968, one of us asked a Finnish bank officer what was the most influential book he had read dealing with management. He answered, "*The Achieving Society,* by David McClelland."

Basic concepts. McClelland stated that a country's economic development depends on the extent to which its citizens have a **need for achievement.**[12] Research by McClelland and others indicates that there is a *high positive correlation between the need for achievement and performance and executive success.* McClelland also discovered that this need *can* be developed in mature people, for an individual's drives or motives are not fixed as a result of childhood experiences.

Characteristics of the achievement-oriented. Achievement-oriented persons have certain characteristics that can be developed. In general, such people do the following:

1. Enjoy *moderate risk taking* as a function of skill, not chance; enjoy a *challenge;* and want *personal responsibility* for outcomes.

2. Tend to set *moderate achievement goals* and take calculated risks. One reason many companies have moved into a management by objectives (MBO) program is that there is a positive correlation between goal setting and performance levels.

3. Have a *strong need for feedback* about how well they are doing.

Jim Harris's pet peeve is instructors who fail to return tests or exams within one or two class meetings. Strongly achievement oriented, he has an intense need to receive rapid feedback about his performance. He cannot understand how some fellow students fail to get upset about professors who take up to two or three weeks to return exams.

4. Have *skill in long-range planning* and possess *organizational abilities.* Both successful students and successful managers are adept at looking at future objectives and considering alternative ways of reaching those objectives. Many companies recruiting college graduates look very carefully at their extracurricular activities and particularly their leadership positions in student organizations. They know from experience that this activity enhances their organizational abilities and leadership skills.

In a "Business Career Development" contest sponsored by Executive Women International, high school seniors were evaluated on the basis of leadership, good citizenship, communication skills, office skills, and career planning. Each entrant wrote an autobiography, and local finalists were judged in a regional and then an international competition.

   The autobiographies of three finalists reflected their needs, desires, and drives for achievement in their lives. They had difficult—but attainable—career objectives and had already made long-range plans to achieve their objectives.[13]

The need for power. More recently, McClelland has gone further with his research and studied the needs people have for affiliation and power. Since the need for affiliation is essentially the same as Maslow's social need, we will focus on the power need. Although all of us have degrees of all three needs—achievement, affiliation, and power—one is usually stronger than the other two.

In one study, McClelland and Burnham discovered that male managers with a higher need for power had more productive departments than managers with a high need for affiliation.[14] While the word *power* has a negative connotation for many people, it should be kept in mind that power is closely related to leadership and results in influencing people, events, and decisions within an organizational framework.

McClelland's research has found that managers with a high need for power in the majority of instances use it for the benefit of the organization rather than for self-aggrandizement. They use power to increase the power of others through participation, support, and the positive reinforcement of accomplishments. They view their role as manager as a way to expand power for themselves and for other members of the organization rather than to hoard power.

PROCESS THEORIES OF MOTIVATION

The previous theories focus on the *needs* that drive or spur behavior and the *incentives* that attract or induce behavior. The *process theories* focus on *how behavior originates and operates.* We will look at (1) expectancy theory, (2) operant conditioning, and (3) equity theory.

Expectancy Theory

Some of the most important modern process theories rely on what is called **expectancy theory.** This concept is related to motivation as follows. Individuals are predicted to be high performers when they see (1) a high probability that their efforts will lead to high performance, (2) a high probability that high performance will lead to favorable outcomes, and (3) that these outcomes will be, on balance, positively attractive to them.

Basic concepts. Expectancy theory states that much work behavior can be explained by this fact: Employees determine in advance what their behavior may accomplish and the value they place on alternative possible accomplishments or outcomes. Notice in the Opening Case that Brown expected certain positive outcomes from the good work she was doing on her report.

Some writers have termed this a "payoff" or "what's in it for me" view of behavior. Yet this approach does partially explain the causes of behavior. For example, Figure 11.8 shows that if you expect hard work and performance to lead to superior pay and promotion, you will place a high value on both receiving superior pay and eventually earning a promotion. In this situation, assuming that you have the ability to do the work, you would probably be inclined to put forth a strong effort to receive the superior pay and promotion.

Let's complicate the situation, though, by introducing some other variables. Assume that you are starting your first job in a firm that has a piecework pay plan that pays additionally for each item produced over standard. If you and your family adhere to the blue-collar work ethic, your expectations regarding the work would probably approximate those shown in Figure 11.9.

You would probably consider the three output options of (1) top performance, (2) average performance, and (3) low performance. Then, on a subjective basis, you would assess the relative attractiveness of the three outcomes: (1) superior pay, (2) acceptance by the work group, and (3) not causing the standard to be raised. From the employer's standpoint, it would be desirable for you to select the first option. The Hawthorne studies indicate, however, that acceptance by the group is sometimes valued above superior pay when there is peer group pressure to resist high standards. (This was true even during the Great Depression.) Nevertheless, it can be predicted that superior performance will tend to result if there is a positive employer environment that rewards superior performance.

Vroom's value-expectancy theory. According to Victor Vroom, people are motivated to work if they (1) expect increased effort to lead to reward and (2) value the rewards resulting from their efforts.[15] Thus, from management's point of view, the following results:

$$
\text{Motivation} = \begin{bmatrix} \text{expectancy that} \\ \text{increased effort will lead} \\ \text{to increased rewards} \end{bmatrix} \times \begin{bmatrix} \text{value to the individual} \\ \text{of the rewards resulting} \\ \text{from his or her efforts} \end{bmatrix}
$$

FIGURE 11.8
How expectations affect performance.

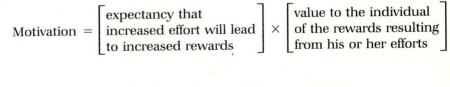

FIGURE 11.9
How options affect expectations.

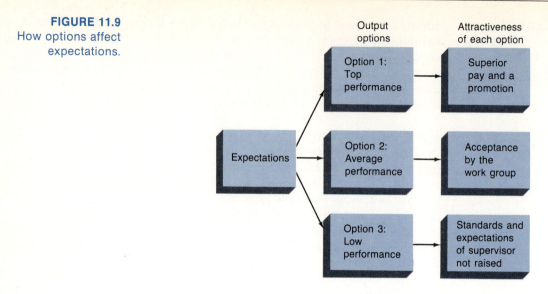

Let's take a look at how Vroom's theory operates. Suppose that Bill's boss says, "If you are able to complete the maintenance work by this Saturday, Bill, I'll recommend you for promotion to supervisor. I realize that it will mean your putting in some overtime, but think about it, and let me know your answer." There are two important factors involved: (1) the *value* Bill places on being promoted to supervisor (suppose the last thing in the world he wants is a promotion!) and (2) Bill's *expectancy* that (*a*) he will be able to realistically complete the work by Saturday and (*b*) if he completes the work, he will actually be named supervisor. (In other words, does Bill's supervisor really have the influence to get him promoted?) The answers to these questions explain Bill's decision whether to exert the necessary effort to complete the work by Saturday.

Evaluation of the theory. Researchers testing the theory have found some difficulties with its application. Yet the most consistent finding supports the notion that there *is* a cause-effect relationship between expectancy, performance, and extrinsic rewards such as pay or advancement.[16] Another finding is that *motivation is more powerful when a person is internally motivated.*

What is your view?

In what ways can expectancy theory explain the different motivations you and your fellow students have to study the material in this book?

Operant Conditioning

Another theory that is receiving attention as having potential to influence and change work behavior is **operant conditioning,** largely based on the work of psychologist B. F. Skinner.[17] Other terms used to describe this approach are **positive reinforcement** and **behavior modification.** Many managers have been using some of these principles for a long time, but only recently has there been a systematic examination and application of the principles in work settings.

How the theory operates. Operant conditioning is based primarily on the outstanding educator Edward Thorndike's **law of effect,** which says that behavior followed by satisfying consequences tends to be repeated, whereas behavior followed by unsatisfying consequences tends not to be repeated.[18] Thus, in operant conditioning the rewards—or possibly punishment—are conditional on the person's response (behavior) or lack of response. In this way, behavior is influenced or shaped in the way the environment (the organization) desires.

Skinner distinguishes between **reinforcement,** the presentation of an attractive reward following a response or the removal of an unpleasant or negative condition following a response, and **punishment,** the reverse of reinforcement.

Suppose a worker's attendance has been spotty recently. Operant conditioning can work in two ways:

1. *You can reinforce (praise, reward) the worker's favorable behavior (showing up on time), thereby encouraging him or her to repeat it.*
2. *You can discourage (scolding, written disciplinary warning) the worker's unfavorable behavior through punishment, thereby encouraging him or her not to repeat it.*

Operant conditioning proponents feel that the consequence of the absences is a key factor in determining the worker's future behavior.

Training, development, and growth occur through reinforcement or focusing behavioral responses on what should be done. As shown in Chapter 5, MBO is based on this principle, for it relies heavily on the behaviorist model of motivational principles.

Evaluation of the theory. There are many criticisms of operant conditioning. Yet the theory does seem to operate when standards are clearly set, and improvement results from the frequent application of positive feedback and from recognition for satisfactory behavior. It is assumed that the employees' desire for the rewards of positive feedback and recognition will in large measure motivate them to perform satisfactorily in anticipation of such rewards.

What is your view?

In what way, if any, was the operant conditioning theory involved in the Opening Case?

Equity Theory

Another theory that has received support from research studies is **equity theory** (or, as some term it, the *inequity theory*). This theory predicts that people will compare (1) the *inputs* they bring to the job in the form of education, experience, training, and effort with (2) the *outcomes* (rewards) they receive as compared to those of other employees in comparable jobs.[19]

Role of perceived inequity. The belief, on the basis of comparison, that an inequity exists, in the form of either underpayment or overpayment, will have possible adverse motivational and behavioral effects on performance. It should be kept in mind that the key factor is whether an inequity is *perceived,* not whether it actually exists.

An associate professor was satisfied with her status and income, even though she knew that she could receive a higher salary elsewhere. This fact did not bother her because the cost of living was much lower in the small university community where she lived, the lifestyle and quality of life were attractive, and she was making contributions to her field through publications.

Things were fine until she heard that another associate professor was earning a much higher salary than she was. She was greatly upset because she considered herself a much better teacher and had contributed more to her field in publications than he had. A discussion with the department head failed to resolve the "inequity" by providing an increase in salary. She therefore sought another position and left the university the next year.

Although the equity theory seems to explain motivation, most of us can identify individuals who don't conform to the equity theory model.

For example, an international accounting firm manager in New Zealand told the following story. Two accountants were hired at the same time, and at the end of the year one was given twice the raise of the other, based on her performance. When the high-performing accountant discovered that her raise was twice what her friend had received, she talked privately with her manager and requested that her raise be lowered to the level of her friend's.

ROLE OF MONEY AND OCCUPATION IN MOTIVATION THEORY

Money and occupational level complicate the study of motivation. In fact, they may modify the previously mentioned theories in actual situations.

How Money Affects Motivation

Money can be a powerful force in motivation if—and some say *only* if—it is related directly to achievement and performance. We saw earlier that many employees expect hard work and accomplishment to lead to promotions and increases in pay. Organizations that enforce such policies can benefit from an environment where productivity, achievement, and excellence are valued. There are, however, many motivational factors influencing employee behavior, and it is impossible to identify and isolate any one variable as the specific stimulus to motivated behavior.

The motivational role of money is based on the law of effect mentioned earlier: Behavior followed by satisfying consequences tends to be repeated, whereas behavior followed by unsatisfying consequences tends not to be repeated.

Some conflicting research findings. Many classical and contemporary management theorists have emphasized the motivational value of money. Many argue that there is a direct and positive relationship between expected compensation and employee productivity. Research studies on this subject have shown that compensation is a strong stimulus to production. Yet there are also many contrary findings.

Money *does* motivate. One research project showed that when people believe that their efforts will lead to the desired reward, they will produce. It also showed that few individuals would engage in extended activities unless they believed that there was a connection between what they did and the rewards they received.[20]

A researcher in England found that when a group of employees were not satisfied with their wages they turned to overtime, slowdowns, and other means of meeting their needs.[21] In China, many methods of increasing employee productivity have been tried, but material rewards seem to be the major method of motivating workers.[22] Similarly, the one-acre private plots in the USSR (the proceeds of which the farmers can keep), which account for only 3 percent of the total land area cultivated, provide almost 60 percent of all eggs and 40 percent of all the meat and milk produced in that country.[23]

Ford Motor Company found that employees at one of its plants were primarily concerned with wages, job security, and employee benefits rather than with having more job responsibility. The employees were ready to swap their "enriched" jobs for "another nickel an hour."[24] Similarly, a survey of sewing machine operators in 17 plants found more concern with pay and job security than with any other factor. The study concluded that the cause of workers' discontent might be their compensation instead of dull jobs. The Civil Service Reform Act tries to apply financial incentives to federal performance-based pay systems.[25] Finally, the previously mentioned BLS survey found that, while only a "few workers" would trade a reduction in income for more leisure or family time, about a quarter of them would "like a longer work week if it meant more money" (see Table 11.1).

Money does *not* motivate. Many researchers conclude that the economic motive is no longer important, for employees have risen above the mundane demands of a physical existence and now have higher desires.

"No doubt about it," said Frank Walsh, general manager of a large paper mill in the Midwest, "our people are just too well-off to take overtime. We can't ever get all the people we need. Money doesn't mean anything like it did 20 or 30 years ago. These workers have hobbies, recreation, family, and social interests that are more important to them than making time-and-a-half overtime pay."

**TABLE 11.1
Time and Money:
Worker Preferences**

SOURCE: Bureau of Labor Statistics, as reported in *The Wall Street Journal*, December 30, 1986, p. 19.

Occupation	Same hours, same money	Fewer hours, less money	More hours, more money
Managerial and professional	72.3%	9.7%	18.0%
Technical, sales, and administrative support	66.1	8.3	25.6
Service	56.6	4.5	38.9
Precision production, craft, and repair	63.5	6.4	30.1
Operators, fabricators, and laborers	59.4	5.6	35.0
Farming, forestry, and fishing	49.4	5.0	45.6

A British sociologist concluded that it was impossible to find a direct statistical relationship between the application of incentive schemes and increased outputs.[26] Psychological rewards may be more significant than material incentives in actual organizations and in experimental laboratories. Also, from an anthropological point of view, people in many cultures work for some reason other than material rewards.

A study done by Korn/Ferry International and the UCLA Graduate School of Management found that love of work—not money—motivates top executives. The study of vice-presidents of major companies found that money was secondary to love of work. It should be pointed out, however, that their average salary was $215,000 a year,[27] so they already had the money.

Conclusions about money and motivation. There is no simple *yes* or *no* answer to the question "Does money motivate?" Instead, the conclusion is reached that until employees satisfy their physiological needs, compensation does serve as a motivator. Wages and employment security may even motivate through the safety needs. Above that level, money tends to decline in importance as a stimulant to performance, and other stimulants acquire greater significance. At all levels, money serves as a symbol of success or achievement. It also represents the higher-order needs, such as status, esteem, and even self-fulfillment.

It can be summarized that people who have high achievement needs will be high producers with or without financial incentives; those with low achievement needs must have the monetary stimulus. Recent research indicates that women now tend to be much more concerned about money than men.[28]

What is your view?

Men tend to make more money than women. Using Maslow's hierarchy of needs, explain women's concern for money.

How Occupational Level Affects Motivation

It has been shown that motivation is different for different individuals. Yet some generalizations can be made about motivation at various occupational levels (see Figure 11.10).

A study comparing employee needs at the professional, managerial-official, service, clerical, and trades-manual levels found that self-actualization,

FIGURE 11.10
The relationship between occupational level and job needs.

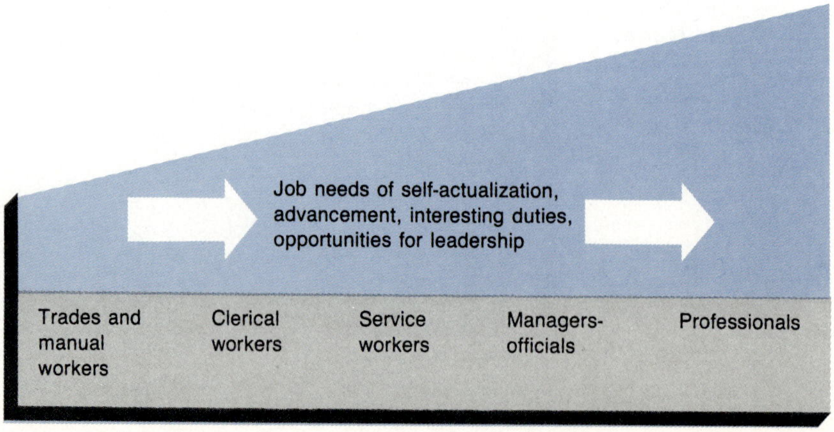

Job needs of self-actualization, advancement, interesting duties, opportunities for leadership

| Trades and manual workers | Clerical workers | Service workers | Managers-officials | Professionals |

advancement, interesting duties, and leadership were selected with increasing frequency from the trade group up to the professionals.[29] Conversely, the needs for respect, money, security, congeniality, and job security were selected more frequently by those in the lower socioeconomic groups (trades and services) and least often by the managerial-official and professional groups. We can conclude from this study that *needs and occupational levels have a fairly consistent relationship.*

A study of scientists and managers of pharmaceutical laboratories found general agreement among scientists and managers concerning the incentive value of promotions, merit salary increases, and more complex and challenging job assignments.[30] These professionals felt that recognition of performance is the most effective of nonfinancial incentives. This study seems to indicate that *self-fulfillment is the prevalent need among scientists.*

> **What is your view?**
>
> How does this finding compare with Brown's needs in the Opening Case?

Self-employed professionals seldom have any problem with motivation; they seem to be "self-motivated." Yet problems commence when they are placed on a company payroll. Then the common motivational elements for most people who are ambitious and have initiative become important. Professional employees have still another problem related to motivation: their **dual allegiance**—loyalty to both their employer and their professional colleagues. Management must learn how to motivate professional employees to satisfy organizational needs as well as to satisfy the requirements of their professional society.

Generally speaking, executives are motivated to a high degree by money—not as a means of satisfying their basic physiological needs but as *recognition* of their status and position. Once this need for status is satisfied, executives usually seek the rewards of egoistic satisfaction and self-fulfillment. Therefore, they will often remain with an organization that cannot afford higher salaries just to satisfy these higher needs.

MOTIVATION IS MORE THAN MERE TECHNIQUES

One of the best statements of the need for motivation was expressed by Clarence Francis when he was chairman of General Foods. Francis said: "You can buy a man's time; you can buy a man's physical presence at a given place; you can even buy a measured number of skilled muscular motions per hour or day; but you cannot buy enthusiasm. You cannot buy initiative; you cannot buy loyalty; you cannot buy devotion of hearts, minds, and souls. You have to earn these things."[31] This truth is evident in practice at the most successful U.S. companies, as shown in MAP 11.2.

This statement illustrates the need to consider motivation as more inclusive than the mere application of some specific tool or device to stimulate increased output. It is a philosophy, or way of life, founded on the needs and desires of employees.

Management Application and Practice 11.2 Motivational Practices at America's Best-Managed Companies

Many organizations and their managers are quite adept at penalizing employees for mistakes or poor performance. A recent best-selling book, *In Search of Excellence: Lessons from America's Best-Run Companies,* concluded that "the dominant culture in most big companies demands punishment for a mistake no matter how useful, small, invisible." The book goes on to say that the dominant culture in the *best-managed companies* is just the opposite. These companies develop "winners" by constantly reinforcing the idea that employees are winners. The performance targets are set so that they provide a challenge—but are attainable. The effective manager continually gives recognition for effective employee performance.

Organization psychologists have long been advocating certain company actions to increase the motivation of individuals. According to one authority, many of America's best-managed companies have implemented these actions, which include: (1) tying extrinsic rewards (such as pay) to performance; (2) setting realistic and challenging goals; (3) evaluating employee performance accurately and providing feedback on performance; (4) promoting on the basis of skill and performance rather than personal char-

acteristics, power, or connections; (5) building the skill level of the work force through training and development; and (6) enlarging and enriching jobs through increases in responsibility, variety, and significance. These actions demonstrate the practicality of the theories presented in this chapter.

On a more all-encompassing basis, a book on employee practices at the best-managed companies shows that these companies place considerable emphasis not only on the rights and responsibilities of employees but also on the value of employee contribution through participative management. Specifically, these companies provide stakeholder status for unions, employee stock ownership, a fair measure of job security, lifelong training, benefits tailored to individual needs, participation in decision making, freedom of expression, and incentive pay.

SOURCE: Thomas J. Peters and Robert H. Waterman, Jr., *In Search of Excellence: Lessons from America's Best-Run Companies* (New York: Harper & Row, 1982), p. 48; Barry M. Stow, "Organizational Psychology and the Pursuit of the Happy/Productive Worker," *California Management Review* 29 (Summer 1986): 48; and James O'Toole, "Employee Practices at the Best-Managed Companies," *California Management Review* 29 (Fall 1985): 35–66.

This philosophy should permeate the whole organization, beginning at the top, and attempt to create an environment in which all employees can apply themselves willingly, as individuals, to the task of increasing productivity. The details of motivation are relatively unimportant if this philosophy is adhered to. The success of the Japanese system is largely based on this philosophical style, as we see in Chapter 17.

We want to point out, however, that motivation theories must be used wisely. Some of the theories are not mature enough to justify widespread application and could result in negative consequences. Employees who receive rewards based on performance tend to perform better than employees in groups where rewards are not based on performance.

SUMMARY

The primary purpose of this chapter has been to develop an understanding of the "why" of human behavior in order to help managers create a climate of positive motivation. We have examined some of the prominent theories of motivation, such as Maslow's hierarchy of needs, Herzberg's motivation-maintenance theory, McClelland's achievement theory, expectancy theory, and equity theory. Moreover, we have looked at the role managers play in satisfying the human needs of their subordinates at work. We hope that as you have read this chapter you have seen the interrelations between the theories.

We described the three primary purposes of motivation and discussed the need for positive motivation. Then we showed how human behavior affects motivation and developed a model to show that motivation is goal directed.

Let us build a few bridges in this summary by using Maslow's hierarchy of needs as the basic building block. In most industries, lower-level needs are relatively well satisfied but can be reactivated if threatened. The big challenge, however, is to create an environment to motivate people through higher-level needs—esteem, achievement, recognition, competence, self-fulfillment, and advancement.

As was indicated, Herzberg's theory supports Maslow's concept of a hierarchy of needs: The motivators relate to the highest levels (esteem and self-fulfillment), and the maintenance factors relate to the lower-level needs, primarily the security needs. Equity theory has a similar relationship in that feelings of inequity trigger feelings of insecurity and injustice that can cause demotivation, whereas feelings of equity cause one to strive even more diligently for accomplishment.

In the section dealing with expectancy theory, you saw that employees assess in advance what their behavior may accomplish and consider possible outcomes. Thus the actions of the supervisor and the organization significantly influence the behavior chosen by subordinates. Ideally, one would hope to create the cause-effect relationship shown in Figure 11.11.

You also saw that workers have certain expectations of their immediate supervisors and organizations. Workers not only expect fair treatment from superiors, equitable wages, and decent conditions of employment, but they also want to work in an environment in which there is a knowledge base, an atmosphere of approval, and consistent discipline.

Today, people expect to be treated fairly by managers. They expect good working conditions and fair pay that is comparable to that of people doing similar work in other firms, and they expect company policies to be consistently and equitably applied to all employees. People are negatively motivated when these expectations are not realized. Usually, these negative feelings are reflected in inefficiency and a high turnover rate.

Money can be a powerful motivator if income is directly related to achievement and performance. Research shows that people are willing to work more for more money. Also, occupation affects motivation.

FIGURE 11.11
Ideal cause-and-effect relationship in motivating employees.

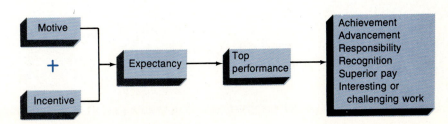

Finally, the best-run U.S. companies use positive motivational tactics to improve performance.

REVIEW QUESTIONS

1. What is motivation?
2. Why is motivation important to management?
3. For what purposes do managers use motivation?
4. What are the human needs according to Maslow?
5. What are some (a) motivating and (b) maintenance factors according to Herzberg?
6. What is expectancy theory?
7. What is operant conditioning, and how does it affect motivation?
8. What is the equity theory of motivation?

DISCUSSION QUESTIONS

1. What do you think is the relationship among performance, ability, and motivation?
2. What theory do you think most nearly explains how you *really* motivate someone? Explain.
3. Are there self-motivated people? Explain.
4. What do you see as the relationship between occupational level and motivation?
5. Does money really motivate people? Explain.
6. What is meant by the statement that "motivation is more than mere techniques"?

LEARNING EXERCISE 11.1

A Motivation Survey

Recently, 19 first-level supervisors with a large manufacturing company responded to the statement "Rank the following factors in order of importance for the typical hourly employee in your company." The rankings of each supervisor are shown in the vertical column in Figure 11.12.

FIGURE 11.12
Rankings of selected employment factors by 19 first-level supervisors.

Factors	Rankings of individual supervisors																		
Higher wages	2	9	8	5	7	1	8	2	1	4	2	1	1	2	3	1	2	2	1
Better job security	1	8	2	1	8	3	7	1	2	1	1	2	2	1	1	6	1	1	6
Better chance for advancement	8	6	1	4	2	6	4	3	4	2	7	3	7	5	2	2	3	5	7
Improved benefits	3	7	7	9	9	4	9	6	6	3	4	4	4	3	5	4	6	3	2
Better working conditions	6	3	4	7	6	2	5	5	3	5	4	5	9	4	4	5	7	4	5
More challenging work	9	5	5	3	1	5	3	9	8	6	8	8	8	9	6	8	8	8	9
Better chance to grow and develop job skills	4	4	3	2	5	7	6	4	7	9	6	6	6	6	7	3	5	6	8
Better supervision	5	1	9	8	4	9	1	8	5	8	9	7	3	7	8	9	9	9	3
Better interpersonal relationships	7	2	6	6	3	8	2	7	9	7	5	9	5	8	9	7	4	7	4

Questions

1. What accounts for the broadly different rankings of individual supervisors?
2. Do any concepts studied in the chapter help to clarify these results? Explain.
3. Assume that you are a management trainee with a company that has just obtained the data above from its supervisors. Prepare an oral or written report for top management that presents your interpretation of the data.

LEARNING EXERCISE 11.2

School Teacher Bonuses: Motivator or Demotivator?

Assume that you have been called in as a consultant by the president of the Harris County school board. He has asked you (or your group) to evaluate a bonus plan that the school board is considering initiating this year. He has also stated that if the proposed plan has too many problems, he would like you (or your group) to recommend an alternative bonus and/or pay plan.

The president indicates that the board was impressed with the recommendations of President Reagan's National Commission on Excellence in Education. They were specifically impressed with the conclusion that "performance-based" teacher salaries were among the ways to push back the "rising tide of mediocrity" threatening U.S. education.

The board is considering paying $1000 bonuses to 25 of its 233 teachers. Principals and department heads would select the 25 meritorious teachers who would serve as role models for the other teachers. The plan calls for the 25 teachers selected to have their names and pictures published in the local paper.

Some additional information:

Teachers' salaries average $20,000 a year.
Starting pay begins at $12,000 a year.
Pay raises in the past have been primarily across-the-board increases. This year the proposed across-the-board increase is 5 percent.

Questions

1. Develop a profile of strong points and weak points of the proposed bonus system.
2. Develop a report to the president of the school board stating whether or not you endorse the plan and why. If you do not endorse the plan, what do you recommend in its place?

NOTES

1. Based on "The Value of Recognition," in Leon C. Megginson, *Personnel Management: A Human Resources Approach*, 4th ed. (Homewood, IL: Irwin, 1981), pp. 575–576.
2. Warren Bennis and Burt Nanus, *Leaders* (New York: Harper & Row, 1985), p. 7.
3. Tom Peters and Nancy Austin, *A Passion for Excellence* (New York: Random House, 1985), p. 204.
4. Cathy Trost, "All Work and No Play? New Study Shows How Americans View Jobs," *The Wall Street Journal*, December 30, 1986, p. 19.
5. Quoted in Alfred J. Marrow, *Behind the Executive Mask* (New York: American Management Association, 1965), p. 7.
6. Abraham H. Maslow, *Motivation and Personality* (New York: Harper & Row, 1954). Maslow's theory was popularized by Douglas McGregor in "The Human Side of Enterprise," *Management Review* 46 (November 1957): 22–28 and 88–92.
7. Although this list of needs is the most popular for teaching purposes, there are many other classifications. For example, John Schindler, a practicing psychiatrist, calls the needs (1) physiological and (2) psychogenic or basic psychological needs. The latter include love, security, creative expression, recognition, self-esteem, and new experiences. See John Schindler, *How to Live 365 Days a Year* (Englewood Cliffs, NJ: Prentice-Hall, 1954), for further details.

8. Frederick Herzberg, Bernard Mausner, and Barbara Snyderman, *The Motivation to Work* (New York: Wiley, 1959).

9. Frederick Herzberg, "One More Time: How Do You Motivate Employees?" *Harvard Business Review* 46 (January–February 1968): 53–62.

10. Donald Mosley, "What Motivates New Zealanders?" *Management* (New Zealand Institute of Management, October 1969), p. 37.

11. D. A. Ondrock, "Defense Mechanisms and the Herzberg Theory: An Alternative Test," *Academy of Management Journal* 17 (March 1974): 79–89.

12. David C. McClelland, *The Achieving Society* (New York: Van Nostrand, 1961).

13. Paula Stringfellow's autobiography, Davidson High School, Business Career Development Program, Mobile, Alabama, 1979.

14. David C. McClelland and David H. Burnham, "Power Is the Great Motivator," *Harvard Business Review* 54 (March–April 1976): 100–110.

15. Victor H. Vroom, *Work and Motivation* (New York: Wiley, 1964).

16. A. C. Filley, R. J. House, and S. Kerr, *Managerial Process and Orgnizational Behavior*, 2d ed. (Glenview, IL: Scott, Foresman, 1976), p. 200.

17. B. F. Skinner, *About Behaviorism* (New York: Knopf, 1974); and B. F. Skinner, *Beyond Freedom and Dignity* (New York: Knopf, 1971).

18. See Edward L. Thorndike, *Human Learning* (New York: Century, 1931), for a discussion of how this law operates in education, training, and development.

19. J. Stacy Adams and S. Freedman, *Equity Theory Revisited: Comments and Annotated Bibliography* (New York: Academic Press, 1976).

20. Melvin J. Lerner, "Evaluation of Performance as a Function of Performer's Reward and Attractiveness," *Journal of Personality and Social Psychology* 1 (April 1965): 355–360.

21. Sylvia Schiammin, "Extramural Factors Influencing Behavior at Work," *Occupational Psychology* 36 (July 1962): 124–131.

22. Charles Hoffman, "Work Incentives in Communist China," *Industrial Relations* 3 (February 1964): 81–98.

23. Charlotte Saikowski, "Soviets Wink at Private Farms," *Christian Science Monitor*, December 1, 1970, p. 7.

24. Richard D. Denzler, "People and Productivity: Do They Still Equal Pay and Profits?" *Personnel Journal* 53 (January 1974): 59–63.

25. Richard A. Stimson, "Performance Pay—Will It Work?" *Defense Management Journal* 15 (July–August 1979): 23–27.

26. Hilde Behrend, "Financial Incentives as the Expression of a System of Beliefs," *British Journal of Sociology* 10 (June 1959): 137–147.

27. "Labor Letter," *The Wall Street Journal*, May 6, 1986, p. 1.

28. Mildred Golden Pryor and R. Wayne Mondy, "How Men and Women View Their Jobs—And What This Means to the Supervisor," *Supervisory Management* 23 (November 1978): 17–25.

29. Boris Blai, Jr., "An Occupational Study of Job and Need Satisfaction," *Psychological Reports* 1 (February 1964): 82.

30. Albert B. Chalupsky, "Incentive Practices as Viewed by Scientists and Managers of Pharmaceutical Laboratories," *Personnel Psychology* 17 (Winter 1964): 385–401.

31. From *Management Methods Magazine*, 1952.

SUGGESTIONS FOR FURTHER STUDY

ACKERMAN, LEONARD, and GRUNEWALD, JOSEPH P. "Help Employees Motivate Themselves." *Personnel Journal* 63 (July 1984): 54–57.

BLANCHARD, KENNETH, and JOHNSON, SPENCER. *The One Minute Manager*. New York: William Morrow and Company, 1984.

COOK, CURTIS W. "Guidelines for Managing Motivation." *Business Horizons* 23 (April 1980): 61–69.

FEDOR, DONALD B., and FERRIS, GERALD R. "Integrating OB Mod with Cognitive Approaches to Motivation." *Academy of Management Review* 6 (January 1981): 115–125.

ROBERTS, KARLENE H., and SAVAGE, FREDERICK. "Twenty Questions: Utilizing Job Satisfaction Measures." *California Management Review* 15 (Spring 1973): 82–90.

YOUNG, PATRICK. "Men, Women's Attitudes Toward Work Similar." *Mobile Register* (Newhouse News Service), September 2, 1987, pp. 20-A, 21-A.

12

Leadership in Action

Learning Objectives

After studying the material in this chapter, you should be able to do the following:

□ Define what leadership is.
□ Present a logical argument in favor of an ideal leadership style and the contingency-situational approach to leadership.
□ Relate some of the traitist ideas about leadership.
□ Explain what the behavioral approach to leadership is and discuss some of the more popular theories.
□ Describe what the contingency-situational popular theory is.
□ Present some insights into diagnosing the proper leadership style to use in various situations.

Outline of the Chapter

What is leadership?
Leadership defined
Ways of classifying types of leaders
Leadership is not the same as management
The traitist approach
Research on traits
Limitations of the traitist approach
The behavioral approach
Lewin's research
McGregor's Theory X and Theory Y
Likert's System 4
Blake and Mouton's Managerial Grid®
The Ohio State studies
Japanese style leadership
Is there an ideal leadership style?
Support for an ideal leadership style
Support for contingency-situational leadership styles

The contingency-situational approach
Examples of contingency-situational approach
Tannenbaum and Schmidt's leadership continuum
Fiedler's contingency theory
Hersey-Blanchard's life-cycle theory
Factors affecting leadership behavior
General factors
Specific factors
Applying leadership theory
Inspiring and developing people
Becoming a transformative leader
Summary

Some Important Terms

autocratic (authoritarian) leaders
democratic (participative) leaders
laissez-faire (free-rein) leaders
task-oriented (production-oriented) leaders
people-oriented (employee-centered) leaders
leadership
management
traitist approach
behavioral approach
Theory X
Theory Y
System 4
Managerial Grid®
initiating structure
consideration
Theory Z companies
contingency-situational approach
leadership continuum
law of the situation
contingency model
least preferred coworker (LPC) scale
life-cycle theory
maturity
task behavior
relationship behavior
transformative leaders

OPENING CASE

Kenny—An Effective Supervisor

Kenny was a maintenance supervisor in a chemical plant of an international corporation.[1] The plant was suffering from problems caused by the ineffective and autocratic leadership of the former plant manager. This poor management had adversely affected the entire plant, resulting in low morale at all levels and losses from plant operations. However, one crew seemed to have escaped the adverse effects—it had very high morale and productivity. This was the maintenance crew that was under Kenny's supervision.

Kenny was in his early thirties, with a two-year associate degree from a community college. He had a very positive attitude, especially in light of the overall low morale and productivity. In Kenny's mind, the plant was one of the finest places he'd ever worked and the maintenance people had more know-how than any other group he'd worked with. Kenny believed that his crew did twice as much work as other crews, that everyone worked together, and that participative management worked.

Kenny's boss reported that Kenny's crew did not do twice as much work as other crews—actually, it did *more* than twice as much. He claimed that Kenny was the best supervisor he had seen in 22 years in the industry.

Why did the pressure and criticism from the old, autocratic manager seem to have no effect on Kenny's crew? According to the crew members, Kenny had the ability to act as an intermediary and buffer between upper management and the crew. He would get higher management's primary objectives and points across without upsetting his people. As one crew member described it:

> The maintenance supervisors will come back from a "donkey barbecue" session with higher management where they are raising hell about shoddy work, taking too long at coffee breaks, etc., etc. Other supervisors are shook up for a week and give their men hell. But Kenny is cool, calm, and collected. He will call us together and report that nine items were discussed at the meeting, including shoddy work, but that doesn't apply to our crew. Then he will cover the two or four items that are relevant to our getting the job done.

Unfortunately, Kenny did have one real concern. He was being transferred from the highest-producing crew to the lowest-producing one. In fact, it was known as the "Hell's Angels crew." The crew members were considered renegades who were constantly fighting with production people as well as with each other. The previous supervisor had been terminated because he could not cope with the crew members.

After Kenny was assigned to the "Hell's Angels crew," he had to decide on the leadership strategy he would use in dealing with its members. His initial diagnosis was that the crew had the ability to do the work, but lacked the willingness because of a poor attitude.

On his first day with the crew, Kenny called a meeting, shut the door, and conducted a "bull session" that lasted over two hours. Among other things, Kenny told the crew about his leadership philosophy and the way he liked to operate. He especially stressed that he was going to be fair and treat everyone equally. Kenny allowed the crew members to gripe and complain about matters in the plant as long as they liked, and he listened without interrupting. In the course of the session, Kenny expressed his expectations of the crew. In response, they told him they would do it his way for two weeks to see if he "practiced what he preached."

341

How do you think Kenny's leadership worked with the new crew? Before the year was out, it was the most productive in the plant. ■

THIS CASE ILLUSTRATES that effective leadership is found in many levels of our society and not simply with the more glamorous top-level positions. We agree with John W. Gardner that effective leadership is dispersed "from the most lofty levels of our national life down to the school principal, the local union leader, the shop foreman."[2]

On the other hand, there is an unfortunate amount of ineffective leadership in our society. Although no single model of leadership exists that everyone agrees with, this chapter should help you identify the need for leadership and how to nurture and use it.

WHAT IS LEADERSHIP?

It is important to clarify some terms that you'll be reading throughout this chapter. So, let us point out the distinction between management and leadership and define different kinds of leadership characteristics.

Leadership Defined

Like management, *leadership* has been defined in many different ways by many different people. Nevertheless, the central theme running through most of the definitions is that leadership is a process of influencing individual and group activities toward goal setting and goal achievement. As a leader, you work to ensure balance between the goals of the organization, yourself, and your group. In the final analysis, the successful leader is one who succeeds in getting others to follow. A leader has to work effectively with many people, including superiors, peers, and outside groups. But in working with followers, he or she is the spark that lights the fire and keeps it burning.

Without Jerry Ayres in the lineup, the City Junior College Wildcats are just another mediocre basketball team. But Jerry makes the team click. Only 5'6", he's not a high-scoring player, but as a leader he's unequaled, and his presence in the game helps his teammates play better. According to his coach, Jerry's playmaking and leadership on the floor are the major factors in the team's 20–6 record, which ranks them in the state's top 10 teams.

Ways of Classifying Types of Leaders

There are many ways to classify leaders or leadership styles. The two most important, however, are (1) by the approach they use and (2) by their orientation toward getting the job done.

Approach used. One common way of studying leadership is in terms of the basic approaches used by leaders: autocratic, democratic, or laissez-faire.

Autocratic leaders—often called **authoritarian leaders**—make most decisions themselves instead of allowing their followers to make them. These leaders are usually thought of as "pushers," somewhat like the image of a military drill instructor.

"How do you know the fault is in my 'leading'? Maybe the fault is in your 'following'!"

(Reprinted by permission of the Saturday Evening Post. *Copyright 1966 by the Curtis Publishing Company.)*

Democratic or **participative leaders** involve their followers heavily in the decision process. They use group involvement in setting the group's basic objectives, establishing strategies, and determining job assignments.

Laissez-faire leaders—also called **free-rein leaders**—are "loose" and permissive and let followers do what they want. You might think of this approach as similar to teachers who handle classes loosely, with few homework assignments, class sessions that seem to drift from one issue to another as they arise, and little direction or discipline.

Orientation toward job. Another way to categorize leaders is to examine their attitudes toward getting the job done. Some leaders emphasize the task; others emphasize followers or subordinates; as you will find out later in the chapter, some can emphasize both.

Task-oriented or **production-oriented leaders** focus on the "work" aspects of getting the job done. They emphasize planning, scheduling, and processing the work, and exercise close control of quality. Another term used in describing this approach is *initiating structure*.

People-oriented or **employee-centered leaders** focus on the welfare and feelings of followers, have confidence in themselves, and have a strong need to be accepted by their team members. Other common terms used to describe people-oriented leaders are *relationship centered* and *considerate*.

Leadership Is Not the Same as Management

People often equate management and leadership. Reporters, for example, comment on the U.S. president's "exercise of leadership." They refer to such things as new programs (planning), organizational changes (organizing), quality of advisers (staffing), ability to inspire confidence (leading), and ability to make changes quickly when things go wrong (control). Perhaps one explanation for such a broad interpretation of leadership is that we sometimes use the term *leader* when referring to managers. Although the two are similar, there are some significant differences.

Leadership is the ability a person has to influence others to work toward goals and objectives. **Management** involves leadership, but it also includes the other functions of planning, organizing, staffing, and controlling. Here is an example of outstanding leadership but poor management.

> *Coach Jones has the most highly motivated, committed group of players in the league. "We'd run through a brick wall if he asked us to," said one of the players. But the team has been very unsuccessful to date. The offense is poorly conceived, consisting of some very simple, fundamental plays, and the defensive system is outdated. Moreover, the recruited players are just not that good. But the players respect the coach and really put out for him. If a "spirit" award were given, the Bay High football team would certainly get it.*

Coach Jones may be highly effective in getting commitment from his players and inspiring them—that is, in leading—but his inability to perform the other management functions negates the effectiveness of his leadership skills.

What is your view?

Do you think that the reverse may also be true—that is, that someone may be an effective manager but a poor leader? Explain.

Leading, then, is an important part of management, but it is not the same as management.

Leadership research and theories can be classified as *traitist, behavioral,* and *contingency-situational* approaches. We present these to you chronologically, since they have evolved from studies of leadership that have been emphasized over the years, as follows:

traitist → behavioral → contingency-situational

THE TRAITIST APPROACH

According to the **traitist approach,** leaders possess certain traits or characteristics that cause them to rise above their followers. Lists of such traits could be very long but tended to include one's height, energy, looks, knowledge and intelligence, imagination, self-confidence, integrity, fluency of speech, emotional and mental balance and control, sociability and friendliness, drive, enthusiasm, and courage.

Research on Traits

Most of the early research on leadership attempted to (1) compare the traits of people who became leaders with those who were followers and (2) identify characteristics and traits possessed by effective leaders. Studies comparing the traits of leaders and nonleaders often found that leaders tended to be more intelligent, somewhat taller, more outgoing, and more self-confident than others and to have a greater need for power. But specific combinations of traits have not been found that would distinguish the leader or potential leader from followers. The underlying assumption of the trait researchers seems to have been that *leaders are born, not made.* But research has still *not* shown that certain traits *can* distinguish effective from ineffective leaders. Yet respected research is still being done in this area.

One of the earliest trait researchers was Ralph Stogdill, who was doing such studies during World War II.[3] As late as 1974, Stogdill found several traits to be related to effective leadership. These included social and interpersonal skills, technical skills, administrative skills, and leadership effectiveness.

A later researcher, Edwin Ghiselli, found that certain characteristics do seem to be important to effective leadership.[4] The most important of these are:

1. *Supervisory ability,* or performing the basic functions of management, especially leading and controlling the work of others.
2. *Need for occupational achievement,* including seeking responsibility and desiring success.
3. *Intelligence,* including judgment, reasoning, and reactive thinking.
4. *Decisiveness,* or the ability to make decisions and solve problems capably and competently.
5. *Self-assurance,* or viewing oneself as capable of coping with problems.
6. *Initiative,* or the ability to act independently, develop courses of action not readily apparent to other people, and find new or innovative ways of doing things.

Limitations of the Traitist Approach

There are some obvious limitations to the traitist approach. For example, we know that people such as Alexander the Great, Napoleon, Joan of Arc, Abraham Lincoln, Florence Nightingale, Geronimo, Mahatma Gandhi, Mao Zedong, Adolf Hitler, Winston Churchill, Vince Lombardi, and Martin Luther King, Jr., were somehow different from others. Yet there appear to be no particular leadership traits found in all of them. In fact, some of them, such as Hitler and Lincoln, had quite different traits! Thus, in summary, the traitist approach did not yield significant findings as to what attributes are the hallmark of a leader. Moreover, there are many cases in which a leader is successful in one situation but may not be in another. For example, Winston Churchill was the brilliant World War II leader who led Great Britain to victory over Hitler's German forces. Yet he was defeated for Prime Minister by a relatively unknown politician in the spring of 1945.

Before leaving the traitist approach, you might wish to complete TIPS 12.1, to see what characteristics are found in effective leaders.

> **TIPS 12.1   Using Effective Leaders as Role Models**
>
> Think of two of the most effective leaders you have had direct contact with and who have had an influence in your life. These leaders can be anyone, such as a parent, a teacher, a coach, a boss, a student leader, a religious leader, or a relative or friend.
>
>   Write a list of at least six characteristics and/or beliefs that made these people such outstanding leaders. Next, do a self-assessment on a scale of 1 to 5 as to how you measure against their characteristics and beliefs.
>
> | 1 | 2 | 3 | 4 | 5 |
> |---|---|---|---|---|
> | Poor | | Average | | Excellent |
>
>   On points where your self-assessment is not 4 or 5, develop an action plan that will improve your self-assessment (1) six months from now, (2) one year from now, and (3) five years from now.

THE BEHAVIORAL APPROACH

It became obvious that the traitist approach could not explain what _caused_ effective leadership; thus attention shifted to the **behavioral approach,** which involved studying the behavior of leaders. Behaviorists assume that leaders are not born but developed. There are some important implications of this approach. First, by focusing on what leaders _do_, rather than on what they _are_, it could be assumed that there is a "best" way to lead. Second, although traits are stable—many are in us at birth—behavior is learned. Many of the traits found by Stogdill are not innate, but are learned.

The behavioral approach, considering the orientation or identification of the leader, assumes that the leader will be (1) employee oriented, (2) task or production oriented, or (3) some combination of the two, as shown in Figure 12.1. Thus the behavioral view is that the leadership process must focus not only on the work to be performed but also on the need satisfactions of work group members.

The most popular behavioral research and theories are (1) sociologist Kurt Lewin's studies, (2) author Douglas McGregor's Theory X and Theory Y, (3) social psychologist Rensis Likert's Michigan studies, and (4) Blake and Mouton's Managerial Grid.® (The Managerial Grid is more of a diagnostic tool than a theory, but we will discuss it here.)

Lewin's Research

Lewin's research on small group behavior in the 1930s greatly influenced the thinking of later researchers, causing them to focus on the notion of an ideal leadership style.[5]

For Lewin's study, four boys' teams were organized and structured with democratic, autocratic, and laissez-faire styles of leadership. (Refer to the definitions at the beginning of the chapter if you need to review these styles.) In the autocratic environment, the boys did no long-range planning, and there was considerable aggression. Work proceeded as intensely as in the democratic group when the leader was present, but the quality was not as good. Moreover, work stopped whenever the adult leader left the work group.

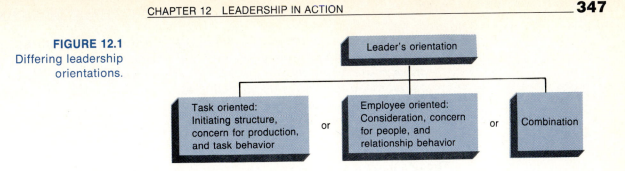

FIGURE 12.1
Differing leadership orientations.

Work continued in the democratic environment even when the leader was not present. Productivity was the lowest in the laissez-faire leadership climate, where everyone did as he pleased, and the boys became frustrated. Two of the boys in the autocratic environment quit because they were being made scapegoats. The results of this experiment clearly demonstrated that, at least in this situation, the participative-democratic leadership style produced the best outcome.

One of the more interesting discoveries was that when the groups were assigned new leaders and the leaders kept their leadership styles, the results were similar to the original designs after a short period of adjustment. For example, when the autocratic leader was moved to the team originally organized along democratic lines, the boys became quite dependent on the leader and lost the favorable outcomes that had been observed under democratic leadership.

What is your view?

As a child, you probably belonged to a club or scouting organization. Think for a minute about the club leaders. What leadership styles did they use? Were the results similar to those in Lewin's study?

McGregor's Theory X and Theory Y

The leadership strategy of effective use of participative management proposed in Douglas McGregor's classic book, *The Human Side of Enterprise,* has had a tremendous impact on managers.[6] The most publicized concept is McGregor's thesis that leadership strategies are influenced by a leader's *assumptions about human nature.* As a result of his experience as a consultant, McGregor summarized two contrasting sets of assumptions made by managers in industry.

The assumptions of Theory X. According to the first set of assumptions, **Theory X,** managers believe that:

1. The average human being has an inherent dislike of work and will avoid it if possible.

2. Because of this human characteristic, most people must be coerced, controlled, directed, or threatened with punishment to get them to put forth adequate effort to achieve organizational objectives.

3. The average human being prefers to be directed, wishes to avoid responsibility, has relatively little ambition, and wants security above all.

A first-line supervisor in a recent training program said: "My first feeling is that people are lazy, don't like responsibility, and have no ambition. If

I didn't really push my group, threaten to put the screws to them, and often do it, nothing would get done around here. I'm sort of like the circus master who gets into the cage with those animals. He's got to really stay on those cats and crack that whip to get them to perform their tasks effectively. If they don't perform, they get popped. That's about how my job as supervisor is. I've got to stay on top of my crew just like that animal trainer does."

The assumptions of Theory Y. Managers who accept **Theory Y** assumptions believe that:

1. The expenditure of physical and mental effort in work is as natural as play or rest, and the average human being, under proper conditions, learns not only to accept but to seek responsibility.

2. People will exercise self-direction and self-control to achieve objectives to which they are committed.

3. The capacity to exercise a relatively high level of imagination, ingenuity, and creativity in the solution of organizational problems is widely, not narrowly, distributed in the population, and the intellectual potentialities of the average human being are only partially utilized under the conditions of modern industrial life.

You can readily see that a leader holding Theory X assumptions would prefer an autocratic style, whereas one holding Theory Y assumptions would prefer a more participative style.

Participants in the Summer Case Workshop at the Harvard Business School in July 1958 heard the late Douglas McGregor say he wished he had never written the two theories, since they had been misunderstood. Most workers did not fit into either the X or the Y category but had some characteristics of each, and the workers' behavior tended to vary from one to the other over periods of time. He said he intended to write "Theory Z," a combination of the two theories. Unfortunately, he died before accomplishing this.

McGregor's concepts have had a significant influence on practicing managers, as the following example shows.

Robert Townsend became president of Avis when it was floundering and had not made a profit for 13 years. He was advised that the top management team was incompetent and should be fired. But three years later the company had grown in sales and had made successive annual profits of $1 million, $3 million, and $5 million. The amazing thing is that this success was achieved with the same management that had been labeled incompetent! Townsend attributes this success to the use of a Theory Y, participative style of leadership and to removing undesirable aspects of bureaucracy.[7]

What is your view?

In the Opening Case, which of these assumptions did Kenny hold concerning his people? What if the renegade crew decides not to cooperate with Kenny and its members continue to be poor performers? Should Kenny continue to be supportive and use his usual leadership style? Why or why not?

Likert's System 4

Some very effective research into the behavioral approach to leadership has been carried out over a number of years by the Institute for Social Research at the University of Michigan. Likert and his associates have studied leadership in several different work settings to see whether valid principles or concepts of leadership could be discovered.

Basically, they found that supervisors who *practiced general supervision and were employee centered* had higher morale and greater productivity than supervisors who *practiced close supervision and were more job centered*.[8] Essentially, the leadership style of close supervision generally reflects Theory X assumptions about people, whereas general supervision reflects Theory Y assumptions.

Close supervision. Close supervision is based largely on Theory X assumptions; that is, close supervisors do not trust people. They believe in detailed instructions and "keeping an eye on things," often doing the same type of work as the workers they are supervising.

Achievement-oriented employees find it frustrating and demoralizing to work under close supervision, especially for prolonged periods. Consequently, departments in which close supervision is practiced tend to have high turnover of personnel.

Close supervision is not very effective when the work requires any type of initiative or creativity in subordinates. It might work well, however, with new employees or those with low IQs or in the short run in a department where costs have been excessive or where an emergency job must be accomplished.

Several years ago on a national television talk show, a well-known retired National Football League football player was relating his experiences as a teacher in a public elementary school. He was explaining that he had started out intending to be open and participative with his class. What these kids needed, he felt, was an opportunity to show that they could respond to a teacher who treated them like mature adults and valued their judgment and ability to direct themselves. "I tried it for about two days," he recalled. "And that classroom was a total disaster. I had no choice but to run that class like a rookie football camp or basic training in the military to get on top of them and stay there, which was the only style those kids understood, given the circumstances of their backgrounds."

General supervision. Likert found that, when asked to give the most important feature of their jobs, leaders practicing general supervision stressed human relations and the development of subordinates. Therefore, these supervisors were called employee centered. This does not mean that these leaders ignored the production or task requirements of their departments. Instead, the leaders emphasized working with and through people in such a way that effective results would naturally follow.

From published research and our own experience, we see four main characteristics of managers using general supervision. They (1) supervise by results, (2) emphasize training and development of subordinates through the process of delegation of authority and supervision by results, (3) spend half or more of their time planning and organizing the work of the department and coordinating with other departments and supervisors, and (4) are more accessible to talk over departmental or personal problems of subordinates.

Likert's four management systems. Likert's greatest contribution was to identify four management systems operating in organizations. He and his team of researchers were strongly convinced that leadership was a causal variable that over time affected end results of factors such as productivity, profits, turnover, and absenteeism. The four management systems, arranged along a continuum, are shown in Figure 12.2.

Likert developed a Profile of Organizational Characteristics questionnaire that provided descriptive ratings in seven areas: leadership processes, motivational forces, communication, interaction-influence process, decision making, goal setting, and control. Although only one of the seven areas specifically focuses on leadership, it is a causal variable that affects the others. Likert and his team strongly implied that the closer an organization is to System 4 (Participative Groups), the more effective it will be in achieving its end results. A number of studies have since been published documenting successful shifts from Systems 1 and 2 to Systems 3 and 4, with accompanying improvements in performance and satisfaction.[9] Following is a brief description of these four leadership styles.

System 1 (Exploitative-Authoritative). Top management primarily uses an autocratic style, makes all the decisions, and relies on coercion as the primary motivating force.

System 2 (Benevolent-Authoritative). Higher management makes most of the decisions, although some minor implementing decisions may be made at lower levels. A condescending attitude is usually displayed in communicating with subordinates, which results in a subservient attitude toward superiors.

System 3 (Consultative). Although higher management still reserves the tasks of direction and control, ideas are at least solicited from lower levels. As a result, up-and-down communications are superior to those in Systems 1 and 2. Although there is very little cooperative teamwork, certain delegated specific operating decisions are made at lower levels.

System 4 (Participative Groups). Under **System 4,** higher management views its role as that of making sure the best decisions are made through a decentralized participative-group structure. These groups overlap and are coordinated by multiple memberships. There is a high degree of trust, which allows both superiors and subordinates to exercise greater control over the work situation.

A key concept of System 4 is the use by managers of group decision making and supervision in the management of the work group. It should be noted that System 4 is similar to the type of management found in many Japanese firms. Perhaps the biggest distinction is that in System 4, each

FIGURE 12.2
Likert's four
management systems.

System 1	System 2	System 3	System 4
Exploitative authoritative	Benevolent authoritative	Consultative	Participative

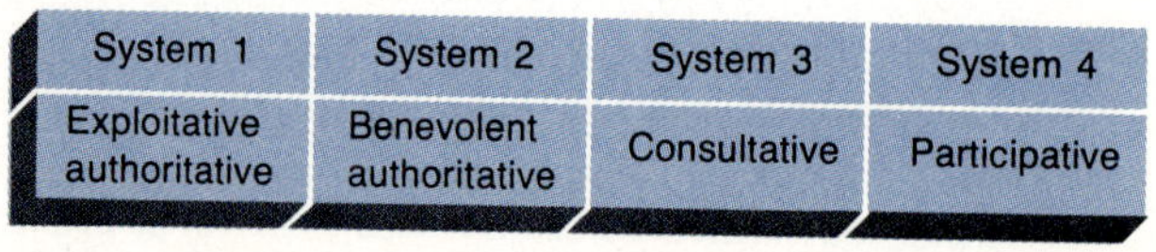

individual manager is still held accountable for his or her decisions and executions even though decision making is a group process.

Blake and Mouton's Managerial Grid®

The **Managerial Grid®** developed by Robert Blake and Jane Mouton focuses on task (production) and employee (people) orientations of managers, as well as combinations of concerns between the two extremes.[10] Figure 12.3 shows a grid with concern for production on the horizontal axis and concern for people on the vertical axis; it plots five basic leadership styles. The first number refers to a leader's production or task orientation; the second, to people or employee orientation.

The *9,1-oriented manager* is described as a stern taskmaster, an autocrat, with some of the characteristics of the close supervisor described in the previous sections. The emphasis is on getting the job done.

The *1,9-oriented manager* uses permissive leadership, with an emphasis on keeping employees happy and satisfied, and tends to avoid the use of pressure in getting work done.

The *1,1-oriented manager* has been described as an abdicator. This is an extreme of the laissez-faire management style identified by Lewin, as discussed in an earlier part of this chapter.

The *5,5-oriented manager* places some emphasis on production but also realizes that people cannot be ignored. Sometimes he or she will use an

FIGURE 12.3
The Managerial Grid®.

SOURCE: Robert R. Blake and Jane S. Mouton, *The Managerial Grid III: The Key to Leadership Excellence* (Houston: Gulf Publishing Co., copyright © 1985), p. 12.

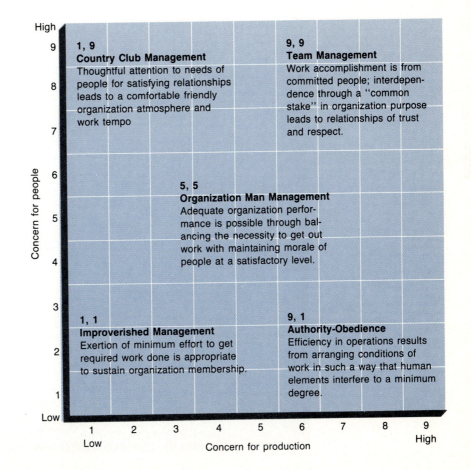

implicit bargaining approach ("You scratch my back, and I'll scratch yours") to get work accomplished.

The *9,9-oriented manager* believes that mutual understanding and agreement regarding the organization's goals—and the means of attaining them—are at the core of work direction. He or she has a high concern for both people and production and uses a participative, team approach in getting work accomplished.

Unlike the Michigan researchers, who found that employee-centered supervisors were more productive than production-centered supervisors, Blake and Mouton emphasize that a high concern for both employees *and* production is the most effective type of leadership behavior.

The Ohio State Studies

Like the earlier researchers at the University of Michigan, the Ohio State researchers identified two sets of behavior that influenced leadership effectiveness—**initiating structure** (task or production emphasis) and **consideration** (employee emphasis).[11] Notice in Table 12.1 how the behavior differed.

The researchers identified four primary leadership styles, as shown in Figure 12.4. Notice the similarity between the Ohio State quadrants and the managerial grid. They also developed two different questionnaires to diagnose the leader's style as perceived by subordinates and by the leader.

A study of Air Force bomber crews during training showed that the subordinates preferred a leader who used a style of high consideration and low structure. This is interesting in that a different preference is observed in

TABLE 12.1 Leader Behavior That Demonstrates Initiating Structure and Consideration

Initiating structure (task- or production-oriented) behaviors	Considerate (employee-centered) behaviors
Establishing policies, rules, and procedures	Praising and rewarding employees for good performance
Seeing that deadlines and schedules are met	Exhibiting friendliness and willingness to listen
Communicating goals and work assignments	Staying informed about employees' needs and concerns
Emphasizing the need to keep on schedule	Encouraging social relations in the department
Recommending ways to improve performance	Keeping employees informed about the department and organization
Emphasizing need for high-quality work	Helping members resolve job and interpersonal conflicts
Delegating necessary authority to accomplish tasks	Making people feel comfortable in the leader's presence
Exerting pressure on subordinates to perform to capacity	Asking for group's opinions and suggestions
Seeking more efficient ways of doing things	Giving attention to employees who are new or feel neglected
	Explaining the reasons for decisions
	Allowing employees to do work in their own way at their own pace

FIGURE 12.4
The Ohio State
leadership quadrants.

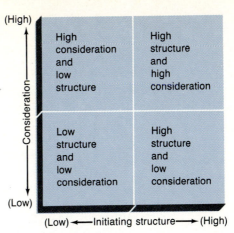

(High)

High consideration and low structure	High structure and high consideration
Low structure and low consideration	High structure and low consideration

Consideration →

(Low)

(Low) ← Initiating structure → (High)

combat situations, when subordinates indicate a preference for a leader who operates with high structure and high consideration. This finding indicates that *employees desire a change of behavior on the part of the leader as circumstances change.* It is also interesting that superiors in both training and combat situations believed that the most effective commanders were the ones who used a style of high structure and low consideration.

What is your view?

Sometimes we find that there is a conflict between subordinates' expectations of a leader and the superior's expectations of the leader. How can an effective leader deal with these sometimes conflicting expectations?

Japanese Style Leadership

In 1981, William Ouchi published a book entitled *Theory Z,*[12] which compared Japanese and American industry and concluded that some Japanese corporations can serve as models for American firms. Ouchi felt that Japanese industrial success was a result of better management and that some American companies had characteristics similar to those of Japanese companies. Invariably, it turned out that these were among the best managed in the world; they included IBM, Procter & Gamble, Hewlett-Packard, and Eastman Kodak. Ouchi referred to these organizations as **Theory Z companies.**

It is becoming quite apparent that the Japanese leadership style discussed by Ouchi is one of the most significant factors in their success in the industrial world. Also, experience with this leadership style in the United States, where Japanese managers are responsible for managing American workers, shows that these techniques are as effective here as they are in Japan—and in some instances more effective. (See Chapters 17 and 20 for more detail.)

IS THERE AN IDEAL LEADERSHIP STYLE?

For some time, there has been a debate about whether there is a normative or ideal leadership style. This debate usually centers on the idea that an ideal style does exist: It is a style that actively *involves* employees in goal setting through the use of participative management techniques and focuses on people *and* task. The essence of this approach is captured by a worker's comment about her supervisor:

> *"Jim Bunting is great to work for," said Joclair Leslie. "He's implemented a management by objectives (MBO) system in which we help to set our own departmental objectives, and he values our inputs greatly. He'll always consult us on big decisions and he tries to get a consensus before deciding. Other regional managers seem to make a lot of decisions on their own. The thing I like best is that he lets us do our jobs without constant pressure. We know our objectives, and he has confidence in us; so he gives us lots of latitude. But he's certainly no 'softie'—don't get that impression. Our performance goals are high, and he expects us to produce. When somebody's not cutting the mustard, Jim'll be wanting to know why. Although he's very much what you'd call a 'people' manager, he's very results oriented, too."*

Support for an Ideal Leadership Style

Researchers in leadership in the 1940s and 1950s, and even into the 1960s (such as Lewin, McGregor, and Likert), gave considerable support to the idea that there is an ideal leadership style—one which incorporates a participative management approach. Early research in motivation theory also supported the participative management approach as the ideal. The concept has both intellectual and moral appeal, especially in developed countries where lower-level needs are relatively well satisfied. Many management practitioners feel that this concept makes sense, and in numerous cases both performance and attitudes improved when participative management was introduced.

The most recent work supporting an ideal leadership style comes from Japan. Jyuji Misumi evaluated 34 studies covering a 35-year period beginning in 1949. Misumi argues that there are four genotypic leader types: (1) the performance oriented (P), (2) the group maintenance oriented (M), (3) the performance and maintenance oriented (PM), and (4) neither performance nor maintenance oriented (pm). The book concludes that performance maintenance (PM) is superior to the other types and results in high levels of both performance and satisfaction.[13] The PM style appears to be quite similar to Blake and Mouton's 9,9 team style and Likert's System 4.

Support for Contingency- Situational Leadership Styles

In recent years, several research studies have challenged the viewpoint that there is one ideal leadership style. Essentially, they say that under various conditions a directive approach may actually get better results and that a participative approach may not work effectively in all situations.

A 1970s study challenged the assumption that leaders who are high in both task and interpersonal behavior will have more satisfied and productive subordinates than those who are not.[14] Another study, judging the leadership effectiveness of 100 managers by three criteria—need fulfillment, salary level, and career progress—concluded that there was a lack of empirical support for Blake's 9,9 leadership style.[15] In this study, the more desirable style seemed to be 1,9, or a leader's behavior of low initiating structure and high consideration.

Another argument against trying to mold all managers into one ideal style is reflected in the following statement:

In managerial grid terms a person should appear to be a 9,9 leader. A 9,1 is too autocratic, a 1,9 never gets work out, a 5,5 lacks drive, and a 1,1 sits around waiting for somebody to notice he died. Thus, regardless of how a person truly thought, there was pressure to see oneself as the ideal and to convince others that he or she was doing well. The added subterfuge and self-delusion necessary to put an image across added confusion for everyone. For instance, a "promotable" manager should appear to hold McGregor Theory Y assumptions and treat people democratically. But this imperative produced lines of people being called on to participate in decisions that were already made.[16]

What is your view?

Can you identify situations in which each of the four approaches mentioned would be appropriate for a leader to adopt? Why would they be appropriate? When would they not be appropriate?

Finally, leadership experience reveals that in some situations an autocratic approach might be best, in others a participative approach; in some a task-oriented approach, in others an employee-oriented approach. This conclusion emphasizes that leadership is complex and that the most appropriate style depends on several interrelated variables, as shown later.

THE CONTINGENCY-SITUATIONAL APPROACH

Just as the traitist approach was inadequate to explain leadership, so was the behavioral approach. Instead, most researchers today conclude that no one leadership style is right for every manager under all circumstances. Instead, the **contingency-situational approach** prescribes that the style to be used is contingent on factors such as the situation, the people, the task, the organization, and other environmental variables.

Examples of Contingency-Situational Approach

Fortune magazine ran a story on the corporate world's 10 *toughest* bosses.[17] Among the traits these leaders had in common were an overriding dedication to their jobs and an insistence that subordinates be equally dedicated. Among the top 10 were Robert Stone and Robert Abboud. Stone, who was known as "Captain Queeg" when he ran Hertz in the 1970s, was a galley master who, hearing that the rowers would die if the beat was raised to 40, would say, "Make it 45." But during his term at Hertz, profits multiplied fourfold. Abboud, former chairman and chief executive officer of First Chicago Bank, was nicknamed "Idi" (for Idi Amin) because he was so tough. During Abboud's reign, top managers left the bank in droves, profits dropped 40 percent in 1979, and shortly after the *Fortune* article appeared in April 1980, Abboud was fired by the bank's executive committee.

So you see that although a hard-nosed, tough leadership style may get results in one situation, it may not in another.

The most popular contingency theories to be discussed are (1) Tannenbaum and Schmidt's leadership continuum, (2) Fiedler's contingency theory, and (3) Hersey and Blanchard's life-cycle theory.

Tannenbaum and Schmidt's Leadership Continuum

In a 1958 issue of *Harvard Business Review*, there appeared an article entitled "How to Choose a Leadership Pattern," by Robert Tannenbaum and Warren Schmidt. The article was so popular with practicing managers that it was reproduced in 1973 as a "classic," along with a retrospective commentary by the authors.[18] The original article had been so well received because it sanctioned a range of behavior instead of offering a choice between two styles of leadership, democratic and authoritarian. It helped managers analyze their own behavior within a context of other alternatives, without labeling any style right or wrong.

What it involves. Tannenbaum and Schmidt's concept is presented as a **leadership continuum,** as shown in Figure 12.5. The continuum is based on Mary Parker Follett's **law of the situation,** which states that there are several alternate paths managers can follow in working with people. Therefore, in making leadership decisions, managers must consider forces in themselves, their subordinates, and the situation.[19] These forces are interrelated and interacting, as shown in Figure 12.6.

Forces in the manager include his or her (1) value system, (2) confidence in subordinates, (3) own leadership inclinations, and (4) feelings of security or insecurity.

Forces in subordinates include (1) their need for independence, (2) their need for increased responsibility, (3) whether they are interested in and have the knowledge to tackle the problem, and (4) their expectations with respect to sharing in decision making.

Forces in the situation include (1) the type of organization, (2) the group's effectiveness, (3) the pressure of time, and (4) the nature of the problem itself. The key point is that the successful manager is the one who has a high batting average in assessing the appropriate behavior for a given situation.

FIGURE 12.5
Continuum of manager-nonmanager behavior.

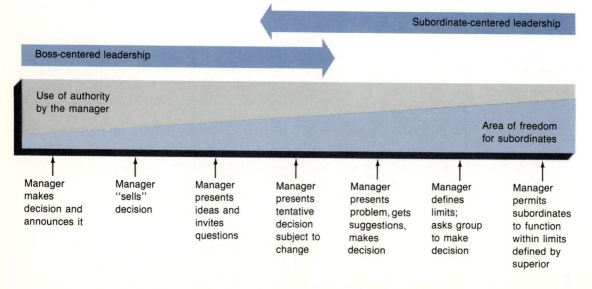

Boss-centered leadership			Subordinate-centered leadership			
Use of authority by the manager						Area of freedom for subordinates
Manager makes decision and announces it	Manager "sells" decision	Manager presents ideas and invites questions	Manager presents tentative decision subject to change	Manager presents problem, gets suggestions, makes decision	Manager defines limits; asks group to make decision	Manager permits subordinates to function within limits defined by superior

FIGURE 12.6
The relationship among the leader, subordinates, and the situation.

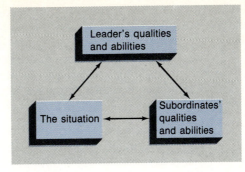

Subordinates must understand what is expected of them. An important warning, though, is that a leader must communicate clearly to subordinates just what degree of involvement they will have in a given situation. Will the workers *make* the decision? Does the supervisor only want to *consider* subordinates' inputs before making the final decision? One mistake leaders make is to "fake" a high degree of involvement, already knowing what the decision will be. In other words, the manager thinks, "I know their thinking on this will be identical to mine, so I'll let them feel that I've involved them in my decision." Beware! *You* do not like to feel manipulated, and the leader who plays such a human-relations "game" may eventually be hurt or surprised by it. The leader will find that thinking can be more varied than he or she ever dreamed.

The department chairperson called in four of her junior faculty members who were teaching principles of management and said, "It is time for us to change textbooks, and these are the four I would like for us to consider. Since we are the ones teaching the course, we will not involve other members of the department in the decision. Will each of you review each book and write me a report ranking them in order of your recommendation? Your recommendations will be of major importance; so take this assignment seriously."

The newest junior faculty member read each book, turned in a list of the pros and cons of each, and made his recommendations. He was surprised when the chairperson adopted the text he had ranked the poorest. He thought, "Hey, I really blew this one. I need to talk with the other instructors and see what I missed in that text she chose."

The four faculty members were upset and dismayed to discover that all of them had ranked the adopted text the poorest of the four. They later learned that the chairperson and the author of the adopted text were close friends.

Primarily as a result of this incident, three of the four junior faculty members sought and obtained positions at other universities.

What is your view?
Where on the leadership continuum did the junior faculty *think* they were operating? Where were the junior faculty *actually* operating? What would have been a more appropriate leadership behavior on the chairperson's part?

Fiedler's Contingency Theory

A complex and interesting leadership theory is Fred Fiedler's **contingency model.**[20] Basically, the theory holds that the effectiveness of a group or an organization depends on the interaction between the leader's personality and the situation. The situation is defined in terms of two characteristics: (1) the degree to which the situation gives the leader power, control, and influence over the situation and (2) the degree to which the situation confronts the leader with uncertainty.

Components of the model. Understanding the contingency model is similar to fitting together a puzzle. Let us first examine the pieces or components and then put them together so that we can see the picture and understand Fiedler's conclusion.

The leader's personality. Fiedler believes that an excellent predictor of one's personality in a leadership situation is a simple test, the **least preferred coworker (LPC) scale.** This test measures the leader's motivation from the standpoint of whether he or she is relationship oriented or task oriented. You might find it interesting to take the test, as provided in TIPS 12.2, to see what your leadership orientation is. Add each of your values and divide by 16. This average gives you your LPC score. A high LPC ranges from 4.1 to 5.7 and a low LPC from 1.2 to 2.2. A high LPC indicates a more relationship-oriented leader, whereas low LPC characterizes a more task-oriented leader.

The situation. The components making up the situation are (1) leader-member relations (To what extent do the members support the leader?), (2) task structure (Does the leader know exactly what to do and how to do it?), and (3) position power (To what extent does the organization give the leader the means to reward and punish subordinates?). The situation is assessed in terms of situational favorableness or unfavorableness; then we have a reading on the extent to which the leader has control and influence over the situation and feels that he or she can determine the outcomes of group interaction.

Fitting the components together. In Figure 12.7, the puzzle is put together. The vertical axis shows the organization's performance, and the horizontal axis shows the "favorableness" of the situation—the degree to which the situation provides the leader with control and influence. The broken lines indicate the performance of low LPC leaders, and the solid line shows the performance of high LPC leaders.

As you can see, the relationship-motivated (high LPC) leaders tend to perform best in situations 4 (good relations with subordinates, low task structure, and weak position power) and 5 (poor relations with subordinates, high task structure, and strong position power). Both these situations are of moderate favorableness.

Task-motivated leaders perform best in situation 1 where all three factors that define their control and influence are either high or low.

It can be concluded from this model that for leaders to be most effective they would need to adapt their leadership styles to the situation. In situation 8, an autocratic approach would probably be most effective. In situations 3, 4, 5, and 6, a more relationship-oriented approach would be called for. Since leaders are limited in their abilities to change their basic personalities and leadership styles, the situation should be changed, or a leader should be chosen whose style matches the existing situation.

Think of the person with whom you can work least well. This person may be someone you work with now or someone you knew in the past. He or she does not have to be the person you like least but should be the person with whom you had the most difficulty in getting a job done. Describe this person as he or she appears to you.

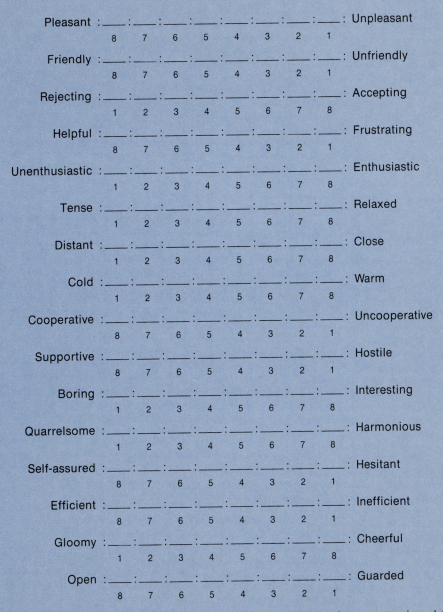

	8	7	6	5	4	3	2	1	
Pleasant									Unpleasant

	8	7	6	5	4	3	2	1	
Friendly									Unfriendly

	1	2	3	4	5	6	7	8	
Rejecting									Accepting

	8	7	6	5	4	3	2	1	
Helpful									Frustrating

	1	2	3	4	5	6	7	8	
Unenthusiastic									Enthusiastic

	1	2	3	4	5	6	7	8	
Tense									Relaxed

	1	2	3	4	5	6	7	8	
Distant									Close

	1	2	3	4	5	6	7	8	
Cold									Warm

	8	7	6	5	4	3	2	1	
Cooperative									Uncooperative

	8	7	6	5	4	3	2	1	
Supportive									Hostile

	1	2	3	4	5	6	7	8	
Boring									Interesting

	1	2	3	4	5	6	7	8	
Quarrelsome									Harmonious

	8	7	6	5	4	3	2	1	
Self-assured									Hesitant

	8	7	6	5	4	3	2	1	
Efficient									Inefficient

	1	2	3	4	5	6	7	8	
Gloomy									Cheerful

	8	7	6	5	4	3	2	1	
Open									Guarded

After completing the test, "score" yourself as follows: (1) add the values you assigned to each of the elements; (2) divide the result by 16 to find your LPC score.

A "high" LPC ranges from 4.1 to 5.7, while a "low" LPC varies from 1.2 to 2.2. A high LPC indicates that you are a more relationship-oriented leader; a low LPC indicates you are a more task-oriented leader.

SOURCE: Fred E. Fiedler, *A Theory of Leadership Effectiveness* (New York: McGraw-Hill, 1967), pp. 40–41.

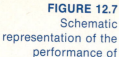

FIGURE 12.7
Schematic
representation of the
performance of
relationship- and task-
motivated leaders under
different situational
favorableness
conditions.

SOURCE: Fred E. Fiedler, *A
Theory of Leadership
Effectiveness* (New York:
McGraw-Hill, 1967), p. 13.

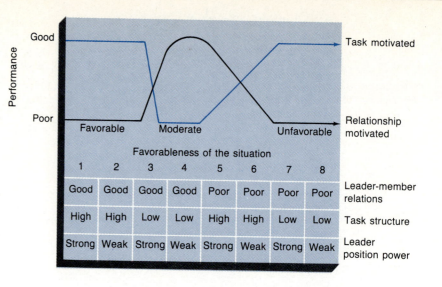

Evaluation of the theory. Fiedler's contingency theory has aroused considerable interest and had a great impact among researchers and academicians.[21] Despite articles in several popular journals read by practicing managers, however, it has not been widely accepted by managers. Two possible reasons are (1) the complexity of the theory and (2) that it reaches conclusions that are different from those of other situational or contingency theorists. In fact, they will probably say that if time is taken to evaluate all these factors in a leadership situation, it may thwart effective teamwork. We believe that leaders *can vary* their styles to meet the requirements of a situation and that they *can learn* to become more effective leaders.

Hersey-Blanchard's Life-Cycle Theory

A leadership theory that has attracted considerable attention is what Paul Hersey and Kenneth Blanchard call the **life-cycle theory.**[22] It draws heavily on previous leadership research, particularly the Ohio State studies (discussed earlier in the chapter) and William Reddin's work.[23] Like Fiedler, Hersey and Blanchard take a situational approach—with one major difference. They emphasize leaders' using an adaptive style depending on the diagnosis they make of the situation.

Basic concepts. The basic concept of the life-cycle theory is that a leader's strategies and behavior should be situational, based primarily on the maturity or immaturity of followers. The following definitions should help you understand the theory.

Maturity is the capacity of individuals or groups to set high but attainable goals and their willingness and ability to take responsibility. These maturity variables, resulting from education and/or experience, should be considered only in relation to a specific task to be performed.

Task behavior is the extent to which leaders are likely to organize and define the roles of their followers, to explain what activities each is to do and when, where, and how tasks are to be accomplished. It relies on establishing well-defined patterns of organization, channels of communication, and ways of accomplishing jobs.

Relationship behavior deals with the leader's personal relationships with individuals or members of his or her group. It involves the amount of support provided by the leader and the extent to which the leader engages in interpersonal communication and facilitating behavior.

Figure 12.8 shows the relationship between the maturity of followers and the leadership style based on task and relationship behavior of leaders. The style of the leader should change as the maturity of the followers increases.

The chart can be used as follows. First, determine the maturity level of the members of a group (mature or immature). Then, trace a line upward until it intercepts the curved line. That intersection determines which of the four basic leadership styles is most effective for that situation. The Q number represents a given quadrant of leadership style.

The theory in practice. Hersey and Blanchard used the example of parents' relationship with their children to illustrate their theory. Negative consequences will probably result if parents tend to use only one leadership style during their children's developmental years. For example, children may either run away or engage in many rebellious, antisocial behaviors if parents tend to use only a very directive leadership style (high task and low relationship). The point at which children are likely to rebel is probably in the early teen years. On the other hand, if parents use primarily a permissive style, the result is frequently children who warrant the label of "spoiled brats," with little regard for rules, regulations, or the rights of others. The key is to use more directive behavior in the early periods and as the child (worker) matures, to provide less direction and control, as shown in the following examples.

"My relationship with my boss has changed a lot, I guess, in the four years I've been here," said John Dixon, a lab technician. "She was constantly checking my work when I first started, giving me detailed instructions, making sure I understood what was expected of me [Q1 in Figure 12.8].

FIGURE 12.8
Situational leadership
theory.

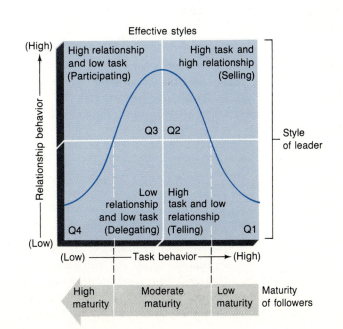

Then, as I began to learn the ropes, she opened up a bit and seemed to be more personal, more interested in me and my feelings [Q2] as well as the work. In a year or so, after I had proved myself as her best technician, she pretty much let me handle the work side of things—I knew as much about them as she did—and most of our discussions were on the social side or about what a good job I was doing [Q3]. Now that I've been here four years and have proved what I can do, I only see her once or twice a week [Q4]. She spends more of her time with the new people."

A key point to remember in either a family or a work environment is that, in regard to a specific task, leaders may have to modify their strategies and shift backward in the maturity cycle when circumstances change.

What is your view?

Assume that for some time you have been operating a high-relationship, low-task style [Q3] with your 16-year-old son with respect to school homework. Your son's grades have been As and Bs; then one quarter his grades drop to Cs and Ds. According to this theory, would you need to shift your leadership style? If so, which style would you shift to?

Our conclusion is that, of the various leadership theories, the contingency-situational approach probably best explains what is required for effective managerial leadership. Let us therefore see some of the many factors affecting leadership behavior.

FACTORS AFFECTING LEADERSHIP BEHAVIOR

Research has shown that leadership is so complex that there are many interrelated variables affecting a leader's behavior. The most significant ones can be classified as general and specific factors, as shown in Figure 12.9.

General Factors

There are at least four general factors that, while they do not influence leadership behavior directly, do have a great indirect effect over a period of time. These factors are (1) the economic situation, (2) the historical and cultural environment, (3) the industry, and (4) the organization.

Economic factors. The economic situation plays an important part in determining the acceptability of a given leadership approach. For example, during periods of economic downturn, there is a tendency to reduce costs, even by laying people off. The concern for reducing costs sometimes causes an emphasis on tighter controls, more centralization, and a shift toward emphasizing 9,1 management.

During the depression of the 1930s, for example, thousands of people would show up on the basis of a rumor that a firm might be hiring. Workers who were employed at that time would be much more likely to respond to a 9,1, or highly autocratic, approach that held their jobs over their heads and said, "Produce or else." Today, more enlightened man-

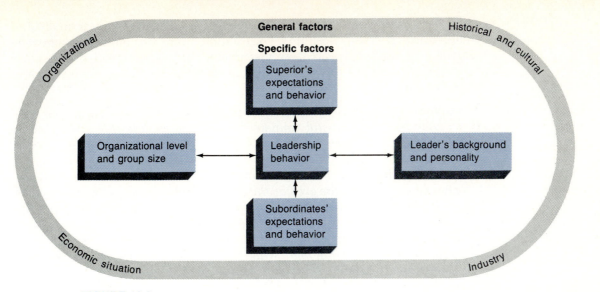

FIGURE 12.9
Factors that influence a
leader's behavior.

*agement and various unemployment benefits make it more likely that
employees' response to such an approach would be: "Take this job and
shove it!"*

Historical and cultural factors. These factors largely determine the acceptability of a given leadership style. For example, after World War II, American
companies establishing operations in West Germany discovered that, because
of cultural and historical factors, authoritarian leadership behaviors were
expected. Over time, the internationalization of business has lessened the
impact of individual countries in this regard. For example, West Germany
has been a leader in more democratic leadership innovations in recent years.

The industry. The industry's influence is due not only to historical factors
but also to the technology of the industry and the nature of the jobs to be
done. We would expect leadership behavior in an industry with a history of
union-management conflict to be different from that in an industry in which
union-management cooperation is the rule.

 What is your view?
What do you think the leadership behavior of a platoon leader in an infantry unit
in combat should be?

The organization. Closely related to the influence of the industry is the
particular organization. Not only does the nature of the work to be done
play a part, but the philosophy of top management is also important. Earlier,
we discussed the example of Avis's experience with Robert Townsend's
philosophy.

Specific Factors   There are many specific factors that influence a leader's behavior, but we
will discuss only a few to illustrate the point.

Background and personality. Background and personality affect one's preference for a leadership style. Certainly, people's personalities are shaped by

their early family environment and experience before they are formally appointed to leadership positions. For example, were you given love, encouragement, praise, approval? Were you treated fairly and provided with consistent discipline? All these can significantly affect the choice of a leadership style later on.

> *Authors Margaret Henning and Anne Jordin, in research regarding successful and unsuccessful women executives, conclude that a daughter's relationship with her father had a major influence on her later success as a manager. Did he spend time with her, take her on camping trips, and encourage her to participate and excel in sports? The better the relationship between them, the greater the chances of her success as a manager.[24]*
>
> *In the case of a son, if the two past leaders he admires most were his high school football coach and his army company commander—both stern disciplinarians who nonetheless achieved effective results—it is possible that the young man, when placed in a supervisory position, will pattern his leadership style after these men.*

Supervisor's behavior and expectations. Management consultants have long been aware that the supervisory behavior and expectations of upper- and middle-level managers also influence the leadership style of managers and supervisors who report to them. As shown in the Opening Case, a major strategy of a consultant is to change a higher-level manager's inappropriate and ineffective style to a more suitable approach that will cause changes in lower-level managers.

> *Ann Holmes had just returned from a week-long management program at State University. She had had no prior classes in management, having been a history major in college. But now, after working her way up to department head in a federal agency, she found the classes extremely stimulating.*
>
> *"I was surprised to learn how many of the other managers attending the course were so open with their employees and would get help from their workers in making management decisions. And, in most of the cases and role playing in the course, the best approaches seemed to reflect a participative approach with employees.*
>
> *"I would prefer to use that approach in my department, because I have some seasoned, experienced employees. But Tom Hayes, the section chief, who's my boss, would blow a fuse. Tom thinks the best leadership approach is what they used at marine boot camp—he's a retired marine officer. If he caught me asking my workers for suggestions about running the department, he'd—well, I don't know exactly what he'd do, but I know what he'd say! He'd say, 'Ann, you're being paid to run the department, not them. If you don't think you can handle it, let me know and we'll find someone else.' And since he is my boss and fills out my performance evaluation, I naturally want to please him. So I guess now's not the time for me to quit being somewhat autocratic."*

What is your view?

What would *you* do if you were Ann?

Organization level and group size. The organization level has a tendency to influence leadership behavior. There seems to be a greater tendency to use participative management in the higher levels than in lower levels. This phenomenon occurs because in most organizations the low-level jobs are simply more structured or more detailed. We have observed that companies using MBO have difficulty in taking it to the lowest levels in the organization because the jobs are too structured.

APPLYING LEADERSHIP THEORY

In discussing leadership, many textbooks present too many theories and not enough summary or nuts-and-bolts usefulness. This section will show how to *apply* leadership theory. We have discussed several leadership theories and shown that no one of them has all the answers. We agree with the contingency theorists that the real challenge for those in leadership positions is to take time to make a thorough diagnosis of the situation and then plan their leadership strategies carefully, based on that situation. Moreover, leadership strategies must be oriented toward carrying out the organization's mission and achieving its objectives.

Some managers ignore ideal leadership models such as 9,9 and System 4. We think that viewpoint is a mistake because there is an increasing number of situations where the appropriate action is to shift toward these leadership styles. More will be said on this point in Chapter 13. Notice in the Opening Case that Kenny dealt with the ''Hell's Angels crew'' that way.

Of the many ways of applying leadership theory, we have selected two— (1) inspiring and developing people, and (2) becoming a transformative leader—because they emphasize the concepts that work successfully in actual practice.

Inspiring and Developing People

The following are concepts leaders can apply to increase their effectiveness.

Say ''thank you.'' It has been shown that productivity can be drastically increased simply by saying ''thank you.'' ''Thank yous'' can vary from financial rewards for good performance to simply writing letters of recommendation.[25] One approach is to look for positive contributions and give people feedback on the spot, as recommended in *The One Minute Manager*. The book's authors suggest one-minute techniques such as:

1. Telling people up front that you are going to let them know how they are doing.
2. Praising people immediately.
3. Telling people what they did right—specifically.
4. Telling people how good you feel about what they did right and how it helps the organization and the other people who work there.
5. Stopping for a moment of silence to let them ''feel'' how good you feel.
6. Encouraging them to do more of the same.

7. Shaking hands or touching people in a way that makes clear that you support their success in the organization.[26]

Expect the best of people. Essential to effective leadership is the awareness that, to bring out the best in people, you must assume the best about them. If you expect the best from people and develop realistic yet difficult performance objectives, your expectations will act as a self-fulfilling prophecy. But you must trust your work team and do what you say you will. A study of school teachers has revealed that having high expectations of students can increase their IQ scores up to 25 points.[27]

What is your view?

As indicated in the Opening Case, Kenny gained the trust of his renegade work team. They gave him two weeks to prove that he would supervise them as he said he would, and he did.

Maintain a positive self-regard. A study of nearly 100 outstanding leaders in different fields revealed that having a good feeling about oneself is one key to effective leadership.[28] We are not talking about cockiness or self-worship, but a sincere self-respect, based on awareness of one's strengths and weaknesses and the desire to improve one's talents.

Develop the entire team. Kenny made a conscious effort to sit down once a month and talk with each member of his crew. But he went beyond focusing on developing individual crew members and developed the entire team by holding regular crew meetings and emphasizing the importance of working together. As a result, the crew thought and acted as a team, helping one another. For example, one team member was afraid of heights; so other members covered for him when there was an assignment involving heights.

Develop the desire to achieve. While the most effective leaders have a strong desire to achieve excellent results, they will be less effective if they become so task oriented that they slight the human-relations aspects of working with people. Kenny did not fall into this pitfall, nor did he go to the opposite extreme of emphasizing human relations at the expense of achievement. For the very reason that he was very achievement oriented, Kenny used a contingency-situational strategy: If his initial approach had not worked, he would have shifted to a more directive style to turn things around.

Becoming a Transformative Leader

Transformative leaders are those who can shape and elevate the motives and goals of followers. This type of leadership considers the interests of both leaders and followers and emphasizes the need to work toward a common goal.[29]

This concept was first introduced by James MacGregor Burns in his award-winning book, *Leadership.*[30] Although Burns was primarily studying world leaders, other writers have noted that the concept applies to leaders at all organizational levels. One study evaluated transformative leadership by assessing three factors: (1) charismatic leadership, (2) individualized consideration, and (3) intellectual stimulation.[31] Does the leader instill pride and respect and a sense of mission? Does the leader provide learning opportunities and treat each subordinate individually? Does the leader provide ideas

Management Application and Practice 12.1 Treating People as Individuals

There was a time when people were [treated as] "factors of production," managed little differently from machines or capital. No more. The best people will not tolerate it. And if that way of managing ever generated productivity, it has the reverse effect today. While capital and machines either are or can be managed toward sameness, people are individuals. They must be managed that way. When companies encourage individual expression, it is difficult for them not to renew. The only true source of renewal in a company is the individual.

SOURCE: Robert H. Waterman Jr., "The Renewal Factor," *Business Week*, September 14, 1987, p. 100.

resulting in rethinking of issues and enabling subordinates to deal with old problems in new ways? If so, she or he is a transformative leader.

What is your view?
Was Kenny a transformative leader? Support your position.

As you can see from the preceding discussion—and MAP 12.1—an essential ingredient of effective leadership is *treating people as individuals*, not as "factors of production."

SUMMARY

You have seen in this chapter that leadership is a process of influencing individual and group activities toward goal setting and goal attainment. The successful leader is able to get others to follow in achieving organizational goals. It has also been shown that leadership is complex and that there are various factors affecting the leadership style used in different countries, organizations, and situations. We have presented several examples and applications to illustrate effective and ineffective leadership.

The case for an ideal leadership style was presented, along with the case for the contingency-situational approach to leadership.

The findings of Stogdill and Ghiselli, supporting the traitist theory of leadership, were presented. Then the research and theories of the behavioral approach were given. Included were ideas by Lewin, McGregor, Likert, Blake and Mouton, and William Ouchi. The general conclusion of these was that participative, employee-centered leadership is the ideal.

The contingency-situational leadership concepts of Tannenbaum and Schmidt, Fiedler, and Hersey and Blanchard were also presented. The general conclusion was that leaders must be prepared to adapt their leadership styles according to forces in the followers, the situation, and the leader. Fiedler believed that because leadership varies in different situations the best solution is to match the leader with the appropriate situation or to change the forces in the situation. We also examined some concepts that leaders can apply to inspire self-confidence and develop people.

We believe that leadership is situational. That is, the style to be used is contingent on many factors, including the manager, the subordinates, and the situation. It is important, however, for you to be keenly aware that there are forces in most organizations that create many situations for which the most effective leadership style is participative.

REVIEW QUESTIONS

1. How would you characterize the leadership style of Kenny in the Opening Case?
2. How would you define (a) autocratic leaders, (b) democratic leaders, and (c) laissez-faire leaders?
3. What is the difference between leadership and management?
4. How would you describe the traitist approach to studying leadership?
5. How would you describe the behavioral approach to studying leadership?
6. How would you describe the contingency-situational approach to studying leadership?
7. How would you describe the general and specific factors that affect leadership behavior?
8. What are the three basic concepts of the life-cycle theory?

DISCUSSION QUESTIONS

1. Do you believe there is an ideal leadership style? Explain.
2. Should a supervisor use one leadership style with certain workers, another with other workers, and perhaps a third with others? Defend your answer.
3. Can you correlate McGregor's Theory X and Theory Y with two leadership styles? How?
4. Which one of the various leadership theories and approaches discussed in this chapter do you think is the most applicable in the real world? Support your position.
5. Discuss Fiedler's contingency theory and contrast it with Hersey and Blanchard's life-cycle theory. What is the primary difference in the conclusions reached in using the two theories?
6. How valid is the "law of the situation"?
7. Do you agree with the concepts presented at the end of the chapter for inspiring confidence, developing people, and increasing productivity? Explain.

LEARNING EXERCISE 12.1

Which Leadership Style?

Mr. Paul received his B.S. degree in accounting from a major university in the Midwest and began his career at the Chicago office of Jones & Jones (J&J), a large accounting firm, in 1961. Nine years later he became a partner in the firm, one of the youngest ever. The firm's executive committee spotted Mr. Paul's leadership potential and aggressive style, and, in 1973, called on him to open a new office in a suburb of New York. The work was predominantly doing audits that required considerable judgment and self-control on the part of subordinates. Mr. Paul was quite task oriented; yet he used a democratic leadership style. He insisted that the entire office be on a first-name basis and encouraged the subordinates to participate in decision making.

The task at J&J was very unstructured. Long-range goals and objectives were known by everyone, but the methods of achieving the goals were very unstructured.

The office grew rapidly, and the professional staff had grown to over 30 by 1978. Mr. Paul was considered to be a highly successful leader and manager.

Mr. Paul was then transferred to Dallas, Texas, to try to salvage an office that had been losing money and whose employees seemed to lack both ability and motivation.

Mr. Paul took over as managing partner in Dallas in early 1979. He started out with the same aggressive managing style that had worked so well in New York. He immediately replaced nearly the entire professional staff of 25 people. Short- and long-range client development plans were made, and the staff was expanded quite rapidly to insure that a sufficient number of employees were available to accommodate the expected growth. Soon there were about 40 professional staff members.

But the aggressive style that had worked in New York did not work well at all in Dallas. The office lost two of its best clients within one year. Mr. Paul soon realized that the office was badly overstaffed and decided to fire 12 staff members, whom he had hired only one year earlier, to minimize losses.

He was convinced that the setback was temporary and continued with his strategy. The staff was increased by six professionals over the next few months to again accommodate the expected increased workload. The expected new business did not materialize, so the staff was again trimmed by 13 professionals on "Black Tuesday" in the summer of 1981.

Following these two layoffs the remaining staff members were insecure and began to question Mr. Paul's leadership ability. The firm's executive committee sensed the problem and transferred Mr. Paul to a New Jersey office.

Questions

1. What were the sources of Mr. Paul's power as a leader?

2. To what extent does this case illustrate the contingency approach to leadership?

3. Where does Mr. Paul belong on Fiedler's contingency model? Explain.

LEARNING EXERCISE 12.2

Sensitive Roughnecks

During summer vacation last year, I worked with an oil well drilling crew in the swamps of southern Louisiana.*

One night we were pulling up drill pipe from about 12,000 feet to change the bit. We were uncomfortable and tired. Hot drilling mud (lubricant) sprayed over us as we broke the connection on each stand of pipe. One of the joints had sealed tight, so we took turns hitting it with a 16-pound sledgehammer. "Hot Rod," the driller (supervisor), was yelling at us to hurry up. I guess he thought he could scare us or make us so angry that we would work harder on the pipe. Finally, while Joe was taking his turn with the sledgehammer, Hot Rod yelled, "You yellow-bellied coward, you couldn't beat your way out of a wet paper bag."

Joe was trying his best, like the rest of us, but Hot Rod was trying to ridicule him before the crew to get him to work harder. That was all Joe could take. He started for Hot Rod with the sledgehammer in his hand, blood in his eye, and who knows what in his heart. We grabbed him before he could use the hammer, but it took a long time for everyone to calm down and get back to work. We felt so much resentment toward Hot Rod that we worked at less than maximum for the rest of the shift.

Several days later, we were drilling through shale, which is, at best, a slow job. Hot Rod, however, told Jim to push the mud pump pressure up to 500 pounds so that we would work faster. Jim said that the pump wouldn't take that much pressure and would blow a gasket, but Hot Rod said, "Push it up to 500 or draw your pay and get off this rig. I'm running things here."

We became apprehensive as the floor trembled from the increasing pressure, for there were 93 feet of pipe in the derrick, waiting to be moved to the hole. Hot Rod connected the pipe too quickly, and the ton of steel began to swing like a pendulum. It caught me off guard, hit me in the chest, and knocked me to the deck. One of the crew flatly told Hot Rod that we would not work unless he slowed down.

* This case was prepared by Gerald A. Rhea, formerly of Louisiana State University. See L. C. Megginson, *Human Resources: Cases and Concepts* (New York: Harcourt Brace Jovanovich, 1968), pp. 160–167, for background material and more details.

As this argument was going on, one of the men went down to check on the mud pumps, a gasket blew out, and mud was blown all over him. After an hour of eyewash treatment, he returned to work. Fortunately, the sun was rising, and a fresh crew was on hand to relieve us. We left the rig feeling pretty shaky, wondering who would be hurt next and how badly.

The poor morale was decreasing productivity. We knew we were good roughnecks, but Hot Rod cursed us like common laborers and made fun of us in front of anyone who visited the rig. All the regular crew had requested transfers to other rigs. Since the driller had to approve such transfers, all were denied.

Word of the accidents and bad feelings reached the field superintendent, who bawled Hot Rod out. This didn't seem to help, for he just became more difficult to work with.

We soon developed a strategy to use whenever Hot Rod got "horsey" with us. When he started to yell and curse, we ignored him and continued what we were doing, as though we hadn't even heard him. This got under his skin as badly as his harsh remarks got under ours. We took great pleasure in watching his face turn purple with rage at us. If he speeded up the draw works more than we thought was safe, we slowed down our own rhythm.

When this didn't work, the boiler tender would adjust the power and water supply. With less water cooling the brakes, Hot Rod could not afford to speed. As a last resort, we would use the tools and machines roughly so that we would have to shut down and make time-consuming repairs. Hot Rod went on vacation about a month after our strategy had been perfected, and Jim, the derrick and mud man, became the driller. He had been a regular driller himself at one time, but an unfortunate accident had caused his demotion.

Jim was well liked and respected. Still, when it became known that Jim would be the relief driller, one man said, "All drillers are bad news, and Jim will probably be the same when he takes over."

Soon afterward, we were assigned to do a "triple completion" of a well that had been drilled. This was the first time this very difficult type of work had been tried, so we had no experience with it and no special tools with which to do the job.

Jim called us together and said, "This job is new to us, so we will have to pull together to get it done. I know we have been goofing off with Hot Rod, but we can't have that now. There's an important job to be done, and I need everyone's cooperation." He asked for suggestions on how the job might be done, and several were made. Jim said they sounded good and by using them we could probably get the job done.

Each man was allowed to choose the job he thought he could do best. If he tired of one job, he could rotate to another one. Jim told us that he would operate the draw-works at a fast but safe speed. We set our goal at 20,000 feet of pipe to be put into the well in the next 12 hours.

After many backbreaking hours, we were dead tired and were falling behind schedule. Jim stopped all work for a few minutes and said, "It's about time we showed the other crews that we are the best. You all know we can outwork any other crew.... Let's get to it!" Then the crew really pitched in and labored for the next four hours.

When the shift ended, we were 150 feet short of our objective. The day crew had arrived and was ready to take over, but we wouldn't leave the derrick floor. We stayed a few minutes extra until the 20,000-foot mark had been achieved.

When we finally quit working, we were exhausted, but we were laughing and joking and seemed to feel satisfied for the first time in weeks about the job we had done.

Questions

1. Using what you have learned in this chapter, explain the behavior and attitude of this crew, first under Hot Rod's leadership and then under Jim's.

2. Which theory or theories in this chapter best explain(s) Hot Rod's leadership style? Jim's?

3. What factors affected Hot Rod's leadership style? Jim's?

4. Would Jim's leadership style work in all situations? Explain.

NOTES

1. Donald C. Mosley, "System Four Revisited: Some New Insights," *Organization Development Journal* 5 (Spring 1987): 19–24.

2. John W. Gardner, *Self-Renewal: The Individual and the Innovative Society* (New York: Harper & Row, 1964), Chapter 11.

3. Ralph M. Stogdill, "Personal Factors Associated with Leadership," *Journal of Applied Psychology* 32 (January 1948): 35–71.

4. Edwin Ghiselli, *Explorations in Managerial Talent* (Pacific Palisades, CA: Goodyear, 1971).

5. *Experimental Studies and the Social Climates of Groups*, film from the Media Library, East Hall, Audio Visual Center, University of Iowa.

6. Douglas McGregor, *The Human Side of Enterprise* (New York: McGraw-Hill, 1960).

7. Robert Townsend, *Up the Organization* (New York: Knopf, 1970), p. 141.

8. Rensis Likert, *New Patterns of Management* (New York: McGraw-Hill, 1961), p. 9; and *The Human Organization* (New York: McGraw-Hill, 1967).

9. The best known of these studies is found in Alfred J. Morrow, David G. Bowers, and Stanley E. Seashore, *Management by Participation* (New York: Harper & Row, 1967).

10. Robert R. Blake and Jane S. Mouton, *The Managerial Grid III: The Key to Leadership Excellence* (Houston: Gulf Publishing Co., 1985), p. 12.

11. See Wayne R. Wheeler and Louis S. Csoka, "Leader Behavior—Theory and Study," in *A Study of Organization Leadership* (Harrisburg, PA: Office of Military Leadership, Stackpole Books, 1976), p. 311.

12. William Ouchi, *Theory Z* (Reading, MA: Addison-Wesley, 1981).

13. Robert J. House, "The 'All Things in Moderation' Leader," *Academy of Management Review* 12 (January 1987): 164.

14. J. L. Larsen, J. G. Hunt, and R. N. Osborn, "The Great Hi-Hi Leader Behavior Myth: A Lesson from Occam's Razor," *Academy of Management Journal* 19 (December 1976): 628.

15. Paul C. Nystrom, "Managers and the Hi-Hi Leader Myth," *Academy of Management Journal* 21 (June 1978): 330.

16. Samuel A. Culbert, "The Real World and the Management Classroom," *California Management Review* 19 (Summer 1977): 65–78.

17. Milton Moskowitz, Michael Katz, and Robert Levering, *Everybody's Business* (New York: Harper & Row, 1980), p. 524.

18. Robert Tannenbaum and Warren H. Schmidt, "How to Choose a Leadership Pattern," *Harvard Business Review* 51 (May–June 1973): 166.

19. Fred E. Fiedler, *A Theory of Leadership Effectiveness* (New York: McGraw-Hill, 1967), p. 36.

20. Lyndall Urwick, ed., *Freedom and Coordination: Lectures in Business Organization by Mary Parker Follett* (New York: Pitman, 1949).

21. See J. Timothy McMahon, "The Contingency Theory: Logic and Method Revisited," *Personnel Psychology* 25 (Winter 1972): 697–710.

22. Paul Hersey and Kenneth H. Blanchard, *Management of Organizational Behavior*, 3d ed. (Englewood Cliffs, NJ: Prentice-Hall, 1977), p. 161.

23. William J. Reddin, *Managerial Effectiveness* (New York: McGraw-Hill, 1970).

24. Margaret Henning and Anne Jordin, *The Managerial Woman* (Garden City, NY: Doubleday/Anchor Books, 1977).

25. Jack Falvey, "Manager's Journal," *Wall Street Journal*, December 6, 1982, p. 22.

26. Kenneth Blanchard and Spencer Johnson, *The One Minute Manager* (New York: William Morrow & Co., 1982), p. 44.

27. Warren Bennis, *The Unconscious Conspiracy: Why Leaders Can't Lead* (New York: AMACOM, 1976).

28. Warren Bennis and Bert Nanus, "The Leading Edge," *Ideas* (Ernst & Whinney), Fall–Winter 1985–1986.

29. Warren Bennis and Bert Nanus, *Leaders: The Strategies for Taking Charge* (New York: Harper & Row, 1985), p. 217.

30. James MacGregor Burns, *Leadership* (New York: Harper & Row, 1978).

31. Bernard M. Bass, Bruce J. Avlio, and Laurie Goodheim, "Biography and the Assessment of Transformational Leadership at the World-Class Level," *Journal of Management* 13 (Spring 1987): 10.

SUGGESTIONS FOR FURTHER STUDY

FLAX, STEPHEN. "The Ten Toughest Bosses in America." *Fortune*, August 6, 1984, pp. 18–23.

GRAEFF, CLAUDE L. "The Situational Leadership Theory: A Critical View." *Academy of Management Review* 8 (1983): 285–291.

HOUSE, ROBERT J., and BAETZ, MARY L. "Leadership: Some Empirical Generalizations and New Research Directions." In *Research in Organizational Behavior*, pp. 341–423. Edited by Barry M. Staw. Greenwich, CT: JAI Press, 1979.

KARMEL, BARBARA. "Leadership: A Challenge to Traditional Research Methods and Assumptions." *Academy of Management Review* 3 (July 1978): 475–482.

LOMBARDO, M. M., and MCCALL, M. W. "Boss." *Psychology Today*, January 1984, pp. 45–48.

NORMANN, RICHARD. *Service Management: Strategy and Leadership in Service Businesses.* New York: Wiley, 1984.

PUTNAM, L., and HEINEN, J. S. "Women in Management: The Fallacy of the Trait Approach." *Michigan State University Business Topics* (Summer 1976): 47–53.

SCHEIN, VIRGINIA E. "The Relationship Between Sex Role Stereotypes and Requisite Management Characteristics." *Journal of Applied Psychology* 57 (April 1973): 99.

WATSON, C. M. "Leadership, Management, and the Seven Keys." *Business Horizons* 26 (March–April 1983): 8–13.

WILSON, MARILYN, and ADKINS, LYNN. "How the Japanese Run U.S. Subsidiaries." *Economy*, October 1983, pp. 32–40.

13

Organizational Culture and Change

Learning Objectives

After studying the material in this chapter, you should be able to do the following:

- Explain the role and functions of organizational culture.
- Appreciate the impact of change and development on individuals and organizations.
- Describe some ways to cope with and manage the changes that inevitably occur in organizations.
- Define organization development, name its objectives, and show how the process works.
- Discuss how to manage conflict.

Outline of the Chapter

Why study organizational culture?
Definition of organizational culture
The role of values
Elements of organizational culture
Problems for the organization related to organizational culture
Participative management and organizational culture
Functions performed by organizational culture
Managing organizational change
Forces causing change
Results of ignoring change
Ways of dealing with change
What should be changed?
Reactions to change
The process of managing change
Ensuring that the change is permanent

Using organizational development (OD) to promote change
What is OD?
A basic OD model
Selected OD intervention strategies
Promise and limitations of OD
Conflict management
Causes of conflict
Conflict resolution: What works?
Summary

Some Important Terms

organizational culture
values
participative management
external change forces
internal change forces
reactive process
proactive process
planned change
organizational effectiveness
resistance to change
change agent
unfreezing
changing
refreezing
organizational development (OD)
synergy
action-research model of OD
confrontation meeting
quality of work life (QWL) programs
quality circles (QC)
conflict management
conflict

I became personally convinced that in order to enlist the support of our entire organization in quality improvement, we had to radically change our entire corporate culture.

—DAVID T. KEARNS, CHAIRMAN, XEROX CORPORATION

Can Ford Stay on Top?[1]

Ford Motor Company is the most profitable car company in the world, earning $3.3 billion in 1986 on $62.7 billion in sales as compared to GM's $2.9 billion on $102.8 billion in sales. And for the first half of 1987, Ford's $2.9 billion in profits topped the combined earnings of GM and Chrysler Corporation, while its market share rose 2.2 percentage points, to 20.1 percent. Ford, whose Escort is the nation's best-selling car, has stolen styling leadership from GM with its line of sleek, European-looking cars, including the Taurus and Sable. What's more, Ford has taken a big leap in improving manufacturing quality.

Yet, as recently as the early 1980s, Ford was losing billions of dollars. According to Thomas F. O'Grady, president of the analytical firm Integrated Automotive Resources Inc., "Ford in 1980 and '81 was really looking at the end of the earth"; it was a company "running scared." So Ford management went on simultaneous cost-cutting and quality-improvement campaigns and has not let up since then. In the process, the company closed 15 plants worldwide and cut 49,800 blue-collar jobs.

The cuts went hand in hand with a drastic change in Ford's culture. Under its founder, Henry Ford, and his grandson, Henry Ford II, Ford had an autocratic, nearly militaristic, top-down organizational structure. But when Henry II resigned as chairman in 1980, the company became team oriented. Now, executive promotions are based on teamwork and performance, and bonuses are tied to companywide improvements in quality. Much of the credit for replacing Ford's stifling hierarchical structure belongs to Philip Caldwell, chairman from 1980 to 1985. He initiated Ford's Project Alpha, which probes business and manufacturing methods throughout the company in search of inefficiencies.

In 1985, Donald E. Petersen took over as chairman and further developed the new corporate culture. One of the first things he focused on was quality. When he closed three North American assembly plants, he didn't shutter the ones with the oldest equipment or the poorest productivity; he axed those that "made the lousiest cars."

As chairman, Petersen inspires people to listen to each other. To develop Taurus, a team of stylists, engineers, and manufacturing types worked together to search for the best possible car. Ford even drew in assembly workers, customers, and the competition. It combed over 50 comparable cars and queried customers in search of the "best in class" characteristics of everything from the effort required to turn the steering wheel to the ease of resetting the car's clock. Ford then matched or bettered 80 percent of these characteristics. And when it came time to produce the cars, workers had the authority to stop the line if quality was being compromised. In fact, the Taurus debut was delayed several months while Ford worked out quality glitches. At a company that used to rush out slipshod cars for the sake of sales, that delay hammered home the new regime's priorities, gave credibility to its slogan, "Quality is Job 1," and reinforced its emphasis on employee involvement groups (Figure 13.1).

But a change in corporate culture can't involve just the top executives; it must permeate the entire organization. And that's true for Ford, where the change has been accepted by all levels of management. For example, Joe Kordick, who heads Ford's Parts and Service division, supervises 7,600 employees with the guiding principles of "love" and "trust."[2]

FIGURE 13.1
Members of a Ford
Motor Company
Employee Involvement
Group.
SOURCE: Ford Motor Company
advertisement.

An essential element in fostering Ford's atmosphere of teamwork is international experience. Petersen himself headed international operations before becoming president in 1980. By now, virtually all top Ford executives have worked abroad. Teams, quality, listening to customers, and international experience are now key concepts at Ford.

What does this case illustrate about the role of organizational culture and change? ■

IT WAS SHOWN in Chapter 3 that organizations can have life cycles similar to those of civilizations. They can go through a period of growth and ascendancy and then a period of stagnation and decline—and even death. The decline process can be reversed, however, by a process of renewal and a new cycle of growth and ascendancy. The Opening Case highlights the fact that Ford has successfully undertaken such a process of renewal and development. In doing so, the company has changed its culture and ways of doing things.

This chapter examines the role organizational culture and change play in the process of organizational renewal and the development of excellence. It also looks at the management of conflict.

A word of caution is appropriate at this time. As you study this chapter, remember that some managers with more traditional views think change and conflict are undesirable and something to be resisted. It is important for new and younger managers to recognize this tendency and be prepared to deal with it if necessary.

WHY STUDY ORGANIZATIONAL CULTURE?

An organization's effectiveness is greatly influenced by its culture, which affects the way the managerial functions are performed. Managerial leadership is particularly influenced by the organization's culture.

Peters and Waterman, in their search for excellently managed companies, found that such companies have a "coherent culture."[3] Managers and employees generally prefer to work in an organization where (1) communication channels are open in all directions, (2) they can participate in decision making, (3) they have the opportunity to exercise considerable self-control, and (4) their work is evaluated on specific performance criteria, rather than on some arbitrary basis.

Definition of Organizational Culture

A definition that is widely accepted is that **organizational culture** is the set of values, beliefs, and behavior patterns that forms the core identity of an organization.[4] Marvin Bowen, for years managing director of McKinsey Company, defines it more succinctly as "the way we do things around here."[5]

The Role of Values

As indicated above, personal values, as reflected in beliefs and behavior patterns of managers and employees, influence most aspects of management. Thus, they define what the organization really is.

Values are those principles and qualities that are intrinsically desirable to us. They are the abstract ideals that shape our thinking and behavior. Values can be classified as (1) *instrumental values*, which are enduring beliefs that certain behaviors are appropriate at all times, and (2) *terminal values*, which are beliefs that certain more tangible objectives are worth striving for. TIPS 13.1 is a survey you may want to complete in order to evaluate your own value system.

Several years ago, a group of McKinsey consultants studied the question "What makes for consistently outstanding performance?" The group concluded that companies that did the best over the long haul were "those that believed in something." The members then offered slogans of outstanding companies that identified something they believed in and carried out in practice, including the following:

General Electric: "Progress is our most important product."

Du Pont: "Better things for better living through chemistry."

Chubb Insurance: "Excellence in underwriting."

IBM: "IBM means service."

What is your view?

Do you agree or disagree with the conclusion of the McKinsey consultants? What are the core values of Ford Motor Company as seen in the Opening Case?

Shortly after the McKinsey survey, an informal survey by the consultants of organizations with which they were familiar found the results shown in MAP 13.1. This is a profile of about 80 organizations.

TIPS 13.1   **The Rokeach Value Survey: Identifying Your Values**

Instructions

Study the two lists of values presented below. Then rank the instrumental values in order of importance to you (1 = most important, 18 = least important). Do the same with the list of terminal values.

Instrumental values	Terminal values
_____ Ambitious (hard-working, aspiring)	_____ A comfortable life (a prosperous life)
_____ Broadminded (open-minded)	_____ An exciting life (a stimulating, active life)
_____ Capable (competent, effective)	_____ A sense of accomplishment (lasting contribution)
_____ Cheerful (lighthearted, joyful)	_____ A world at peace (free of war and conflict)
_____ Clean (neat, tidy)	_____ A world of beauty (beauty of nature and the arts)
_____ Courageous (standing up for your beliefs)	_____ Equality (brotherhood, equal opportunity for all)
_____ Forgiving (willing to pardon others)	_____ Family security (taking care of loved ones)
_____ Helpful (working for the welfare of others)	_____ Freedom (independence, free choice)
_____ Honest (sincere, truthful)	_____ Happiness (contentedness)
_____ Imaginative (daring, creative)	_____ Inner harmony (freedom from inner conflict)
_____ Independent (self-sufficient)	_____ Mature love (sexual and spiritual intimacy)
_____ Intellectual (intelligent, reflective)	_____ National security (protection from attack)
_____ Logical (consistent, rational)	_____ Pleasure (an enjoyable, leisurely life)
_____ Loving (affectionate, tender)	_____ Salvation (saved, eternal life)
_____ Obedient (dutiful, respectful)	_____ Self-respect (self-esteem)
_____ Polite (courteous, well-mannered)	_____ Social recognition (respect, admiration)
_____ Responsible (dependable, reliable)	_____ True friendship (close companionship)
_____ Self-controlled (restrained, self-disciplined)	_____ Wisdom (a mature understanding of life)

SOURCE: Copyright 1967 by Milton Rokeach. Reproduced with permission from Halgren Tests, Sunnyvale, California.

Elements of Organizational Culture

The area of organizational culture has a rich vocabulary, including such terms as *heroes, rites, rituals, storytellers, priests, whispers, gossips, spies, myth,* and *legend.* For our purpose of understanding the importance of culture and its impact on performance, we will focus on the first three: heroes, rites, and rituals.

Heroes. *Heroes,* or those who provide role models and make attaining success and accomplishment human and possible, are essential to a strong organizational culture. They symbolize the values of the organization not only internally but also to the outside world. Not only do they preserve what makes the organization special, but they also set high standards and are masterful at creating a motivating environment. In an organization with a long history of a strong culture, some of the most notable heroes may still have significant influence even when they are no longer with the organization. Perhaps the most influential heroes are the ones who create an environment where many ordinary members can become heroes.

> ### Management Application and Practice 13.1   Belief Systems of Selected Outstanding Companies
>
> Of the companies surveyed by a group of McKinsey company consultants, only about a third (25) had clearly articulated beliefs.
>
> Of this third, nearly three-quarters (18) had qualitative beliefs or values, such as "IBM means service." The other third had financially oriented goals that were widely understood.
>
> Of the 18 companies with qualitative beliefs, all were uniformly outstanding performers. But no such correlations of any relevance were found among the other companies: Some did okay, some poorly; most had their ups and downs. The consistently high performers were characterized as "strong-culture companies."
>
> SOURCE: Terrence E. Deal and Allen A. Kennedy, *Corporate Culture* (Reading, MA: Addison-Wesley, 1981), p. 7.

The legendary Mary Kay Ash of Mary Kay Cosmetics is an example. She trains her salespeople not only to represent the firm but also to believe that they could do what she has done. To inspire them with her own confidence, Mary Kay awards diamond bumblebee pins to outstanding performers and explains that, according to aerodynamic engineers, the wings of the bumblebee are too weak to support its heavy body in flight. But bumblebees don't know this, and so they fly anyway. The message is clear: Anyone can be a hero given the confidence and persistence to try.[6]

Rites. At one time, Napoleon was criticized for awarding so many Legion of Honor medals. His reply was, "You lead men by baubles, not words." Napoleon understood that achievement deserves recognition and that recognition is a powerful motivator. Both rites and rituals call attention to and reinforce what is desired from organization members. *Rites* may be defined as relatively elaborate, dramatic, planned activities that combine various forms of cultural expressions and that often have both practical and expressive consequences.[7]

Rituals. *Rituals* are detailed methods and procedures faithfully or regularly followed. Among other things, a ritual can be the way an awards rite is carried out or the way a quality circle ideally functions. Rites and rituals can be designed for such activities as work, play, recognition, and management meetings.

Tandem corporation is a successful high-technology company without a long cultural history. Yet, in a relatively short time, it has developed a strong culture that has a tremendous impact on "the way we do things around here." Tandem's turnover rate is only a third of the national average, and it is known as a good place to work. Among other factors making Tandem a good place to work is a widely shared philosophy and an emphasis on people. There is no formal organizational chart, no reserved parking places, but instead an open-door policy at all levels. Many people participate in selecting new employees, and prospective candidates may be called back several times. They are also required to accept the position before salary is discussed. The message conveyed is: "We take longer, and we take care of the people we hire, because we really care."[8]

Tandem is also known for its play rituals, such as Friday afternoon beer busts and companywide celebrations on important holidays.

What is your view?

In your opinion, does the Tandem approach echo the paternalism of some firms of the 1920s—"Daddy will take care of you"? Why or why not?

Problems for the Organization Related to Organizational Culture

One major problem with emphasizing organizational culture is the risk of falsifying the corporate culture, or not doing what you say you will do. Employees are quite conscious of hypocrisy and will react negatively if management tries to practice it.

A classic example was a microcomputer manufacturer that was featured in several magazines, including Time, *as one of the rising stars of Silicon Valley. It hired a management consulting firm to meet behind closed doors with the president and vice-president to develop "Falcon Culture." These meetings were referred to as "culture meetings" and later as "values meetings." Eventually, a two-page culture document espousing—among other things—open communication, participative decision making, and ethical behavior toward customers was issued.*

The basic problem was that the firm did not practice what it preached. One of the values was: "Attention to detail is our trademark; our goal is to do it right the first time." However, even though employees at lower levels reported that a shipment of computers was defective, two members of the executive group decided to ship it anyway.

As a result of this type of performance, sales began slipping, and other aspects of the values statement were violated—secret meetings, firings without just cause, and so on. Yet, even as the firm declined into bankruptcy and the "culture statement" had become a joke to the employees, top management continued to hold "culture meetings." Today the firm is no longer in existence.[9]

Another pitfall of emphasizing corporate culture is that the culture may become rigid and not change when the outside environment changes. A related problem is having policies that may be impossible to carry out. For example, Procter & Gamble has historically had a strong corporate culture emphasizing customer satisfaction and employee relations. One of their employee relations values is a policy not to lay off employees. Although the odds are against a prolonged recession similar to the Depression of the 1930s occurring, such a situation would force Procter & Gamble to either reconsider this value or jeopardize stockholders' interests by rigidly adhering to it.

Participative Management and Organizational Culture

Drawing on survey and performance data for 34 corporations, a study covering five years showed that organizations that used participative management and had well-organized workplaces had better performance records than those that did not. Figure 13.2 compares return on sales for those firms that were high in participative decision making and those that were low. Initially the differences were small, but they grew progressively larger as participative management concepts were implemented. Marshall Sashkin also makes a strong case for participative management as an ethical imper-

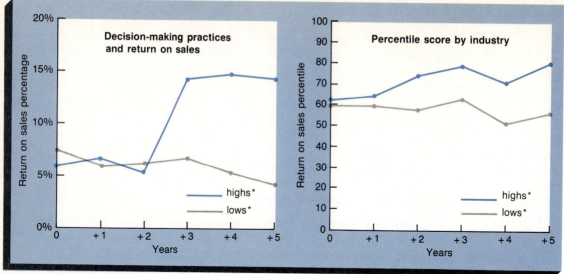

*Participation rates.

FIGURE 13.2

Comparison of return-on-sales rates for companies with high and low participative management (by percentage and percentile for a five-year period).

SOURCE: Daniel R. Denison, "Bringing Corporate Culture to the Bottom Line," *Organizational Dynamics* 13 (Autumn 1984): 16.

ative and asserts that over 50 years of action research "has demonstrated that participative management is, when properly applied, effective in improving performance, productivity, and job satisfaction."[10]

But another study, by Locke, Schweiger, and Latham, argues that "participation is not an ethical imperative but simply a managerial technique that is appropriate only in certain situations." These authors cite 50 studies in which the effects of job changes on decisions introduced participatively were compared with autocratic decisions. The results, shown in Table 13.1, highlight that 26 percent of participative decisions led to higher productivity, 26 percent of authoritarian decisions were superior, and in 49 percent of the cases studied, the results were the same or contingent on other factors.[11]

We believe that the difference in research findings results from varying definitions of "participation" and whether it was properly introduced. And we are convinced that there are an increasing number of situations in which participative management is appropriate for improving bottom-line performance. For example, A&P's 300 Super Fresh Food Markets, which trimmed wages but gave workers some say in running the stores, plus a bonus when sales revenues increased, are "the most successful part of our company," according to A&P's vice-president, Michael Rourke.[12]

What is participative management? **Participative management** is not permissive leadership, nor is it even democratic management in the sense of wholesale involvement of employees in decision making. Rather, it is a philosophy that states that under proper conditions employees should have the opportunity to make a significant contribution to solving problems, controlling costs, contributing to objectives, and assisting in managing and controlling the organization. Thus, not all situations call for participation, for people have to be developed and trained before they can effectively participate. Moreover, if the process is to be successful, key line managers and supervisors must be committed to and involved in it.

**TABLE 13.1
Results of 50 Studies of
Participation**

SOURCE: Edwin A. Locke, David
M. Schweiger, and Gary P.
Latham, "Participation in
Decision-Making: When Should
It Be Used?" *Organizational
Dynamics* 14 (Spring 1985): 65.

	Participative superior to authoritative methods		Authoritative superior to participative methods		No difference or differences only in certain groups within the study	
	Number	**Percent**	**Number**	**Percent**	**Number**	**Percent**
Participation in decision making	9	26%	9	26%	17	49%
Participation in goal setting	1	7	1	7	13	87
Total	10	20	10	20	30	60

Note: Percentages across first two columns are calculated from the bases of 35 studies and 15 studies, respectively.

According to many analysts—as well as employees and managers—of People Express airline, the inappropriate use of "democratic" and "participative" management led to its downfall and sale to Texas Air Corporation.*

Its policy of rotating all employees and managers and involving them in major decisions—such as acquiring Britt Airways, a commuter airline, and money-losing Frontier Airlines—added to People's other problems. According to Gerald Gitner, People's co-founder and former president, management's biggest mistake was letting participative management become "an end unto itself, rather than a means to execute strategy and make money."[13]

On the other hand, the participative management system used at GE's Bromont, Canada, compresser airfoil plant is given credit for the plant's "competitive edge." Under the program, three semi-autonomous teams have considerable voice in determining the best means of achieving production goals. The teams participate in important activities such as hiring, setting compensation methods, improving quality, and cutting costs and production time. The results: Labor costs were dropping at a rate of 20 percent in 1986, and only 16 parts were defective, out of more than 500,000 shipped.[14]

Where can participative management be used? Keeping in mind that this type of involvement should be implemented only when conditions are appropriate, it can be used (1) in setting goals; (2) in making decisions or choosing among alternative courses of action; (3) in solving problems, a process that includes the definition of issues and the generation of alternative courses of action as well as choice among the alternatives; and (4) in making changes in the organization (that is, in "organization development" activities).

---

* See the Chapter 5 Opening Case, "People Express—Growing Too Fast, Too Soon," for more details.

Rosabeth Kanter has developed a set of guidelines for the effective use of participative management. They are shown in Figure 13.3.

When should participative management not be used? Clearly, participative management should not be used if one person has greater expertise and there is no need for the others to have a degree of ownership in the decision. It would not be used in emergencies or when there is little time. It would not be used for routine matters, or when people do not have the ability or the inclination for participation.

TIPS 13.2 provides a questionnaire to help you estimate whether or not you are inclined to use the participative management culture.

Functions Performed by Organizational Culture

Organizational culture performs a number of important functions. Some of the most important of these are:[15]

1. To specify the goals and values toward which an organization should be directed and by which its success and worth should be evaluated.

2. To prescribe the appropriate relationships between individuals and the organization—that is, the psychological contract that indicates what the organization can reasonably expect from its people—and vice versa.

3. To indicate how behavior in the organization should be controlled, and the kinds of controls that are legitimate and those that are not.

4. To depict which qualities and characteristics of organization members should be valued or disapproved, as well as how they should be rewarded or punished.

5. To show members how they should treat one another—competitively or collaboratively, honestly or dishonestly, closely or distantly.

6. To establish appropriate means of coping with the external environment—aggressive exploitation, responsible negotiation, or proactive exploration.

FIGURE 13.3
When to use participative management.

SOURCE: Rosabeth Moss Kanter, "Dilemmas of Managing Participation," *Organizational Dynamics* 11 (Summer 1982): 25–26.

Participative management works best when the following conditions are met:

- A clearly designed management structure and involvement by the appropriate line people.
- Assignment of meaningful and manageable tasks with clear boundaries and parameters.
- A time frame, a set of accountability and reporting relationships, and standards that groups must meet.
- Information and training for participants to help them make participation work effectively.
- A mechanism for involving all of those with a stake in the issue in order to avoid the problems of power and to make sure that those who have input or interest have a chance to get involved.
- A mechanism for providing visibility, recognition, and rewards for teams' efforts.
- Clearly understood processes for the formation of participative groups, their dissolution, and the transfer of the learning.

TIPS 13.2 Am I Inclined Toward a Participative Management Culture?

If you were the newly appointed manager of an autonomous or semi-autonomous division, how prepared psychologically would you be to create a culture of participative management? The answers to the following questionnaire will give you some insight. Circle the number that fits you best.

	Strongly disagree	Disagree	Don't know	Agree	Strongly agree
1. Philosophically, I agree more with Theory Y assumptions about people than Theory X assumptions (discussed in Chapter 11).	1	2	3	4	5
2. When a difficult problem develops that affects the entire division, I would appoint a small task force to develop action planning recommendations as opposed to solving the problem alone or assigning it to one individual.	1	2	3	4	5
3. I feel comfortable with a shared leadership philosophy and using participative management with the managers reporting directly to me.	1	2	3	4	5
4. I sincerely believe that internally team cooperation is a stronger force than individual competition in achieving effective results.	1	2	3	4	5
5. I would tend to ask employees' opinions when a problem comes up that involves their work.	1	2	3	4	5
6. If the home office recognized our division as the top-producing division in the company, I would be generous in sharing the credit and providing recognition to others as opposed to claiming the credit myself.	1	2	3	4	5

Scoring

Add up the numbers for the six statements. If you scored from 24 to 30, your self-assessment indicates that you are psychologically inclined to create a climate of participative management. Of course, a way to validate your self-assessment is to have the people reporting to you complete the questionnaire on the basis of their perception of how you operate in practice.

The organizational culture that is most effective is one that is receptive to change. So let's look at the problem of managing organizational change.

MANAGING ORGANIZATIONAL CHANGE

You've heard the adage that nothing is certain but death and taxes. But a third term could be added—*change.* In management, change is expected as part of everyday life. Some examples are (1) a new method of doing the work, (2) a new product or service, (3) a new organization structure, and (4) changes in personnel policy or employee benefits. Change is now occurring at an explosive rate, and it may accelerate in the 1990s to the point of becoming impossible to predict.

Forces Causing Change

As discussed in previous chapters, numerous factors affect an organization, and most of these are continuously changing. These forces leading to or causing change originate both outside and within the organization, as shown in Figure 13.4.

You might compare this situation to yourself as a human organism. You respond to external stimuli, such as the temperature outside, whether it's raining or sunny, the work schedule for the day, and situations that arise during the day. You also respond, however, to internal stimuli, such as your need for food, whether you feel alert and well rested, whether you have a cold or fever, or your mood. Substitute an organization for yourself, and we have a very similar situation.

External change forces. Although it is difficult to generalize, it seems that **external change forces** have a greater effect on organizational change than internal stimuli, since management has little control over them and they are so numerous. Yet an organization depends on and must interact with its external environment if it is to survive; its resources are obtained from outside, as are the clients and customers for its products and services. Therefore, anything that interferes with or modifies that environment can affect the organization's operations and cause pressure for change.

Certainly, organizational change occurs because of changes in external variables such as political systems, economics, markets, technology, and values. Who, for example, would have predicted the soaring rate of inflation and mortgage interest rates or the far-reaching effects of deregulation on banking, transportation, and communication we experienced in the early 1980s? Could anyone have foreseen that the rising cost of petroleum products would combine with antipollution legislation to force automobile manufacturers to concentrate on improving the gas mileage and reducing the size of their cars? Now these trends are changing businesses that cater to the tourist trade. Airlines are changing their equipment, routes, speeds, and altitudes to reduce fuel costs. Or, who foresaw the stock market plunge of October 19, 1987? In summary, there is an enormous variety of external forces, from technological discoveries to changing life-styles, that can pressure the organization to change its goals, structure, and methods of operation.

What is your view?

Suppose you were the director and owner of a 30-bed nursing home. What are some kinds of external change factors that might have an impact on your organization?

Internal change forces. Pressures for change may also come from within the organization. These **internal change forces** result from factors such as new organization objectives and cultures—such as that at Ford Motor Company—managerial policies, technologies, and employee attitudes. For example, top-management's decision to shift its goal from long-term growth to short-run profit will affect the goals of many departments and may even lead to reorganization. The introduction of automated equipment and robots to perform work that was previously done by people will cause changes in work layout and routine, incentive programs, and personnel policies and procedures. Worker attitudes may also lead to many changes in management policies and practices.

FIGURE 13.4
External and internal
change forces.

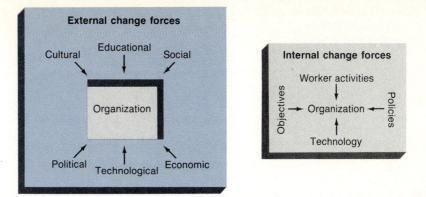

External and internal forces for change, however, are not found in isolation, but are often interrelated. This linkage often results from changes in values and attitudes that affect people in the system. Some of these people enter the organization and cause it to change from within. For example, many of the changes now occurring in organizations are the result of the activist attitudes of the 1960s and early 1970s concerning pollution, equal employment opportunity, product safety, and equal rights for women.

**Results of
Ignoring Change**

Institutions in our society, including business organizations, help preserve many things of worth from the past. These include values and social, cultural, and technological innovations. This role of institutions is important in connecting the past, present, and future and allowing the continuation of a high standard of living. On the other hand, to protect themselves against further change, institutions harden their resistance by formalizing rituals, customs, and traditions. This resistance sometimes leads to inability to cope with a new environment and paves the way for stagnation, decline, and failure. Thus, unless an organization plans for and copes effectively with the challenge of change, the results can be disastrous. The same reasoning applies to managers and employees, who face change at an even more accelerated pace. An example is the Itel Corporation, a computing and transportation leasing company on the West Coast.

> *At the beginning of 1979, Itel Corporation was booming. Its stock had risen from $18.00 to $39.00 a share in six months, it had reached its first billion-dollar year, and its marketing employees were, as the Wall Street Journal reported, "living high on the hog."[16]*
>
> *The newspaper continued, "Itel Corp.'s 1979 junket to Acapulco feted its hottest marketing men with fireworks and bugle fanfares, champagne, and showers of rose petals. 'It was like Fantasy Island,' recalls a former Itel man. [It was] an extravaganza that wined and dined some 1,300 employees and spouses at a month-long show that cost the company some $3 million."*
>
> *By the end of 1979, Itel had lost $226 million in six months, slashed employees from 7000 to 1000, and seen its stock drop 79 percent, to $5.00 a share. What happened? According to the Wall Street Journal article, "Itel's expansion ran on heedless of bad news in the market and almost unchecked by any controls until it was too late." Particularly damaging*

FIGURE 13.5
Two organizational
change approaches.

Proactive process (Takes place before the problem occurs)	Problem	Reactive process (Takes place after the problem occurs)

was a new computer model marketed by IBM in 1979 that took business away from Itel. In short, the company had ignored changes occurring in the marketplace and had failed to develop contingency plans to adapt to a changing environment.

Ways of Dealing with Change

Management is often defined as the art and science of getting things done through people. Thus, favorable change can be brought about only by working through people.

There are two major ways of dealing with organizational change, as shown in Figure 13.5. The first is a **reactive process** of change, whereby management adapts in a piecemeal, one-step-at-a-time manner in order to deal with problems or issues as they arise. The second is for management to use the **proactive process** of change and develop a program of **planned change.**

The reactive process. The reactive process tries to keep the organization on a steady course by solving problems as they come up. For example, if you are a department store manager and complaints about sales clerks suddenly increase, you might set up a short training program to correct the problem. If one of your major suppliers goes bankrupt, you quickly search for another source of supply. If new government regulations require you to have better fire protection, you buy more and better extinguishers. In each of these cases, you initiate change by *reacting* to something that has already happened.

This approach involves little planning and is usually not viewed by managers as "threatening," since it is aimed at solving a current, visible problem. Over a period of time, however, a series of small, incremental problems can add up to a significant change in an organization. And sometimes the end result is not desirable.

Planned change. On the other hand, planned change involves deliberate actions to modify the status quo. It is *proactive* in that it sets out to change things by setting a new course rather than correcting the current one. Also, planned change seeks to anticipate changes in the external and internal environments and deals with ways of coping with those predicted new conditions. Because of the rapidity and complexity of changes in today's world, we feel that managers must understand and utilize planned organizational change.

What is your view?

Take a moment to review the Opening Case. What type of action did the new management take? Why?

What Should Be Changed?

If management wants to plan for change, then it must decide what needs to be changed in the organization. In general, managers seek to change those elements that are preventing greater organizational effectiveness. **Organizational effectiveness** is the result of activities that improve the organization's structure, technology, and people.

All elements must be changed. The choice of the particular technique used to achieve organizational change depends on the nature of the problem that is causing the organization to be less than ideally effective. Management must determine which alternative is most likely to produce the desired outcome. The diagnosis of the problem includes specifying the outcome that management desires from the change. In general, the desired outcome is improved employee behavior that will result in improved performance. This can be achieved by changing the organization's structure, technology, and people.

This classification of organizational elements in no way implies a distinct division among them. According to the systems concept, a change in one element will likely affect other elements. In general, the more change that is required, the more likely it is that management will change all three elements.

As you can see from Figure 13.6, management must decide (1) the desired outcomes and (2) the type of change programs to use to (3) change the specific organizational element.

Changing the structure. Changing the organization's *structure* involves modifying and rearranging the internal relationships. It requires modifying variables such as authority-responsibility relationships, communications systems, work flows, and size and composition of work groups.

Changing technology. Changing the organization's *technology* may require altering or modifying such factors as its tools, equipment, and machinery; research direction and techniques; engineering processes; and production system, including layout, methods, and procedures. Changing technology may result from, or contribute to, changing tasks to be performed. For example, mechanization changes the very nature of the work that employees do.

FIGURE 13.6
Organizational effectiveness results from changing structure, technology, and people.

Changing people. Changing the organization's *people* may include changing (1) recruiting and selection policies and procedures; (2) training and devel-

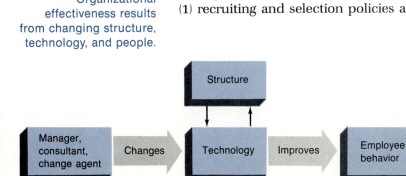

opment activities; (3) reward systems; (4) managerial leadership and communication.

Structure and technology are covered elsewhere in the text; therefore, at this point we will emphasize the people factor in this discussion. We will try to illustrate how changing the organization's structure, technology, and people improves employee behavior, leading to greater organizational effectiveness, as shown in Figure 13.6.

Reactions to Change

When change occurs, both managers and employees will react—whether positive or negative, there will be some reaction. In fact, **resistance to change** _can always be expected when a substantial change is proposed._ Notice that this reaction is almost universal. The change may be for the better or for the worse, may help or harm employees; but the initial reaction tends to be resistance. Gradually, however, as its benefits become known, positive change is accepted. People tend to react to the social, or human, aspects of change more than to the technical aspects.

Here are some typical reactions to change.

1. _People may deny that change is taking place._ The organization will probably continue to lose its effectiveness when this happens.

    For example, many American and Swiss watchmakers did not believe that people would buy digital watches when they were first introduced. Most firms, instead of offering the public a choice of regular and digital watches, either were forced out of business or introduced the new watches only after such firms as Texas Instruments had taken away most of their market.

2. _People may ignore the change._ Managers may simply put off decisions in the hope that the problems will go away.

What is your view?

Consider the initial reaction of domestic auto firms to the increased sale of small foreign cars resulting from the increased cost and decreased availability of gasoline. Have you seen other evidence of situations in which organizations choose to ignore change? Explain.

3. _People tend to resist the change._ As indicated, people almost always resist change at first. Reasons for this resistance may be (1) emotional, (2) economic, or (3) social, or it may be due to (4) fear of failure, (5) fear of the unknown, or (6) unwillingness to give up existing benefits or programs.

4. _People may accept the change and adapt to it,_ recognizing it as a new way of life.

"I don't like the new organization structure much," said Anne Simon, the director of nursing at City Hospital. "Under the new setup, I report to the assistant administrator instead of the administrator, as in the past. But things weren't all that good before, either, because the administrator was always so tied up that it was tough to get in to see him. I feel like I've lost some status now, though, and so do the others who'll be reporting to the *assistant. But it might turn out to be a good thing if the assistant is more accessible. I'll give it a try, anyway, before I make any waves."*

5. *People may also anticipate change and plan for it*, as the more progressive firms do.

Managers and employees are likely to support change if it is directed at the *real* cause of the problem, is *an effective solution*, and doesn't affect them adversely. A neutral response—a "wait and see" attitude—is probably the most frequent response of employees.

Most managers consider resistance bad. But is it? What if the employees see problems in the changed policies that the manager hasn't anticipated? How will the change affect the organization's "social system"? When there is resistance, managers should reexamine the proposed change to see whether they can find a solution acceptable to all. And that change must be brought about through people.

The Process of Managing Change

The management of change requires the use of some systematic process that can be broken down into steps or subprocesses. Many models can be used for this process, but one of the most logical and popular ones emphasizes the role of the change agent. A **change agent** is the individual, usually from outside the unit or organization being changed, who takes a leadership role in initiating and introducing the change process. As you study this change process, notice that it must involve two basic ideas if the change is to lead to organizational effectiveness. First, there is a redistribution of power within the organizational structure. Second, this redistribution results from a developmental change process.

Phases of the change process. The proposed change process, as you can see from Figure 13.7, goes through six phases:

1. Pressure and arousal.
2. Intervention and reorientation.
3. Diagnosis and recognition of problem(s).
4. Invention of and commitment to new solutions.
5. Experimentation and search for results.
6. Reinforcement and acceptance.

Phase 1: Pressure and arousal. The process begins when top management begins to feel a need or pressure for change. This is usually caused by some significant problem(s), such as a sharp decline in sales or profits, serious labor unrest, and/or high labor turnover.

Phase 2: Intervention and reorientation. An outside consultant or change agent is often brought in to define the problem and begin the process of getting organization members to focus on it. Internal staff people may be capable of managing the process if they are perceived as expert and are trusted.

Phase 3: Diagnosis and recognition of problem(s). Information is gathered and analyzed by the change agent and management. The most important problems are recognized and given attention.

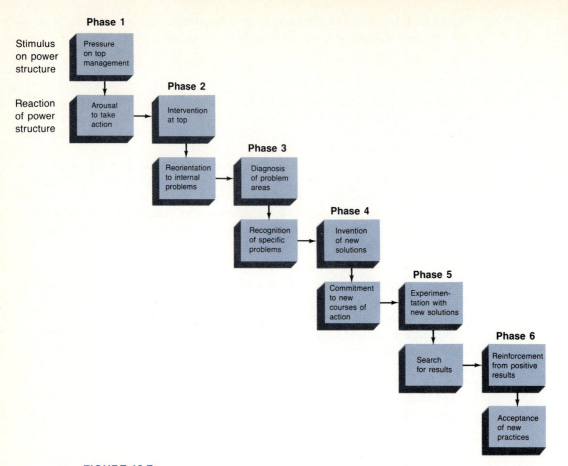

FIGURE 13.7
Model of the change process.

Phase 4: Invention and commitment to solutions. The change agent should stimulate thought and find solutions by creatively developing new and plausible alternatives. If subordinates are encouraged to participate in this process, they will probably be more committed to the course of action finally chosen.

Phase 5: Experimentation and search for results. The solutions developed in Phase 4 are usually tested in small-scale pilot programs and the results analyzed. One unit, or a certain part of a unit, may try out an idea before it is tried in the organization as a whole.

Phase 6: Reinforcement and acceptance. If the course of action has been tested and found desirable, it should be accepted more willingly. Improved performance should be a source of reinforcement and thus should lead to a commitment to the change.

Ensuring That the Change Is Permanent

Change requires that organization members modify the ways in which they usually behave or work. Therefore, managers must be able not only to improve the structure-technology-people relationships in the organization but also to make the changes in such a way that other related human behavior is changed most effectively. Effective change occurs only when organization members modify their behavior in the desired direction. The change may be permanent if behavioral changes are properly made. Otherwise, they may be only temporary.

Sociologist Kurt Lewin noticed that change often lasted only a short time before people and conditions reverted to their former state.[17] According to Lewin, behavioral change, if it is to be effective, involves three related conditions experienced by an individual: unfreezing, changing, and refreezing, as shown in Figure 13.8.

Unfreezing. Unfreezing is the state in which you would become ready to acquire or learn new behavior. You would recognize the ineffectiveness of your present behavior patterns and be ready to attempt to learn new behavior that would make you more effective. It might be difficult, though, for you to "thaw out" because of positive attitudes you associate with your past behavior.

Changing. Changing occurs when you begin experimenting with new behavior. You try the new behavior patterns in the hope that they will increase your effectiveness.

Refreezing. Refreezing has occurred when you see that the new behavior patterns you have experimented with during "changing" are now part of you. You feel comfortable performing the new behavior and now see it as part of your normal method of operation. Any rewards you receive as a result of performing the new behavior are very instrumental in refreezing.

What is your view?

Can you think of an instance in your own life when you have gone through the unfreezing, change, and refreezing processes?

USING ORGANIZATIONAL DEVELOPMENT (OD) TO PROMOTE CHANGE

Many institutions attempt to cope with changes by developing innovative ways not only to deal with change but also to promote it. One of these

FIGURE 13.8
Behavioral changes involve unfreezing, changing, and refreezing.

innovative methods is a management concept and approach called *organizational development (OD)*. This approach is not perceived in the same way by all its practitioners and experts, but we feel that the concept shows great promise for helping organizations go through a process of change and revitalization, especially in shifting to a more participative culture.

What Is OD?   **Organizational development** (**OD**) may be defined as a planned, organizationwide effort, managed from the top, to increase organizational effectiveness through planned interventions in the organization's processes, using behavioral-science knowledge.[18] While the effort should be "managed from the top," this does not necessarily mean by the chief executive officer. Instead, "the top" could be the dean of a college in a university or, in a large corporation, the manager of a branch plant or even the head of a major department. Some OD experts give the impression that OD cannot occur in an organization without the aid of either an outside or an internal consultant. However, a healthy organization can develop itself using regular managers and employees as the primary OD practitioners.

What is your view?

Would you characterize the change in Ford Motor Company as OD?

The objectives of typical OD efforts include the following:

1. To increase the level of trust and support among organization members.

2. To create an environment in which the authority of an assigned role is increased by personal authority based on expertise and knowledge.

3. To increase the level of personal—and group—responsibility in planning and implementation.

4. To increase the openness of communication between organization members.

5. To find synergistic solutions to problems with greater frequency. (**Synergy,** as discussed in Chapter 8, is the action of two or more organisms working together to achieve an effect of which each alone is incapable.)

A Basic OD Model   As with other aspects of planned organizational change, it is important to have models to keep in mind when we are reading and thinking about and discussing OD. Perhaps the most popular model is the **action-research model**—Figure 13.9—which can be used in several contexts, organizations, or organizational units.

In one way, the *research-diagnosis phase* is similar to a doctor's diagnostic method. Like a doctor learning the patient's medical history and present symptoms, the manager or change agent gathers information from members of the organization. Often this information encompasses organizational strengths, problems, and opportunities or more specific questions. The difference between the doctor's diagnosis and the change agent's is that the change agent often provides feedback to organization members so that they can help in developing plans that are concerned with specific actions to be

FIGURE 13.9
Action-research model
of OD.

SOURCE: Wendell L. French, Cecil H. Bell, Jr., and Robert A. Zawocki, *Organization Development Theory, Practice, and Research* (Dallas: Business Publications, Inc., 1978), p. 15.

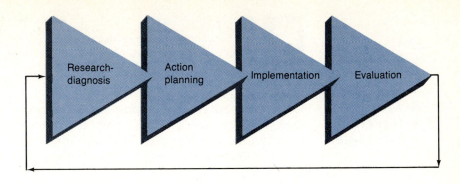

taken. In other words, organization members help to write their own prescriptions.

The data gathered by the change agent are assembled, synthesized, and summarized, with members of the organization helping to develop action plans *(action-planning phase)* that are then implemented *(implementation phase)*. The *evaluation phase* sometimes employs the same methods used in the research-diagnosis phase so that OD becomes an ongoing process. Let us illustrate the action-research model with a class in principles of management taught by a young, inexperienced instructor.

Two weeks into the semester, Professor Clark noticed that students were beginning to cut class, and some were even sleeping during lectures. She decided to try the action-research and feedback process in an effort to improve class performance and to create a more effective learning environment.

She asked members of the class to respond, anonymously and in writing, to two questions: What are the strengths of this class? What are the problems that are preventing this class from reaching its potential effectiveness? In summarizing the responses, she was dismayed to find that very few strengths were given and the top-ranked problem was that "the class was dry and boring."

Professor Clark reported the findings to the class and divided them into teams to analyze the problem. The consensus of the teams was that it was dry and boring because (1) it was offered at 1:00 in the afternoon, when most of the students had just eaten lunch and were sleepy; (2) the text was highly theoretical, with few examples of practical applications; and (3) the lectures were primarily a rehash of the text, and a course that uses lectures exclusively is a very passive form of learning.

When the groups were asked to make recommendations on what could be done to make the class more effective, they suggested (1) using more real-world management examples and bringing in executives as guest lecturers; (2) using short cases, critical incidents, and experiential learning exercises to illustrate the text; and (3) requiring students to work occasionally in their groups to develop case reports and presentations.

The text could not be changed, and time did not permit bringing in guest lecturers, but the other suggestions were implemented. At the end of the semester, students evaluated the course as "excellent" and indicated that the change in approach had created an effective, stimulating learning environment.

Selected OD Intervention Strategies

While there are many OD intervention strategies that can be used, we shall limit our focus to examining three that are particularly useful in changing an organization's effectiveness. These interventions are (1) Likert's System 4, (2) confrontation meeting, and (3) quality of work life (QWL) programs and quality circles (QC).

Likert's System 4.[19] Recall that we discussed Likert's System 4 (Participative Group) in Chapter 12. This OD intervention strategy emphasizes democracy and participation in organizations, together with a focus on goal attainment. It is particularly useful in changing an organization's culture from a System 1 or 2 to a System 3 or 4. There is one large paper company that is attempting to shift many of its mills from an environment of Benevolent Autocracy to System 3 and 4. It has an outside consulting firm that is working with one division at a time before shifting to another division, since the transformation takes time. One General Motors assembly plant successfully used this method to move from System 2 to System 4. It conducted training sessions about System 4 management, held team-building sessions at all organizational levels, and improved both hourly workers' and foremen's jobs. Performance increased dramatically, while grievances and costs decreased.[20]

Confrontation meeting. The confrontation meeting was developed by Richard Beckhard and is particularly useful for organizations that don't have time to spend on a more in-depth OD program. A **confrontation meeting** resolves problems of organization performance by generating and analyzing data about group problems and then formulating action plans to respond to them. These are usually one-day meetings and generally follow this procedure:

1. A top manager introduces the issues and goals.
2. Operating in small groups, participants gather information about organizational problems.
3. A representative from each group reports on its findings.
4. Formed into natural work groups, participants set priorities for the problems and determine early action steps.
5. A top-management team continues to meet to plan follow-up action.
6. The group reconvenes four to six weeks later to report on progress.

A key point to note is that although natural work groups are involved, top management plays a key role in initiating and continuing the process.

Qualify of work life (QWL) programs and quality circles (QC). In response to Japanese competition in the automobile industry, Ford Motor Company and General Motors Corporation have worked with the United Automobile Workers union to implement **qualify of work life (QWL) programs.**[21] Although commitment to a QWL program comes from top management, action plans are developed by employee and supervisory groups from below. Essentially, a QWL program systematically studies factors such as working conditions, jobs performed, supervision, company policy, and others that affect the conditions of the work environment. Under the programs at GM and Ford (see Figure 13.1 in Opening Case), teams of 3 to 12 workers from different departments focus on diagnosing and recommending solutions to various QWL problems.

In one reported study from two plants, the programs resulted in substantial dollar savings and greatly increased supervisor and employee participation in job-related problem solving.

An integral part of most QWL programs are quality circles. **Quality circles** (QC) are small groups of workers, along with a supervisory leader, who belong to the same division or unit of the plant. For best results, membership in a QC should be voluntary. The group meets regularly, say once a week or twice a month, to identify problem areas, investigate the causes of the problems, and recommend solutions for management. TIPS 13.3 gives some suggestions for the most effective use of quality circles. Problems and opportunities can be brought up by QC members, operating managers, or staff personnel. QC sessions are neither gripe nor bull sessions, and the groups usually receive training in decision-making techniques.

Promise and Limitations of OD

OD is not a panacea for all organizational problems. It requires the support of top management and has worked much better in some environments than in others. For example, it seems to be more effective in organizations with an existing climate that favors a participative, problem-solving approach to achieving effective results.

Promise. The ultimate promise of OD is that when successfully applied it enables the organization to remove obstacles to individual and organizational development and renewal. Certainly, more and more organizations are now using OD. For example, there has been widespread use in the military. The U.S. Army, with the full support of its chief of staff, has trained over 400 OD consultants to work with various units on a decentralized basis.[22] The navy's program is more centralized and relies heavily on action research and survey feedback.

TIPS 13.3   How to Implement Effective Quality Circles (QC)

1. Managers at all levels, especially at the top, should be committed to the concept and give it their unqualified support.
2. Only volunteers should be allowed to participate in the program.
3. Projects undertaken should relate directly—or at least indirectly—to participants' work.
4. Projects should be team efforts, not individual activities.
5. Participants should be trained in effective quality control and problem-solving techniques.
6. Circle leaders should also be trained in group dynamics and leadership of workers as a group.
7. QC groups should be given feedback regarding their recommendations and solutions.

SOURCE: Donald C. Mosley, Leon C. Megginson, and Paul H. Pietri, Jr., *Supervisory Management*, 2nd ed. (Cincinnati: South-Western Publishing, 1989), Chapter 16.

Limitations. Perhaps you are wondering, "If OD is so promising, why aren't more groups and organizations practicing it?" There are several reasons for this. First, we have only begun to learn within the last three decades how to use the process of change and growth within organizations. Second, OD is a complex process and requires considerable organization. Third, it has not always been successful.[23]

One study that has examined most of the research in this area concluded that change efforts succeed most often in the following:

1. Profit-seeking organizations.
2. Task environments that are long-term stable and short-term unstable.
3. When the parties involved are willing to collaborate.
4. When the change agent has a participative orientation.
5. If the solution is focused on a mix of organizational relationships.
6. If change efforts are directed at the total organization.
7. If change efforts employ standardized strategies that involve high levels of participation.[24]

CONFLICT MANAGEMENT

A chapter on change and development would not be complete without a discussion of **conflict management.** One problem often encountered in OD programs is excessive conflict between either individuals or departments. Even more significant is the amount of time a manager spends in dealing with conflict. A few years ago, a survey of middle- and higher-level managers indicated that approximately 20 percent of their time was spent dealing with

VIETOR'S **FUNNY BUSINESS**

"Hang on, Griswold! Don't give up the turf!"

(Copyright 1987, USA TODAY. Used with permission.)

conflict, and conflict management skills were becoming increasingly important to their effectiveness.[25]

Conflict can be defined as any kind of opposition or antagonistic interaction between two or more parties. Thus it can be viewed as a range of
possibilities. At one extreme, there is no conflict; the other extreme is conflict's highest state, the act of destroying or annihilating the opposing party.
All types of interpersonal, intragroup, and intergroup conflicts would fall
somewhere along this continuum.

There are two significant points that should be made before we go any
further. First, *conflict is inevitable in organizations*. Whenever people interact,
there will be some negative interactions. Second, *conflict is not inherently
negative or destructive*. Rather, it often leads to desirable change.

Causes of Conflict

Conflicts usually arise in an organization as a result of problems in communication, organizational structure, or personal relationships. Let us briefly
examine each of these causes.

1. *Communication:* misunderstandings due to semantics, unfamiliar language, or ambiguous or incomplete information.
2. *Structure:* power struggles between departments with conflicting objectives or reward systems, competition for scarce resources, or inter-
   dependence of two or more groups to achieve their goals.
3. *Personal:* incompatibility of personal goals or social values of employees
   with the role behavior required by their jobs.

Certain personality characteristics, such as authoritarianism or dogma-
tism, may also lead to conflict.

*Mark Johnson, president and chief executive of ABC National Bank, was
worried about his two chief executive officers, Jim Smith and Jackie
Jones, who were barely speaking to each other. The two officers' antagonistic behavior toward one another was beginning to affect morale and
the bank's effectiveness. Personnel throughout the bank were choosing
sides, and even some bank customers were aware of the conflict.*

*Three months earlier, Mark had called Jim and Jackie into his office
and requested that they settle their differences and work more effectively
together. Unfortunately, Mark's request had not been heeded, and more
decisive action must now be taken.*

What is your view?

What do you see as some alternative ways Mark Johnson could proceed in
dealing with the conflict between Jim and Jackie? What do you think would be
the best alternative?

The situation just presented was triggered by a combination of structural
and personal factors. Before the conflict erupted, several changes had occurred. The bank had employed a management consulting firm that had
recommended a reorganization of the bank that was implemented by the
president and the board of directors. Jackie Jones, under the old organization, had had 70 percent of the departments and employees reporting to
her. Now, Jim Smith, under the new organization, wound up with 70 percent

under his jurisdiction, including some key departments that had previously reported to Jackie Jones. The personalities of the two officers were entirely different in that Jackie was much more autocratic and authoritarian in her relationships with others. This fact was a primary reason for the consulting firm's recommendation to shift key departments in the reorganization.

The conflict was aggravated because Mark Johnson was retiring as president in two years, and both vice-presidents wanted to succeed him. Under these conditions, both officers were competing intensely for the top job, and the resulting power struggle was causing dysfunctional consequences in the bank.

Conflict Resolution: What Works?

A study focusing on approaches managers use to resolve conflict identified four methods—forcing, problem solving, compromise, and avoidance.[26] The two preferred methods were *forcing* (one party uses superior power to impose a solution) and *problem solving* (parties to the conflict seek a solution that will satisfy the goals of each). The study revealed that if one approach did not work, a fallback approach was then used. The study concluded that each approach has its merits in certain situations. It found that problem solving was more successful in settling conflicts caused by communication difficulties, whereas forcing was the only method used with any success in conflicts of personal values or personality.

Table 13.2 shows some situational indicators that can be used to help choose the appropriate method of managing a conflict.

TABLE 13.2 Situational Indicators to Be Used in Choosing a Resolution Method

SOURCE: Eleanor Phillips and Ric Cheston, "Conflict Resolution: What Works?" *California Management Review* 21 (Summer 1979): 82.

Indicator	Use problem solving	Use forcing
Conflict issue	Goal agreement Joint work relationship Good communication	"One best way" Values conflict Scarce resources Subordinate discipline
Power relationships	Peers, equal power Coalition Power not an issue	Superior-subordinate Unequal political power Control of resources
Existing procedures	Review committee Objective criteria Equal representation of involved parties	Arbitration method Adjudication committee No agreement on criteria Unequal representation of parties
Climate for resolution	Trust, regard for others Open-mindedness History of problem solving No previous history of conflict Group goals oriented to corporate goals	Personal antagonism History of forcing Continuing and bitter conflict Strong adversary relationship
Potential for recurrence of conflict	Conflict inherent in structure of situation Need for ongoing conflict resolution	Eliminate recurrence by task change or removal or transfer of personnel

SUMMARY

This chapter has examined the role organizational culture plays in the process of organizational renewal and development. We defined organizational culture as the set of values, beliefs, and behavior patterns that forms the core identity of an organization. Values especially play an important role in the development of a strong culture, and companies with strong qualitative beliefs and values tend to be consistently strong performers. Other elements that make up a company's culture include heroes, rites, and rituals. Some problems with organizational culture are falsifying the corporate culture—not doing what you proclaim to do—and becoming rigid and not changing the culture when the outside environment changes.

Today participative management is an ethical imperative, and although it is not appropriate in all situations, there is an increasing number of situations where it is appropriate. We developed a viewpoint of what participative management is and suggested guidelines for its use.

We then showed that, unless organizations cope effectively with challenge and change, the results can be disastrous, for institutions are inclined to become bureaucratic and to resist change. There are internal and external forces affecting change, and they must be considered in any change program. There are two ways of dealing with change—reacting to it or being proactive and planning for it.

The process of managing change includes six phases: (1) pressure and arousal, (2) intervention and reorientation, (3) diagnosis and recognition of problem(s), (4) intervention of and commitment to solutions, (5) experimentation and search for results, and (6) reinforcement and acceptance of new practices. The change process involves unfreezing old attitudes and behavior, changing these, and refreezing them.

Next, we defined organizational development (OD) and named the objectives of typical OD efforts. After explaining the action-research model of OD, we discussed three popular intervention strategies. We noted that in many change programs there is a need to shift an organization to a more participative, problem-solving orientation. So we examined Likert's System 4, confrontation meetings, and quality of work life (QWL) programs and quality circles (QCs) to see how they could be used to achieve that objective. Then we examined some promises and limitations of OD.

We also discussed conflict management. It was noted that a survey indicated that managers spend approximately 20 percent of their time dealing with conflict. The three primary sources of conflict are problems in communication, personal relationships, and organization structure. There are several ways to manage conflict, and two of the most widely used are forcing and problem solving. Problem solving seems to be the most successful in dealing with conflicts caused by communication difficulties, whereas forcing is necessary in dealing with conflicts of personal values and personality.

REVIEW QUESTIONS

1. What is organizational culture?
2. What roles do values play in developing a strong culture?
3. What are some of the problems with organizational culture?

4. What is participative management and what is it *not*?
5. What are some significant external change forces that have had an impact on organizations in the 1980s?
6. What are the two major ways of dealing with change? Explain each.
7. What are some typical reactions to change?
8. What are the usual phases of the change process?
9. What are some of the objectives of typical OD efforts?
10. Briefly identify what takes place in each phase of the action-research model of OD.
11. How can quality circles be used to change an organization's effectiveness?

DISCUSSION QUESTIONS

1. How could an OD approach be used to convert a highly structured system with an autocratic style of management to a more open system with a participative style of management? Assume that the change is necessary because of low morale and declining profits.
2. Discuss the reasons why participative management seems to be effective in an increasing number of situations. Does this trend negate the contingency theory of management?
3. Discuss the role a strong culture plays in an organization's development.
4. Do you agree that "change" should be added to the old adage "Nothing is sure but death and taxes"?
5. What are some of the primary reasons people resist change? What are some of the ways a manager can ensure that change is accepted or at least not resisted?
6. Discuss the limitations and promise of OD as a change strategy to move an organization from one state of development to an improved state.
7. Is all conflict undesirable? Explain.

LEARNING EXERCISE 13.1

You as an Entrepreneur

Assume you start your own business sometime after graduation. It can be any business of your choice that has a good opportunity for growth. After 10 years, the business has become quite successful and now employs 102 people.

1. Identify the business you have chosen.
2. Assume that initially you believed there is a positive correlation between having a strong culture and business success. Identify the specific actions you have consequently taken over a 10-year period to develop a strong organizational culture.

LEARNING EXERCISE 13.2

The Participative Management Debate

Debate the issue: *Participative management is an ethical imperative that will pay dividends on the bottom line.*

Divide the class into three groups, one debating the affirmative side and one the negative; the third group determines who has won the debate and why.

LEARNING EXERCISE 13.3

Organizational Development in Action*

Several years ago, one of us was contacted by the vice-president and division manager of a chemical division of a large corporation to help with an unprofitable plant in

---

* This case was first reported in Donald C. Mosley, "System Four Revisited: Some New Insights," *Organization Development Journal* 5 (Spring 1987): 19–24.

FIGURE 13.10
Profile of Organizational Characteristics.

SOURCE: *Organization Development Journal* 5 (Spring 1987): 23.

May 1985		June 1986		
System 1	System 2	System 3	System 4	
Virtually none	Some	Substantial amount	A great deal	1. How much confidence and trust is shown in subordinates?
Not very free	Somewhat free	Quite free	Very free	2. How free do they feel to talk to superiors about job?
Seldom	Sometimes	Often	Very frequently	3. How often are subordinate's ideas sought and used constructively?
1, 2, 3 occasionally 4	4, some 3	4, some 3 and 5	5, 4 based on group-set goals	4. Is predominant use made of (1) fear, (2) threats, (3) punishment, (4) rewards, (5) involvement?
Mostly at top	Top and middle	Fairly general	At all levels	5. Where is responsibility felt for achieving organization's goals?
Very little	Relatively little	Moderate amount	Great deal	6. How much cooperative teamwork exists?
Downward	Mostly downward	Down & up	Down, up & sideways	7. What is the usual direction of information flow?
With suspicion	Possibly w/ suspicion	With caution	W/ a receptive mind	8. How is downward communication accepted?
Usually accurate	Often inaccurate	Often accurate	Almost always accurate	9. How accurate is upward communication?
Not very well	Rather well	Quite well	Very well	10. How well do superiors know problems faced by subordinates?
Mostly at top	Policy at top; some delegate	Broad policy at top; more delegation	Throughout but well integrated	11. At what level are decisions made?
Almost never	Occasionally consulted	Generally consulted	Fully involved	12. Are subordinates involved in decisions related to their work?
Not very much	Relatively little	Some contribution	Substantial contribution	13. What does decision-making process contribute to motivation?
Orders issued	Orders, some comment invited	After discussion, by orders	By group action, except in crisis	14. How are organizational goals established?
Strong resistance	Moderate resistance	Some resistance at times	Little or none	15. How much covert resistance to goals is present?
Very high at top	Quite high at top	Moderate delegation to lower levels	Widely shared	16. How concentrated are review and control functions?
Yes	Usually	Sometimes	No— same goals as formal	17. Is there an informal organization resisting the formal one?
Policing, punishment	Reward punishment	Reward some self-guidance	Self-guidance problem solving	18. What are cost, productivity, and other control data used for?

his division. The problem was due in part to marketplace conditions and in part to the autocratic leadership style of the plant manager.

Morale was so bad at this nonunion plant that employees bypassed the plant's management and contacted the division manager to complain about their treatment at the plant. After an investigation, the division manager concluded that the autocratic leadership style of the plant was a major factor in poor results.

The vice-president had been a follower of Rensis Likert for 20 years, and he appreciated the potential benefits of participative management. He concluded that the solution would be to shift the plant from an autocratic management system in the direction of a consultive (System 3) or participative (System 4) system. Toward achieving this objective, he (1) removed the plant manager and placed him in a staff role elsewhere in the corporation, (2) replaced him with a new plant manager he believed shared his philosophy about participative management, and (3) asked the author to meet with him and the new manager to explore how to shift to a participative management system and culture.

Entry and approach

In the meeting, we decided to use an OD action-research approach that would serve as the basis for a tailored management development program. In the action research, a strength/problem profile was developed; several questionnaires were used to develop "before" measurements that could be compared with "after" measurements a year later. The research was carried out through interviews with all managers, supervisors, and engineers. Group meetings with operative personnel were held to gather data using a technique called nominal grouping. We also decided that after

FIGURE 13.11
"Before" and "after" scores on communication flows.

SOURCE: *Organization Development Journal* 5 (Spring 1987): 24.

Communication

On a scale of 1–10, in your opinion, how effective is each of the three basic communication flows in your organization compared to a year ago? Please write in the appropriate number in each of the three spaces provided.

1	2	3	4	5	6	7	8	9	10
Very weak									Excellent

May 1985	June 1986	
3.9	7.1	Downward communication—the effective transfer of information, including goals, objectives, policies, changes, performance feedback, etc., from top management to lower levels of organization.
4.8	6.9	Upward communication—the effective transfer of information such as performance reports, problems, suggestions, feelings, attitudes, gripes, etc., from lower levels to top management of the organization.
3.7	6.5	Lateral or diagonal communication—the effective transfer of ideas and information between and among departments, including interdepartmental cooperation, interdepartmental service relationships, committees, task forces, etc., comprising members of different departments.

training had been given in group dynamics and team building, task forces would be established to develop action planning recommendations regarding key problems.

The outcome

In June 1986, a year after the program was initiated, the plant was producing at its top performance level and making a profit for the first time in its history. Although improved market conditions were a factor, it was concluded that the style of the new plant manager and his effective use of the OD program played a key role in the turnaround.

At the start of the OD program in May 1985, the Profile of Organizational Characteristics questionnaire revealed that the plant was being operated essentially as a benevolent autocracy (System 2 in Figure 13.10). But the information was ignored and no action was taken. At the end of the first cycle of the OD program, completed in June 1986, the questionnaire revealed that the management system had shifted from a benevolent autocracy to a consultive management system (System 3). A new cycle of the OD program was initiated to focus on shifting the plant even further, to a participative-group management system (System 4). Figure 13.11 shows the "before" and "after" measurements using the Profile of Organizational Characteristics questionnaire.

In addition, two tailored instruments were used in the May 1986 evaluation phase of the OD program. The instruments and results are shown in Figures 13.11 and 13.12. Again, there has been significant improvement in one year's time. It is worth noting that the top two ratings in June 1986 were downward communication and the confrontation of problems and opportunities. This highlights the role of the new plant manager and his effective use of task forces to work on problems and opportunities.

Questions

1. Evaluate the OD approach used in this situation.
2. Would you have handled the assignment differently? Explain.
3. What does this case illustrate about the potential for the effective use of OD?

FIGURE 13.12
"Before" and "after" scores on cooperation, teamwork, morale, and confrontation of problems and opportunities.

SOURCE: *Organization Development Journal* 5 (Spring 1987): 24.

Plant Survey

On a scale of 1–10, in your opinion, how effective is each of the following areas compared to a year ago? Please write in the appropriate number in each of the spaces provided.

1	2	3	4	5	6	7	8	9	10
Very weak									Excellent

May 1985	June 1986	
3.5	6.7	Cooperation between production and maintenance.
3.9	6.7	Teamwork between all departments.
3.1	6.9	Attitudes and morale within the plant.
3.5	7	The confrontation of problems and opportunities rather than "sweeping them under the rug and allowing them to grow and fester."

NOTES

1. Adapted from "Can Ford Stay on Top?" *Business Week*, September 29, 1987, pp. 78–86; Leonard M. Apcar, "A Management Style Passes with Death of Henry Ford II: The Last of the Old Scions, He Autocratically Ruled His Grandfather's Domain," *Wall Street Journal*, September 30, 1987, p. 1; and other sources.

2. See Eric Gelman, "Ford's Idea Machine," *Newsweek*, November 24, 1986, p. 66.

3. Thomas J. Peters and Robert H. Waterman, Jr., *In Search of Excellence: Lessons from America's Best-Run Companies* (New York: Harper & Row, 1982).

4. Daniel R. Denison, "Bringing Corporate Culture to the Bottom Line," *Organizational Dynamics* 13 (Autumn 1984): 4–22.

5. Terrence E. Deal and Allen A. Kennedy, *Corporate Culture* (Reading, MA: Addison-Wesley, 1982), p. 3. The following discussion has been adapted from this book.

6. *News Information* packet from Mary Kay Cosmetics, Inc.; and H. Rudnitsky, "Flight of the Bumblebee," *Forbes*, January 22, 1981, pp. 104–106.

7. Janice M. Beyer and Harrison M. Trice, "How an Organization's Rites Reveal Its Culture," *Organizational Dynamics* 16 (Spring 1987): 6.

8. Deal and Kennedy, p. 12.

9. Peter C. Reynolds, "Imposing a Corporate Culture," *Psychology Today* 21 (March 1987): 33–38.

10. Marshall Sashkin, "Participative Management Is an Ethical Imperative," *Organizational Dynamics* 13 (Spring 1984): 5.

11. Edwin A. Locke, David M. Schweiger, and Gary P. Latham, "Participation in Decision-Making: When Should It Be Used?" *Organizational Dynamics* 14 (Spring 1985): 67.

12. *Wall Street Journal*, January 6, 1987, p. 1.

13. Steven Prokesch, "Offbeat System Blamed for People's Distress," *Minneapolis Star and Tribune*, October 5, 1986, p. 10D.

14. Gregory T. Farnum, "An Experiment in Management," *Manufacturing Engineering*, March 1986, pp. 91–92.

15. Michael Beer, *Organization Change and Development: A Systems View* (Glenview, IL: Scott, Foresman, 1980), p. 33.

16. Marilyn Chase, "How a Red-Hot Firm in Computer Business Overheated and Burned," *Wall Street Journal*, February 22, 1980, p. 1.

17. Kurt Lewin, "Frontiers in Group Dynamics: Concept, Method, and Reality in Social Science," *Human Relations* 1 (June 1947): 5–14.

18. D. D. Warrick, ed., *Academy of Management OD Newsletter* (Winter 1978).

19. Rensis Likert, *The Human Organization* (New York: McGraw-Hill, 1967), pp. 26–29.

20. Judith R. Gordon, *A Diagnostic Approach to Organizational Behavior* (Boston: Allyn & Bacon, 1983), p. 612.

21. For greater detail, see Donald C. Mosley, Leon C. Megginson, and Paul H. Pietri, Jr., *Supervisory Management*, 2d ed. (Cincinnati: South-Western Publishing, 1989), Chapter 18.

22. Denis D. Umstot, "Organization Development Technology and the Military: A Surprising Merger?" *Academy of Management Review* 5 (April 1980): 194.

23. Lyman K. Randall, "Common Questions and Tentative Answers Regarding Organization Development," *California Management Review* 21 (Summer 1979): 77.

24. William N. Dunn and Frederic W. Swierczek, "Planned Organization Change: Toward Grounded Theory," *Journal of Applied Behavioral Science* 13 (April–June 1977): 135.

25. Kenneth W. Thomas and Warren H. Schmidt, "A Survey of Managerial Interest with Respect to Conflict," *Academy of Management Journal* 19 (June 1976): 315–318.

26. Eleanor Phillips and Ric Cheston, "Conflict Resolution: What Works?" *California Management Review* 21 (Summer 1979): 77.

SUGGESTIONS FOR FURTHER STUDY

BENNETT, AMANDA. "What Went Wrong: Experts Look at the Sudden Upheaval at Allegis." *Wall Street Journal*, June 24, 1987, p. 29.

CAMERON, KIM S. "Domains of Organizational Effectiveness in Colleges and Universities." *Academy of Management Journal* 24 (March 1981): 25–47.

FIELD, ANNE R. (with Richard Brandt, Julie Flynn, and Alex Beam). "The Free-for-All Has Begun." *Business Week*, May 11, 1987, pp. 148–151, 155, 159.

FLAX, STEVEN. "Boot Camp." *Inc.*, September 1987, pp. 99–104.

GELMAN, ERIC (with John McCormick and Carolyn Friday). "Let's Not Have Lunch." *Newsweek*, June 30, 1986, pp. 44–45.

GROSSMAN, JOHN. "Burnout." *Inc.*, September 1987, pp. 89–96.

GUYON, JANET. "Culture Class: GE's Management School Aims to Foster Unified Corporate Goals." *Wall Street Journal*, August 10, 1987, p. 29.

JONES, GARRETH R. "Organization-Client Transactions and Organizational Governance Structures." *Academy of Management Journal* 30 (June 1987): 197–218.

KERR, JEFFREY, and SLOCUM, JOHN W., JR. "Managing Corporate Culture Through Reward Systems." *Academy of Management Executive* 1 (May 1987): 99–107.

MAIN, JEREMY. "Wanted: Leaders Who Can Make a Difference." *Fortune*, September 28, 1987, pp. 92–94, 99–100, 102.

MEMMOTT, MARK. "Tips for Handling Executive Stress." *USA Today*, October 7, 1987, p. 5B.

PROKESCH, STEVEN. "Offbeat System Blamed for People's Distress." *Minneapolis Star and Tribune*, October 5, 1986, p. 10D.

QUICK, JAMES CAMPBELL; NELSON, DEBRA L.; and QUICK, JONATHAN D. "Successful Executives: How Independent?" *Academy of Management Executive* 1 (May 1987): 139–146.

RANDALL, DONNA M. "Commitment and the Organization: The Organization Man Revisited." *Academy of Management Review* 12 (July 1987): 460–471.

REIBSTEIN, LARRY. "Crushed Hopes: When a New Job Proves to Be Something Different." *Wall Street Journal*, June 10, 1987, p. 31.

UTTAL, BRO. "The Corporate Culture Vultures." *Fortune*, October 17, 1983, pp. 66–70.

WALDMAN, PETER. "Motivate or Alienate? Firms Hire Gurus to Change Their 'Cultures.'" *Wall Street Journal*, July 24, 1987, p. 23.

PART FIVE

Controlling Organizational Operations

IN PREVIOUS PARTS, we have shown that *planning* is effective when people put together the right combination of activities; *organizing* is effective when the proper structure and relationships are *used; staffing* is effective when the appropriate people are employed; and *leading* is effective when employees' performance is properly supervised. In this part, we will show that the performance of these functions is of limited value unless they are properly controlled.

Controlling essentially ensures that planned performance is achieved with a minimum of disruptions and disorder. It assures that plans are carried out and objectives are reached.

As you can see from the opposite page, there are certain fundamentals that are necessary for effective control. These, along with types of controls, steps in the control process, elements of managerial control, characteristics of effective control systems, and functional areas needing control, are covered in Chapter 14.

Some of the more popular control methods and techniques are discussed in Chapter 15. These include budgets, audits, ratio analysis, break-even analysis, and time charts—especially the Gantt chart and other time-related techniques.

Chapter 16 explores managing operations, examining important subjects such as the elements of an operations system, designing facilities to be used in operations, planning and controlling operations, materials and energy management, the automation revolution, and the use of management science.

14. Fundamentals of control

What is control?	Total and partial control systems How control relates to other functions
Types of control	Feedforward, concurrent, and feedback
Steps in the control process	1. Establishing performance standards 2. Determining performance measurements 3. Measuring performance 4. Comparing standard and actual performance, and analyzing variations 5. Taking corrective action if needed
Elements of managerial control	Management by exception (MBE) Management information systems (MIS)
Characteristics of effective control systems	Control the proper activities Timely Cost-effective Accurate Accepted
Controlling key functional areas	Financial Inventory Quality

15. Control techniques and methods

Types of controls	Nonquantitative methods Quantitative methods
Budgets and budgetary control	Benefits and limitations Types of budgets Variable budgets How budgetary control operates
Specialized budgetary control methods	Planning-programming-budgeting systems (PPBS) Zero-base budgeting
Using audits to control	
Using ratio analysis for control	Most popular ratios Examples of ratios
Using break-even analysis for control	Computing the break-even point How to use break-even analysis Limits on its use
Using time-performance charts and techniques	The Gantt chart Program evaluation and review technique (PERT) Critical path method (CPM) Evaluating their effectiveness

(continued)

16. Managing operations

Competitiveness of U.S. operations	Improvements in manufacturing Services need improving Japanese competition
Elements of an operations system	Definition of operations Universality of operations management Types of operations Timing of operations
Designing operations facilities	Determine product to be produced Determine output Determine space needs Provide best layout
Planning and controlling operations	Master operations plans Operations planning and control Improving operations
Materials and energy management	
The robotics revolution	Description of the revolution Advantages of automation and robotics Results of the revolution Future of the revolution
Management science and operations	Management science tools Limitations

14

Fundamentals of Control

Learning Objectives

After studying the material in this chapter, you should be able to do the following:

□ Explain what is meant by management control.
□ Identify and describe the steps in the control process.
□ Explain the relationship between planning and controlling.
□ Define what is meant by a management information system (MIS).
□ Discuss how return on investment (ROI) and ratio analysis (RA) are used to control financial performance.
□ Recognize the characteristics of effective controls.

Outline of the Chapter

What is control?
Total and partial control systems
How controlling is related to other management functions
Types of controls
Feedforward control
Concurrent control
Feedback control
Steps in the control process
Step 1: Establishing performance standards
Step 2: Determining performance measurements
Step 3: Measuring performance
Step 4: Comparing performance with standards and analyzing deviations
Step 5: Taking corrective action if needed

Elements of managerial control
Management by exception (MBE)
Management information systems (MIS)
Characteristics of effective control systems
Proper activities should be controlled
Controls should be timely
Controls should be cost-effective
Controls should be accurate
Controls must be accepted
Controlling key functional areas
Financial control
Inventory control
Quality control (QC)
Summary

Some Important Terms

control
cybernetics
feedforward control
concurrent control (steering control *or* screening)
feedback control (post-action control)
standard
management by exception (MBE) *or* exception principle
management information system (MIS)
statistical quality control (SQC)
ratio analysis (RA)
return on equity (ROE) *or* return on investment (ROI)
"just-in-time" inventory system
quality control (QC) *or* quality assurance
quality control (QC) circle
zero defects (ZD) *or* do it right the first time program

I. If anything can go wrong, it will.

II. Of the things that can go wrong, the one that will is that which will do the most damage.

III. If you think nothing can possibly go wrong, you have obviously overlooked something.

IV. Left to themselves, things go from bad to worse.

—MURPHY'S LAWS

Apple Computer—The Apple III Fiasco

In 1976, two high school buddy college dropouts, Stephen Jobs and Stephen Wozniak, formed Apple Computer out of a garage by building their first circuit board from scrounged parts. By 1982, just six years later, Apple had broken into the *Fortune* 500, with sales in excess of $580 million and the largest market share (26 percent) of the personal computer market.

In a previously buttoned-down industry, Apple was remarkable for a corporate culture in which many key people were in their twenties and the chairman of the board wore jeans. This highly informal, creative environment, where innovation seemed to flourish, was considered a central key to Apple's success. Apple I and Apple II products had proven highly successful, and the company anticipated similar, or even greater, success for the Apple III, introduced in late 1980. It was described as the first microcomputer designed specifically for professional and small business users and included more than 30 hardware and software items. As it turned out, the Apple III provided a major test for the fledgling firm, since its introduction turned into a fiasco. These were the early pratfalls:

1. Apple III software, especially the word processing package, was seven to eight months late in getting to dealers.
2. About 20 percent of the first computers shipped arrived at their destinations inoperable because loose chip sockets had allowed chips to slip out during shipping.
3. A clock/calendar chip purchased from National Semiconductor failed to live up to specifications.
4. Connectors that attached the printed circuit board to the computer suffered a variety of mechanical problems.

During this period, Apple was suffering from so much internal chaos that some referred to it as "Camp Run-Amok." To overcome its problems, the company recalled 14,000 Apple IIIs, several key managers were relieved, and a top-level team of vice-presidents began running the company. Apple ultimately surmounted the difficulties it experienced in launching the Apple III, but not without considerable damage to its reputation.[1]

How could this fiasco have been prevented?

ORGANIZATIONAL LIFE IS REPLETE with daily examples of poor control such as those in the case of Apple Computer. Poor control may be reflected in project cost overruns, schedules not being completed on time, poor-quality service or products, botched opportunities, and so forth. Fortunately for Apple, the company was able to overcome its control problems and learn from its experience. Managerial control consists of the things that management does to see to it that plans *are* accomplished as intended.

WHAT IS CONTROL?

In this chapter, you should gain a broad, general understanding of the concept of control. There are many names for the control function. It is often called *monitoring, evaluating, appraising,* or *correcting.* We choose to call it *control* because none of the other terms carries the connotation of setting standards, measuring actual performance, and taking corrective action. Chapter 15 focuses on some specific control techniques and methods.

Have you ever driven on an unfamiliar highway, come to an unmarked fork in the road, selected a route, and then driven miles and miles before you found a highway marker? How relieved you were to find yourself on the right road—and how annoyed you were if it was the wrong one! Managers in many organizations find themselves in a similar situation. They do not have assistance from periodic road markers along the way, because no markers have been established.

What is your view?

Should Apple have known in advance the problems associated with the Apple III as described in the Opening Case? Why?

You might think of controlling as being similar to the road markers on a highway. The road markers tell you whether you are on the right track. If you are not on the right track, you take corrective action to get on it. **Control** can be defined as the process of assuring that organizational and managerial objectives are accomplished. It is concerned with ways of making things happen as they were planned to happen.

FIGURE 14.1
Common examples of
control.

Hotel. Automatic sprinkler system

Auto. Oil pressure gauge on dashboard

Human body. Production of white blood cells to combat infection

Home. Electrical circuit break system

Highway. Radar system designed to detect speeders

School. Detention hall after school

In 1985, the Bank of Boston Corporation pleaded guilty to a charge of failing to report $1.22 billion in cash transactions with foreign banks. It was fined and paid $500,000 to the U.S. government. The Bank Secrecy Act of 1980 requires banks to report cash transactions of $10,000 or more; the purpose of the law is to prevent banks from laundering money as an aid to organized crime. Bank of Boston chairman William L. Brown vigorously denied that the bank's actions were linked to crime and labeled the bank's misdeeds a result of "systems failure." He said that those responsible for seeing that the bank complied with federal laws "failed to notice the new requirement."[2]

Organizations that don't exercise proper control run tremendous risks. The Bank of Boston Corporation received much adverse publicity as a result of its control oversight. Or consider the consequences of Union Carbide's poor control at its plant in Bhopal, India, where toxic fumes escaped and killed over 2000 people in 1984. Certainly, these events were not supposed to happen, but a breakdown in the control function allowed them to occur.

We live in a world of controls and control systems. Some common, non-business examples of controls with which you might be familiar are listed in Figure 14.1.

What is your view?

Can you think of some other examples of control with which you are familiar, including those associated with your home, driving, school?

Total and Partial Control Systems

Some control systems are total systems; that is, they are designed not only to detect the problem but also to correct it. When there is a self-correction feature, the system is often referred to as **cybernetics.** A sprinkler system is a total control, or cybernetic, system because it not only detects a fire but also puts it out. On the other hand, a smoke detector is a partial system, since it only *warns* of trouble; another step must then be taken to remedy the situation.

A good example of a total control system, with all the necessary steps for control, is probably found in your classroom, office, or home in the form

(Copyright 1981 by NEA, Inc.)

of a thermostatically controlled air conditioning or heating system. Figure 14.2 shows that the standard (or your plan) is established when you set the thermostat at, say, 68 degrees. The temperature in the room is monitored constantly by the system. When the temperature falls to 66 degrees, this information activates the burners, and the system produces heat. When the room reaches 70 degrees, the thermostat deactivates the burners, and the room cools. When the room reaches 66 degrees again, the heater is again activated. The process repeats itself continuously and may be thought of as a total self-regulating control system.

How Controlling Is Related to Other Management Functions

Controlling is related to, is affected by, and affects the other managerial functions. This is especially true of planning.

Controlling complements planning. Planning sets an airplane's course, and the control process keeps the plane on course. When the navigator finds the plane to be off course, he or she takes corrective action by having the pilot make some adjustments. Otherwise, locating the landing area on schedule would depend largely on luck. Some organizations and managers lay out careful and elaborate plans, but unless they use effective controls, they find that accomplishing the plans becomes just what we've said—a matter of luck. You might even think of planning as being "incomplete" unless good controls are also established.

Planning and controlling are so closely linked that, as stated in Chapter 5, they have been called *the Siamese twins of management.* In fact, as you will see shortly, the initial step of the control process is actually a planning step—establishing a goal, standard, or performance objective. Thus you might think of control as answering the question, "How are things going?" This implies that the basis for the answer lies in comparing the actual results with what you would *like* to accomplish ideally—in other words, your plan.

Sometimes, in fact, it is difficult to distinguish between a plan or standard

FIGURE 14.2
A self-regulating total control system.

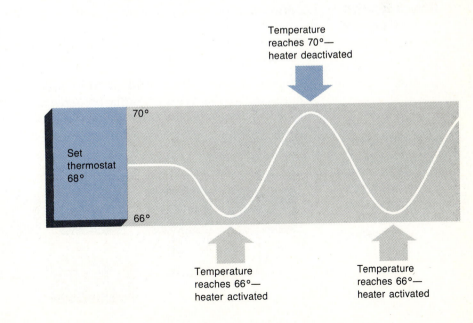

Temperature reaches 70°— heater deactivated

70°

Set thermostat 68°

66°

Temperature reaches 66°— heater activated

Temperature reaches 66°— heater activated

and a control. Earlier in the book, we labeled targets, objectives, goals, policies, and procedures as plans.

What is your view?

Is a four-way stop sign at a busy intersection a plan or a control? What about the red traffic light? What about a "no smoking" sign in a room containing flammable materials?

Each of these represents a standard or a target for behavior. As such, these are examples of plans rather than controls. What would more likely be considered a control is the police officer who monitors the intersection, detects offenders who violate the laws, and writes a ticket. The officer's task is to ensure that the standard or plan is carried out. And that is the essence of control—*to assure that plans are effectively executed.*

Controlling is linked to other functions. The control function of management is related closely to the other managerial functions also, as shown in Figure 14.3. It helps assess whether planning, organizing, staffing, and leading are being performed effectively. In fact, the control function itself must be controlled. Is the system providing timely information? Are the control reports accurate? Is performance measured at sufficiently frequent intervals? These are aspects of controlling the control function.

TYPES OF CONTROLS

There are three basic types of controls. These types, as shown in Figure 14.4, are (1) feedforward, (2) concurrent, and (3) feedback controls.

Feedforward Control

Feedforward control attempts to anticipate problems or deviations from the standard *in advance* of their occurrence. It is thus a more active, aggressive approach to control, allowing corrective action to be taken in advance of the problem.

The Loril Corporation, with 17,000 employees, was by far the largest employer in the county. Traffic bottlenecks at plant quitting time were especially bothersome, since there was only a four-lane highway access to the entrance and exit. Traffic lights were installed and seemed to help.

FIGURE 14.3
Relationship of control to other management functions.

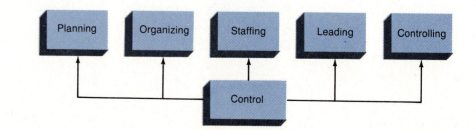

FIGURE 14.4
Three types of control.

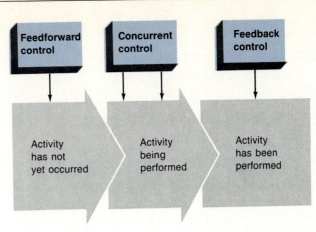

The company also staggered its working hours so that operative personnel left in four different shifts, beginning at 4:00 P.M. and ending at 6:00 P.M. Still, traffic jams often occurred, leading to short tempers as well as accidents.

One day the local police received a call from the plant superintendent, who indicated that, because of a work stoppage earlier, most of the plant's employees would not be leaving until 6:00 P.M., which would cause a severe traffic problem without police assistance. Accordingly, police were on hand at 5:45 P.M., and the traffic flow went exceptionally well. But, as one police officer remarked, "It would have been a total disaster without anyone here directing traffic. I've never seen such a line of cars trying to get onto that highway."

Feedforward control thus *anticipates* problems and permits action to be taken *before* a problem occurs. Caterpillar Tractor Company, for example, introduces a new product only after it has built up a two-month supply of spare parts. It also maintains tight control over its parts inventories so that it can provide 48-hour delivery of any part to any customer anywhere in the world.[3] Tips 14.1 identifies four key steps in establishing feedforward control.

What is your view?

How might Apple Computer have utilized feedforward control over the quality of chips received from National Semiconductor?

Concurrent Control

Concurrent control, also called **steering control,** or **screening,** occurs *while* an activity is taking place. For example, the navigator of an aircraft who adjusts the plane's movements is performing concurrent control. When you ride a bicycle, you must adjust your steering constantly, depending on turns in the road, obstacles, and changes in terrain to keep your bicycle upright and move toward your objective.

What is your view?

Notice the grade progress report in Figure 14.5. In what ways is this an example of concurrent control?

TIPS 14.1   How to Establish Feedforward Controls

1. Identify major goals. These might be such things as production, service, quality, costs, and profitability.
2. Identify factors most critical to accomplishing the goals identified in (1). Examples might include *weather* for transportation carriers, *availability of high-quality raw materials* or *smoothly functioning manufacturing equipment* for manufacturers, *availability of key personnel at a job site* for construction contractors, and so on.
3. Determine those circumstances most likely to threaten the critical factors. Using the examples in (2), these could be circumstances such as ex-

tended severe weather conditions, major equipment malfunctions, or a strike by local construction unions. Past experience and asking "What if?" questions allow identification of any number of potentially negative scenarios.
4. Develop a plan for preventing such circumstances as those in (3) from occurring, or for minimizing their negative impact. Delta Air Lines, for example, certainly can't control the weather. But having well-thought-out contingency plans, such as predetermined rerouting schedules, along with extra personnel at passenger information counters, can certainly help smooth the effects.

Feedback Control

Feedback control, also known as **postaction control,** is historical. That is, the measured activity has already occurred, and it is impossible to go back and correct performance to bring it up to standard. Instead, corrections must occur after the fact. Examples of feedback controls are disciplinary situations, performance appraisal interviews, financial and budgetary results, and final inspections. An example is shown in Figure 14.6.

Perhaps you are thinking, "Since feedback controls occur *after* the fact, why even bother? Isn't it too late to do anything about the past?" For a partial answer, consider the following situations, which illustrate that feedback control is also future oriented.

FIGURE 14.5
Parental control of son's academic performance.

Performance standard. Bill is to have an overall B average on his final report card.

Performance measure. Progress reports every 5 weeks; report card every 10 weeks.

Results. First progress report shows 3 Bs, 2 Cs, and 2 Ds.

Evaluation of deviations. Bill was out one week for a tonsillectomy that put him behind. The Ds are in algebra and history. Discussion with teachers shows entire class is having difficulty in algebra; history grade will improve when he makes up missed work.

Corrective action. None for now. Bill is getting off to a slow start, apparently resulting from some missed classes. He should have time to pick up his grades before the first report card. Corrective measurement—such as loss of television privileges, cutback of allowance, limiting overnights with friends, and mandatory study hours—will be considered if Bill fails to improve his grades.

FIGURE 14.6
Example of feedback
quality control in a
restaurant.

Management Encourages Your Comments

Date _5/19/8–_

Waiter or waitress _Phyllis_

Please circle meal   Breakfast (Lunch) Dinner

	Yes	No
1. Were you greeted by host or hostess promptly and courteously?	✓	
2. Was your server prompt, courteous, and attractive in appearance?	✓	
3. Was the quality of food to your expectations?		✓
4. Was the table setting and condition of overall restaurant appearance pleasing and in good taste?	✓	
5. Will you return to our restaurant?		✓
6. Will you recommend our restaurant to your friends and associates?		✓

Comments

Food was overcooked. Potatoes were left-overs. Meat was tough. This was my second visit and I brought a friend with me. We were both very disappointed.

Name and address
(if you desire)

_____

_____

_____

Please drop this in our quality improvement box provided as you exit room.

Thank you and have a good day.

Suppose that a quality control inspector in a garment factory finds that in a completed batch of shirts one sleeve of each shirt is three inches longer than the other. What can be done? Most or all of the material in the shirts will be scrapped. Thus, the inspection occurred too late to salvage the shirts. But detecting the errors at a final control point is still better than having the shirts bought by a customer in damaged condition!

Suppose Bill's first-term report card (Figure 14.5) had four Ds and an F. That's past history and can't be changed. But Bill's parents will certainly expect him to improve his performance in the second term and will probably take steps to ensure this!

Likewise, when the Tacoma National Bank falls 20 percent short of its profit objectives for the first quarter, that's history. But the hope of feed-

back controls lies in finding out why performance was poor and taking the steps necessary to remedy the situation in the future.

What is your view?

When Apple Computer recalled 14,000 Apple IIIs, what form of control was it using?

All three forms of controls—feedforward, concurrent, and feedback—are useful. Feedforward and concurrent controls are sufficiently timely to allow management to make corrective changes and still achieve objectives. But there are several other factors involved, despite the appeal of these two forms of controls. First, they are costly. Second, many activities do not lend themselves to frequent or continuous monitoring. Third, at some point excessive control becomes counterproductive, as in the case of sales representatives who spend their time filling out control reports for the home office instead of making customer calls. Management must therefore use the control system that is most appropriate for the given situation.

STEPS IN THE CONTROL PROCESS

The controlling process usually consists of at least five steps, as shown in Figure 14.7. These steps are (1) establishing standards of performance (planning), (2) determining performance measurements, (3) measuring actual performance, (4) comparing performance with standards and analyzing variances, and (5) taking corrective action if necessary. Notice how these steps were used in Figure 14.5.

Step 1: Establishing Performance Standards

The first step in controlling is establishing standards of performance. You have already read in Chapter 4 how important it is for managers to set clear objectives that channel the entire organization's efforts. In fact, we spent considerable time discussing goal setting and management by objectives (MBO). For our purposes, we define a **standard** as a unit of measurement that can serve as a reference point for evaluating results. Accordingly, goals,

FIGURE 14.7
The process of control.

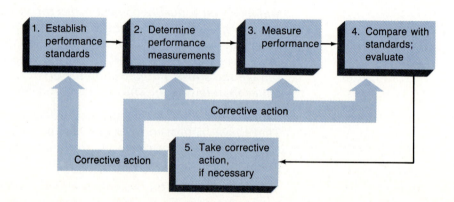

objectives, quotas, and performance targets will all be considered "standards" in this discussion. Some specific standards are sales quotas, equal employment opportunity (EEO) targets, budgets, job deadlines, market share, and profit margins.

Three common types of standards are physical, monetary, and time.

1. *Physical standards* might include quantities of products or services, number of customers or clients, or quality of product or service.

2. *Monetary standards* are expressed in dollars and include labor costs, selling costs, materials costs, sales revenue, gross profits, and the like.

3. *Time standards* might include the speed with which jobs should be done or the deadlines by which jobs are to be completed.

Each of these types of standards can be expressed in terms of quantifiable results. This enables managers to communicate their performance expectations to subordinates more clearly and permits the other steps in the control process to be handled more effectively.

What is your view?
Which types of standards were not met in the Apple III case at the beginning of the chapter?

Nonquantifiable, or qualitative, standards also play an important role in the control process. Sometimes managers and subordinates are not as much aware of the nonquantifiable standards, but these are still very important. The applicant-counselor relationship is a difficult one to quantify. So are other qualitative standards, such as appropriate dress on the job, personal hygiene, cooperative attitudes, hiring good personnel, promoting the best person, and so on. Indeed, control over qualitative standards is more difficult to achieve, but it is still important to try to control them.

> *Manager Helen Leyden of the State Employment Office overheard one of the newer employment counselors in the department, David Hoffman, berating a job applicant. The tone of Hoffman's voice was loud and strident, as though he were scolding a child, although the applicant was perhaps 30 years his senior. She heard Hoffman conclude the interview with, "Now don't come back here and bother us until you've had someone fill this form out properly for you. That's not what we're paid to do!"*
>
> *After the applicant left, Helen listened to Hoffman's explanation of what had just happened. Acknowledging his curtness with the applicant, Hoffman said he'd had a lot of pressure that day and had grown very impatient. Helen told him that he hadn't handled himself in a professional manner and discussed what he should have done differently. Later in the day, David was to call the applicant, apologize, and offer to be of further help.*

Step 2: Determining Performance Measurements

Setting standards is futile unless there is some way to measure actual performance. Therefore, the second step in control is to determine the appropriate measurement of performance progress. Some of the important considerations in doing this are found in these questions: *How often* should performance be measured—hourly, daily, weekly, yearly? *What form* will the measurement take—a phone call, a visual inspection, a written report? *Who* will be involved—the manager, an assistant, a staff department? (See MAP 14.1.)

Another consideration is that the measurement must be easy to do and relatively inexpensive. Also, it must be capable of being easily explained to employees and others.

Step 3: Measuring Performance

Performance itself is measured once the frequency and form of the monitoring system are determined. There are many ways of doing this. They include (1) observation; (2) reports, both oral and written; (3) automatic methods; and (4) inspections, tests, or samples. Most large firms, and many small ones, are now using internal auditors who make use of all these methods.[4]

Some examples of observation are a supervisor overseeing the activities of subordinates, a basketball coach studying the players during a game, and a floorwalker in a department store.

Some automatic measuring devices are a car's speedometer, counters on machines that indicate the number of units produced, and the buzzer that comes on when the clothes in the dryer are dry.

Traffic police, final examinations, and spot checking of units being produced are examples of inspections, tests, and samples.

Step 4: Comparing Performance with Standards and Analyzing Deviations

A critical control step is comparing actual performance with planned performance; facts about performance, standing alone, are relatively worthless.

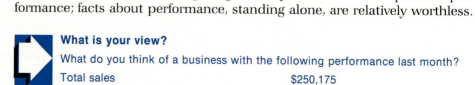

What is your view?

What do you think of a business with the following performance last month?

Total sales	$250,175
Number of finished products produced	1,100
Number of customer calls	1,112
Number of new customers	87
Number of new salespersons hired	3
Average shipping time to customer	5 days
Employee turnover	18
Number of lost-time accidents	7

Does this list contain any significant information about the company's progress? Is the company doing well? You can't tell, can you? To judge performance, you must be able to *compare* the results cited with other pertinent data. What was the company's sales goal? How many customer calls is considered "good"? How many new customers was the company attempting to gain? How many new salespersons had the company sought to hire? What "norm" is there for the average shipping time? It is only when you compare *actual* performance to established performance *standards* that you are in a position to exercise control.

Deviations must be analyzed to determine why the standard is not being met when performance falls short of the standard. Chapter 6 showed how important it is in decision making to identify the real causes of performance problems rather than just the symptoms. Managers frequently use staff as-

Management Application and Practice 14.1 Mr. Marriott Reads the Complaint Cards

Tom Peters, coauthor of *In Search of Excellence,* has stated that J. Willard Marriott, Sr., founder and senior executive officer for over 50 years of the hotel and food chain empire that bears his name, read every single complaint card sent in by his customers. In fact, it's said he read the original, raw, unedited cards, rather than typewritten summaries of them.

According to Peters, one senior Marriott officer summed up the impact of Marriott's control: "You had 100 or so property managers working 26 hours a day, 8 days a week to make sure the boss had a very, very light reading load."

SOURCE: Thomas J. Peters, "An Excellent Question," *Inc.* 6 (December 1984): 158.

sistance and third parties to aid them in analyzing deviations, especially in important matters.

Step 5: Taking Corrective Action If Needed

If corrective action is needed, it is taken. The action may take any of many forms. The standard may be modified, steps may be taken to improve performance, or both may be done concurrently, as shown in the following example.

> *Harold Brown, the director of manufacturing at Central City Iron Works, usually starts his morning with a conference of key managers from production and production-related staff sections, such as metallurgy, quality control, and industrial engineering. The meeting is held at the company's scrap pile, where the previous day's rejects are inspected, the causes of the defects jointly determined, and the responsibility for correcting the defects assigned.*

As shown earlier in Figure 14.7, the corrective action may be to alter the planning or control system in any of the following ways:

1. Change the original standard (perhaps it was too low or too high).

2. Change the performance measurements (perhaps inspect more or less frequently or even alter the measurement system itself).

3. Change the manner in which deviations are analyzed and interpreted.

A practical example of the total control process in action is shown in Figure 14.8.

ELEMENTS OF MANAGERIAL CONTROL

There are many techniques that can aid managers in exercising control. Two of the more popular ones are management by exception (MBE) and management information systems (MIS).

FIGURE 14.8
Executive control of division financial performance.

SOURCE: See Lester R. Bittel, *Management by Exception* (New York: McGraw-Hill, 1964).

Performance standard. Division X should have a net profit of 9 percent of sales for the fiscal year.

Performance measure. Quarterly net profit figures.

Results. Net profit for first quarter was only 3 percent.

Evaluation of deviations. Low profit resulted primarily because (1) salespeople failed to push a new product recently added to the product line and (2) a computer malfunction caused excessive downtime of machinery and equipment. This required overtime work that caused labor costs to increase substantially for the period.

Corrective action. Arrange for a series of weekly on-site meetings with division manager and his or her staff. Get report from division manager on how he or she plans to get the salespeople moving. Send Hal Abrahams and corporate electronic data processing troubleshooters to develop plan to prevent computer breakdowns in the future.

Management by Exception (MBE)

Do you remember the story of Moses and his father-in-law, Jethro, from Chapter 7? Jethro advised Moses to choose "capable men" and give them control over groups of people. The persons chosen were to govern their groups, and only the exceptional cases were to come to Moses. This is the first recorded example of **management by exception (MBE),** or the **exception principle.**

How the technique operates. MBE enables managers to direct attention to the most critical control areas and permits employees or lower levels of management to handle routine variations (see Figure 14.9). It can be practiced

FIGURE 14.9
Management by exception (MBE).

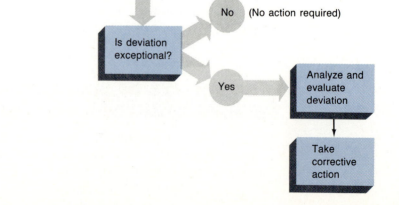

by managers in sales, production, finance, personnel, purchasing, quality control, and other functional areas. Even first-line managers can use this principle in their daily supervision.

Example of MBE. The following example shows how this principle works in actual practice.

The president of Jones Boat Trailers was studying the sales volume plan for the present year, as shown next.

Sales Forecast

MONTH	VOLUME
January	$ 100,000
February	125,000
March	135,000
First quarter total	$ 360,000
April	150,000
May	155,000
June	150,000
Second quarter total	$ 455,000
July	150,000
August	135,000
September	130,000
Third quarter total	$ 415,000
October	220,000
November	110,000
December	110,000
Fourth quarter total	$ 440,000
Year total forecast	$1,670,000

On February 3, the sales report for January came across the president's desk. The actual volume of sales for the month was $95,000, or 5 percent below the forecast figure. What action should the president take?

Should she call in her vice-president of sales and find out what he thinks? Should she increase advertising, hire additional salespeople, tell the sales vice-president to write a report explaining the problem, or tell the vice-president that his February quota will be $130,000?

Of course, there is another alternative. If the president practices MBE, she may well do absolutely nothing.

Analysis of the example. The key to this example is whether a 5 percent deviation from the sales target for the first month is an exceptional one. Perhaps the president has agreed with the sales vice-president that so long as sales fall within 10 percent of the forecast the matter of exercising control will be delegated to the vice-president. But sales deviating from target by more than 10 percent would be considered an exceptional deviation from standard, and the president herself would need to be notified and would become active in the control process. She might want to be briefed by the sales vice-president, find out what is causing the problem, and take the action necessary to recoup the lost ground so that the quarterly performance target could still be attained.

Note also that if sales performance exceeded expectations and was $110,000.00, the president would also become active in the control process. What caused the overage? What did the company do right? Was it the result of the new dealer incentives or the new line of models? Was the quota too low, and should the standards for the year be raised? (This probably wouldn't be very good news for the sales vice-president!)

A final note: Managers who practice MBE must temper the process with various methods of remaining visible to and communicative with their personnel, for, as indicated in Chapter 11, it is important for employees to receive recognition for making things go right.

Management Information Systems (MIS)

Perhaps some of you will be, or already are, employed in situations related to the "management information" needs of an organization. These include a broad variety of positions, including market researchers, accountants, auditors, computer analysts and programmers, and many others. A **management information system (MIS)** plays an important role in management's effective performance of the planning and controlling functions of management. From a control standpoint, a MIS is most helpful in providing timely, relevant information so that managers can make greater use of feedforward and concurrent controls.

"It's the most expensive computer in our industry, but it's far and away the most functional"

What is a MIS? A definition of a MIS that you might find useful is this: A management information system (MIS) is a planned system of gathering, processing, storing, and disseminating information so that effective management decisions can be made.

The concept of MIS today is linked closely to computer technology, including computer capacity, programs and program language, remote terminals, storage disks, and the like. The giant computer, however, did not make its business debut until 1954, when General Electric (GE) installed a Univac at its new household appliance plant at Appliance Park, Kentucky. Until then, organizations had MIS, but what they had was something considerably less sophisticated than the systems we have today and was mechanically rather than electronically operated. Today, organizations may have a MIS without a computer, but the system will be less sophisticated without such assistance.

Firms today process information at incredible rates. Think of the payroll checks, orders placed, bills paid, personnel files updated, purchase requisitions, and cost and revenue data. A soft drink bottler with $50 million in sales and 300 employees will process between 4000 and 5000 separate items *daily*. This adds up to over 1 million items yearly! You might think of MIS as an attempt to deal with such a deluge in an orderly, timely manner so that needed information is placed in management's hands in the right form and at the right time. A MIS, then, serves management by providing the right person with the right amount of the right information at the right time.

Figure 14.10 illustrates the major information outputs available from the Medical University of South Carolina's integrated hospital information system. The system uses the latest in computer technology to assist operating and management personnel in achieving the hospital's objectives.

But a computerized control system, by itself, is not an effective safeguard. There is a need for other information-gathering devices. For example, in 1981 the Wells Fargo Bank in Beverly Hills lost $21.3 million to embezzlement. The bank's operations officer, the prime suspect, disappeared. "Any kind of decent auditing system should have turned this up," said the chairperson of a competing bank. But Wells Fargo's chairperson said of the computer, "We discovered a hole in the system and had to change the system."[5]

Example of how a MIS operates. TIPS 14.2 shows just a few of the many applications of MIS. There is no question that management information systems have advanced the quality and timeliness of the data available to help managers make better decisions.

Sales manager William Owens had just received a call from one of the company's best customers. The customer inquired about the progress of an order placed with the company just over two weeks ago. She is planning a big sales promotion and wants to make sure that if she advertises the items she'll have them on hand.

Turning his chair, Owens sits in front of a small computer monitor and types in the customer's name. A listing of all the orders placed by the customer in the past year flashes on the screen. Owens keys in the customer's order number. Immediately, the status of the order appears on the screen, showing the various stages of production, with the anticipated delivery date.

FIGURE 14.10

The information outputs of the Medical University of South Carolina hospital information system. The common data base is held in the hospital computer.

SOURCE: Barton Hodge, Robert Fleck, Jr., and C. Brian Honess, *Management Information Systems* (Reston, VA: Reston Publishing Co., 1984), p. 487. Used by permission.

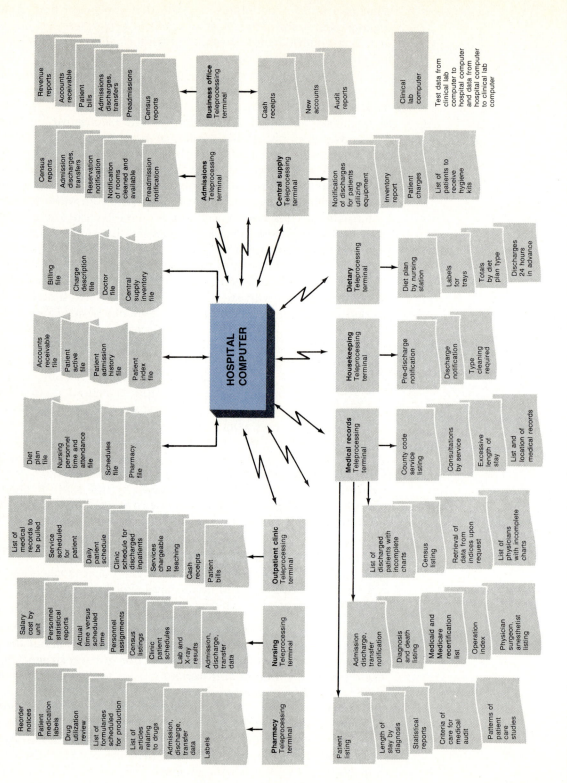

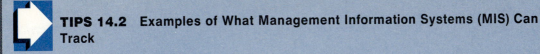

TIPS 14.2   Examples of What Management Information Systems (MIS) Can Track

You may be surprised by some of the things a MIS can keep track of. Here are just a few examples.

Sales status by product, territory, salesperson, and customer, with deviations and projections

Production status by product, department, and plant, including orders behind schedule and reasons for the deviations

Profit position compared to past performance and future expectations

Inventory position, both in terms of units or dollars and in comparison with budgeted figures

Personnel skills inventory for all employees, by demographic characteristics

Budget deviations of expenses, such as capital expenditures and labor and materials costs, compiled by budget center

Automatic compilation of all financial ratios, with indicators comparing this information to industry norms and trends

Hospital bed occupancy, types and quantities of drugs issued, and cost per patient of meals served

Professional athletes' past and present performance record in various categories

Owens can give this information to the customer directly over the telephone, without even leaving his chair. "In the old days," he thinks, "it might have taken me at least an hour to track down the status of that order, and even then I might not have been sure of my information!"

CHARACTERISTICS OF EFFECTIVE CONTROL SYSTEMS

To be effective, any control system must meet certain criteria. For example, the system should (1) control the proper activities, (2) be timely, (3) be cost-effective, (4) be accurate, and (5) be acceptable to those concerned with it. The more nearly these criteria are met, the more likely it is that effective control will result.

Proper Activities Should Be Controlled

Control systems influence where job energies are directed; therefore, managers must assure that the proper activities are "controlled." When people recognize that certain activities will be monitored and compared to some standard, their behavior is likely to be channeled toward the standards set.

Management must frequently balance control systems to assure that controlling one activity does not cause another one to get out of control. To meet a production standard, for example, a supervisor may overtax machinery and equipment. A sales manager may cut prices drastically to reach the sales quota for the division; unless he or she is also working under a profit standard, reaching the sales standard, in itself, isn't necessarily good. Managers must therefore make sure to control the proper balance of activities in the system.

> *It is now believed by some experts that top managers' overconcern with details is due not so much to government regulation as to their own accounting and budget directors. These directors are pushing such detailed financial reports at chief executives that long-range planning gets lost in the shuffle.*[6]

Controls Should Be Timely

We have pointed out that for controls to be effective they must report deviations in time to allow management to take corrective action.

> *One shipyard had its contractors determine a basic price for ship repair and maintenance before beginning work and then negotiate the final price when repairs were almost completed. Cost controls in the company were so slow, however, that frequently the ship had been delivered to its owner and the final, negotiated price already billed and received by the company several weeks before the internal cost system allowed management to know whether it had made a profit or suffered a loss. Streamlining the cost control system allowed the company to arrive at a final price that included a reasonable profit above costs incurred for the work.*

In some cases, timely information is needed constantly—hourly, daily, weekly, quarterly, annually, or at longer intervals. The more information management has at a realistic time, even though performance may be past history, the more rapidly it can respond.

What is your view?

Assume that you are the owner of five clothing stores in a large metropolitan area. Each store has its own manager and anywhere from four to ten employees. What control information do you need as owner, and how often do you need it?

Controls Should Be Cost-Effective

Control systems are not free or even inexpensive. Control costs include such factors as (1) monitoring and processing systems—such as computers and cash registers; (2) personnel to operate the system—such as inventory controllers, inspectors, and accountants, as well as supervisors and managers of these groups; and (3) line personnel's time in working with control personnel and providing data to them—such as cost, scrap, production, and personnel reports.

For example, should a company inspect each item it produces? At first glance this seems desirable, but sometimes it is impractical and uneconomical. Surely, this procedure will differ for a manufacturer of parachutes compared to a manufacturer of notebook paper or pistons for an automobile engine. Mass manufacturing processes often use **statistical quality control (SQC)** techniques in which control is based on inspection of random samples rather than every item. With the high costs of sophisticated control systems, equipment, and personnel, it is easy to control an organization right into bankruptcy! Management must always raise the question of cost versus the benefits of control systems.

Controls Should Be Accurate

Control systems are important indicators of progress and are the basis for corrective reactions; thus care must be taken to assure that control mea-

"I was a victim of computer accuracy."
(Source: Management Review 70 [August
1981]: 4. Copyright 1981 by Punch/Rothco.)

surements are accurate. Yet measurements are often imprecise, and honest errors can be made in interpreting and reporting control results. And occasionally falsified or misleading reports or attempts to make the results "look good" will occur.

> *Some time ago, the Boy Scouts of America revealed that membership figures coming in from the field had been falsified. In response to the pressures of a national membership drive, people within the organization had vastly overstated the number of new Boy Scouts. To their chagrin, the leaders found out something that other managers have also discovered: Organizational control systems often produce unintended consequences. The drive to increase membership had motivated people to increase the reported rather than the actual number of new Boy Scouts enrolled![7]*

Controls Must Be Accepted

People resent controls, especially those they consider excessive. Excessive controls give the impression that people are not trusted to act on their own. Sometimes, too, the standards set by management may be perceived as being unreasonable or unfair. We show our resentment by rebelling—finding ways to beat the system. A classic example of this tendency is found in the *Grace Report*, by Peter Grace, on government waste. It gives numerous examples of the clever ways employees of the federal government circumvent established control mechanisms.

If controls are to be accepted, it is important that people clearly understand the purpose of the system and feel that they have an important stake in it. This is especially true when new systems are established.

> *Frances Johnson, the new computer analyst, was perplexed. She had been hired by the president of the company to implement a new control system in the warehouse and local stores and was highly enthusiastic about her new job. There was no question in her mind that a cost-benefit analysis would show that she could save the company several hundred thousand*

dollars annually and improve profits at the stores. But she had received an icy reception when introduced at the annual management meeting, and questions from the floor had seemed downright hostile, especially those coming from several store managers. After the meeting she overheard one manager saying, "We've been operating successfully for 60 years. We don't need one of these computer people around here to tell me how to run my store!"

CONTROLLING KEY FUNCTIONAL AREAS

We now look at the control process as it applies to three key functions: finance, inventory, and quality. This will give you a better view of how the control function operates.

Financial Control

Financial controls are important for several reasons. First, financial data have been the traditional index of a firm's success and prestige (see Tables 14.1 and 14.2 for examples). Financial results give a broad picture of a firm's overall success, since profitability is a broadly visible signal to other firms in the industry and also the investment community. The most popular financial control techniques are budgetary control, auditing, and ratio analysis (RA). While these methods are discussed in detail in Chapter 15, ratio analysis will be briefly discussed here.

Ratio analysis (RA).

Ratio analysis (RA) involves selecting two or more components of a firm's financial statement and expressing their relationship as a percentage or ratio. Management can determine which "red flags" need to be watched more closely by comparing these ratios to those of other firms in the industry.

One such ratio is **return on equity (ROE),** often called **return on investment (ROI),** which is the net profit owners receive on their investment in a firm. The technique's use was developed by Du Pont. Its major value is that it permits a common evaluation of the performance of different organizational units.

Preoccupation with ROE (or ROI) can lead to problems. For example, Du Pont once used a 20 percent ROI as a minimum for approving new product projects. This control technique caused the firm's management to forgo expansion into xerography and instant photography. Yet a disregard for ROE may also be harmful over a period of time.

In 1981, Chrysler Corporation, in an effort to survive, sacrificed ROE by giving large rebates and other concessions to increase output. The company's share of the domestic market rose from 9.9 percent in 1980 to 12.5 percent in 1981. The firm met its volume objectives but then changed its objectives to "becoming more cost-effective."[8]

Financial performance of the large manufacturers.

The *Fortune* 500 is a popular listing of the 500 largest U.S. industrial firms, based on sales revenues. Table 14.1 gives you a good idea of the relative performance of the 20 largest

TABLE 14.1
The 20 Largest U.S. Industrial Corporations, 1987

(Ranked by sales)

SOURCE: Fortune, April 25, 1988, pp. D11 and D12. Reprinted by permission.

Rank 1987	Rank 1986	Company	Sales $ Millions	Sales % Change from 1986	Profits $ Millions	Profits Rank	Profits % Change from 1986	Assets $ Millions	Assets Rank	Stockholders' equity $ Millions	Stockholders' equity Rank	Profits as percent of Sales %	Sales Rank	Assets %	Assets Rank	Stockholders' equity %	Stockholders' equity Rank
1	1	General Motors (Detroit)	101,781.9	(1.0)	3,550.9	4	20.6	87,421.9	1	33,225.1	3	3.5	307	4.1	336	10.7	314
2	2	Exxon (New York)	76,416.0	9.3	4,840.0	2	(9.7)	74,042.0	2	33,626.0	2	6.3	165	6.5	217	14.4	213
3	3	Ford Motor (Dearborn, Mich.)	71,643.4	14.2	4,625.2	3	40.8	44,955.7	4	18,492.7	4	6.5	161	10.3	75	25.0	50
4	4	International Business Machines (Armonk, N.Y.)	54,217.0	5.8	5,258.0	1	9.8	63,688.0	3	38,263.0	1	9.7	66	8.3	144	13.7	227
5	5	Mobil (New York)	51,223.0	14.2	1,258.0	11	(10.6)	41,140.0	5	16,783.0	5	2.5	369	3.1	360	7.5	366
6	6	General Electric (Fairfield, Conn.)	39,315.0	11.7	2,915.0	5	17.0	38,920.0	6	16,480.0	6	7.4	127	7.5	181	17.7	148
7	8	Texaco (White Plains, N.Y.)	34,372.0	8.7	(4,407.0)	480	—	33,962.0	9	9,171.0	12	—		—		—	
8	7	American Tel. & Tel. (New York)	33,598.0	(1.4)	2,044.0	6	1,370.5	38,426.0	7	14,455.0	9	6.1	172	5.3	278	14.1	221
9	9	E.I. du Pont de Nemours (Wilmington, Del.)	30,468.0	12.2	1,786.0	8	16.1	28,209.0	10	14,244.0	10	5.9	181	6.3	229	12.5	261
10	11	Chrysler (Highland Park, Mich.)[a]	26,257.7	16.6	1,289.7	10	(8.1)	19,944.6	15	6,502.9	15	4.9	224	6.5	219	19.8	102
11	10	Chevron (San Francisco)	26,015.0	6.8	1,007.0	19	40.8	34,465.0	8	15,780.0	7	3.9	284	2.9	365	6.4	376
12	12	Philip Morris (New York)	22,279.0	7.7	1,842.0	7	24.6	19,145.0	17	6,823.0	14	8.3	100	9.6	100	27.0	42
13	15	Shell Oil (Houston)[b]	20,852.0	23.9	1,230.0	13	39.3	26,937.0	11	14,842.0	8	5.9	180	4.6	320	8.3	357
14	13	Amoco (Chicago)	20,174.0	10.4	1,360.0	9	82.1	24,827.0	12	12,107.0	11	6.7	147	5.5	270	11.2	298
15	17	United Technologies (Hartford)	17,170.2	9.6	591.7	37	713.6	11,928.6	28	4,292.6	31	3.4	317	5.0	303	13.8	226
16	19	Occidental Petroleum (Los Angeles)	17,096.0	11.4	240.0	95	32.5	16,739.0	20	5,164.0	25	1.4	401	1.4	403	4.6	395
17	18	Procter & Gamble (Cincinnati)[c]	17,000.0	10.1	327.0	69	(53.9)	13,715.0	23	5,990.0	19	1.9	382	2.4	381	5.5	384
18	20	Atlantic Richfield (Los Angeles)	16,281.4	11.6	1,224.3	14	99.0	22,669.9	14	5,877.5	20	7.5	122	5.4	275	20.8	84
19	14	RJR Nabisco (Atlanta)	15,868.0	(6.6)	1,209.0	15	13.6	16,861.0	19	6,038.0	17	7.6	117	7.2	192	20.0	97
20	16	Boeing (Seattle)	15,355.0	(6.0)	480.0	46	(27.8)	12,566.0	26	4,987.0	29	3.1	337	3.8	345	9.6	340

[a] Figures include American Motors (1986 rank: 113) acquired August 5, 1987.
[b] Owned by Royal Dutch/Shell Group (1986 International 500 rank: 1).
[c] Figures are for fiscal year ended June 30, 1987.

TABLE 14.2
Top Industrial Performers and Industry Medians, *Fortune 500 Directory of Industrial Firms,* **1987**

SOURCE: *Fortune,* April 25, 1988, p. D9. Reprinted by permission.

Return on stockholders' equity		
The ten highest	Sales rank	% Return
Affiliated Publications	486	62.1
Georgia Gulf	392	57.4
Ralston Purina	70	54.4
Fairchild Industries	346	49.5
Magnetek	419	49.5
GAF	356	46.7
Merck	80	42.8
Jefferson Smurfit	301	42.2
Union Texas Petroleum	274	42.2
Goodyear Tire & Rubber	35	42.0
The 500 median		**13.2**

Return on sales		
The ten highest	Sales rank	% Return
Newmont Mining	450	61.0
Affiliated Publications	486	41.0
Hercules	150	30.5
GAF	356	28.4
Homestake Mining	471	28.4
UST	445	23.2
Cray Research	397	21.4
Asarco	255	20.6
Himont	292	19.5
Merck	80	17.9
The 500 median		**4.6**

firms of the *Fortune* list for 1987. Table 14.2 shows the best performers of the entire 500, so far as return on equity and return on sales are concerned. Notice that the best performers among the top 500 are Affiliated Publications (Sales Rank 486), with 62.1 percent *return on stockholders' equity;* and Georgia Gulf (Sales Rank 392), with 57.4 percent. As for *return on sales,* Newmont Mining (Sales Rank 450) had the best—61 percent—while Affiliated Publications had 41 percent.

Inventory Control

Inventory represents a substantial part of many organizations' capital investment. These costs include inventories of raw materials to be used in producing goods, inventories of finished goods, and inventories of spare parts for machinery and equipment. Inventory costs result from the cost directly associated with the items. They also include costs of financing warehouse space, financing the purchase of the items, and other "administrative costs," as well as lost interest and "opportunity costs."

Inventory that sits idle and doesn't move is very expensive. Estimates of the costs of carrying inventory range from 15 percent to over 100 percent of the average inventory investment for a year. Recent high interest rates warrant the use of a 30 percent to 35 percent figure for valuing inventory costs. It is also costly not to have inventory on hand when a customer needs it or when an important production run is scheduled or to have a key machine shut down because it will take several days for a spare part to arrive.

Purpose of inventory control. Inventory control systems are basically designed to (1) establish the maximum and minimum amounts of inventory to have available, (2) provide feedback about the movement of inventory and changes in inventory levels, and (3) signal management when items reach or fall below the minimum level.

Example of an effective inventory control system. In 1987, Wall Street was bullish on Circuit City Stores, the largest specialty retailer of audio and video products and appliances in the country. While other such companies were in the doldrums, Circuit City was having an 83 percent rise in earnings over 1986. Why? According to an analyst for Goldman, Sachs & Company, Circuit City's automated distribution centers in Atlanta and Richmond give it important cost advantages, such as lower inventory requirements, less storage space—and more selling space—in its stores, quicker turnaround of inventory, less pilferage, and lower labor costs. These benefits result from Circuit City's having "the strongest control system, lowest cost structure, and unmatched depth of management," as compared with its competitors.[9]

Just-in-time inventory. A recent new approach called a **"just-in-time" inventory system** is described in MAP 14.2.

Quality Control (QC)

As consumers, you have undoubtedly experienced your share of products that didn't work, were missing key parts, or had extremely poor workmanship. The same also holds true for services you may have received that were provided in an unsatisfactory manner by restaurants, hospitals, or educational institutions. Quality control is designed to overcome this problem.

Quality control (QC) or **quality assurance** is the process by which an organization insures that its finished products or services meet the expectations of clients and consumers. These expectations may take the form of taste (of a fast-food hamburger), cleanliness (of a room in a motel), noise (of a ceiling fan), durability (of an automobile part), quantity (of a canned soft drink), and so on.

What is your view?

Think of a "poor quality" experience you've recently had with a product or service. What was it about the product or service that fell below your expectations?

Reasons for renewed interest. Organizations have become more quality conscious than ever before for several reasons. One is the activity of consumer

Management Application and Practice 14.2   Inventory, Coming Up!

In quest of decreased inventory management costs, many large U.S. manufacturers have adopted what have been called "just-in-time" (JIT) inventory systems. Basically, the goal of JIT is to minimize storage and handling costs associated with stockpiles of raw supplies, parts, and materials, fabricated parts, subassemblies, and finished goods. Among JIT inventory practices:

1. Manufacturers rely on fewer suppliers with longer-term contracts and strong buyer-vendor trust relationships.
2. Suppliers may agree to locate facilities close to major buyers, assuring quick delivery of ordered supplies and materials.
3. Suppliers may submit their manufacturing practices to certification and even periodic inspection by buyers so as to assure product reliability and reduce or even eliminate the need for buyer in-

spections when products arrive. Ford Motor Company, for instance, awards its highly valued "Q1" designation to those suppliers who meet Ford's criteria for practicing effective statistical quality control techniques.

4. Manufacturers' unloading docks are workstation oriented so as to move materials directly to workstations rapidly. Whirlpool requires transporters to unload through a plant door onto a conveyor that directly feeds the assembly line. Such trucks are called "warehouses on wheels."
5. Manufacturers allow suppliers to have direct on-line computer linkage to production schedules and inventory levels so that orders for parts or supplies can be automatically triggered within the supplier's system.

SOURCE: A. T. Sadhwani and M. H. Sarhan, "The Impact of Just-In-Time Inventory Systems on Small Business," *Journal of Accountancy* 164 (January 1987): 119–132.

groups and the Consumer Protection Agency of the U.S. government. You've all read about massive product recalls and the increased number of lawsuits for product reliability, safety, and performance. Another factor is the high quality of products being made in other countries that have cut deeply into U.S. markets. This is especially true of Japan's high-quality products in the

fields of electronic and photographic equipment and automobiles. Table 14.3 shows one example of the result of this trend.

Activities involved. Basically, quality control activities are performed by departments that fall under the title of "Quality Control," "Quality Assurance," or "Inspection." The quality control function involves some or all of the following fundamental steps:

1. Standards and specifications are set to establish the quality objectives to be measured or evaluated.

2. Materials, parts, products, and services are inspected to compare them to established standards.

3. Statistical techniques, including sampling and analysis, are used to indicate whether quality is sufficiently under control.

4. Measuring instruments or inspection devices are used for objective and measurable comparison of actual quality to the established standards.

Some organizations are quite relaxed about quality and its control; others are very concerned. They commit themselves to *making* the product or service in the desired way instead of focusing on reworking and inspections that weed out undesirable goods. The cost of reworking faulty parts alone may run as high as 2 percent of sales for American industries. This estimate does not include those items that are totally scrapped and whose cost will not be recouped!

Calculating that up to 25 percent of manufacturing assets were tied up in reacting to quality problems, Hewlett-Packard president and CEO John Young implemented a bold objective of reducing tenfold by 1990 the failure rates for Hewlett-Packard products. The core of the HP approach was the timely information system that would show on a computer screen the latest parts-failure data, process schedules, and rework information. Managers and quality-oriented personnel would thus have ready access to information reflecting poor quality and could experiment and receive rapid feedback on their decisions. At one HP division, the cost of service and repair of desktop computers was reduced 35 percent. At another, production time for the popular HP oscilloscopes dropped 30 percent, defects substantially declined, and prices could be reduced by 16 percent.[10]

TABLE 14.3
Defects per Million
Components

In a select group of Japanese and American plants)

SOURCE: Courtesy of Gordon A. Heath, Rochester Community College.

Component type	Japanese	American
Integrated circuit	183	1,500
P.C. boards	60	6,000
Diodes	4	400
Resistors	1	150
Transistors	12	1,000
CRT	1,000	10,000
Connectors	10	4,000

Feedforward, concurrent, and feedback quality controls. *Feedforward quality control* involves quality checks of purchased raw materials prior to their use. For example, a manufacturer of clothing will first examine the fabric that has been purchased from the mills to assure that costly work will not be performed on an item that will eventually be rejected because of poor-quality material. Apple Computer, in response to the many problems encountered by customers who bought early Apple IIIs, realized that recalling 14,000 of the computers wasn't the answer to effective control. Today, Apple has agreements with major suppliers to place Apple employees at supplier manufacturing sites to assure that items being manufactured and shipped will meet Apple specifications. *Concurrent controls* use inspection points during production so that unsatisfactory items can be reworked. *Feedback quality control* occurs after the item has been completed; there is a strong probability that the overall item will have to be scrapped if it fails to meet standards.

Statistical quality control (SQC) different. It may surprise you to learn that for many products there is no "final inspection." Frequently goods are produced in such great quantities that inspection of each is not feasible because of the cost of inspecting individual nails, paper clips, or envelopes.

It is very costly to inspect each component, or each finished product. Therefore, organizations commonly use *statistical quality control (SQC)*, which uses the laws of probability to draw generalizations about entire batches of products; that is, they draw conclusions based on samples. This is a form of management by exception: No action is taken as long as the variations in product quality fall within the tolerance limits for the items being produced. If, say, 6 of a batch of 1000 fail to meet specifications, then the entire lot will be pulled and examined, and the cause of the deficiency will be investigated.

Quality control circle. A relatively recent approach to quality control is the quality circle, also known as the **quality control (QC) circle,** that originated in Japan. As indicated in Chapter 13, a QC circle is a relatively autonomous work unit with a small group of workers (ideally about 10) led by a supervisor or senior worker. Typical efforts include reducing defects, scrap, rework, and machinery and equipment downtime. The circles may also view quality in a broader sense and focus on improved morale, working conditions, and recognition of worker achievements.[11] A poll of 1566 companies in Japan showed that 91 percent have QC circles.[12]

Introduced in the United States in 1974 by Honeywell and Lockheed, quality control (QC) circle programs are now increasing in popularity in U.S. firms, including American Airlines, Ford Motor Company, Rockwell International, and others. A recent estimate claims that over half of the Fortune 500 companies have some form of QC circle program.

Zero defects. Zero defects (ZD) programs were introduced in the aerospace industry in the early 1960s. They enjoyed considerable success in several other organizations but fell into disrepute when the federal government required that contractors have such programs as a condition of getting a contract. Now they are regaining popularity.

A **zero defects (ZD)** or **do it right the first time program** focuses on high quality attainment by emphasizing prevention rather than cure, or doing the job right the first time, hence the name *zero defects*. Employees are encouraged to sign pledge cards signifying an intent to reduce errors and to contribute their suggestions for eliminating mistakes. Supervisors and specialists rapidly follow up on suggestions, and pins, plaques, dinners, and awards honor those who contribute most. Ford is a leading company with such an effort. Avondale Mills also has a ZD program.

Role of employees in quality control. Although quality control departments or inspection departments play an important part in controlling quality, there is no doubt that individual workers play the key role. Some organizations, though, seem to ignore one fact: workers who are poorly trained or qualified or who lack pride and dedication in their work must have a severe effect on the quality control picture. QC circles and ZD programs exist in only a very small percentage of U.S. industrial firms. Some firms, such as National Cash Register (NCR), American Telephone & Telegraph Company (AT&T), GE, and others, have created key executive positions with substantial clout that head up quality assurance programs. But the key to effective quality control is undoubtedly the line worker.

> Fortune *recently highlighted several products known for their high quality. At Baccarat Crystal in France, a worker who sees a flaw smashes the goblet: There is no such thing as a "second." At Cross Company, any employee on the line can reject a pen or pencil he or she thinks is unacceptable. At Remington Arms, although a computer controls many metal-forming and wood-shaping machines that make rifle parts, experienced gunsmiths hammer their individual marks on the barrel and put the entire gun together. At Dunhill Pipes in London, a pipe maker may turn as many as 50 "bowls" to produce a single perfect one, and it takes a month to make and season each pipe.*[13]

SUMMARY

Control is defined as the process of assuring that organizational and managerial objectives are accomplished. Controlling is related closely to each of the other management functions, especially planning.

The basic types of controls are feedforward, concurrent, and feedback. Feedforward control attempts to anticipate problems *before* they occur, allowing corrective action to be taken before the problem situation arises. Concurrent or steering control occurs *during* an activity. Feedback control takes place *after* performance has occurred. Each of these control types plays an important part in an organization's overall control system.

The five steps in the control process are (1) establishing standards of performance, (2) determining performance measurements, (3) measuring actual performance, (4) comparing performance with standards and analyzing deviations, and (5) taking corrective action if necessary.

The first step in the control process is to establish performance standards or target behaviors. Physical standards, monetary standards, and time standards are common examples of quantifiable control standards. But nonquantifiable, or qualitative, standards are also important.

Management by exception is a control technique in which a manager focuses attention on exceptional deviations from standard, allowing subordinates to control routine variations.

The basis for much organizational control, especially in larger organizations, lies in its management information system. A MIS is a planned system of gathering, processing, storing, and disseminating information so that effective management decisions can be made.

To be effective, control systems must meet several criteria. First, the standards of performance that are the focus of the system must reflect the true, significant objectives of the organizational unit: Appropriate activities should be controlled. Second, the controls should be sufficiently timely to allow management to take corrective action and still accomplish its objectives. Third, control benefits should outweigh the costs of the system: Control should be cost-effective. Fourth, an effective system must provide accurate information. Fifth, controls must be accepted by those involved with or affected by the control system.

Three functional areas of control discussed were finance, inventory, and quality. Financial controls include return on investment and ratio analysis, which enable a firm to compare the relative performance of its divisions from a profit perspective and provide insight into management's performance. Inventory control tries to balance the cost of carrying inventory with the cost of being out of needed stock. Just-in-time inventory systems are now being used to reduce inventory costs. Quality control is again becoming important because of lawsuits and product recalls. Quality control circles and zero defects programs are two techniques gaining popularity. Yet ultimately all employees are responsible for maintaining quality standards.

REVIEW QUESTIONS

1. What is control?
2. Distinguish between total and partial control.
3. How is control related to the other functions?
4. What steps are involved in the control process?
5. What is the distinction between feedforward, concurrent, and feedback controls?
6. What is management by exception?
7. What is a management information system?
8. What are two techniques commonly used for financial control?
9. How does a just-in-time inventory system work?
10. What is statistical quality control? How is it like management by exception?

DISCUSSION QUESTIONS

1. One manager who owns a chain of sporting goods stores in a large metropolitan area states: "The best control I have for each of my stores is their net profit picture at the end of each month. That's the overriding reason we're in business, and the only real information I need to know is whether my store managers are doing their jobs." What is your reaction to this statement?
2. Feedforward control *anticipates* problems and takes corrective action to prevent problems from occurring. Feedback controls occur *after the fact* and let manage-

ment know if a problem has occurred. Why is feedback control used by so many organizations when nothing can be done about past performance? Discuss.

3. It is sometimes said that if the planning function is done correctly there is little need for the controlling function. Do you agree or disagree? Why?

4. Does a small business such as a nursery (eight employees) or a women's dress shop (five employees) need a MIS? Discuss.

5. In what ways is control of governmental or nonprofit organizations different from control of profit-seeking firms?

6. In a newly purchased garment, you have probably found a slip of paper that says something like "Inspected by No. 17." Can you think of at least two ways in which this is a control device? Discuss.

LEARNING EXERCISE 14.1

Eastern Out of Control*

Eastern Air Lines had long been plagued by poor financial performance when, in October 1986, Texas Air chairman Frank Lorenzo merged it with his own airline. Lorenzo immediately installed in Eastern a new top management team charged with slashing costs in an effort to return the airline to respectable profitability.

By June 1987, just eight months later, Eastern was reeling. Among the reasons:

1. Eastern pilots reported that the company's attempts to trim costs compromised airplane safety. Two cost-saving measures—reduced parts inventories and fewer maintenance personnel—meant that scheduled maintenance work was being delayed or cleared from logbooks when it wasn't actually performed.

2. In the eight-month period, almost 10 percent of Eastern's pilots had either retired or quit.

3. U.S. Representative Newt Gingrich (R-GA), a member of the U.S. House of Representatives Aviation Subcommittee, had received over 1000 letters critical of the company's new methods from employees who worked at Atlanta's Hartsfield Airport, Eastern's largest hub.

4. Formal grievance cases filed by employees during the eight-month period since Texas Air's merger jumped to over 3000, compared to 1353 for the same period in 1986.

5. Eastern's problems weren't only internal ones—as shown in Table 14.4, consumer complaints against Eastern had risen steadily to where it ranked second only to its Texas Air sister, Continental.

These results led many to question the effectiveness of the new profit-driven control system that Lorenzo had pledged to establish.

Questions

1. Identify the major control issues involved in the case.

2. What recommendations do you have for better controlling Eastern's customer satisfaction problem?

LEARNING EXERCISE 14.2

The Missing Speech

The president of Acme Engineering, C. G. Barrington, picked up the phone and called Charlie Halston, his public relations director. When Charlie answered, the following conversation took place:

BARRINGTON: Charlie, where is that environmental speech I'm supposed to deliver to that national conservation group's convention at noon today? You said you'd

* Adapted from Bert Roughton, Jr., "Eastern May Cut Safety with Costs, FAA Fears," *Atlanta Journal-Constitution*, June 21, 1987, p. 1A.

**Table 14.4
The Unsatisfactory Skies—Monthly Consumer Complaints Rankings for Selected U.S. Airlines in 1987**

SOURCE: U.S. Department of Transportation, as reported in Bert Roughton, Jr., ''Eastern May Cut Safety with Costs, FAA Fears,'' *Atlanta Journal-Constitution*, June 21, 1987, p. 1A.

Airline ranked by complaints	Number of complaints	Complaints per 100,000 passengers
January 1987		
1. Continental*	149	8.62
2. Pam Am	62	6.21
3. Northwest	166	6.20
5. TWA	93	5.42
7. Eastern*	109	3.07
8. United	105	2.62
11. American	56	1.53
16. USAir	18	.99
17. Delta	22	.68
19. Piedmont	11	.56
February		
1. Continental	372	11.23
2. Pam Am	64	6.10
3. TWA	112	5.91
4. Northwest	177	5.78
6. Eastern	140	3.86
7. United	159	3.72
11. American	70	1.75
14. Piedmont	21	.99
17. USAir	17	.91
18. Delta	18	.79
March		
1. Continental	717	25.49
2. Pan Am	53	14.52
3. Northwest	181	7.50
4. Eastern	220	6.28
6. TWA	92	5.34
8. United	135	3.54
13. American	58	1.66
14. Piedmont	22	1.26
16. Delta	34	1.08
17. USAir	17	1.05

Airline ranked by complaints	Number of complaints	Complaints per 100,000 passengers
April		
1. Continental	767	25.40
3. Eastern	261	6.98
4. TWA	114	6.82
5. Pan Am	67	6.81
6. Northwest	179	6.32
9. United	125	3.07
12. USAir	39	2.23
13. American	74	2.13
17. Piedmont	30	1.09
19. Delta	30	.74
May		
1. Continental*	793	21.39
2. Eastern	445	10.11
3. TWA	194	8.68
4. Pan Am	99	8.06
5. Northwest	283	8.01
9. United	224	4.25
12. American	107	2.37
14. USAir	42	1.99
15. Piedmont	44	1.97
16. Delta	93	1.78

* Continental and Eastern are both owned by Texas Air. Northwest includes Republic Airlines; TWA includes Ozark; Continental: beginning in February, includes New York Air and People Express, beginning in April, data also includes Frontier Air Lines; Delta: beginning in April, data includes Western Air Lines; and USAir and Piedmont are awaiting approval to merge.

have it for me on Wednesday so that I could go over it, but I've been out of town. I'd like to go over it a few times before I give it. Can you get it to me right away?

HALSTON: *(Surprised)* Mr. Barrington, you mean you haven't gotten that speech yet? I gave your speech situation and facts to Fred Osbourne, who's really knowledgeable about this group and also knows our position well. He was supposed to have gotten something to you by Wednesday.

BARRINGTON: Well, Charlie, today is *Friday,* and all I know is that in exactly two hours I'll be standing on a podium giving that speech to 500 people who are not exactly sympathetic with our position. Call Fred and see what the problem is. I want that speech on my desk right now! *(Hangs up.)*

HALSTON: *(Immediately dialing Fred Osbourne's office)* Fred, this is Charlie. Barrington just called me, and he's supposed to give that environmental speech at noon today. He can't find it. Didn't you get it to him?

OSBOURNE: That environmental speech? I finished it on Tuesday and left it with your secretary to type up. He was supposed to give it to you.

HALSTON: Hang on, Fred!

At this point, Charlie rushed into his secretary's office and uncovered a 10-page roughly handwritten draft in the bottom of his secretary's in-basket, under several routine items. On it was a note: "Please type and give to Mr. Halston by Wednesday." It was the first time Ed Winston, Halston's secretary, had seen or even heard about the speech.

Questions

1. Was either feedforward or concurrent control used in this case? Explain.
2. What standards existed in the task that Barrington assigned to Halston?
3. Whom would you hold accountable for the breakdown? Why?
4. What action do you recommend to Barrington to prevent a reoccurrence of this sort of situation?

NOTES

1. Adapted from Arthur A. Thompson, Jr., and A. J. Strickland, *Strategic Management,* 3d ed. (Plano, TX: Business Publications, 1984), pp. 377–408.
2. "An All-Out Attack on Banks That Launder Money," *Business Week,* February 25, 1985, p. 30.
3. "Caterpillar: Sticking to Basics to Stay Competitive," *Business Week,* May 4, 1981, p. 74.
4. Laurel Leff, "Watchdogs Wanted: Internal Auditors Find Themselves Loved as Rules Stiffen for 'Clean' Sets of Books," *Wall Street Journal,* January 15, 1980, p. 46.
5. Hal Lancaster and G. Christian Hill, "Anatomy of a Scam: Fraud at Wells Fargo Depended on Avoiding Computer's Red Flags," *Wall Street Journal,* February 26, 1981, p. 1.
6. Thomas H. Naylor, "Management Is Drowning in Numbers," *Business Week,* April 6, 1981, pp. 14–16.
7. Cortlandt Cammann and David Nadler, "Fit Control Systems to Your Managerial Style," *Harvard Business Review* 54 (January–February 1976): 65–72.
8. "What is Fueling Chrysler's Comeback?" *Business Week,* June 1, 1981, p. 49.
9. Jeffrey A. Tannenbaum, "Circuit City Stores Wins Praise of Analysts as Competition Grows During a Shake-Out," *Wall Street Journal,* June 24, 1987, p. 57.
10. John Young, "One Company's Quest for Quality," *Wall Street Journal,* July 25, 1983, p. 17.
11. See Robert E. Cole, "Learning from the Japanese: Problems and Pitfalls," *Management Review* 69 (September 1980): 23.

12. James Riggs et al., *Industrial Organization and Management* (New York: McGraw-Hill, 1979), p. 366.
13. "Things Made Well," *Fortune*, December 1980, pp. 35–41.

SUGGESTIONS FOR FURTHER STUDY

ALEXANDER, C. PHILLIP. "A Hidden Benefit of Quality Circles." *Personnel Journal* 63 (February 1984): 54–58.

BURNS, WILLIAM J., JR., and MCFARLAN, F. WARREN. "Information Technology Puts Power in Control Systems." *Harvard Business Review* 65 (September–October 1987): 89–94.

DAFT, RICHARD L., and MACINTOSH, NORMAN B. "The Nature and Use of Formal Control Systems for Management Control and Strategy Implementation." *Journal of Management* 10 (Fall 1984): 43–66.

GARVIN, DAVID A. "Quality Problems, Policies and Attitudes in the United States and Japan: An Exploratory Study." *Academy of Management Journal* 29 (December 1986): 653–674.

MALONE, STEWART C. "Computerizing Small Business Information Systems." *Journal of Small Business Management*, April 1984, pp. 10–16.

"The Meanest and Leanest Sit Down to Just Desserts." *Business Week*, February 9, 1987, pp. 30–31.

MERCHANT, KENNETH A. "The Control Function of Management." *Sloan Management Review* 23 (Summer 1982): 43–55.

MILLS, PETER K. "Self-Management: Its Control and Relationship to Other Organizational Properties." *Academy of Management Review* 8 (July 1983): 445–453.

NEWMAN, WILLIAM H. *Constructive Control: Design and Use of Control Systems.* Englewood Cliffs, NJ: Prentice-Hall, 1975.

WALDON, BARRY. "The Human Side of Control." *Supervisory Management* 30 (April 1985): 10–16.

WALLEIGH, RICHARD C. "What's Your Excuse for Not Using JIT?" *Harvard Business Review* 64 (March–April 1986): 38–45.

YOUNG, WILLIAM J. "Have Computers Revolutionized Sales Management?" *Management Review* 75 (April 1987): 54–55.

15
Control Techniques and Methods

Learning Objectives

After studying the material in this chapter, you should be able to do the following:

☐ Recognize some of the methods and techniques most frequently used in controlling managerial activities.
☐ Explain what budgets are and how they are used to control activities.
☐ Discuss some of the special aspects of budgeting and controlling, such as the planning-programming-budgeting system (PPBS), zero-base budgeting (ZBB), and human-resource accounting (HRA).
☐ State how internal, external, and management audits are used for control purposes.
☐ Describe break-even analysis and show how it is used in controlling activities.
☐ Identify the more popular time-related charts and techniques—the Gantt chart, Program Evaluation and Review Technique (PERT), and the Critical Path Method (CPM)—and show how they are used in controlling.

Some Important Terms

nonquantitative control methods
quantitative control techniques
budgets
budgetary control
capital budgets
operating budgets
production budgets
personnel budgets
variable (flexible, step, sliding-scale) budgets
fixed costs
variable costs
variances
planning-programming-budgeting systems (PPBS)

zero-base budgeting (ZBB)
audits
management audit
ratio analysis (RA)
break-even analysis
break-even point (BEP)
scheduling
Gantt chart
Program Evaluation and Review Technique (PERT)
PERT network
critical path
Critical Path Method (CPM)

I claim not to have controlled events but confess plainly that events have controlled me.
—ABRAHAM LINCOLN

"Blueprint Perfect"

The U.S. Navy's plan to build 27 Trident submarines and to arm them with powerful nuclear weapons ran nearly three years behind schedule and $13 billion over budget. Each Trident is a seaborne launching pad for 24 nuclear missiles, each five times more powerful than the atomic bomb that devastated Hiroshima.

The Navy wrote to the General Dynamics Corporation, contractor for 8 Tridents, that if the program could not be put back on schedule by the end of 1981, plans for 19 additional Trident subs might be dropped.

The Trident fiasco resulted from a bitter feud between Adm. Hyman G. Rickover, the most influential figure in the nuclear Navy, and the secretary of the Navy, as well as from the collapse of communication between the Navy and one of the nation's well-known shipyards and a command structure with at least 10 officials in charge but none with overall responsibility.

Electric Boat, a division of General Dynamics, was already busy building a series of attack submarines, and, despite a history of turning out first-class submarines, it soon ran into deep trouble with the *Ohio,* the first Trident. The hastily hired work force lacked the necessary expertise: Welders couldn't weld, managers couldn't manage, the quality controllers couldn't control the quality of materials or workmanship.

As a result of a "serious breakdown in workmanship and quality control," 2,772 welds had to be repaired, and the wrong kind of steel was used in 126,000 locations, and much of it had to be replaced. A faulty turbine was installed in the first sub and had to be removed piece by piece. Drug abuse and fistfights were common in the shipyard. The firm was losing so much money on the attack submarines that it threatened to stop all Navy work including that on the Tridents.

The third shipyard manager in the three years since construction had begun on the Trident fired a quarter of the yard's 28,000 workers and made many sweeping production changes. This manager's improvements led to a settlement between the Navy and Electric Boat on the cost of the attack submarines, whereby the company absorbed a $359 million loss.

Not since the early 1970s has the Navy had a single person as overall manager of the Trident program. Responsibility has been spread among at least 10 officials in a chain of command in which Rickover, a four-star admiral, is subordinate to officers lower in rank and 30 years his junior.

Rickover insisted that the *Ohio* be completed "blueprint perfect." Company officials say this added months to the delivery time of all the Tridents, for many small imperfections could have been fixed after the *Ohio* was in service.

Rickover's insistence on performance contributed to a virtual breakdown in communication between the Navy and the shipyard so that it became increasingly difficult to deal with Electric Boat on a day-to-day basis at the working level.[1]

What caused this impasse, and what can now be done about it?

IMPORTANCE OF CONTROL TECHNIQUES AND METHODS

We tend to think of large organizations as succeeding in spite of anything they do. Yet this is far from true, as shown by the Trident case. Do you remember—or have you even heard of—Baldwin Locomotive, the Franklin National Bank, W. T. Grant, or the Penn Central Railroad? Many other large organizations have failed. In fact, of the 100 largest firms in 1900, only American Sugar Refining and the Standard Oil companies (such as Exxon) remain.[2]

There are many reasons for the failure of these and other organizations. But one recurring problem in all of them was a lack of adequate control, as shown in the following example.

> *Lack of control was given as a primary reason that W. T. Grant neared collapse in 1975. Managers were not granted authority to control the stock in their own stores. They often had to ask their suppliers for figures on their inventories, since management had no data. Further, about 20 percent of all credit purchasers' bills were never paid, and the delinquencies were not detected.*[3]

These events illustrate the need for prompt, adequate, and effective application of the principles of control discussed in the previous chapter. In this chapter, we will see how some of those control techniques operate in actual practice.

DIFFERENT TYPES OF CONTROL METHODS

There is an interesting paradox inherent in the control process. Control implies maintaining stability and equilibrium. To achieve balance, however, managers must continually change what they are doing or change the preset standard used to measure performance. In either case, it is difficult to reach a state of stability or equilibrium, but it is a desirable goal to strive for.

Nonquantitative Control Methods

Nonquantitative control methods are those used by managers in performing the other management functions of planning, organizing, staffing, and leading. In general, these lead to control of *overall* organizational performance. Most of these control employees' attitudes and performance.

The more frequently used control techniques include (1) observation, (2) regular or "spot" inspections, (3) oral and written reports, (4) performance evaluations, and (5) discussions between the manager and employees involved in performing an activity. In general, these measures are used in leading or supervising the work force. Some examples of these controls that were discussed in the previous chapter are:

Control by observation. The supervisor assigns custodial employees the job of cleaning your classroom after classes. She goes with the employees while they are working to see that the work is being done properly. She tells employees how to correct work done improperly.

Control by regular inspection. A maintenance supervisor has people working all over the campus. He can't be with all of them all of the time. Instead, he will go to different places after his workers are supposed to be finished to see that the work is satisfactory. He tells employees how to correct work done improperly.

Control by spot inspection. The heat-absorbing tiles on the space shuttle were supposed to be inspected as they were installed. Yet a later inspection, done at an irregular time, found thousands of the tiles to be defective, and they had to be replaced.

Control by reports. Most sales representatives must make *written* reports to the home office on a regular basis. These reports usually tell the number of calls made, the number and amounts of sales made, and other pertinent information. Sometimes the rep makes an *oral* report on his or her return.

Performance evaluation. You may have had the opportunity to evaluate your teacher's performance at the end of a course. This type of evaluation usually includes an appraisal of the teacher's knowledge of the subject, how well the material was covered, and whether the tests were fairly designed and graded. The teacher's evaluation of your performance is another example.

Some other management systems and methods that are used for control purposes include management by objectives (MBO), management by exception (MBE), and management information systems (MIS). MBE and MIS were discussed in the previous chapter, and MBO was covered in Chapter 4.

Quantitative Control Techniques

Quantitative control techniques tend to use specific data and quantitative methods to measure and correct the quantity and quality of output. Those more popular with managers, as shown in Figure 15.1, are as follows:

1. Budgets, such as (1) the regular operating, capital expenditure, sales, and cash budgets; and (2) specialized budgets, such as planning-programming-budgeting systems (PPBS), and zero-base budgeting (ZBB).
2. Audits, such as (1) internal audits, (2) external audits, and (3) management audits.
3. Ratio analysis (RA).
4. Break-even (BE) analysis.
5. Time-performance charts and techniques, such as (1) the Gantt chart, (2) Program Evaluation and Review Technique (PERT), and (3) the Critical Path Method (CPM).

USING BUDGETS AND BUDGETARY CONTROL

The budget is the most widely used control device in both business and government.[4] In fact, it is used so extensively that for many people the word *budget* means control. Yet the preparation of budgets is an integral part of the planning process, and the budget itself is the end point of the planning

FIGURE 15.1
Quantitative control
techniques.

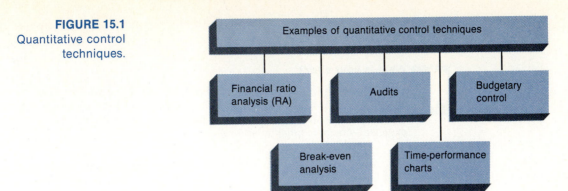

process, that is, the statement of plans. To avoid the negative reactions often associated with the concept of control, some managers refer to their budgetary controls as *profit plans.*

In our discussion of budgetary controls, we first examine the nature of budgets and budgetary controls, review the types of budgets used most frequently, and study the advantages and disadvantages of budgetary control.

Nature of Budgetary Control

Budgets express plans, objectives, and programs of the organization in numerical terms. Thus budgets are statements of planned revenue and expenditures—by category and period of time—of money, time, personnel, space, buildings, or equipment. Obviously, planning is an integral part of any budget. That is, preparation of the budget is an integral part of the planning function. Yet, as with MBO, the *administration* of the budget is an integral part of the control function.

Once the budget is planned, measures of expenditures are periodically made and compared with budgeted amounts. Management may then ob-

"Oh, it's great here, all right, but I sort of feel uncomfortable in a place with no budget at all." (Drawing by D. Reilly, copyright 1976 by the New Yorker Magazine, Inc.)

serve over, under, or "on target" expenditure levels and take corrective action if warranted.

What is your view?

If you buy more clothes than expected, you are "over" on your clothing budget. Consequently, you must spend less (be "under") on food and drink. You are probably "on target" for tuition most of the time, since it tends to be a "fixed expense." Are there other items on which you are consistently "over" or "under"?

Budgets can also be used for improving machinery, equipment, personnel, time, space, and material resource utilization. These forms of budgets substitute nondollar numbers for financial figures. Items such as worker hours, capacity utilization, and units of production can be planned for daily, weekly, monthly, or annual appraisal.

Budgetary control is a system of using the target figures established in a budget to control managerial activities by comparing actual performance with planned performance. So planning the budget is really setting standards, the first step in control.

Budgetary control is a simple and direct application of the essentials of the control process. Budget figures are set; then records of actual receipts and expenditures are made. Each budget item is then compared with the actual performance, and variances can be noted—over or under budget. The manager then has the information needed to take corrective action, such as (1) to increase receipts, (2) to reduce expenditures, or (3) to revise the budget. This process enables the manager to check continually and to locate problems early, before they become so large they threaten the very existence of the organization. Note that the budget in the Trident case permitted the Navy to see early that the program was in trouble. Later, the Navy was able to take corrective action.

Figure 15.2 shows how budgetary control is related to planning. Notice that the budget provides the feedback for changing plans (that is, the budget).

Benefits and Limitations of Budgets

That most organizations—profit or nonprofit—operate within the framework of budgets is evidence of the benefits of budgeting. Budgets are used widely by managers to plan, monitor, evaluate, and control various activities and operations at every level of the organization. There are several important advantages of preparing and using budgets, but there are also many limitations regarding their use.

We noted earlier that the word *control* has negative connotations for many people. The same holds true for the terms *budget* and *budgetary control*. Like other types of controls, however, budgets have many features that are potentially helpful to organizations and their members in reaching their goals. Just how effective budgetary controls turn out to be in actual practice depends on how well managers receive and carry out the budgeting process. It is particularly important that the budgeting process, like other types of controls, be clear and acceptable to the people whose activities it is intended to control.

Benefits of budgetary control. The most obvious advantage of budgetary control is that a comparable statement of goals, in uniform financial terms, is provided for all organizational units. Also, the budget serves as a standard

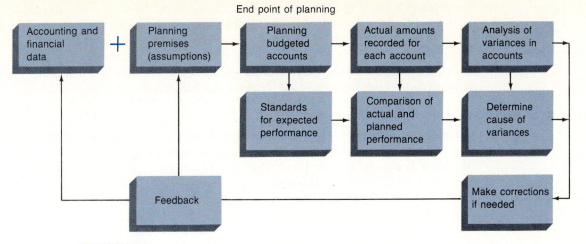

End point of planning

FIGURE 15.2
How the budget relates
to planning and control.

of performance, and deviations from this standard are readily measurable and provide the basis for necessary corrective action.

There are also many indirect benefits resulting from the proper use of budgets:

1. The consistent and uniform application of budgets results in a more clearly defined organizational structure, since budgets measure the performance of organizational units.

2. More significant information systems and terminology are developed. Traditionally, accounting has been concerned with preparing historical and tax records rather than reporting current operations and forecasting future performance.

3. Better planning of all phases of operations results from the use of budgets. Budgets are plans that serve to emphasize the continuous nature of the planning-control-planning cycle.

4. A clearer statement and understanding of organizational goals comes from the use of budgets because managers are forced to develop and state attainable goals for organizational units.

Limitations on the use of budgetary control. Paradoxically, one of the strengths of budgets—translating all aspects of organizational performance into a single comparable monetary unit of measurement—can become their greatest weakness. This practice may result in measuring only easily measurable items—for example, those aspects of organizational performance that are readily converted into monetary terms. Other important factors, such as manager performance and plans for organizational development, may be ignored because achievement in these areas is not easily converted into financial terms. Also, there is the danger of confusing symptoms with causes. A decline in revenue from sales may not necessarily call for greater sales effort. Instead, the real problem may be a poor product, the actions of competitors, or general economic conditions. Further, there is the danger that staff people will exercise autocratic control instead of leaving it to line managers. The function of the controller or the budget director is to coordinate and guide the development of budgets, but the actual control of performance must remain in the hands of operating managers. Finally, budgets tend to become static and not reflect changing conditions.

Many government budgets tend to remain fixed for the budgeted period. This is particularly true of those states and municipalities that require a balanced budget. Also, many not-for-profit organizations (see Chapter 18) operate on a fixed budget. Most religious institutions use this type of budget.

Types of Budgets

Most organizations have a budget for each of their major activities. **Capital budgets** are for purchasing equipment and facilities; **operating budgets** are for forecasting sales and allocating financial resources and supplies; **production budgets** are for producing the organization's basic products or service; and **personnel budgets** are for securing and developing human resources. Table 15.1 provides a more detailed explanation of these different types of budgets.

These budgets are discussed as if they were separate and distinct units, but they are in fact part of a comprehensive system. The sales budget tends to be the focus of the system, since it shows the main function of the organization. The production budget is based on the sales budget, and all the others are derived from and related to these two.

Using Variable Budgets

As stated earlier, budgets tend to become static once they are established. Yet this need not be true. Instead, a **variable budget** (sometimes called a **flexible budget, step budget,** or **sliding scale budget**) can be used for control purposes. This is a technique involving standard costs tied to the volume of revenues that permits managers to exercise control over the expenditure of funds depending on volume of sales.

What is your view?

Suppose you are the production manager of a shoe manufacturing firm. What additional costs will your department have if production is raised from 1000 to 1500 pairs of shoes per month? Would it make sense for you to have a "variable" budget to work with that would reflect the different levels of production required of your department?

**TABLE 15.1
Types and Purposes of Budgets**

Type of budget	Brief description of purpose
Sales budget	Provides an estimate of the amount and source of expected revenues
Production budget	Expresses physical requirements of expected production, including labor, materials, and overhead requirements for the budget period
Expense budget	Provides details for allocation of various expenses, such as selling, general, and administrative
Cash budget	Forecasts the flow of cash receipts and disbursements
Capital budget	Outlines specific expenditures for office, plant, equipment, machinery, inventories, and other capital items
Balance sheet budget	Forecasts the financial status of assets, liabilities, and net worth at the end of the budget period

Essentially, a variable, or "flexible," budget shows expected costs of production at various levels of activity. The prerequisite for flexible budgeting is the separation of fixed and variable costs. Certain costs, such as some utilities, rent for the building, insurance, and salaries for supervisors, would be the same in the shoe example cited above, even if production were increased by 50 percent. These are called **fixed costs** (see Figure 15.3). **Variable costs** are those that vary according to the level of output. Variable costs might be the cost of some utilities, raw materials, extra workers' wages, or extra supplies needed (see Table 15.2).

The basic idea is to allow material, labor, advertising, and other related expenses to vary directly with changes in the volume of output. The actual level of sales or output is not known in advance; therefore, variable budgets are more useful for evaluating what the expenses should have been under the circumstances but have limited value for providing planning information to the overall budgeting program.

Notice in Table 15.2 that as monthly sales increase from 10,000 to 12,000 to 14,000 units, revenue goes up from $100,000 to $120,000 to $140,000. Total variable costs also rise from $48,000 to $57,600 to $67,200, but total fixed costs remain at $40,000. Therefore, income from operations increases from $12,000 to $22,400 to $32,800. You can see that profits increase much more rapidly than output because the fixed overhead costs are allocated to more units produced. Therefore, the unit cost of production declines, and the profit margin is greater.

How Budgetary Control Operates

Budgets are control devices in that they are designed to guide the actions of management by providing feedback when the budget is exceeded. They become the standard by which actual expenditures are measured.

The amount needed for each item is projected and budgeted. The amounts actually expended are recorded. Then the **variances,** that is, the amounts over or under budget, are computed. The results indicate areas that are "over" or "under" and should be corrected by (1) increasing the

FIGURE 15.3
Variable and fixed costs.

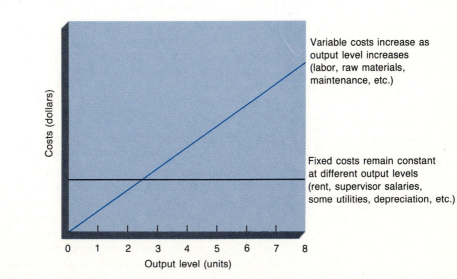

Variable costs increase as output level increases (labor, raw materials, maintenance, etc.)

Fixed costs remain constant at different output levels (rent, supervisor salaries, some utilities, depreciation, etc.)

Costs (dollars)

Output level (units)

TABLE 15.2
Example of a Variable Budget

SOURCE: W. W. Pyle, J. A. White, and K. D. Larson, *Fundamental Accounting Principles,* 8th ed. (Homewood, IL: Irwin, 1978): p. 847.

	Fixed budget	Flexible budget — Price and variable cost per unit	Flexible budget — Total fixed cost	Flexible budget for unit sales of 12,000	Flexible budget for unit sales of 14,000
Sales: In units	10,000			12,000	14,000
In dollars	$100,000	$10.00		$120,000	$140,000
Variable costs					
Raw materials	$ 10,000	$ 1.00		$ 12,000	$ 14,000
Direct labor	15,000	1.50		18,000	21,000
Factory supplies	2,000	0.20		2,400	2,800
Utilities	3,000	0.30		3,600	4,200
Sales commission	9,000	0.90		10,800	12,600
Shipping expenses	4,000	0.40		4,800	5,600
Office supplies	5,000	0.50		6,000	7,000
Total variable costs	$ 48,000	$ 4.80		$ 57,600	$ 67,200
Contribution margin	$ 52,000	$ 5.20		$ 62,400	$ 72,800
Fixed costs					
Depreciation of machinery	$ 8,000		$ 8,000	$ 8,000	$ 8,000
Supervisory salaries	11,000		11,000	11,000	11,000
Insurance expenses	1,000		1,000	1,000	1,000
Depreciation of office equipment	7,000		7,000	7,000	7,000
Administrative salaries	13,000		13,000	13,000	13,000
Total fixed costs	$ 40,000		$40,000	$ 40,000	$ 40,000
Income from operations	$ 12,000			$ 22,400	$ 32,800

budgeted amount, (2) reducing expenses, or (3) using a combination of these two procedures. The following example illustrates this control process. It shows that although the concept may be simple, the application of budgetary control is complex and requires managerial expertise.

Table 15.3 is the March 1989 budget of a hypothetical department. The major expense items include direct labor, postage, supplies, and materials, indirect labor, utilities, maintenance, and administrative expense. Actual expenditures for each item are compared to the budgeted amounts at the end of the month. Then the reasons for the variances are determined, and corrective action is taken.

What is your view?

Examine Table 15.3 before reading further. What do you think might account for the 50 percent overage in postage costs for the mail room?

Answer: The $1200 overage for direct labor resulted from overtime to get out special mailings before a postal increase went into effect March 22. This activity also accounted for the increased postage, supplies and materials, and utilities. The savings in subsequent months will compensate for the increase.

Most of the utility increase was accounted for by costs associated with decontrol of oil prices and increases in imported oil. The amount budgeted for utilities must be increased to $3000, since this is considered to be a permanent increase.

TABLE 15.3
A Hypothetical
Departmental Operating
Budget

(Mail room operating
budget, March 1–31, 1989)

Budget account	Amount budgeted	Actual expenditure	Over	Under
Direct labor	$15,000	$16,200	$1,200	—
Postage	8,000	12,000	4,000	—
Supplies and materials	1,875	2,250	375	—
Miscellaneous expenses (phone, coffee, and so on)	300	240	—	$ 60
Applied overhead				
Indirect labor	2,750	2,750	—	—
Utilities	2,500	3,000	500	—
Maintenance	2,700	2,100	—	600
Administrative expenses	2,000	2,000	—	—
Other	1,200	900	—	300
Totals	$36,325	$41,440	$6,075	$960
			−960	
Net overage			$5,115	

Maintenance costs were down because of contracting with an outside maintenance firm. Therefore, the budgeted figure can be reduced to 2100 in future months.

SPECIALIZED BUDGETARY CONTROL METHODS

Two innovative developments in the budgeting process have come largely from government. The *planning-programming-budgeting system* (PBBS) was developed by the Rand Corporation in the 1950s and introduced into the Department of Defense in 1961.[5] In 1965, it was mandated for the entire executive branch by President Johnson. Jimmy Carter used *zero-base budgeting (ZBB)* as governor of Georgia. Later, as president, he ordered ZBB used in the executive branch of the federal government.[6]

**Planning-
Programming-
Budgeting
Systems (PPBS)**

Planning-programming-budgeting systems (PPBS) were developed to aid management in identifying and eliminating costly programs that tend to duplicate other programs and to provide a means of analyzing the benefits and costs of each program or activity.

Essential elements. The essential elements of PPBS include the following:

1. Analyzing and specifying the basic *objectives* in each major activity or program area. The starting point for PPBS is to answer such questions as, "What is our basic purpose or mission?" and "What, specifically, are we trying to accomplish?" As you will see in Chapter 18, the objective of the Polio Foundation for many years was to eliminate polio. When this goal had been achieved, the organization then made minimizing birth defects its objective.

2. Analyzing the *output* of each program in terms of the specific objectives. In other words, "How effectively are we achieving our goals?"

3. Measuring the *total costs* of the program for several years ahead. For example, in budgeting for additional schools, you would need to consider not only the initial costs of construction but also the costs of operating and maintaining the facilities in future years.

4. Determining *which alternatives are most effective* in achieving the basic objectives at the least cost. The Salk polio vaccine, for example, was the most effective method of preventing polio.

5. Implementing PPBS in an organized and systematic manner so that future budgetary decisions are subject to similar rigorous analysis.

A modified version of these elements is shown in Figure 15.4. Notice that it emphasizes the control aspects of (1) planning, programming, and budgeting; (2) working, operating, and implementing; and (3) evaluating and controlling.

Implementing PPBS. PPBS has not been implemented successfully. What were some of the reasons for the federal government's failure to implement what appears to be an improved approach to budgeting during the 1960s? Probably the most important reason was the opposition of the agencies and departments involved. Such resistance to change seems to develop whenever a new program is introduced, especially when it is done without prior consultation with those affected by the change.

Zero-Base Budgeting (ZBB)

The traditional approach to budgeting is *incremental budgeting*, whereby an organization bases budgets upon certain increases (or decreases) from the amounts granted for the previous period. Thus you hear of a budget increase of 5 percent to 10 percent, based on the allocation in the previous budget period. In contrast, **zero-base budgeting (ZBB)** divides an organization's programs into "decision packages," consisting of goals, activities, and resources needed; costs are computed "from scratch," as if the program had never existed. This technique is simple in concept, but in practice it is much more complex and difficult to apply. For example, the state of Georgia was able to identify around 11,000 "decision packages" in its 1972 to 1973 budget.[7]

Figure 15.5 shows that ZBB requires management to take a fresh look at programs and activities each year instead of merely adding an increment to the previous year's budget. In other words, the *previous* year's budget allo-

FIGURE 15.4
Steps in implementing PPBS.

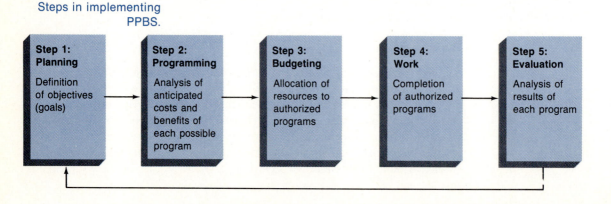

Step 1: Planning	Step 2: Programming	Step 3: Budgeting	Step 4: Work	Step 5: Evaluation
Definition of objectives (goals)	Analysis of anticipated costs and benefits of each possible program	Allocation of resources to authorized programs	Completion of authorized programs	Analysis of results of each program

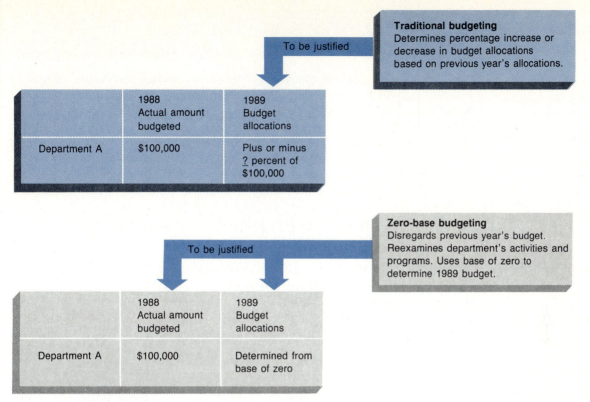

FIGURE 15.5
Comparison of traditional and zero-base budgeting (ZBB).

cations are not considered as a basis for *this* year's budget. Each program or decision package must be justified on the basis of a cost-benefit analysis. Under a modified ZBB system, a base other than zero may be used. For instance, if a 60 percent base budget system were used, a department would be assured of automatically receiving 60 percent of the previous year's budget as its base; amounts in excess of that would require documentation as in a normal ZBB system.

ZBB cannot solve all the problems associated with budgetary control, for organizations may have problems in implementing it. Among its several disadvantages are that (1) it is expensive to implement, requiring much time of line and staff managers, (2) there is an exceptionally large amount of paperwork required, and (3) managers still have a tendency to subvert the system by inflating the benefits of pet projects in order to have them funded.

A survey conducted in the late 1970s found that ZBB was used at that time by 54 of the largest companies in the United States, by 11 state governments, and by many municipalities.[8] But the federal government abandoned ZBB in 1981, declaring that the program was cumbersome and did not materially affect the level of agency spending.[9]

But ZBB does establish a system whereby an organization's resources are allocated to the higher-priority programs. Under this system, programs of lower priority can be reduced or eliminated. On balance, the benefits of ZBB appear to outweigh its costs. Ironically, though, it is the companies that are well managed that are best able to implement ZBB. Those in weak shape do not have the internal management skills to use it effectively.[10]

USING AUDITS FOR CONTROL

Another effective control method is the use of **audits,** which are efforts to examine activities or records to verify their accuracy or effectiveness. Traditionally, auditing has been thought of as an independent appraisal of an organization's financial records. It sought to test the reliability and validity of financial records by determining the degree of accuracy and the extent to which financial statements reflected what they purported to represent. Hence, these programs are often regarded as a way of encouraging honesty on the part of employees and safeguarding the organization's financial resources.

This concept of auditing, the verification of financial records, is limited in scope and is associated with an *external audit* that is conducted by outside agencies such as bank examiners or certified public accountant (CPA) firms. An *internal audit* can be an effective means of control as well as a means of verifying financial records when conducted by a specialized group of company personnel. The internal audit is wider in scope and considers the control system and its performance.

It is also possible to apply auditing techniques as a way of determining the overall effectiveness of management. When the technique is used for this purpose, it is referred to as a **management audit.** This type of audit studies the present and looks to the future. It considers programs, policies, organization, operating methods and procedures, financial procedures, personnel practices, and physical facilities and reports on the organization's overall effectiveness.

The information generated by a management audit helps top executives insure that current policies and procedures relate to the overall objectives of the organization. It highlights major areas needing attention, improves communication by informing all employees of the state of the organization, and acts as a test of the effectiveness of the current management control system. Management audits are usually used by large organizations, but they can also be used by small firms.

USING RATIO ANALYSIS (RA) FOR CONTROL

As shown in the previous chapter, **ratio analysis (RA)** is studying the relationships between financial statement data expressed as ratios or percentages. Managers can better observe relative changes in the organization's performance over a period of time by using ratios rather than comparing absolute figures. The use of RA also facilitates comparisons of the performance of different organizations.

Most Popular Ratios   Depending on its purpose and objectives, particular operating problems, the general economy, competition, and similar factors, an organization's management will use different ratios. The desired values of these ratios tend to be similar among managers of firms in the same industry, but these values may differ significantly from industry to industry.

Ratios can be computed for practically any financial measurements, but the most commonly computed ones are liquidity, asset management, debt management, and profitability. These ratios are used as follows:

1. *Liquidity ratios* indicate how well a firm is prepared to meet its short-term obligations, such as payrolls, creditor payments, and interest; that is, whether cash and accounts receivable will cover current debts.

2. *Asset-management ratios* measure how well a firm uses its assets.

3. *Debt-management (leverage) ratios* indicate a firm's ability to meet its long-term obligations, such as bonds, mortgages, and notes payable.

4. *Profitability ratios* measure management's overall performance as shown by profits on sales and investments.

Examples of Ratios

The more popular ratios have been computed for a large aluminum producer, as shown in Table 15.4. You will note that the ratio results become significant in comparisons to other firms in the industry. The major ratios that appear to need attention are these:

1. *Fixed-asset turnover*, which is poor compared to the industry. This means that National is not using its plant, equipment, and land to as high a capacity as other firms in the industry.

2. *Total-asset turnover*, which suggests that National is not generating sufficient sales for a firm with as many assets as it has. Perhaps low sales is the culprit or perhaps some assets should be disposed of.

3. *Total debt to total assets*, which is high for the industry. The company would find it difficult to borrow additional funds without improving this ratio.

4. *Times interest earned*, which shows that National runs the risk of financial embarrassment if its earnings decline because it may not have sufficient funds to make interest payments on its debt.

5. *Return on total assets*, which is one-third below that of the industry. It may result from a low profit margin on sales, low utilization of assets (shown by the first two ratios), and National's above-average debt that causes high interest payments and reduces profits.

USING BREAK-EVEN ANALYSIS FOR CONTROL

What is your view?

As a child, did you ever go into business selling lemonade or cookies? Did it feel good to sell the fifth or sixth item that recouped your out-of-pocket "cost" and permitted every other item sold to be "profit"?

Ratio	Formula for calculation	Calculation ($millions)	Ratio	Industry average	Evaluation
Liquidity					
Current	$\dfrac{\text{Current assets}}{\text{Current liabilities}}$	$\dfrac{\$\ 700}{\$\ 300} =$	2.3 times	2.5 times	Slightly low
Quick or acid test	$\dfrac{\text{Current assets} - \text{Inventory}}{\text{Current liabilities}}$	$\dfrac{\$\ 400}{\$\ 300} =$	1.3 times	1.0 times	Okay
Asset management					
Inventory turnover	$\dfrac{\text{Sales}}{\text{Inventory}}$	$\dfrac{\$3,000}{\$\ 300} =$	10 times	9 times	Okay
Average collection period	$\dfrac{\text{Receivables}}{\text{Sales}/360}$	$\dfrac{\$\ 350}{\$8,333} =$	42 days	36 days	Poor
Fixed-asset turnover	$\dfrac{\text{Sales}}{\text{Fixed assets}}$	$\dfrac{\$3,000}{\$1,300} =$	2.3 times	3.0 times	Poor
Total-asset turnover	$\dfrac{\text{Sales}}{\text{Total assets}}$	$\dfrac{\$3,000}{\$2,000} =$	1.5 times	1.8 times	Poor
Debt management (leverage)					
Debt to total assets	$\dfrac{\text{Total debt}}{\text{Total assets}}$	$\dfrac{\$1,100}{\$2,000} =$	55 percent	40 percent	High
Times interest earned	$\dfrac{\text{Earnings before interest and taxes}}{\text{Interest charges}}$	$\dfrac{\$\ 266}{\$\ 66} =$	4.0 times	6 times	Low
Profitability					
Profit margin on sales	$\dfrac{\text{Net income after taxes}}{\text{Sales}}$	$\dfrac{\$\ 120}{\$3,000} =$	4 percent	5.0 percent	Low
Return on total assets	$\dfrac{\text{Net income after taxes}}{\text{Total assets}}$	$\dfrac{\$\ 120}{\$2,000} =$	6 percent	9.0 percent	Low
Return on common equity	$\dfrac{\text{Net income after taxes}}{\text{Common equity}}$	$\dfrac{\$\ 120}{\$\ 900} =$	13.3 percent	15.0 percent	Low

[a] Figures used to make these calculations came from National Metals Company's balance sheet and profit-and-loss statement.

**TABLE 15.4
Summary of National Metals Company's Ratios**[a]

SOURCE: Eugene F. Brigham, *Fundamentals of Financial Management*, 4th ed. (New York: Dryden Press, 1986), p. 229. Based on compilations by *Quarterly Financial Report*, published by the Federal Trade Commission.

The objective of most private firms is to make a profit—or at least not to suffer a loss. Break-even analysis is a useful tool that allows firms to visualize more clearly the revenue-cost relationship. It uses the same concepts used in preparing a variable budget (see Figure 15.3 and Table 15.2). With **break-even analysis,** revenues and costs are charted and analyzed to determine at what volume (of sales or production) an operator's total costs equal total revenues so that there is neither profit nor loss. This shows where marginal operations occur.

What is your view?

Suppose the ingredients to make a given quantity of lemonade cost you $0.54 and cups cost $0.01 each. How many cups must you sell to ''break even'' if you sell the lemonade for $0.10 a cup?

Computing (or Plotting) the Break-Even Point (BEP)

The **break-even point (BEP)** is that point on a chart at which total revenue exactly covers total costs, including both fixed and variable costs. Figure 15.6 illustrates this relationship in a simplified form. Figure 15.7, using figures from Table 15.2, presents a more comprehensive example of how the BEP is computed. Notice in Table 15.2 that the total fixed costs are $40,000, regardless of the level of output, from 1 unit to 14,000 units. Notice also that the variable cost per unit produced is $5.20. The sales price is $10.00 per unit. There are several ways of computing the BEP. Mathematically, the BEP can be computed by dividing fixed costs by the difference between the sales price (revenue) and the variable cost per unit.

$$\text{Break-even point (in units)} = \frac{\text{fixed costs}}{\left(\begin{array}{c}\text{sales price}\\\text{per unit}\end{array}\right) - \left(\begin{array}{c}\text{variable}\\\text{cost per unit}\end{array}\right)}$$

Therefore

$$\text{BEP} = \frac{\$40,000}{\$10.00 - \$5.20} = \frac{\$40,000}{\$4.80} = 8,333 \text{ units}$$

The BEP can also be found graphically (see Figure 15.7) by doing the following:

1. Calculating the total fixed costs (A) for a given period.
2. Computing all variable costs for each unit produced (B).
3. Plotting the total cost line (C) by drawing in the fixed costs and adding the variable costs, which are then plotted above the fixed costs. (This line is computed by adding the variable cost per unit, times the units produced, to the total fixed costs.)
4. Plotting the total revenue line (D) by multiplying the number of units sold by the unit price.

FIGURE 15.6
How the break-even point (BEP) shows relationships.

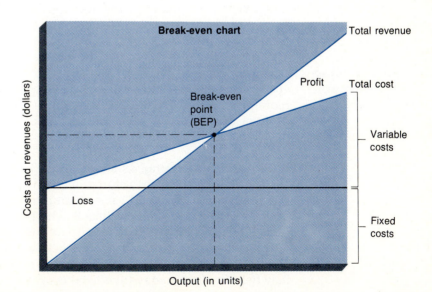

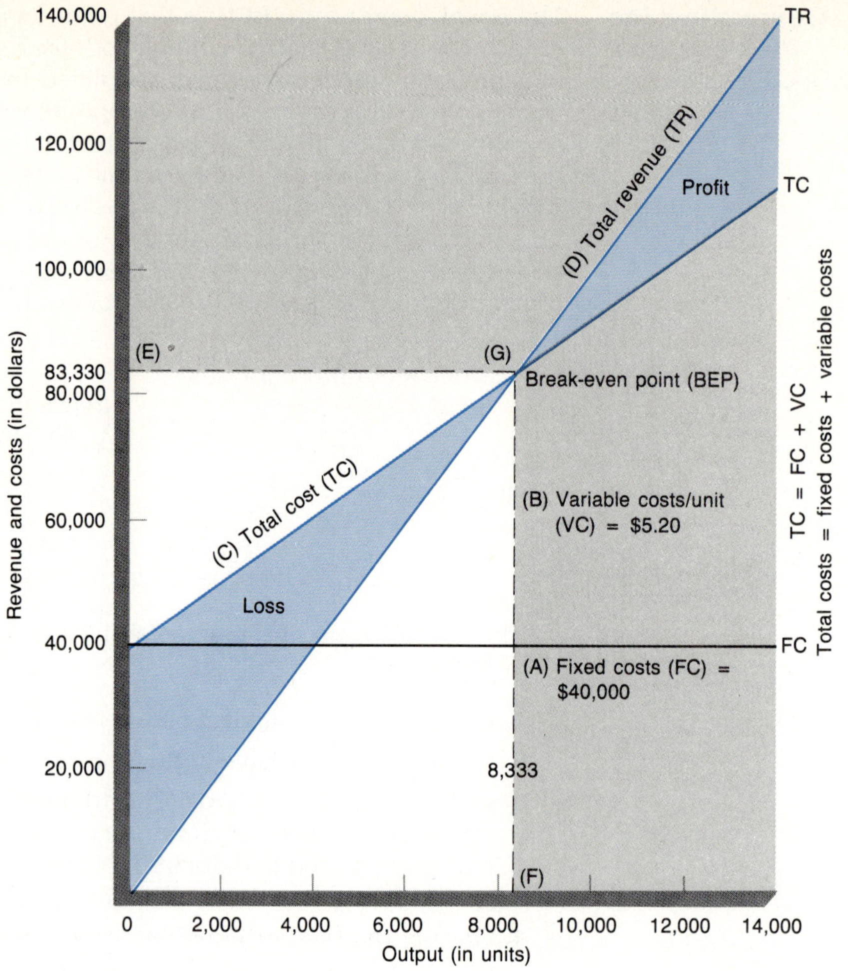

FIGURE 15.7
An example of BEP
analysis.

FIGURE 15.7
An example of BEP analysis.

The BEP is the point on the revenue line (E) or output line (F) that is perpendicular to the point (G) where the total revenue line (D) and the total cost line (C) intersect.

How to Use Break-Even Analysis

Managers can use break-even analysis to study the relationships between costs, sales volume, and profits. Thus output must be shifted to the right if more profit is desired. Break-even analysis also provides a rough estimate of profit or loss at various sales volumes. Also, it can be used both as an aid to decision making and as a control device.

Aid to decision making. As an aid to decision making, break-even analysis can (1) identify the sales volume needed to prevent a loss, (2) identify the minimum production and sales volume needed to meet established objectives, (3) provide data to help decide whether to add or drop a product line, and (4) help decide whether to raise or lower prices.

Yet sometimes firms will operate below the break-even point for a short period of time if the variable revenue exceeds variable costs. This decision may help to affect some of the fixed costs that already exist.

Control device. As a control device, break-even analysis provides one more objective measurement by which to evaluate the organization's performance and provides a basis for possible corrective action. One primary reason for a high BEP is high investment in fixed assets. Management can approximate this point before investing in a new building or machine. Another cause of losses is inadequate control of expenses. This type of analysis can help management detect increases in variable costs before they get out of control.

> *In 1979, Chrysler had to sell 2.3 million cars and trucks to break even. By 1982, under Lee Iacocca's stringent cost saving and selling off of inefficient operations, the "new" Chrysler's break-even point had been reduced to 1.1 million units.*[11]

Limitations on Its Use

The very simplicity of break-even analysis is one of its limitations. Break-even analysis assumes that variable and fixed costs can be separated and classified and that variable costs per unit, fixed costs, and selling price per unit are fixed.

All these assumptions are questionable. It is often difficult to determine whether a cost is fixed or variable. For example, machinery is considered a fixed expense, but if it is operating at capacity and production is to be increased, it is no longer fixed. You must buy or rent additional machinery to increase production. Also, variable costs change greatly as prices and wages fluctuate.

In spite of these difficulties, this type of analysis is valuable to management.

USING TIME-PERFORMANCE CHARTS AND TECHNIQUES

Scheduling is the term used for planning the timing and sequencing of the use of physical and human resources used in the operational activities of an organization. There are many scheduling techniques available. These range from simple devices, such as appointment books, reservation forms for the use of space and equipment, and rough, longhand memos, to mathematical programming of complex and sophisticated activities such as building a nuclear submarine, planning and conducting moon landings, and building and operating the space shuttle.

Managers need better scheduling and control techniques as the expected use of equipment, space, or human resources approaches maximum capacity. Also, when one operation cannot start until a previous operation or sequence of operations is completed, scheduling and controlling are more important—and more difficult.

Fortunately, several useful analytical techniques have been developed to aid in these planning and controlling processes. The primary purpose of such techniques is to permit managers to see how the various segments of operations interrelate and to evaluate the overall progress being made. The best known of these techniques are the Gantt chart and two network analysis techniques, PERT and CPM. While these techniques are often applied to operations or production situations, we have chosen to discuss them in this chapter so that you will better grasp their implications as a planning, scheduling, and controlling tool.

The Gantt Chart

The best-known and most popular of the older methods is the Gantt chart, which was developed by Henry L. Gantt in the early 1900s (see Chapter 3). This relatively simple chart has made a significant contribution to all forms of operations management and is still a valuable and widely used control technique, especially in firms with many unrelated projects. It is also the foundation on which the more sophisticated types of time-related charts and control techniques, such as network analysis using PERT and CPM, are based.

The **Gantt chart** has output on one axis and units of time on another and shows work planned and work accomplished in relation to each other and in relation to time. Figure 15.8 presents a Gantt chart in its simplest form. For each project listed on the left of the chart, the upper (white) bar records the production schedule; the lower (solid) bar records the part of the schedule that has been finished.

What is your view?

Examine the Gantt chart shown in Figure 15.8. Assume that today is March 5, 1989. Which activities are ahead of scheduled completion? Which are behind?

On most Gantt charts, the bars are movable strips of plastic, with different colors to indicate scheduled and actual progress. Mechanical boards with movable pegs or cards can be used. At a glance, the manager can see whether a project is on time, ahead of time, or behind time. Action must be taken to put a project back on schedule.

Program Evaluation and Review Technique (PERT)

The **Program Evaluation and Review Technique (PERT)** was developed in the 1950s by the U.S. Navy Bureau of Ordnance, with the assistance of the management consulting firm of Booz, Allen & Hamilton. It was first used in developing the Polaris Fleet Ballistic Missile and is credited with saving two years on that project.[12] It aids in scheduling sophisticated, nonrepetitive technical projects by (1) focusing management's attention on key program steps, (2) pointing to potential problem areas, (3) evaluating progress, and (4) giving management a reporting device.

A **PERT network** expresses in a line chart the relationships of events and activities and their timing, under conditions of uncertainty. Thus *time* is the central control element.

Fundamentals of PERT. Timing and sequencing are the primary concerns in PERT's use of a network or flow plan. The flow plan consists of a series of related events and activities. An *event* is a significant, specified performance milestone (physical or mental) in the program plan, accomplished at a particular instant of time, that represents the start or finish of an activity. It does not consume time or resources. An event is usually represented by a circle or *node*:

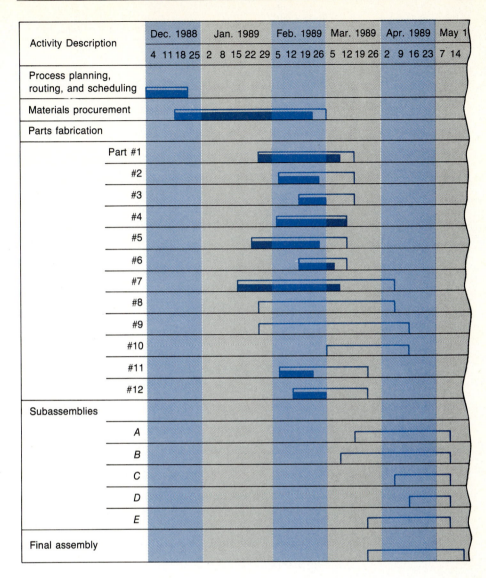

Activity Description	Dec. 1988	Jan. 1989	Feb. 1989	Mar. 1989	Apr. 1989	May 1
	4 11 18 25	2 8 15 22 29	5 12 19 26	5 12 19 26	2 9 16 23	7 14
Process planning, routing, and scheduling						
Materials procurement						
Parts fabrication						
Part #1						
#2						
#3						
#4						
#5						
#6						
#7						
#8						
#9						
#10						
#11						
#12						
Subassemblies						
A						
B						
C						
D						
E						
Final assembly						

Your turning in a completed term paper for this course is an event.

An *activity* is a time-consuming element of the program. It represents the work needed to complete a particular event. It is usually represented by an arrow:

→

Your library research for the term paper is one activity, your writing a rough draft is another, and typing the final draft is a third.

Two events, connected by an activity, are shown in Figure 15.9. Event 1 could represent the point in time when the project "began," and event 2

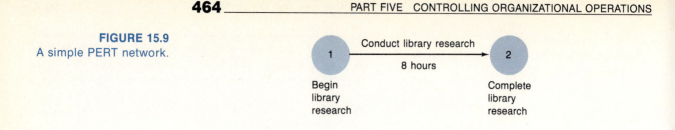

could represent the point when it was "completed." The figure "8 hours" represents the elapsed time the activity, shown by the arrow, required. Figure 15.9 thus represents the beginning of the activity, how long it took to do the activity, and completion of the activity.

The elapsed time that will be budgeted to complete an activity is estimated on the basis of past experience or anticipated progress. For example, in Figure 15.9, eight hours was the estimated time required for you to start and complete your library research. In most uses of PERT, the "8 hours" estimate would be determined in a more scientific manner than mere guesswork. Three possible completion-time estimates are submitted: (1) an *optimistic time estimate* (T_o) based on minimal difficulties (say, 6 hours); (2) a *pessimistic time estimate* (T_p) based on maximum potential problems (say, 14 hours); and (3) the *most likely completion time* (T_m) under "normal" conditions (say, 7 hours).

The formula for computing *estimated PERT time* (T_e) is:

$$T_e = \frac{T_o + T_p + (4)T_m}{6} \text{ or } \frac{6 + 14 + (4)7}{6} = 8$$

Note in the formula that the most likely time (7 hours) is weighted by a factor of four. There is a total of six times to be averaged in the formula.

Steps in constructing a network. In constructing a PERT network, emphasis is placed on identifying events and activities with enough precision to permit monitoring accomplishments as the project proceeds. The basic steps in PERT are the same regardless of the type of project. They include at least the following:

1. Identifying and defining the *component activities* that must be performed.
2. Defining the *order* in which those activities in the *network* will be performed.
3. Analyzing the *estimated time* required to complete the individual activities and the entire project.
4. Finding the **critical path**—that is, the longest path—in terms of time, from the beginning event to the ending event.
5. Improving on the initial plan through *modifications*.
6. *Controlling* the project.

There are numerous computer programs available to perform the mechanics of computing the critical path.[13]

All events and activities must be sequenced in the network under a strict set of logical rules; for example, one rule may be that no event can be considered complete until all predecessor events have been completed. This permits the critical path to be determined. Figure 15.10 is an example of a PERT chart for building a house.

Dealing with uncertainty. Because PERT projects are usually one-time projects, they are subject to a great deal of uncertainty. PERT is designed to deal with this problem in determining the time estimates.

Figure 15.11 shows a simple project represented by both a Gantt chart and a project network. Notice that the project network has two distinct advantages over the Gantt chart: (1) the way the activities depend on each other is noted explicitly, and (2) the activities are shown in greater detail.

What is your view?

What is the critical path in Figure 15.11(b):

(1) 1–3–4–6–7, (2) 1–2–4–6–7, or (3) 1–5–6–7?

Path 1 is 18 + 11 + 8 + 4 = 41.

Path 2 is 10 + 15 + 8 + 4 = 37.

Path 3 is 30 + 11 + 4 = 45.

This presentation of PERT has been limited to its basics. There is much more about PERT that could be presented,[14] but this is best left to more advanced courses such as management science and production and oper-

FIGURE 15.10
PERT chart for building a house.

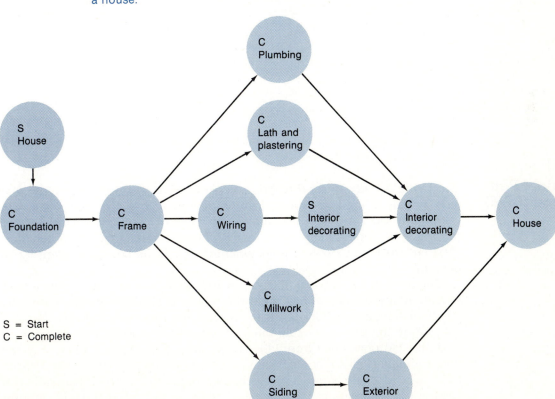

S = Start
C = Complete

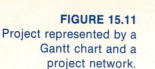

FIGURE 15.11
Project represented by a
Gantt chart and a
project network.

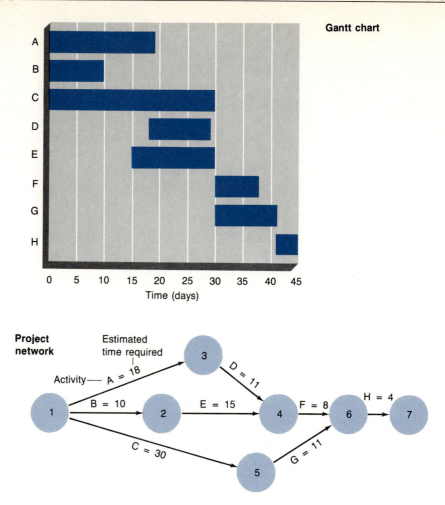

ations management. For most practicing managers, however, the basic model provides the greatest benefits.

Critical Path Method (CPM)

The **Critical Path Method (CPM),** a scheduling and control technique that aids in scheduling sophisticated, nonrepetitive technical projects, was developed by Du Pont, with the aid of experts from Remington Rand Univac, to reduce downtime for periodic construction, overhaul, and maintenance. CPM cut Du Pont's downtime for maintenance in its Louisville plant by 26 percent.

The differences between PERT and CPM are more a matter of degree than of kind. Many writers, in fact, treat the two as basically identical, with only subtle distinctions.[15] PERT tends to emphasize time and to provide a way of computing the most probable time, whereas CPM emphasizes cost as well as time. CPM does differ from PERT in at least three respects. First, only *one* time estimate is given for each set of activities leading up to a given event in CPM instead of the *three* time estimates required by PERT. Second, with CPM, a cost estimate can be included, along with each estimated time for both normal and "crash" conditions. Third, CPM assumes at least some previous experience with the work involved in completing each event. Otherwise, it would not be practical to state a single time and cost estimate.

These differences help to explain why PERT is used primarily for one-of-a-kind projects involving an extensive amount of research and development prior to the building of a prototype and for similar projects in which time is of greater importance than cost. CPM, on the other hand, is used widely in complex construction and maintenance projects in which cost is a significant factor and prior experience offers some basis for making reliable estimates of both time and cost.

> **What is your view?**
> Would PERT or CPM be effective control techniques for the Trident submarine project discussed at the beginning of this chapter?

Evaluating the Effectiveness of Network Analysis

There are many varied users and uses of network analysis. There must, apparently, be many benefits from its use. There are also some limitations.

Benefits. The benefits of PERT and CPM include the following:

1. By providing a graphic representation of how each task depends on others, networks offer an advantage over simpler methods.
2. Drawing up a network requires the project manager to plan the project better from start to finish.
3. Bottlenecks and potential trouble spots are discovered early enough for preventive measures to be applied or corrective action to be taken.
4. Network analysis provides a common frame of reference for all the different parties involved in a project.
5. Managers are provided with a means of comparing different methods for reaching the project goal.
6. By identifying critical tasks, network analysis allows managers to give attention where it is most needed and at the same time indicates where other tasks are falling behind, allowing managers to take immediate corrective action.
7. In a complex project, the critical path may change as time estimates prove inaccurate, but PERT and CPM provide the means of identifying the current critical path on a continuing basis.

Limitations. There are a few limitations to network analysis. They include the following:

1. The costs of setting up such systems are extensive.
2. These systems will not help managers solve all their problems.
3. These systems are not a substitute for managerial planning and control. Instead, if the systems are to be effective, they must be carefully planned and tightly controlled throughout a project.
4. The network schedules must always be regarded as tentative.

In spite of these limitations, however, network analysis, when properly constructed and used, can provide valuable aids for planning and control,

Management Application and Practice 15.1   Who Uses PERT/CPM?

PERT and CPM, because they facilitate planning and controlling, have a wide variety of potential uses in all types of organizations. Ford Motor Company, for instance, uses them for retooling assembly lines; Chrysler Corporation recently used them in building a new assembly plant. A variety of other organizations also use them regularly, including Brigham and Women's Hospital in Boston, Procter & Gamble, Walt Disney Corporation, and the San Francisco Opera Association. The U.S. Department of Defense actually *requires* the use of PERT or CPM by its major contractors.

Project management (see Chapter 7) has been developed to coordinate and control large, complex, one-time projects, such as a hospital's physical move to another location, a civic group's sponsorship of a large pops concert, or even a department store's special one-time sale. Because of the need to schedule, coordinate, and control the many phases of these types of projects, PERT or CPM concepts are especially useful.

SOURCE: Based upon Lee J. Krajeski and Larry P. Ritzman, *Operations Management* (Reading, MA: Addison-Wesley Publishing Co., 1987), p. 678; and various other sources.

but it should not be regarded as a substitute for effective management. MAP 15.1 shows how selected organizations use PERT and CPM.

SUMMARY

This chapter showed how control principles operate in actual practice. We grouped various control methods into two categories: nonquantitative methods and quantitative control techniques. The most frequently used general control methods include (1) observation, (2) regular or "spot" inspections, (3) oral and written reports, (4) performance evaluations, and (5) discussions between the manager and employees involved in performing an activity.

Quantitative control techniques tend to use specific data and quantitative methods to measure and correct quantity and quality of output. The more popularly used ones include budgets and budgetary control, audits, ratio analysis, break-even analysis, and time-performance charts and techniques.

Budgets are particularly widely used as both a planning and a control device. The primary benefit of budgetary control is that it allows comparable goals expressed in uniform financial terms to be provided for all organizational units. Equally important, since the budget serves as a standard of performance, deviations from this standard are readily measurable and provide the basis for corrective action. In addition, there are several indirect benefits that result from the proper use of budgets.

There are also some potential limitations on the use of budgetary control. First, long-run planning and development such as managerial planning and organizational development may be slighted because it is difficult to convert these areas into financial terms. Second, there is a danger of confusing symptoms with causes. A decline in revenue from sales may not necessarily call for greater sales effort. The real problem may be a poor product or general economic conditions. Third, a budget tends to become static and not reflect changing conditions in a dynamic environment.

We discussed different types of budgets and how budgetary control operates and noted that, although the concept is simple, the application of budgetary control is complex and requires managerial expertise.

Two innovative developments in budgeting were discussed: planning-programming-budgeting systems and zero-base budgeting. PPBS has not had tremendous success in application, but ZBB has been more widely adopted.

Audits, ratio analysis, break-even analysis, and time-performance techniques are all used widely and for different purposes. For example, auditing is used to verify financial records and can also be helpful in assessing the overall effectiveness of management. On the other hand, break-even analysis can be used as a planning, decision-making, and control device. It is especially useful for a firm considering a new venture or deciding whether to add or drop a product line or to raise or lower prices.

Finally, we discussed three of the most widely used time-performance charts—the Gantt chart, Program Evaluation and Review Technique (PERT), and the Critical Path Method (CPM). All these assist in planning the timing and sequencing of the use of physical and human resources for the operational activities of an organization. Although there are additional slight differences in the two, the primary difference between PERT and CPM is that PERT tends to emphasize time, whereas CPM emphasizes cost as well as time. We concluded the chapter with a discussion of the benefits and limitations of PERT and CPM.

REVIEW QUESTIONS

1. What are some of the nonquantitative control techniques? Explain.
2. What are the *(a)* benefits and *(b)* limitations of budgets and budgeting control?
3. How does budgetary control operate?
4. What are the objectives of PPBS and ZBB?
5. In what way does ZBB differ from incremental budgeting?
6. *(a)* What are audits? *(b)* How can audits be used for control?
7. *(a)* What is break-even analysis? *(b)* How can break-even analysis be used for control?
8. *(a)* What is PERT? *(b)* How can PERT be used for control?
9. What is the difference between PERT and CPM?

DISCUSSION QUESTIONS

1. Assume that you are a student attending college away from home. You will live in a campus dormitory, will purchase a 7-day meal ticket, and will drive your 4-year-old fully paid-for automobile as a means of transportation. Identify the likely fixed and variable costs that you will incur during the next semester of school. Is it helpful to differentiate these? Why?
2. The text states that a budget is both a planning and a controlling tool. How can this be so? Explain.
3. In what way(s) are Gantt charts and PERT networks similar? Different? Discuss.
4. A survey of *Fortune* 500 companies showed that only 55 percent of them made "moderate or more" use of network analysis. Why do you think this figure is so low?

LEARNING EXERCISE 15.1

The Birthday Cake Venture

"It's got to work," said Fred Gerald to Irene Sawyer and Bill Haskins, two of his good college friends and classmates at State University. "We get the birth dates of the 5000 entering first-year dorm students, send letters to the parents offering to deliver a birthday cake to the kid's room, with a personal message written by their parents, and even sing 'Happy Birthday' to the student if he or she is present when we deliver the cake. It's a natural."

"But how will we get the names of the new students and their birthdays?" asked Bill.

"No problem," replied Irene. "I have a friend who works part-time in the university computer center, and I bet she'd be able to do this without any trouble."

Fred continued: "It's simple: we just give the campus bakery our orders a day or two in advance. We pick up the cakes and deliver them ourselves. Or, if business is too good, we can even hire someone to help us. I figure the cakes would cost us about $6.00 apiece with 'Happy Birthday' and the person's name on top of it. My guess is that we could sell our service for $15.00 per cake, which would give us a pretty good margin to work with after we determine our costs."

Questions

1. What are the fixed-cost items involved in the project?
2. What are the variable-cost items? What problems are involved in establishing precise variable costs?
3. Suppose fixed costs were projected to amount to $1500.00 and variable costs were placed at $7.50 per cake. Calculate the break-even point.
4. Does the venture sound like one that would be feasible? Discuss.

LEARNING EXERCISE 15.2

Drawing a PERT Network*

Assume that your company is a manufacturer of auto equipment and has just purchased a patent for an antismog auto muffler. In order to make this new product, your firm must complete the following major steps:

A. Decision to add product.
B. Engineering work completed.
C. Financing arranged.
D. Material purchase orders placed.

E. Production started.
F. Sales campaign arranged.
G. Initial orders received.
H. Initial orders shipped.

Analysis indicates the following necessary sequences between the above events and the estimated time required to perform the work to advance from one event to the next. (Work cannot move forward until all necessary preceding work is completed.)

Necessary sequence	Estimated time	Necessary sequence	Estimated time
A to B	60 days	C to F	2 days
B to C	20 "	D to E	40 "
B to D	30 "	E to H	45 "
B to E	75 "	F to G	60 "
B to F	30 "	G to E	2 "
C to D	2 "	G to H	10 "

---

* Adapted from William H. Newman and James P. Logan, *Strategy, Policy and Central Management*, 8th ed. (Cincinnati: South-Western Publishing, 1981), pp. 541–542. Used by permission.

Questions

1. Prepare a PERT diagram showing the network of the above events.
2. What is the critical path?
3. In what ways are your answers to questions (1) and (2) helpful in *(a)* planning and *(b)* controlling the project? Explain.

NOTES

1. "Inside Story of the Trident Debacle," *U.S. News & World Report*, March 30, 1981, pp. 21–22.
2. See Robert G. Murdick et al., *Business Policy: A Framework for Analysis*, 2d ed. (Columbus, Ohio: Grid Publishing, 1976), pp. 4–6, for further details.
3. For more details, see "How W. T. Grant Lost $175 Million Last Year," *Business Week*, February 24, 1975.
4. This section has been heavily influenced by W. W. Pyle, J. A. White, and K. D. Larson, *Fundamental Accounting Principles*, 8th ed. (Homewood, IL: Irwin, 1978).
5. Robert N. Anthony and Regina E. Herzlinger, *Management Control in Nonprofit Organizations* (Homewood, IL: Irwin, 1975), is the definitive authority on this subject.
6. See James E. Carter, *Memorandum for Heads of Executive Departments and Agencies* (Washington, D.C.: White House, February 14, 1977).
7. George S. Mimmier and R. H. Hermanson, "A Look at Zero-Base Budgeting—The Georgia Experience," *Atlanta Economic Review* 27 (July–August 1976): 5.
8. Graeme M. Taylor, "Introduction to Zero-Base Budgeting," *Bureaucrat* 6 (Spring 1977): 33–55.
9. "Zero Based Budgeting Is Abandoned by Reagan," *Wall Street Journal*, August 10, 1981, p. 8.
10. Daniel F. McCarthy, Robert J. Minichiello, and Joseph Curran, *Business Policy and Strategy* (Homewood, IL: Richard D. Irwin, 1983), p. 417.
11. Lee Iacocca, *Iacocca: An Autobiography* (New York: Bantam Books, 1984), p. 278.
12. Donald G. Malcolm et al., "Applications of a Technique for Research and Development Program Evaluation," *Operations Research* 7 (September–October 1959): 646.
13. A survey of available PERT-packaged programs is provided by Ann B. Pushkin and Jim Wynne, "A Survey of Computerized PERT/CPM Related Packages," *Review of Industrial Management and Textile Science* (Fall 1976): 15–34.
14. Joseph J. Moder and Cecil R. Phillips, *Project Management with CPM and PERT* (New York: Van Nostrand Reinhold, 1970).
15. See, for instance, Sang M. Lee, Lawrence Moore, and Bernard W. Taylor, *Management Science* (Dubuque, IA: Wm. C. Brown, 1981), pp. 261–278.

SUGGESTIONS FOR FURTHER STUDY

BHADA Y. K., and MIMMIER, GEORGE. "Integrate ZBB into Your MBO Framework." *Financial Executive* 48 (June 1980): 42–47.
CAMP, ROGER A. "Multidimensional Break-even Analysis." *Journal of Accountancy* 154 (January 1987): 132–133.
COX, JAMES F.; ZMUD, ROBERT W.; and CLARK, STEVEN J. "Auditing an MRP System." *Academy of Management Journal* 24 (June 1981): 386–402.
DODIN, BAJIS M., and ELMAGHRABY, SALAH E. "Approximating the Criticality Indices of the Activities in PERT Networks." *Management Science* 31 (February 1985): 207–224.
EVANS, JAMES R.; ANDERSON, DAVID R.; SWEENEY, DENNIS J.; and WILLIAMS, THOMAS A. *Applied Production and Operations Management.* 2d ed. St. Paul, MN: West Publishing Co., 1987. See especially Chapter 17, "Project Planning and Management."
GARRISON, RAY H. *Managerial Accounting.* 4th ed. Plano, TX: Business Publications, 1985. See especially Chapter 10 for an excellent discussion of budgeting.

LINDQUIST, STANTON C., and MILLS, K. BRYANT. "Whatever Happened to Zero Based Budgeting?" *Managerial Planning* 29 (January–February 1981): 31–35.

MOREHEAD, R. D., and MYERS, D. W. "Audit Management and Control." *Internal Auditor* 37 (February 1980): 58–68.

RALSTON, BILL. "Application of ZBB: North American Private Sector." *Managerial Finance* 12 (Spring 1986): 7–10.

UMPATHY, SRINIVASAN. "How Successful Firms Budget." *Management Accounting* 69 (February 1987): 25–27.

VISCIONE, JERRY A. "Small Company Budgets: Targets Are Key." *Harvard Business Review* 62 (May–June 1984): 42–50.

16

Managing Operations

Learning Objectives

After studying the material in this chapter, you should be able to do the following:

- Explain the importance of operations in making U.S. industry more competitive with foreign industry.
- Explain what operations are.
- Describe the elements of an operations system and the various kinds of operations and explain each one.
- Describe the process of materials management and explain how it can contribute to profitability.
- Suggest some ways to improve energy management and conservation.
- Give some reasons for, and advantages and disadvantages of, the automation revolution.
- Explain the use of management science in operations.

Outline of the Chapter

Competitiveness of U.S. operations
Reasons for the declining position
Improvements in manufacturing
Need for improvements in services
Competition from Japan
Elements of an operations system
What are operations?
Operations management is universal
Operations provide utility to customers
Types of operations
Timing of operations
Designing facilities needed for operations
Determine the product to be produced
Determine the volume to be produced
Determine parts, operations, and activities needed
Determine space requirements
Decide on the best layout
Implement plans

Planning and controlling operations
Master operations plans
Operations planning and control
Improving operations
Materials management
Determining needs
Deciding whether to make or buy a part or component
Energy management
The robotics revolution
Automation is tending to replace manual operations
Reasons for growing use of automation and robotics
Results of the revolution
Future of the revolution
Using management science in operations
Types of management science tools
Limitations of management science tools
Summary

Some Important Terms

productivity
just-in-time scheduling (JIT)
operations
production
services
synthetic *or* assembly process
analytic *or* disassembly process
continuous process
job shop processing
computer-assisted design (CAD)
computer-aided manufacturing (CAM)
master operations plan (MOP)
scheduling
control and follow-up
zero defects
materials
automation revolution
robotics revolution
steel-collar workers
linear programming (LP)
queuing theory
simulation
Monte Carlo
network analysis
regression analysis

Being good just isn't good enough any more. We must be better.
—R. E. HECKERT, CHAIRMAN, DU PONT

Quality is our best assurance of customer allegiance, our strongest defense against foreign competition, and the only path to sustained growth and earnings.
—JOHN F. WELCH, JR., CHAIRMAN, GENERAL ELECTRIC COMPANY

Registering by Remote[1]

Tired of long registration lines? Let your fingers do the waiting: register by telephone, as queue-weary students are doing from Iowa State to Union Community College in New Jersey. Computerized registration is in use or about to be installed at 30 colleges across the country, according to Perception Technology, the Massachusetts firm that introduced the system in 1983.

Armed with a complex packet of course code numbers, students gain access to their school's computerized registration system by punching the appropriate keys on a Touch-Tone telephone. A student can choose, add, or drop courses simply by entering the right codes. If the course is full, or if another problem arises, touching a button can bring a live operator on for assistance. "This is really a 'have it your way' kind of thing," says Perception Technology's product-management director, John E. Haldeman. "You're doing it where and when you want."

The process has not been entirely glitch-free, however. For example, when close to 20,000 students first used the system last fall at Texas A&M, the most common complaint was a frequent busy signal. "You have to get in by luck," said Michael Buck, a freshman aerospace engineering major, who tried to get through to the computer for two hours and then was cut off twice. But most students surveyed loved the convenience. As A&M junior David White put it, "Even when you're waiting with a busy signal you *still* can eat or watch TV." That's not easy to do in most registration lines.

Do you think this system would improve your school's registration procedure? Would you like to use it?

THREE SIGNIFICANT POINTS are illustrated by this case. First, it shows that operations are involved in services such as education as well as in producing goods through manufacturing. Second, it emphasizes that the computer is increasingly being used to improve service-type operations. Third, it gives you some idea of what is involved in managing operations. These three points will be covered in this chapter.

As shown in Chapter 3, F. W. Taylor made his first studies of improving productivity in the shops of a steel company. Although many of the principles of management were developed by studying manufacturing, now they are being applied on a much broader scale to other types of managerial activities. Since "production" is usually thought of as occurring in manufacturing industries, the term *operations* is used in this book to include the production function in manufacturing and most other types of economic activities, including services. In other words, all types of organizations require some form of operations to attain their goals.

This chapter looks at what is involved in managing these operations. But first we need to see why improving operations is so important.

COMPETITIVENESS OF U.S. OPERATIONS

Until recently, U.S. business led the world in developing, producing, and selling a broad range of goods and services. Its inventiveness, willingness to improve and invest in new processes, and emphasis on effective marketing created a business environment that tended to be well ahead of the rest of the world. In recent years, however, many factors have caused an erosion in this favorable position. Foreign businesses are now producing and selling an increasing volume of goods and services (relative to our producers) in this country as well as in their home countries. This trend has progressed to the point where many industries, such as textiles, are migrating overseas, and we are losing a large percentage of our manufacturing.

What is your view?

Look around you at the many products you own that were produced in foreign countries. Why might a U.S. firm choose to manufacture its products outside the United States, then import them for sale inside the country?

Reasons for the Declining Position

Many factors—both here and abroad—led to this problem. The amount invested in plant and equipment did not grow as fast in the United States as in some other countries. Private and public research and development expenditures increased slowly—or even declined in many instances. **Productivity,** which is the amount of goods or services produced by a worker in a given period of time, with due consideration to quality, lagged behind that of competitors. And U.S. labor costs—made up of wages and employee benefits—rose much more rapidly than in other countries.

Improvements in Manufacturing

A reversal of this trend apparently occurred in 1986, when our manufacturing productivity was the highest of 10 leading industrial nations for the first time in 37 years. As Figure 16.1 shows, the growth in U.S. manufacturing productivity was 3.5 percent, while Great Britain showed only 2.9 percent growth, Japan 2.8 percent, and France and West Germany 1.9 percent.[2] The improvement resulted from variables such as improved operations techniques, job cutbacks, and wage restraints here, while industrial output overseas was slowing because of the falling value of the dollar. U.S. labor costs declined 0.6 percent, while they were rising 10 to 43 percent in other countries.[3]

Need for Improvements in Services

A productivity problem still exists in the services, which account for about three-quarters of the U.S. economy. Since 1979, services have registered average productivity gains of "a few tenths of a percent" annually.[4] And most of that improvement came from the recently deregulated industries, especially airlines, railroads, and telecommunications, where efficiency rose 5 to 10 percent per year during the 1980s. But productivity has plunged in retailing and financing. And the much-acclaimed "information revolution" has not budged white-collar productivity among office workers.

Competition from Japan

In the past, products made in Japan were considered to be of poor quality. Even during the post–World War II reconstruction period, the Japanese were

FIGURE 16.1
Growth in U.S. and
foreign productivity.
SOURCE: *Fortune*, September 28,
1987, p. 62.

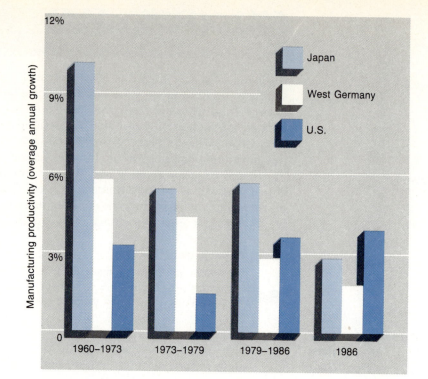

embarrassed by the shoddiness of their goods.[5] During the war, they had recognized the superior quality of American-made products and carefully studied disassembled American products in order to copy—and improve—them. Some of the foremost Japanese industrialists recognized, in the years after the war, that they had their backs to the wall, with no place to turn except to American experts who were willing to help.

About 1950, W. Edwards Deming, an American educated and trained in the value of quality—especially statistical quality control—tried to help U.S. companies improve quality and increase output. But American managers wouldn't listen to him. Instead, he found an audience of top management in Japan. He convinced Japanese managers that true quality demanded a totality of commitment that began at the very top. If top management was committed to the idea of quality, and if executive promotions and salary increases were tied to quality, emphasis on it would seep down into the middle and lower levels of management and eventually trickle down to the workers. Above all, he said, quality had to be central to the purpose of a company. He was concerned about the apathy of top American management toward quality, as compared to their short-term interest in profits.

The Japanese success did not come from technological superiority but from manufacturing skills. The Japanese moved ahead of America when they were at a distinct disadvantage in technology. They moved ahead by slowly and systematically improving the process of their manufacturing in thousands of small ways. They did it by being there, on the factory floor, as the Americans were not.

Don Lennox, a former Ford manufacturing executive, explained the Japanese success as "two decades of Japanese manufacturing engineers coming to work every day, busy, serious, being taken seriously by their superiors, being filled with the importance of their mission, improving the manufacturing in countless small ways. It was not that they had made one giant breakthrough . . . ; they had made a thousand and one quite modest ones."[6]

Two production innovations, however, have contributed to the Japanese advantage. Japanese manufacturers use **just-in-time scheduling (JIT),** which is planning for materials, parts, and goods to arrive just when they are needed for operations, to keep inventory costs down. Also, they have developed many new robots, producing over 60 percent of the robots in the world, and have large numbers installed and operating in their industries.

The Japanese spurt ahead in productivity adds to the difficulty that U.S. businesses have in competing with them. Our firms are now recognizing the loss in competitiveness and are making changes, including copying some of the Japanese methods. Major changes are being made in production methods, operations, and management to help offset the effect of our high labor costs, poor management, and low employee motivation. Substantial positive effects are being directed toward improving this situation.

ELEMENTS OF AN OPERATIONS SYSTEM

What are operations, and what elements are found in all operating systems? Those questions are answered in this section.

What Are Operations?

Simply stated, **operations** include designing, operating, and controlling a production system to convert human, financial, and physical resources into needed goods and services. Although the terms *production* and *production management* can be used for this process, we prefer the term *operations*, or *operations management*, which emphasizes not only the production of physical goods but also the performance of various types of services. In fact, as shown earlier, the performance of services is now more prevalent than the production of goods.

Production usually means performing a series of activities that result in a physical good being made. **Services,** on the other hand, involve performing activities that result in some type of tangible or intangible satisfaction.

Notice that the definitions of production and service do not clearly differentiate them. It would help to have a dividing line between them, but there is a gray area instead. It is even harder to distinguish production and service *firms*. For example, is a laundry a producing or service firm? What about a restaurant, a print shop, a hospital, or an air conditioning repair firm? How about CPA firms? Even retailing has aspects of both types of business. A company may be structured to be mainly a producer, but it cannot function without some service aspects. Even if it is designed to be primarily a service supplier, it has some aspects of production.

Operations Management Is Universal

In summary, operations involves the use of the *systems concept* (see Chapter 3, especially Figure 3.9, for a fuller discussion of this concept). Figure 16.2 shows that this systems concept of operations is found in all types of organizations, including those that are both goods-producing and service-performing.

Why can the operating methods used by industrial firms be applied to all types of firms? Because the processes of changing inputs to outputs have some characteristics that are common to all situations. These include:

1. Systems of transformation as related to form, place, or time utility.
2. A sequence of steps or operations to convert the inputs to outputs.
3. Special skills, tools, machinery, or equipment to make the transformation.
4. Instructions to identify work to be performed and units to be produced.
5. Some time frame in which the work is to be completed.
6. Standards and maximum rates of input and output.
7. Exceptions and errors that must be handled.

Operations Provide Utility to Customers

Operations are performed to create some type of *utility*, which is the ability of a good or service to satisfy the wants and needs of consumers. Operations may provide one or more types of utility, such as form, time, and place utility, but must provide them at a cost that the customer is able and willing to pay. For example, a transistor has little or no utility by itself, but when it is assembled into a radio, it has value in that it provides news and entertainment. Service companies provide other utilities—for example, plumbers by repairing water lines, moving firms by transporting household goods, and computer services by providing stock market information.

What is your view?

Discuss the utility provided by the following products or services: computerized registration, automatic teller machines at banks, car rentals, veterinarians, billboards, cable TV, and VCRs.

Most organizations try to meet customer needs for variety and at the same time use standard products and parts. Products may be the same except for some small detail, such as color. For example, radios that do not look the same on the outside may have the same parts on the inside. When you have your television repaired, the repairer may replace a unit or module that is a standard assembly. This combination allows for part of production to follow the continuous form.

Types of Operations

Each organization arranges its operations in the sequence that is needed to produce its goods or services effectively. A study of the process needed can determine the operations processes required and establish the sequence that will result in the best transformation. Some processes just change the input without additions or subtractions, such as providing place and time utility in retailing and delivery of goods. Other processes put together (assemble) materials into airplanes, autos, computers, camcorders, jeans, and

Inputs	**Transformation through**	**Outputs**

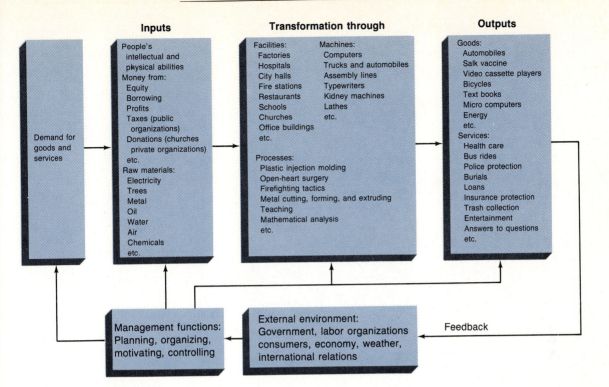

Demand for goods and services

Inputs
People's intellectual and physical abilities
Money from:
  Equity
  Borrowing
  Profits
  Taxes (public organizations)
  Donations (churches private organizations)
  etc.
Raw materials:
  Electricity
  Trees
  Metal
  Oil
  Water
  Air
  Chemicals
  etc.

Transformation through
Facilities:
  Factories
  Hospitals
  City halls
  Fire stations
  Restaurants
  Schools
  Churches
  Office buildings
  etc.

Machines:
  Computers
  Trucks and automobiles
  Assembly lines
  Typewriters
  Kidney machines
  Lathes
  etc.

Processes:
  Plastic injection molding
  Open-heart surgery
  Firefighting tactics
  Metal cutting, forming, and extruding
  Teaching
  Mathematical analysis
  etc.

Outputs
Goods:
  Automobiles
  Salk vaccine
  Video cassette players
  Bicycles
  Text books
  Micro computers
  Energy
  etc.
Services:
  Health care
  Bus rides
  Police protection
  Burials
  Loans
  Insurance protection
  Trash collection
  Entertainment
  Answers to questions
  etc.

Management functions: Planning, organizing, motivating, controlling

External environment: Government, labor organizations consumers, economy, weather, international relations

Feedback

FIGURE 16.2
Universality of production and operations management: Inputs are transformed into outputs.

SOURCE: Thomas E. Hendricks and Franklin G. Moore, *Production/Operations Management*, 9th ed. (Homewood, IL: Irwin, 1985), p. 13.

sandwiches (see Figure 16.3) to provide form, place, and time utilities for customers. This is called the **synthetic** (or **assembly**) **process.**

Other processes start with one material and disassemble it to produce many and varied products from it. This is the **analytic** (or **disassembly**) **process.** Trees provide lumber, pulp, bark, and sawdust; catalytic cracking and refining is used to produce a variety of products from crude oil (Figure

"Get a waiter to that table immediately!"

(Used by permission of The Wall Street Journal.*)*

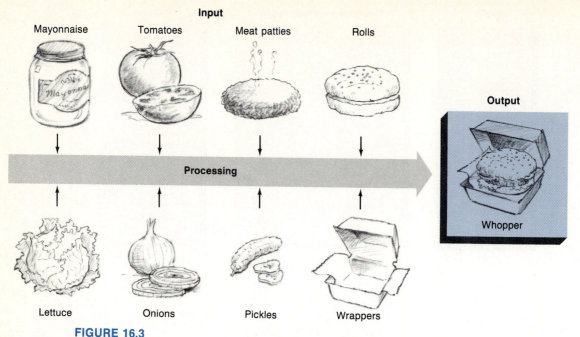

Input

Mayonnaise   Tomatoes   Meat patties   Rolls

Processing

Output

Whopper

Lettuce   Onions   Pickles   Wrappers

FIGURE 16.3
The synthetic production (assembly) process.

SOURCE: Leon C. Megginson, Lyle R. Trueblood, and Gayle M. Ross, *Business* (Lexington, MA: D. C. Heath, 1985), p. 202.

16.4). The wide variety of processes requires customized design for each, but basically the same approach can be made for all. Improvement in service processes has lagged behind that of manufacturing.

Advances in technology are changing the roles of machines and employees. Historically, machines have been developed to replace routine manual operations. Mechanization has changed processes by providing more consistency, faster processing, less worker fatigue, and—usually—lower costs.

Now computers and electronic information processing systems are being designed and used to direct machines and employees. This has accelerated changes and has provided the means for making service firms more efficient. Electronic answering machines reduce employee time in this activity. Customer addresses and other data stored in computers help reduce the costs of mailings and can provide information for market research and other analyses. Computers connected to cash registers can process sales, make inventory changes, provide credit information, and order merchandise. This reduces employee time in these activities, improves accuracy, and provides more current—and accurate—information.

These changes have increased the need for special skills and more precise scheduling. Also, rapid changes in products and demand for special characteristics of products require greater flexibility to meet changes. Computers are causing these changes while at the same time helping to handle them.

Timing of Operations

Currently, manufacturing companies may produce only one standard product or—at the other end of the spectrum—produce individual products to the special order of each customer. The former process tends to be auto-

FIGURE 16.4
The analytic production
(disassembly) process.

SOURCE: Leon C. Megginson,
Lyle R. Trueblood, and Gayle M.
Ross, *Business* (Lexington, MA:
D. C. Heath, 1985), p. 202.

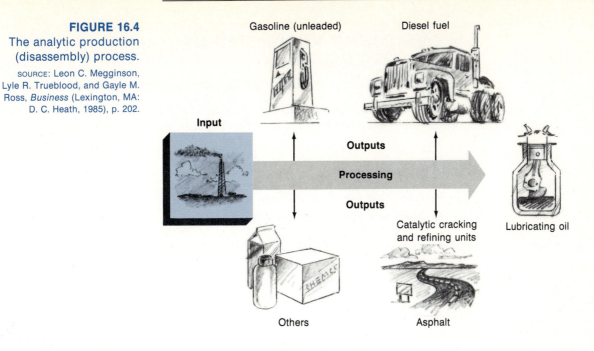

mated and continues to produce the same product for long periods of time. This is called a **continuous process** and is a type of operation that is relatively easy to run and tends to have the lowest costs per unit. Most companies try to establish their processes with these characteristics, but there are very few that entirely fit this category. For example, we think of the automobile assembly lines being continuous, but they frequently stop and start, to get parts, assemblies, or subassemblies to the lines.

The **job shop processing** of goods to special order is based on meeting the special demands or needs of specific customers. A customer designs a special house, a transistor must have a special set of characteristics for a product, a car of a certain style and color is "loaded" with specific options, a suit is made to fit a person, or a bridge is to be constructed over a river. Each job must have its own set of instructions to be processed properly.

Job processing is used primarily in service industries to try to satisfy the needs of individual customers. Retail stores work with individual customer needs, with similar products grouped together in one section of the store. For example, in department stores, the electronic products are in one location where specialists can serve the customers. Ideally, other departments have sales clerks knowledgeable in other specific areas. Meat in a supermarket is located for ease of selection and for specialized service. The location and arrangement within the building depends on the desired path of customers in search of goods.

What is your view?

Can you think of some service organizations that use job shop processing? Give some examples.

DESIGNING FACILITIES NEEDED FOR OPERATIONS

Good selection and arrangement of physical facilities is essential for effective operations. Planning physical facilities requires the following steps:

1. Determine the product to be produced.*
2. Determine the volume to be produced.
3. Determine parts, operations, and activities needed.
4. Determine space requirements.
5. Decide on the best layout.
6. Implement plans.

Determine the Product to Be Produced

This step raises a question for top management. What product should management provide? The good or service may be new to the company and require new processes, or revision of an existing good or service may warrant revising the processes.

Designing the product. The product must be designed to attract customers and to fulfill their needs and wants—at a cost low enough to assure that customers will be willing and able to buy it.

Goods, services, ideas, and processes are changing and will continue to change very rapidly. For example, look around in a video rental store, new within the last few years, to see how the tapes and their packaging and marketing have been changing. Do you notice ways in which the store environment has changed from the past?

What is your view?

Since you have been in school, have you ever been challenged to develop new ideas? What were the results?

Computer assistance. **Computer-assisted design** (CAD) has become a great aid in the design and improvement of products. Computers and software are available for displaying a wide range of designs and sketches, for rearranging lines using an electronic pen, for matching parts, and for processing data for the "paperwork" needed. Computers expand the scope of designer thinking by fostering the "what if?" approach, to determine, for example, what would happen if shaft A were enlarged. The computer can be programmed to answer questions of this type.

---

* The end result of operations is a usable *product* to satisfy customer needs. The product may be (1) a good, (2) a service, or (3) an idea. To avoid unnecessary repetition, we will use the word *product* to refer to any one—or all—of these.

For example, General Motors has been able to shorten its design cycle because of computerization of production. The time between the start of design of an auto and its production is expected to drop from about eight years to three years. Thus the end product will more nearly follow consumer tastes.

Operations are being increasingly mechanized and automated. With mechanization has come mass production—large numbers of like units produced in a stream through special machines. Automated machines and robots are increasing in number at a geometric rate. Flexibility is achieved for the machines by attaching them to computers for **computer-aided manufacturing (CAM).** Computers can be programmed to adjust and change tools to produce a variety of sizes, shapes, textures, and other characteristics desired. Thus, specially ordered products can now be produced at mass production prices.

For example, Coleco was able to create the illusion of "mass produced individuality" by having computers make slight adjustments on each Cabbage Patch Kid® produced.

Determine the Volume to Be Produced

This step depends on the forecast of expected sales during future years and the level of operations desired. Market research can be done to determine the demand for the goods or services planned. Potential sales can be determined for the industry and your share of the market computed. Estimates of the investment needed and costs for this volume can be related to the money that is available in order to determine what reasonable volume is needed. Many times, it is best to set capacity on the low side. Overtime, subcontracting, and arrangements to delay delivery can give a company flexibility so that investment can be delayed, but overinvestment in physical plant can be disastrous if sales do not match expectations.

(Source: Coleco Industries, Inc.)

Determine Parts, Operations, and Activities Needed

Goods and services require parts, materials, or supplies; entail one or more operations; and involve activities. In order to plan for each of these properly, the process must be detailed to determine the physical facilities and workers required to produce the desired volume.

Determining the sequence of operations. During the design stage, specifications, operations, and the sequence of operations are developed in enough detail for production to be planned.

Operations are the steps or segments of work performed to transform the material into the finished product. Each operation requires a worker and/or a machine for its performance. Thus, a printing press was needed to print the text on this page. A salesperson may be used to make a sale, a computer to process it, and a griddle to cook a meat patty. Figure 16.5 shows the sequence of operations for assembling a car using machines and workers.

Determining number of machines and operators needed. Using the volume of output planned and the rate of output of each machine and/or worker required, the number of machines and workers can be determined. Since there are many ways to perform an operation, and the cost and rate of output of the methods vary, several analyses are usually needed to find the best selection.

A similar analysis should be done by service-type organizations. As the following example shows, it is easy to plan incorrectly for the number of customers expected at a given period of time.

> *Ken Hoffman, operations manager of Four Seasons amusement and theme park, had just spent the busiest day of his life. On the Easter weekend of 1985, the park had broken the single-day attendance record of 40,000 and also the weekend record, with over 100,000 people churning through the turnstiles. But what should have been good news for Hoffman wasn't. Top management had vetoed Hoffman's request to add another 75 part-time employees to the weekend staff, and, as a result, the weekend had been an operational nightmare. The maintenance crew was overwhelmed and was not available when repairs were needed on some of the equipment, resulting in longer-than-usual shutdowns. Lines for some of the popular events, such as the Whiplash and roller coaster, were so long that it took patrons nearly 30 minutes to reach the head of the line. Moreover, the concessions were overcrowded, restrooms were overtaxed, and parking was a disaster. The normally neat grounds were blighted with waste paper and debris, and many patrons personally complained, demanding and receiving a refund of their admission fee. "Our system was just plain overloaded," stated Hoffman, who bore the brunt of the pressure-packed, stressful weekend.*

Determining other activities. Other activities arise from the operations. Material must be moved from operation to operation or to display shelves, tools must be stored and moved to machines, service personnel must be dispatched to a customer's residence, maintenance must be performed, and supervisors must be present to advise and control operations. Nonactivities also occur as a result of variations in actual performance: delays in delivery, unbalanced operations, breakdowns, and unplanned inventory. While every effort should be made to minimize such nonactivities, they will occur to some extent and so should be taken into account in planning.

What is your view?

What specific steps or segments are involved for a university when it conducts each of the following operations: *(a)* admisssion, *(b)* registration, *(c)* freshman orientation, and *(d)* processing of final grades?

Determine Space Requirements

Physical facilities—such as a plant, office, TV station, or retail store—are designed to house an organization's operations. Space should be available for operations, including space for machines, employees, and materials. Also, other uses, such as for offices, for service functions, for movement of inventory, and for storage, may require as much space. Space must be provided for unloading and loading of incoming and outgoing materials near transportation sidings.

Much emphasis is being placed now on *just-in-time scheduling* (JIT), which has been emphasized for assembly lines in the auto industry but is now being applied on a broader basis. An obvious example is the serving of hot food in fast-food establishments, but the technique can be applied also in service activities such as airports and florist shops.

Space requirements may be designed only for today's operations or for operations at some future date. Finances and costs are among the factors limiting the size. Larger facilities can take care of future expansion at a low cost, but meanwhile the added space requires a heavy initial investment and higher energy costs. Costs of adding to buildings are less if planned for when the original building is constructed. But addition of machines can be delayed.

Decide on the Best Layout

The arrangement of facilities and workstations is called the *layout*. The type and importance of layout varies with the type of business. An electrical repair company into which customers call and crews report and leave for the jobs needs at least an office and a storeroom. The layout of the storeroom is designed for ease in finding parts, and the office can be fairly simple in design. Supermarkets, department stores, and other retail establishments are planned to make it easy for customers to find what they need and to foster additional sales. The layout will vary according to the size of goods, types of service (whether self-service or salesperson-assisted), volume of business, security needs, and desired flexibility of movement.

The planning of layouts in manufacturing is basically the same as for service businesses except that the orientation is more toward processing material than toward dealing with customers. The processing involves machines, workers, and materials. It must be efficient, meet time requirements, and produce output that meets customer demands.

Some specific questions to ask when doing layout planning are shown in TIPS 16.1.

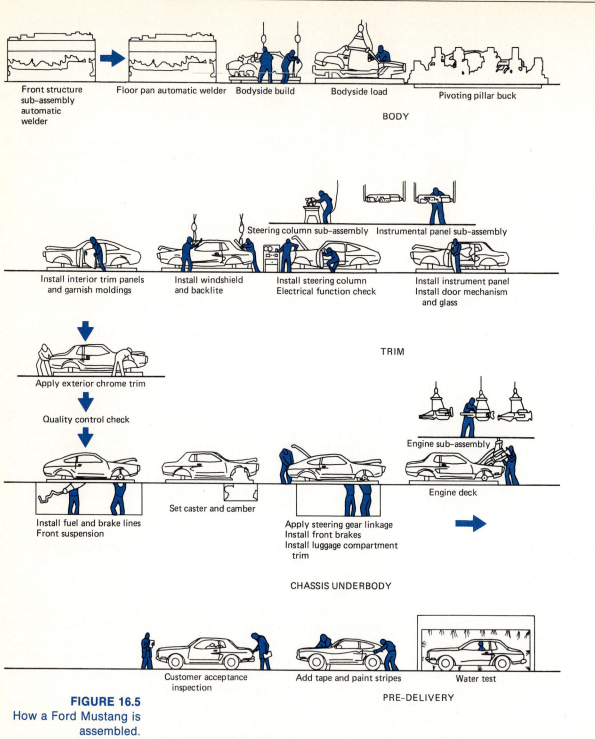

Front structure sub-assembly automatic welder

Floor pan automatic welder

Bodyside build

Bodyside load

Pivoting pillar buck

BODY

Steering column sub-assembly

Instrumental panel sub-assembly

Install interior trim panels and garnish moldings

Install windshield and backlite

Install steering column Electrical function check

Install instrument panel Install door mechanism and glass

Apply exterior chrome trim

Quality control check

TRIM

Engine sub-assembly

Engine deck

Install fuel and brake lines Front suspension

Set caster and camber

Apply steering gear linkage Install front brakes Install luggage compartment trim

CHASSIS UNDERBODY

Customer acceptance inspection

Add tape and paint stripes

Water test

PRE-DELIVERY

FIGURE 16.5
How a Ford Mustang is assembled.

SOURCE: Leon C. Megginson, Lyle R. Trueblood, and Gayle M. Ross, *Business* (Lexington, MA: D. C. Heath, 1985), p. 200. Reprinted by permission of the Educational Affairs Department, Ford Motor Company.

What is your view?

Study the plan of your room, apartment, and/or home. Could it be better arranged? Are electric outlets conveniently located? Make blocks for rooms and templates for furniture and see what choices you have when planning a new layout for it.

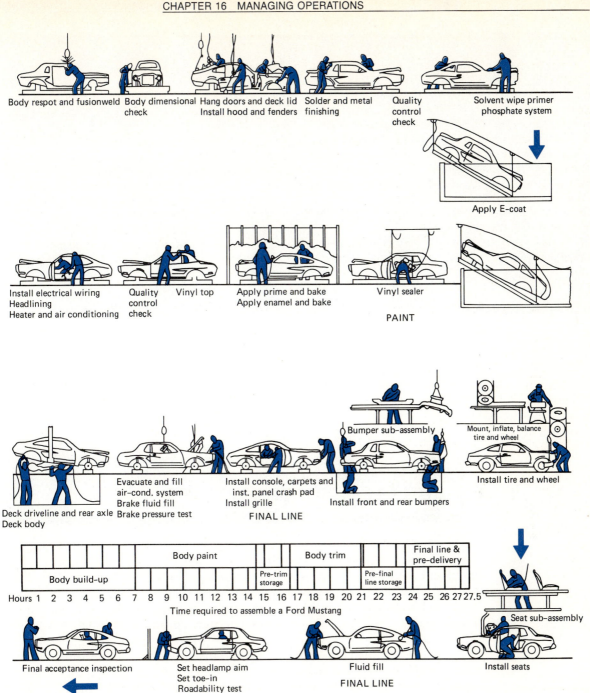

Body respot and fusionweld   Body dimensional   Hang doors and deck lid   Solder and metal   Quality   Solvent wipe primer
                              check   Install hood and fenders   finishing   control   phosphate system
                                                                                               check

Apply E-coat

Install electrical wiring   Quality   Vinyl top   Apply prime and bake   Vinyl sealer
Headlining   control   Apply enamel and bake
Heater and air conditioning check

PAINT

Bumper sub-assembly   Mount, inflate, balance
                           tire and wheel

                                                                         Install tire and wheel

Deck driveline and rear axle   Evacuate and fill   Install console, carpets and   Install front and rear bumpers
Deck body   air-cond. system   inst. panel crash pad
                               Brake fluid fill   Install grille
                               Brake pressure test   FINAL LINE

Body build-up						Body paint								Pre-trim storage		Body trim					Pre-final line storage		Final line & pre-delivery			

Hours 1 2 3 4 5 6 7 8 9 10 11 12 13 14 15 16 17 18 19 20 21 22 23 24 25 26 27 27.5

Time required to assemble a Ford Mustang

Seat sub-assembly

Final acceptance inspection   Set headlamp aim   Fluid fill   Install seats
                              Set toe-in   FINAL LINE
                              Roadability test

Implement Plans

A review of all the steps taken may reveal a need for further improvement. The availability of a computer makes simulation of the whole process reasonably easy. Introduction into the model of some mishaps that are likely to occur can suggest changes in the layout. It might be well to design the operations plan to be used and try it out on a computer to see what happens. Any tests that find bugs in the process may be valuable.

TIPS 16.1   Sample Questions to Ask About a Production Layout

1. *Space for movement.* Are aisles wide enough for cart and truck movement? Is there enough room for lines that form at machines and checkout stations? Can material be obtained easily and shelves restocked conveniently?

2. *Utilities.* Has adequate wiring and plumbing, and provision for changes, been planned? Has provision been made for proper temperature? Does the area meet EPA standards?

3. *Safety.* Is proper fire protection provided and are OSHA standards being met? Are proper guards on machines, in aisles, and around dangerous areas planned?

4. *Working conditions.* Do workers have enough working space and light? Is there provision for low noise levels, proper temperature, and elimination of objectionable odors? Are workers safe? Can they socialize and take care of personal needs?

5. *Cleanliness and maintenance.* Is the layout designed for effective housekeeping and waste disposal at low cost? Can machinery, equipment, and the building be maintained easily?

6. *Product quality.* Has provision been made to assure proper quality and to protect the product as it moves through the plant or stays in storage?

The planning of the building to house the layout is beyond the scope of this discussion. However, care should be exercised to make sure that the building has features that will make the layout work.

PLANNING AND CONTROLLING OPERATIONS

Planning and controlling functions have been covered in Part II and this part of the text. This section uses the basic processes shown in those parts to aid in operations activities. Some planning would already have been done during the layout of the operating units. The layout then becomes one of the determining factors in designing a system for ordering the operations process. For example, if a conveyor will move products through the operations and no variation is to occur during the process, no information beyond the initial training is needed to prepare employees to work on the conveyor. Directions are needed at the start of the process about loading the conveyor and at the end of the conveyor about delivery of the products. Also, if processing varies from one unit to another on the conveyor (as in customizing an automobile), directions must be provided.

All operations systems need some sort of *master plan* to inform management when the plant is to be running, how much to produce, and who is to do the work. Sales demand varies from time to time, which means that operations activities may vary. Decisions on how to handle these situations require economic analysis, consideration of the workers, and consultation between the marketing and operations departments.

Master Operations Plans

Variations in demand for a company's products occur over a period of time. A major cause is the change in seasons and styles. Changes in weather influence the demand for a wide variety of products, such as air conditioners, footballs, clothing, agricultural products, and recreation equipment. Changes in fads, styles, technology, and government regulations also influence what is produced and when.

To make a master plan, a forecast for about a year ahead must be developed. Usually, the marketing department and its market research branch make forecasts of demand for the product. Some changes can be predicted with reasonable certainty, some can only be estimates, and some are based on whether or not a certain activity occurs.

> *For example, forecasters can be reasonably sure that most people will not buy air conditioners in the winter or blankets in the summer. It is anybody's guess what books will become best sellers and what records will make the Top 40. On the other hand, a manufacturer can probably expect that products featuring the logos of successful NFL teams will outsell those of teams at the bottom of their divisions, and Olympics souvenirs will sell better if the U.S. team wins many gold medals.*

Using the forecast, the alternative plans that might be used for operations can be evaluated. The following are some possible alternative operations plans (OPs):

1. *Meet customer demand as it arises.* As demand increases, workers are hired, work overtime, or both; as demand drops, workers are laid off, lose overtime, or work short weeks. These changes result in high employee benefits, unemployment, absenteeism, severance pay, and related costs. Morale may drop and quality suffer. Investment in facilities is high. This plan is costly but must be used when others are not feasible.

2. *Meet demand through inventory and processing.* As demand drops below operations, the excess output is placed in inventory; as sales rise above operations, items are pulled out of inventory and sent to customers. A relatively constant work force, low machine investment, and low information-processing requirements make this plan attractive. However, high interest rates and rapid production innovation make carrying inventory very expensive (low inventory is one of the advantages that many Japanese companies have over some U.S. companies). Many service companies, such as electric utilities, cannot inventory their services.

3. *Counterbalance demand to level total demand.* Under this plan, the sum of the demands for one month is the same as that for another month, but the demand is for different products. This is one of the reasons some companies produce, sell, or service both furnaces and air conditioners; equipment for football, basketball, baseball, and other seasonal sports; or both winter and summer clothing. If the company's machines and workers' skills can be used for both products, and if the demand is such as to balance the load, relatively constant operations can be achieved. This type of plan is highly favored because it levels

out operations and lowers operating costs, and the wider product line makes marketing easier.

4. *Meet high demand by subcontracting or buying.* This plan keeps the company capacity—number of employees and/or machines—low. However, it may be difficult to find a good, reliable supplier who can effectively meet the desired requirements.

5. *Raise low demand by using sales inducements.* The inducements might be special promotions, extra advertising, lower prices, or a combination of these. This type of marketing activity may help even out demand, but its application is limited.

The **master operations plan** (**MOP**) provides a general operations guide extending for about a year ahead. From this plan monthly, weekly, and daily plans can be prepared. The amount of detailed planning depends on the variations in demand. Then, as time passes, actual performance can be compared to plans so as to make needed revisions.

Operations Planning and Control

Operations planning and control can be generally divided into four functions: routing, scheduling, dispatching, and control and follow-up.

Routing. *Routing* is the paperwork needed to define the order of operations so that it can be scheduled, dispatched, and followed up on. A system exists to assure proper performance of the functions. Forms are completed when a sale is made. Instructions for activities such as design, selection of item, operations, inventory, shipment, quality, and time must reach the right people at the right time. The information, transmitted orally, on paper, or by computer, is used to direct the people performing the operations. Routing is performed for each special order, but for standard items continuously ordered, all the information can be stored and retrieved when necessary— usually only when a model change occurs.

Scheduling. As shown in Chapter 15, *scheduling* is planning the timing and sequencing of the use of physical and human resources used in the operational activities of an organization. Figure 16.5 showed an automobile assembly line, which requires very close scheduling to avoid delays and pileups. *Just-in-time scheduling* has been reemphasized successfully by the Japanese to approximate *zero inventory*. Gantt and PERT charts, discussed and shown in Chapter 15, can be used effectively to develop schedules for complex work such as large construction work. The person doing the scheduling usually determines when the product is to be completed. Then, the separate operations, or component activities, are scheduled according to the time and sequence necessary to have each completed in time. The earlier operations are scheduled so as to perform work efficiently and meet delivery dates.

Dispatching. Although routing and scheduling have been completed, no production has yet occurred because these steps have been planning ones. Now resources must be made available and operations performed. This step, called *dispatching*, transmits the instructions for performing the work to operating personnel. The routing instructions and schedules are sent to dispatchers so that materials, parts, and tools are issued at the proper time, items are moved to the proper stations, and the proper operations are performed. Also, items are identified, standards are provided, and inspections are performed.

For example, dispatching can be seen at airports just before the departure of a plane. A taxi is dispatched to a customer when a call is received asking for one. Most people have seen these activities but not the behind-the-scenes activities required for baggage handling, food and beverage provision, and employee scheduling.

Control and follow-up. **Control and follow-up** have been discussed in Chapters 14 and 15. As stated, feedforward controls attempt to anticipate problems or deviations from standards in advance of their occurrence. In fact, all systems should be designed and people trained to prevent deviations. The ideal of **zero defects,** or no deviations from the standard, is being emphasized more than in the past. The success of Japanese quality control efforts has awakened a desire for perfection, both to reduce costs and to enhance a company's reputation for quality. Much of the data used for control can be entered into a computer, which then provides the information for follow-up by company personnel.

Follow-up action may be in the form of revising methods, machines, tools, schedules, and plans; retraining personnel; responding to customer queries and complaints; or a combination of these. Reaction time should be short to minimize the effects of poor performance. Without question, a control system is expensive: Repairing, reworking, or scrapping units is costly and delays operations. Moreover, delays in resource availability can cause confusion. Still, passed defective output can damage the company's reputation for quality or result in suits for damages. The amount of control and follow-up is based on balancing the system's costs against its value.

Improving Operations

As in the design of products, continued effort is needed to find and apply the best operating methods. The steps used to study activities for improvement follow those for problem solving. Specialized charts, diagrams, statistics, and other techniques are used to collect and interpret information. Process, multiactivity, computer, and other charts are used to show operations, moves, delays, storage times, conflicts, and other data. Each item in such an operation is checked for possible change. A sample of the questions that can be asked follows:

1. What operation is being performed? Can it be combined with another one? Can it be eliminated?
2. Where is it being performed? Is there a better place?
3. When is it being performed? Should it be done sooner or later?
4. Who is performing the operation? Does he or she need more training or retraining?
5. How is it being performed? Can the operation be simplified?
6. Why is it being performed? Can it be eliminated?

What is your view?

Apply the above questions to some of your daily activities. Can you use the answers to improve your grades or enjoyment of life?

MATERIALS MANAGEMENT

The cost of **materials** (supplies, parts, and goods) to most companies is about half the total revenue from their products. This means that labor costs, plus manufacturing, selling, and administrative costs, plus profits, just about equal the total bill for materials purchases. Consequently, a substantial increase in purchased items may wipe out a company's profit. Management must therefore exercise great care in purchasing and managing materials.

Materials management usually includes the following:

1. Determining needs.
2. Deciding whether to make or buy a part or component.
3. Timing and quantity of purchasing and processing.
4. Analysis of inventory and operations.
5. Materials requirements planning (MRP).
6. The purchasing process.

Only the most important of these are discussed in this chapter.

Determining Needs

Operations, whether performing a service or producing a good, start with purchases of materials from another company. Retailers, wholesalers, and manufacturers must determine the products they will produce or sell. The design of the products and processes determines the specifications and quality level for the items to be purchased. Sales forecasts and production plans set the schedule from which the volume of material needed is determined. The changes in the amount of inventory planned, plus the amount needed for expected sales or production, indicate the amount to be purchased.

Deciding Whether to Make or Buy a Part or Component

Thinking about this question can be helpful to most organizations. For example, should a restaurant buy prepared foods? Should a hotel train its managers or hire from other hotels? Should a professional sports team develop its players in a farm system or trade for experienced players? Should auto companies produce all their parts or depend on subcontractors? Are the decisions the same for boom times and slow times?

What is your view?

Under what situations should a company's decision be to ''make''? To ''buy''? During slack times, when sales are low, should an auto company lay off workers and leave the machines idle, or should it produce and sell the excess parts to outsiders?

If a company plans to supply its own needs, resources must be invested in facilities to produce them and cannot be invested elsewhere. If it decides to buy, it does not have as much control over the quality, cost, and timing as it does when making them. Therefore, trade-offs such as the following must be considered when making the make-or-buy decision.

Advantages of *making* your own are:

1. The company has more control over the process and quality.

2. There is less idle machine and personnel time.

3. More growth is possible.

Advantages of *buying* are:

1. Both capital investment (in machines) and personnel costs are lower.

2. Management can specialize, devoting company time to producing its main product.

3. Planning, directing, and controlling are less complex.

MRP starts with the demand for one or more products. The delivery date is set, the time for the last operation is deducted, and the operation's starting time is set. Prior operations, including those to produce parts, are handled in the same manner—set date needed, process time, and starting time. By repeating this for all operations, the schedule for all material movement is planned. As can be seen, a computer is essential for processes of any size.

ENERGY MANAGEMENT

With only 5 percent of the world's population and 7 percent of its land area, we in the United States use about a third of all the energy consumed each year. And our industry accounts for around 36 percent of that energy consumption—much of it for production and operations.

Actually, industry is doing quite well in energy conservation and management. But more care is still needed, and everyone in the organization needs to help, not just the production people. While operations managers and employees may find ways to decrease the use of energy through better design of products and production processes, no program of energy conservation will succeed unless all employees become energy conservers.

There are many ways of conserving energy by reducing the use of natural gas, oil, electricity, and other energy sources. But the most frequently used ones are:

1. *Improving housekeeping*—by turning lights and machines off when not in use. For example, Raytheon has inspectors who roam the production areas giving out citations to people guilty of wasteful energy practices.

2. *Energy recycling*—such as using heat, steam, and other energy generated by operating processes to fulfill other energy needs.

3. *Improving building design*—including more and better insulation and more efficient heating and cooling systems.

4. *Using more effective lighting*—switching from incandescent light to fluorescent systems.

THE ROBOTICS REVOLUTION

Many technological developments are occurring in operations management, especially in the areas of automation, resulting from the application of computers and robotics. This **automation revolution** is the growing tendency for work to be performed by machines that are, in turn, computer controlled. At the present rate of growth, the trend seems to be toward a **robotics revolution,** with assembly work being performed by machines that are computer controlled and with parts and assemblies being handled automatically. For example, computers and robots at General Electric's Erie, Pennsylvania, plant can assemble a locomotive engine frame in one day, whereas it previously took 16 days for 68 skilled machine operators to do the same. Computers run all the operations, and no humans are involved until a control (executive) computer is satisfied with the work and asks an employee to take over.

In the past, technological growth created more jobs than it eliminated, but it now appears that automation may be capable of replacing whole groups of workers in many work situations. Automatic systems are being used almost entirely to produce goods and perform services, as shown in MAP 16.1.

 What is your view?

Have you visited an automatic teller machine (ATM) lately and conducted your banking business with a machine? Studies of banking show that ATMs are the wave of the future and by 1990 will surpass human tellers in share of deposit and withdrawal transactions processed. From the financial institution's viewpoint, what are the advantages of such a system? Disadvantages? What are the advantages and disadvantages to you as a customer?

Automation Is Tending to Replace Manual Operations

The character and volume of activities determine the skills and machines needed. Industry is moving from the use of manual operations to robotic machines. This change is forcing management to perform its functions better because *humans are better able to:*

1. Perform work that does not fit some preprogrammed pattern, such as reacting to breakdowns and answering grievances.

2. Use their experience to handle the variations in situations that require modifications of the work being done.

3. Analyze, make judgments, and develop entirely new solutions to problems.

Reasons for Growing Use of Automation and Robotics

A primary reason for using automation and robotics is that Japan and our other trading competitors are doing it. Because we operate in global markets, we must be able to match or surpass competitors' effective use of advanced technology. We can no longer use inefficient and ineffective operating methods of production and service.

Management Application and Practice 16.1   Punching Up the Ads with Robots

Robots aren't yet co-anchoring the evening news, but automation is making strides in television studios. At some TV stations, a jukeboxlike robotic system is replacing the people who pick and play pretaped commercial sequences. In April 1987, the National Broadcasting Company (NBC) became the first to use the system to play taped sequences on national news programs.

The machines are produced by Odetics Inc., an Anaheim, California, company that also makes specialized robots and tape recorders for the space program. In Odetics' $300,000 TV system, as many as 280 tapes are arranged in slots in a cabinet that surrounds a four-armed carousel equipped with a barcode reader to identify tapes. Robot arms can simultaneously select and play a tape, retrieve a finished tape from a playback machine, and return another tape to its storage spot. An IBM personal computer directs traffic and tallies which tapes have been aired.

According to Odetics Vice-President David E. Lewis, stations that use this equipment can play 15-second air spots in rapid succession without missing a beat. Another advantage, says Lewis, is the freedom to change the ad lineup at the last minute. "You can replace a promotional tape with something you're getting paid for," he notes.

SOURCE: Adapted from "Tonight's News: Brought to You by Tom Brokaw, and a Robot," *Business Week*, April 13, 1987, p. 99.

Another reason for using robotics is that *machines are more effective than people when used to:*

1. Perform repetitive tasks, such as printing newspapers, washing clothes, or keeping routine records.

2. Apply great force smoothly and evenly, as in shaping metal, doing heavy construction work, or drilling holes.

3. Count or measure physical quantities more precisely than would be possible for humans, as do odometers, weighing scales, and counting machines.

4. Store information and data for quick, accurate, and consistent retrieval and use, as is done with computer-assisted registration and grade reports. Also, in many retail store checkout stations, electronic sensors connected to computers and cash registers are being used to read the bar codes on packages and enter prices and other information automatically. Computers can update inventory and sales records, too, routinely, rapidly, and accurately, using data stored in their memory banks.

5. Do tiring and dirty work.

Results of the Revolution

Some of the *favorable results* of this trend are (1) increased productivity, (2) reduced costs, (3) more and better products, (4) higher quality, and (5) increased competitiveness. For example, productivity increased almost 20 percent when robots replaced 200 welders at Chrysler's plant in East Detroit, where it produces its K-cars. About 50 small robots are carefully fitting light bulbs into car radios and dashboards at one Ford Company plant. It has been predicted that by 1990 half the workers in U.S. factories will be specialists trained to repair and service robots.[7]

But there are also some *unfavorable consequences* of this trend. These include (1) job displacement—that is, that people who might have been able to perform the more technically advanced jobs have been displaced by machines, and (2) strained group relations, since there is less interaction between workers when machines run by people are replaced by machines run by other machines. Also, robots are quite costly to buy and operate, and they have not always proved satisfactory in actual operations.

Future of the Revolution

The robotics revolution will probably lead to improved productivity and quality, since robots do not need rest periods, never take vacations, and ask for no holidays—with or without pay (although there is a cost for downtime for maintenance and repairs). They can be more efficient to operate, can perform more effectively, and can be cheaper. These robots, which cost from $30,000 to $150,000 each and usually work two or more shifts a day, can displace workers who would together earn over $700,000 a year in wages and benefits.[8]

But there is a limit to what robots can do. Increased and cheaper production? Yes! But when it comes to reasoning and making informed decisions, these **steel-collar workers** are still machines and infinitely inferior to frail, fallible human beings!

USING MANAGEMENT SCIENCE IN OPERATIONS

In Chapter 3, we showed how *management science*, which involves decision-making techniques and mathematical models, was developed during World War II. Chapter 15 showed how it could be used to improve control. Now let us see how these techniques can be applied to operations.

Types of Management Science Tools

The purpose of this section is to give you a basic understanding of some of the applications of the techniques called *management science techniques.* The actual techniques are complex, but you should develop a feel for the types of decisions that lend themselves to management science approaches.

Linear programming. **Linear programming (LP)** is a management science tool that is used to solve "optimization" problems, or problems in which there is one "best" answer from a set of alternatives. LP lends itself to operations problems such as capital budgeting, selection of advertising media, pricing, warehousing, and others.

Let us consider an example in which the objective is to find the best distribution locations and routes.

A company buys goods from suppliers and distributes them through warehouses to customers (retailers) located around the country. Because of changes in the market, the company must periodically check its warehouse locations and its distribution routes for possible changes. The

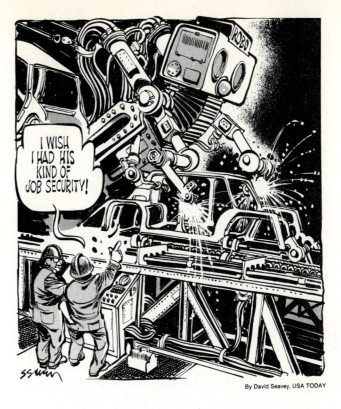

By David Seavey, USA TODAY

(Source: USA Today, *July 30, 1987, p. 8A. Art by David Seavey.)*

company has choices in both locations and routes. Transportation and operating costs and prices vary. The company wants to minimize its costs.

A special type of LP can be used to find the locations and routes that minimize costs. This method uses rules to establish alternatives, check for a better solution, find that solution, and make the change; it repeats the process until the optimum solution is found. The method is tedious, but a computer can process the LP easily.

Queuing theory. Supermarket managers often have to decide how many clerks to employ at given times to work the store's checkout counters. To have cashiers on duty at, say, 10 stations when only three are needed will make employee costs unnecessarily high. Yet to have only two or three on duty when there is heavy customer traffic will mean long checkout lines and disgruntled customers! **Queuing theory** permits a decision to be made that will balance out the costs of providing customer service and maintaining employees at the checkout stations. To solve these problems, data on characteristics of server performance and customer arrival are collected. From these, a model of customer use can be developed. From this point, the model can be manipulated to reflect variables such as number of customers, time required to check out customers, number of checkout stations available, and so on.

Queuing theory has application to a wide variety of waiting line problems, such as:

1. How many bank tellers to assign to various teller stations throughout the day.

2. How many unloading stations to construct and operate at a warehouse docking facility.

3. How many collection booths to construct and operate at a highway toll station.

4. How many people to work in various service capacities at various times (pharmacists, hotel desk clerks, driver's license examiners, cafeteria servers, and so on).

5. How much machinery and equipment to make available to have smooth production and operations work flow.

What is your view?

What are some other activities that lend themselves to the use of queuing theory?

Simulation. Simulation is the act of performing experiments on a model (rather than the real thing) in some planned, orderly fashion. **Monte Carlo,** which takes its name from the roulette wheel, is one form of simulation, relying on the laws of probability to simulate actual experience. For example, some queuing problems fall into the simulation category if there are no trends known in the frequency of the variables involved. Simulation can be used, according to the laws of probability, to predict what behavior will occur when there is no apparent trend in such behavior.

Examples of problems that can be solved by simulation include the following:

1. How much inventory should a store carry when demand fluctuates unpredictably?

2. What is the necessary capacity a power company should have on hand to meet peak loads when energy use occurs in no predictable pattern?

What is your view?

What other activities are you familiar with that could use simulation?

Network models. Network analysis is a management science tool used to help management plan and control nonroutine, complex projects. Two common types of network models are the Program Evaluation and Review Technique (PERT) and the Critical Path Method (CPM). Network models as control techniques were explored in greater detail in Chapter 15.

In general, network models express graphically and quantitatively the overall network of events to be completed. Through computer manipulation, network models measure the impact on the overall project of changing the schedule (for example, getting one activity done by "rushing" it) in the completion of any of the various events.

Consider these two examples in which network analysis would prove helpful.

1. An aircraft manufacturer must submit bids on a new jet aircraft for the Department of Defense, including not only prices but also well-supported estimates of completion dates for various phases of the project.

2. A company uses a CPM model to help plan and schedule construction of a large office building requiring the coordination and completion of over 20,000 separate activities.

What is your view?

In what other situations should network models be of help?

Regression analysis. Regression analysis is a statistical technique that is used to determine the nature of an association or relationship between variables. For example, a relationship may be shown to exist between the following:

1. The speed of a machine and the percentage of defective parts it produces.

2. Rate of pay and sex (used as the basis of many discrimination cases against organizations).

3. The amount of money spent on advertising and a store's total sales.

The particular model constructed is called a "linear regression model" and can be used for predictive purposes in decision making.

What is your view?

Can you think of any examples of regression analysis that might be useful to a small business such as a florist, shoe store, or hobby shop?

Limitations of Management Science Tools

Generally, the use of management science techniques has been limited primarily to larger firms and has not yet lived up to the promises of its early advocates. Why haven't these techniques caught on more quickly? In part, the answer is that the field is still very new. In fact, refinements of the techniques involved continue to be made. As advancements in computer technology occur, the use of management science techniques should also increase.

But there are also other problems to be overcome. Some of these were pointed out by C. Jackson Grayson, the academician trained in management science who was named to head the commission to monitor the price controls imposed by President Richard Nixon in 1971. Grayson had done research in the area, had written a book urging the use of management science in oil well drilling, and had taught various courses in the subject—for example in statistics, management control systems, and quantitative analysis. Yet he later said, "In the most challenging assignment of my life—putting together the Price Commission—I used absolutely *none* of the management science tools explicitly."[9] The reasons Grayson gave for not using management science techniques included (1) shortage of time, (2) data inaccessibility, (3) resistance to change by the managers involved, (4) long response time, and (5) oversimplification.

Grayson feels that management scientists must develop a greater appreciation of the real-world constraints of operating managers. Management scientists are going to have to think in terms of the manager's perceptions, needs, expectations, and pressures if they want to have a real impact in the real world of the manager. If not, Grayson says, they will continue to miss the mark. But top management in organizations should also take steps to help make management scientists become more real-world oriented. Grayson recommends spreading management scientists around in the organization instead of grouping them in a centralized department so that they can become better identified with line management and perhaps be more likely to develop approaches that affect bottom-line results of lower costs and greater profits.

SUMMARY

This chapter has dealt with the management of operations—that is, those activities that convert inputs to outputs, bringing together material, financial, and human resources to create the product, which may be either a good or a service. Improving the efficiency of operations, or productivity, is especially important now when U.S. industry is suffering in competition for foreign industry.

Although the operations of goods-producing and service-performing industries may seem very different, it is hard to draw a dividing line between them. Both have systems designed to process inputs into outputs, providing form, place, or time utility at an acceptable cost. Both require a certain sequence of steps; use specific skills, tools, machinery, or equipment to effect this transformation; require instructions about what is to be processed and how it is to be done (as well as when it is to be completed); set standards for operations; and are subject to variations from standard that must be dealt with.

Some operations during the conversion process just change the input to produce output, others assemble items, and still others "disassemble" inputs. These types of operations are carried out either in a straight-line, invariable sequence, a continuous process, or a varying sequence, different for each product, which is job shop processing.

Designing the facilities needed for operations requires the following steps: (1) determining the product to be produced, (2) determining the volume to be planned for, (3) determining parts, operations, and activities needed, (4) determining space requirements, and (5) deciding on the best arrangement of machines and workstations.

Planning and control operations are major activities of a company. Variations in demand force decisions on whether to vary operations with demand, to vary inventory, to counterbalance, to subcontract, and/or to induce favorable sales patterns. Routing, scheduling, dispatching, and follow-up are functions used to direct and control operations. Operations can sometimes be improved by asking the basic questions of what is being done and where, by whom, and—especially—why.

Materials management, which includes purchasing and storage, is another crucial management area because the cost of materials to most manufacturing companies is about half the total revenue from their products. Often, management must decide whether to make or buy materials, and this decision may vary according to the level of operations. Just-in-time scheduling will reduce inventory carrying costs and is therefore desirable, but some inventory is necessary to decouple consecutive operations. The most efficient method of materials management is materials requirements planning (MRP), which, usually using a computer, carefully plots the exact amount of materials needed on a given date so that they may be ordered to arrive just in time.

Energy management is important to the nation as well as to management. Energy may be conserved by improving housekeeping, recycling energy, improving building design, and using more effective lighting.

The robotics revolution is found in industry worldwide. Fully automated systems, often under computer control, are being used in many types of production operations. Such machines are especially useful for performing repetitive tasks, applying great force smoothly and evenly, counting or measuring precise physical quantities, storing data for quick, accurate, and consistent retrieval, and doing tiring and dirty work. They can greatly increase efficiency in some operations. However, robots and computers will never replace people, who are still needed to do work that does not fit a preprogrammed pattern, apply their experience to novel situations, or analyze, make judgments, and develop entirely new solutions to problems.

Management science, which evolved from the operations research (OR) developed in World War II, usually involves the use of a mathematical model, often requires the use of a computer, and can be a great help in operations management. Some management science tools are linear programming (LP), queuing theory, simulation, network models, and regression analysis. Although these techniques can be helpful, they are usually available only to very large companies and even there may not be used because of shortage of time, inaccessibility of data, resistance to change, long response time, and oversimplification.

REVIEW QUESTIONS

1. Define *operations*. Be sure that your definition is applicable to service-performing as well as goods-producing industries.
2. List the elements of an operations system.
3. How valuable is inventiveness to an organization? What happens when management does not foster it?
4. Distinguish continuous and job shop processing and give examples of operations for which each is especially suited.
5. List the steps in designing facilities needed for operations. In which of these steps can a computer be especially helpful?
6. What is just-in-time scheduling, and why is it important for production operations?
7. Distinguish product and process layouts, and tell what kinds of operations each is especially suited for.
8. *(a)* What is involved in materials management? *(b)* Why is it so important to manufacturing companies?
9. List some ways to *(a)* improve operations and *(b)* conserve energy.
10. Why is use of robots on the rise? What functions do they *not* perform well?
11. List and describe some management science techniques.

DISCUSSION QUESTIONS

1. Why do you think U.S. industry is suffering in competition with the Japanese? What are some of the things they are doing right?
2. Think of a business that performs a service, and discuss the elements of an operations system as seen in the operations of that business.
3. Think of a small business that you might go into while still in college. Discuss the pros and cons of (1) starting small and (2) planning for expansion.
4. For the same business discussed in question 3, list the sequence of operations involved. Would you use continuous or job shop processing? A product or process layout? How would you determine the space requirements for these operations?
5. Develop a master operations plan for your business. Will demand vary seasonally? If not, why?
6. Will you produce your product (or perform your service) to customer demand, or will you stockpile an inventory? How can you apply the concept of just-in-time scheduling and zero inventory?
7. Will you make your materials "from scratch" or purchase some partially assembled components?
8. Will you use a computer in any way in your business? If so, how?

LEARNING EXERCISE 16.1

Observing Operations Layouts

a. Visit a local grocery store and observe the layout, including shelves, storage, aisle space, traffic flow, and other aspects that you consider important from an operations point of view. Be prepared to discuss this in class.
b. Visit a Wendy's (or some other fast-food restaurant where hamburgers are prepared to order), and do the same as above.
c. Visit a McDonald's (or other fast-food restaurant where the hamburgers are prepared in advance), and do the same as above.

LEARNING EXERCISE 16.2

Coke Cools It

Coca-Cola is a product that is bottled in many locations convenient to population centers and distributed promptly to customers by truck through a distribution network. About seven years ago, the Coca-Cola Company bought three wine-producing companies, thinking that wine, as a beverage, would fit into the Coca-Cola line. However, the company had difficulty applying to wine some of the techniques used in producing and distributing Coke.

Wine must be aged to give it the flavor consumers like. Aging requires that each bottle of wine be kept in inventory for a year or more. The high investment in inventory increased costs and reduced the capital available to the company for other purposes. Also, profits from wine sales did not meet the company's minimum return on investment goal.

Several years ago, the company vastly overestimated the amount of grapes needed, resulting in a large inventory of grapes. Soon after, it came out with an inexpensive wine that would compete at the low end of the market and use the excess inventory of grapes. Sales, expected to be one million gallons, did not meet expectations because of competitive action, and the company lost about $8 million.

The Coca-Cola Company subsequently sold the wine business.

In 1985, management made another decision that had unexpected consequences. After months of exhaustive research and market testing, it introduced "New Coke" with an elaborate and expensive sales promotion campaign. After nearly 100 years, the secret formula was changed. The reaction was immediate, violent, and largely negative. Management's response was to bow to popular opinion and bring back "the real thing" as "Coca-Cola Classic," which required new labels and advertising, not to mention adjustments in bottling schedules, shipping plans, and shelf distribution in retail outlets.

Questions

1. Could inventory problems have made the wine and "Coke" business incompatible? Explain.
2. Compare the effects that inventories of wine and "Coke" had on the company. How does a company take into consideration the costs of inventory?
3. Did the company make the right decision when it found itself with the large inventory of grapes? Were there other alternatives? Discuss.
4. What are some production problems resulting from the Coca-Cola Company's present diversity of products: New Coke, Classic Coke, Diet Coke, Caffeine-Free Coke, Caffeine-Free Diet Coke, Tab, Sprite, Diet Sprite, Crush, Sugar-Free Crush, and Cherry Coke?

LEARNING EXERCISE 16.3

Line Up or Scramble?

Some university cafeteria layouts are designed to have students move along a line that displays food items. As students move, they pick up items they want and carry them on trays to tables where they eat. The cash register is located at one end of the line.

Other universities use the "scramble" system in which different types of food are located in modules at the sides of a square room and in a circle in the center of the room. A student wanting hot vegetables and meat goes to one module, to another side for hamburgers and sandwiches, for drinks and salad to the center module, and so on. The students come from one corner and go out the opposite corner; in the process, they go by the cash register.

Questions

1. What are the operations involved? Would you call this a production process? Explain.
2. What kind of layout is each of these? Explain.
3. What are the advantages and disadvantages of each type of layout? Are there limitations to each? Explain.
4. Which type of layout does your school use? Should it change to the other layout? Explain.
5. Do you believe the "scramble" system layout is best limited to use on campuses? Explain.

NOTES

1. Based upon "Registering by Remote," *Newsweek on Campus*, February 1987, p. 36; and other sources.
2. "Productivity Rises 1.7%," *USA Today*, May 5, 1987, p. 1B.
3. *Wall Street Journal*, June 23, 1987, p. 1.
4. Sylvia Nasar, "Productivity Perks Up," *Fortune*, September 28, 1987, p. 62.
5. David Halberstam, *The Reckoning* (New York: Wm. Morrow & Co., 1986), p. 314.
6. Ibid., p. 693.
7. Ernest Cronine, "Industrial Robot Race under Way," *Tulsa World*, January 24, 1982, p. 2.
8. Hidehiro Tanakadate, "The Robots Are Coming and Japan Leads the Way," *U.S. News & World Report*, January 18, 1982, p. 47.
9. C. Jackson Grayson, Jr., "Management Science and Business Practice," *Harvard Business Review* 51 (July–August 1973): 41–48.

SUGGESTIONS FOR FURTHER STUDY

BIRCH, DAVID L. "Is Manufacturing Dead?" *Inc.*, June 1987, pp. 35–36.

BUSSEY, JOHN, and SEASE, DOUGLAS R. "Speeding Up: Manufacturers Strive to Slice Time Needed to Develop Products." *Wall Street Journal*, February 23, 1988, pp. 1 and 24.

CASE, JOHN. "Zero-Defect Management." *Inc.*, February 1987, p. 17.

CLARK, LINDLEY, H., JR. "Manufacturers Grow Much More Efficient, But Employment Lags." *Wall Street Journal*, December 4, 1986, p. 1.

EGAN, JACK. "Companies That Refused to Rust." *U.S. News & World Report*, July 27, 1987, p. 50.

FARNUM, GREGORY T. "An Experiment in Manufacturing." *Manufacturing Engineering*, March 1986, pp. 91–92.

FINEGAN, JAY. "Uncle Sam, Research Director." *Inc.*, February 1987, pp. 23–24, 26.

LUBOVE, SETH H. "In Computer Age, Certain Workers Are Still Vital to Success," *Wall Street Journal*, August 3, 1987, p. 9.

MAMIS, ROBERT A. "Taking Control." *Inc.*, February 1987, pp. 82–84, 86, 88.

MILLER, MICHAEL W. "Computers Keep Eye on Workers and See If They Perform Well." *Wall Street Journal*, June 3, 1985, p. 1.

MITCHELL, CONSTANCE. "A Growing Shortage of Skilled Craftsmen Troubles Some Firms." *Wall Street Journal*, September 14, 1987, p. 1.

PALFRAM, DIANE. "Hewlett-Packard Chief Calls for Manufacturing Overhaul." *Manufacturing Engineering*, January 1987, p. 33.

REESE, K. M. "CAD/CAM Being Employed to Make Dental Crowns." *Chemical & Engineering News*, July 27, 1987, p. 88.

SASSER, W. EARL, et al. *Management of Service Operations* (Boston: Allyn & Bacon, 1978), pp. 92–93.

WHIPPLE, CHARLES. "Small Business: Gambling on a Dream." *PHP Intersect*, September 1986, pp. 6–10. (*PHP Intersect*, "Where Japan Meets Asia & the World," is published by PHP Institute, founded in 1946 by Konosuke Matsushita "in the belief that frank communication and a deeper understanding of human nature are indispensable to the realization of our common goals of peace, happiness, and prosperity." This English-language publication, printed in Japan, is intended to further international cooperation and understanding.)

WORK, CLEMENS P., with Evelyn Bankhead. "Flying on the Razor's Edge." *U.S. News & World Report*, August 3, 1987, p. 38.

PART SIX

Current Issues and Challenges Facing Managers

The world hates change, yet it is the only thing that has brought progress.
—CHARLES F. KETTERING

Far better it is to dare mighty things, to win glorious triumphs, even though checkered by failure, than to take rank with those poor spirits who neither enjoy much nor suffer much, because they live in the gray twilight that knows not victory nor defeat.
—THEODORE ROOSEVELT

UP TO THIS POINT, this book has dealt primarily with current aspects of management in business firms in the United States. Now the main thrust shifts from managing such firms in the United States to managing not-for-profit organizations and international operations in the future, as shown on the opposite page.

Chapter 17 emphasizes the role of international business and how it has grown, the requirements for success in cross-cultural movement, and selecting and preparing managers for international assignments.

Private firms still employ the majority of workers, but not-for-profit organizations are requiring an increasing proportion of all managers. Some unique aspects of managing these institutions are covered in Chapter 18.

Chapter 19 emphasizes the concepts of social responsibility and managerial ethics. It is important to know how each concept has evolved and its relationship to management.

You will be employed and work as a manager in the world of tomorrow. You will work in an environment that is being shaped by current events and ideas. Chapter 20 covers this important subject.

17. Managing international operations

Importance of international operations	To the nation, organization, and individual Reasons for international operations Some problems involved Changing nature of international operations Future expectations
The universality of management principles in operation	Management principles are the same everywhere Management styles and activities are different Cultural determinants of managerial effectiveness
Development of international operations	Colonialism and mercantilism Trend toward nationalism Growth of multinational corporations (MNCs)
Causes and effects of cultural conflicts	
Staffing international operations	With U.S. nationals, local nationals, and nationals of third countries
Factors leading to managerial success	Criteria for selecting international managers Different perceptions of foreign assignments

18. Managing not-for-profit organizations

Classification and roles of organizations	Profit-oriented versus not-for-profit organizations
Differences between profit and not-for-profit organizations	Mission and objectives Strategies Fund-raising and budgeting Use of volunteers Management selection
Difficulties of not-for-profit organizations	
Concepts applicable to the not-for-profit sector	Strategic planning and MBO Marketing Newer leadership styles
Contingency management and the not-for-profit sector	Community leadership programs Outside reviews
Improving local and state government productivity	

(continued)

19. Social responsibility and managerial ethics

What social responsibility is	Examples Two perspectives
Emerging views of social responsibility	Profit maximization period Trusteeship management period Period of activism Social responsiveness period
Social responsibility in action	Employee relations; public and community service; environmental protection; consumerism; educational and other assistance; urban renewal and development; culture, arts, and recreation
Social responsibility and financial performance	Leads to profitability Does not lead to profitability Synthesis of opinion
Maintaining managerial ethics	Bribery, industrial theft, and espionage; conflict of interest; advertising abuses; collusion and fraud
Developing ethical standards	
Evaluating ethical and social performance	Improving managerial skills Use of social audits and codes of ethics

20. Your future in management

Management career opportunities	White-collar Service industries Clerical, technical, and professional
Improving managerial opportunities	For women For minorities
Characteristics of successful managers	Intelligence; education; broad analytical interests; favorable personal characteristics; ability to manage own personal affairs
Initial management position	First-line management positions Identifying managerial talent Possible career problems
The role of organizations in career planning and development	Career planning and development Dual aspects of career planning Providing career paths Management and career development
Becoming an entrepreneur	Opportunities Rewards and challenges
Management and the future	Continuing trends Changes in management functions The Japanese experience

17

Managing International Operations

Learning Objectives

After studying the material in this chapter, you should be able to do the following:

□ Recognize the importance of international operations, including their changing nature.
□ State how the concept of universality of management operates in actual practice.
□ Trace the development of international business.
□ Describe some of the cultural determinants of managerial effectiveness.
□ Discuss some of the causes and effects of cultural conflict.
□ Explain some of the problems involved in staffing international operations, including sources of personnel and preparing personnel for their assignments.
□ List some of the factors leading to managerial effectiveness in international operations.
□ Identify some of the valid criteria for selecting international managers.
□ Recognize why people accept or reject foreign assignments.

Outline of the Chapter

Importance of international operations
Importance to the nation, organization, and individual
Reasons for international operations
Some problems involved
Changing nature of international operations
Future expectations

The universality of management principles in operation
Management principles are the same everywhere
Management styles and activities are different
Cultural determinants of managerial effectiveness
Development of international operations
Colonialism and mercantilism
Trend toward nationalism
Growth of multinational corporations (MNCs)
Causes and effects of cultural conflicts
Causes of cultural conflicts
Effects of cultural conflicts
Staffing international operations
Staffing with U.S. nationals
Staffing with local nationals
Staffing with nationals of third countries
Factors leading to managerial success
Criteria for selecting international managers
Different perceptions of foreign assignments
Summary

Some Important Terms

expropriate
ethical standards
culture
cross-cultural conflict
nationalism
multinational corporations (MNCs)

cultural conflict
ethnocentrism
perception
third culture
cultural determinants

OPENING CASE

Rudolph Carter—International Manager

Rudolph Carter, a young electrical engineer in a dead-end job with a small-town utility firm, received an attractive job offer from the SEMA Company, a major sugar company in the tropics. Although the job offer represented a "very substantial increase in salary, good promotional promise, and numerous fringe benefits," it did have certain drawbacks. Carter was well aware of these, having been born, reared, and educated (through his high school years) on a similar tropical plantation where his father had worked until his death five years earlier. He knew well that one of the chief difficulties was getting to know the local engineers—working with them and winning their acceptance—and coping with other cultural problems.

Carter accepted the job and within two months reported for his first assignment. The first few days on the job proved to be very difficult because of the human-relations problems resulting from the chief engineer's sudden return to the States for medical treatment. The electrical plant was being run by the senior electrical engineer, Señor José Gonzales, a national who was a graduate of the technical college on the island. Gonzales, about 45 years old, had 16 years' service in the department. The chief engineer had left full, written instructions with Gonzales (with a copy for Carter) outlining Carter's job assignments and responsibilities. The instructions left little doubt that Carter was to assume full responsibility and authority for operating the electric plant.

The beginning of the crop-grinding season was only two weeks away, and Carter found himself in a crush of people rushing around trying to put all the facilities into operating condition. The plant's work force consisted of about 40 locals, most of whom could understand some English but could not speak it well. This was true even of Gonzales.

Carter saw that Gonzales, a competent engineer, had, in fact, been efficiently running the entire operation for many years. Gonzales's word was law as far as the workers were concerned, for they respected him highly. Moreover, Gonzales was highly ambitious, with a strong desire and motivation to become the chief electrical engineer.

Gonzales quicky and definitely let Carter know that his presence was resented; he offered no cooperation, advice, or help. The only factor creating some rapport between the two men was Carter's ability to speak Spanish, which kept him from being totally ineffective.

Three days before the grinding season began, the plant manager requested a detailed report on the start-up status of all equipment. Carter requested a report from Gonzales, who replied that everything was "completely OK and ready to go" and that he had never before prepared such a detailed status report, since the chief engineer had always been content with his word alone.

Carter located in the files the status report submitted by the chief engineer the previous year—with copies to no one. The report went into considerable detail, listing all electrical items and showing everything in a ready-to-go condition.

Carter wondered whether he should simply duplicate the previous report, showing everything as satisfactory—thus relying on Gonzales's verbal assurance—or take the list to Gonzales and insist on witnessing the testing and operation of all components. Carter did not want to antagonize Gonzales this early in the game, and yet he wanted to be certain that his first report to the plant manager would be correct and accurate.

He decided to show the report to Gonzales, who was surprised to see it and immediately became defensive. But, after Carter emphasized his willingness to accept Gonzales's assurance that all items were ready to go and made it clear that he wanted merely to recheck the equipment listing, Gonzales cooperated graciously.

During the check, the two men found numerous items that had been physically deleted in the field and a few new installations. Gonzales even pointed out that one major piece of equipment had not checked out to his satisfaction, since his men were having trouble hooking up test instruments to check it out. Gonzales seemed relieved when Carter suggested that they work together to see if they could find the difficulty.

Carter quickly spotted the difficulty, but, instead of pointing it out directly, he guided Gonzales's analysis so that he was able to spot the problem. The workers were most impressed that their man had located and corrected the difficulty. Carter could tell that Gonzales realized that he had been allowed to save face with his men.

This was the beginning of a very pleasant and cooperative relationship, with Gonzales slowly but surely recognizing and accepting Carter's position and authority over him.

Could Carter have done anything differently to ensure success? If so, what? ■

A VERY IMPORTANT DIMENSION of management is illustrated by this case—managing international operations. Today there is a growing emphasis on international activities, and persons interested in management must appreciate some of the opportunities and problems associated with management practices in international activities.

IMPORTANCE OF INTERNATIONAL OPERATIONS

As Heywood Broun says in the opening quotation, we cannot ignore the fact that "we are citizens of the world." When Iran and Iraq fight each other, we pay higher prices for gasoline; when South Korea's Daewoo introduced the Leading Edge personal computer for $1195, it affected the demand for U.S.-made PCs; when Japanese exports to us far exceed purchases from us, the resulting dollar imbalance results in their investing "around $100 billion" in our stock market;[1] and when there is political unrest in South Africa, there is disinvestment by the United States. In other words, we are involved, directly or indirectly, in what happens almost anywhere in the world.

Since this book deals with the overall subject of management, we do not attempt to solve the functional problems associated with international operations. This section, however, tries to present an overview of the subject and emphasizes the importance of selecting suitable managers for international activities.

Importance to the Nation, Organization, and Individual

More and more American organizations, both businesses and others, are engaged in international activities. And an increasing number of Americans will work in some aspect of international operations during their productive lives. We estimate that up to one-half of all college graduates will work with international activities in one way or another.

Reasons for International Operations

MAP 17.1 summarizes some opportunities available in international operations and the risks involved. In explanation of the listing, one of the first reasons for U.S. firms to expand their operations overseas is that they can usually obtain a higher percentage of earnings from foreign operations than from domestic activities, because wages are cheaper and costs lower. Notice in Table 17.1 that U.S. labor costs are among the highest in the world.

A second major reason is that there is still an effective demand abroad for many American goods, especially food, the export of which helps to pay for imported goods, especially petroleum. Thus, foreign operations are quite important to many U.S. firms. For example, Pfizer has over 55 percent of its assets in other countries; around 75 percent of Exxon's sales and 64 percent of its assets are in foreign countries; and Coca-Cola receives about 60 percent of its net earnings from such operations.

Third, U.S. investments can benefit the host country by providing the needed capital and technology to produce economic development in those countries. In fact, foreign companies, once thought of as "capitalistic exploiters," now are being viewed as a means of building and developing the economies of other countries rather than taking from them.

For example, McDonald's, which expects to receive about 40 percent of its earnings from foreign operations by the end of this decade, is planning to open soon in the Soviet Union. Also, Pepsi, which has been serving the Soviets since the 1970s, is trying to get its Pizza Huts into the country. A recent Soviet TV broadcast implied that one reason for letting McDonald's in is that the "fast" in "fast foods" is bound to appeal to the Soviets, who spend much of their time waiting in lines for food.[2]

Many Third World countries are now buying used U.S. factories that are obsolete here because of their size, environmental problems, or high energy or labor costs. The seller gets rid of unwanted equipment, and the buyer gets a bargain.

▷ Management Application and Practice 17.1   Opportunities and Risks in International Operations

Opportunities and challenges available

1. Expansion of markets.
2. Lower labor costs in most countries.
3. Availability and lower cost of certain desired natural resources.
4. Potential for higher rates of return on investment.

Problems and risks involved

1. Higher possibility of loss of assets by nationalization, war, or other disturbances.
2. High potential for loss of earnings, or difficulty or impossibility of retrieving the earnings from investment.
3. Favored treatment usually given to local organizations by the host government.
4. Rapid change in political systems, often by violent overthrow.
5. Lower skill levels of workers in underdeveloped countries.
6. Difficulties in maintaining communication and coordination with home office because of distance, time difference, and poor communication systems.
7. Unfair competition, particularly from state-subsidized firms.
8. Fluctuating foreign exchange rates, possibly resulting in lower profits (or a loss).

TABLE 17.1
World Labor Costs

(Average hourly compensation, including fringe benefits, for workers.)

SOURCE: *Wall Street Journal*, October 17, 1986, p. 31. Data from Business International Corp.

Country	Hourly compensation
Switzerland	$14.01
West Germany	13.85
United States	13.29
Sweden	12.53
Italy	10.82
France	10.49
Japan	7.76
United Kingdom	7.67
Greece	4.04
South Korea	1.53

For instance, a used alkali plant was shipped from Canada to India, where it was put in operation for only $4 million, compared to the $10 million a new one would have cost.

Venezuela bought a used cement plant from Pennsylvania for $30 million, at a saving of $20 to $30 million.[3]

What is your view?

Can you think of other reasons for U.S. firms to engage in international operations? How about nonbusiness operations, such as the YMCA, which is active in many countries?

Some Problems Involved

As shown in MAP 17.1, there are risks and problems involved in international operations. For example, recent economic activities around the world, including recession and new restrictions, may be reducing opportunities abroad. In fact, some American businesses that have gone international are now finding that the domestic market is often more important because of the increasingly competitive international activities. There are four other problem areas that we will discuss.

Danger of expropriation. What are some of the problems in a foreign environment? First, the host government may **expropriate** the firm's assets, as shown in the following examples.[4]

Mexico ordered all foreign oil companies out during the 1930s and converted their facilities into the Mexican national oil company, Pemex.

Chile took over the holdings of large numbers of foreign firms (e.g., International Telephone and Telegraph [ITT]) during the Allende regime, as did Fidel Castro in Cuba.

U.S. and other foreign firms currently have many billions of outstanding claims against Iran.

Differing attitudes and policies. Often, the attitudes and policies of the host government may be difficult to deal with. For example, having the host government as a "partner" is in many cases a condition of entry. Or the host government may require that the foreign firm enter into joint-venture partnership with a local firm. Sending profits back to the firm's home country is usually restricted, sometimes severely. Sometimes the host government's foreign policy can be a problem, as shown by these examples.

> *Some time ago, a GM truck assembly plant in Argentina was caught in a bind between the Argentine government's insistence that it sell 5000 trucks to Cuba and the United States embargo on all trade with Cuba. Eventually, the U.S. State Department decided to advise GM to let the deal go through rather than create an unpleasant international incident.*
>
> *Many U.S. firms have to contend with the state of Arab-Israeli relations and with the peculiar international status of the Republic of South Africa.*

Another general problem may be the weakness of the host country's infrastructure, including variables such as transportation networks, power and energy supplies, communication services, quality of education, and water and sewer systems.

Some staffing problems. Constraints are usually imposed on the staffing of the foreign firm. A frequent pattern for U.S. firms is to start with a cadre of U.S. managerial-professional-technical people, gradually hire and train native operating personnel, and ultimately turn the entire operation over to local personnel or staff hired from third countries. A few Americans do take up permanent residence and play monitoring roles. The reason the host country insists on such a pattern is no mystery: It wants the job for its people, as well as the local control that can be made to go with it.

Local workers may be less productive or not motivated in the fashion U.S. managers expect, or they may present other kinds of management problems. In some cases, the American concepts of regular job attendance, punctuality, adhering to the work schedule, and so on, are simply not part of the local norms. In other cases, native work forces have had little prior involvement with a money economy and with the idea of accumulating some wealth and consequently are not motivated by monetary compensation.

Furthermore, cultural differences in the host environment may be so great as to lead to culture shock. For example, American executives working in Japan, for example, have complained that their Japanese opposites stall endlessly before getting down to business. Two different value systems with respect to the use of time are being used.

Violence and terrorism. Unfortunately, violence and terrorism are all too prevalent in many overseas positions. For example, because of kidnappings and killings, there are no American teachers left at the once-great American University in Beirut, Lebanon. Passengers and bystanders were wantonly massacred in Rome's airport, and the first Kuwaiti ship carrying oil under the U.S. flag struck a mine in the Persian Gulf.

Different values. Values differ from country to country. First, **ethical standards** differ, and in many countries bribes are not only accepted, but expected. For example, Lockheed had to pay out about $12 million—most of it in bribes, including a $1.7 million secret payment—in order to sell TriStar jets to Japanese airlines.[5] And Boeing had to pay $7.3 million in "commissions" to sell 35 planes to Spain, Honduras, Lebanon, and the Dominican Republic.[6] In both cases, the payments not only were considered unethical in the United States but were also illegal.

Second, the way different nations treat people according to race, sex, age, and other demographic characteristics varies.

Changing Nature of International Operations

It was once thought that successful managers of foreign operations were "shrewd Yankee traders," notorious for their salesmanship or showmanship. Showmanship is still important in foreign operations, but today's overseas personnel must possess other qualities as well. There are many complicating factors, as shown in Figure 17.1, that should be judged carefully by an international organization, the host nation, and the U.S. government.

One most impressive factor to consider is that the character of international operations has changed from the eighteenth and nineteenth centuries' colonial imperialism to the present philosophy of mutual benefit to the participating countries. Today's international business firm is expected to contribute to the host nation's economic growth as well as produce a profit for the owners.

Philosophical changes are also occurring. Organizations are expected to accept the ideas that (1) world peace will result only from international trade, (2) wealthier nations should help feed starving people in less fortunate areas, and (3) they should support individual freedom in all parts of the world. For these and similar reasons, many areas considered good investment opportunities 20 to 25 years ago are no longer so regarded. For example, many areas in Africa, South America, the Middle East, and Eastern Europe are no longer favored.

Foreign buyers are investing more in the United States. As the U.S. trade deficit has grown, the U.S. dollar has become cheaper, so that foreign holders of those dollars are using them to buy up U.S. assets. According to the U.S. Department of Commerce, foreign investments in the United States totaled $1312 billion in 1986, up from $1060 billion in 1985. Of that amount, $183 billion was in direct investments in assets such as plants, companies, and real estate holdings, while $877 billion was in portfolio holdings of items

FIGURE 17.1
Primary groups
influencing foreign
operations.

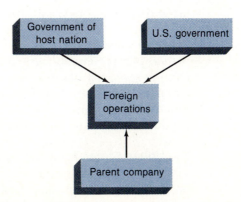

TABLE 17.2
Foreign Investment in
U.S. Assets
SOURCE: U.S. Department of
Commerce.

	($ billions)
Portfolio investment	**$876.9**
Bank deposits, other assets	380.5
U.S. government securities	227.6
Stocks, corporate and other bonds	207.8
Miscellaneous	61.0
Direct investment	**183.0**
Manufacturing	60.8
Petroleum	28.1
Wholesaling	27.5
Real estate	18.6
Banking	11.5
Insurance	11.1
Miscellaneous industries	9.9
Retailing	6.7
Nonbank finance	4.7
Mining	4.1

NOTE: Figures are year's end, 1985.

such as bank deposits, U.S. government securities, and corporate stocks and bonds (see Table 17.2 for more detail). In 1987 alone, foreign buyers bought 316 U.S. corporations, worth $40.7 billion.[7]

Some well-recognized American firms now have foreign accents in their home offices. For example, Carnation Company is owned by Nestlé, a Swiss firm; RCA Records belongs to a German company; the Exxon building in Rockefeller Center and the Tiffany building on Fifth Avenue have Japanese landlords; and Brooks Brothers Clothiers is owned by Canadians.

Which countries are the largest purchasers of U.S. corporations? Companies from Great Britain bought 122 companies in 1987; from Canada, 43; from Australia, 24; France, 17; and from West Germany, 9.[8]
What are the results of these changes? First, these investors have created around 3 million new jobs, paying more than $75 billion annually in wages and benefits. Second, by one measure of productivity, foreign-owned factories averaged sales of $131,430 per worker in 1984, compared to $118,846 for U.S.-owned plants.[9] Finally, new management and production methods are becoming standard practice. For example, Japanese companies are becoming a dominant factor in U.S. manufacturing (see Figure 17.2). And in many cases, Japanese managers of these companies, using American workers, are more productive and have higher quality than their counterparts in Japan.

The United States is exporting entrepreneurship. One U.S. productive factor that is still preeminent is our vaunted free-enterprise system and its entrepreneurship. This spirit is now being imported by many countries—even by some Socialist economies.

FIGURE 17.2
How Japanese affect
U.S. manufacturing:
number of Japanese
factories in the United
States.
*(Figures are for
manufacturing plants
operated by Japanese firms
or their subsidiaries as of
May, 1987. All figures are
estimates.)*
SOURCE: Adapted from *U.S.
News & World Report,* February
1, 1988, p. 73. Reprinted by
permission. Basic data from
Japan External Trade
Organization.

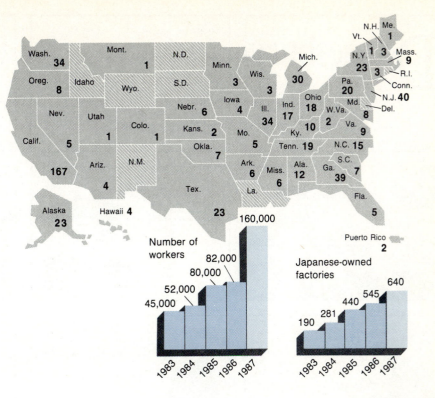

Britain started the trend by reducing the top rate for income taxes from 90 percent to 60 percent and providing tax breaks for small businesses. The result? The number of self-employed people escalated from 1.8 million in 1979 to 2.6 million in 1986.

Entrepreneurship is also popular in Japan, especially with young people who fear their careers will falter as do the larger firms. According to one venture capitalist, some 70,000 to 80,000 new ventures are created each year—up from almost none just a few years ago.[10]

The United States is exporting technology. A large percentage of students in U.S. graduate schools are from other countries. The knowledge they acquire is helping their countries improve their standard of living and making them more competitive in the world's markets. Countries in Southeast Asia predominate—especially Taiwan, whose 24,000 students form the largest international bloc on U.S. campuses.

**Future
Expectations**

The advantages and benefits derived from international operations far outweigh the problems involved, even with the many difficulties and conflicts encountered. Therefore, opportunities in this area will probably become even more attractive.

It is therefore estimated that the volume and number of international business operations will continue to increase in the future. More people in the United States and more nationals in other countries will be involved in the international arena.

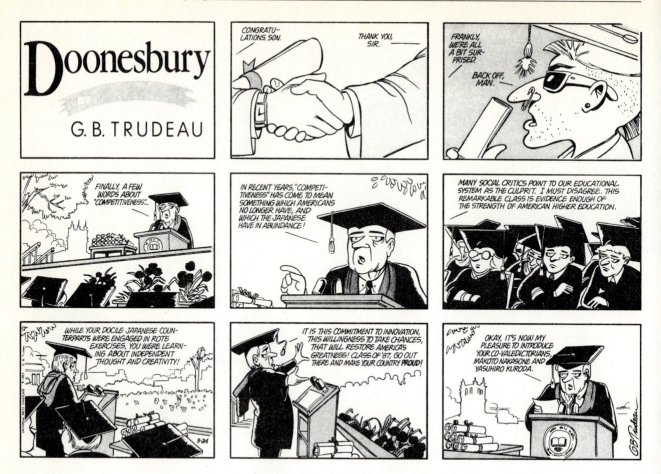

(Copyright 1987 by Universal Press Syndicate.)

THE UNIVERSALITY OF MANAGEMENT PRINCIPLES IN OPERATION

It was shown in Chapter 1 that management tends to be universal, since many of its activities are the same everywhere. The reasons for this conclusion are given first. Then it will be shown that management *styles* and *practices* are different in different cultures.

Management Principles Are the Same Everywhere

Human nature is the same among people everywhere. Because management principles tend to be universal, differences in behavior tend to be cultural differences. **Culture** is defined as the knowledge, beliefs, art, morals, law, customs, and any other capacities and habits acquired by a person as a member of society (see Figure 17.3). People who are born—and learn—in a given cultural system will therefore have a different behavioral pattern from others who grow up in another society. This assumption, however, does not deny that every individual is born with a different physical makeup and

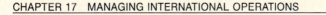

FIGURE 17.3
Major components of
culture.

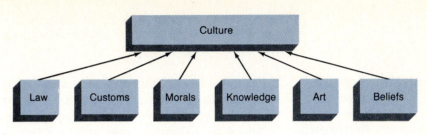

mental capacity. Rather, it means that an individual's hereditary differences are worked on by the same cultural influences as the capacities of other members of the same cultural set.

People can learn to accept another culture. If a person cannot learn to adjust to another culture, he or she finds that the cultural differences, or **cross-cultural conflict,** may lead to ineffective management of international operations. Although cross-cultural conflict is inevitable in the process of adjusting to international operations, it can be eliminated, or at least minimized, in time through the social learning process.

Management principles and functions are applied differently. Management principles and functions are assumed to be similar whether used in a small business or a large one, whether in a stateside organization or in an international one. That is, management is management whether you are in Lisbon, London, or Los Angeles. Differences do exist, however, in carrying out the management functions and applying the principles to given situations. These differences depend on the different situations and the different cultural backgrounds of the personnel involved. Different cultural backgrounds, managerial resources and skills, managerial philosophies, and business environments may cause variations in management's performance of business activities. Yet the functions managers perform and the principles they are based on are still universal.

It is known, for example, that automatic operations tend to be more efficient than manual ones. Yet, when USAID installed automatic grade-crossing signals on certain Indian roadways, each one eliminated nine jobs, which increased the poverty level in the area. The use of the signals was soon discontinued.

Managerial effectiveness depends on professional competence and adaptability. Managerial effectiveness depends on one's ability to adjust and adapt to the cultural environment in which one operates and performs the managerial functions, provided that one's technical proficiency and managerial philosophy remain the same. But a particular culture may determine a given pattern of human behavior; consequently, a manager's technical knowledge and philosophies, which are appropriate to his or her own culture, may not be adequate in a different culture. The manager who is unable to apply the management principles effectively in another culture may not be able to perform the managerial functions, but those who do so will succeed. Notice in the Opening Case that Carter was technically proficient.

Moreover, Carter's managerial philosophy of respecting local personnel permitted him to adjust to the new environment that was similar to the one in which he had grown up.

Management Styles and Activities Are Different

It has always been difficult to transfer management styles and practices to another culture, and this is now becoming more complex because of nationalism. Overall attitudes toward employees, consumers, suppliers, and distributors are different, as are organizations and staffing. Host country skills are replacing U.S. methods in many instances.

Cultural Determinants of Managerial Effectiveness

While the management functions are universal, in carrying out these functions, activities, practices, and philosophies, one finds that certain factors have a modifying effect. For example, the principle of standardization is applicable in all cultures, but different environments determine how the principle will be applied.

In the United States, for example, the best way to standardize automobiles has been to have a higher-powered engine using automatic features. But the best way to do the same thing in other countries has been to have less horsepower and to use fewer labor-saving devices to achieve a more economical engine. That is one reason Japan is now the largest auto producer in the world.

The knowledge of management, if the foregoing observation is true, is not automatically transferable into efficiency unless the manager develops his or her own managerial philosophy and practices that can be applied to, and accepted in, another cultural background.

To be most effective, then, a manager operating in another culture must be able to understand the cultural variables and adapt to them. Notice how Carter was able to adapt to the local culture so that Gonzales was able to maintain his sense of self-worth, something that is very important in Latin cultures.

DEVELOPMENT OF INTERNATIONAL OPERATIONS

If you are to understand the international dimension of management, you should understand the changing characteristics of international operations.

Colonialism and Mercantilism

During the period of European colonization, international operations were merely an extension of domestic operations and was based primarily on the concept of *mercantilism*. Under it, international enterprises operated almost as agencies of the government. The firm would buy—at a very low price—the raw materials produced in other countries and build up the position of the home country. To that end, the cost of production in the home country was to be held low, raw materials were to be imported and converted into finished products, and the finished goods were to be exported to other countries at a substantial profit to the firm and government. In return, the importing countries were to send the industrial nation additional raw materials.

Under this arrangement, personnel sent to other countries were simply the sales agents of domestic producers or agents to exploit the raw materials in the foreign countries. These individuals tended to carry their own culture with them and to create a small extension of the mother culture in the countries to which they went. Because of their superior products and the imperialistic power behind them, the firms from the developed nations were able to do this, and the managers were accepted in the other nations. Yet the managers did not accept the local people.

England's experience in India is an example. The English built roads, railroads, schools, and hospitals and developed agriculture, industry, and commerce. Yet, even in 1948, when India got her independence, there were many clubs that the Indians could not enter as either members or guests.

Trend Toward Nationalism

The trend toward **nationalism,** or a nation's maintaining and protecting its natural resources, as well as its socioeconomic, cultural, and political systems, is on the rise. It has drastically changed since the shift away from colonialism and imperialism. Emerging nationalistic power tended to counteract economic imperialism to protect the host country's resources and economy. Emerging countries in Asia, Africa, and Latin America, as well as some relatively well-developed countries in Europe, were fearful of economic domination by the stronger countries. However, these countries needed the investment capital and the advanced technology provided by the powerful nations. This necessity justified and induced the importation of the foreigners' investment and business operations, even in nationalistic countries.

During the 1950s and 1960s, China adopted the Soviet system of enterprise management (see Figure 17.4). But many parts of the system did not fit the Chinese culture. Now China is learning about the U.S. free enterprise system, and workers are demanding more from the system. Still, says the head of the National Center for Industrial Science and Technology Management Development, "We can't simply graft the U.S. system to China. We have to see how it can be applied to China."[11]

Now, capable personnel who can adjust to foreign cultures are being sought and encouraged to pursue international careers. Because of expanding foreign operations, however, the demand for capable overseas personnel is far greater than the available supply, as subsequently shown.

Growth of Multinational Corporations (MNCs)

Change in the form of the international business organization is expected to occur. Replacing the strong, dominant companies that merely extended their national operations into the international arena to exploit raw materials are **multinational corporations (MNCs),** which use investments from owners in three or more countries to secure resources to produce and sell goods or services in several countries. Their top-level personnel tend to come from several different countries. Their intention is not to exploit the host country as an international company might. Instead, they operate, produce, and distribute the goods or services to the mutual benefit of the host and home countries. This is accomplished by creating more jobs, increasing the stan-

FIGURE 17.4
Under enterprise management, Chinese workers expect better pay, more incentives to increase factory productivity.
SOURCE: *U.S. News & World Report*, May 22, 1978, p. 43. Reprinted by permission.

dard of living, and often providing managerial opportunities for citizens of the host country.

CAUSES AND EFFECTS OF CULTURAL CONFLICTS

When managers enter a different cultural system, they encounter human traits and behavior that are alien to their own, and these often result in **cultural conflict.** The different cultural environment may cause frustration and insecurity until the manager becomes accustomed to the new environment.

The Japanese perceive time very differently from Americans. To them, months and years may be required to make important decisions. Americans interpret this as lack of interest, when in actuality it is not.

French managers are much more likely than their American counterparts to use space as a network of influence. American managers cherish their private corner offices, whereas French managers will normally be found in the center of their subordinates' work areas, where these managers feel that they can exert control.

In the Middle East and Latin America, the American businessperson feels overcrowded. People get uncomfortably close, violate our sense of personal space, and are more physical with each other. Unless the businessperson reciprocates, he or she is perceived as cold and distant.

In India, it is considered highly improper to discuss business in the home on social occasions. To invite someone to one's home to further a business relationship violates sacred hospitality rules.[12]

Let us look at some of the causes and effects of cultural conflicts.

Causes of Cultural Conflicts

Some of the causes of cultural conflicts are (1) ethnocentrism, (2) inappropriate use of one's own managerial philosophies and practices, (3) different perceptions, (4) miscommunications, and (5) cultural attitudes.[13]

Ethnocentrism. **Ethnocentrism** is the tendency to believe and act on the belief that one's own cultural value system is superior to all other cultural value systems. If an overseas executive persists in such self-centered viewpoints in dealing with people in a new culture, his or her behavior will probably be resented by the host country and may lead to rejection or conflict.

There are several reasons this type of behavior is found in managers operating abroad. First, the managers have feelings of pride and superiority that do not allow them to accept a different way of living, thinking, or managing other people. Second, even if they wanted to adjust to the new culture, they do not always know how to do it because of their lack of understanding, training, and experience. The cure for the first problem may be to avoid hiring that type of individual or at least to avoid sending him or her overseas. The second problem may be solved with additional time and training.

Inappropriate use of management customs. The best way to apply a given management principle in one culture is not necessarily the best way to use it in another, as shown by the following illustration.

A Ford Foundation resident adviser on management development in Pakistan would sharpen half a dozen pencils to use at his desk. He noticed that his Pakistani counterparts used only one pencil and would ring for the "peon" to come and sharpen it. The advisor considered this quite inefficient until he learned that his failure to use the peon would "break the rice bowl" of seven people. That is, if the peon were fired, he and six family members would go hungry. The adviser learned to use the services of the peon.

Another obstacle to the use of the best management philosophies and practices is the lack of management education. Management, to most of the world's managers, is more an art than a science and so cannot be learned at school—even if it were considered desirable to do so. This, too, is now changing. For example, in Shanghai, 16 colleges have started to offer management courses. A National Center for Management Development has been established at China's Datien Institute of Technology.[14]

Different perceptions. **Perception** is the frame of reference in which we see the world around us. People see what they want to see and act on the basis of what they see or think they see. Thus the frame of reference or perception we have is influenced by environmental factors such as our reference group, our role, our interaction with others in the organization, our organizational and social environments, and our cultural backgrounds. A person's unique set of perceptions is acquired and developed through experience in a particular cultural system. One study has shown that Japanese cultural elements have influenced Japanese workers' perception of the manager-employee relationship, personal involvement in management, status, and sources of information.[15] Japanese workers' perceptions of these areas differ sharply from those of American employees.

Miscommunication. *Communication,* as shown in Chapter 10, is the transfer of meaning from one individual to another, and many barriers filter the sender's meaning. Differences in languages, customs, feelings, and cultures may cause miscommunication. The entire complex of human life, with its individual variations, offers opportunities for misunderstandings. Language, however, is the most serious source of miscommunication because it is the means of communication most often used. In addition to his or her lack of knowledge of the language itself, the manager's intonation, pronunciation, and facial expressions may also cause misunderstanding. Notice that Carter's knowledge of Spanish led to rapport with Gonzales, which ultimately led to Carter's acceptance by the other workers.

An American executive may find many English-speaking people in the culture in which he or she operates but may also find that reliance on them still leads to problems. First, nationals are often unfavorably impressed when a foreign manager makes no attempt to learn their language. Hence, citizens of the host country are less receptive to the manager's ideas. Second, the chances of misunderstanding may be greater if the executive does not learn the new language, because the actual capacity of the nationals to understand English may be small. Dealing through translators may also create problems, as shown in MAP 17.2.

Cultural attitudes. Personality is developed through interactions between people and their environments; thus a given individual's personality will be

---

Management Application and Practice 17.2 "How's That Again?"

The following are some examples of mistakes and infelicities of translation.

Macy's New York
Headline: "Macy's Introduces the Fabulous Fall Faces by PUPA." (cosmetics)
Polish translation: *pupa* = "behind, buttocks"

American Manufacturer
Product: hydraulic ram
Arabic translation: "water goat"

General Motors
Product: Chevy Nova
Spanish translation: "Chevy does not go."

American Manufacturer
Product: touch-toe industrial drill, instruction manual
Italian translation: "The dentist takes off his shoe and sock and presses the drill with his toe."

PepsiCo
Advertisement: "Come alive with Pepsi."
Chinese translation: "Pepsi brings your ancestors back from the grave."

SOURCE: Unknown.

unique even in his or her own culture. This difference is compounded when an individual moves into another culture. It is difficult to generalize, but an observable difference of personality and attitude among different cultures may be caused by cultural variables. Thus, a person's cultural attitudes are important in determining his or her effectiveness as a manager in another culture.

Effects of Cultural Conflicts

The manager's unfamiliarity or inability to cope with these problems emotionally and psychologically often results in (1) extreme conservatism, (2) communication breakdown, and (3) irrational reactions and resultant behavior, as shown in Figure 17.5.

Extreme conservatism. Cultural conflicts interrupt harmonious relationships between the manager and the local personnel; thus the manager may tend to rely on rigid rules and regulations to ensure control over local operations. The manager cannot trust the workers, who, in turn, do not respect the manager. Consequently, the manager becomes more alienated from the local personnel, and the social distance between the two parties will increase, as shown in the following example.

> *Production suddenly started falling behind schedule at an American-controlled plant in Bangladesh. The newly arrived manager noticed that the workers were listless and apparently uninterested in their work. He tried speeding up the operations, which resulted in a strike. Then he found out that it was a religious holiday called* Ramadan, *during which the Muslims fast from before dawn until after dark.*

Communication breakdown. The increased social distance will naturally hamper favorable communication, especially upward communication, between the manager and workers. The result is that the manager has no grasp of what is going on in the local operations, and this will probably lead to further misunderstandings on both sides. This lack of knowledge of local conditions is apparently what happened at the U.S. embassy in Teheran after the fall of the Shah and before the U.S. diplomatic personnel were taken hostage in 1979. The embassy personnel seemed to be unaware of the magnitude and severity of deteriorating American-Iranian relations.

Irrational reactions. The inability of the manager to cope with the conflicts may result in an emotional or irrational response to the local personnel. This may also lead to irrational reactions from the local personnel. Thus there is

FIGURE 17.5
Causes and effects of cultural conflict.

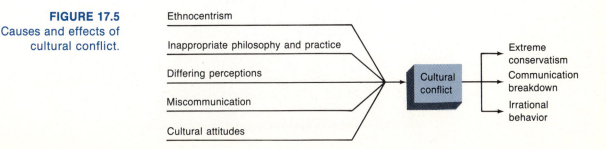

the beginning of a vicious cycle of irrational responses. One area where this tendency is prevalent is the problem women managers often have in dealing with global clients, especially in some Third World countries.

STAFFING INTERNATIONAL OPERATIONS

The United States and other developed nations have expanded their international operations, and the demand for qualified personnel to staff these operations has far exceeded the supply.

The experience of the most active firms in international operations indicates that there are three sources of employees for such activities: (1) employees who have been educated and trained and have gained experience in the American firm, (2) individuals who have gotten their education, training, and experience in the host country, and (3) individuals who are citizens of a country other than the United States or the country of operation (see Figure 17.6).

No specific figures are available for the proportionate degree of use of these three types of employees; it can be generalized, however, that top management comes from the parent firm, middle and lower management comes from nationals of the host country and of third countries, and other employees are nationals of the host country.

Staffing with U.S. Nationals

This first alternative—staffing with U.S. nationals—is desirable because it protects the parent company's interest; yet it has limitations. The number and quality of capable Americans that can be trained in this way are limited, because the training is costly and because many countries have legislation requiring employment of nationals.

FIGURE 17.6
Sources of employees for international operations.

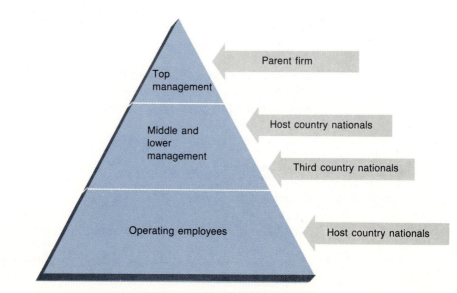

Qualities sought in personnel. Selecting individuals for international operations is more difficult than selecting them for domestic operations. The persons selected must have not only professional skills but also certain traits that help them understand the complex world in which they must operate.

Ideally, international employees should be individuals who can move from one culture to another without much difficulty. In fact, they should be from a "third culture." This **third culture** is defined as the behavior patterns that are created, shared, and learned by people of different societies who are in the process of relating their cultural systems to those of people from a second culture. In essence, this third culture is a world-encompassing culture.

Preparing them for international operations. These employees need predeparture training that exposes them to the customs, language, and living conditions of the country in which their operations will be situated. This training can be done by the company itself, in one of the government's training centers for overseas diplomatic personnel, or by an educational institution.

Many colleges and universities have instituted curricula in international business. These curricula usually include courses in the individual's specialized functional area, other business courses, at least two foreign languages, cultural anthropology, sociology, international economics, geography, and others—with special emphasis on the "cultural" courses.

Staffing with Local Nationals

Willingly or otherwise, almost all firms today employ nationals of the host country to fill their vacancies. This source is limited, for the supply of capable personnel is limited if operations are located in a relatively undeveloped economy. Notice in the opening case that the top personnel had to come from outside the country, since the skills required were not available locally. Yet Gonzales aspired to the chief engineer's position and thought he was in line for it.

Reasons for using local nationals. These employees are used because (1) it is less costly; (2) it is good politics, because it helps the local employment situation; (3) it may facilitate cultural understanding between the company's home country and local personnel; and (4) their employment creates purchasing power that serves to enhance demand for the firm's product. Also, local laws often require that nationals be employed to fill the majority of the managerial positions and all the supervisory positions. For example, Mexico has a law decreeing that 90 percent of the employees of a foreign firm's operations in Mexico must be Mexican citizens.

Reasons for not using local nationals. This source of supply also has many drawbacks. First, the shortage of qualified personnel also exists in other countries. Second, national pride restricts employment of qualified local managerial and technical personnel when the top positions are restricted to foreign personnel. Third, there is a strong, paternalistic urge that restricts the layoff and dismissal of employees in these countries. Brazil had a law requiring that all employees with 10 years' seniority be given lifetime employment. Both foreign and domestic firms got around this by firing employees in their ninth year and then rehiring them later.

Preparing them for international operations. Once the nationals are hired, they must be prepared to work for the foreign firm. One persistent problem is the amount to pay those individuals. In general, it is necessary to determine a wage that is consistent with what the foreigners are making and yet is not too far out of line with local earnings.

Also, in underdeveloped countries, some foreign firms will draw local people from their rural setting and introduce them to the western economic system. This may necessitate major social and psychological adjustments.

Staffing with Nationals of Third Countries

The alternative of employing nationals of third countries has been used extensively since World War II. The breaking up of large colonial empires such as those of Great Britain, France, Belgium, and the Netherlands has resulted in freeing many qualified nationals of those countries who have been engaged in international operations. Hence these persons have been hired by U.S. firms and by the host nations.

Other reasons for hiring those individuals are their fluency in languages, their ability to move from one culture to another with a minimum of disruption, and the popularity of this system in certain countries.

FACTORS LEADING TO MANAGERIAL SUCCESS

Figure 17.7 shows that all managers, especially international managers, are in the center of at least four partially conflicting systems. These managers must be able to adjust to the systems to an even greater extent than people working in their native land alone. Therefore, it is highly desirable to be able to predict if a manager is likely to succeed in such assignments.

Research has shown that there are positive relationships between some cultural variables and a manager's effectiveness, as shown by his or her performance rating.[16] These are called **cultural determinants.** A few of these variables that have been found to be positively related to managerial productivity and their value to potential executives are as follows:

1. The ability to move and adapt one's culture to another plays an important role in the adjustment process. The more similar the cultural elements in two or more societies, the less effect culture has on managerial effectiveness. One reason Rudolph Carter was able to adjust so readily to his new job in the environment was his upbringing in a similar culture.

2. Overseas executives need the ability to understand the inner logic of another society's cultural variables and way of life.

3. While a knowledge of the language in itself is important, one's willingness to learn the language is even more important.

4. Technical personnel, such as engineers, chemists, physicists, and the like, have more difficulty adjusting to another culture than less-specialized individuals.

5. It is easier for a manager to move from a lower level of technology to a higher level and remain effective than the reverse.

6. Executives' spiritual and religious values have great influence on their managerial effectiveness because their behavioral assumptions and managerial decisions will be based on them.

Criteria for Selecting International Managers

There are certain factors in a potential international manager's background that can be used to forecast his or her effectiveness in operating in another culture.

First, managers must have *professional competence* in their chosen field to be successful in international business activities. The engineer must be a good engineer, the chemist a good chemist, and the manager must understand and know how to use the body of knowledge that constitutes the science of management.

Second, managers must possess an *adventurous attitude*, an *optimistic outlook*, a *broad liberal education*, a mind that is more attuned to cultural similarities than differences, and a personal philosophy that accepts value differences in other people. Therefore, they should conceive of people, places, cultures, and so forth, as being similar rather than different; dealing with similarities leads to cooperation among people, whereas an overemphasis on differences leads to competition and ultimately to conflict.

Third, people are needed who have a history of *success in various activities* other than their professional activities. In other words, a person who has been successful in sports, or extracurricular, church, or social activities, has a greater chance for success in international operations than one who has not.

FIGURE 17.7
Four intermeshing systems in which the international manager must function.

SOURCE: C. Wickham Skinner, "Management of International Production," *Harvard Business Review* (September–October 1964):132.

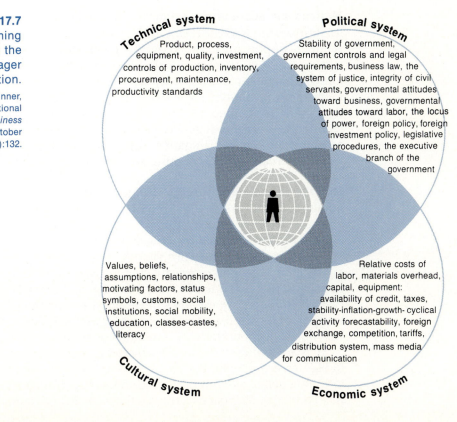

Technical system
Product, process, equipment, quality, investment, controls of production, inventory, procurement, maintenance, productivity standards

Political system
Stability of government, government controls and legal requirements, business law, the system of justice, integrity of civil servants, governmental attitudes toward business, governmental attitudes toward labor, the locus of power, foreign policy, foreign investment policy, legislative procedures, the executive branch of the government

Cultural system
Values, beliefs, assumptions, relationships, motivating factors, status symbols, customs, social institutions, social mobility, education, classes-castes, literacy

Economic system
Relative costs of labor, materials overhead, capital, equipment: availability of credit, taxes, stability-inflation-growth- cyclical activity forecastability, foreign exchange, competition, tariffs, distribution system, mass media for communication

Fourth, people with *greater self-reliance* have more chance of success than those who depend on others; managers in another culture are on their own more than those engaged in domestic activities.

Fifth, *experience in overseas assignments* such as the military, diplomatic corps, Peace Corps, or similar activity helps. Unfortunately, qualified female managers often lack such experience and even the opportunity to get it.[17]

Sixth, one of the basic problems encountered in the intercultural movement is learning to trust others, but probably more important is the *ability to instill in others*, by your actions, *a trust in you*. An overgeneralization is that one's perception of and sensitivity toward the values found in another's culture are important to success as an international manager.

What is your view?

Do you think you have the qualities needed to be an international manager? What do you lack? How could you acquire the qualities you lack?

Different Perceptions of Foreign Assignments

Employees engaged in international operations may be viewed as either heroes or martyrs. In the eyes of their colleagues at home, they are heroes living "romantic" lives in "faraway place." To themselves, they may be heroes "helping to better people's standard of living." But at the same time, they, and certainly their spouses, may also see themselves as martyrs, for they may be ill equipped to deal with cross-cultural operations. An individual accustomed to living in a given cultural setting (consisting of customs, norms, value judgments, language, and other factors) may find it difficult to become comfortable with a new pattern of life.

Motives for accepting foreign assignments. An individual may feel some frustration and insecurity and may make some personal sacrifices, but there is much opportunity to "enjoy the good life" while experiencing another culture in depth. Research has shown that the usual motives for choosing foreign assignments are greater administrative responsibility, experience for more rapid promotion, personal satisfaction from living abroad (U.S. executives overseas attained considerably more job satisfaction than their domestic counterparts), higher net income, desire for adventure, less competition from other personnel, and a chance to widen one's horizons. TIPS 17.1 provides you some reasons for accepting and rejecting foreign assignments.

Motives for refusing foreign assignments. The usual reasons for refusing foreign assignments are children of school age whom you would like to have educated in their own country, spouse's reluctance to live abroad, and fear of severing connections for career opportunities at home. Change of habit and routine are also negative factors.

An increasingly important factor in refusing a foreign assignment is the social and political unrest in many foreign countries. For instance, it is more difficult for energy companies to get employees to go to Iran or Saudi Arabia today than it was just a few years ago. And the American University in Beirut was once an option for U.S. teachers, but no more.

It is extremely difficult for American firms to protect their workers in foreign environments. For example, several years ago, Lockheed employees in Iran usually were not permitted to use their personal cars and had to use U.S. banks for all financial transactions. In Saudi Arabia, workers were not

TIPS 17.1   To Do or Not to Do?

Reasons for accepting and rejecting foreign assignments.

For accepting

Chance for greater authority and responsibility

Less competition from others in the organization

Source of greater sense of achievement and personal satisfaction

High after-tax income

Chance for travel and adventure

Chance for broadening experience

For rejecting

Fear that children of school age will not receive a good education

Spouse's reluctance to live abroad

Fear of losing career opportunity contacts in own country

Reluctance to change customs

Fear of or inability to learn another language

Reluctance to leave familiar surroundings, entertainment, and recreational opportunities

able to bring their families with them until they had attained permanent status. And one of the authors was a Ford Foundation adviser in Pakistan during the political upheavals between 1968 and 1970. We had instructions to head for our compounds immediately if we saw the metal windows of a centrally located American airline closed. It meant trouble was brewing or in progress.

Returning to the home-based organization after the overseas tour is over is another problem. Loyalties and positions have been realigned while you

were away. Unfortunately, "out of sight, out of mind" is truer of those overseas than "absence makes the heart grow fonder." For example, one of the authors was in a preferred position at his university before becoming a Fulbright Research Scholar in Spain. When he returned a year later, someone else occupied the prominent position, and he was just another professor.

On balance, though, the benefits of accepting an overseas assignment tend to outweigh the disadvantages.

What is your view?

In what country would you be most willing to accept a foreign assignment? Why? In what country would you be least willing to accept a foreign assignment? Why?

SUMMARY

There's a growing emphasis on international business, and persons interested in management must understand some of the opportunities and problems involved.

International operations are very important to the nation as a whole, to individual firms, and to you as a future manager. Some of the reasons why U.S. firms seek overseas opportunities are: (1) the possibility of higher return on investment, (2) the high effective demand for American goods—especially food—abroad, and (3) that U.S. investments can provide needed capital and technology to produce development and growth in host countries.

But there are problems involved. Recent economic activities—such as recession and new trade restrictions—may be reducing opportunities. There are also (1) the danger of expropriation, (2) differing attitudes and policies, (3) staffing problems, and (4) violence and terrorism. Operations may be staffed with (1) U.S. nationals—but such capable people are limited, and it's very costly to maintain them overseas; (2) local nationals—but, again, the supply of capable people is limited, and it's often difficult to discipline or terminate them; and (3) nationals of third countries available with the breakup of English, French, Dutch, and Belgian colonial empires.

Some criteria for selecting managers to operate in another culture are: (1) professional competence, (2) an optimistic outlook, (3) success in various activities in addition to professional activities, (4) greater self-reliance, (5) the ability to trust others and gain their trust, and (6) previous overseas experience in the Peace Corps, diplomatic corps, or military.

Finally, while increased nationalism is causing conflicts with international business operations, it is the function of international executives to enhance the material well-being of their own and the host country through stimulating international operations while living within the environmental framework caused by the search for nationalism. If these managers can achieve greater material well-being for the nations concerned, they will enhance our economic status. If, at the same time, they can accomplish this with a minimum of friction and conflict, they should be able to enhance our cultural well-being.

This idealistic objective is admittedly difficult to achieve. Yet it is a responsibility that must be accepted by international executives in the future. One of the hopes for the future is that many nations, working together to achieve a common goal, namely, economic advancement, without conflict and friction, should achieve a better understanding in noneconomic areas as well.

REVIEW QUESTIONS

1. (a) What are the reasons for increasing international business operations? (b) Discuss the reasons from (1) an American point of view and (2) the other nation's point of view.
2. How has international business changed over a period of time?
3. What are some of the problems involved in international operations? Explain each.
4. What are some of the differences between (a) colonialism and mercantilism and (b) nationalism?
5. (a) What are some of the factors causing cultural conflicts for executives abroad? (b) What are some of the effects of such conflict?
6. What cultural factors lead to managerial effectiveness, especially when managers operate in another culture?
7. What qualifications should be sought in a person for an overseas managerial position?

DISCUSSION QUESTIONS

1. (a) Do you agree with the authors' projections of the future trend of international business and its management? (b) Explain.
2. (a) Do you think the universality of management principle is valid? (b) If so, how do you explain the divergence of management practices in different cultures?
3. Why is the study of cultural variables important for cross-cultural business operations?
4. What are some problems international business firms may face when trying to staff overseas operations with their own nationals?
5. What are some of the problems associated with staffing with local and foreign nationals in an international business firm?
6. Why does the United States have an "Ugly American" image abroad? What can be done about it?

LEARNING EXERCISE 17.1

Money Does Not Always Motivate

Les Rogers, an American, had been enchanted with New Zealand since his days as a high school exchange student in that country. After graduation from college in the United States, he sought and accepted a job with a New Zealand accounting firm. After several years of experience, Les was appointed manager of the firm.

Although New Zealanders have the deserved reputation of being energetic and talented people, their attitude toward work differs from that of Americans, since they are not as materialistic. In fact, New Zealanders have a saying that "Americans live to work, but New Zealanders work to live."

Les ran up against this difference in attitude in granting merit pay increases to two women working as accountants under him. The women had started work for the firm together a year earlier and were good friends, both on and off the job. Les perceived Betty's performance as clearly superior to Mary's and accordingly gave her a raise at the end of the year that was twice as much as Mary's.

Much to Les's surprise and dismay, Betty came in to see him after the pay raise had been instituted and requested that her increase be the same as Mary's.

Questions

1. Analyze the reasons why Betty would accept the job initially.

2. How would you handle this situation if you were Les Rogers? Explain your reasons.

NOTES

1. Rand Araskog, "We Just Can't Sell to Japanese Market," *USA Today*, April 7, 1987, p. 11A.

2. Kenneth R. Sheets, "How About a Big Mcski?" *U.S. News & World Report*, June 22, 1987, p. 43.

3. *Wall Street Journal*, February 26, 1981.

4. Thomas M. Calero, Illinois Institute of Technology.

5. Milton Moskowitz, Michael Katz, and Robert Levering, eds., *Everybody's Business* (New York: Harper & Row, 1980), pp. 688–689.

6. Larry Margasak, "Boeing Admits Guilt in Payments Case: Fined $400,000," *Mobile Register*, July 1, 1982, p. 6E.

7. Anne Kates, "Foreign Corporations Increase Stake in USA," *USA Today*, January 19, 1988, pp. 1B and 2B.

8. Ibid.

9. Cindy Skrzycki, "America on the Auction Block," *U.S. News & World Report*, March 30, 1987, pp. 56–58.

10. Pamela Sherrid, "America's Hottest Export," *U.S. News & World Report*, July 17, 1987, p. 39.

11. Frank Ching, "China's Managers Get U.S. Lessons," *Wall Street Journal*, January 23, 1981, p. 25.

12. Edward T. Hall, "The Silent Language in Overseas Business," *Harvard Business Review* 38 (May–June 1960): 87–96.

13. Richard J. Fleming, "Cultural Determinants of the Effectiveness of American Executives Abroad," (Ph.D. dissertation, Louisiana State University, 1966), pp. 49–64.

14. "China Seeks a New Management Cadre," *Business Week*, June 16, 1980, pp. 142–147.

15. A. M. Whitehill, Jr., "Cultural Values and Employee Attitudes: United States and Japan," *Journal of Applied Psychology* 48 (February 1964): 69–72.

16. Fleming, "Cultural Determinants," p. 157.

17. N. L. Thal and P. R. Cateora, "Opportunities for Women in International Business," *Business Horizons* 22 (December 1979): 21–27.

SUGGESTIONS FOR FURTHER STUDY

CHIPELLO, CHRISTOPHER J. "Matter of Honor: Japanese Top Managers Quick to Resign When Trouble Hits Firm." *Wall Street Journal*, July 10, 1987, p. 25.

DRUCKER, PETER F. "Beyond the Japanese Export Boom." *Wall Street Journal*, January 6, 1987, p. 28.

GRAY, MARGARET A. "Japanese Management Systems: Some Critical Questions." In *Proceedings of the Southwest Division of the Academy of Management* (March 17–20, 1982), ed. Rickey W. Griffin, pp. 200–204.

GUMBEL, PETER, and SEASE, DOUGLAS R. "Unwelcome Mat: Foreign Firms Build More U.S. Factories, Vex American Rivals." *Wall Street Journal*, July 24, 1987, p. 1.

KAMINARIDES, JOHN, and MULLINS, ROLAND. "International Business: The Challenge to Business Schools in the Next Decade." *Collegiate News and Views* 35 (Fall 1981): 15–18.

KELLEY, LANE, and WORTHLEY, REGINALD. "The Role of Culture in Comparative Management: A Cross-Cultural Perspective." *Academy of Management Journal* 24 (March 1981): 164–173.

LEWYN, MARK. "Korean Firms Seek Bigger USA Market." *USA Today*, December 22, 1986, p. 1B.

LUTHANS, FRED; MCCAUL, HARRIETTE; and DODD, NANCY. "Organizational Commitment: A Comparison of American, Japanese, and Korean Employees." *Academy of Management Journal* 28 (March 1985): 213–219.

MARCOM, JOHN, JR. "Warm Welcome: Spain's New Openness to Foreign Investment Is a Boon to Consumers." *Wall Street Journal*, July 29, 1987, p. 1.

MCCORMICK, JOHN. "A New Brain Drain." *Newsweek on Campus*, February 1987, p. 24.

SAFAVI, FARROKH. "A Model of Management Education in Africa." *Academy of Management Review* 6 (April 1981): 319–331.

TUNG, ROSALIE L. "Expatriate Assignments: Enhancing Success and Minimizing Failure." *Academy of Management Executive*, May 1987, pp. 117–125.

18

Managing Not-for-Profit Organizations

Learning Objectives

After studying the material in this chapter, you should be able to do the following:

□ Explain that not-for-profit organizations are among the largest employers of managers.

□ Describe how management concepts, principles, and ideas apply to not-for-profit organizations as well as private firms.

□ Discuss some of the differences between the two types of organizations.

□ Identify some of the difficulties facing these not-for-profit organizations.

□ Name and discuss some management concepts or techniques that are particularly applicable to not-for-profit organizations.

Outline of the Chapter

Classification of organizations
Profit-oriented organizations
Not-for-profit organizations
Role of not-for-profit organizations
Profit and not-for-profit organizations are similar
Profit and not-for-profit organizations are different
Differences between types of organizations
Mission and objectives
Strategies
Fund-raising and budgeting
Use of volunteers
Management selection

Difficulties of not-for-profit organizations
Concepts particularly applicable to the not-for-profit sector
Strategic planning and MBO
Marketing
Newer leadership styles
The not-for-profit sector's use of contingency management
Community leadership programs
Outside reviews by volunteer task forces
Improving local and state government productivity
Summary

Some Important Terms

not-for-profit organizations
professional corporations (PCs)
not-for-profit service organizations
mutual benefit and protective societies
commonweal groups
public sector
third sector

Some 50 percent of the country's national income now goes to or through . . . public-service institutions.

—PETER DRUCKER

The Family Planning Clinic[1]

The board of directors of a family planning clinic in a major American city assembles to review the facility's performance. In looking at the clinic's year-end data, board members note with some dismay that fewer women have received family planning services this year than last. The clinic director points out, however, that the services provided have expanded dramatically. Not only are the women receiving birth control services, but each client also receives a Pap smear, a breast examination, minor gynecological treatment, and, where appropriate, such ancillary services as menopause counseling.

This report sends the board into total disarray. "I thought we were in the family planning business," says one. "What about the teenage pregnancy problem?" asks another. "Gynecological services are fine," adds a third, "but is that what we're here for?" Time runs out, and the meeting breaks up before any agreement can be reached. The clinic's director leaves the meeting with a confused and contradictory sense of direction. The clinic drifts.

Scenarios like this are all too common in the not-for-profit world. The key reason is that most such organizations fail to agree on clearly defined objectives. Instead, they accept without rigorous discussion a broad and unquantifiable "idea" as a goal. In addition, managers and board members who do agree on goals usually fail to quantify them and to develop yardsticks for measuring progress toward them.

The solution to both problems is simple to state but stubbornly difficult to implement: Key managers and board members of not-for-profit organizations must define—and periodically redefine—exactly what it is they are in business to achieve. Further, they must define their goals with enough precision to be able to develop yardsticks that will tell them when they are making progress and when they aren't.

Does this problem sound familiar? Is it substantially different from the problems facing profit-oriented organizations?

THIS CASE EMPHASIZES the need for effective management in not-for-profit and public service organizations. As Drucker points out, 50 percent of the country's national income goes to or through public service institutions. Before proceeding further, let us examine how organizations are classified according to profit orientation.

CLASSIFICATION OF ORGANIZATIONS

Throughout this book, you have read about "organizations," but no attempt has been made to distinguish them according to purpose, mission, or objective, or to point out that different types of organizations are managed differently.

Classification of organizations is difficult and at best arbitrary. The grouping shown in Table 18.1 has two dimensions: (1) the primary motivation of the organizers, whether or not to try to make a profit, and (2) the primary

537

Purpose	Primary beneficiaries	Common examples	Overriding management focuses
Profit-oriented organizations			
Business	Owners Employees Consumers	Automobile manufacturers Newspaper publishers Fast-food restaurant chains Railroads Parcel delivery firms	Make a profit Provide purposeful jobs Produce goods or services efficiently
Professional corporation	Partners Clients	Physicians Lawyers Architects	Provide needed services Have a satisfactory income
Not-for-profit organizations			
Not-for-profit service	Clients Public	Private universities Welfare agencies Church schools Not-for-profit hospitals	Selectively screen large numbers of potential clients
Mutual benefit and protection	Members	Unions Clubs Political parties Trade associations Professional associations	Satisfy members' needs
Commonweal	Public at large	U.S. Postal Service Police departments Fire departments Public schools Public universities	Provide standardized services to large groups of people

**TABLE 18.1
Organizations,
Classified According to
Primary Purpose**

SOURCE: Based on Robert Kreitner, *Management*, Third Edition. Copyright © 1986 by Houghton Mifflin Company. Adapted with permission.

purpose or orientation of the organization. One classification, according to the motivation of the organizers, distinguishes between (1) organizations whose survival depends on making a profit, in which the profit motive is therefore paramount, and (2) organizations operating primarily to provide a service, whether profitably or not. This does not mean that **not-for-profit organizations** do not think about profitability, but that it is not their primary motivation.

Profit-Oriented Organizations

The primary *profit-oriented organizations* are (1) businesses and (2) professional corporations.

Businesses. A person (or group of persons) organizes a business to produce and/or sell goods or to perform a service for customers. This is to be done at a price that will cover costs (including taxes) and yet provide a profit for the owner. Such an organization is usually called a *business, firm, corporation,* or *enterprise,* and the owners are private citizens of a state that grants them a charter or permit to operate the business. They are primarily profit seeking; the owners know they must perform the service and attain social objectives if they expect to make a profit.

Professional corporations (PCs). Until recently, professionals were not permitted to incorporate, since this was assumed to weaken their professional integrity and personal liability. Now, primarily for tax and estate planning purposes, professionals such as physicians, psychologists, counselors, lawyers, and architects are permitted to form **professional corporations (PCs)** that are profit oriented.

Not-for-Profit Organizations

The primary classifications of not-for-profit organizations are (1) not-for-profit service, (2) mutual benefit and protection, and (3) commonweal.

Not-for-profit service organizations. The primary objective of **not-for-profit service organizations** is service to the public (or clients). They must be cost effective, and, even though they do not seek to make a profit, in the long run, these organizations' revenues must cover expenses. Their primary problem is to be selective in the clients served and judicious in expenses incurred, since profit is not the main performance criterion. Some examples of not-for-profit service organizations are city orchestras, museums, churches, and hospitals run by religious groups.

Mutual benefit and protection societies. Some groups are run for the benefit of their client members. The main problems for these **mutual benefit and protection societies** are (1) determining and satisfying members' needs, (2) protecting members' interests, and (3) speaking up for the members. Private clubs, employee associations, trade associations, and professional associations are examples of this type of organization.

Commonweal groups. Commonweal groups are governmental bodies that provide service to *all* members of the public. The main problems of these groups are (1) to identify their clients and (2) to provide the needed services in a manner that is as cost effective as possible. Public health units, public libraries, and public parks and recreational areas are examples of commonweal groups. Table 18.2 shows how business and government organizations compare in terms of market situation, personnel system, production system,

Dimension	Business organizations	Government organizations
Market situation		
Nature of service or product	Clear, "hard"	Ambiguous, "soft"
Market test: measurability of performance	Yes. High measurability	No. Low measurability. Little or no market test
Competitive situation: client or consumer options	Existent, although variable by industry and economic sector	Nonexistent in most government agencies; they are monopolies
Client relations: vulnerability to outside political pressures	Increasing but still limited	Very high, turbulent setting Functions in uncertain political environment
Personnel system		
Extent of constraint of management resulting from personnel and collective bargaining policies	Increasing but no civil service	Very high, civil service and union work rules. Cities constrained more by collective bargaining agreements
Limits on having incentives, rewards related to performance	Some, but competence and high performance likely to be rewarded through salaries, promotions	Strong limits. Seniority and conformity to informal group norms determine promotion. Competence and performance not as likely to be rewarded
Production system and institutional setting		
Extent of autonomy and control over production or service delivery-related activities	Very high. Much vertical, horizontal, and conglomerate integration. Much control over production and distribution	Very low. Part of interdependent, intergovernmental system that includes many state and federal agencies
Extent of fragmentation of the production or service delivery system	Low, because of patterns just noted	Very high
Financing arrangements	Internal financing from profits	Completely dependent on external bodies or agencies
Internal structure		
Line manager authority	High	Low. Rule by expert practitioners
Status of "management" relative to "expert and staff" functions	High	Low. Management downgraded to secondary activity
Promotion from within versus outsider recruitment via lateral entry	Much variability but many outsiders	High recruitment from within. Few outsiders, except at very top
Term of service of top management	Long. Much continuity, allowing for more long-range planning, research and development, innovations, and so forth	Short. High turnover and discontinuity
Prospects for decentralization	High, with capacity to measure performance, market test, use of "profit center" concept	Low. Few existing criteria for evaluating, monitoring, and controlling
Management traditions and culture		
Time horizons	Longer term	Very short term
Extent of management tradition	High	Very low

TABLE 18.2

Characteristics and Environment of Business and Government Organizations

SOURCE: David Rogers "Managing in the Public and Private Sectors: Similarities and Differences," *Management Review* 70 (May 1981): 51.

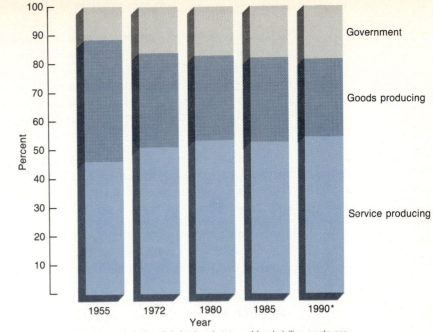

FIGURE 18.1
Percentage distribution of total employment (counting jobs rather than workers) for selected years.

Note: Government includes all federal and state and local civilian employees. Goods producing includes agriculture, mining, construction, and manufacturing. Service producing includes transportation, communication, public utilities, trade, finance, insurance, real estate, and other services.
*Estimated.

institutional settings, internal structure, and management traditions and culture.

What is your view?

Do you remember from Chapter 1 who the largest single employer in the United States is? Is it American Telephone & Telegraph (AT&T), General Motors (GM), U.S. Steel? Read on for the correct answer.

You can see from Figure 18.1 that government employment has grown very rapidly during recent decades. During the 1960s and 1970s, it grew faster than the goods-producing industries. Now, nearly one of five workers is employed in some type of government organization. In fact, the biggest employer in the United States is the federal government, which employs around 3 million civilians and 2 million military personnel. Probably as many people are employed in not-for-profit service organizations as in governments.

ROLE OF NOT-FOR-PROFIT ORGANIZATIONS

Management expert Peter Drucker emphasizes the role of public and not-for-profit types of organizations in the opening quotation. He shows that the not-for-profit sector is one of the fastest growing in the society, despite having encountered many difficulties in recent years. This growth sector encompasses not only the **public sector,** composed of federal, state, and local governments, but also the **third sector,** consisting of many not-for-profit service organizations that are private or semipublic, such as hospitals, churches, schools and universities, trade associations, orchestras, museums, dance and opera companies, the United Fund, the YMCA and YWCA, scouting organizations, and municipally owned utilities. In fact, many of you will choose a career in a not-for-profit public service institution.

Profit and Not-for-Profit Organizations Are Similar

Most of the concepts, principles, and ideas in this book are just as applicable and relevant to managing not-for-profit organizations as they are to managing private business firms. And, as will be shown later, the similarities are becoming greater.

Similar problems and functions. All large organizations face the same general management problems and perform the same functions, regardless of whether they are in the profit-seeking or non-profit-seeking sector. All must develop (1) an appropriate product and/or service mix, (2) a workable organizational structure, (3) professional human-resources management techniques, (4) the capacity to finance their operations, (5) an efficient production process, and (6) excellent marketing. While these have long been important to profit-oriented organizations, they are now becoming more important to not-for-profit groups as they move toward more professional management.

Also, the differences between the private and public sectors are becoming increasingly blurred. For example, as big corporations merge and diversify, they assume a much more federated and loosely structured form because the products are so diverse. These changes cause the corporations' management to resemble fragmented government bureaucracies. Also, as pressure from activist groups and the government have led to increased social accountability, private-sector organizations have become more vulnerable to outside pressures and begun to act more like public-sector organizations.

At the same time, governments have been increasingly subjected to demands for better management and improved performance, since finances have become tighter.

And as restrictions on government spending tighten, the profit motive is becoming stronger in the not-for-profit sector, as institutions expand their money-making activities. For example, YMCAs run profit-making exercise centers; colleges organize tours and run catering services; and hospitals sell eyeglasses and hearing aids and operate commercial pharmacies and laundries. What especially galls business people is that these sidelines are tax-exempt.[2]

Another example is the not-for-profit Children's Television Workshop, which, by licensing toy manufacturers, book publishers, and others to use its characters and trademark, earns profits that are used to develop new educational programs for children.[3]

Similar objectives. In Chapter 5, we covered the objectives set by businesses, according to Drucker. To what extent do Drucker's objectives for business also apply to not-for-profit organizations, such as the city government of Washington, D.C., a city hospital, or a state university?

A university, for example, produces a service. And the organization itself will diminish if the demand for the service diminishes. That is, if student enrollment at the university level begins to drop off, then the university, like the company that sees its sales decreasing, will have to reduce its staff. Accordingly, universities set market share goals and revamp programs to attract students; that is, they offer more services and put more hype into recruiting. For example, a school might distribute coupons that waive the application fee if the application is returned within a specified period.

The objectives of productivity, innovation, physical and financial resources, and management and employee performance would certainly apply to the university as well.

The only objective on Drucker's list that would not have direct application to not-for-profit organizations is *profitability*, which is the usual result of doing the other things well. When a city hospital stays within its budget or even accomplishes its objectives at a surplus, it has achieved something comparable to "profit." Such "profits" can be used to expand the organization and increase its services to the public. But some public departments are actually in business to make a profit, such as state facilities, like toll roads and state docks, and some city facilities, like a city wharf or a municipal auditorium. These profits are returned to the "owners" (i.e., taxpayers) in the form of other services, such as public education or highway maintenance.

Similar control. Public utilities such as Con Edison and the Tennessee Valley Authority (TVA) are public monopolies. Because they have no competition, does this mean that they can neglect new products, new services, or greater efficiency? Certainly not! We constantly complain about our rising bills and demand that these organizations show greater efficiency. If we knew precisely what percentage of the taxes deducted from our paychecks (federal, city, and state) went to which particular agency (Department of Health and Human Services, Department of Agriculture, Department of Defense, city police and fire departments, etc.) we would probably be quite concerned about increased efficiency and service on their part!

Profit and Not-for-Profit Organizations Are Different

Nevertheless, there are certain differences between not-for-profit and profit-oriented organizations that a manager should be aware of to manage effectively.[4] There are also certain concepts that are particularly useful in managing not-for-profit organizations but have not been used to full advantage. Let us examine some of the differences between the not-for-profit sector and the private sector, after which we will briefly consider some of the difficulties facing not-for-profit organizations.

DIFFERENCES BETWEEN TYPES OF ORGANIZATIONS

The essential differences between private, profit-oriented firms and public and not-for-profit organizations are (1) mission and objectives, (2) strategies, (3) fund-raising and budgeting, (4) use of volunteer workers, and (5) management selection.

Mission and Objectives

One difference between profit and not-for-profit organizations is the assumptions underlying their mission and objectives. As shown in Chapter 4, the bottom line for most businesses is to *optimize long-term profits* for the owners while *performing a needed service* for the public. For most not-for-profit organizations, the bottom line is to provide services that improve their clients' quality of life.

> *The mission of a city police department, for example, is to use its budgeted funds in such a way that it maximizes the service it provides to the community, within its cost constraints. The department's efficiency is measured not in profits but in the quality of service delivered compared to the amount of money allocated and expended.*

As discussed earlier, there are some not-for-profit organizations that do attempt to make a profit (revenue received in excess of all costs), not to pass on to stockholders but to reinvest in the organization to further improve service to their clients.

What is your view?

What do you think should be the mission and objectives of the family planning clinic in the Opening Case?

Strategies

In Chapter 5, we defined *strategies* (or *strategic plans*) as long-range plans that establish the nature of the organization. You can see, therefore, that the strategies of profit and not-for-profit organizations would differ. Although both types of organizations produce a good or provide a service, sell or market it, deal with financing, and staff the organization with employees, they use different strategies.

In general, not-for-profit organizations tend to give less attention to strategies than do privately owned firms. Instead, more emphasis is given to short-range plans or tactics.

Fund-raising and Budgeting

While most government organizations are financed largely by taxes, other not-for-profit organizations must raise funds through voluntary giving. And this activity is becoming more difficult, partly because the 1986 tax reforms made charitable donations less valuable on tax returns. MAP 18.1 shows how one not-for-profit organization improved its fund raising.

The budget is both a *planning* vehicle and a *control* device in profit-oriented organizations. It is primarily a control device in non-profit-oriented groups. There is an incentive in profit organizations to economize by reducing costs and so contribute more to profits. The opposite incentive is in effect in not-for-profit organizations; frequently, if a government or United Fund agency does not spend its entire budget allocation, it receives a reduced amount the next year.

Use of Volunteers

With the possible exception of the government, not-for-profit organizations make widespread use of volunteers. For example, several years ago, a national survey indicated that 6 billion hours of labor were volunteered each year. This is equivalent to the hours put in by 3 million full-time workers. In monetary terms, the market value of this voluntary time was $29 billion.[5] Candy stripers and Grey Ladies work in hospitals and nursing homes, and

Management Application and Practice 18.1   American Express's James Robinson Raises Funds for United Way

James Robinson, CEO of American Express, has been volunteer chairman of United Way for two years. During that time, he's been working to infuse United Way—second only to the U.S. government in funding social services—with new fund-raising techniques and marketing know-how. He's encouraged UW and its affiliates to double their intake of money and volunteer help by 1991. The main funding technique at the grass-roots level is still employer payroll deductions. He notes that for the first time in decades,

average Americans gave more than 2 percent of their annual income to charity. In addition, he's emphasized reaching out to small businesses, which accounted for only 2.8 percent of UW's funds in 1983. Pensioners on company retirement funds are also to be solicited, and corporate contacts are to be tapped more rigorously.

SOURCE: Andrea Gabor, "Fund Raising in Trying Times." Reprinted from *U.S. News & World Report*, May 4, 1987, p. 53. Published by the American Marketing Association.

retired senior citizens work with charitable organizations such as churches, the Red Cross, the United Fund, and others.

Although the use of volunteers makes it possible for the nonprivate sector to perform its services, it also complicates the job of managing for the paid professional staff. It raises the accountability issue in that volunteers assume management responsibilities on the board; yet "seldom do they have a direct reporting relationship with the paid administrative staff."[6] Thus they're usually not held accountable for their actions. In addition, when volunteers are working directly for or in cooperation with the paid staff, the paid staff cannot use the usual monetary incentives to deal with poor performance. Instead, they must appeal to the higher-level needs, such as achievement, altruism, responsibility, and creative and challenging work.

What is your view?

Why are volunteers willing to spend so much time with not-for-profit organizations? Compare your view with the authors', as presented below.

Daniel Yankelovich, a prominent futurist and writer, has argued that we need a new ethic in searching for self-fulfillment in a world that is different from the time when the Protestant ethic was a major motivator. His thesis is that many people, particularly in America, are attempting to achieve self-fulfillment in a hedonistic, selfish manner, thinking primarily of themselves and not the needs of others. The ethic he espouses is an ethic of commitment to and involvement in making the world a better place.

In the opinion of the authors, this is a primary drive for most of the people who are volunteers in not-for-profit organizations. These people are committed to and involved in trying to improve things in their small part of the world. They are reaching beyond their own selfish interests in trying to help others.

Management Selection

Many not-for-profit organizations support the activities of professionals such as doctors, lawyers, educators, social workers, and scientists. So it is not surprising that many times the top management of these enterprises is selected on the basis of professional competence rather than managerial expertise.

Moreover, political influences are associated with all organizations, but politics appear to be much more involved in the selection of higher managers in not-for-profit organizations than in profit-oriented concerns. For example, Clyde Kirkland, the administrator of the Capital City Hospital (Opening Case in Chapter 2), was selected as administrator by the hospital because he had close ties to prominent citizens in the area and was a leader—at the state and local levels—of the religious group that supported the hospital.

Some of the major differences between profit and not-for-profit organizations are summarized in Table 18.3.

What is your view?

We have identified five differences between profit and not-for-profit organizations. What other differences can you think of?

DIFFICULTIES OF NOT-FOR-PROFIT ORGANIZATIONS

Not-for-profit organizations are a growth sector in the United States, but there is increasing pressure from citizens to curtail some of the growth. Two related reasons account for this trend: (1) opposition to increased taxes at the local, state, and federal levels and (2) a more conservative mood in the country.

It is the not-for-profit organizations, however, which specialize in meeting needs not adequately provided for by either government or business, that appear to be in real difficulty. These organizations depend on the support of private citizens and grants from the other two sectors to achieve their

**TABLE 18.3
Differences Between
Private, Profit-Oriented
Organizations and
Public, Not-for-Profit
Organizations**

	Private, profit-oriented organizations	Not-for-profit organizations
Measure of effectiveness	Profit and service to customers	Services provided to clients and society
Strategies	Primarily emphasize long term	Emphasize short term
Budget	Planning and control tool	Primary control tool
Tangible compensation	Pay, benefits for all employees	Psychic satisfaction, since most volunteers receive no financial compensation
Top-manager selection	More likely based on managerial expertise	Often based on technical, professional competence

social and service-oriented mission. The following examples indicate the extent of the difficulties.

> *More than 170 private colleges have closed their doors since 1965. Some have been unable to attract enough students, others have failed to find sufficient funds, and some have had both problems.*
>
> *Hospital costs are continuing to soar so that daily room rates of $300 or more are found in some large hospitals. Many hospitals are experiencing underutilization—especially in the maternity and pediatric sections as the birthrate drops.*
>
> *Many performing groups, such as orchestras, opera and ballet companies, and chamber ensembles, cannot attract large enough audiences to break even. Even those that have seasonal sellouts face huge operating deficits at the end of the year.*
>
> *Many third-sector organizations—such as the YMCA, Salvation Army, Girl Scouts, and Women's Christian Temperance Union—that prospered at one time are presently reexamining their mission in an effort to reverse membership declines.[7]*

CONCEPTS PARTICULARLY APPLICABLE TO THE NOT-FOR-PROFIT SECTOR

Many concepts and principles from profit-oriented organizations are applicable to the not-for-profit sector. We have selected three that are especially relevant to, and can make a significant difference in, organizational effectiveness. These concepts are (1) strategic planning and management by objectives (MBO), (2) marketing, and (3) newer styles of leadership.

Strategic Planning and MBO

Drucker has stated that the starting point for increasing organizational effectiveness is to define the organization's mission. The mission statement affects all that follows—strategic planning, goal setting, marketing strategy, evaluation, and other factors, just as we discussed in Chapters 4 and 5.

> *Take, for example, the YMCA. As a result of the urban crisis and the social upheavals of the 1960s, the YMCA decided to take a new look at its mission and market. Specifically, the YMCA directors began with a general statement of mission: "The YMCA will be significantly influencing domestic and international conditions which affect the quality of human life."[8]*

Need for clear statement of mission. Not-for-profit organizations, like profit-seeking organizations, must do the following if they are to be effective:

1. Define what their mission is and what it should be. They need to bring alternative definitions into the open and consider them carefully.
2. Derive clear objectives and goals from their definition of function and mission.
3. Set priorities that enable them to select targets, to set standards of accomplishment and performance—that is, to define the minimum

acceptable results, to set deadlines, to go to work on results, and to make someone accountable for results.

4. Define measurements of performance.

5. Use these measurements to provide feedback on their efforts.

6. Make an organized review of objectives and results to weed out those objectives that no longer serve a purpose or have proved unattainable.

7. Identify unsatisfactory performance and activities that are outdated or unproductive or both.

8. Provide a mechanism for dropping such activities instead of wasting money and human energies when the results are poor.

Need for tangible goals. A common explanation for the failure of not-for-profit organizations is that they lack tangible goals. According to this point of view, businesses have definite profit goals that they can point their members toward, and profit also becomes the measure of the business firm's success or lack of it. Recall, however, that profitability is only *one* measure of success for a business organization and that this profit results only from the provision of a quality service to society. For example, Honeywell proudly states, "Our business is making your business more productive through automation and control." And Mercedes-Benz says its cars are "engineered like no other car in the world." These are intangible definitions of purpose— just as intangible as a church's goal of "saving souls" or a charitable organization's purpose of "serving the needy."

Profitability is not the only way business firms measure progress toward their purpose. Firms also measure profitability indirectly through customer satisfaction, new product development, implementation of new programs, and so on. For example, church attendance is measurable; so is tithing by parishioners; so are Bible school enrollment and test scores, and so are hospital visits and other specific ways to measure the extent of a church's performance.

What is your view?
Can you think of some ways to measure the effectiveness of your city government and your school?

Remember: The mission statement must be translated into specific, tangible goals, stated in quantitative terms, with target dates. One study involving 192 hospitals indicated that using MBO improved accountability and performance effectiveness in 93 percent of the hospitals.[9] In only 2 percent of the hospitals did its use result in a "change for the worse," while in the other 5 percent it resulted in "no change."

Marketing   Phillip Kotler, a marketing expert, indicates that of all business functions, marketing has been the last to arrive on the not-for-profit scene. One reason is that many not-for-profit organizations operated in a seller's market for many years—colleges and hospitals in the 1960s, for example. Another reason is that many not-for-profit organizations assume that the quality of the service will sell itself, and so they fail to develop a marketing plan and delivery

---

➡️ **TIPS 18.1** Questions Colleges and Universities Should Raise in Marketing Planning

Market analysis

1. What important trends are affecting higher education? (Environmental analysis)
2. What is the primary market? (Market definition)
3. What are the major market segments in this market? (Market segmentation)
4. What are the needs of each market segment? (Need assessment)
5. How much awareness, knowledge, interest, and desire is there in each market segment concerning the college? (Market awareness and attitude)
6. How do key public groups see us and our competitors? (Image analysis)
7. How do potential students learn about the college and make decisions to apply and enroll? (Consumer behavior)
8. How satisfied are current students? (Consumer satisfaction assessment)

Resource analysis

1. What are the major strengths and weaknesses in faculty, programs, facilities, and so forth? (Strengths and weaknesses analysis)
2. What opportunities are there to expand the financial resources? (Donor opportunity analysis)

Mission analysis

1. What business are we in? (Business mission)
2. Who are the customers? (Customer definition)
3. Which needs are we trying to satisfy? (Needs targeting)
4. On which market segments do we want to focus? (Market targeting)
5. Who are the major competitors? (Competitor identification)
6. What competitive benefits do we want to offer to the target market? (Market positioning)

SOURCE: Phillip Kotler, ''Strategies for Introducing Marketing into Nonprofit Organizations,'' *Journal of Marketing* 43 (January 1979): 39.

---

system for the service. Today, as a result of reduced support, this thinking has changed drastically.

TIPS 18.1 summarizes the questions that must be answered for effective university marketing planning. A similar profile should be developed for other not-for-profit organizations.

All organizations have a product or service that they want to sell or provide to a given market or customers. To do this, they use a wide variety of marketing techniques to induce their customers to accept what they have to offer. In other words, many not-for-profit organizations are coming to the conclusion that they need to be profit minded in a not-for-profit world. The object is not to make a profit for stockholders but to reinvest money to increase services or, in some cases, simply to survive. As a result, questions are being raised regarding new markets for existing services. For example, in a recent year, the Metropolitan Museum of Art in New York City netted $1.6 million ''profit'' from the sale of such items as art reproductions, greeting cards, and calendars.

Organizations such as colleges, universities, and hospitals are using marketing strategy as never before. One study involving hospitals indicates that the application of marketing techniques can make significant contributions in the areas of objectives, health care environment, problem definition, consumer analysis, and market segmentation.[10] Ten years ago, the marketing of health care was unheard of; now it is estimated that there are over 10,000 marketing health care professionals in the United States.

What is your view?
Can you think of some recent television commercials, newspaper ads, or other forms of promotion that have been used by universities or hospitals to promote their programs? Just a few years ago it would have been difficult to find these.

Newer Leadership Styles

Managers in not-for-profit institutions tend to use different leadership style than those in profit-oriented organizations. Yet there is also a difference between the commonweal not-for-profits and the others.

Use of bureaucracy. In commonweal or governmental groups, there tends to be greater use of the bureaucratic approach. There is greater reliance on the use of rules, regulations, and "red tape"—that is, on doing things according to established procedure—than in private, profit-oriented firms. The leadership is less receptive and responsive to change.

Use of participative leadership. The not-for-profit service and mutual benefit associations, using large numbers of volunteers, have a more relaxed, laissez-faire type of leadership. Greater use is made of shared leadership, subordinate decision making, public committees, and the participative approach to management. These groups are quite receptive to change, including changing their mission.

> *For example, the Polio Foundation used the "March of Dimes" drive, primarily carried on by mothers, to raise funds to combat polio. When a successful vaccine was found, the organization changed its objectives and strategies to combat "birth defects."*

Use of organization development (OD). The use of the action-research model of organization change and development (see Chapter 13) is especially useful in improving the effectiveness of not-for-profit organizations.

As noted earlier, this approach uses a participative approach to diagnose and effect needed change. When successfully applied, OD not only increases the level of trust and support among organization members but also enables the organization to find synergistic solutions to problems with greater frequency.

For several reasons—not the least being the large number of volunteers used—authority in many not-for-profits is fragmented and diffuse. Moreover, there is a strong "ethos of equality" among organization members. OD is especially helpful in this area, since it tends to increase personal satisfaction and enthusiasm, in addition to creating an environment where assigned authority is augmented by personal authority based on expertise and knowledge.

Use of different motivators. Remember that the motivational process (Chapter 11) begins when a person has a *need* for something, which causes a *desire* to satisfy that need. When the appropriate *stimulus*, in the form of an *incentive*, is applied, the person *responds* by *performing* an activity. This results in achieving personal and organizational goals. This is what happens in not-for-profit groups. In general, a sense of common purpose among the volunteers and staff aids in motivating the volunteers.

Further, to motivate staff, not-for-profit managers must decentralize power and do things to make the staff not only *feel* important but also *be* important. Obviously, money is not the primary motivator in nonprofit organizations, but managers can create a highly committed, loyal staff by sharing power and letting the staff influence decisions and actions.

These motivational techniques are some ways for not-for-profit managers to share power and improve effectiveness without losing control.

What is your view?

What are some other management concepts that would be especially helpful in managing not-for-profit organizations?

THE NOT-FOR-PROFIT SECTOR'S USE OF CONTINGENCY MANAGEMENT

Contingency management emphasizes that different conditions and situations require the application of differing management techniques. Yet, as shown, many not-for-profit organizations have difficulty because of the widespread use of volunteers and the fact that volunteer leaders are not permanent members of the organization or the board of directors. Moreover, many of the permanent managers in the not-for-profit sector do not have education and training in the use of advanced management principles, concepts, and techniques. It is difficult for them to diagnose problems and apply the proper management techniques and concepts because they are unfamiliar with what solutions are available.

There is a great need for managers of not-for-profit groups to interface with various constituencies. Fortunately, there are two developments taking place in this country that address this issue. The first is the widespread use of community leadership programs. The second is the increasing use of management audits and reviews by volunteer task forces that have exceptional knowledge regarding management concepts and applications. Let us examine each of these developments.

Community Leadership Programs

There has been increasing interest and activity in *community leadership programs* in the last 15 years. Over 100 cities are now members of the National Association of Community Leadership Organizations (for example, Leadership Atlanta and Leadership Philadelphia). Each year, additional cities initiate such programs, and their success in developing leaders and improving the quality of a community's life has been rather dramatic.

These programs feature instruction in the development of "contingency leadership" and "team building" skills as well as "action research" and "field work and project implementation." Then, after the training phase is over, some programs require the participants to research a real problem within the community or region and develop a plan of implementation to solve it. They also motivate participants by (1) increasing their awareness of community or state issues and problems, (2) involving them in in-depth research on issues of current interest, and (3) providing a network of leaders who are actively involved in improving the area's quality of life.[11]

Outside Reviews by Volunteer Task Forces

Not-for-profit organizations do not have the accountability of the marketplace and the discipline of being measured by "bottom line" results. Yet they should be accountable for how effectively and efficiently the organization serves its clients. One way to ensure this accountability is to have an outside review by a knowledgeable task force of volunteers.

The United Way of Albuquerque, New Mexico, has developed such a review process, which has been adapted for use by the United Way in many other cities. For example, all United Fund agencies in Mobile, Alabama, are reviewed by different volunteer task forces every five years. The review process examines the programs, operations, mission management, and functioning of each agency. The process consists of the following steps:

1. A questionnaire is completed by the agency being reviewed.
2. Interviews are conducted with board members and agency executives.
3. A preliminary report is developed and discussed with the board and agency executives.
4. The agency develops action plans to deal with recommendations.
5. A followup meeting with the board president and agency executive director is conducted about three years later to monitor results.

Many of the recommendations involve improving the management process of the agency. For example, in a recent review of a United Fund agency in Mobile, seven recommendations were made, including the following two to improve the agency's planning and control functions:

1. The agency should formalize an ongoing planning process incorporating strategic and operational planning. These plans should include a series of simple, realistic agency goals, with immediate staff objectives, and be stated in such terms as to allow an annual measure of progress.
2. The agency should conduct an annual self-evaluation to determine its effectiveness in dealing with clients and the extent to which it has an impact on the community.[12]

IMPROVING LOCAL AND STATE GOVERNMENT PRODUCTIVITY

During the past decade, both state and local governments in various sections of the country have been charged with operating at much less than expected effectiveness. The research and policy committee of the Committee for Economic Development has made several recommendations that address this issue. Some of these recommendations are as follows:

1. State governments should encourage and assist small local governments in enlisting professional management (by a circuit city manager or other manpower-pooling arrangements), and help larger government

agencies to provide management training for top administrators and to create full-time administrative units staffed by personnel professionally trained in management.

2. The personnel systems of state and local governments should be modified to allow employees to move among local and state agencies without loss of rank, seniority, or pension rights.

3. State governments should establish and enforce minimum standards for local government accounting, budgeting, and performance and reporting systems in order to provide data on level, quality, results, and costs of services.

4. The governor of each state should establish a high-level commission with state, local, and nongovernment representation to identify and suggest permanent procedures to evaluate and improve state and local government productivity.

5. State governments should provide technical and financial assistance to local governments in order to (a) develop and implement performance measures, (b) experiment with, or implement, techniques or programs that have greatest likelihood of success, and (c) undertake other programs that would improve productivity.[13]

SUMMARY

The management of not-for-profit organizations is similar to that of private, profit-oriented groups. Yet there are some significant differences that are discussed in this chapter.

Different types of organizations may be classified according to the motives of their organizers. Profit-oriented groups include (1) businesses and (2) professional organizations. Not-for-profit institutions may be grouped as (1) not-for-profit service, (2) mutual benefit and protection associations, and (3) commonweal organizations.

The role of organizations in the not-for-profit sector is to provide service to their members.

The primary differences between profit-seeking and not-for-profit organizations include (1) mission and objectives, (2) strategies, (3) fund raising and budgeting, (4) use of volunteer workers, and (5) management selection.

New pressures facing these institutions include (1) opposition to new taxes and contributions and (2) a more conservative mood.

Some concepts that are particularly applicable to the not-for-profit sector include (1) strategic planning and management by objectives (MBO), (2) marketing, and (3) the newer leadership styles.

The use of contingency management is also applicable and has been enhanced by community leadership programs and the use of reviews by volunteer task forces.

Several recommendations for improving the productivity of local and state government operations are included to encourage interest and involvement for principals and constituents.

REVIEW QUESTIONS

1. The primary not-for-profit institutions are: *(a)* not-for-profit service, *(b)* mutual benefit and protection, and *(c)* commonweal. Define and list the characteristics of each of these.
2. How do private, profit-oriented firms differ from public, not-for-profit organizations in terms of *(a)* mission and objectives, *(b)* strategies, *(c)* fund raising and budgeting, and *(d)* management selection?
3. Is it important that not-for-profit organizations use many volunteers? Why is this so?
4. Why are not-for-profit institutions now having difficulties?
5. Why are the concepts of strategic planning and MBO particularly relevant to not-for-profit institutions?
6. Is the marketing concept becoming more or less important to not-for-profit institutions? Explain.
7. Not-for-profit organizations tend to use the newer leadership styles, such as *(a)* bureaucracy, *(b)* participative leadership, and *(c)* organization development, extensively. Explain why and how this is done.

DISCUSSION QUESTIONS

1. "Incompetent managers are much less likely to be identified in not-for-profit organizations because it is difficult to measure their performance." Discuss this statement.
2. An argument frequently made to differentiate between profit and not-for-profit organizations is that the latter do not have to worry about competing organizations. Do you agree with the statement? Explain.
3. The Management Club at a university has as its statement of mission " . . . to serve our student members' professional needs as future managers." Evaluate this statement of mission.
4. What would be some examples of tangible goals that the Management Club (of question number 3) could establish? Try to come up with at least three examples.
5. Some religious group leaders, such as Billy Graham and Oral Roberts, have established highly visible marketing and promotion techniques through newspapers, magazines, and television. Other organized religious groups, however, have not used such techniques. What do you think accounts for these differences in marketing? Discuss.
6. In the text, we stated "not-for-profit service and mutual benefit associations . . . have a more relaxed, laissez-faire type of leadership." Does this mean that an autocratic leader will not be a successful manager in these organizations? Discuss.
7. What is your estimation of the value of community leadership programs?

LEARNING EXERCISE 18.1

The New Director

James Hankins, a successful business executive, had taken early retirement at age 55. At age 57, he found that he missed the fast pace of the world of profits, budgets, standard costs, inventory, performance appraisal, recruiting, landing big contracts, and the like. That's why he was anxious to become the director of the United Support Office (USO), the city's major coordinating center for dispersing funds to community charitable and service organizations.

Last year, the USO had generated over $450,000 through fund raising that was used to provide grants to 17 different organizations such as the Boy and Girl Scouts of America, Home for Abused Children, Northvale Mental Retardation Center, Salvation Army, American Cancer Society, and others. Amounts given to a particular agency last year ranged from $500 to $50,000.

After his first week on the job, James was very distressed by what he found. Each year the annual fund-raising goal had been easily met. In some cases the goal had even been set lower than the amount collected the previous year! There was no apparent reason why certain amounts were awarded to various agencies. These amounts varied each year by as much as 75 percent from the previous year. Moreover, no accounting was made by the agencies to explain specifically how the funds were spent.

James, with his strong business background, had set as his number-one priority the goal of "changing some policies around here so that we're run more like a business."

Questions

1. Is James correct in wanting to change the policies of the USO? Explain.
2. What changes, if any, would you make? Be specific in your recommendations.
3. How can USO know if it's "doing a good job?"
4. How would you go about establishing objectives for the USO?

LEARNING EXERCISE 18.2

Managing a Not-for-Profit Organization

River View Church has over 5000 members, around 25 full-time and 30 part-time employees, and an annual budget of over $1 million. Sue Weatherford, one of the full-time workers, has the title of business administrator. She reports to, and is directly responsible to, the pastor. Yet she also takes orders about some activities from the chairperson of the board of deacons and the chairperson of the administrative committee. She has one professional assistant and a secretary (see Figure 18.2).

FIGURE 18.2
Partial organization chart for River View Church.

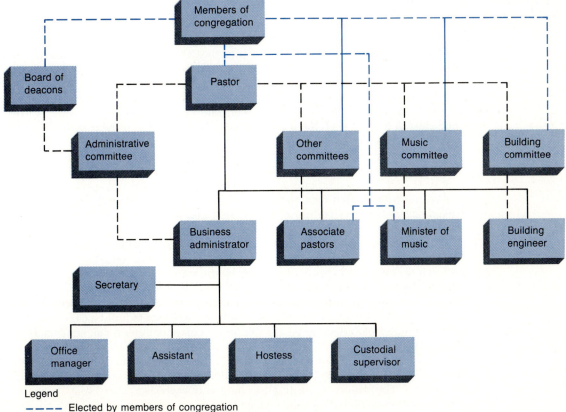

Legend
- - - - Elected by members of congregation
———— Elected by and reports to members of the congregation
———— Day-to-day supervision of routine activities
- - - - Reports to and receives suggestions from the person or committee shown

Sue prepares the annual budget for presentation to the administrative committee, which defends it before the deacons, who then take it to the church for approval. She determines the personnel needs, except for the ministerial staff, which is decided by the church members. The sources and uses of funds are also Sue's responsibility. The organization structure is planned and modified by Sue, subject to approval by the committee.

All employees except the pastor, two associate pastors, the minister of music, and the building engineer are hired, trained, supervised, paid, and terminated by Sue.

Sue sees that the offerings are collected, counted, taken to the bank, and accounted for. She prepares and presents monthly financial statements and explains them to the deacons. She can borrow money within defined limits.

She helps manage the property, except for the actual maintenance. Most supplies, food, equipment, and literature are purchased, received, stored, and issued under Sue's supervision.

She has an office manager, hostess, and custodial supervisor helping her manage the church's secular activities.

Questions

1. To what extent is Sue performing the managerial functions?
2. What are the differences between her managerial activities and those of managers in private business?

LEARNING EXERCISE 18.3

Private Prisons*

For almost ten years, the Bay County Correctional Center (BCCC) in northern Florida was a typical jailhouse—one of ill repute. The cells were overcrowded, and there were too few guards. Those days are over. BCCC is now clean and orderly. This reformation was accomplished by turning the county jail over to a private firm, Corrections Corporation of America, Inc.

The county pays about $30 per day per inmate to CCA for maintaining the facility. In just 20 months, CCA converted a local dump into a showplace. A new warden kept most of the old staff, hired more guards, and distributed them throughout the building.

To overcome the crowding problem, the county contracted with CCA to build a $4.5 million work camp to house women, juveniles, and sentenced prisoners. The facility is very high-tech, complete with closed-circuit cameras, motion detectors, and sound sensors that alert the corrections officers of any problems in the glass-walled cells. These devices allow for less staff and therefore lower labor costs. CCA officials say they are turning a small profit.

Private prisons such as Bay County are slowly finding a niche in the United States. By the summer of 1987, there were about 3000 private adult jail beds in the nation, and that number was expected to double by the summer of 1988 as Texas, Arkansas, and Oklahoma put more than 3000 beds out for bids. And a subsidiary of the Bechtel Group, Inc., construction company has joined with Daewoo Corporation, a South Korean conglomerate, and American Correctional Systems to build a 512-bed private prison in Ault, Colorado. It is being built on speculation, hoping that some state will flood it with inmates.

The benefits at BCCC are numerous. CCA thoroughly cleaned the place, hired a doctor and lawyer for regular inmate consultations, and reinstated exercise periods in the gym. The results, according to one guard supervisor, show that "Respect is our aim and obligation. You earn respect by doing a good job."

* Prepared by Teresa W. Blakney, Mobile College. Condensed from "A Person, Not a Number," *Newsweek*, June 29, 1987, p. 63.

By the summer of 1987, CCA, headquartered in Nashville, remained the industry leader. With nine contract facilities, including the Santa Fe, New Mexico, county jail and the workhouse in Chattanooga, Tennessee, CCA runs a first-rate operation. According to CCA chairman, Thomas W. Beasley, "We deliver a service very quickly, very efficiently."

Even with all its success, though, CCA has run into opposition in many states. The American Federation of State, County, and Municipal Employees has mounted an effective campaign against privatization of services in general—and jail cells in particular. There have been many arguments. Among them: The contracts invite cost overruns and corruption; states may not delegate the power to punish; and, as a shooting incident in one private Texas holding pen showed, officials who transfer control still can be held liable for fouled operations.

One very important aspect to remember is that at Bay County and at other private prisons, an inmate is "a person, not a number."

Questions

1. What do you see as Bay County's mission?

2. What effects will private prisons have on the nation in the future?

3. What are some benefits (other than the ones listed in the exercise) that inmates may receive from private prisons?

4. What are some possible benefits to society of using private firms to run government activities, such as prisons?

NOTES

1. Phillip D. Harvey and James D. Snyder, "Charities Need a Bottom Line, Too," *Harvard Business Review* 65 (January–February 1987): 14.

2. Janice C. Simpson, "Nonprofit Groups' Push for Profits Riles Many Small-Business Owners," *Wall Street Journal*, May 12, 1987, p. 35.

3. Paul B. Firstenberg, "Profit-Minded Management in the Non-Profit World," *Management Review 65* (July 1976): 8.

4. See "Reflections of a Businessman in Washington: An Interview with Secretary of the Treasury W. Michael Blumenthal," *Fortune*, January 29, 1979, for one person's perception of how great the differences are.

5. Burton A. Weisbrod, "The Forgotten Economic Sector: Private but Nonprofit," *Challenge*, September–October 1978, p. 34.

6. Cecily Cannon Selby, "Better Performance from Nonprofits," *Harvard Business Review 56* (September–October 1978): 93.

7. Phillip Kotler, "Strategies for Introducing Marketing into Nonprofit Organizations," *Journal of Marketing* 43 (January 1979): 37.

8. Selby, "Better Performance from Nonprofits," p. 97.

9. Fred Luthans and Jerry L. Sellantin, "MBO in Hospitals: A Step Toward Accountability," *Personnel Administrator* 21 (October 1976): 44.

10. L.B. Fox III, B. Seaton, and R.H. Vogel, "The Application of Marketing to Hospital Management," *Proceedings of the 1976 Conference of the Southern Marketing Association*, pp. 130–132.

11. "Leadership and Community Development: An Innovative Approach," *Proceedings of the Southwestern Management Association*, 1984.

12. Agency Review Report, conducted by United Way volunteer task force, Mobile, Alabama, October 23, 1984.

13. *Improving Productivity in State and Local Government* (Committee for Economic Development, 477 Madison Avenue, New York, NY, March 1976), pp. 69–71.

SUGGESTIONS FOR FURTHER STUDY

ALLAN, PETER. "Managers at Work: A Large-Scale Study of the Managerial Job in New York City Government." *Academy of Management Journal* 24 (September 1981): 613–619.

Cox, Meg. "Fund Raising, Computers and Low-Tech: Memos on a Major Meeting of Museums." *Wall Street Journal*, June 12, 1987, p. 39.

Drucker, Peter F. "Managing the Third Sector." *Wall Street Journal*, October 3, 1978, p. 26.

Fottler, Myron D. "Is Management Really Generic?" *Academy of Management Review* 6 (January 1981): 1–12.

Gabor, Andrea. "Fund Raising in Trying Times." *U.S. News & World Report*, May 4, 1987, p. 53.

Modic, Stanley J. "Associations: Shaking Foundations." *Industry Week*, September 21, 1987, pp. 18–19.

Ricklefs, Roger. "Campus Cutbacks: Some Colleges Drop Whole Departments to Meet Fiscal Crunch." *Wall Street Journal*, September 11, 1981, p. 1.

Simpson, Janice C. "Nonprofit Groups' Push for Profits Riles Many Small-Business Owners." *Wall Street Journal*, May 12, 1987, p. 35.

Waldholz, Michael. "Financial Cure? Some Hospitals Are Entering Diverse Businesses, Often Unrelated to Medicine, to Offset Losses." *Wall Street Journal*, August 12, 1981, p. 46.

Whorten, Joseph W., and Worthley, John A. "A Perspective on the Challenge of Public Management: Environmental Paradox and Organizational Culture." *Academy of Management Review* 6 (July 1981): 357–361.

19
Social Responsibility and Managerial Ethics

Learning Objectives

After studying the material in this chapter, you should be able to do the following:
□ Tell what social responsibility is.
□ Discuss how the concept of social responsibility has evolved.
□ Describe what types of action plans are needed to fulfill management's social responsibility.
□ Explain the need to balance social responsibility and profits.
□ Describe what managerial ethics are and discuss some aspects of management in which they are involved.

Outline of the Chapter

What is social responsibility?
Examples of social responsibility
Two perspectives of social responsibility
Emerging views of social responsibility
Profit maximization period
Trusteeship management period
Period of activism
Social responsiveness period
Social responsibility in action
Employee relations
Public and community service
Environmental protection
Consumerism
Educational and other forms of assistance
Urban renewal and development
Culture, arts, and recreation

Social responsibility and financial performance
Evidence that social responsibility is profitable
Evidence that social responsibility is not profitable
Synthesis of opinion
The growing problem of maintaining managerial ethics
Bribery
Industrial theft and espionage
Conflict of interest
Advertising abuses
Collusion
Fraud
Developing ethical standards
Evaluating ethical and social performance
Responsible behavior requires improvements in managerial skills
Use of social audits and codes of ethics
Summary

Some Important Terms

social responsibility
Protestant (work) ethic
trusteeship management
equal employment opportunity (EEO)
consumerism
affirmative action (AA)
handicapped

environmental protection
ecology
conservation
recycling
pollution
managerial ethics
social audit
code of ethics

Business has a soul, and management has social responsibilities as a major partner in the community, alongside capital and labor.

—OLIVER SHELDON,
The Philosophy of Management, 1923

Merck Gives Away "Miracle Drug"[1]

Merck and Company, a New Jersey pharmaceutical giant, announced on October 21, 1987, that it was giving away what has been called a "miracle drug" to virtually rid the world of a disease threatening to blind millions in the Third World. The drug was said to offer a cure to millions of people, in more than 30 developing countries, for "river blindness," spread by blackflies, which thrive near fast-flowing rivers. The sickness causes intense itching, weight loss, disfiguring skin irritations, and blindness.

The company's announcement of its discovery, ivermectin, was praised by the U.S. and French governments and the head of the World Health Organization as an act of generosity. Merck chairman P. Roy Vagelos said the drug, bearing the brand name Mectizan, was approved for human use by French drug officials on October 21, clearing the way for Merck to begin making it available worldwide. It was expected that this socially responsible act would restore and preserve the joy of sight for millions of human beings.

The drug, which is one of the truly extraordinary health discoveries of our times, was discovered by Merck scientists in 1975 during research on animal parasites.

Why do you think Merck officials took this extraordinary step? ■

THIS CASE ILLUSTRATES the present tendency of U.S. managers—to act ethically and to be socially responsible. To be sure, companies have exercised social responsibility for a long time. For example, the Carnegie Foundation, with resources from Carnegie Steel, has endowed libraries and made numerous grants to colleges and universities since the turn of the century. The Ford Foundation, with resources from Ford Motor Company, has provided consulting assistance for agricultural and management development programs in many developing countries.

But the meaning of the term *social responsibility,* as well as its importance to those managing profit and not-for-profit organizations, has changed significantly in recent years. Business firms have historically been asked to use their resources efficiently to produce goods and services that customers want and to sell them at prices customers are willing and able to pay. It was felt that if this was done effectively, profits would be made, and the material well-being of society would be the greatest. This view meant that managers were permitted to optimize profits within the rules of the game set up by custom and the law. Now the view is changing, as we'll see.

WHAT IS SOCIAL RESPONSIBILITY?

There are many widely differing explanations of what is meant by the term **social responsibility.** Essentially, however, it means management's obligation to set policies, make decisions, and follow courses of action that are desirable in terms of the values and objectives of society. Some other terms for this concept are *social action*, *public affairs*, *community activities*, *social challenges*, and *social concern*.

Examples of Social Responsibility

No matter what term they use, however, most managers seem to have adapted to the changed thinking about their responsibility to society. In fact, many corporations have set up committees, special offices, or departments for this purpose.

> *For example, Aetna Life & Casualty has a Corporate Social Responsibility Department; Allied Corporation has a senior vice-president to oversee public and government affairs; General Electric has a Public Issues Committee of the Board; INA, a major insurance firm, has the position of Executive Vice-President, Legal and Government Affairs; and GM has appointed a full-time executive, Dr. Betsy Ancker-Johnson, just to handle environmental and safety problems.*

Many firms have unique programs for dealing with the public's demand for socially responsible actions. Sperry Rand, for example, encourages operating managers to help the community with social development. Allied Corporation includes managers' community service in performance evaluations for bonuses. Procter & Gamble encourages its executives to participate in student groups, such as Junior Achievement. IBM sponsors a management training program for executives of not-for-profit organizations. The five-day program, taught by IBM's own management development personnel, tries to improve skills in people management and leadership, planning, and finance. IBM also gives executives paid leave to perform community service, and it was the lead company for Summer Jobs '87, a youth summer employment program sponsored by the New York City Partnership, Inc., a coalition of businesses, educational institutions, and not-for-profit organizations to improve social and economic conditions in the city.[2]

Two Perspectives of Social Responsibility

There are many perspectives on the extent to which management should practice social responsibility. While no reputable management authority argues *against* social responsibility itself, there is disagreement as to the extent to which it should be carried. The views vary from the *limited*, or *restricted*, view to the *unlimited*, or *extensive*, view.

The limited view. The best-known proponent of the limited view of social responsibility is Milton Friedman, the Nobel Prize–winning economist. He argues that making business managers responsible both to business owners—for reaching profit objectives—and also to society—for enhancing the general welfare—represents a conflict of interest that has the potential of causing the death of business as it is known today. According to Friedman, this will almost certainly happen if business is continually forced to perform acts that are in direct conflict with private organizational objectives. Finally, he argues that managers are employees of the owners, not the public, and so should act for the owners. Moreover, the costs of social responsibility are passed on to consumers as higher prices, and this is "taxation without representation."[3]

The extensive view. The argument for the extensive, or unlimited, view begins with the premise that business is a major segment of society and exerts a significant impact on the way society exists. Moreover, since business is so influential, it is responsible for helping maintain and improve the overall welfare of society. Since society asks no more and no less of any of its members, why should business be exempt from such responsibility?

Some authorities also argue that business should perform socially responsible activities because profitability and growth go hand in hand with responsible treatment of groups such as employees, customers, and the community.[4] In essence, this argument implies that being socially responsible is a means of earning greater organizational credibility and profit.

What is your view?

Do you think the action of Merck and Company will give it greater credibility as an ethical company in the medical and pharmaceutical communities?

Arguments for and against social responsibility. There are many more arguments for and against social responsibility. Some of these are presented in TIPS 19.1. They should help you to determine your own beliefs as to what role social responsibility should play.

What is your view?

Which perspective do you think is the more desirable? Which is the more defensible in a free-enterprise system?

EMERGING VIEWS OF SOCIAL RESPONSIBILITY

It is now assumed that managers—especially of large firms—have an obligation to see that employees, consumers, and the general public—as well as the owners—are treated fairly. This is quite a change from the philosophy held by the Supreme Court of Michigan in 1919 when Henry Ford wanted to use his large profits to reduce the prices of his cars so that more people could buy them. The Court ruled against him, saying that "a business corporation is organized and carried on primarily for the profit of the stockholders."[5]

Today, the judicial system, and the government as a whole, are strong advocates of social responsibility, often forcing business owners and managers to act more responsibly.

The concepts of social responsibility have evolved through four periods, namely, (1) profit maximization, (2) trusteeship management, (3) activism, and (4) social responsiveness.[6] Because it is difficult to date these periods precisely, the following time periods are only approximations.

Profit Maximization Period

This period actually started in antiquity. Even then, however, efforts were made to enforce responsiveness. For example, in Sumer (present-day Iraq), the government tried nearly 5000 years ago to enforce minimum wages and improve employee working conditions. Nearly 4000 years ago, the Code of Hammurabi (king of Babylon) contained several laws relating to business, especially employer liability and minimum wages for workers.

TIPS 19.1   Some Arguments FOR and AGAINST Business Performing Socially Responsible Activities

Major arguments FOR

1. It is the ethical thing to do.
2. It is in the best interest of a business to promote and improve the communities where it does business.
3. It improves management's public image.
4. It may increase the viability of the business system. Business exists because it gives society benefits, and society can amend or take away its charter.
5. Sociocultural norms require it.
6. It is necessary in order to avoid government regulation.
7. Society should give business a chance to solve social problems that government has been unable to solve.
8. Business is considered by some groups to be the only institution with the financial and human resources needed to solve social problems.
9. Prevention of problems is better than cures—so let business solve problems before they become too great.
10. Laws cannot be passed for all circumstances, so business must assume responsibility for maintaining an orderly legal society.
11. It is in the stockholders' best interest. It will improve the price of stock in the long run because the stock market will view the company as less risky and open to public attack and therefore award it a higher price-earnings ratio.
12. Social actions can be profitable.

Major arguments AGAINST

1. It might be illegal.
2. Business plus government equals tremendous power.
3. Business already has too much power, and such involvement might make business too powerful.
4. The cost of social responsibility is too great, and it would increase prices too much.
5. Business managers tend to lack the skills to solve social problems.
6. It would dilute business's primary mission or purpose, which is to balance the interests of customers, employees, the public, and owners, in order to survive.
7. It would weaken the U.S. balance of payments because the price of goods might have to go up to pay for social programs.
8. Business lacks accountability to the public; so the public would have no control over its social involvement.
9. Such business involvement lacks broad public support.
10. Social actions cannot be measured, and so it is difficult to control their cost.
11. Social responsibility violates profit maximization.

SOURCE: Adapted from Joseph W. McGuire, *Contemporary Management* (Englewood Cliffs, NJ: Prentice-Hall, 1974), p. 616. Reprinted by permission of Prentice-Hall, Inc.

Later, during the Industrial Revolution, restrictions on business declined, especially in England. The principles guiding managers were John Locke's philosophy of ownership of private property—which was to be protected by government—and Adam Smith's belief that the well-being of society is enhanced when business acts on its own, guided by the "invisible hand" of the marketplace. These principles were later incorporated into the U.S. Constitution.

These principles, plus the **Protestant (work) ethic,** which emphasizes hard work and industry, productivity, thrift, and frugality, guided U.S. business owner-managers from about 1800 to the early 1930s. Entrepreneurs like John D. Rockefeller, Andrew Carnegie, and Henry Ford concentrated on increasing efficiency to lower prices—so more people could afford their products—and to maximize profits for owners. Those profits were then used to foster economic growth and help society. These capitalists were enlightened to the point of improving products, working conditions, and wages.

For example, Ford doubled his workers' wages in 1914—from $2.50 to $5.00 a day—in order to attract the best workers, improve productivity, and lower the cost/price of his "Tin Lizzie" so more people could buy them.

Other capitalists, however, known as "robber barons," weren't so socially aware. Many of them believed that employees, like other resources, were to be hired, exploited, and then discarded when no longer productive. These entrepreneurs felt they were not accountable to anyone, especially not to consumers. Railroad tycoon William H. Vanderbilt best expressed this thought in 1882 when he said, "The public be damned. I'm working for my stockholders."[7]

These and other abuses led to a concentration of wealth and power that caused the public to demand government regulation. Thus, the Interstate Commerce Act (1887) prohibited unjust and unreasonable shipping rates, as well as kickbacks and favorable rates to favored customers. The Sherman Anti-Trust Act (1890) restricted combinations and conspiracies to monopolize and restrict trade. The Pure Food and Drug Law (1906) was a direct result of Upton Sinclair's book *The Jungle*, which vividly described the unsanitary and unsafe working conditions in the meat-packing industry.[8]

Trusteeship Management Period

The second period, **trusteeship management,** during which the government and professional business managers began to be concerned for employees, customers, and the community while protecting the interests of stockholders, began in the 1930s following the Great Depression. Just a few of the laws passed at that time to protect employees were the Wagner Act (1935), which gave employees the right to join unions and bargain collectively against management; the Social Security Act (1935), which provided for unemployment insurance and old-age and survivors' and disability benefits; and the Wage and Hour Law (1938), which set minimum wages and maximum hours to be worked and restricted child labor.

Many laws were also passed to protect consumers. Some of these were the Wheeler-Lea Act (1938), which enlarged the power of the Federal Trade Commission (FTC) to prevent unfair competition and false advertising, and amendments to the Pure Food and Drug Act (1938), which added cosmetics to the list of products covered.

The Securities Act (1933) and Securities Exchange Act (1934) gave a measure of protection to investors.

Period of Activism

This third period began with the activism of the early 1960s. There were several streams of activities, or movements, during this period that drastically and permanently changed the way managers operate. The main movements were in the areas of equal employment opportunity, environmental protection, and consumerism.

Equal employment opportunity. The civil rights marches in the early 1960s were reinforced by the Civil Rights Act (1964), as amended, and a series of other remedial laws. These resulted in **equal employment opportunity**

(EEO), which means that employment opportunities are fully available to anyone, including minorities, women, Vietnam veterans, and older and disabled workers. The Equal Employment Opportunity Commission (EEOC) is the primary guardian of these rights.

Environmental protection. The Clean Air Act (1963) really started the movement toward environmental control, although there were environmental laws as far back as 1899 (the Refuse Act). Later, all aspects of the environment—air, solid waste, toxic substances, nuclear energy, and water—were to be included for protection. The National Environmental Policy Act (1969) set up the Environmental Protection Agency (EPA) to guard the public's interest.

Consumerism. In 1962, President John Kennedy, in a special message to Congress, asked for protection of the following consumer rights:

1. The right to safety, or protection against goods that may be hazardous to health or life.

2. The right to be informed, or protection against fraudulent, deceitful, or grossly misleading information, advertising, labeling, and other practices, and to the receipt of facts needed to make an informed choice.

3. The right to choose, including the assurance of access to a variety of products and services at competitive prices.

4. The right to be heard, including the assurance that consumer interests will receive full and sympathetic consideration in the creation of government policy.

These rights became the basis of the consumerism movement.

Consumerism is the organized effort of independent, government, and business groups to protect consumers from undesirable effects resulting from poorly designed and produced products. In 1966, Congress passed the Traffic and Motor Vehicle Safety Act, which is administered by the National Highway Traffic Safety Administration (NHTSA). The act required manufacturers to notify new car purchasers of safety defects discovered after manufacture and delivery. Next came the Child Protection and Toy Safety Act (1969), which provided greater protection from children's toys with dangerous mechanical or electrical hazards. The Consumer Product Safety Act (1972) empowered the Consumer Product Safety Commission (CPSC) to set safety standards, require warning labels on potentially unsafe products, and order recalls of hazardous products.

Social Responsiveness Period

As indicated earlier, because large modern businesses have become such power centers in the economic, social, and political realms, their managers have a special responsibility. Most indications are that managers now accept that responsibility and are responsive to the needs of all groups, and "stockholders have no special priority."[9] This social responsiveness was exemplified by Johnson & Johnson during the "Tylenol scare," as shown by MAP 19.1.

To what extent are U.S. managers socially responsive? A recent survey of 116 corporate CEOs found broad and deep support for some basic social responsibility assumptions. Table 19.1 shows the percentage of CEOs agreeing strongly or mildly with six basic assumptions.

Management Application and Practice 19.1   The Tylenol Scare—Social Responsibility in Action

McNeil Consumer Products Company, a subsidiary of Johnson & Johnson (J&J), introduced Tylenol as a prescription drug in 1955 when aspirin was found to be potentially harmful, especially to children. In the mid-1960s, J&J converted Tylenol into an over-the-counter consumer product to compete with Anacin, Bufferin, and Bayer.

Tylenol had 7 to 8 percent of the painkiller market by 1975 when Datril, a competing product, was introduced at a lower price by Bristol-Myers. J&J retaliated by reducing prices, increasing advertising, and resorting to several lawsuits to beat out its competition. In three years, Tylenol had become the best-seller. After spending over $85 million on advertising from 1978 to 1982, Tylenol had 37 percent of the painkiller market and was increasing that share by 2 to 3 percent each year.

Then tragedy struck. In October 1982, seven people died in Chicago from cyanide-laced Extra-Strength Tylenol capsules. Although it was proven that the tampering was done on retail store shelves and not at the factory, Tylenol's sales dropped 80 percent—to 12 percent of the market—by November.

J&J's management immediately stopped producing Tylenol, recalled 22 million bottles of capsules, offered a $100,000 reward for information leading to the arrest of the guilty party or parties, and opened up toll-free lines to answer customer concerns. Since 80 percent of its customers bought Tylenol on the recommendation of their doctors, J&J also used telegrams, telephone calls, and visits by sales representatives to reassure physicians and pharmacists all over the country.

At that point, management had three alternatives: (1) do nothing and hope that people would buy the product again after the crisis was over, (2) bring the product out under another name, and (3) do everything possible to protect J&J's good reputation and recover Tylenol's lost customers. Since sales of Tylenol totaled $400 million a year and profits were $80 million—17 percent of J&J's earnings—management committed itself to rebuilding Tylenol's name.

First, a three-way safety-sealed package was designed. Then, at news conferences and on television talk shows, the chairmen of McNeil and J&J demonstrated to the public how safe and secure the product was. They explained that Tylenol would cost no more because of the new packaging and that the U.S. Food and Drug Administration had cleared J&J of any imputation of negligence or wrongdoing. Retailers and customers were reimbursed for any capsules thrown away, and a 25 percent discount was given to retailers for Tylenol purchases at or above precrisis levels. Also, $1.00 discount coupons on the new safety-sealed capsules appeared in newspapers, magazines, and mailboxes. These coupons went out before customers had had a chance to replace their discarded Tylenol with a competing brand.

The company paid the entire cost of these activities—over $100 million—but the effort paid off. Within 15 months, Tylenol had recaptured over 30 percent of the total market. Later, after another scare, J&J quit making Tylenol capsules altogether. Now it produces only tablets and caplets.

SOURCE: Various sources, including correspondence with Johnson & Johnson.

SOCIAL RESPONSIBILITY IN ACTION

Social responsibility can best be illustrated in terms of specific action programs that management undertakes. These programs usually include—but are not limited to—activities in such areas as (1) employee relations, (2) public and community service, (3) environmental protection, (4) consumer-

**TABLE 19.1
Top Management
Support for Selected
Social Responsibility
Assumptions**

SOURCE: Based on Robert Ford
and Frank McLaughlin,
''Perceptions of Socially
Responsible Activities and
Attitudes: A Comparison of
Business School Deans and
Corporate Chief Executives,''
*Academy of Management
Journal* 27 (September 1984):
670.

Assumptions about social responsibility	Percentage of corporate chief executive officers agreeing with each assumption
Responsible corporate behavior can be in the best economic interest of the stockholders.	92%
Efficient production of goods and services is no longer the only thing society expects from business.	89
Long-run success in business depends on its ability to understand that it is part of a larger society and to behave accordingly.	87
Involvement by business in improving its community's quality of life will also improve long-run profitability.	78
A business that wishes to capture a favorable public image will have to show that it is socially responsible.	78
If business is more socially responsible, it will discourage additional regulation of the economic system by government.	71

ism, (5) educational and medical assistance, (6) urban renewal and development, and (7) culture, the arts, and recreation.

Companies participating in these programs have received national acclaim from the president (see MAP 19.2), and employees who have made substantial contributions may be recognized by their management.

For example, Levi Strauss & Company publishes a monthly volunteer newsletter. Its 75 employee "community involvement teams" figure out charitable fund-raising schemes during work hours.

In 1886, Richardson-Vicks Inc. began honoring its five best volunteers. Each recipient now gets a $1000 check for a favorite social-service group.[10]

Employee Relations

American managers are now much more employee oriented than before the 1960s. There is a growing interest in and concern for employee rights, especially regarding employment, promotions, pay, and safety.

Equal employment opportunity. As discussed in Chapter 9 and earlier in this chapter, employees' rights are now protected by the Equal Employment Opportunity Commission (EEOC) and the U.S. Department of Labor. Current EEO regulations make it unlawful for any employer to discriminate against any person because of race, creed, color, religion, sex, nation of origin, age, or disability. These laws cover all aspects of employment from recruiting to termination or retirement. Managers must do more than just *not* discriminate; they must take **affirmative action (AA)** to actively seek out members of these protected groups, hire them, train and develop them, and move them into better positions in the firm.

Women and minorities. Much progress has been made in this area, especially in the employment of women, but much more is needed. More than

◖ **Management Application and Practice 19.2 Firms Hailed for Heart**

President Reagan honored 100 USA corporations and associations for community involvement.

Among recipients of presidential citations:

Trailways for a year-old Home Free program that has provided 4000 runaway youngsters free rides home.

Safeway for printing pictures of missing children on milk cartons and bags; in five months three kids were found.

Mobil Oil Corp. for a $1.5 million summer job program that employed 2000 low-income youths.

American Automobile Association for training and buying gear for school safety patrol officers around the country.

B. Dalton Booksellers for a $3 million four-year literacy program now involving 16,000 volunteers in 105 communities.

Trailways Chairman Jim Kerrigan says, "It's great for morale; for people to see . . . that as corporate strategy we do something besides pursuing the dollar."

SOURCE: Lorrie Lynch, "Firms Hailed for Heart," *USA Today*, June 14, 1985, p. 1A.

half the women in the United States are now working or looking for work outside the home. During the last three decades, two out of every three new jobs have been filled by women. But women are still concentrated in sex-stereotyped jobs.

For blacks, the figures are also mixed. Nearly 14 percent of blacks in the work force (as compared to 17 percent of whites) are in professional and technical jobs. But only 6 percent of blacks are managers, and only 4 percent of all corporate officials and managers are black. Yet it has been nearly 20 years since the Reverend Leon H. Sullivan became the first black member of GM's board of directors in 1971.[11]

Although discrimination still exists, most firms now accept and implement EEO. For instance, in 1983, Coca-Cola sold part of its stock in its New York bottling company to Bruce Lloweyn, a black businessman, and to entertainer Bill Cosby and Philadelphia '76ers forward Julius Erving.[12]

The handicapped. The Vocational Rehabilitation Act (1973) was passed to prevent discrimination against the **handicapped,** which includes anyone with a physical or mental disability that substantially restricts major normal activities such as walking, seeing, speaking, working, or learning. The more progressive firms are responding positively. For example, Eastman Kodak has over 75 deaf employees in its apparatus-manufacturing arm, and there is at least one deaf tool-and-die maker in its U.S. Equipment Division.[13]

Older workers. During the 1960s, there was a decline in hiring and an increase in firing and forced early retirement of older workers to make room for younger ones. The Age Discrimination in Employment Act (1962), as amended, tries to prevent discrimination against people over the age of 39. Mandatory retirement is now prohibited, and employers must continue contributing to pension plans for those continuing to work beyond age 65.

In order to encourage older managers to leave and make room for younger ones, many employers are offering lucrative early retirement plans. In fact, 16 of the largest industrial firms made such offers in 1986. But several lawsuits have been filed charging that these plans are a form of age discrimination.

> *For example, T. W. Brehmer, the 65-year-old director of Du Pont Company's Thailand office, thought his 43 years of service should make him eligible for Du Pont's "lucrative early retirement plan." But he was told that, as a more senior executive, he wasn't eligible for it. Now, he is among a group of older employees suing the firm, charging that its plan is in effect a form of age discrimination.*[14]

Maintaining safety and health. An important aspect of employee relations is maintaining employee safety and health. While management has been active in this area for a long time, the Occupational Safety and Health Act (1970) forced even speedier action. The law is enforced by the Occupational Safety and Health Administration (OSHA), which concentrates inspections in those industries with the highest accident rates.

Public and Community Service

Some business managers feel that their services belong to the community as well as to their employer. While this concept is not new, the extent to which employers are formalizing such programs to permit their personnel to help in civic and community activities, such as the United Way, Girl and Boy Scouts, and the Red Cross, is new.

Employee volunteerism—which, as shown in Chapter 18, is the lifeblood of not-for-profit organizations, is now on the rise as business managers escalate their public service efforts. For example, Volunteer—The National Center, an Arlington, Virginia, nonprofit group, found that more than 500 companies have organized programs to encourage worker involvement in community service, up from about 300 in 1979.[15] This movement polishes corporate images despite scarce funds for other forms of philanthropy. Some companies maintain employee skill banks for community groups, while others give workers time off to help out. Corporate volunteer councils participate in joint projects in many cities.

> *Xerox has a Social Service Leave Program that pays an employee full salary for a year to perform public service. Peter Neidecker, a senior marketing executive who lived and worked in a plush area of Portland, Oregon, left it for the city's streets, alleys, night shelters, and soup kitchens, helping the poor and homeless. He found jobs for the unemployed, helped train people for work, gave counseling, and visited the poor.*[16]

Another form of public service is making and paying for ads or announcements contributing to public safety and security. For example, Barber Milk Company, a Birmingham, Alabama, firm, puts National Child Safety Council messages on cartons of milk likely to be used by children (see Figure 19.1). Photographs and descriptions of missing children also appear on many grocery bags, milk cartons, and other containers.

Environmental Protection

Environmental protection is maintaining a healthy balance between elements of the **ecology,** which is the relationship between living things—especially people—and their environment. These relationships are complex

FIGURE 19.1
Example of social
service type ad.

and fragile. While almost everyone believes that they should be preserved, the real problem is how to maintain a balance between the use of natural resources now and conservation of them for future generations.

Unfortunately, we don't always know when we're upsetting that balance. For example, scientists tell us that the carbon dioxide generated by burning fossil fuels—coal, gas, oil, and wood—may be holding in the earth's heat and causing the polar ice caps and glaciers to melt, the so-called greenhouse effect. And even after becoming aware of problems, it's difficult to balance economic needs with ecological ones.

For example, while coal is a relatively cheap energy source, there are two problems with its use. First, much of eastern U.S. coal is high in sulfur, and burning it can result in acid rain. While western coal is purer, the best way to extract it is by strip mining, which destroys terrain that then must be returned to its original state at a high cost.

A socially responsible environmental protection program involves two steps: conserving natural resources and preventing pollution. Such programs may be difficult and expensive to implement.

Conservation. **Conservation** is practicing the most effective use of resources, considering society's present and future needs. Conservation can be achieved by limiting the exploitation of scarce resources. We are trying to do this with energy sources. For example, automakers are producing more fuel-efficient cars, and we are using our cars less, so petroleum use is increasing only slightly.

Recycling, which is reprocessing used items for further use, is another form of conservation. Many companies use recycled paper letterheads. Reynolds Aluminum, which began its recycling program in 1968, and Alcoa pay for the return of used cans, from which new aluminum products can be made much more cheaply than from raw materials. As shown in Figure 19.2, 51 percent of all new cans come from recycled ones. This is now a $93

FIGURE 19.2
Aluminum recycling is growing in popularity.

SOURCE: The Aluminum Association, Inc., Alcoa, as reported in *USA Today*, March 7–9, 1986.

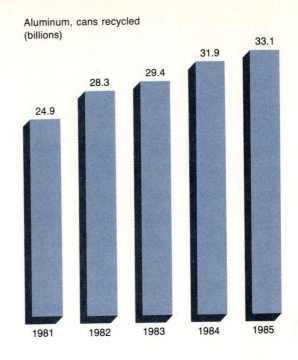

Aluminum, cans recycled (billions)

million-a-year business. Companies are now experimenting with machines that automatically weigh the cans and dispense the correct cash reward.[17]

Although trees are called "our renewable resource," prudent forest management is required to assure their most efficient use. The U.S. Forestry Service and state forestry agencies protect national and state timberlands from unwise cutting or extraction of minerals. The U.S. Department of the Interior shares responsibility for conservation of natural resources, especially on government-owned land.

Pollution control. Pollution, which is the contamination or destruction of the natural environment, is one of our greatest problems. Management efforts to prevent or control air, land, water, and noise pollution are major goals of responsible companies.

The Environmental Protection Agency (EPA) is responsible for protecting the air and water and regulating chemical and toxic waste disposal and seeing that these wastes are cleaned up when accidents or violations occur. The Nuclear Regulatory Commission (NRC) licenses nuclear power plants and sets standards for their construction and use. When there is an accident, such as the release of radioactive matter at Three Mile Island, the NRC sees that it is cleaned up and that action is taken to prevent recurrence.

Companies and governments have taken actions to reduce pollution. For instance, Mobil Oil Corporation spent $25 million on a state-of-the-art water treatment system so that the water returned to the Delaware River by Mobil's Paulsboro, New Jersey, refinery was of better quality than the water entering it.[18]

Sometimes, however, a cost-benefit analysis convinces management that antipollution measures are too costly—or impossible to implement—and the facilities are closed. For example, Phelps Dodge Corporation operated a copper smelter at Douglas, Arizona, for nearly 80 years. But after failing to meet clean-air laws for more than a decade, the company closed the smelter in 1987 rather than spend the millions of dollars required to control sulfur dioxide emissions. The closure left many of the 347 employees and 13,000 town residents saddened—and left a $10 million hole in the town's economy.[19]

Consumerism

The old saying that "the customer is always right" may not be true, but at least managers are now truly concerned about consumers' needs and wishes. The movement to protect the interests of consumers is a major force in the world of business and government. Over 500 state and local groups, as well as over 100 national ones, have sprung up around the nation to speak for—and support legislation to protect—consumers. And since President Kennedy's previously mentioned 1962 speech, consumers have more rights to know what is in products as well as more protection against mislabeling and false advertising.

(Copyright 1987 by Universal Press Syndicate.)

For example, on June 24, 1987, Chrysler Corporation and two of its senior executives were hit with a federal indictment charging them with selling as new more than 60,000 cars and trucks whose odometers had been tampered with. The company faced a maximum fine of $120 million if convicted on all 16 counts of conspiracy to commit mail fraud, wire fraud, and odometer fraud.

While the indictment was only for the 18-month period beginning in July 1985, it charged that the practice went back to 1949 and that "millions of cars were sold to consumers under the same circumstances."[20]

Many of the cars had been driven up to 400 miles, for periods ranging from "a few days to five weeks," with their odometers disconnected.[21] Some of the cars had even been involved in accidents and repaired before the odometers were reconnected. They were sold as "new models."[22]

Chrysler maintained that it had done nothing wrong but, on the contrary, was helping consumers by seeing that its cars were built up to quality standards. The executives were only subjecting the cars to even more rigorous testing, and the odometers were disconnected to prolong the customers' warranty.

Under existing consumer protection laws, you have the right to know your true interest rate (APR) on loans and to see your credit rating and have factual errors corrected. Consumers also have more rights and protection against dangerous or contaminated food and drugs.

In 1987, a big consumer issue was delayed airline flights, overbooking, and lost baggage. Many passengers viewed the airlines as antagonists rather than providers of a useful service for customers.

Educational and Other Forms of Assistance

Business managers continue to cooperate with educational institutions to set up new programs and upgrade old ones. While graduates are giving large amounts of money to colleges and universities, they may not realize that the business community, including their own employers and related foundations, gives almost as much. The private business sector gave $7.4 billion in gifts to colleges and universities in 1985 and 1986, as shown in Figure 19.3.

Another example of educational assistance was given by such corporations as Apple, Control Data, Data General, Digital Equipment Corporation (DEC), and IBM, which donated about $100 million worth of computer hardware to schools in one year.[23]

Entrepreneurs and managers are increasingly helping provide medical assistance to those who can't afford it. For example, Scott Paper Company has created a complete line of seven products, a portion of whose sales *always* goes to charity. A nickel of the purchase price of Helping Hand toilet paper, napkins, and other products is designated for groups such as the March of Dimes. Scott expects to give $1 million to these groups each year.[24] Actor Paul Newman is a high-profile corporate owner setting an example by helping people with medical problems. From the $9 million profit he had made from Newman's Own, the salad dressing and spaghetti sauce business he and writer A. E. Hotchner started in 1982, Newman and his wife, actress Joanne Woodward, built the $8 million "Hole in the Wall Gang" camp in Connecticut in 1986 and 1987. The camp, complete with log cabins, music halls, corrals, and canoes, is for children ages 7 to 17 with "life-threatening diseases."[25]

FIGURE 19.3
Business and other contributions to colleges and universities. Since 1976, total giving to colleges has tripled, and business contributions have risen four times over.

SOURCE: "Education: A Capital Investment." Advertisement by the Council for Aid to Education (CFAE).

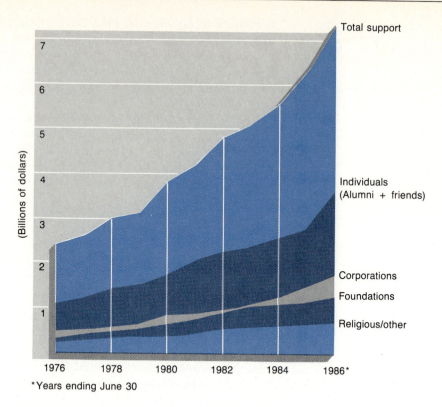

Urban Renewal and Development

Many responsive companies also help with urban renewal and development. For example, Ralston Purina Company, the giant agribusiness firm, spent $4.5 million to help the city of St. Louis rehabilitate the area around its headquarters, with favorable reaction from the community.

Culture, Arts, and Recreation

Companies have been contributing to culture, the arts, and recreation for a long time. For example, Mobil Oil sponsors many cultural and news programs on public TV, and Texaco has sponsored *The Metropolitan Opera on the Air* since the 1930s. Also, when the Eastern Shore Chamber of Commerce made plans to convert a scenic overlook on Interstate 10 into a welcome center in 1987, See Coast Manufacturing Company, Inc., of Fairhope, Alabama, offered to donate two coin-operated telescopes and return the revenue to the welcome center.

SOCIAL RESPONSIBILITY AND FINANCIAL PERFORMANCE

The relationship between social responsiveness and profitability is difficult to establish because (1) it is difficult to define socially responsible actions, and (2) it is practically impossible to measure the consequences of social responsiveness. For example, is management only being socially responsible

Paul Newman and Joanne Woodward. With business profits from Newman's Own, they built a camp for children with medical problems.

in replacing a dangerous machine with a newer and safer one, or may the action also improve productivity and profits and reduce taxes?

What is your view?

While the management of Johnson & Johnson acted quite responsibly in the Tylenol crisis (see MAP 19.1), wasn't it also acting to protect profits by minimizing losses? Did it have to choose between acting profitably and acting responsibly?

Evidence That Social Responsibility Is Profitable

There is much evidence that acting responsibly does "pay off" financially. For example, a poll of nearly 6000 executives by *Fortune* on the "community and environmental responsibility" of the 10 largest U.S. companies in the 20 largest industries found Eastman Kodak, IBM, and Johnson & Johnson the top three. On ratings of financial soundness, the survey found IBM and J&J among the top three companies, thereby matching their high social responsibility rating.[26] Other enthusiastically responsible entrepreneurs have similarly found that social responsibility is profitable.

For example, Jeno Palucci has built a fortune on the concept of combining philanthropy and business. It is difficult to separate his private business actions from his public philanthropy. The Duluth vegetable peddler converted a field of bean sprouts into Chun King Foods, which he then sold to R. J. Reynolds Industries Inc. for $60 million. Next, Pillsbury Company offered him about $200 million for his frozen pizza business, Jeno's. So he launched Pizza Kwik, a chain of pizza delivery shops.

These ventures made him a fortune. At the same time, he has spent much of his time using his business skills and the force of his personality to perform unorthodox socially responsive activities, such as handing out pizzas to the unemployed on a frozen New Year's Eve, selling moccasins to a Sears, Roebuck buyer on behalf of a struggling Indian tribe, inaugu-

rating and participating in a statewide program to aid the hungry in St. Paul, Minnesota, and lobbying for the rights of the homeless in Washington.

Despite this enlightened attitude toward social responsibility, he also admits that he does nothing that isn't a very good business decision.[27]

Other companies have also found that good business practice, social responsibility, and profit are inseparable.

Evidence That Social Responsibility Is Not Profitable

Of course, some social programs may not provide a profit—or may even reduce profits. For example, if a firm installs expensive antipollution devices and the costs can't be passed on to consumers, its profits will probably be lower than before.

A recent study of mutual funds indicated the problems involved in relating social responsibility to financial performance. First, there's the question, "What are the determining characteristics of social responsibility?" The answers are often ambiguous and inconclusive. Second, the answer to the question, "Can fund managers apply criteria of social responsibility in buying stocks and still make money?" is often no. For example, a study of eight mutual funds using social and ethical criteria in selecting stocks for their portfolios found that none performed as well in 1986 as the Dow Jones Industrial Average, which rose 22.6 percent. As shown in Figure 19.4, only two funds did better than typical mutual funds, which gained 15.1 percent.[28]

In some instances, socially desirable activities are made possible by more efficient operations. For example, Scott Paper Company could afford the previously mentioned donations to charity because of marketing efficiencies in advertising the entire line as one brand.

Either way, however, the public often winds up paying for activities such as cleaning up the environment. When the EPA imposed further air pollution controls in 1987, motorists had to pay modest price increases. For example, modifications to the automobiles coming out in 1991 would make them cost $19 to $20 more, and it would cost the refineries around 2 cents more per gallon of gas to reduce the pollution, which has been found to result in smog.[29]

Synthesis of Opinion

A definitive study of the relationship between corporate social responsibility and profitability by three reputable scholars concluded that "this study has not been able to corroborate the claims of either advocates or critics as to the value social responsibility may have for industrial organizations."[30] First, the researchers reviewed the literature dealing with this subject from 1972 to 1979 and found that the studies produced varying results. The studies that appeared to be the most methodologically sound did not find a relationship between responsibility and profitability.

Then the authors conducted an in-depth, rigorous questionnaire survey of 241 CEOs listed in the *Forbes 1981 Annual Directory*. "No statistically significant relationship" was found when social responsibility, as shown by "a concern for society," was correlated with "profitability."

The only conclusion we can reach at this time is that there is no definitive

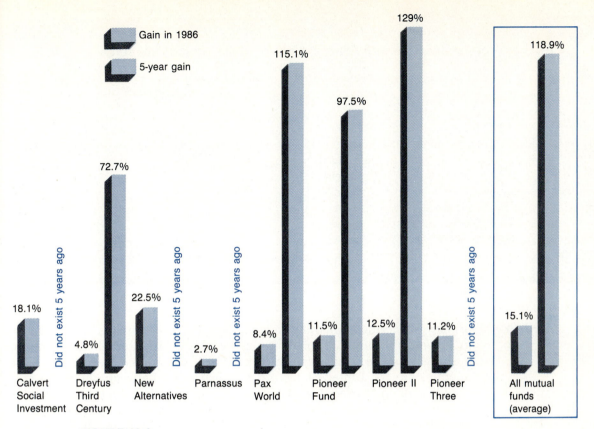

FIGURE 19.4
Performance of ethical funds. Over time, few ethical funds have matched the gains of the typical mutual funds.

SOURCE: *U.S. News & World Report*, January 26, 1987, p. 50. Basic data from Lipper Analytical Services.

answer one way or the other as to whether social responsibility "pays off" financially, but it does help management in other ways.

THE GROWING PROBLEM OF MAINTAINING MANAGERIAL ETHICS

Interest in managerial ethics is increasing at a rapid rate. Business ethics courses are now a growth industry at colleges and universities, and business executives are also displaying more interest in the study of ethics. There are few management development programs that don't cover the subject to some degree. The extent of the ethics problem in the United States is shown in MAP 19.3. Figure 19.5 shows that maintaining ethical behavior is a worldwide problem, not restricted to just the United States.

Managerial ethics are the standards used to judge the rightness or wrongness of a manager's relations to others. Just a few of the managerial activities related to ethical decisions are (1) bribery, (2) industrial theft and espionage, (3) conflict of interest, (4) false and/or misleading advertising, (5) collusion, and (6) fraud.

Management Application and Practice 19.3 Shaky Ethics Widespread

You're not alone if you think the person in the next office is a little shaky when it comes to ethics. Of 722 executives polled by the executive search firm McFeely Wackerle Jett, 84 percent agreed that most people are at large occasionally unethical in their business dealings. Partner Charlie Jett says that reflects the world of business today. "We live in an extremely competitive world, and there are a lot of people who are willing to bend a little bit to get ahead," he says.

Other results from the firm's survey of *Fortune* 1000 professionals at the level of executive vice president or above:

56 percent said people have become less ethical in the past 20 years. Only 8 percent saw an improvement. The remaining 36 percent reported no change.

87 percent agreed that ethics should be taught in every business course.

84 percent said companies should provide all employees with some ethics training.

SOURCE: "How Do Your Office Ethics Compare?" *USA Today*, September 30, 1987, p. 4B.

Bribery

Bribery is offering something of value to a person to influence his or her judgment or conduct. Though it may be part of the normal way of doing business in some foreign countries, bribery is considered illegal, or at least unethical, in the United States. Yet the distinction between gift giving and bribery is often blurred. For instance, a salesperson has the chance to get a big order from a large firm, and the firm's buyer hints that she needs a new motor for her boat. The cost of the boat motor is hidden in the selling company's accounts. Is it bribery or a gift?

Yet managing in foreign countries may be more effective if bribes are involved. For example, in 1975, it was disclosed that in order to sell the TriStar jet to Japanese airlines, Lockheed paid out about $12 million, most of it in bribes. A $1.7 million secret payment was made to Japan's prime

FIGURE 19.5
Ethics in business.

SOURCE: Survey by The Conference Board, as reported in *USA Today*, November 27, 1987, p. 1B.

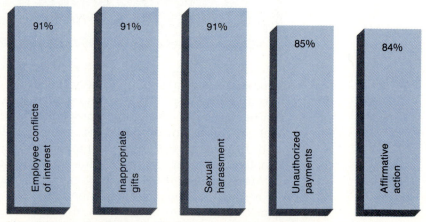

The top ethical issues facing businesses*

Employee conflicts of interest	Inappropriate gifts	Sexual harassment	Unauthorized payments	Affirmative action
91%	91%	91%	85%	84%

*According to more than 80 percent of the CEOs and senior managers surveyed by the International Survey of Corporate Ethics; October survey of 300 companies worldwide.

minister.[31] Although tried and convicted, he was later reelected to Japan's Diet, or Parliament. And Boeing concealed $7.3 million in "commissions" to sell 35 airplanes to Spain, Honduras, Lebanon, and the Dominican Republic.[32]

Industrial Theft and Espionage

In the past, corporate spies have been known to break into an office or plant and steal blueprints or formulas for a new product or process. Now such theft may be more subtle: A rival firm may hire the victim's computer programmer away with a fabulous offer. But espionage is still a fact of management life.

The sale of highly classified robotized milling machines to the Soviets to make propellers for their submarines so they are harder to hear and track is a good example. In 1980, a Soviet official visited the trade representative of Wako Koeki Company, a Japanese firm trading exclusively with Communist countries, and asked them to find such a milling machine. Despite their suspicions, Wako Koeki went ahead and helped Toshiba Machine Company sell the machines that U.S. intelligence sources believe make Soviet submarines quieter and thus harder to track.[33]

Conflict of Interest

Conflict of interest is one of the most difficult ethical problems for managers to cope with because it occurs so often and in so many forms. It is easy for managers to rationalize an action that to them is good business but which may be a conflict between company needs and personal needs. One form of this conflict occurs when a company issues its own stock to its employees' pension fund in order to conserve cash. For example, Harcourt Brace Jovanovich used $25.5 million of its employee pension fund to build its corporate headquarters in Orlando, and the fund is administered by trustees who are all Harcourt executives.[34] It is legal for a firm to put up to 10 percent of its assets into such a fund. But the practice is questionable, for employees already rely heavily on the company for their pensions. The companies rationalize their action by assuming that the stock will grow in value and the pensions will benefit.

What is your view?

Is it ethical for members of the U.S. Congress to accept fees and other benefits from companies, unions, environmental groups, and others with legislation pending before them?[35]

Business managers are not the only ones who act unethically.

For example, the Internal Revenue Service (IRS) took Gary D. Keefer's life savings of $10.35 out of his bank account without his knowledge because his parents owed the IRS $900. Keefer, aged 12, did not owe the IRS, which took the money anyway to help pay his parents' delinquent tax bill. The IRS also took $700 from Gary's father's account and $7.00 from his mother's account. Gary wrote a letter to President Reagan complaining about the problem, and the decision was reversed.[36]

Advertising Abuses

There is currently much concern about advertising abuses, such as false and misleading advertising. Other questions are related to the ethics of advertising to children, especially during Saturday morning cartoon shows. Also, is it really ethical for Bic to use John McEnroe's reputation for "ranting and raving and [being] out of control on the court" to sell its razor blades?[37]

Collusion

Another worrisome ethical area is *collusion*, which is a secret agreement or cooperation between two or more individuals or companies to help or harm another one. Collusion may also be found between employees within companies as well as with people outside the company.

In 1987, the U.S. Transportation Department investigated charges that the computerized reservation systems owned by the major airlines were unfairly discriminating against other airlines. They were accused of putting competing airlines' schedules at the bottom of the computerized list of flights, giving misleading arrival times, and displaying more complete information on seats available for the system's owner than for competitors. The problem is worrisome because two-thirds of all airline tickets are sold by travel agencies, over 70 percent of which use the American and United Airlines systems.[38]

In August 1985, R. Foster Winans, a financial writer for the *Wall Street Journal*, a broker, and several others were convicted of collusion. Winans gave the others advance information as to whether his column in the *WSJ* would contain favorable or unfavorable information about certain stocks. With this advance knowledge, the broker and other persons made $700,000 by anticipating the market's reaction to Winans's column. He received $30,000 as his share of the arrangement. He was tried, convicted, and sentenced to 18 months in prison, a $5000 fine, five years' probation, and 400 hours of community service for collusion and for securities and mail fraud.[39]

Fraud

Fraud is intentional perversion of the truth in order to induce someone to part with something of value or surrender a legal right. It often involves deceit and trickery. While many cases of fraud are illegal, as in the Foster Winans case, there are others that take on an ethical implication. An example of this occurred when six employees of Volkswagen's foreign exchange department in Frankfurt, a former Volkswagen exchange dealer, and independent dealers defrauded VW and others out of about $268 million through foreign exchange manipulation.[40]

Also, the Consumer Federation of America (CFA) charged that financial advisers in the United States were involved in over $540 million of fraud in 1986. The CFA estimated that they also gave bad advice in at least the same amount because of incompetence or conflict of interest.[41]

Fraud is found in other areas, including research laboratories. For example, the Civil Aeromedical Institute (CAMI), the premier drug-testing lab of the U.S. Transportation Department, was found to be acting unethically in its testing program. Transportation Department officials became suspicious that the researchers at CAMI had done a sloppy job of testing whether drug use was a factor in the worst railroad accident in Amtrak's history, in January 1987. Investigators found that CAMI's forensic toxicology department had fabricated the results of 17 train-wreck blood tests during a nine-month period in 1986. In fact, no one in the lab knew how to use the sophisticated equipment needed to perform such a test.[42]

DEVELOPING ETHICAL STANDARDS

From the previous discussion, you can see that there is a real problem in maintaining ethical behavior on the part of managers today. The true problem, though, is in defining ethical behavior. Is adherence to the law enough to constitute ethical behavior? Or does ethical behavior mean going beyond the law?

Figure 19.6 provides a framework for analyzing the relationship(s) between legal and ethical issues. Quadrant I shows management behavior that is both legal and ethical, for producing a high-quality product, at low cost, is ethically desirable *and* legally acceptable. Quadrant II shows behavior that might be regarded as ethical but is unfortunately illegal. Legal but unethical behavior is exemplified in Quadrant III. Finally, polluting the environment and discriminating against minorities and women is both illegal and unethical (Quadrant IV). This framework can be used by management to help understand whether behavior is legal and/or ethical.

A second problem is the conflict between job demands and personal ethics. A study by Archie Carroll found that 50 percent of top managers, 65 percent of middle managers, and 84 percent of lower-level managers perceived conflicts between their personal ethics and job demands.[43]

Many situations in today's business world cannot easily be labeled "right" or "wrong." Instead, they fall into the gray area of "maybe." To show how difficult these ethical dilemmas can be, Learning Exercise 19.1 provides an ethics test for you. You might want to give it a try!

FIGURE 19.6
Framework for determining legal and ethical behavior.

SOURCE: Adapted from V. E. Henderson, "The Ethical Side of Enterprise," *Sloan Management Review* 23 (Spring 1982): 42.

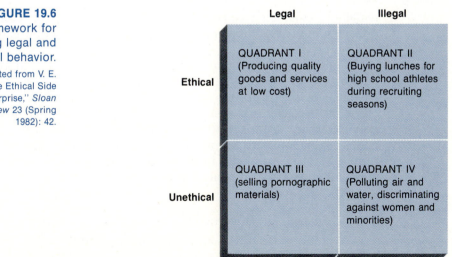

EVALUATING ETHICAL AND SOCIAL PERFORMANCE

While the public is demanding higher levels of social and ethical behavior, management faces the difficult task of implementing and evaluating that behavior. This behavior requires new managerial skills and the use of social audits and codes of ethics.

Responsible Behavior Requires Improvements in Managerial Skills

As the need for greater organizational effectiveness increases (see Chapter 13) and as the demands for more ethical and socially responsible behavior grow, the managerial skills discussed in Chapter 2 must be improved to cope with the changes.

For example, managers must improve their communication skills so that, particularly at the top level, the spokesperson for the organization will be able to give more truthful and meaningful information to external groups. Therefore, those managers will need to be persuasive, effective representatives in order to promote their organizations' best interest to outsiders.

Managers will need to develop more cooperative problem-solving skills. Instead of being confrontational, managers will find it beneficial to work with those social forces that are demanding ethical and socially responsible changes, instead of working against them.

Finally, managers must not only have, but must exhibit, more open-mindedness in their approach to social issues. They will need to see problems from other points of view, rather than just from their own short-run perspectives, in order to deal with increasing social pressures.

Use of Social Audits and Codes of Ethics

Some progressive firms measure their social performance by using a **social audit,** which is a formal procedure for evaluating and reporting on actions with social implications. While there is no generally accepted format, subjects usually covered include equal employment and training, conservation and pollution control, educational assistance, and contributions to culture, the arts, and recreation.

In addition, many organizations and groups have adopted a **code of ethics,** which is a formal statement that serves as a guide to action in problems involving ethical questions. There are many such codes for regulating the behavior of professions or occupational groups, business associations, advisory groups, and individual organizations and managers. Such codes can be long and formal or as short as that of the late J. C. Penney: "Do unto others as you would have them do unto you." Probably the best such code is Rotary International's Four-Way Test:[44]

1. Is it the truth?

2. Is it fair to all concerned?

3. Will it build goodwill and better relationships?

4. Will it be beneficial to all?

SUMMARY

When management acts in a socially responsible manner, it sets policies, makes decisions, and follows courses of action that are desirable in terms of the values and objectives of its customers, employees, and people in the community, as well as its stockholders. Companies act responsibly because (1) if they do not, the people may take away their right to operate; (2) it is in their long-run best interest to do so; (3) if they don't, adverse legislation may result; and (4) it helps them maintain their credibility with the public.

Social responsibility has evolved through four stages. In earlier days, government and religious groups tried to force business owner-managers to act responsibly, but business was primarily operated for the benefit of owners. Most U.S. business grew as a result of applying the work ethic of hard work, thrift, and savings to the principles of private property and unfettered competition. But abuses by some shortsighted owners around the turn of the century led to legislation to protect customers.

This period of profit maximization ended with the Great Depression. Trusteeship management began by emphasizing concern for all four groups and gave meaning to that concern through the passage of many significant pieces of social legislation. However, primary emphasis was still on the owners.

The third phase blossomed during the 1960s and 1970s. It was a period of activism, with movements fostering equal employment opportunity, environmental protection, and consumerism.

The present stage includes—but is not restricted to—(1) maintaining effective but humane employee relations programs, (2) supporting public and community service, (3) assuring environmental protection, (4) encouraging consumerism, (5) providing educational and medical assistance, (6) investing in urban renewal and development, and (7) subsidizing culture, the arts, and recreation.

There is a need for business managers to balance social responsibility and profits. While social responsibility may even increase profits in many cases, in others it may reduce them. In still other cases, however, companies are able to balance gains from effective operation with the costs of social action so that there is no net loss to themselves. While social responsibility is now generally accepted, some authorities think management's primary social responsibility is to make a profit for the owners. But the prevailing belief is that business must balance the interests of customers, employees, the public, and stockholders in order to survive.

There is a growing problem in maintaining managerial ethics, namely, what standards to use in judging the rightness or wrongness of a manager's relations to others. There is growing interest in this subject among students, faculty members, business owners, managers, and the public. Just a few of the areas of concern are (1) bribery, (2) industrial theft and espionage, (3) conflict of interest, (4) advertising abuses, (5) collusion, and (6) fraud.

Many efforts are currently being made to develop some ethical standards of behavior. This chapter reviewed some of these efforts, especially one providing a framework for understanding legal and ethical behaviors.

Management now faces the difficult task of implementing and evaluating social and ethical behavior. New managerial skills will be needed, and managers need to perform social audits and adhere to codes of ethical conduct.

REVIEW QUESTIONS

1. What is social responsibility?
2. What are some other terms used instead of *social responsibility?*
3. What does Milton Friedman think management's social responsibility is?
4. "Management must be socially responsible in order to survive." What is meant by this statement?
5. What are the four main stages through which managerial social responsibility has evolved?
6. Name the three main movements during the "period of activism." What were some of the laws or events shaping each movement?
7. What are the main specific action programs found in socially responsive organizations?
8. What are managerial ethics?
9. What are some of the managerial activities involving ethical decisions?
10. What are some of the new skills required to cope with the increasing demands for more ethical and socially responsible behavior?

DISCUSSION QUESTIONS

1. What is the rationale for social responsibility?
2. Can management really practice social responsibility and still make a profit for the owners? In other words, do you think the odds favor trying to earn a profit or maintaining social responsibility? Explain.
3. How can you explain the evolution of the four stages of managerial social responsibility: profit maximization, trusteeship management, activism, and social responsiveness?
4. How effective do you think social audits are—or will be?
5. Your firm needs a new employee, and you have a friend who needs a job. You think the friend is qualified, but there are probably some better qualified people available if the firm keeps looking. What would you do? Why?

LEARNING EXERCISE 19.1

A Simple Ethics Test*

Put your value system to the test in the following situations:

Scoring Code: Strongly Agree = SA   Disagree   = D
**   Agree   = A   Strongly Disagree = SD**

	SA	A	D	SD
1. Employees should not be expected to inform on their peers for wrongdoings.	—	—	—	—
2. There are times when a manager must overlook contract and safety violations in order to get on with the job.	—	—	—	—
3. It is not always possible to keep accurate expense account records; therefore, it is sometimes necessary to give approximate figures.	—	—	—	—
4. There are times when it is necessary to withhold embarrassing information from one's superior.	—	—	—	—

*Adapted from Lowell G. Rein, "Is Your (Ethical) Slippage Showing?" *Personnel Journal* 59 (September 1980): 59. Reprinted with the permission of *Personnel Journal*; all rights reserved.

	SA	A	D	SD

5. We should do what our managers suggest, though we may have doubts about its being the right thing to do. — — — —

6. It is sometimes necessary to conduct personal business on company time. — — — —

7. Sometimes it is good psychology to set goals somewhat above normal if it will help to obtain a greater effort from the sales force. — — — —

8. I would quote a "hopeful" shipping date in order to get the order. — — — —

9. It is proper to use the company WATS line for personal calls as long as it's not in company use. — — — —

10. Management must be goal-oriented; therefore, the end usually justifies the means. — — — —

11. If it takes heavy entertainment and twisting a bit of company policy to win a large contract, I would authorize it. — — — —

12. Exceptions to company policy and procedures are a way of life. — — — —

13. Inventory controls should be designed to report "underages" rather than "overages" in goods received. [The ethical issue here is the same as that faced by someone who receives too much change from a store cashier.] — — — —

14. Occasional use of the company's copier for personal or community activities is acceptable. — — — —

15. Taking home company property (pencils, paper, tape, etc.) for personal use is an accepted fringe benefit. — — — —

Score Key: (0) for Strongly Disagree (1) for Disagree (2) for Agree (3) for Strongly Agree

If your score is:

0 Prepare for canonization ceremony	**16–25 Average ethical values**
1– 5 Bishop material	**26–35 Need moral development**
6–10 High ethical values	**36–44 Slipping fast**
11–15 Good ethical values	**45 Leave valuables with warden**

Question

1. What do you think is "right" or "wrong" with each of these actions? Explain your answers.

LEARNING EXERCISE 19.2

$10 Buys Sapphire Worth $2 Million*

It was announced in November 1986 that a gem broker, Roy Whetstine, had bought the world's largest star sapphire from an unwitting amateur for $10 in February 1986. The uncut, lavender-gray, potato-sized stone has since been appraised for $2.28 million. Whetstine's agent, jeweler Jim Griffin, who's trying to sell the stone, said the purchase was kept secret for eight months for "security reasons," but he didn't say what they were.

Whetstine had decided not to attend the Tucson, Arizona, gem show but changed his mind and arrived on the last day of the ten-day show. Ignoring the hotel where the better gems were kept, he went to the hotel where most of the amateurs displayed their wares. Spotting the stone, which was covered with dust, he immediately knew

* Based on "What a Bargain? $10 Buys Sapphire Worth $2 Million," *Atlanta Journal*, November 13, 1986, pp. 1A and 16A.

what it was. He said to the seller, "You want $15 for this rock?" The seller answered, "Tell you what—I'll let you have it for $10. It's not as pretty as the others."

The L. A. Ward Gem Laboratory in Fullbrook, California, valued the 1905-carat gem at $1200 per carat, for a total of $2.286 million. Whetstine planned to sell it uncut for $1.5 million because of the risk involved in cutting such a stone.

When asked if he had any qualms about paying so little for so precious a gem, Whetstine replied, "When a man places a price on something he sells, that's what it's worth to him."

The gem dealer's two young sons put up $5 each for him to buy the stone; if he sells it, he plans to put the money in a trust for them.

Questions

1. Did the gem dealer act legally? Ethically?
2. What, if anything, should he have done differently? Why?
3. What would you probably have done?

NOTES

1. " 'Miracle Drug' to Be Given Away," _Mobile_ (Alabama) _Register_, October 22, 1987, p. 5A; and other sources.
2. International Business Machines Corporation, _Stockholders' Report_, Second Quarter 1987, p. 8.
3. Milton Friedman, _Capitalism and Freedom_ (Chicago: University of Chicago Press, 1962), p. 133.
4. See Keith Davies et al., _Business and Society_, 4th ed. (New York: McGraw-Hill Book Co., 1980).
5. _Dodge_ v. _Ford Motor Company_, 204 Mich. 459 (1919).
6. Robert Hay and Ed Gray, "Social Responsibilities of Management," _Academy of Management Journal_ 17 (March 1974): 142.
7. From letters to the _New York Herald_, October 1, 1918.
8. Upton Sinclair, _The Jungle_ (1906; repr. Cambridge, MA: R. Bentley, 1972).
9. U.S. Congress, Subcommittee of the Joint Committee on the Economic Report, _Hearings on Profits_, 80th Congress, December 1949.
10. _Wall Street Journal_, March 4, 1986, p. 1.
11. Susan Dentzer and Renee Michael, "They Shall Overcome," _Newsweek_, May 23, 1983, p. 60.
12. "A Minority Stake in Coke," _Business Week_, August 1, 1983, p. 32.
13. "Technology Is Opening More Jobs for the Deaf," _Business Week_, May 9, 1983, pp. 134–135.
14. Jeanne Saddler, "Playing Favorites? Older Workers Sue Over Early Retirement Plans," _Wall Street Journal_, August 14, 1987, p. 17.
15. _Wall Street Journal_, March 4, 1986, p. 1.
16. Government Street Presbyterian Church (Mobile, Alabama), _Newsletter_, July 23, 1986, p. 1.
17. WALA-TV Channel 10 (Mobile, Alabama), "News 10 Early Edition," November 21, 1987.
18. Mobil Corporation advertisement, _Parade_, June 12, 1983, p. 17.
19. Tom Shields, "Smelter's Billows Depart Ariz. Sky," _USA Today_, January 15, 1987, p. 3A.
20. Pete Yost, "Chrysler Execs Accused of Selling Used Cars as New," _Mobile_ (Alabama) _Register_, June 25, 1987, p. 7A.
21. "Advice to Lee," _Wall Street Journal_, July 8, 1987, p. 18.
22. Andy Pasztor, "U.S. Charges Chrysler Fudged Mileage on Cars," _Wall Street Journal_, June 25, 1987, p. 3.
23. "The Struggle to Go to the Head of the Class," _Business Week_, June 20, 1983, p. 68.
24. _Wall Street Journal_, February 19, 1987, p. 31.

25. "Newman's Own Brand of Class," *USA Today*, December 23, 1986, p. 2D.

26. Claire Makin, "Ranking Corporate Reputations," *Fortune*, January 10, 1983, pp. 34ff.

27. Ellen Wojahn, "Little Big Man," *Inc.*, June 1986, p. 85.

28. Jill Rachlin, "A Question of Principle: Can Do-Gooders Do Well?" *U.S. News & World Report*, January 26, 1987, p. 50.

29. Rae Tyson, "EPA Order to Pump Gas, Auto Prices," *USA Today*, July 23, 1987, p. 1A.

30. K. E. Aupperle, A. B. Carroll, and J. D. Hatfield, "An Empirical Examination of the Relationship Between Corporate Social Responsibility and Profitability," *Academy of Management Journal* 28 (1985): 446–463.

31. Milton Moskowitz, Michael Katz, and Robert Levering, eds., *Everybody's Business* (New York: Harper & Row, 1980), pp. 688–689.

32. Larry Margasak, "Boeing Admits Guilt in Payments Case: Fined $400,000," *Mobile* (Alabama) *Register*, July 1, 1982, p. 6E.

33. Damon Darlin, "The Toshiba Case: Japanese Firms' Push to Sell to Soviets Led to Security Breaches," *Wall Street Journal*, August 4, 1987, p. 1.

34. Daniel Hertzberg and Daniel Machalaba, "Harcourt's Use of Pensions Is Criticized," *Wall Street Journal*, May 25, 1983, p. 33.

35. Brooks Jackson and Edward Pound, "Legislative Lucre: Fees for Congressmen from Interest Groups Doubled in Past Year," *Wall Street Journal*, July 28, 1983, pp. 1 and 14.

36. Stephan Stern, "Taxing Problems of Youth," *USA Today*, July 27, 1987, p. 1A.

37. Howard Rosenberg, "Sex and Snooty Behavior Sell: Are TV Ads Going Too Far?" *Tulsa World*, March 18, 1983, p. 2E.

38. Doug Carroll, "Reservation Computers Undergoing Scrutiny?" *USA Today*, July 14, 1987, p. 8A.

39. "Crime and Punishment," *Business Week*, June 15, 1987, p. 85.

40. Robert Ingersoll, James B. Trice, and Rose Brady, "Can Volkswagen Pull Itself out of the Mud?" *Business Week*, June 22, 1987, pp. 60–61.

41. Barbara Rosewicz, "U.S. Financial Advisors Were Blamed in $540,000,000 of Fraud During 1986," *Wall Street Journal*, July 16, 1987, p. 6.

42. Walt Bogdanich, "Testing Debacle: Federal Lab Studying Train, Airline Crashes Fabricated Its Findings," *Wall Street Journal*, July 31, 1987, p. 1.

43. Archie B. Carroll, "Managerial Ethics: A Post-Watergate View," *Business Horizons* 18 (April 1975): 77.

44. "Four-Way Test." Copyright 1946 by Rotary International.

SUGGESTIONS FOR FURTHER STUDY

BARTLEY, ROBERT L. "Business Ethics and the Ethics Business." *Wall Street Journal*, May 18, 1987, p. 30.

BUSSEY, JOHN. "Pretested or Used? Some Products Bought as New May Have a History." *Wall Street Journal*, July 27, 1987, p. 19.

CHALLENGER, JAMES E. "If You Sue Your Boss, You May Not have Another." *Wall Street Journal*, March 28, 1988, p. 22.

HERZLINGER, REGINA E. "Nonprofit Hospitals Seldom Profit the Needy." *Wall Street Journal*, March 23, 1987, p. 24.

NASSER, HAYA EL; KATES, ANNE; and LANDIS, DAVID. "Shad Helps Promote Ethics." *USA Today*, April 1, 1987, p. 2B.

OTTEN, ALAN L. "Ethics on the Job: Companies Alert Employees to Potential Dilemmas." *Wall Street Journal*, July 14, 1986, p. 23.

PAUL, BILL. "Utility Aids Customers' Welfare Needs." *Wall Street Journal*, July 8, 1987, p. 6.

RASPBERRY, WILLIAM. "The Money Chase." *Washington Post*, June 15, 1987, p. A13.

TOFFLER, BARBARA LEY, compiler. *Tough Choices: Managers Talk Ethics.* New York: Wiley, 1986.

20

Your Future in Management

Learning Objectives

After studying the material in this chapter, you should be able to do the following:

□ Discuss the future outlook for jobs in the management field.

□ Describe the characteristics of successful managers.

□ Explain how companies identify managerial talent in nonmanagerial employees.

□ Relate some problems encountered by individuals in their first management positions.

□ Explain how organizations help individuals in their career development.

□ Prepare yourself to adapt to future management developments.

Outline of the Chapter

Management career opportunities
Growth of white-collar positions
Growth of service industries
Growth of clerical, technical, and professional occupations
In summary: increasing managerial opportunities
Increasing managerial opportunities for women and minorities
Improving opportunities for women
Improving opportunities for minorities
Characteristics of successful managers
Intelligence
Education
Broad analytical interests
Favorable personal characteristics
Ability to manage own personal affairs

Initial management position
Filling first-line management positions
How organizations identify managerial talent
Career problems you might face
How organizations help in career planning and development
Reasons for career planning and development
Dual aspects of career planning
Providing career paths
How management helps with career development
Career opportunities as an entrepreneur
Where the opportunities are
Rewards and challenges of being an entrepreneur
Concluding comments: management and the future
Continuing management trends
Changes in performing the management functions
The future now: the Japanese experience
Summary

Some Important Terms

white-collar work
blue-collar work
assessment centers
organizational career planning (OCP)
individual career planning (ICP)

career planning
career development
career paths
Theory Z

The shaping of our own life is our own work. It is a thing of beauty or a thing of shame, as we ourselves make it.
—HENRY WARE

The golden age is before us, not behind us.
—COMTE DE SAINT-SIMON

Mary Marshall's Quandary

Mary Marshall was in a quandary. It had been five days since she had joined Midvale Cafeteria. Midvale was one of over 300 cafeterias in the Johnson, Inc., chain, with most units located in the western United States. Mary had been impressed with the company during her interviews on the school campus and on a later visit to the company headquarters in Los Angeles. She had accepted a position with the understanding that she would join the company's management trainee program, which would eventually prepare her to manage her own cafeteria. The normal lines of progression included a trainee position in one of the company's cafeterias for four to six months, sandwiched around six to ten weeks of formal schooling at the company's headquarters in L.A. She would then become an "advanced trainee" and be moved to two or more other cafeterias over a period of two to three years. Depending on her progress, Mary could then expect to become an assistant cafeteria manager and to qualify as a full-fledged cafeteria manager within five to seven years.

From her first day at work at the Midvale Cafeteria, Mary's disillusionment had grown. Walter McRae, the cafeteria manager, had largely ignored her, as had Cal Drummond, the assistant manager. McRae had assigned Mary to only routine chores, such as mopping, serving customers on the food line, cleaning tables, unloading trucks, and making salads. He had not mentioned anything about inventory systems, cost accounting, cash register codes, menu planning, interviewing prospective employees, or other management concerns. Moreover, Mary felt unaccepted by the employees, 85 percent of whom were minority workers. Although not a quitter, Mary was wondering if she had really made a mistake in joining Johnson Cafeterias.

What would you do if you were Mary?

Is it possible that Mary was being tested to determine how serious she is about managing her own cafeteria?

Is it normal for management trainees to start their careers on the bottom rung, performing routine tasks?

CAREER PLANNING AND DEVELOPMENT are important to both the organization and its present—and potential—employees. So in this chapter we discuss several topics that are relevant to preparation for managerial careers.

Although you may not aspire to become a manager, after studying this chapter, you will better understand many career-related issues that affect all people in organizations. Therefore, before reading further, complete the career decision-making exercise in TIPS 20.1. This activity should give you an insight into your career interests.

MANAGEMENT CAREER OPPORTUNITIES

A career in management has much to offer. Generally, managerial pay and benefits are good, and managerial jobs offer status and prestige, are interesting and nonroutine. Managerial positions entail the use of judgment and

TIPS 20.1 Career Decision-Making Exercise

According to one career expert, a college student has some 40,000 career opportunities from which to choose. But how do you go about the job of narrowing down the choices? Tom Jackson, an author and career consultant, suggests several step-by-step tactics that you may find helpful and that may indicate an area of management interesting to you.

1. Make a list of 25 things you like to do, even though some may seem insignificant. You may like to hunt, cook, play sports, work on cars, read books, and so on.
2. Separately, list 25 things you do that produce good results—what you *do* that receives compliments from others. This might result in a list that includes singing, sewing, making others feel relaxed, handling children, and the like.
3. Select the top 5 from categories (1) and (2), and make a grid with horizontal and vertical categories. This gives you 25 different possible categories. Select 10.
4. On 10 separate sheets, list 3 or 4 jobs that could fit in each category. For example, if you like indoor

plants and feel that one thing you do well is grow plants, jobs to consider might be working in a nursery, owning a plant shop, becoming a horticulturist, and so on.

5. Grade each job from A to C, with A giving you the maximum degree of satisfaction and C the least. Then rank each in terms of practicality, such as additional education that may be required, the probability of your finding such a position, financial considerations, and so on. Ask yourself, "Am I willing to take the necessary action to get such a job?" If you're not, eliminate it from consideration.

Completing this exercise should result in a list of realistic possible careers, many of which might include managerial positions.

SOURCE: Tom Jackson, *Guerilla Tactics in the Job Market* (New York: Bantam Books, 1978). Copyright 1978 by Tom Jackson. Reprinted by permission of Bantam Books, Inc. All rights reserved. Another excellent book on career planning is Richard Nelson Bolles, *What Color Is Your Parachute?* (Berkeley, CA: Ten Speed Press, 1977).

the exercise of responsibility and offer the social satisfaction of working closely with others. Moreover, effective managers will continue to be in demand in the 1990s, as you will find in reading this chapter.

There are, however, some negatives in a management career that we should point out. If you dislike the pressure of responsibility and like to work independently rather than with others, then a management career is probably not for you. Also, as a manager you will tend to put in longer hours (without overtime pay!) and have to make several career moves within management ranks as you progress up the ladder, and both of these conditions require family-life adjustments.

The pros and cons of a management career presented here are broad generalizations; specific management positions vary greatly within firms and industries, ranging from first-line supervisor to chief executive officer. As you will see, the greatest opportunities for future management careers will be in white-collar positions in service-performing industries.

Growth of White-Collar Positions

White-collar and blue-collar work is a general classification of jobs used by the U.S. Department of Labor. **White-collar work** includes that done by technical and professional personnel, managers and administrators, salespeople, and clerical workers. **Blue-collar work** includes that performed by

FIGURE 20.1
White-collar and service positions are increasing, whereas blue-collar and farm jobs are declining.

SOURCE: *Employment and Training Report of the President* (Washington: Government Printing Office, various years.)

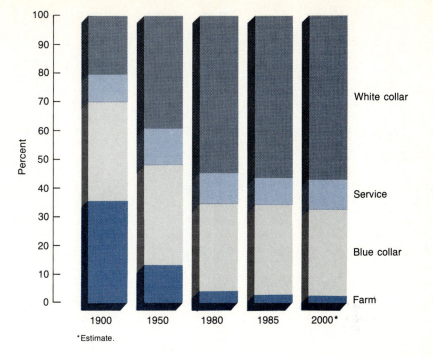

*Estimate.

(1) craft workers, such as mechanics, carpenters, electricians, and pipe fitters; (2) operative workers, such as machine tenders and assemblers; and (3) laborers.

Until the end of World War II blue-collar workers in the United States outnumbered white-collar workers. Since that time, however, the number of white-collar jobs has increased so that they now outnumber blue-collar positions (see Figure 20.1). The trend is expected to continue through the 1990s, when close to 55 percent of all employees will have white-collar jobs, and only about 30 percent will have blue-collar jobs.

Growth of Service Industries

Much of the growth in the number of white-collar jobs is explained by the growth of service-related industries. These industries have accounted for some of the fastest employment growth over the past few decades, a growth that is expected to continue through the 1900s (see Figure 20.2). This industry sector includes organizations involved in health care; wholesale and retail trade; education; banking; food service; hotels; federal, state, and local government; and numerous others. By 1990, around 74 percent of all employees will work for service-performing industries.

Growth of Clerical, Technical, and Professional Occupations

The Labor Department forecasts that the two occupational areas that will experience the largest increases in new job positions through the 1990s are (1) clerical work and (2) technical and professional work. Note that these involve white-collar work.

Included among clerical workers would be bank tellers, cashiers, file clerks, postal clerks, secretaries and stenographers, and bookkeepers. Future

FIGURE 20.2
Industries providing services will continue to employ many more people than those producing goods.

SOURCE: U.S. Department of Labor, Bureau of Labor Statistics, *Occupational Outlook Handbook for 1986–1987*, Bulletin 2250 (Washington: Government Printing Office, 1986), p. 17.

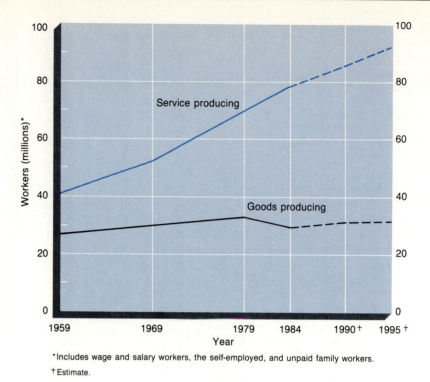

*Includes wage and salary workers, the self-employed, and unpaid family workers.
†Estimate.

clerical positions will be more likely than in the past to require a high school diploma, some college, or even a college degree.

As you can see from Figure 20.3, the number of technical and professional positions has increased tremendously since 1950. And the proportion of the work force performing those jobs has increased from around 8 percent to around 18 percent—and this trend is expected to continue into the next century.

This trend is reflected in changes in the Department of Labor's Dictionary of Occupational Titles. *When it was first published in 1939, it contained around 17,000 job definitions. The third edition, published in 1965, listed around 35,000 definitions. The 18,000 new job titles were mostly connected with new technologies such as computers, electronics, information processors, and space exploration.*

In Summary: Increasing Managerial Opportunities

Managers held about 8.8 million U.S. jobs in 1984, and the job outlook for managers is expected to increase faster than average through the mid-1900s as organizations become more numerous and complex.[1] The bulk of the new positions forecast for managers, officials, and proprietors will involve management of the increasing number of new positions created in the ranks of clerical, technical, and professional fields. The outlook, then, for strong career opportunities in management is exceptionally bright. But since the levels of education and training among professionals, technicians, and clerks will increase, increasing levels of managerial education and sophistication will also be required.

FIGURE 20.3
Technical and
professional jobs will
continue to multiply.

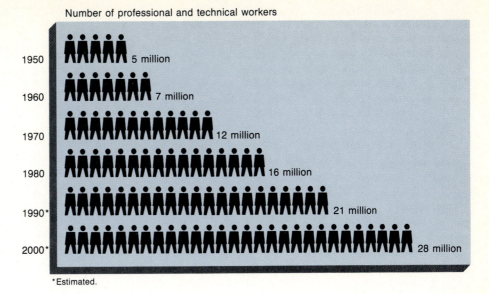

FIGURE 20.3
Technical and professional jobs will continue to multiply.

Number of professional and technical workers

1950 5 million
1960 7 million
1970 12 million
1980 16 million
1990* 21 million
2000* 28 million

*Estimated.

INCREASING MANAGERIAL OPPORTUNITIES FOR WOMEN AND MINORITIES

One of the most significant trends in career development during the last decade was the improving position of women and minorities, especially the higher-level jobs.

Improving Opportunities for Women

At present, women make up close to 46 percent of the total work force, but it is expected that they will account for 60 percent of employment in new jobs that will open up through the mid-1990s (see Figure 20.4). While women hold 37 percent of management and administrative jobs, they occupy only about 5 percent of middle management and only 1 percent of top management jobs. In 1985, only 29 of 1362 senior executives of *Fortune* 1000 companies were women, according to a survey by Korn, Ferry, International, management consultants.[2] Moreover, women are overrepresented in service, retail, and clerical jobs; the large proportion of management jobs they do hold are in areas such as education, public administration, and health care—not necessarily the highest-paying fields.

What is your view?

In 1984, only one company on *Fortune's* list of the 500 largest U.S. industrial companies had a woman chief executive officer. That was Katherine Graham of the *Washington Post*. According to *Fortune*, Graham readily admits that she's in the top spot only because her family owns a controlling interest in the corporation. Why do you suppose so few of the top firms had women CEOs at that time? To what extent do you think the situation has changed?

FIGURE 20.4
Through the mid-1990s, women will account for over three-fifths of the growth in the labor force.

SOURCE: Bureau of Labor Statistics.

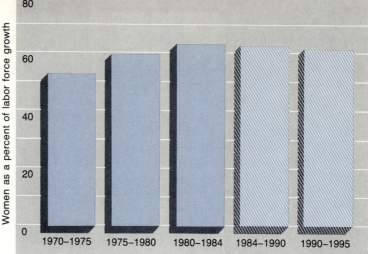

As you read in Chapter 9's Opening Case ("Corporate Women—Breaking Through to the Top"), the 37 percent figure for women holding management and administrative jobs today is a huge improvement over the 20 percent figure for those who held such positions in 1972. And today, nearly half of MBA degrees go to women, while at top business schools such as Stanford, Yale, and Harvard, half the graduates are women. A recent *Harvard Business Review* survey found that only 5 percent of executives felt that women did *not* make good managers, down from 41 percent in 1965.[3] From a career standpoint, women are definitely on the move.

Improving Opportunities for Minorities

Minorities, especially blacks, have made considerable progress up the organizational ladder in the past three decades. Although still underrepresented relative to whites in professional and managerial jobs, they have made increases in clerical, technical, and sales positions. Because of EEO laws and more enlightened management, minorities are now progressing into the higher technical, professional, and managerial positions.

The proportion of black men in the more desirable and higher-paying jobs has increased most significantly. Black men have shown much progress especially in moving upward within the same occupation. Black women have shown more progress moving from one occupation to another, especially from service jobs (primarily domestic) to clerical, sales, and technical positions.

The proportion of blacks in white-collar jobs has increased from one in five in 1964 to two in five today. The greatest gains made by blacks have been in the retail and clerical fields, where they have more than doubled their share of the market since 1964. The proportion of all male employees who are black has more than doubled in accounting, drafting, engineering, and medicine.

Although Hispanic workers now represent slightly over 5 percent of the U.S. working population, they are fast becoming the largest group of minority workers in the near future. Because of their relatively lower levels of education and lack of facility in the use of English, Spanish-speaking workers are concentrated in occupations with high unemployment and low incomes.

"All in favor of getting more women into management positions please raise your hands."
(Copyright 1979. Reprinted by permission of Changing Times, The Kiplinger Magazine, *and David Harbaugh.)*

The rapidly growing numbers of Asians are also making an impact on U.S. management. People from Japan, Vietnam, South Korea, Taiwan, Hong Kong, Malaysia, and Indonesia are swelling the ranks of management.

CHARACTERISTICS OF SUCCESSFUL MANAGERS

Perhaps you have started thinking, "Do I have the personal characteristics to become a successful manager?" We cannot directly answer whether you have the necessary qualities, although an attribute barometer for measuring management potential is available.[4] But we can at least show you what qualities research has found in successful managers.

There is no list of the qualities necessary to be a successful manager that all experts would agree on. Remember also that managerial positions vary from the presidents of large companies to supervisors directing the work of only one other worker. However, research does show that some characteristics are generally considered plus factors when people are evaluated for managerial positions. These plus qualities, which are discussed later in detail, are listed here.[5]

1. Intelligence.
2. Education, including rank or class standing and leadership in extracurricular activities.
3. Broad analytical interests and capabilities.

4. Certain personality traits, especially the ability to relate to people.

5. Ability to manage own personal affairs.

Intelligence

You needn't be a genius to be an effective manager. Research does show, however, that on intelligence tests people in management positions usually score above the average for our society as a whole.[6] Moreover, managers at higher levels score higher than lower-level managers. You needn't interpret these findings, however, as meaning that managers should necessarily be more intelligent than every person they supervise. It is not at all unusual for some or even *all* (in the case of a research group, for example) individuals to have higher intelligence levels than their immediate supervisor! It does mean that you must have a certain minimum level of intellect that will permit you to learn and develop your managerial abilities. So intelligence is a reflection more of your ability to learn than of what you know.

Education

Managers also tend to be more highly educated than nonmanagers. When different variables are compared with measures of success in management, the extent of education has been found to be an important predictor of success. Generally, studies also tend to show that class rank, leadership experience in extracurricular activities, and being a graduate of an above-average college substantially increase promotability. However, a recent comprehensive study by AT&T of 422 college graduates who were placed in the company's general management training program found no correlation between grade point average and subsequent advancement over a period of years.[7] The message here is that grades are critical in landing the first managerial job, but on-the-job performance determines future promotability.

We must point out, moreover, that *age, motivation, initiative, self-study, and good performance help to overcome a lack of formal education.* This is especially true of owner-managers of small businesses.

> *John was intelligent, inquisitive, and ambitious, but he did not like school. He dropped out of high school after his junior year. Later, he passed the equivalency test for his high school diploma with the highest grades ever made in the district.*
>
> *He was bored with the required college courses and was not permitted to take the courses he liked. After a year, he dropped out of college, too, and worked for several building contractors.*
>
> *After six years, he owned his own construction firm and had three crews working for him.*

Broad Analytical Interests

In general, upper-level managers seem to have significantly broader interests than nonexecutives. These interests may range from hobbies to community or church activities. These broader and more intense interests are indicated by top executives who score higher on computational, literary, and persuasive tests than others do. This would seem to indicate that they are capable of comprehending and dealing with a wider range of problems.

Favorable Personal Characteristics

There are other differences between managers and nonmanagers in other personality variables. For example, managers tend to have these qualities:

1. *Ability to communicate.* Since such a large part of a manager's job involves interpersonal relationships, possessing effective verbal communication skills is an important requirement. This ability is even more crucial as managers move upward through lower, middle, and top management ranks.

2. *Superior skill in dealing with people.* The lack of this skill is a prime cause of managerial failure. For example, one survey of 177 organizations revealed that for every manager who failed through lack of technical job knowledge, seven failed because of personality problems in dealing with other people effectively.[8]

3. *Self-confidence and self-esteem.* How can managers instill confidence in others if they don't have it themselves?

4. *Tolerance for ambiguity, frustration, and pressure.* The manager's job deals with uncertainties, unknowns, and pressures.

5. *Innovativeness and ingenuity rather than conformity.* Successful managers tend not to be conformists.

6. *Integrity.* This is increasingly needed, since people now seem to show less trust and faith in all institutions.

7. *Physical, mental, and emotional health.* Managers work in a fast-paced, often stressful environment. Successful managers frequently follow a regular health program.

What is your view?

Suppose that you were being interviewed for a management position with an organization of your choice. How would you answer these questions:

1. What do you consider your strengths, the things going for you to make you a successful manager?
2. What do you consider your weaknesses, the things working against you in your attempt to become a successful manager?

Ability to Manage Own Personal Affairs

How you manage your own personal affairs is an important factor in your effectiveness as a manager. When worry and strife are present in your personal life, you can't effectively devote yourself to your job. In general, college graduates who have been successful in management positions tend to have much better relationships with their spouses and children, socialize more with friends, and have more time for public-spirited activities than their unsuccessful counterparts.

Figure 20.5 shows the profile of 1700 key executives in some of the largest U.S. corporations. Generally, you see that these executives display high educational attainment, are results oriented, and feel that integrity has been vital to their success.

INITIAL MANAGEMENT POSITION

Most management jobs are in first-line supervisory positions. These managers supervise the doers in organizations—that is, the nonmanagerial assembly line workers, salespeople, tellers, clerks, and office personnel. This section focuses on some key career aspects related to these positions.

FIGURE 20.5
Profile of 1700 key
executives.

SOURCE: See John A. Sussman,
"A Career Profile of the Senior
Executive," *Management
Review* 68 (July 1979): 15–21,
for more details.

A study was made of 1700 key executives in 750 of the largest U.S. corporations. These executives were vice-presidents, senior vice-presidents, and other executives who reported directly to their organization's chief executive officer. You will find the background of these individuals most interesting.

Education. Graduate degrees were held by 43 percent of the executives. Eighteen percent had MBAs, 11 percent had LL.B. or J.D. (law) degrees. Other graduate degrees were in specialized fields such as engineering, chemistry, math, and so on.

Traits enhancing success. Traits for improving an executive's chances for success mentioned by the sample were concern for results (74 percent), integrity (66 percent), desire for responsibility (58 percent), and concern for people (49 percent). Traits mentioned least often included social adaptability (16 percent) and personal appearance (15 percent).

Political philosophy. Sixty-eight percent of the executives were registered Republicans; 13 percent were Democrats, and 18 percent were independents. Ninety-two percent considered themselves conservative or moderate on social issues, and 74 percent had conservative leanings on fiscal issues.

Hours and travel. The average work week for the executives was 50 hours, and they spent about 10 weeks of the year out of town on business trips.

Executive mobility. The average executive had worked for his present firm for the past 19 years! Three-fourths of the executives had had only three or fewer job changes in their *entire* careers. In fact, one-fourth had worked *only* for their present companies. For those who had worked with more than one employer, the most frequently mentioned reasons for changing jobs were increased responsibility (44 percent), increased challenge (42 percent), and increased compensation (32 percent).

Future routes to the top. These executives felt that the single fastest routes to top management in the late 1980s would be in finance and accounting positions (named by 30 percent of the executives), general management (division management, branch management; 23 percent), and marketing-sales (20 percent). Few executives named production and manufacturing, personnel administration, or the international area as particularly "fast tracks" in climbing to top management positions.

Filling First-Line Management Positions

The supervisor's position is quite a difficult task for recent college graduates. It is the only management position that does not have other managers reporting to it. Moreover, many employees do not even consider it a management position.

The help-wanted section of almost any newspaper lists several positions advertised as "manager trainee." These may be positions with a bank, a fast-food chain, a retail company, or others. You may wonder why these organizations do not attempt to fill these positions by promoting from within.

Many firms do try to fill initial managerial positions through internal promotion. Many operative-level employees in the firm, however, do not have the educational requirements (frequently a college degree) needed for management positions. Also, many operative employees are not capable of becoming good managers.

Many of these organizations are experiencing very rapid growth. In addition to expansion, turnover and promotion have caused many of these vacancies. Thus, it may not be possible to fill all the vacancies through internal promotion, nor is it always necessarily advisable.

What is your view?
What are some of the other reasons firms would seek their managerial personnel from outside the firm instead of promoting from within?

How Organizations Identify Managerial Talent

Most large firms, such as General Electric, Ford, and IBM, have established methods of identifying managerial talent in their operating employees. One of the more effective ways of selecting managers is the use of an assessment center. Basically, **assessment centers** are places where personnel spend a period of time to determine whether they have the skills to succeed in a management position. Assessment usually consists of such things as personal interviews and the completing of various lingual, interest, and personality tests. Consider the following example.

Sara Albright, age 27, had been a telephone operator with the New England Telephone Company for three years, was well liked by her peers, and had been recommended by her superiors for the company's training program for potential supervisors. One week Sara spent two days at the company's assessment center, where she took a variety of tests, had interviews with the company's human-resources department personnel, and participated in a series of exercises, cases, and games.

One exercise involved Sara and five other operators who were also being assessed at the center. The group was asked to decide what were the 10 most important skills for an effective supervisor in the company. The team was then to rank these items in their order of priority. It was up to the team to decide how to do this and to finish in 35 minutes.

While team members worked on the assignment, several evaluators sat in, observed the sessions, and rated each person's leadership, contribution of ideas, communication skill, sensitivity toward other members, and so on.

At the end of the two days, Sara was given an overview of the results and the probability of her moving soon into a supervisory position.

Many organizations now have formal management training programs that prepare individuals for their first managerial position. If you are accepted for a manager trainee position with an energy company such as Exxon, you may begin your career pumping gas in a service station or working on an offshore oil rig. With Wal-Mart, J. C. Penney, or other retail firms, you might rotate through several premanagement positions, taking warehouse inventory, handling customer complaints, or working as a salesperson in one of the store's departments. Many programs provide a rigorous blend of classroom training and on-the-job assignments, as shown in MAP 20.1.

What is your view?
Note in the Opening Case that management trainee Mary Marshall had spent her first week with Midvale Cafeteria doing simple, menial work. What value can a management trainee receive from such tasks as mopping floors, peeling potatoes, or unloading trucks?

Management Application and Practice 20.1 **The Ten Best Company Training Programs**

Many U.S. companies have outstanding management training programs for newly hired personnel. One expert, Marian Salzman, identifies her top ten as:

1. *R. H. Macy.* New management trainees begin with several months' classroom instruction, after which the first job assignment is a highly challenging one involving much responsibility, such as sales manager or assistant buyer.
2. *May Department Stores.* A strong college recruiter, May reputedly offers the highest starting salaries in retailing. With over 150 stores, May believes in on-the-job training and places new hires directly into a high-pressure department manager or group sales manager position.
3. *Jordan Marsh.* This New England department store chain has a highly structured 12-week program in which trainees shadow sales managers and buyers to learn the technical aspects of the business.
4. *Grey Advertising.* The largest New York agency leans toward liberal arts graduates who are high achievers. In its account management training program, entrants on the first day are assigned a brand; through constant dialogue with colleagues and supervisors, they learn the nuts and bolts.
5. *Olgilvy and Mather, International.* With over 1800 clients, this advertising firm annually hires a number of assistant account executives. Their training starts at a country retreat where they meet key officers. They are immediately assigned an account, attend seminars on subjects such as agency finance and media strategy, and receive a detailed perspective on managing a major account.
6. *Procter & Gamble.* It's said that two to four years of brand management experience at P&G is stronger on a résumé than an MBA from a top business school. Entry-level hires are placed on brand management teams, work with specialists in copy, media, and sales promotion, and sit in on meetings with executives from sales and product development.
7. *SmithKline Beckman.* This leader in health care believes strongly in centralized training at the corporate level. The 18- to 28-month program grooms trainees for leadership positions and features a strong mentoring system. Those chosen for the program receive four challenging assignments.
8. *Morgan Guaranty Trust Company.* With most attention focused on corporate and government clients, MGT's program features six months of formal classroom training followed by three months in the financial analysis department, focusing on number crunching and loan portfolio analysis.
9. *First National Bank of Chicago.* Their First Scholar Program is a 30-month general management program combining bank employment with evening graduate courses at the University of Chicago and Northwestern University. First Scholars take two courses each semester and get on-the-job exposure to a broad range of bank functions, rotating periodically. They receive priority assignments within the bank.
10. *McKinsey & Company.* This large consulting firm is highly selective, hiring B.A.s for two-year research jobs in the $30,000 and higher range. Trainees are assigned to various client cases with teams of two to three experienced consultants. As team members, they receive an insider's view of the problems faced by clients.

The message should be clear to you if you're interested in examining job opportunities and are considering a management trainee position. Questions to ask of your prospective employer include: What does the training consist of? How long will it last? What's the range of specific jobs likely after completing my training?

SOURCE: Marian L. Salzman, "The 10 Best Company Training Programs," *Careers* 3 (Spring–Summer 1985): 25–29; based on her book, *Inside Management Training: The Career Guide for College Graduates* (New York: New American Library, 1985).

Career Problems You Might Face

What are the most important problems that young managers face in their first jobs? In this section, several problems that have been identified are discussed. They are the following:

1. Feeling of lack of progress.
2. Lack of challenge.
3. Insensitivity to organizational politics.
4. Failure to reconcile loyalty dilemmas.
5. Problems with the first supervisor.

Feeling of lack of progress. New managers, especially recent college or junior college graduates, come from an environment in which they have made steady, sequential progress over several cycles. For example, you will soon make a grade in this course and the others you are taking, and you will move 12 or 15 credit hours closer to a degree. After you have passed a certain number of courses, you move from freshman to sophomore or sophomore to junior and then to senior standing. Then you graduate, and so on.

But in your first job, you may feel a distinct lack of perceptible progress, with fewer events changing your basic status. Compared to a school environment, with its rapid progress and feedback of results, the new work environment will probably have a much slower timetable, and it will take a while for you to feel a sense of progress and increased status.

Lack of challenge. A study of 1000 college graduates who had been hired by a large company disclosed that about half of them had left the company over a period of three years. The major reason given was the lack of job challenge.[9] Reasons managers change companies are shown in Figure 20.6.

Entry-level jobs often do not require a person to have a college education to function. Therefore, college graduates must compete for the roughly 20 percent of jobs that do require some college. Indeed, many college graduates experience frustration in their initial job assignments because they are placed in dull jobs that do not entail much responsibility. In reality, though, many employers consider young people's expectations too lofty and unrealistic. Therefore, you will probably have to endure a period during which you have to earn the right to have greater authority and responsibility.

What is your view?

Do you think beginning professional and managerial positions with small organizations are *more* or *less* challenging and satisfying than similar positions in large firms? Why?

Insensitivity to organizational politics. Employees in most organizations face established codes of behavior and interrelationships. New personnel may be idealistic or choose to ignore these codes. Sometimes they are just too naive or unseasoned to be able to recognize them. These failures can lead to reprimand, discipline, or at least a poor record, as shown in the following example.

Joe Bronson, a young assistant manager of a branch bank, considered the branch manager incompetent, an opinion shared by other branch personnel. Bigham, the manager, chewed tellers out in front of customers

FIGURE 20.6
Why do managers change jobs?

SOURCE: Thomas C. Amory, "Why Executives Quit," *MBA Executive*, November–December 1979, pp. 3–14. Copyright 1979 Association of MBA Executives.

Thomas C. Amory, chairman of William H. Clark Associates, a 20-year-old executive search firm, cites several major reasons why executives leave their present companies to embark on careers with other firms.

1. **Lack of challenge.** Many executives find their jobs too easy, too undemanding. Projects, even crises, begin to look the same—very routine.

2. **Management style or personality incompatibility.** Often highly innovative, creative executives are stymied by conservative top management. They possess creativity, imagination, and boldness—all of which produce results that move them up the ladder quickly, but on nearing the top they may find that their styles differ dramatically from a conservative top management. Personality clashes or poor rapport also lead to turnover.

3. **Blocked or retarded career.** Many aspiring managers make a career move when they see future progress blocked or stymied. Some roadblocks may be that the company is family owned, or that "policy" dictates a wait of 4 or 5 years between promotions, or that only certain backgrounds (say, finance or marketing) make it to the top.

4. **Acquisitions and mergers.** Many uncertainties occur when one company acquires or merges with another. The grapevine fuels rumors of transfers, firings, job shifts, and so on. Many executives make a decision to join another company rather than face a state of corporate limbo.

5. **Inadequate compensation.** Compensation, far from being just an economic consideration, is also a form of status. When compensation is more attractive with a competitor, or managers feel unfairly treated in relation to others in the company, they may look for and find work elsewhere.

6. **Company relocation.** Managers who have strong ties to the local community may choose to change companies rather than be relocated by their own companies.

7. **Ignored personal needs and aspirations.** Managers vary in their values and needs, and these often change during a career. An executive may place higher value on time spent with family, on a hobby, or performing a specific type of work. When organizations fail to recognize or leave room for these needs, turnover occurs.

and failed to act on several issues brought up by his employees, including job changes, merit raises, and vacation scheduling. Employee turnover was high. It was not uncommon for employees to learn about new developments in the branch from customers rather than from Bigham.

Joe was torn by three issues: (1) he hated working for Bigham; (2) other employees looked to Joe to represent their interests with higher management; and (3) Joe sincerely wanted the bank to do well. After much thought, he tactfully communicated the branch's problem to the vice-president in charge of the bank's branches.

The vice-president's reaction shocked Joe. The vice-president lectured him about learning to "roll with the punches" of an assistant manager's job. Moreover, he said that if Bronson wasn't able to work in his present

position, it would be in his best interest to leave the bank! "What a turn of events!" thought Joe.

What Joe had failed to realize was that Bigham's family was highly influential in the community and his father was on the bank's board of directors. While top bank management recognized Bigham's ineffectiveness, they chose to ignore the problem. And nobody needed a young upstart to make them feel guilty about not dealing with the problem, which was a taboo subject at higher management levels!

Power coalitions, although they don't show up on the organization chart, are still important ways of accomplishing goals. New employees must learn the organization's behavioral norms, dress codes, and modes of thinking. To fail to understand these realities or to ignore them may lead to misunderstandings, friction, and disillusionment for the new employee.

Failure to reconcile loyalty dilemmas. Most managers in positions of authority greatly value their subordinates' loyalty to them—and expect it. Some unspoken views on loyalty that supervisors expect of subordinates are related to obedience, success, protection, and truthfulness, and present "loyalty dilemmas" for new employees. Some of these are listed here:

1. Obey me.

2. Be successful, whatever it takes.

3. Protect me.

4. Tell me the truth.

Obey me. Managers strongly value their subordinates' general obedience. Excessive obedience, however, creates a "yes-person" atmosphere that may not be in the employee's or organization's best long-run interests. The Bay of Pigs and Watergate traumas serve as excellent examples of the obey-me or group-think loyalty dilemmas that many of President Kennedy's and President Nixon's subordinates faced. Many individuals were asked to make decisions or to take actions they did not agree with, but they felt compelled to comply because of the obey-me atmosphere created by the presidents and their key advisers.

Be successful, whatever it takes. Many executives are shocked to learn that subordinates have given bribes or "cooked the books," but they have only themselves to blame for creating the "success at any cost" dilemma. Honest effort is a legitimate managerial request, but to demand "success at any price" encourages unethical, immoral, and illegal behavior by subordinates in efforts to reach goals that may be unrealistic. Stated another way, this dilemma results from the philosophy that "the end justifies the means."

Protect me. How far should you go to protect your boss? E. Howard Hunt refused to incriminate his commander-in-chief, President Nixon, in the Watergate break-in and cover-up, even though his refusal resulted in a long prison sentence. So did G. Gordon Liddy. Both steadfastly maintained their loyalty by protecting their superior. There was also much evidence of such protection by various subordinates regarding the Iran-*contra* matter during President Reagan's last term.

Gloria Hodges was shocked. As secretary to Dave Donnelly, the director of purchasing for a medium-sized company, she had accidentally overheard a conversation between Donnelly and a sales representative for a local equipment firm. The sales rep had offered Dave a $1000 bonus if Dave bought a large piece of equipment from his company. In fact, the two had talked as if this were not the first time that such a deal had been worked out. Gloria had thought that such a kickback was against company rules.

Gloria had an excellent relationship with Dave Donnelly, who was highly thought of by everyone in the company. What would you advise her to do?

Tell me the truth. One management axiom states the following: Tell your bosses what they need to know so that they will not be caught by surprise. As a supervisor, you would expect your workers to keep you informed, even though reports might reflect negatively on their—or your—performance. One problem is getting employees to tell you what you *need to know* rather than what they think you *want to hear*. It is difficult, though, to admit one's mistakes freely or to convey unpleasant facts to a supervisor, even though that supervisor should be kept informed of important matters. Loyalty, then, is reflected in communication practices. For example, in ancient times, there was an Oriental king who hated to hear bad news. Whenever a courier reported bad news or an unfortunate event to him, the courier was beheaded. Soon, he heard no bad news at all.

As shown in Figure 20.7, each of the concepts just discussed requires a delicate balancing act to maintain loyalty (1) to your boss, (2) to your organization, and (3) to yourself. Many new employees fail to identify properly which of these loyalties their superiors most expect from them. Although all these loyalties may be legitimate, to pursue them to extremes may jeopardize your own, your boss's, or your organization's best interests.

Problems with the first supervisor. Another initial career problem that confronts new managers is a supervisor who doesn't support them. Essentially,

FIGURE 20.7
Balance of loyalties
needed in a managerial
career.

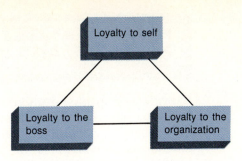

you will expect your supervisor to give you a feeling of progress by providing feedback about your performance, working with you as you improve your job skills and learn new job concepts, and so on. Also, you will expect the supervisor to relay your ability, potential, and promise to higher-level managers. Supervisors are often less than happy about communicating a subordinate's ability and potential to higher management because of (1) their own job insecurity (the supervisor may see an outstanding subordinate as a threat to the security of his or her own position) or (2) the desire to retain an outstanding employee whose performance would help insure the success of the department's results.

> *For example, Bobbie Brough, an outstanding young nursing supervisor trainee, had done excellent work on the first shift of City Hospital's large pediatrics department. Bobbie and many of her peers were surprised when she wasn't promoted to nursing supervisor when the position became vacant. Instead, the job was awarded to another, seemingly less capable trainee.*
>
> *Behind the scenes, though, May Anderson, the head nurse to whom Bobbie reported, had not strongly supported her for the position. May depended heavily on Bobbie's outstanding ability to relate with the nurses on her shift and to perform an increasingly large part of her own administrative duties.*
>
> *Privately, May remarked, "Bobbie's only been with me for six months, and I don't want to go through the process of breaking in another trainee right now. She's the best I've had, and she will make a fine head nurse. Her time will come. She just needs to be patient and put in her time, and then I'll push her more forcefully for a promotion to supervisor."*

Bobbie may not wait, especially if she feels that her own supervisor is not helping to advance her cause fairly. Ambitious, competent personnel depend heavily on their supervisors to report their talents. Supervisors who jealously safeguard their personnel by keeping them "under wraps" may impede, stall, or even derail many promising careers. If this happens, or if your boss is corrupt or incompetent, you ought to consider changing jobs within or outside the organization.

What is your view?
Do these thoughts help to explain Gloria Hodge's problem in the loyalty-dilemma case on page 604?

HOW ORGANIZATIONS HELP IN CAREER PLANNING AND DEVELOPMENT

Individuals and organizations have recently become more interested and active in *career planning and development.* This is a change, for organizations traditionally have done relatively little along these lines—especially in planning for managerial personnel.

It has long been accepted that professional and managerial careers are highly desirable because people in those positions are more satisfied with the professional and personal aspects of their lives. It was assumed that these people had greater social prestige, jobs with greater range and challenge, and greater autonomy. Recent research indicates that this may no longer be true.[10] Therefore, midlife career changes are becoming more frequent, orderly, and rational.

Reasons for Career Planning and Development

Today, *career planning* and *career development* are popular in larger organizations, where it is much more likely than a decade earlier that formal career planning systems exist. If it is in an organization's best interest for its employees to visualize clearly a path or track along which their careers will progress, it is also in a firm's best interest to attempt a reasonable linkage of an employee's talents and interests with the organization's needs.

You, for example, have certain skills and potential skills that you take with you to work. Ideally, a match of your skills and interests with those required by the job should be made. A mismatch costs an organization in at least two ways:

1. You may be ignored and unchallenged, thereby limiting your performance of tasks.

2. Your talents to accomplish a higher-level task effectively are not being developed fully.

For these and other reasons, organizations are now becoming more concerned about career planning and development. Operative employees are not as likely to become chief executive officers as in the past, but today's organizations are better equipped to recognize talent within their ranks.

Dual Aspects of Career Planning

There is much confusion over just what career planning in organizations is. Career planning must be an integral part of overall organizational planning if it is to succeed. Career planning cannot succeed without *organizational career planning,* nor can it be as effective without *individual career planning.* One useful way of understanding the relationship between these two forms of planning is to examine the following relationship:

Organizational career planning (OCP) focuses on the needs of the organization; **individual career planning (ICP)** focuses on the needs of the individual. As shown in Figure 20.8, an important phase of OCP is making sure that the organization's career planning will match the known and projected needs for personnel and talents in the future. Thus, determining and planning the career moves of individuals that will help them develop and prepare for advancement and greater responsibility in the organization is an example of OCP.

On the other hand, ICP focuses on individuals and their particular needs. Figure 20.8 shows how these two types of career planning actually operate in an organization.

Consider the case of Bill Andrews, a talented young geologist with a large petroleum company. Bill had a graduate degree in geology and was identified as a comer who the company felt would be able to take on greater responsibility at higher organizational levels. But when approached about this possibility, Bill felt great uncertainty. He enjoyed the technical work in geology and felt unsure about leaving his specialty. But his company practiced ICP, and Bill was given tests and diagnostic measures by the human-resources department of the company, as well as in-depth counseling with the company psychologist. These results helped Bill clarify his identity, his interests, and his aspirations. Six months later, Bill accepted a transfer to another division of the company, taking on managerial responsibilities. Five years later, he was one of the most successful project managers the company had.

FIGURE 20.8
An example of career pathing.

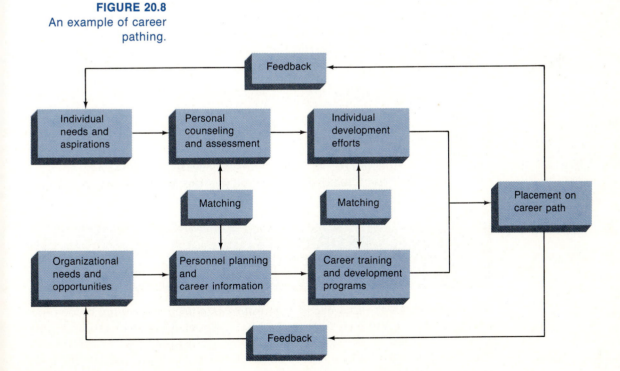

Employers more often practice OCP than ICP. Those who embark on an ICP program usually employ professional specialists to assist individuals in examining themselves and their career goals. But suppose that the outcome of ICP is that individuals realize that the present organization is not the place for them—that their career needs will not likely be met and that another organization is more likely to allow them to reach their goals? It is probably in the organization's best interest to help individuals reach such a conclusion.

ICP is still in its infancy in U.S. organizations, but as organizations take on more social identity, ICP will be more frequently used and be seen as a logical complement of OCP.

Providing Career Paths

Career planning involves helping employees to (1) choose their goals and (2) identify the means of attaining those desired objectives. **Career development** is (1) providing the means of attaining objectives and (2) encouraging employees to use those means.

An important aspect of career planning and development is providing **career paths,** or the sequence of jobs that can be expected to lead to career goals and the ways of preparing for, and moving into, those jobs. A recent survey shows that it took an average of 23 years for a person to climb the ladder to the chief executive's position.[11]

Regardless of the chosen career path, the basic management principles discussed in this book should apply. And since job requirements change, you must develop your skills as you move up the organizational ladder.

How Management Helps with Career Development

Most employers are now making more formal efforts to help employees with their career development. A recent survey by Columbia University's Graduate School of Business reflected the extent of career planning activities undertaken by 79 major corporations. As indicated in Figure 20.9, tuition aid programs, in which the organization paid for all or part of an employee's tuition costs for additional education, were the most popular programs listed.

What is your view?

Examine Figure 20.9. Can you identify those activities that might reflect the following?

1. OCP activities.   **2.** ICP activities.   **3.** A combination of both.

Which of these activities or programs do you think should be most effective?

CAREER OPPORTUNITIES AS AN ENTREPRENEUR

A fast-growing area of career opportunities is *entrepreneurship,* or owning and managing your own business. This is especially true in retailing and services. Around 96 percent of the 15 million business firms in the United States have less than $1 million in sales each year. Also, around 700,000 new businesses open each year.[12] Although many new companies fail, nine new

FIGURE 20.9
What companies do: 15
common career
development activities of
79 top firms.

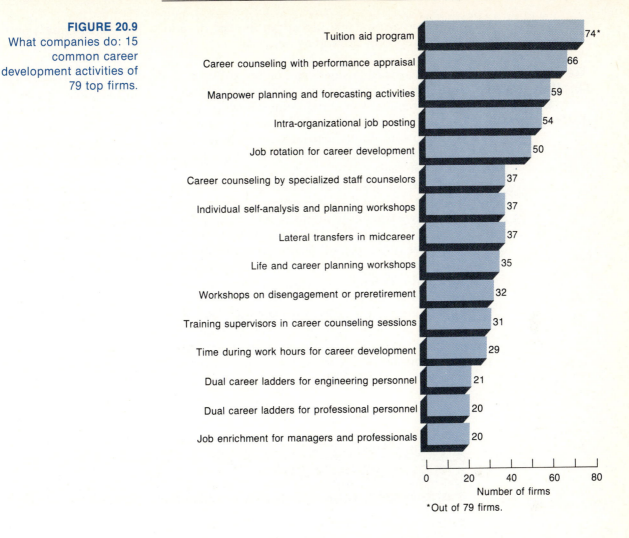

FIGURE 20.9
What companies do: 15 common career development activities of 79 top firms.

businesses are organized for every one that fails, and they account for nearly half of our gross national product during a typical year.[13]

Where the Opportunities Are

The growth rate of entrepreneurs is greater than that of the general work force. For example, while the work force grew 21 percent from 1974 to 1984, the number of self-employed individuals grew 24 percent.[14]

Entrepreneurial opportunities are particularly favorable for women. The number of companies owned by women grew 71 percent from 1980 to 1986, making the 1980s "the decade of women entrepreneurs."[15] Women are starting new firms at three times the rate of men, and they are expected to own half the nation's small businesses by the year 2000.[16]

Entrepreneurship also offers many opportunities for minorities. For example, from 1976 to 1986, the number of businesses owned by blacks grew from 225,000 to about 340,000.[17] Black entrepreneurs are now moving into areas such as advertising, electronics, insurance, computers, and real estate development.

The number of businesses owned by Hispanics in the United States increased around 200 percent in the last decade, while the Hispanic population grew only around 64 percent.[18]

Rewards and Challenges of Being an Entrepreneur

Owning a small business can be rewarding in many ways. First, managing a firm that you have created brings a certain satisfaction that does not come from directing a business others have built. Second, a small business can win its owner a position of prestige in the community. The owner can become active in community activities, which in turn may help the business. Finally, it provides the opportunity to make a great deal of money and offers certain tax advantages.

There are also some challenges that small business owners must face. The first is inadequate management. During the early life of a small business, some owner-managers tend to rely on one-person management. These persons tend to guard their positions jealously and may not select qualified employees. The second challenge is the shortage of working capital, which makes it difficult to keep new facilities, equipment, and processes in line with those of larger competitors. The final challenge is that of government regulations and paperwork. These regulations are unlimited, complex, and often contradictory, which explains why small business managers find it so difficult to comply with governmental requirements.

So, if you have a strong need for independence and for being your own boss, and are a risk taker, you may want to investigate a career in small business (see TIPS 20.2).

CONCLUDING COMMENTS: MANAGEMENT AND THE FUTURE

We feel that an appropriate final section for this book is one that draws some conclusions about the management process as it will exist in organizations of the future. There is no question that there are significant trends occurring that will have a distinct impact on you and your organizational career.

Over ten years ago, Dr. Steve Fuller, vice-president of human resources for General Motors, made some startling predictions about managing organizations in the future. He predicted that many of the following would occur:

1. Operative and production employees will serve on boards of directors.
2. All employees will be salaried and the time clock eliminated.
3. Employment will be guaranteed for life, from the date of becoming a permanent employee to retirement.
4. Employees in operating departments will schedule their own work and approve plant changes and modifications.
5. Supervisors will be elected by—and their actions will be subject to the approval of—the people they supervise.
6. Employees will determine who will be laid off when it becomes necessary to do so (for employers not providing lifetime employment).

TIPS 20.2   Career Considerations with a Smaller Company

David Burch, a professor at MIT, the author of *Job Creation in America,* and the man *Fortune* magazine considers the nation's leading authority on how jobs are created, sees tremendous career opportunities with small companies in the decade ahead. Burch notes that *Fortune* 500 firms have cut employment by 2.8 million since 1980, while smaller firms have continued to account for the new jobs created in our economy. He points out that over 700,000 new entrepreneurial companies are formed each year, in contrast to the 200,000 start-ups in 1965.

Burch recently identified the best locations for beginning and nurturing new companies, based on such factors as telecommunications, quality of labor force, cost effectiveness, efficiency of government, quality of life, and a strong university or corporate research climate. His choices of the 15 best locations:

1. Austin, Texas
2. Orlando, Florida
3. Phoenix, Arizona
4. Dallas/Fort Worth, Texas
5. Tucson, Arizona
6. San Antonio, Texas
7. Raleigh/Durham, North Carolina
8. Manchester/Nashua, New Hampshire
9. Atlanta, Georgia
10. Huntsville, Alabama
11. Washington, D.C.
12. Albuquerque, New Mexico
13. San Diego, California
14. Charleston, South Carolina
15. Nashville, Tennessee

On the basis of Professor Burch's opinion, then, you should consider the following pointers in choosing a career:

1. Don't rule out employment with smaller firms that are not household names, since many opportunities are available in firms of this type. But be sure you ask the right kinds of questions and do the proper research in evaluating the future performance potential of such firms.
2. Some parts of the country—and perhaps of each state—are more attractive than others for employment opportunities and career growth. If you're mobile, consider a job search in high-growth locations such as those identified above.
3. Is starting your own business one of your career goals? If so, there's a high risk of failure. So first try to get some experience with another employer—such as a consultant firm, an investment banking firm, or a smaller company where you can get a good feel in advance for the types of problems you'll face.

SOURCE: Vasil J. Pappas, "How Will You Fare in the New Economy?" (an interview with MIT professor David Burch), *National Business Employment Weekly,* College Edition, "Managing Your Career," Fall 1987, pp. 4–9.

7. Sabbaticals for educational and development purposes will be granted to employees who desire them.
8. Yearly surveys will be made to determine employee attitude and behavior.
9. Bonuses for executives will be based partly on employee attitudes.

Continuing Management Trends

All of these predicted developments, and many other new and innovative practices, are now being seen in organizations in the United States and Canada. But let us now point to some broader patterns that are emerging to shape management in the future.

New leadership and management styles. A primary management challenge in the future will be managing a more diverse work force. As shown in Figure

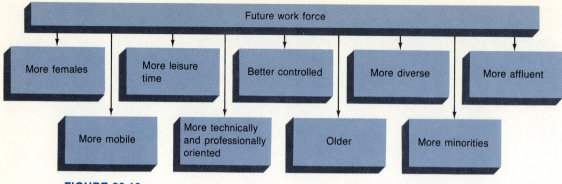

FIGURE 20.10
Changes in employees
of the future.

20.10, employees in general will be better educated, more independent, more professional and technical, more mobile, more affluent, and more inclined to challenge preexisting structures of authority. They will continue to demand significant work and more participation in decision making. We believe that *contingency management* and *situational leadership* are the appropriate management styles today and in the future, with emphasis on results. We feel strongly, however, that *more and more situations will require participative management*, where managers are sensitive to the needs of employees and help to integrate employee objectives with the organization's objectives. We feel equally strongly that there will be fewer situations in which authoritarian management practices and strategies will be effective.

Tendency toward decentralization and appropriate scale. John Naisbitt, in his best-selling *Megatrends*, predicted a continued power flow toward the individual rather than toward large organizations or government.[19] While organizations have always seemed to value the notion that "bigger is better," there is evidence that the trend toward "appropriate scale" is catching on. Many organizations, including Johnson & Johnson and Hewlett-Packard, constantly monitor their divisions, product groups, and other organizational units so as to prevent them from becoming too unwieldy. New units, each with its own relative autonomy, are spun off from larger divisions to eliminate complexity and bulk.

Broader measures of management performance. Alvin Toffler, the futurist, in his book *The Third Wave*, forecasts the following scenario for management in the future.[20] He sees a world in which the performance of managers will be evaluated against many criteria—some newly developed—rather than simply by productivity, sales, and profits. The areas measured will also include environmental, informational, and ethical measures, all of which will be interrelated and interdependent.

Increased attention to external variables. Because of the impact of such rapid change and the increased vulnerability of organizations to external pressures, management will become much more externally focused in the future. There will be increased attention to political, economic, social, and cultural factors and their potential impact on organizations.

Changes in Performing the Management Functions

Many of the trends that we have discussed will affect the ways managers will perform the management functions. Some of the ways these functions will be different in the future are as follows:

Planning will profit from better techniques for adjusting to a more technological environment, the use of more sophisticated decision models, greater reliance on the computer, and the need for more precise planning premises.

Management Application and Practice 20.2   How the Best Get and Stay There

Robert Waterman, consultant, coauthor of *In Search of Excellence,* and recent author of *The Renewal Factor,* sees the major challenge facing organizations as their need to constantly renew themselves in order to stay on top of today's complex, constantly changing environments. On the basis of his extensive study of top corporations (such as IBM, GE, and Morgan Guaranty Trust), Waterman identifies eight characteristics of firms that successfully practice *renewal:*

1. *Informed opportunism.* Renewing companies understand uncertainty. So, in establishing direction, they leave plenty of room for maneuvering. With information as their primary competitive weapon and flexibility as their major strategic weapon, they are able to grasp subtle and difficult-to-recognize opportunities.
2. *Direction and empowerment.* Employee initiative is central to renewing firms. Thus, while managers establish direction, employees have considerable latitude to make their own decisions—within boundaries. In an effort to push decisions to lower levels, renewers have reduced layers of management and have smaller percentages of staff personnel, who are located close to actual operations.
3. *Friendly facts, congenial controls.* Renewing firms don't value data for its own sake, but do prize information that is useful and allows intelligent analysis. Moreover, financial controls, rather than negative strangleholds, are viewed as essential checks and balances.
4. *A different mirror.* Curiosity is a key attribute to top managers, who constantly listen to customers, competitors, suppliers, directors, employees, and critics. The mirror they look into to check themselves out isn't dominated by voices inclined to reinforce how well things are going.

5. *Teamwork, trust, politics, power.* Renewers stress the values of teamwork and trust, based on strong informal relationships. They minimize bureaucracy and power politics and seek to eliminate any "we/they" orientations. But they are aware of the important positive role that power and politics, properly implemented, can play.
6. *Stability and motion.* Renewing organizations have a fluidity, a rhythm that enables them to change while still maintaining a stable base. While policies, rules, and procedures play a stabilizing role, they and other organizational processes are not permitted to hamper functioning or prevent finding better ways of doing things.
7. *Attitudes and attention.* At renewing companies, top managers understand the *Pygmalion effect,* which says that if I expect you to do well, you will. Thus, they try to establish and nurture strong, positive self-images for their people.
8. *Causes and commitment.* Commitment by employees throughout the organization results from management's ability to turn grand causes into small actions so that all levels feel active in pursuing the cause. Renewing companies have the ability to create an environment where even shop floor operators feel their jobs play a key role in contributing to the cause.

Because management of today's organizations is so much more complex than in past environments, Waterman feels that it will be more essential than ever for future managements to follow the patterns that allow for constant organizational renewal.

SOURCE: Robert Waterman, *The Renewal Factor* (New York: Bantam Books, 1987).

Organizing will be affected by greater reliance on task forces and project management, newer uses of staff and service personnel, greater use of decentralization, reduced levels of hierarchy, and broader spans of management as control systems are perfected.

Staffing will involve more intensive use of personnel planning and career management (especially providing more precise career paths); reduced working time and more leisure time; greater use of scientific, technical, and professional personnel; and lifetime employment.

Leading will require greater use of motivational tactics designed for creativity, achievement, prestige, and self-expression; more emphasis on personal dignity and worth, security, recognition, and participation; and improved communication, based on listening.

Controlling will be influenced by more efficient systems for instantaneous and simultaneous control, greater reliance on computers, and an emphasis on all types of controls, not just financial.

Note how the functions of management are reflected by Robert Waterman's characteristics of "renewing" organizations in MAP 20.2. You should look for these characteristics when choosing your future employers, as you plan your career.

The Future Now: The Japanese Experience

If the projections we have in mind are correct, we are certain that management in the future will be characterized by innovation and more involvement of employees through team decision making.

Actually, as shown in Chapter 17, the future is here now and flourishing in Japan. William Ouchi, in his classic book *Theory Z*, contrasts Japanese and American industry and concludes that several Japanese corporations can serve as models for American firms. Ouchi feels that Japanese industrial success is the result of better management, which he calls a **Theory Z** approach. Ouchi's research highlights the contrasts between Japanese and American organizations, as shown in Figure 20.11.

In his book, Ouchi describes the management philosophy and commitment necessary to make Theory Z work. Among other practices, this approach emphasizes long-range planning, consensus decision making, and strong, mutual worker-employer loyalty. The key to increased productivity is to get employees involved by using such techniques as quality circles (discussed in Chapters 13 and 14), developing interpersonal skills, and broadening career path opportunities and development.

FIGURE 20.11
Contrast between Japanese and American organizations.

SOURCE: Adapted from William G. Ouchi, *Theory Z* (Reading, MA: Addison-Wesley, 1981), p. 58.

Japanese organizations

Lifetime employment
Slow evaluation and promotion
Nonspecialized career paths
Implicit control techniques
Collective responsibility
Concern for the whole organization

American organizations

Short-term employment
Rapid evaluation and promotion
Specialized career paths
Explicit control techniques
Individual responsibility
Concern for parts of the organization

Another major difference between Japanese and American companies is the organization structure. According to one report, "It takes twice as many people to produce a U.S. car as a Japanese one. The typical U.S. company has 12 layers of management, while the average Japanese maker has seven."[21] Moreover, the Japanese minimize staff positions and emphasize line positions, where profits are made. As author William Newman has noted, "The Japanese will train their smartest engineers to identify problems, then put them on the shop floor. In the U.S. they'd be sitting at a desk reviewing things."[22]

Ouchi and others note that not all Japanese management techniques can be used in American settings. The forecast for the future, however, is that more American firms will move in that direction.

SUMMARY

This chapter has focused on several key aspects of planning a management career. One of these was the extent of management career opportunities. Much growth will occur in white-collar clerical, technical, and professional positions, which will require an expansion in the number of managers needed to supervise the positions.

While there is no generally accepted list of qualities necessary to be a successful manager, several characteristics considered a plus are intelligence, education, broad analytical interests, and certain personality traits, including skill in communicating and dealing with people.

First-line managers supervise hourly or operative-level employees and constitute the largest group of managers. Some firms look for outsiders to fill these positions, but many companies actively seek to identify operative-level personnel who possess the necessary skills to be effective in a management position.

Newly appointed managers face many problems in their first management jobs. These include (1) their feeling of lack of progress, (2) lack of challenge, (3) insensitivity to organizational politics, (4) failure to reconcile loyalty dilemmas, and (5) problems with their own supervisors.

Two main parts of career planning are organizational career planning (OCP) and individual career planning (ICP). OCP focuses on the needs of the organization in attempting to make sure the organization's future needs for manpower and various talents are met. ICP focuses on the individual employee in helping him or her map out career objectives and interests. Ideally, OCP and ICP merge so that individuals follow career patterns that are in their own interests and simultaneously meet their organization's manpower and career development needs. Career paths are the sequences of jobs employees can follow to reach their career objectives.

There are growing opportunities in entrepreneurship, and owning and managing your own business offers many challenges and rewards. Small business ownership is particularly attractive to women and minorities— especially Asians.

Regarding management practices in the future, a number of trends are evolving. Among these are (1) greater application of participative management styles and use of situational or contingency approaches, (2) emphasis on decentralization and optimum, rather than maximum, size of organizational units, (3) measures of management performance that include social, ethical, and environmental concerns as well as profitability, (4) increased management attention to external environmental variables when making decisions, and (5) changes that will have an impact on the performance of the management functions of planning, organizing, staffing, leading, and controlling.

William Ouchi's *Theory Z* contrasts Japanese and American approaches in areas such as career paths, employment tenure, and evaluation and promotion. It is felt that American firms will in the future incorporate a number of Japanese approaches.

REVIEW QUESTIONS

1. What is meant by "white-collar" work? "Blue-collar" work?
2. What are the three occupational areas that the Labor Department forecasts will have the largest increases in new job positions in the 1980s?
3. What are the five characteristics of successful managers as listed in the text? Can you think of any other factors that could be added?
4. What is meant by the "loyalty dilemma" that managers face in an organization?
5. What is the difference between organizational career planning (OCP) and individual career planning (ICP)? Give some examples of each.
6. Why would you consider owning or managing a small business?
7. What are some differences between the management approaches of Japanese and American companies?

DISCUSSION QUESTIONS

1. Which type of work do you think offers greater advantages as a career—blue-collar work or white-collar work? Why?
2. How do women fare in management positions? What can be (or is being) done to change this situation?
3. Search the want ads of your local newspaper and see how many positions are advertised for managers. What kinds of skills, if any, are indicated as being desirable? How are the required qualifications described?
4. How would you set up OCP and ICP programs for a local firm of your choice?
5. How would you develop a managerial career plan for yourself (see TIPS 20.1: Career Decision-making Exercise)?
6. Of those items shown in Figure 20.11, "Contrast Between Japanese and American Organizations," which have the strongest implications for career development? Explain.

LEARNING EXERCISE 20.1

Henry Blackmon's Dilemma

Henry Blackmon faced a dilemma. As a 26-year-old, he had resolved some difficult career decisions prior to this present problem. Included among these were his decision to attend junior college after graduating from high school, to get married while at junior college, and to postpone receiving his B.S. in business to accept a position as sales representative for National Foods, a large food processing company. His territory included grocery stores within the Kansas City area. Henry and his wife had lived their entire lives in Kansas City, also the home of both their families.

During the six years since joining National Foods, Henry had become the father of two children, completed his bachelor's degree in business through an evening program at a large university in Kansas City, and turned down offers from several other companies.

Henry enjoyed his work as a National salesman, made what he considered a good salary ($31,500), and received other solid benefits, including the use of a company car and liberal medical, dental, disability, and life insurance.

What had happened to shake Henry's neat, comfortable world? On Friday he had been asked by the regional manager to enter the company's sales management training program. As a trainee, Henry would attend a three-month training program in St. Louis and then be assigned a position as assistant to a sales manager, probably somewhere in a larger city in the Midwest. It was explained that Henry would probably remain on that job for one to three years and then take on a sales manager position within the 12-state midwestern region. National was in need of new talent at the sales manager level, and Henry was one of several key young salespersons who had been selected for such training.

Several of Henry's friends in the company said he'd be foolish not to take the promotion, which included a $5000 salary increase. If he turned it down, they said, he'd not likely get another chance later on. But the thought of leaving his and his wife's family and other ties to the Kansas City area weighed heavily on Henry's mind. There seemed to be three choices:

1. Accept the position that could start him on a successful managerial career with a strong national company.
2. Reject the offer, continue in the sales work he enjoyed, and retain the social and family roots in Kansas City.
3. Reject the offer and remain in his present job but look for other openings with local companies that would allow him to advance to higher levels without breaking social and family ties.

Questions

1. What are the pros and cons of a decision by Henry to enter the company's sales management training program?
2. What are the pros and cons of a decision by Henry to reject the opportunity to enter the company's sales management training program?
3. What would you do if you were in Henry's shoes?

LEARNING EXERCISE 20.2

Career Insight*

Part I

Assume that a large party is being held, and the guests are grouped in six rooms according to their personality traits and skills, as shown below.

ROOM A   People who enjoy learning, analyzing, investigating, evaluating, and/or problem solving.

ROOM B   People who enjoy unstructured situations, are imaginative and creative, and have an artistic, innovative, or creative flair.

ROOM C   People who possess good verbal skills and enjoy working with others to inform, help, train, develop, or cure them.

ROOM D   People who enjoy influencing others by persuading or leading, or managing a process.

ROOM E   People who enjoy working with data, have clerical or numerical ability, pay attention to detail, and follow through on instructions.

---

* This exercise was developed from ideas from several sources, including Richard Bolles, "Career Success Requires We Know More . . . About Ourselves," *Training and Development Journal* 36 (January 1982): 15; John L. Holland, *Making Vocational Choices: A Theory of Careers* (Englewood Cliffs, NJ: Prentice-Hall, 1973), p. 20; and Phillip L. Hunsaker and Curtis W. Cook, *Organizational Behavior* (Reading, MA: Addison-Wesley, 1986), p. 86.

Room F People who have athletic or mechanical ability, prefer to work with objects, machines, tools, plants or animals, often outdoors.

Instructions: Fill in the blanks below; then continue to Part II.

1. The people that I would most enjoy spending the evening with are in Room _____.

2. The people that I would next most enjoy spending the evening with are in Room _____.

3. The people that I would least enjoy spending the evening with are in Room _____.

Part II

An important aspect of career management is identifying the types of work that you feel best about and enjoy doing. This exercise is designed to give you some idea regarding a career match-up of your interests and skills and possible occupational choices available.

According to Richard Bolles, one of the top experts in career planning, an important first step in career planning is deciding what type of job offers a fit with your personality and skills. Thus, you are apt to be attracted to people with similar personality traits and skills and this would likely influence your choice of rooms at the party. The six basic personality types, as found in the rooms at the party (given in parentheses), are described below. As each of these lends itself to potential management careers, this exercise should interest you.

Personality type	Description	Occupational environment
Realistic (F)	Likes work requiring physical strength, co-ordination; tends to avoid interpersonal and verbal types of work; prefers concrete rather than abstract tasks.	Engineering, architecture, mechanics, forestry, and agriculture.
Intellectual (A)	Prefers tasks involving cognitive processes, such as thinking and understanding; tends to avoid work activities that require close interpersonal contact; tends to be more introverted than extroverted.	Biology, math, chemistry, physics, and medicine.
Social (C)	Exhibits skill in interpersonal relations; prefers work activities that help other people; tends to avoid high-stress and intellectual problem-solving work activities.	Social work, counseling, teaching, nursing, clerical, and psychology.
Artistic (B)	Involves self-expression, expression of emotions, and individual activities; tends to disdain high structure.	Art, journalism, music, and photography.
Enterprising (D)	Desires power and status; likes work activities that involve using verbal skills to influence others and to attain power and status.	Law, sales, politics, and management.
Conventional (E)	Prefers structure, rules, and regulated work activities; attentive to detail(s); subordinates personal need for power and status to others in the organization.	Accounting, clerical, data processing, and credit.

Questions

1. To what extent did your choice of rooms match your perceived personality description and occupational environment?
2. Break into groups of four or five students and compare your room choices. To what extent are they similar? Different?
3. Do you feel that this exercise can provide help regarding possible *managerial* career insights? If so, how?

LEARNING EXERCISE 20.3

Japanese Management: Why Not Here?*

In 1982, General Motors' Fremont, California, auto assembly plant had 5000 employees, an average of 5000 grievances outstanding, numerous wildcat strikes, 20 percent absenteeism, and output of 240,000 cars a year. Management closed the plant in frustration. It was later reopened as a joint venture with Toyota as New United Motor Manufacturing, Inc. (NUMMI).

In the fall of 1986, some 18 months after the first Chevrolet Nova rolled off the line, things had changed tremendously. The plant, with about 2500 workers—half the original force—still produced 240,000 cars, but had only two outstanding grievances and less than 2 percent absenteeism. The difference: Japanese management styles. First, only a single model is being built at the facility. NUMMI's Japanese bosses set up a typical Toyota system with just-in-time inventory and a flexible assembly line run by worker teams. Employees, not industrial engineers, decide how to set up their job. Workers have broader classifications than typical U.S. auto workers and perform in a variety of jobs. Responsibility for quality rests heavily on the workers themselves.

Three major Japanese auto assembly plants in the United States—Toyota in California, Honda in Marysville, Ohio, and Nissan in Smyrna, Tennessee—are sending the message that Japanese companies in the United States can obtain the same results with American employees as with Japanese labor.

Japanese management styles, however, differ markedly from those of U.S. managers. At these three plants, there are no privileged parking lots, since Japanese managers seek cooperation by presenting themselves as equals. Honda's executives eat in the employee cafeteria, everyone wears white overalls with his or her first name embroidered on them, and employees are "associates." Honda president Shotchiro Irimajiri has no private office, but occupies the same work area as 100 other white-collar workers.

Questions

1. Critics point out that Japanese management styles are well suited to some organizational situations, but not to others. Do you agree? Discuss.
2. The three Japanese automakers cited in the learning exercise have achieved good short-run results. What factors might make them successful in the short run, but perhaps less so in later years?
3. One of the perks of American organizations is the increased power and status given to managers as they climb the promotion ladder. The Japanese system downplays this. Is the traditional American system wrong? Discuss.

NOTES

1. U.S. Department of Labor, Bureau of Labor Statistics, *Occupational Outlook Handbook* (Washington: Government Printing Office, 1986), p. 25.

* Based on "The Difference Japanese Management Makes," *Business Week*, July 14, 1986, pp. 47–50.

2. Anthony Astrochan, "What to Expect When You Work with Men," *Business Week Careers* 5 (Special Women's Issue, 1987): 18.

3. Ibid., p. 17.

4. S. Van Der Herwe, "What Personal Attributes It Takes in Management," *Business Quarterly* 43 (Winter 1978): 28–35.

5. This list of personal qualities is derived from J. Sterling Livingston, "The Myth of the Well-Educated Manager," *Harvard Business Review* 49 (January–February 1971): 79–89; Edgar Schein, *Career Dynamics* (Reading, MA: Addison-Wesley, 1978), pp. 235–239; and Leon C. Megginson, *Personnel Management: A Human Resources Approach*, 5th ed. (Homewood, IL: Irwin, 1985), pp. 261–262.

6. E. E. Ghiselli, "The Validity of Management Traits Related to Occupational Level," *Personnel Psychology* 16 (Summer 1963): 109–113.

7. Ann Howard, "College Experiences and Managerial Performance," *Journal of Applied Psychology* 71 (August 1986): 530–532. For an earlier study of AT&T managers, see Frederick R. Kappel, "From the World of College to the World of Work," in *Business Purpose and Performance* (New York: Duell, Sloan & Pearce, 1964), p. 186.

8. George E. Vaillant, "The Climb to Maturity," *Psychology Today*, September 1977, pp. 34–49.

9. M. D. Dunnette, R. D. Arvey, and P. A. Banas, "Why Do They Leave?" *Personnel* 50 (May–June 1973): 25–39.

10. Abraham K. Korman, Ursula Wittig-Bergman, and Dorothy Lang, "Career Success and Personal Failure: Alienation in Professionals and Managers," *Academy of Management Journal* 24 (June 1981): 342–360.

11. "Labor Letter," *Wall Street Journal*, December 16, 1980, p. 1.

12. *USA Today*, May 29, 1986, p. 4B.

13. "Millions of New Jobs to Be Created in '86, Survey Shows," *Mobile* (Alabama) *Register*, March 31, 1986, p. 3A.

14. *USA Today*, November 25, 1985, p. 1B.

15. Rusty Brown, "Women Entrepreneurs Dominate '80s," *Mobile* (Alabama) *Register*, January 18, 1986, p. 4A.

16. "Solidarity of the Sexes," *Nation's Business*, October 1986, p. 52.

17. Virginia Inman, "Black-Owned Businesses," *Inc.*, February 1986, p. 18.

18. Susan Antilla, "Hispanic Businesses Flourish," *USA Today*, November 2, 1984, p. 3B.

19. John Naisbitt, *Megatrends: Ten New Directions Transforming Our Lives* (New York: Warner Books, 1982).

20. Alvin Toffler, *The Third Wave* (New York: Morrow, 1980).

21. "A Better Crop for B-Schools," *Business Week*, September 14, 1981, p. 128.

SUGGESTIONS FOR FURTHER STUDY

BOLLES, RICHARD N. *What Color Is Your Parachute?* Berkeley, CA: Ten Speed Press, revised annually.

BYRNE, JOHN A. "Getting Ahead: This Test May Tell You to Switch Careers." *Business Week*, September 21, 1987, p. 125.

FLYNN, W. RANDOLPH, and LITZINGER, JUDITH U. "Strategies for the Dual Career Couple." *Personnel Administrator* 26 (July 1981): 81–85.

INGRAM, EARL II, and GILES, WILLIAM F. "Developing an Information Base for the Career Planning Interview." *Personnel Administrator* 28 (November 1983): 88–90.

JACKSON, TOM, and VITBERG, ALAN. "Career Development, Part I: Careers and Entrepreneurship." *Personnel* 64 (February 1987): 12–17.

KRAM, KATHY E., and ISABELLA, LYNN A. "Mentoring Alternatives: The Role of Peer Relationships in Career Development." *Academy of Management Journal* 28 (March 1985): 110–132.

LOUIS, MERYL L. "Managing Career Transition: A Missing Link in Career Development." *Organizational Dynamics* 10 (Spring 1982): 68–77.

MOSS, DESDA. "Census Survey Shows Higher Education Pays." *USA Today,* October 2, 1987, p. 11A.

POSNER, BRUCE G. "Executive Compensation '87: The Brave New World." *Inc.,* September 1987, pp. 63–76.

SHEERAN, LISA R., and FENN, DONNA. "The Mentor System." *Inc.,* June 1987, pp. 138–142.

STASHOWER, GLORIA. *Careers in Management for the New Woman.* New York: Franklin Watts, 1978.

"Top Black Managers Named [by *Black Enterprise*]." *USA Today,* January 6, 1988, p. 2B.

VEIGA, JOHN. "Mobility Influences During Managerial Career Stages." *Academy of Management Journal* 26 (March 1983): 64–85.

WILHELM, WARREN R. "Helping Workers to Self-Manage Their Careers." *Personnel Administrator* 28 (August 1983): 83–89.

GLOSSARY

Acceptance theory of authority. The theory that subordinates will accept orders only if they understand them and are willing and able to comply with them.

Accountability. The practice of holding subordinates accountable for exercising delegated *authority* in such a way as to fulfill assigned responsibilities and of rewarding or punishing them on the basis of their performance.

Action language. Body movements or actions that, although not specifically intended to replace words, transmit meaning; for example, walking at a rapid pace indicates haste.

Action-research model. A model of organizational change as implemented in four phases: research-diagnosis, action planning, implementation, and evaluation.

Active listening. A listening skill used by people whose professions require a deep understanding of their clients; involves the use of *reflective statements*.

Ad hoc committees. Committees that function similarly to a task force in seeking to accomplish a specific purpose and are then disbanded; they do not have permanency.

Administrative activities. One of four groups of activities engaged in by managers. They include processing paperwork, preparing and administering budgets, monitoring policies and procedures, and maintaining the stability of operations.

Administrative management. The form of management concerned with setting *objectives* and then *planning*, *organizing*, *staffing*, and *controlling* activities in a coordinated manner so that the organization's objectives are attained.

Administrative skills. One of the four types of skills needed by managers. They are associated with *planning*, *organizing*, *staffing*, and *controlling* and in-clude the ability to follow policies and procedures, process paperwork in an orderly manner, and manage expenditures within the limits set by a budget. See also *conceptual skills; human-relations skills; technical skills*.

Affirmative action (AA). Guidelines developed to help firms eliminate discrimination against such groups as women and minorities during their recruitment, promotion, and training.

Affirmative-action programs (AAPs). Employers' programs to seek out women and minorities actively and promote them into better positions as required by the *Equal Employment Opportunity Act of 1972*.

Analytic (disassembly) process. A production process that begins with one material and ends up with many and varied goods.

Anticipatory assignment. See *temporary assignment*.

Assessment centers. Locations where organizations use tests, interviews, and other tools to determine whether selected personnel have the skills to succeed in certain positions.

Audits. Efforts to examine activities or records to verify their accuracy or effectiveness. See also *management audit*.

Authority. The right to command others to act or not act to reach *objectives*.

Autocratic (authoritarian) leaders. Leaders who make most decisions themselves instead of allowing their followers to make them.

Automation revolution. The growing tendency for work to be performed by computer-controlled machines.

Behavioral (humanistic, organic) approach. Emphasizes favorable treatment of employees rather than their output or performance.

Behavioral approach to leadership. A theory based

on the assumption that leaders are not born but developed. It focuses on what leaders do rather than what they are.

Behavior modification. Another name for *operant conditioning,* a process motivation theory in which favorable behavior is reinforced by satisfying consequences and unfavorable behavior is eliminated by unsatisfying consequences.

Benefits. What persons are entitled to because of their employment.

Blue-collar work. Traditionally, work done by workers in blue work shirts. It includes work performed by (1) craft workers, such as mechanics, carpenters, electricians, and pipefitters; (2) operative workers, such as machine tenders and assemblers; and (3) laborers.

Bounded rationality. A concept originated by Herbert Simon that ranks satisfaction in relationships as *maximizing* (most or greatest), *optimizing* (best), and *satisficing* (satisfactory).

Brainstorming. Involves a small group of creative employees in an idea-generating session under rigidly controlled conditions. Employees are encouraged to present ideas and to refrain from criticizing.

Break-even analysis. A method of charting and analyzing revenues and costs to determine at what volume (of sales or production) an operation's total costs equal total revenues so that there is neither profit nor loss.

Break-even point (BEP). That point on a chart at which total revenue exactly covers total cost, including both fixed and variable costs.

Budget. A statement of planned revenue and expenditures—by category and period of time—of money, time, personnel, space, buildings, or equipment, expressed in numerical terms.

Budgetary control. A system of using established quantifiable figures, such as revenues, expenses, or time, as a basis for comparing actual performance with planned performance.

Budgets. Expressions of plans, objectives, and programs of the organization in numerical terms. See also *capital budgets; operating budgets; personnel budgets; production budgets; variable budget.*

Bureaucracy. A highly specialized form of organizational structure designed to provide order and guidance; often characterized as highly restrictive and impersonal.

Capital budgets. Budgets for purchasing equipment and facilities. See also *operating budgets; personnel budgets; production budgets; variable budget.*

Career development. Provision by an employer of the means by which employees may attain their job progression objectives and of encouragement of employees to use those means.

Career management. A process that integrates the individual's career planning and development into the organization's personnel plans. See also *career planning.*

Career paths. The sequences of jobs that can be expected to lead to career goals.

Career planning. The process by which an organization helps employees to choose their career goals and to identify the means of attaining them.

Centralization. Concentration of power and authority near the top, or in the head, of the organization.

Chain of command. The authority-responsibility relationships that link superiors and subordinates throughout the entire organization; may be represented graphically on an organization chart by lines and arrows.

Change agent. The individual, usually from outside the organization being changed, who takes a leadership role in initiating and introducing the change process.

Changing. One of the stages of behavioral change according to Kurt Lewin. It occurs when you begin experimenting with new behavior, trying new patterns in the hope that they will increase your effectiveness. See also *refreezing; unfreezing.*

Closed system. Tends to move toward a static equilibrium.

Coaching. An on-the-job method of employee development whereby superiors provide guidance and counsel to subordinates in the course of their regular job performance.

Code of ethics. A formal statement that serves as a guide to action in problems involving ethical questions.

Coercive power. A form of *power* that derives from people's perceived expectation that punishment (being fired, reprimanded, or the like) will follow if they do not comply with the aims of a potential leader.

Commission. Percentage of sales paid to employees as a financial incentive.

Committees. Groups of persons from more or less the same level whose purpose is to exchange information, advise top management, or even make decisions themselves.

Commonweal groups. Governmental bodies that provide service to *all* members of the public. Public health units, public libraries, and public parks are examples.

Communication. The process of transferring meaning, in the form of ideas or information, from one person to another.

Comparable worth. A *compensation* concept that goes beyond paying equal salaries for equal jobs and requires equal salaries for women performing jobs that are different from, but just as demanding and valuable as, those performed by men. The rating of a given job is arrived at by a formula that considers education, effort, skill, and a responsibility.

Compensation. Financial payment provided to employees as a reward for work performed and as a motivator for future performance; the provision of such a payment.

Computer-aided manufacturing (CAM). Use of computers programmed to adjust and change tools to produce a variety of sizes, shapes, textures, and other characteristics as required.

Computer-assisted design (CAD). Use of computers to display a wide range of designs and sketches, rearrange lines using an electronic pen, match parts, and process data for the "paperwork" needed. Especially helpful when programmed to answer "what if" questions—adjusting all other relevant factors when one factor is changed.

Concentration. Refers to a firm that operates within a single line of business.

Concept. An abstract or generic idea generalized from particular instances that serves as the basis for an action or discussion. See also *principle*.

Conceptual skills. One of the four groups of skills used by effective managers; the mental abilities needed to acquire, analyze, and interpret information received from various sources and to make complex decisions. See also *administrative skills; human-relations skills; technical skills*.

Concurrent (steering, screening) control. A form of *control*, used while an activity is taking place, such as the adjustments made in steering a vehicle.

Conflict. Opposition or antagonistic interaction between two or more parties.

Conflict management. The methods and programs managers use to deal with excessive conflict between either individuals or departments.

Confrontation meeting. An *organization development* technique developed by Richard Beckhard that is particularly useful for organizations that don't have time to spend on a more in-depth OD program. It resolves problems of organizational performance by generating and analyzing data about group problems and then formulating action plans to respond to them.

Connotative meaning. A subjective meaning sometimes associated with a word; contrasted with the *denotative meaning* or dictionary definition.

Conservation. Practicing the most effective use of resources, considering society's present and future needs. Achieved by limiting the exploitation of scarce resources.

Consideration. Employee-centered behavior of managers, such as praising or rewarding employees for good performance.

Consumerism. The organized effort of independent, government, and business groups to protect consumers from undesirable effects resulting from poorly designed and produced products.

Content theories (need theories). Theories of motivation that focus on the internal needs that individuals attempt to satisfy on the job, such as the need for security, achievement, or status; examples are the theories of psychologist Abraham Maslow (*hierarchy of needs*) and Frederick Herzberg (*motivation-maintenance*).

Contingency approach. An approach to management based on the belief that management decisions and actions should be determined by the prevailing situational elements.

Contingency model. A complex and interesting leadership theory developed by Fred Fiedler. The theory holds that the effectiveness of a group or an organization depends on the interaction between the leader's personality and the situation.

Contingency-situational approach. Leadership theories prescribing that no single leadership style is best and that the style of leadership to be used should be contingent on factors such as the situation, the people, the task, the organization, and other environmental variables.

Continuous process. A type of *production process* that continues to produce the same product for long periods of time. It is usually automated and is relatively easy to run and more efficient than *job shop processing*, which is production of goods to special order.

Control. The process of assuring that organizational and managerial *objectives* are accomplished.

Control and follow-up. Feedforward controls attempt to anticipate problems or deviations from standards in advance of their occurrence. Follow-up action may be in the form of revising methods, machines, tools, schedules, plans, and so forth.

Controllable factors. Factors over which the organization has at least some control through the decisions of its managers.

Controlling. One of the basic management functions: devising ways and means of assuring that planned performance is actually achieved.

Control-of-information power. A form of *power* derived from knowledge that others do not have, used by either giving or withholding needed information.

Cottage system. Work that was performed in the homes of the workers in rural areas. An independent merchant would pay the master craftsman on a piecework basis, and he, in turn, would pay the workers who did the actual production in their homes.

Creativity. Uses knowledge, evaluation, innovation, imagination, and inspiration to convert something into something else.

Credibility (in communication). The acceptability of a communication, based on the sender's "expertness" in the subject area being communicated and on the degree of the receiver's confidence and trust that the sender will communicate the truth.

Critical path. In a *PERT network*, the longest path, in terms of time, from the beginning event to the ending event.

Critical Path Method (CPM). A scheduling and control technique that aids in scheduling sophisticated, nonrepetitive technical projects; it uses only one time estimate and a cost estimate for each event.

Cultural conflict. Difficulty in adjusting to differences in another *culture*, which may lead to ineffective management of international operations.

Cultural determinants. Cultural variables that have a positive relationship to managerial productivity, such as the ability to move and adapt to another culture or willingness to learn a new language.

Culture. The knowledge, beliefs, art, morals, law, customs, and any other capacities and habits acquired by a person as a member of society.

Culture, organization. See *organization culture*.

Customer departmentalization. Grouping activities in such a way that they focus on a given use of the product or service; used primarily in grouping sales or service activities.

Cybernetics. A self-correcting control system, such as a thermostat.

Day wages. See *time wages*.

Decentralization. The extent to which upper management delegates *authority* downward to divisions, branches, or lower-level organizational units.

Decision making. The conscious selection of a course of action from among available alternatives to produce a given result.

Decision tree. A decision-making tool that outlines various alternatives and the possible outcomes of each; the Vroom-Yetton decision tree attempts to identify the "optimum" decision style for a given situation.

Delegation. The process by which managers allocate *authority* downward to the people who report to them.

Delphi technique. Involves sending a series of questionnaires to a group of volunteer respondents who do not meet with the other participants—or even know who they are.

Democratic (participative) leaders. Leaders who use group involvement in setting the group's basic ob-

jectives, establishing strategies, and determining job assignments.

Denotative meaning. The literal, dictionary meaning of a word. See also *connotative meaning*.

Departmentalization. The process of dividing large groups into smaller, more workable groupings.

Desire. A goal of which one is fully aware.

Development. As contrasted with *education* and *training*, the broader scope of improvement and growth of abilities, attitudes, and personality traits.

Diagonal communication. Communication that cuts diagonally across an organization's chain of command; often results from *line* and *staff* department relationships. See also *downward communication; informal communication; lateral (horizontal) communication; upward communication*.

Diversification. Involves deciding whether to enter a business different from the present one(s).

Divestment strategy. Selling off the business, or a component of it.

Division of labor. The management *principle* stating that when a job is divided into components more can be accomplished by the group than would be possible if each person tried to complete the entire task individually.

Downward communication. Communication that follows the organization's formal chain of command from top to bottom, including information related to policies, rules, procedures, objectives and other types of plans; work assignments and directives; feedback about performance; general information about the organization, such as its progress or status; and specific requests for information from lower levels. See also *diagonal communication; informal communication; lateral (horizontal) communication; upward communication*.

Dual allegiance. A problem related to *motivation* in professional employees that arises from their loyalty both to their employers and to their professional colleagues.

Eclectic approach. Draws on the best available information from all approaches and disciplines.

Ecology. The relationship between living things—especially people—and their environments.

Economic man concept. The assumption by management that *motivation* and rewards are achieved by providing employees with "a fair day's pay for a fair day's work."

Education. The acquisition of generalized knowledge.

Effectiveness. The managerial ability to "do the right things" or to get things accomplished; includes choosing the most appropriate *objectives* and the proper methods of achieving the objectives.

Efficiency. The ratio of outputs to inputs; an efficient manager is one who achieves higher outputs (results, productivity, performance) relative to the inputs (labor, materials, money, machines, and time) needed to achieve them.

Employee referrals. Current employees' opportunity to recruit a relative or friend for a particular job.

Entrepreneurial role. A phase of managerial activity in which managers actively seek to improve performance by initiating planned changes to adapt to environmental changes.

Entrepreneurs. Persons who conceive of, gather resources for, organize, and run businesses; entrepreneurs tend to be risk takers who are motivated by the profit motive.

Environmental protection. Maintaining a healthy balance between elements of the ecology.

Equal employment opportunity (EEO). Employment opportunities fully available to anyone, including minorities, women, Vietnam veterans, and older and disabled workers.

Equipment departmentalization. See *process departmentalization.*

Equity theory. Predicts that people will compare (1) the inputs they bring to the job in the form of education, experience, training, and effort with (2) the outcomes they receive as compared to those of other employees in comparable jobs.

Ethical standards. Individual standards set by a manager that are higher than those set by law.

Ethnocentrism. The tendency to believe and act on the belief that one's own cultural value system is superior to all other cultural value systems.

Executive development programs. A form of *off-the-job development* that takes place at a university or other educational institution and where managers participate in generalized programs using case analysis, *simulation*, and other learning methods.

Expectancy theory. A theory of *motivation* stating that individuals are predicted to be high performers when they see (1) a high probability that their efforts will lead to high performance, (2) a high probability that high performance will lead to favorable outcomes, and (3) that these outcomes will be, on balance, positively attractive to them.

Expert power. A form of *power* derived from a potential leader's expertise or knowledge in an area in which that leader wants to influence others.

Expropriate. Confiscate another's property, especially for conversion to public use. Governments frequently expropriate foreign holdings in their countries and either give them to their own citizens or nationalize them (convert them to public ownership).

External change forces. Environmental factors outside the organization over which management has little control but with which it must interact if it is

to survive—for example, the cultural, political, economic, social, educational, and technological environments.

Facilitators. Persons who intervene to resolve clashes resulting from conflicting priorities.

Factory system. The system of production, brought about by machines and interchangeable parts, that gave workers the right to contract with their employers, to bargain over terms and conditions of employment, and to choose or decline their jobs.

Feedback. A stage in the *communication* process in which the receiver of a message responds to the sender.

Feedback (postaction) control. A type of *control*, such as financial reports or monthly sales reports, that measures performance *effectiveness* only after the results have been attained.

Feedforward control. A type of *control* that attempts to anticipate problems or deviations from standard in advance of their occurrence.

Feeling. Innate processes that include values and beliefs in arriving at conclusions that take other people's actions or beliefs into consideration.

Feudal system. Designed to be a form of land tenure that was adapted to rural and agrarian production.

Fixed costs. Cost that would be the same even if the production level were changed. These include some utilities, rent for the building, and salaries for supervisors. See also *variable costs.*

Formal authority. As contrasted with the *acceptance theory of authority*, the formal authority view is that *authority* is conferred; it exists because someone was granted it.

Functional authority. *Authority* granted by top management to give a *staff* specialist the right to command *line* units in matters regarding the functional activity in which the staff specializes; the strongest relationship staff can have with line units.

Functional departmentalization. A form of organizational *departmentalization* that groups together common functions or similar activities to form an organizational unit.

Functional managers. Managers responsible for activities of only one of the *primary* or *service functions*, such as production, marketing, finance, personnel, or accounting.

Functional organization. When a staff function or activity becomes so important that its performance is critical to the organization's success.

Gantt chart. A chart developed by Henry Gantt, with output on one axis and unit of time on the other, to show work planned and work accomplished in relation to each other and in relation to time.

General managers. Managers who oversee a total unit

or operating division that includes all the functional activities of the unit.

Goal. A specific end result sought; commonly referred to also as an *objective* that organizations, managers, and employees seek to attain.

Grapevine. Transmission of information by word of mouth without regard for organizational levels, *departmentalization*, or *chain of command;* the best-known type of *informal communication* within an organization.

Grid analysis. See *Managerial Grid®.*

Guild system. In medieval times, an association of workers divided into master craftsmen, journeymen, and apprentices; the beginning of personnel management, since selecting, training, and developing workers were involved.

Handicapped person. Anyone with a physical or mental disability that substantially restricts major normal activities.

Hawthorne effect. A phenomenon discovered in the *Hawthorne studies;* namely, that workers chosen as subjects in a scientific study had a greater incentive toward increased production because they felt important and appreciated.

Hidden agenda. Committee members may appear to be focusing on an item on the agenda, but in reality their attitudes—and possibly their decisions—are being influenced by some other item, issue, or personality that is not mentioned by name.

Hierarchy of needs. In psychologist Abraham Maslow's needs theory, an arrangement of human needs in order of decreasing urgency.

Human-relations movement. Followed the Hawthorne experiments: Managers were more concerned with morale building than with improving operations and outputs.

Human-relations skills. One of the four groups of skills needed by effective managers; the many diverse abilities required to understand other people and to interact effectively with them. See also *administrative skills; conceptual skills; technical skills.*

Human-resource planning. Includes all activities needed to provide the right types and numbers of employees to reach the organization's objectives.

Incentive. An external stimulus that induces one to attempt to do something or to strive to achieve something.

Incentive wage. A form of *compensation* whereby employees' earnings are directly related to the amount they produce or sell above a predetermined *standard.*

Individual career planning (ICP). Career planning that focuses on the needs of the individual, as contrasted with *organizational career planning.*

Industrial Revolution. The changes in production systems in the eighteenth century brought about by machines and a new economic system.

Informal communication. Communication flows that travel along channels other than those formally designed by the organization.

Informal organization. Consists of groupings and relationships of personnel that may be more influential than the formal relationships. They emerge whenever people come together and interact in social groupings.

Informational roles. Roles played by managers acting as monitors, disseminators, and spokespersons.

Initiating structure. Task- or production-oriented behavior of managers, such as establishing *policies, rules,* and *procedures* and seeing that deadlines and schedules are met.

Integration process. According to Mary Parker Follett, a way to make conflict constructive by having the people involved together look for ways to resolve their differences.

Interactional activities. Roles managers play, including interpersonal roles (figurehead, leader, and liaison), informational roles (monitor, information dispenser, and spokesperson), and decisional roles (entrepreneur, disturbance handler, resource allocator, and negotiator).

Intermediate-range plans. Plans having a time span of a few months to three years.

Internal change forces. Pressures for change that result from factors such as new organizational *objectives,* managerial *policies,* technologies, and employee attitudes.

Intrapreneurship. Allowing people the freedom to take an entrepreneurial role in large, bureaucratic groups.

Intuition. The ability to know things without the use of rational thinking processes.

Jargon. Technical vocabulary used by specialists. It can be a barrier to effective *communication.*

Job analysis. The process of determining the skills, responsibility, knowledge, authority, environment, and interrelationships involved in a particular job.

Job burnout. Physical or mental depletion significantly below one's capable level of performance; a major cause of absenteeism, alienation, and work-site antagonisms.

Job descriptions. Outlines of the skills, responsibility, knowledge, authority, environment, and interrelationships invovled in each job. Based on *job analysis.*

Job rotation. An on-the-job development method that moves people through highly diversified and differentiated jobs to give them a variety of experience.

Job shop processing. Based on meeting the special demands or needs of specific customers.

Job specifications. Written statements about the job and the personal qualifications required of a person to perform the job successfully. Based on *job descriptions.*

Jungian Framework. A matrix of four key elements: the present (S), the future (N), things and logic (T), and people and values (F).

Just-in-time inventory system. See *just-in-time scheduling.*

Just-in-time scheduling. A scheduling method whereby materials are received just as they are needed and do not need to be stored, resulting in zero inventory.

Laboratory training. An off-the-job development method whereby participants learn to be more sensitive to other people and more aware of their own feelings.

Laissez faire, laissez passer. The economic doctrine stating that *entrepreneurs*, if left alone to pursue their own self-interests, would be guided toward the interests of the whole society; the forerunner of the free enterprise system.

Laissez-faire (free-rein) leaders. Permissive leaders who give little direction or discipline and let followers do basically what they want.

Lateral (horizontal) communication. Communication between and among departments on the same level; it is coordinative in nature.

Law of effect. A law stating that behavior followed by satisfying consequences tends to be repeated, whereas behavior followed by unsatisfying consequences tends not to be repeated.

Law of the situation. The law, formulated by Mary Parker Follett, stating that three interrelated and interacting variables affect the leader's style. These variables are (1) the leader, (2) the followers, and (3) the situation.

Leadership. The process of influencing individual and group activities toward goal setting and goal achievement.

Leadership continuum. A range of behavior associated with leadership styles from *democratic* to *authoritarian (autocratic).*

Leading. One of the basic management functions: influencing employees to accomplish desired objectives; involves the leader's qualities, styles, and *power*, as well as the leadership activities of *communication, motivation,* and discipline.

Least preferred co-worker (LPC) scale. A tool used in Fred Fiedler's contingency leadership theory to determine whether one is relationship oriented or task oriented.

Legitimate power. A form of *power* derived from internalized values that dictate that a leader has a legitimate right to influence subordinates.

Life-cycle theory. A leadership theory advanced by Paul Hersey and Kenneth Blanchard that holds that a leader's strategies and behavior should be situational, based primarily on the degree of *maturity* of the followers.

Line-and-staff organization. A type of organizational structure in which staff positions have been added to assist and serve the basic line departments and help them accomplish the organization's *objectives* more effectively.

Linear programming (LP). A *management science* tool used to solve "optimization" problems or problems for which there is one "best" answer.

Line authority. The *authority* that superiors exercise over their immediate subordinates; it is directed downward through the organizational levels.

Line organization. The departments in an organization that perform the major activities of the enterprise—production, sales, and finance.

Liquidation strategy. Involves terminating a business's existence by either shutting it down or disposing of the assets.

Logrolling. Lawmakers exchanging assistance, favors, or votes with one another to get support for proposals of interest to each one.

Long-range plans. Plans involving activities from two to five or more years in the future.

Maintenance (hygienic) factors. According to Frederick Herzberg, factors such as security, compensation, and working conditions that, although incapable of providing strong positive motivation, can forestall any serious employee dissatisfaction.

Management. The activity of working with people to determine, interpret, and achieve organizational objectives by performing the functions of *planning, organizing, staffing, leading,* and *controlling;* not necessarily synonymous with *leadership, supervision,* or *entrepreneurship.*

Management audit. The application of auditing techniques as a way of determining the overall effectiveness of management.

Management by exception (MBE) or exception principle. A *control* technique that enables managers to direct attention to the most critical control areas and permit employees at lower levels of management to handle routine variations.

Management by objectives (MBO). A management system in which subordinate managers actively participate with their superiors in establishing quantifiable, measurable performance goals for a given time period; a basis for directing the various departmental efforts and for assessing the performance of each department member.

Management information system (MIS). A planned system of gathering, processing, storing, and disseminating information so that effective management decisions can be made.

Management science (quantitative methods) approach. Decision-making techniques that involve the use of a mathematical model and often a computer to solve production and operations problems.

Managerial ethics. The standards used to judge the rightness or wrongness of managers' relations to others.

Managerial Grid®. A leadership approach developed by Robert Blake and Jane Mouton that uses a leader's concern for production and concern for people as the two "grid" components. Five basic leadership styles are shown on the resulting grid, with the ideal leadership approach (team management) plotted as a 9,9 style.

Managers. High-level employees who identify more closely with other employees than with the owners. As distinct from *entrepreneurs* and *leaders* but including *supervisors*.

Master operations plan (MOP). A general *production* guide extending about a year ahead, taking into account whether production will be level or seasonal.

Materials. Supplies, parts, and goods used by companies.

Matrix departmentalization. A hybrid form of *departmentalization* in which the project manager organization is superimposed on the various functional departments.

Maturity. The capacity of individuals or groups to set high but attainable goals and their willingness and ability to take responsibility.

Maximizing. According to Herbert Simon's concept of *bounded rationality*, achieving the most or greatest satisfaction in a relationship.

Mental revolution. The assumption that managers would want to increase productivity and share those gains with the workers through easier work and improved material well-being; the heart of Frederick Taylor's *scientific management* approach.

Mentor. An individual who will systematically develop and promote a subordinate's abilities through intensive tutoring, coaching, and guidance.

Mission. The function that an organization intends to perform within the social or economic system that defines the character and nature of the organization.

Monte Carlo. A form of *simulation* relying on the laws of probability to simulate actual experience.

Motivation. Inducing a person, or group of people, each with his or her own distinctive needs and personality, to work to achieve the organization's objectives while also working to achieve personal objectives.

Motivators. According to Frederick Herzberg, factors such as achievement, advancement, and recognition that have a strong, positive effect on employee *motivation* and performance.

Motive. An internal stimulus that directs conscious behavior toward satisfying a need or reaching a goal.

Multinational corporations (MNCs). Corporations that operate in more than one country; a relatively new form of business organization whose investments frequently come from several countries.

Mutual benefit and protection societies. Not-for-profit institutions run for the benefit of their client members, including private clubs, employee associations, trade associations, and professional associations.

Myers-Briggs Type Indicator. A questionnaire that helps identify individuals' problem-solving type, showing whether they gain information by sensing or intuition and make decisions based on thinking or feeling.

Nationalism. Devotion to the interests of one's own nation, including maintaining and protecting its natural resources as well as its socioeconomic, cultural, and political systems.

Need for achievement. The major factor in researcher David McClelland's achievement theory of motivation. The theory states that there is a high positive correlation between need for achievement and performance and executive success.

Negative control. A form of control that ensures that unwanted or undesirable activities do not occur or recur.

Network analysis. A *management science* technique of *scheduling* and *control* graphically depicting the linkages between and among the activities that must be performed to complete a given project; a *PERT network* is one example.

Noise. The interference that impedes communication effectiveness.

Nominal grouping technique (NGT). A structured process in which small groups, five to nine members, make suggestions in writing and then discuss all suggestions to reach a decision.

Nonquantitative control methods. Subjective control methods used by managers, including observation, regular or "spot" inspections, oral and written reports, and *performance evaluations*.

Nonverbal communication. Transmission of meaning without the use of words.

Not-for-profit organizations. Organizations whose primary objective is service rather than profit. They include not-for-profit service organizations, mutual benefit and protection societies, and commonweal organizations.

Not-for-profit service organizations. Organizations

whose primary objective is service to the public or clients, such as city orchestras, museums, churches, and hospitals run by religious groups.

Object language. A form of *nonverbal communication* in which physical objects, such as clothes or furniture, convey a message.

Objectives. End results, goals, or targets that an organization, a department, or an individual seeks to reach.

Open system. Tends to be in a dynamic relationship with its environment, receiving various inputs, transforming them in some way, and producing outputs.

Operant conditioning. A process method of motivation in which favorable behavior is reinforced by satisfying consequences and unfavorable behavior is eliminated by unsatisfying consequences; also called *behavior modification.*

Operating budgets. Budgets for forecasting sales and allocating financial resources and supplies. See also *capital budgets; personnel budgets; production budgets.*

Operations. Those activities that convert inputs into outputs, bringing together elements of material, financial, and human resources to be processed into a product, which may be either a good or a service.

Operations research (OR). Refers to several *management science* tools for making operating decisions. Developed during World War II, OR involves pooling knowledge of research team specialists to develop quantitative "models" that behave similarly to real-world situations confronting the decision makers.

Operative management. The aspect of management involved with supervising, motivating, and communicating with employees to lead them to achieve effective results.

Optimizing. According to Herbert Simon's concept of *bounded rationality*, achieving the best satisfaction in a relationship.

Organization. A group of individuals working together to achieve a common mission, purpose, objective, or goal.

Organization culture. The pattern of values, beliefs, and expectations shared by organization members; the shared assumption about how the organization should go about its work and what should be evaluated and rewarded.

Organizational career planning (OCP). Planning that focuses on the needs of the organization, as contrasted with *individual career planning.*

Organizational development (OD). A process of change in an organization's culture through the use of behavioral science technology, research, and theory.

Organizational effectiveness. The result of activities that improve the organization's structure, technology, and people.

Organizational mission. The function that the organization intends to perform within its social or economic system.

Organizational objectives. The targets toward which managers move in order to fulfill the organization's mission.

Organizing. One of the basic management functions: determining what resources and which activities are required to achieve the organization's objectives, combining these into a formal structure, assigning the responsibility for accomplishing the objectives to responsible subordinates, and then delegating to those individuals the authority necessary to carry out their assignments.

Paralanguage. Related to vocal sounds that influence how words are expressed; for example, vocal pitch, tone, volume, pace, and other delivery-related factors.

Participative management. A philosophy that states that under proper conditions, employees should have the opportunity to make a significant contribution to solving problems, controlling costs, contributing to objectives, and assisting in managing and controlling the organization.

People-oriented (employee-centered) leaders. Leaders who focus on the welfare and feelings of followers, have confidence in themselves, and need to be accepted by their team members.

Perception. The process by which individuals select, organize, and give meaning to the world around them; it is influenced by environmental factors such as one's reference group, one's role, interaction with others, and one's cultural background.

Performance appraisal (evaluation, review). The formal system by which managers evaluate and rate the quality of subordinates' performance over a given period of time; a quantifiable or nonquantitative method of *control.*

Personnel budgets. Budgets for securing and developing human resources. See also *capital budgets; operating budgets; production budgets.*

PERT network. A line chart that expresses the relationships of events and activities and their timing under conditions of uncertainty. See also *Program Evaluation and Review Technique (PERT).*

Planned change. Deliberate actions to modify the status quo. They seek to anticipate changes in the external and internal environments and to find ways of coping with predicted new conditions.

Planned progression. An on-the-job method of development whereby subordinates are moved in well-ordered channels through different levels of the organization.

Planning. Choosing or setting organization objectives and then determining the *policies, projects, programs, procedures,* methods, systems, *budgets, standards,* and *strategies* needed to achieve them.

Planning premises. Assumptions about the future settings in which planning is to take place and the total environment in which the plans are to operate.

Planning-programming-budgeting systems (PPBS). Methods developed to aid management in identifying and eliminating costly programs that tend to duplicate other programs and to provide a means of analyzing the benefits and costs of each program or activity.

Policies. Broad, general statements of expected actions that serve as guides to managerial decision making.

Pollution. The contamination or destruction of the natural environment.

Polygraph. Used to conduct "lie detector" tests.

Positive control. Control that tries to see that the objectives of the organization are reached efficiently and effectively.

Positive reinforcement. A key part of *operant conditioning,* a process motivation theory, in which desired employee behavior is followed by pleasant, satisfying consequences.

Power. The ability to influence individuals, groups, decisions, or events.

Primary functions. The three functions that are essential to the survival of economic organizations:
1. *Operations:* production, manufacturing, or the generation of service.
2. *Marketing:* distribution, sales, or service.
3. *Finance:* acquisition of funds, utilization of funds, budgeting.

Principle. A general belief or proposition sufficiently applicable to a situation to provide a guide to thought or action in that situation. See also *concept.*

Principle of the transfer of skill. Developed by Charles Babbage, this principle states that to the extent that a machine becomes more automatic and is able to produce large quantities of goods accurately, the worker using it requires less skill and becomes a machine tender rather than a skilled worker.

Proactive process. The process of dealing with organizational change by setting a new course instead of correcting the current one.

Procedures. A detailed *standing plan* established by management that defines certain steps to be taken in a given sequence to accomplish organizational *objectives.*

Process departmentalization (equipment departmentalization). A form of *departmentalization* that focuses on production processes or equipment as the basis for grouping activities.

Process theories. Theories that deal with how behavior originates and is performed.

Product departmentalization. A form of *departmentalization* that groups together all the functions associated with a single product line.

Production. A type of *operations* that specializes in producing goods.

Production budgets. Budgets for producing the organization's basic product or service. See also *capital budgets; operating budgets; personnel budgets.*

Productivity. A measure of inputs compared to outputs (compare *efficiency*). Designed to convey how efficiently a system utilizes its resources, it is expressed as a ratio, such as the ratio of units produced to labor hours.

Profession. Management is considered a profession if the following criteria are met: (1) a codified body of knowledge; (2) a long period of formal education and training; (3) controlled entry; (4) an enforced code of ethics; and (5) unselfish service to others.

Professional corporations (PCs). Profit-oriented associations of professionals such as physicians, psychologists, counselors, lawyers, and architects.

Profit-sharing plan. A method of *compensation* under which employees receive a definite, prearranged percentage of the firm's profits as extra income.

Program Evaluation and Review Technique (PERT). A scheduling and control technique that aids in scheduling sophisticated, nonrepetitive technical projects by (1) focusing management's attention on key program steps; (2) pointing to potential problem areas; (3) evaluating progress; and (4) giving management a reporting device.

Programmed decisions. Decisions that are routine and repetitive.

Programs. *Single-use plans* that include the objectives of the program and the principal steps that must be taken to achieve the objectives—with the approximate timing of each—as well as the resources required to accomplish the stated objective.

Projects. Individual segments of a general *program.*

Promoting. A method of obtaining employees internally by moving employees from a lower-level job to a higher-level one, which usually brings a higher salary, a new job title, and added duties and responsibilities. See also *transferring; upgrading.*

Protestant (work) ethic. Emphasizing hard work and industry, productivity, thrift, and frugality, it guided U.S. business owner-managers from about 1800 to the early 1930s.

Public sector. The classification of organizations that includes state, federal, and local governments.

Punishment. The reverse of reinforcement, which is the presentation of an attractive reward following a response or the removal of an unpleasant or negative condition following a response.

Pygmalion effect. See *self-fulfilling prophecy.*

Quality circles (QC). Small voluntary groups of workers, along with a supervisory leader, who belong to the same division or unit of the plant. They meet regularly to identify problem areas and recommended solutions for management.

Quality control (QC) or quality assurance. The process by which an organization ensures that its finished products or services meet the expectations of clients and consumers.

Quality of work life (QWL) programs. Programs that systematically study factors such as working conditions, jobs performed, supervision, company policy, and others that affect the conditions of the work environment.

Quantitative control techniques. *Control* techniques that use specific data and quantitative methods to measure and correct the quality and quantity of output.

Queuing theory. A *management science* decision tool that attempts to balance the cost of services provided and the availability of service at various time periods; also called waiting line theory.

Ratio analysis (RA). The use of two or more components of a firm's financial performance whose relationship is expressed as a percentage or ratio.

Reactive process. A management approach to dealing with change by responding to problems or issues one at a time as they arise.

Recruitment. Reaching out and attracting a pool of potential employees from which to select the ones needed to best satisfy the organization's needs.

Recycling. Reprocessing used items for further use.

Red tape. Official routines and procedures marked by excessive complexity, resulting in unnecessary delay.

Referent power. A form of *power* based on people's identification with a potential leader and what that leader stands for or symbolizes; personal charisma, charm, courage, and other traits are important factors in the exercise of referent power.

Reflective statements. An *active listening* technique, a reflective statement paraphrases what the speaker has just said, demonstrating that the listener has heard and understood and returning the initiative to the speaker.

Refreezing. In Kurt Lewin's model of organization change, *refreezing* has occurred when you see that the new behavior patterns you have experimented with during *changing* are now part of you; you feel comfortable with the new behavior and now see it as part of your normal method of operation. See also *changing; unfreezing.*

Regression analysis. A statistical technique used to determine the nature of an association or relationship between variables.

Reinforcement. Presentation of an attractive reward (or removal of an unpleasant or negative condition) following a desired response.

Relationship behavior. The leader's personal relationships with individuals or members of his or her group.

Resistance to change. Managers' and employees' reactions to the occurrence of change.

Responsibility. The obligation that is created when a subordinate accepts a manager's *authority* to delegate tasks or assignments.

Retrenchment strategy. See *turnaround strategy.*

Return on equity (ROE). The net profit a firm earns, expressed as a percentage of the investment required to earn such profits. Often called *return on investment (ROI).*

Return on investment (ROI). See *return on equity (ROE).*

Reward power. A form of *power* derived from the number of positive rewards (money, protection, and the like) a potential leader is seen as controlling.

Robotics revolution. Assembly work being performed by machines that are computer controlled and with parts and assemblies being handled automatically.

Rules and regulations. *Standing plans* that specifically state what can and cannot be done under a given set of circumstances; the result of a *policy* being adhered to in *every* instance.

Satisficing. In *decision making*, selecting an alternative that is reasonably good, although not necessarily perfect or ideal.

Scheduling. Planning the timing and sequencing of the use of physical and human resources for the operational activities of an organization. In production, accomplished by working backward from the date when products are due to be delivered and subtracting the time required for each operation in order to arrive at a starting date.

Scientific approach. Sought efficient operations and regarded workers as just another factor of production, like land or equipment.

Scientific management movement. A mechanistic approach to management that emphasized increasing production efficiency by improving the employees' working methods and procedures and increasing earnings.

Selection. Choosing from a group of potential employees the specific person to perform a given job.

Selective perception. The way one's frame of reference has a limiting effect on the way one sees events, people, objects, and situations.

Self-fulfilling prophecy. The process by which people try to convert their attitudes, beliefs, and expectations into reality. If they predict that something is going to happen, they will try very hard to make it happen.

Sensing. Becoming aware of things through the five senses.

Service functions. Functions necessary to keep the *primary functions* operating effectively—that is, personnel; accounting; maintenance; research and development; legal; clerical; engineering; purchasing; and public, community, and legislative relations.

Services. Performing activities that result in some type of tangible or intangible satisfaction.

Short-range plans. Plans with an effective time span of one day to one year.

Sign language. Nonverbal messages that literally replace words, such as a movement of the head to indicate "yes" or "no," shrugged shoulders and uplifted palms to convey "I don't know," or raised eyebrows to signal shock or disapproval.

Simulation. The act of performing experiments on a model (rather than the real thing) in some planned, orderly fashion.

Single-use plans. Plans used for nonrecurring short-range activities, including *programs*, *projects*, and *budgets*.

Social audit. A formal procedure for evaluating and reporting on actions with social implications.

Social ethic. Concern for the corporate well-being of society and the value of harmony and solidarity in interpersonal and intergroup relationships.

Social responsibility. Management's obligation to set policies, make decisions, and follow courses of action that are desirable in terms of the values and objectives of society.

Span of management (control, authority). The number of subordinates a manager can effectively supervise; also, the number of subordinates reporting to a given supervisor.

Specialization. Another term for *division of labor*, whereby employees (and managers) carry out the activities they are more qualified for and adept at performing.

Staff authority. The right possessed by staff units or specialists to advise, recommend to, or counsel line personnel.

Staffing. One of the basic management functions; includes *selection*, placement, orientation, *compensation*, *development*, and utilization of employees.

Stakeholders. Those who have a stake in the organization's success, including employees, owners, customers, government authorities, creditors, and others.

Standard. A unit of measurement that can serve as a reference point for evaluating results; physical, monetary, and time standards are three common types.

Standing committees. Permanent *committees* in the structure of the organization set up for a specific long-term or repetitive task.

Standing plans. Plans for recurring or long-range activities; including *policies*, *procedures*, and *rules and regulations*.

Statistical quality control (SQC). A method of *control* used in mass manufacturing processes that is based on inspection of random samples rather than every item.

Steel-collar workers. Industrial robots.

Stereotyping. Developing a fixed, unvarying idea about a certain group—women, blacks, students, old people, politicians—and treating all members of the group according to this preconception and expecting predictable action and responses from them.

Strategic business unit (SBU). A unique company business that has its own mission, product or service lines, competition, customers, threats, and opportunities.

Strategic planning. Long-range planning that involves activities two to five years or more in the future.

Strategic plans. Plans that fix the nature of the organization, the *mission* or purpose of the organization, and the organization's *objectives* and *strategies*.

Strategies. Grand plans that management adopts to achieve the organizational goals by considering what management, as well as competitors, will do in a given set of circumstances.

Supervision. Leading and directing lower-level employees in the organization.

SWOT analysis. The process of systematically identifying an organization's strengths, weaknesses, opportunities, and threats.

Synergy. The action of two or more organisms working together to achieve an effect of which each alone is incapable.

Synthetic (assembly) process. A kind of *production process* in which several materials or parts are processed and assembled into a product. See also *analytic process*.

System. An organized or complex whole; an assemblage or combination of things or parts forming a complex or unitary whole. It is made up of (1) inputs, (2) operations (or processes), and (3) outputs.

System 4. One of four management systems operating in organizations, according to *Likert's internal systems model*. Under System 4 (Participative Groups), higher management views its role as that of making sure that the best decisions are made through a decentralized participative-group structure. These groups overlap and are coordinated by multiple memberships. There is a high degree of trust, which allows both superiors and subordinates to exercise greater control over the work situation. Likert believes that the closer an organization is to System 4, the more effective it will be in achieving its end results.

Systems approach. Integrates the universal management functions, the managerial activities approach, and strategic planning with the importance of external factors.

Task behavior. The extent to which leaders are likely to organize and define the roles of their followers and to explain what activities each is to do, and when, where, and how tasks are to be accomplished.

Task forces. Teams that usually consist of volunteers, are of limited duration, and set their own goals.

Task-oriented (production-oriented) leaders. Leaders who focus on the "work" aspects of getting the job done, emphasizing planning, scheduling, and processing the work and close control of quality.

Technical skills. One of the groups of skills needed by effective managers; these include the ability to use the knowledge, tools, and techniques of a specific discipline or field, such as accounting, engineering, production, medicine, or sales. See also *administrative skills; conceptual skills; human-relations skills*.

Temporaries. Part-time employees.

Temporary assignment. An on-the-job training method whereby the subordinate serves in management positions for short periods.

Territorial departmentalization. Grouping organizational activities according to the place where operations are located; sometimes referred to as *regional, area*, or *geographic departmentalization*.

Theory X and Theory Y. Sets of assumptions made by managers in industry, as defined by Douglas McGregor. Under *Theory X*, managers assume that workers dislike work and must be coerced and controlled to achieve company objectives. *Theory Y* assumes that workers accept work as natural, seek responsibility, and will exercise self-direction and self-control to achieve company objectives.

Theory Z approach. As defined by author William Ouchi, a managerial approach used in Japan that emphasizes long-range planning, consensus decision making, and strong, mutual worker-employer loyalty.

Theory Z companies. As defined by William Ouchi in *Theory Z*, American companies with characteristics similar to those of Japanese companies, which result in better management and greater effectiveness.

Thinking. Process whereby one uses a logical process and a rational—or sometimes legalistic—reasoning in arriving at impersonal conclusions.

Third culture. Behavior patterns created, shared, and learned by people of different societies who are in the process of relating their cultural systems to those of other people from a second culture.

Third sector. Nonprofit service organizations that are private or semipublic, such as hospitals, churches, schools and universities, trade associations, orchestras, museums, dance and opera companies, the United Fund, the YMCA and YWCA, scouting organizations, and municipally owned utilities.

Time wages. A form of compensation based on the number of hours worked.

Training. Attaining specific, detailed, and routine job skills and techniques to become a more productive worker.

Traitist approach. A leadership theory based on the belief that leaders possess certain traits or characteristics that cause them to rise above their followers.

Transferring. A method of obtaining employees internally, whereby employees are moved from less desirable or less rewarding jobs in the organization to others that better satisfy their needs. See also *promoting; upgrading*.

Transformative leaders. Those who can shape and elevate the motives and goals of followers.

Trial-and-error approach. An approach used in performing managerial activities. It is increasingly lacking in accuracy and efficiency.

Trusteeship management. The second period of social responsibility whereby the government and professional business managers began to be concerned for employees, customers, and the community while protecting the interests of stakeholders.

Turnaround strategy. A strategy used to bring a poorly performing company back to health. This is done by the replacement of management, attention to cost controls, pruning of unprofitable segments, or shifting resources from some segments to others.

Uncontrollable factors. Factors affecting an organization whose causes cannot be traced directly to the organization, such as population growth, political environment, and social pressure.

Unfreezing. In Kurt Lewin's change model, the state in which one becomes ready to acquire new behavior, recognizing the ineffectiveness of present behavior patterns. See also *changing; refreezing*.

Unity of command. A management principle stating that each individual employee in an organization should report to and be accountable to only one immediate superior.

Universality of management. The principle holding that the functions of management are the same everywhere, in all organizations, and at any time.

Unprogrammed decisions. Decisions that occur infrequently and, because of differing variables, require a separate decision each time the decision situation occurs.

Upgrading. A method of obtaining employees internally, whereby the employee currently holding the position is educated, trained, or developed to perform the job better as the situation demands. See also *promoting; transferring.*

Upward communication. *Communication* that flows up the *chain of command* from lower levels to upper management levels, usually in the form of *feedback.*

Values. Those principles and qualities that are intrinsically desirable to us.

Variable budget (flexible budget, step budget, or sliding-scale budget). A *control* technique involving standard costs tied to the volume of revenues or production; permits managers to exercise *feedforward control* over the expenditure of funds.

Variable costs. Costs that vary with the level of output, including the cost of some utilities, extra workers' wages, or extra supplies needed. See also *fixed costs.*

Variances. Differences between amounts actually budgeted and amounts expended.

Vertical integration. Extending a business's scope by taking on an activity or function backward toward sources of supply or forward toward the end user.

Wages. The reward one receives for working for someone else; they take the form of an hourly wage, salary, bonus, tips, or commission.

White-collar work. Traditionally, work performed by workers wearing white dress shirts. It includes that done by technical and professional personnel, managers and administrators, salespeople, and clerical workers.

Zero-base budgeting (ZBB). A *budgetary control* method that divides an organization's programs into "decision packages" consisting of goals, activities, and resources needed and then computes costs "from scratch," as if the program had never existed.

Zero defects. No deviations from the standard.

Zero defects (ZD) program. A program that focuses on high quality attainment by emphasizing prevention rather than cure, or doing the job right the first time.

INDEX